NO NUKES:

everyone's guide
to nuclear power

by anna gyorgy and friends

SOUTH END PRESS

Library of Congress Catalog Card Number: 78-71203
ISBN 0-89608-006-4 (paper)
ISBN 0-89608-007-2 (cloth)

Printed by Maple Vail, York, PA, U.S.A.
Typesetting and paste-up done by the publishing collective:
South End Press, Box 68, Astor Station
Boston, MA 02123

 9

ACKNOWLEDGMENTS

Writers

Joseph Bowring is a graduate student in economics at U/Mass
Amherst.

Nancy Folbre is an economist and anti-nuke activist now teaching at
the New School for Social Research, New York City,

Anna Gyorgy lives in Montague, MA near nukes and a proposed site.
She has been active with local groups and the Clamshell Alliance.

Tom Harris is a carpenter with the western MA firm, House
Carpenters, and an anti-nuclear activist.

Howard Kohn is a journalist with *Rolling Stone* magazine and is now
working on a book on Karen Silkwood.

Peter Lichtner is a nuclear physicist at the University of Maryland.

Michael Lucas is an American living in West Berlin and is a frequent
contributor to European anti-nuclear and political journals.

Sam Lovejoy fights nukes, starting at home.

Don Michak is an economist and anti-nuke activist now with NIRS
(Nuclear Information Resource Service, Washington, D.C.)

Peter Natti is a woodworker, potter and Montague farmer.

Steve Turner is a freelance writer living in Amherst, MA.

Harvey Wasserman wrote *Harvey Wasserman's History of the United States*
(Harper & Row, 1972) and is active with the Clamshell Alliance.

Graphic Artists

Bonnie Acker is a political artist and activist who is doing community
and women's organizing in eastern Massachusetts.

Peg Averill has done political cartoons, drawings for *WIN* magazine
and others for years; she's working on a book of her collected
drawings.

Lionel Delevingne is a freelance photographer in Northampton,
MA, with a special interest in anti-nuclear/solar subjects.

Candace Kaihlanen is a calligrapher/artist in Amherst, MA.

Susanna Natti is a children's book illustrator (see Charlotte Pomer-
antz's *The Downtown Fairy Godmother*, Addison-Wesley, 1978).

Mike Prendergast, our wonderful mapmaker, is a commercial artist
and anti-nuke activist in Newburyport, MA.

Editorial Help
Richard Asinof; Elizabeth Bell; Phyllis Joffe; Susan Kramer; Martha Miller; Peter Natti; Violet Robison; Bob Rottenberg; Cathy Wolff.

Reviewers
Thanks to the following for their helpful review comments on various sections of **NO NUKES**: Sr. Rosalie Bertell, Larry Bogart, Ken Bossong, Dr. Helen Caldicott, Dr. Barry Commoner, David Holzman, Charles Komanoff, Richard Morgan.

General Support
Peter, Lee, Robert, and Susanna Natti; the Montague Farm home crew; The Bloom Institute of Media Studies; Christina Platt; Ellen Emerson; the Clamshell Alliance Resource Committee; Mary Lea and the South End Press, and many more. Thanks for everything.

Thanks to all our national and international reporters:
National Reports—especially prepared for this book in order of presentation:
Long Island Safe Energy Coalition (LISEC), Tobe J. Carey (Woodstock Nuclear Opponents); Ellen Rocco (Upstate People for Safe Energy Technology); Gertrude Dixon (Wisconsin League Against Nuclear Dangers); Kitty Tucker; Detroit Safe Energy Coalition; Mark Haim (Missourians for Safe Energy); Armadillo Coalition of Texas; Terry Mulcahy and Judi Bartlett-Lagorio (Cactus Alliance); Paul Finley (Crabshell Alliance); Liz Apfelberg, Jane Swanson (Mothers for Peace); Steve Leeds (People Against Nuclear Power).

International reports—prepared for this book by: Michael Lucas (Federal Republic of Germany); Dave Elliott (U.K.), Petra Karin Kelly (Belgium), Peter D. Jones, Alastair Machin (Australia).

TABLE OF CONTENTS

Message to Readers

Since 1945, atomic energy has been widely represented as an almost miraculous future energy source for the United States and much of the rest of the world. But now, as the roots of the nuclear construction program have spread, so have serious questions about the safety and necessity of a fission-powered future.

We wrote this book because we don't want to be "nuclear neighbors." The threat of a giant reactor complex in our own town made us aware of the problems with all atomic power plants. This book's purpose is to present what we have learned simply and clearly. Nuclear power is a huge and complex subject, but one which affects us all. For our own protection, we *have* to understand its basic principles. In order to help along a reasoned public debate and decision on this most crucial issue, we've tried to summarize key information in a way everyone can understand.

This has been a low-budget, mostly volunteer effort. Since the atomic-industrial establishment has tremendous resources at its disposal, we haven't felt it necessary to present its "side" of the debate. That's readily available, and we tell you where to find it. Pro-nuclear propaganda has flowed from government, industry, and utilities for decades now. Most of us learned what little we knew about nuclear power through the eyes of the industry, in their well-funded hype designed to sell rather than inform. We want to help set the record straight.

Until now, information critical of nuclear energy has been scattered—in books, articles, newsletters. In this volume we've distilled information from hundreds of sources to offer a coherent background for making the energy choices we all have to make.

Frankly, it's hard to stop writing! Every day there are new reports and information, studies, accidents, actions to add to the story. There can be no "last word" on nuclear energy. All we can do here is share with you the results of five years of research and participation so that you can have an outline and some basic facts at your fingertips.

In the course of writing this book we have seen the tide of public opinion turning sharply against atomic energy. As the stockpiles of atomic wastes mushroom, as the price of both plant construction and electric bills soar, as the health and environmental dangers become more obvious—so grows the anti-nuclear movement. Of late, because of new information about safe, viable renewable resources, it has also become a pro-solar movement.

This broad movement includes people from all walks of life all over the planet. Some of their reports are included here.

Because the issue is so vast, there are of necessity many simplifications here. We urge you to consult the footnotes and the resource sections and keep on reading. If this project is successful, there will be more editions of *NO NUKES*. In that hope, we invite your participation. Please send comments, corrections, up-dates—and bulk orders!—to *NO NUKES* in care of our publisher.

Thanks go to the many people who have made this book possible, from our kitchen in Montague to Australia and back again.

Yours for a nuclear-free tomorrow.

Anna

October 1978

INTRODUCTION

Where are We Starting From?

We are at an energy crossroads. Since 1960 energy use in the U.S. has more than doubled. The industrialized societies of Japan and the West are based on high energy consumption, more specifically on fossil fuels—oil, natural gas, and coal.

Our economy is based on continued growth, expansion, use of energy. But 40% of the oil we use is imported. It is expensive, a finite resource that we do not and cannot control. It takes dollars overseas and causes inflation at home, as well as air, water, and thermal pollution.

Dependence on fossil fuels has to end, one way or another. What will the future hold? The Brookhaven National Laboratory

U.S. Energy Consumption Trends, 1850-1974

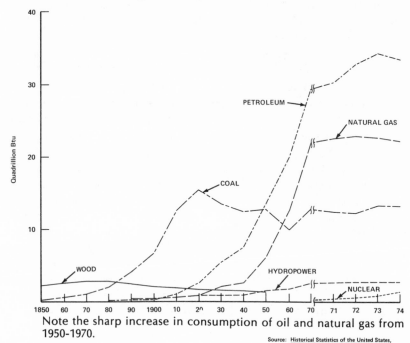

Note the sharp increase in consumption of oil and natural gas from 1950-1970.

Source: Historical Statistics of the United States, Bureau of the Census; U.S. Bureau of Mines.

does frequent studies for the U.S. government. A recent (1978) one presented possible sources of long-term energy supply. In the past, such projections saw nuclear energy taking the place of oil and gas in a never-ending upward curve. In the Brookhaven study, some role is given to solar and geothermal technologies. In the graph, the shaded areas represent amounts of energy that could be met by a choice of either coal or nuclear (lower shaded area) or solar or nuclear (above). The striking thing about this projection is that it assumes that energy use will continue to rise, doubling from a present 75 quadrillion Btu to around 150 by year 2010 (given only "moderate" conservation), and that solar energy will not play a major role until well into the next century.

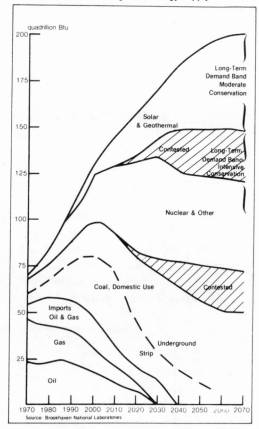

A Perspective on U.S. Long-Term Energy Supply

quadrillion Btu

Long-Term Demand Band Moderate Conservation

Solar & Geothermal

Contested

Long-Term Demand Band Intensive Conservation

Nuclear & Other

Coal, Domestic Use

Contested

Imports Oil & Gas

Gas

Underground

Strip

Oil

Source: Brookhaven National Laboratories

But as we will see, this projection is not the only one. Others have foreseen the possibilities of a much reduced energy budget, provided entirely by renewable and safe energy sources.

Where Do We Go From Here?

This book will explore the choices before us. Do we want to have a nuclear future? What are the dangers, the costs? And what are our alternatives? First we will look at atomic energy, in its "peaceful use" as the power source of what are called in the U.S. nuclear power plants. The story of nuclear power, from its history to its economics, tells us a great deal about the society in which we live. The alternatives hold forth the possibility of another sort of growth.

Finally, we will look at the movement against nuclear power, in the U.S. and in the world. And now, for the "nuclear alternative..."

SECTION 1: WHAT'S A NUKE?

Chapter 1:

History

Human civilization is rapidly approaching a series of crises that can be managed only through some radical departures in man's dealings with the relationship between energy and matter. Nuclear energy holds one key—a crucial one—to the successful resolution of these crises. Without it there is no doubt that civilization, as we know it, would slowly grind to a halt.[1]

> Glenn T. Seaborg, nuclear
> physicist, Chairman, AEC
> 1961-1971

Atomic power—the energy of nuclear fission—has been with us since the first atomic bomb was tested in July 1945, and used in August of that year.

The following is a brief account of the atom's development from weapon to center-stage political issue—its current use as an energy source.

THE 1940s: WAR ROOTS AND PEACEFUL PROMISES

Atomic Roots

In late 1938, European physicists finally succeeded in splitting—fissioning—an atom of uranium. But developments in unlocking the atom's power were completely altered by the approaching war. Many scientists left fascist Germany and Europe and came primarily to U.S. universities. With war approaching, the previously open international world of scientific experimentation and exchange closed.[2]

Many of these emmigrating scientists came to the U.S. and Canada aware that great amounts of energy could potentially be released if an atomic chain reaction could be attained—if enough atoms could be split simultaneously.

Atomic power was born with the arms race. Some of the scientists suspected

1

that Germany was working on development of an atomic fission weapon. In the summer of 1939, three Hungarian physicists convinced Albert Einstein to write President Roosevelt about possible German development of "extremely powerful bombs of a new type."[3] The letter suggested the President obtain a supply of uranium ore for the U.S. (later gotten from the Belgian Congo, now Zaire), and speed up the experimental work then being done by funding university research and getting the cooperation of industrial laboratories.

FDR responded by forming a three-person "Uranium Committee." The decision to undertake an all-out research and development program in atomic energy was made in December 1941, about the time of the Pearl Harbor attack. The next summer, the President ordered that the program proceed, and on 13 August 1942, the Army established the "Manhattan Engineer District" in its Corps of Engineers. Its job was to develop an atomic bomb as soon as humanly possible.

In fact, the Germans were nowhere near building an atomic weapon. Many of their best atomic scientists had left the country, and those who remained were evidently not anxious to develop this weapon for the fascist military regime.[4] When the war was over, Albert Einstein mourned: "If I had known that the Germans would not succeed in constructing the atom bomb, I never would have moved a finger."[5]

The Manhattan Project 1942-45

As the war-time top-secret Manhattan Project began, the various processes used to produce the enriched uranium and plutonium needed for an atomic weapon were at the most elementary, often just theoretical, stages of development. The effort of the Manhattan Project, under the driving leadership of General Leslie Groves, has been described as "the greatest single achievement of organized human effort in history."[6]

The base of U.S. atomic might was put in place during an incredibly fast-paced three years, at a cost of about $2 billion.[7] The atomic-industrial-academic establishment came together as the Army, large companies and universities worked to get basic atomic processes ready for large-scale factory production and final testing.

Several processes for enriching uranium were worked on simultaneously. The gaseous diffusion process of uranium-235 separation was developed at Columbia University labs in New York City. The Berkeley Radiation Lab at the Univ. of California housed Prof. Ernest Lawrence's electro-magnetic method of U-235 separation, which was passed over in favor of the ambitious but apparently more feasible diffusion process. (See separation and the enrichment of uranium, p. 47). Diffusers for the process were made in Detroit by Chrysler, while the Houdaille-Hershey plant in Decatur, Illinois, got ready for industrial production of barriers for the diffusion factory—part of the giant new installation at Oak Ridge, Tennessee. Pumps for the gaseous diffusion plant were manufactured by Allis-Chalmers in Milwaukee.

The scope of the project was massive. Factory sites were carved out of the wilderness in Oak Ridge and around the small village of Hanford in Washington State. Oak Ridge—54,000 acres of open countryside and rolling hills 18 miles from Knoxville—was selected (from an airplane!) as the site for the gigantic gaseous diffusion plant that would produce the enriched uranium for the atom bomb. The plant, known as K-2, covered 44 acres of ground. Each side of the U-shaped building was a half-mile long.[8] It took 20,000 people and $500 million to construct. No one building it or working inside was told what it was for, and security and cleanliness were extraordinarily tight.

The Hanford site was chosen for the production of plutonium, another fissionable material for the bomb—if enough of the rare, newly discovered metal could be produced. The plutonium would be created when enriched uranium was irradiated in a production reactor—a power plant based on the experimental "pile" built by atomic scientists at the University of Chicago (see also pp. 34-35). The plutonium production effort at Hanford was directed by Dupont, asked to engineer this war-job. The plutonium program's scientific base remained in Chicago with Enrico Fermi and others at Arthur Compton's lab.

In December 1944, the first irradiated slugs of uranium reactor fuel were dissolved and the next month the first uranium was separated.

During this period of sustained effort little mention was made of what would later become the nemesis of the atomic program: radioactive contamination and waste disposal. At the time, little thought was given to the aftereffects of possible radioactive contamination, nor to atomic wastes. Military immediacy meant that only crucial problems of the moment were seen and solved. The longer term effects were "unimportant" and ignored.

The enriched uranium and plutonium finally produced at Oak Ridge and Hanford was transported to Los Alamos, New Mexico. There a private boy's camp atop a mesa had been converted to a top secret scientific laboratory under the direction of Nobel prizewinning physicist Robert J. Oppenheimer.[9] The Los Alamos bomb lab was 20 miles from Santa Fe. Here a team of scientists and Army technicians worked for two years on the design, timing and triggering of an atomic weapon.

On 16 July 1945, the first bomb was exploded. The Trinity test explosion took place on flat, unpopulated desert about 200 miles south of Los Alamos, at the Army's Alamogordo bombing range. It was the first full-scale test of an implosion-type weapon (the body of the bomb was triggered by charges set around it). As it exploded, Enrico Fermi estimated that the blast corresponded to roughly 10,000 tons of TNT.[10]

The Bomb is Used

In the month following the Trinity test Los Alamos scientists waited for more nuclear materials to come from Oak Ridge and Hanford, and then built several more bombs in the summer of 1945.

The war would soon be over. Germany surrendered in June 1945 before the Trinity test. By mid-summer the Japanese were sending out secret diplomatic feelers to the U.S., hoping to arrive at a settlement. But the U.S. government, set on an unconditional surrender, refused to negotiate.[11] A land invasion of Japan appeared imminent.

In a document known as the Franck Report, some of the same scientists who urged initial development of the bomb, including Leo Szilard, asked Secretary of War Henry Stimson not to use it against Japan. Just at this point, FDR died and Harry Truman ascended the war throne. He gave the go-ahead for the first bombing.[12]

On the morning of 6 August 1945, the B-29 bomber Enola Gay dropped a uranium bomb on the Japanese city of Hiroshima. More than one hundred thousand people died.

Here is an account of the bombing by Philip Noel-Baker, a British politician born in 1889 who was involved with the creation of both attempts at world peace organization, the League of Nations, and the United Nations.

August 6, 1945. 8:15 a.m.—The streets are full of people; people going to work, people going to shop, children going to school. It is a lovely summer morning, sunshine and blue sky. The aircraft flies across the city. Above the center of town something falls. It is hard to see; the bomb is very small, and appears a little larger than a tennis ball in size. It falls for 10 to 15 seconds. Then there is a sudden searing flash of light, brighter and hotter than a thousand suns. Those who were looking directly at it had their eyes burnt in their sockets...

(People) vanished from the Earth. They were utterly consumed by the furnace of the flash. There were not even ashes on the pavement. Nothing but their black shadows on the stones. Scores of thousands more, sheltered by walls or buildings from the flash, were driven mad by intolerable thirst from the heat. They ran in frenzied hordes toward the seven rivers of the delta on which Hiroshima is built. They fought like maniacs to reach the water. If they succeeded, they stopped to drink the poisoned stream. In a month they, too, were dead.

Then came the blast, thousands of miles an hour. Buildings in all directions for miles flattened to the ground. Lorries, cars, milk-carts, human beings, baby prams, picked up and hurled like lethal projectiles, hundreds of feet through the air.

The blast piled its victims in frightful heaps seven or eight corpses deep. Then the fireball touched the Earth, and scores of conflagrations, fanned by hurricane winds, joined in a firestorm.

And many thousands more trapped by walls of flame, that leaped higher than the highest tower in the town, were burnt to death, swiftly or in long agony. Then all went black as night. The mushroom cloud rose to 40,000 feet. It blotted out the Sun. It dropped its poison dust, its fallout, on everything that still remained non-lethal in Hiroshima. And death by radioactive sickness from the fallout was the fate of those who had survived the flash, the river, the blast, the firestorm.[13]

Three days later, a second bomb, this one constructed with plutonium, was dropped on Nagasaki. The next day Japan sued for peace.

The war was over, but the atomic era had begun. Atomic scientists knew that the technology could not be kept secret long. This was also explained in the Franck Report, which had urged the display rather than use of the Bomb's power. In the report the scientists recognized their feelings of responsibility for what had been created.

Firestorm at Hiroshima—from *Barefoot Gen*, Keiji Nakazawa (see Contacts, p. 366)

"We feel compelled to take a more active stand now because the success we have achieved in the development of nuclear power is fraught with infinitely greater dangers than were all the inventions of the past." They urged "a specific international agreement barring a nuclear armaments race."[14]

Post-War Atomic Development

One chapter of atomic development ended at Nagasaki. Another was about to begin. What would happen to the atomic program after the war?

Truman's announcement of Hiroshima told people about the program for the first time. He asked for a "commission to control the production and use of atomic power within the United States." The goal? To make sure that "atomic power can become a powerful and forceful influence towards the maintenance of world peace."[15]

Atomic scientists aside, there seems to have been little official consideration of stopping atomic development. Suddenly it became an assumption almost of faith that there in fact existed "future peaceful applications" of atomic technology. Gordon Dean, Chairman of the Atomic Energy Commission (AEC) from 1950 to 1953, called it one of the "basic premises on which future policy could be built."[16] The idea that there were peaceful uses of nuclear energy was a political and psychological necessity—a rationale for accepting a continuing atomic military program.

David Lilienthal, the AEC's first Chairman, later wrote that hopes for a peaceful atom were "inflated": "The basic cause, I think was a conviction, and one that I shared fully, and tried to inculcate in others, that somehow or other the discovery that had produced so terrible a weapon simply *had* to have an important peaceful use... We were grimly determined to prove that this discovery was not just a weapon."[17]

During the early fall of 1945 the U.S. and world public were just hearing about what the atomic program was and what it involved. Much material that had been super-secret was quickly declassified.[18] The war-time production teams broke up as scientists returned to academic life. The British and Canadian missions that worked on the bomb departed as well.

The race to be first to build the bomb left the U.S. with a tremendous physical plant geared to the production of uranium, plutonium, and nuclear weapons. By war's end more than 600,000 people had been part of the production of four bombs. But now the whole operation was at a stand-still, without significant amount of fissionable materials on hand. The unleashing of two bombs in three days may have given the impression that the U.S. military had unlimited atomic striking power. In fact, it did not. But the plant and the labor and money involved in building it had made atomic power part of the U.S. economy.

The atom's future development became a major political issue. Of that time Dean says: "...if things were quiet on the laboratory front, political activity in Washington was furious," as "men were wrestling with the decisions that would determine America's course in the atomic age...building a legal structure that would contain the unleashed atom." Immediate official post-war concerns were: developing the "peaceful" applications of atomic energy; controlling the atom nationally and internationally; maintaining the U.S. monopoly until "an effective system of international control could be set up and placed in effect."[19] These points were all covered in Truman's early public pronouncements on Hiroshima and atomic bombs.

BIKINI—Living With the Bomb—

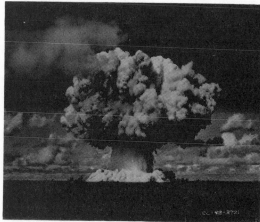

"Baker" Bomb Test, Bikini, 25 July 1946—
From 1946-1958, the U.S. dropped 23 nuclear bombs in the mid-Pacific in a testing program called "Operation Crossroads." The Bikini atoll was a ring of 26 small islands around a central lagoon, part of the Marshall Islands, a U.S. Trust Territory 2,500 miles southwest of Hawaii. (The islands were taken from Japan in 1944.) Several of the islands were blasted away. The lagoon is now filled with twisted wreckage of warships sunk in the tests, which are the largest single source of plutonium pollution in the world.

(Credit: Joint Task Force One, DOE-48-3721)

"Return of Bikinians to Bikini" reads the official caption of this AEC photo. In 1968 the U.S. government decided that the radiation had subsided enough for the people of Bikini to return home. Here they are being given the "good" news by Commissioner Norwood, High Commissioner, U.S. Trust Territories. Most of the 816 Bikinians had been staying in exile on Kili, a remote island 450 miles from Bikini. Some families returned to Bikini in 1972 to replant coconut palms and restore the small island. In 1975, fearing for their health, the people sued for complete radiation tests (not done before) when newly planted coconuts came up orange. Tests showed that the island would not be habitable for another 35-50 years. At the end of August 1978, the Bikinians on the island had to leave, returning to Kili, which they call "the prison." (Credit: U.S. DOE-69-8603)

(Note: How the bikini got its name—The 1954 "Bravo" H-bomb tested at Bikini yielded 15 megatons rather than the expected 6. "It's power so impressed the public that the atoll gave its name to an impressive garment from which the central part vanished." (Inglis, Nuclear Energy, p. 214.)

The U.S. public believed that the bombings of Hiroshima and Nagasaki had brought an end to the long war and had prevented a land invasion of Japan that would have cost many lives, U.S. and Japanese. Feelings of fear, of disgust for the new weapon were evidently eclipsed by the coming of peace.

In the summer of 1946, a year later, the Carnegie Corporation and Rockefeller Foundation funded a study called "Public Reaction to the Atomic Bomb and World Affairs." Around 6,000 people were polled. Half of them said that they were "not at all worried" about the bomb. Three-fourths supported continued bomb manufacture, at least temporarily. Most felt that the U.S. should keep its military secret as long as possible (though they felt that other countries did have or would soon get atomic know-how). One-fifth advocated immediate UN control over atomic development. The report found that: "Though people were not prepared to give the bomb over to the UN at that time the great proportion of them (about 75%) did believe that we should try to work out a system of international control to prevent any nation including the U.S. from using atomic bombs." Only a few more than a third of those asked thought that international control could be successful.[20]

The Atomic Energy Commission

The history of the AEC and JCAE can soberly be described as outrageous.[21]
—Ralph Nader

In early October 1945, Truman urged Congress to establish an Atomic Energy Commission to run all atomic programs, from bomb production to medical uses and research. He called for talks leading to international cooperation on atomic matters.

Congress proceeded to debate two bills that would set up this commission. One allowed for military members (appointed by the President and confirmed by the Senate), the other called for a full-time commission of members with "no conflicting military or business interests."[22] The atomic scientists backed civilian control. After prolonged debate, the civilian commission came into being on 1 August 1946.

The Atomic Energy Act of 1946 established a "five-man" Atomic Energy Commission (AEC) to be appointed by the President for five-year terms, with the advice and consent of the Senate. The law gave the AEC a monopoly in the field of atomic energy. All research, development and production of bombs was to go through the Commission as well as every "peaceful" use of atomic power. The AEC's mission was spelled out in this way:

> ...it is hereby declared to be the policy of the people of the United States, that, subject at all times to the paramount objective of assuring the common defense and security, the development and utilization of atomic energy shall, as far as practicable, be directed toward improving the public welfare, increasing the standard of living, strengthening free competition in private enterprise, and promoting world peace.[23]

Overseeing the AEC was the Joint (Congressional) Committee on Atomic Energy (JCAE), made up of nine Senators and nine Representatives who would be informed of all AEC activities. A civilian nine-member General Advisory Committee would assist the AEC on scientific and technical matters. A Military Liaison committee of representatives from the Army, Navy, and Air Force would advise and consult on military applications of the Commission's work.

As one critic, Roger Rapoport, put it in his excellent book on the U.S. atomic military machine:

> Establishment of the Atomic Energy Commission, and its congressional watchdog, the Joint Committee on Atomic Energy, ranks as one of the nation's major legislative disasters. In their zeal to put atomic energy under civilian control, the legislators merely totalitarianized nuclear power.[24]

There was activity on the international front as well. By mid-1946 the United Nations had an Atomic Energy Commission, too. A U.S. plan for international control was developed by Undersecretary of State Dean Acheson, scientists and atomic luminaries. Issued in March, it was presented to the UNAEC in June 1946 by U.S. delegate Bernard Baruch.

Basically, what became known as the Baruch Plan called for international inspection of all nuclear-related facilities to make sure that no atomic weapons work was being done. Following implementation of such an inspection plan, the U.S. would dispose of its atomic bombs, stop all atomic weapons work and turn over all its atomic energy knowledge to the UN agency.[25]

The Soviet Union refused to go along with the plan, opposing inspection before disarmament. According to Dr. David Inglis, a pioneering nuclear physicist (and wind power expert) much concerned with arms control, "the plan was submitted before the United Nations in modified form by a conservative elder statesman, Bernard Baruch, who placed on it restrictions and a tone of presentation calculated to guarantee Russian rejection."[26]

THE 1950s: ARMS RACE AND COMMERCIALIZATION

The Arms Race

On 23 September 1949, the U.S.S.R. exploded its first atomic weapon. The nuclear arms race was on. In November 1952, the first "clean" bomb—the H-bomb or fusion "super-bomb" which allegedly produced less fallout but was a thousand times more powerful than the A-bomb used at Hiroshima—was tested at Eniwetok by the U.S.

This was the beginning of extensive testing over the South Pacific, testing that would lead to tragedy and disruption for the people of the area. (See p. 6).

The six years following the adoption of atomic power as a national post-war program saw extensive expansion of its atomic materials production and physical plant. In 1951 construction began at Rocky Flats, the plutonium weapons center just 16 miles upwind of Denver.[27]

By 1952, 13 nuclear reactors had been built for weapons production. General Electric built reactors at Hanford, Westinghouse at Argonne, Illinois. Union Carbide ran Oak Ridge. DuPont was chosen to design, build and run a giant facility for plutonium waste reprocessing and storage on South Carolina's Savannah River.

All government work was contracted out to private firms; the government did not do any direct hiring except for the AEC bureaucracy. From research work to weapons construction, the job was—and is now—done by private firms, think tanks, universities. The new infusion of capital ensured the heavy participation and involvement of private industry. Companies that had previously been involved in the war effort naturally tended to have the skills, and the connections, needed for post-war atomic contracts.

Throughout the country, thousands of companies were involved in other weapons production or in developing specialized nuclear equipment. The AEC's contract system of operation slowly built up a powerful industrial alliance that protected it against outside appraisal and political attack.[28]

It is often said that the commercial nuclear power plant program was developed to allay a guilt felt by the atomic establishment as a whole—as if something wonderful had to be made of this awesome power that could be so destructive. The atom-splitters longed to show the peaceful contributions of atomic power, to provide the world with vast, unlimited amounts of electric power.

There are at least two additional reasons. One reason is that the combined existence of vast amounts of nuclear hardware and factories and trained personnel had created an atomic establishment that wanted to insure its continued existence. Building more bombs was one way, meeting future power needs atomically was surely another. Another reason was that the U.S. wanted to keep its edge militarily. The atomic arms race was underway. The commercial program helped justify the huge military expenditures.

Atoms for Peace (and Export)

We need to do something to capture the imagination of the world... Ostensibly, one of the purposes of the program is for the United States to establish itself in the minds of the people of the world as the leaders in the development of the peaceful atom.[29]

—J. Luntz
Editor, *Nucleonics*

The program that Eisenhower outlined before the UN in his famous "Atoms for Peace" speech (December '53) called for agreements with other countries for technical asistance, including the sale of U-235 for peaceful development programs.[30] The speech was rich with U.S. promises of peace, international prosperity and goodwill from the shared development of atomic power.

According to one journalist recorder of the time, the speech and the offer to share peaceful nuclear technology was "part of our cold war strategy. It was first advanced as a key to an increased standard of living for underdeveloped areas."[31]

From the point of view of foreign policy the United States was attempting to alter the image the world had of the United States. We sought to divest ourselves of the stigma with which we had been tagged. Abetted by Soviet propaganda, the world had come to think of us as the nuclear bully preoccupied with the art of dropping megaton size bombs.[32]

For the first time the offer of nuclear technology was introduced as a tool of US foreign policy, a practice that has continued to this day.[33] By the end of 1955, some 25 agreements had been negotiated between other countries and the U.S. State Department and AEC. The international commission urged by Eisenhower was established in 1957: the International Atomic Energy Agency (IAEA). It would supposedly make sure that nuclear material was not diverted to nonpeaceful ends. (See International Section, page 297.)

The Atomic Energy Act of 1954

After Ike's message to the world on sharing the fruits of the peaceful atom, U.S. industry got an invitation too. In 1954 the AEC and President proposed changes in the 1946 Atomic Energy Act that would provide for private ownership of reactors and private patent rights for the production and utilization of fissionable material, previously exclusive rights of the AEC.

The 1954 revisions of the Atomic Energy Act also gave unprecedented powers to the JCAE. According to new provisions, the JCAE would become the only body in Congress that could draft and submit its own legislation and then act as a joint House and Senate "conference committee" to prepare the legislation for final vote.[34]

There was an unusually clear division of support for this move along party lines. Republicans, who controlled House, Senate and JCAE, stood for expanding industry involvement. Democrats and organized labor opposed the changes, seeing them as another government give-away to big business.[35]

In 1954 the AEC began a five year Reactor Development Program with private industry. The first contract was signed in the summer of 1956 with the Yankee Atomic Electric Co., a corporation formed by several New England utilities, for a 185-Mw Westinghouse pressurized water reactor (PWR) in Rowe, Mass. Other permits were issued for Consolidated Edison's PWR at Indian Point, New York, and Commonwealth Edison's G.E. reactor at Dresden, Ill. A construction permit was also sought for the first commercial fast breeder, the Enrico Fermi plant in Monroe, Michigan.

By 1956, when *Atomic Energy for Your Business: Today's Key for Tomorrow's Profits* was published as an atomic primer for businessmen, the atomic energy program had received $14 billion in federal appropriations. The "physical plant and equipment owned by the government of the United States (was) greater than the combined value of plant and equipment of the American Telephone and Telegraph Company, General Motors, and United States Steel altogether... One plant built for the AEC by E.I. DuPont de Nemours Corporation (Savannah River) cost twice as much as the total value of all plants and facilities owned by DuPont at the time."[36]

The Price-Anderson Act

As industry prepared to get financially involved in atomic power, and utilities weighed the costs and benefits, one problem became obvious. Now that industry could legally build nukes and utilities could buy and run them, what would happen in case of an accident? Who would foot the bill? The President of General Electric was one who demanded that Congress adopt legislation that would protect the nuclear industry from liability in case of accident. The Price-Anderson Indemnity Act, first passed in 1957 for a ten-year period, renewed in 1965 and 1976 for additional decades, guaranteed up to $500 million in federal (taxpayer) accident coverage for nuclear accidents. The utilities were to provide for an additional $60 million through joint insurance company pools. Later the figure rose to $125 million.

In passing the legislation, Congress took the spectre of financial responsibility in case of accident away from the utilities and nuclear hardware manufacturers. Unions criticized the act, calling it a further example of government subsidy of the nuclear industry.

In any case, consumers would be the ones to pay. The first report that attempted to give casualty statistics and set dollar figures for losses from a catastrophic accident (a meltdown)—reported that a major accident could cost upwards of $7 billion! And subsequent reports showed that the figure would climb as reactor size grew.

The Fallout Controversy

Man must learn to live with radiation.[37]

—1958 UN Report on Effects of Atomic Radiation

As the pro-atomic forces consolidated their hold on the legislative, administrative and regulatory processes, the AEC met its first big public relations problem—explaining away the dangers of radioactive fallout.

The radiation controversy follows nuclear power from its beginnings to the present. When the bombs were dropped on Japan there was little or no understanding of what the vast amounts of hot fission products (fall-

"Look, Lady-You Don't See Me Worrying"
1957

out) created in the explosion could do. Radiation sickness was seen for the first time following the blast (although numerous scientists had died following contact with radium and other radioactive sources). But this mass affliction was a dreadful scourge, with no known cure. In the interests of science, the U.S. established the American Bomb Casualty Commission at Hiroshima to study the long-term effects of the blast. (They didn't treat people, just examined them, a fact bitterly emphasized by Hiroshima survivors.)

Still radiation was seen as a danger mainly in amounts where immediate damage could be seen—radiation burns, etc. The continuing danger of low levels of radiation was not recognized.

Thus, at first the AEC scientists—like everyone else—knew little of the effects of radiation. Their ignorance continued into the era of the big bomb tests. For instance, at the beginning of the testing, AEC scientists thought that the fallout would disperse itself evenly throughout the earth's atmosphere. Instead, the fission product particles collected in the air streams that circulate around the globe. More fallout was deposited in the north temperate zone than near the equator, and "became far more dangerous than they had originally estimated."

For many years the AEC maintained that the main danger from fallout was radiation that was external to the body. Scientists who were working for the AEC didn't consider the danger of internal radiation caused by taking radioisotopes into the body along with food.

The AEC began a policy—carried out today under its new name—of being the last to accept any new information about radiation dangers.

"Don't Worry. I Don't Think There's Anything in There"

HERBLOCK
DAILY THE WASHINGTON POST CO
1957

Commoner points out (in *Science and Survival*) that in 1953, "the AEC stated that the only possible hazard to humans from strontium-90 (from fallout) would arise from the ingestion of bone splinters which might be intermingled with muscle tissue during butchering and cutting of the meat." No mention was made of the simple biological fact that the milk from such an animal would also contain strontium-90. By 1956 the AEC had acknowledged that milk represented the most important food source of strontium-90.[38]

Radiation danger really "came home" after the summer of 1953, when it was learned that in April heavy rains in Troy, New York had brought to earth radioactive debris from Nevada nuclear tests.[39] One important radioactive fission product was recognized—strontium-90.

Fallout became a campaign issue for Adlai Stevenson when he ran against Eisenhower in 1956. He lost, but concern about fallout grew. In February 1957 the AFL-CIO held a national conference for affiliated unions on atomic radiation hazards.

Covering Up

The AEC's denial of fallout as a health problem and subsequent efforts to deny and contain the problem by harassing dissenting scientists is well known (and in fact continues to this day). Chet Holifield (D. Calif.) was a member of the JCAE who would go on to become the most powerful member of the committee and (with ally Craig Hosmer, also of Calif.) the staunchest advocate of AEC positions on safety, etc. But back in 1957, even he had to say: "I believe from our hearings that the AEC approach to the hazards from the bomb test fallout seems to add up to a party line—'play it down.'"[40]

The fallout cover-up was to be the first of many AEC failures that included unnecessary exposure of miners to cancer-causing radon gas in uranium mines; allowing uranium mill tailings—the radon-rich leftovers of uranium ore milling—to be used as harmless fill for homes, schools, and roads, etc. in several southwestern states; harassing opposition scientists; suppression of evidence that would reflect poorly on the AEC and the nuclear industry.

Atomic power was becoming industrialized and institutionalized. Radioactive tracers were being adapted for a variety of industrial processes for measurement and leak/break detection. Hospital use of isotopes was increasing. Although these uses accounted for a miniscule percentage of the radioactive wastes produced in nuclear reactors, they were used to justify the "peaceful" atomic program. Meanwhile, a variety of new books explained the mysteries of atomic power to the public, almost always in glowing terms.[41]

Project Plowshare:
Planetary Engineering
Although it has dropped from the current vocabulary of federal energy literature, Plowshare ("and they shall turn their swords into plowshares") was a treasured and much acclaimed AEC "Peaceful Atom" program. By 1970, its last funded year, it had received $138 million of federal research and development funds.

Plowshare involved what AEC Chairman Glenn Seaborg termed "nuclear excavation." The builders of the big bombs noticed the weapon's ability to move tremendous amounts of earth, creating vast craters on land and perfectly round holes in the ocean offshore. Plowshare could mean instant harbors; a new, wider, sea level Panama Canal ($17 million and 6 years were spent studying that one); underground caverns for storing natural gas and even water (!), etc. As Seaborg put it: "Large nuclear explosives give us, for the first time, the capability to remedy nature's oversights."[42]

But there were to be problems involved. The 1963 Limited Test Ban Treaty stopped above-ground nuclear explosions. And the danger from radioactive fallout in the project area made it difficult to find sites where people would accept the "excavating."

In 1963, ex-AEC Chairman David Lilienthal would comment: "Without judging the details of these undertakings, the important thing they show is how far scientists and administrators will go to try to establish a non-military use (for atomic power)."[43]

As the 1950s drew to a close, the AEC's propaganda show "Atoms for Peace" was seen by 2.2 million people. Its exhibits were widely shown in U.S. schools and abroad.[44]

The 1960s:
Nuclear Plants and More Fallout
The accumulated power of the AEC began to manifest itself in the 1960s. Electricity was coming from the first commercial nuclear plants, including the Navy-run PWR at Shippingport, Pa. Then in January 1961, three men were killed at the SL-1 reactor in Idaho Falls. However, since this was an "experimental" reactor and not a "commercial" one, their deaths were not attributed to the nuclear program. Meanwhile, the 1958 explosion of stored atomic wastes in the USSR (see page 128) was successfully kept secret by the CIA, and presented no threat to the burgeoning U.S. nuclear program. In 1962, the AEC reported to President Kennedy that nuclear power was on the "threshold" of economic competitiveness. Said the AEC's Chairman Glenn Seaborg: "...relatively modest assistance by the AEC will insure the crossing of that threshold and bring about widespread acceptance by the

"Rock-A-Bye Baby. In The Tree Top—Let's Make Believe The Fallout Will Stop"

1957

utility industry."[45] Looking back on the 1960s Seaborg wrote:

> The years 1963-1967 constituted a crucial period of change for nuclear power. Costs came down further as nuclear power proponents drew up plans for 500-megawatt, and even 1000-megawatt power plants. The first sign of a real economic breakthrough came in 1964 with the selection of nuclear power for the Oyster Creek Plant by the Jersey Central Power & Light Company. More of the new large competitive nuclear plants were selected as other utilities climbed on the nuclear bandwagon. Roughly half of the new large-size commercial power plants ordered in 1966 and 1967 were nuclear. Some analysts saw a turning point; by A.D. 2000, the projections predicted that half of the electric power in the United States would be nuclear.[46]

But others did not see such a rosy situation for atomic power. The dozen atomic plants that were to be built by utilities alone or with AEC help under the Cooperative Power Reactor Demonstration Program all ran into problems. Costs escalated. There were long delays and technical problems. In 1963 a study by economist Phillip Mullenbach concluded that:

> ...eight years after the passage of the 1954 (Atomic Energy) act, (private utilities) had constructed only two full-scale plants without heavy government assistance, and these two were among the very first announced. The evidence raises the question whether the private utilities are prepared even at

this late date to make the large investments called for by full-scale nuclear power.[47]

The industry was "saved" by GE's offer of a 500-Mw BWR to New Jersey Central Power and Light Company at a cost that would make nuclear power cheaper than coal. The offer was a great "economic breakthrough" for atomic power. Actually, GE was trying to improve business by offering reactors at or below cost. Westinghouse made similar offers, and utility orders for nuclear power plants suddenly jumped. By April 1968, about 100 reactors were operable, under construction, or being ordered.[48]

In effect, GE and Westinghouse were taking a calculated risk: that they could afford to lose money initially to get the market for nuclear reactors going. They had to convince private utilities that nuclear power was indeed cost-competitive with coal-fired plants.

The Fermi Fast Breeder

An account of the 1960s is not complete without mention of the Enrico Fermi liquid metal fast breeder reactor. Michigan's Detroit Edison headed the utility group that built the reactor at Lagoona Beach, on the shores of Lake Erie about 20 miles from Detroit.

It was an ambitious project—to build the first commercial fast breeder in the world. The nuke would be fueled with enriched uranium and engineered in such a way that plutonium would be created. (See pp. 11-13). Another big difference in this reactor would be the moderator. Whereas in light-water nukes water is the reactor core coolant, in breeders of this type liquid sodium is used. It is a very volatile substance, exploding on contact with air or water.

The project could not have been considered without extensive government aid. Its sponsors got free design research, cheap uranium fuel, waste storage and a government promise to buy the plutonium produced. When the builders applied for a construction permit from the AEC in January 1956, the project's cost estimate was $40 million. Final costs were $130 million.[49]

The project was a risky one. The EBR-1, an experimental fast breeder reactor built by the AEC at their Idaho Falls testing station had an accident that melted the fuel rods, destroying the model reactor. Fortunately, the mass of the melted fuel had not formed a critical mass and there was no explosion. But the November 1955 accident at this small Fermi-type reactor gave the new plant's builders cause for concern. For Fermi would be 300 times larger than the EBR-1.

In August 1956 the project got an AEC construction license before major health and safety questions had been answered. By the end of the month United Auto Worker President Walter Reuther charged that the AEC had not shown that a meltdown would not lead to an explosion. "Reuther claimed that building such a plant would endanger at least three million people in a thirty-mile radius around the plant."[50]

Spearheaded by Reuther, the AFL-CIO sued to stop construction. In June 1960 the Court of Appeals ruled that Fermi's construction permit was illegal. The AEC and utilities appealed to the Supreme Court. But construction continued with AEC permission.

Reuther's fears seemed confirmed by yet another accident. This one took place at the SL-1 test reactor—not a breeder—also in Idaho Falls. Three men were killed on 3 January 1961 as they moved fuel rods in a "routine" preparation for the reactor start-up. They were so heavily exposed that hands and heads had to be buried separately with other radioactive waste. As construction continued,

Reuther released a study of 40 reactor accidents. Some were minor, but all potentially serious.[51] A growing number of scientists and critics spoke out against the plant.

The Supreme Court did give the plant the go-ahead and it was eventually built, opening for the first time in early 1966. Then on 5 October 1966, it had a major accident—a partial fuel meltdown. (See John G. Fuller's *We Almost Lost Detroit.*) The plant was finally decommissioned in the early 1970s without ever producing a substantial amount of electricity. The Enrico Fermi project represented the highest hopes and lowest results of the program for peaceful atomic power.

The Test Ban Treaty

Meanwhile, the fallout controversy continued. By the early 1960s people were organizing. Women across the country were alarmed. The Women's Strike for Peace was formed; SANE and other groups were also active against continued bomb testing.

The controversy grew until the U.S.-U.S.S.R. Limited Nuclear Test Ban Treaty of 1963 ended super-power atmospheric testing. Now the main fallout danger would come from French and later Chinese above ground testing, from unplanned releases of radiation from underground testing, and from the existing fallout still circling the north temperate zone in the stratosphere.

Estimates of the "human cost of fallout" varied widely. But a UN committee suggested that tests up to 1958 had caused anywhere from 2,500 to 10,000 serious genetic defects.[52]

Intervention

In communities faced with atomic reactor construction small groups of concerned citizens and scientists organized to oppose nuclear plants in their areas: in New York at Indian Point; in California at Bodega Head... They hired lawyers and began the slow, expensive, often frustrating experience of challenging the AEC's regulatory arm. (See Sec. 5, Chap. 1)

Diversion

Theft of nuclear materials—known in the industry as "diversion"—became real in 1965 when it was discovered that 400 pounds of bomb grade uranium was missing from the Zion nuclear plant in Illinois. The AEC accepted the operating company's explanation—that the fuel was used up in the production process or in "gaseous effluence." Although outside investigation pointed to illegal diversion, the FBI refused to get involved. The JCAE challenged the AEC's explanations, but there was evidentally no follow-up action. The missing uranium was never found.[53]

The 1960s in Retrospect

The 1960s marked a time when U.S. government activities became seen and understood in a new light. Americans witnessed their nation's armed intervention in Third World countries, government spying and infiltration, suppression of black liberation movements, police violence, government-Mafia collaboration, media intimidation. The civil rights and peace movements—along with photos, television reports, war casualties—revealed to the public the extent of the problems and the need for action.

The first stirrings of public opposition to the government's atomic program were eclipsed by other social movements going on during the 60s. But a growing ecological awareness at the end of the decade, plus the widespread growth of atomic plants, created the conditions for increased public awareness and opposition in the decade to come.

"You Said It, Pal—We Both Got A Right To Poison The Air"   1956

THE 1970s:

1970-1978: Challenges to Power

In 1975, atomic energy celebrated its 30th anniversary. On that day a declaration was presented to Congress and the President that was signed by more than 2,000 biologists, chemists, engineers, and other scientists. It urged a "drastic reduction" in nuclear construction and a suspension of nuclear plant exports.

On that day also, thousands of people met in Hiroshima—as they do each year on August 6—and demanded world peace with an end to nuclear power, in both its civilian and military forms.

The 1970s saw the end of the Vietnam War, Nixon's Watergate, and the spread of the women's movement. In energy, the decade has so far brought big changes in energy politics as well. The 1973 oil embargo that triggered the U.S.'s first "energy crisis" made people more aware that fossil fuels were on the way out and would be increasingly expensive. The energy corporations knew it too and continued to invest in uranium as well as coal—and, increasingly, solar technology. They would not be "caught short."

The AEC-JCAE's arrogance of power was revealed for all who cared to see. Cover-ups were exposed, along with the now usual gamut of conflict-of-interest cases, character assassination, and more. Although twice reorganized, the government branch of the atomic-industrial complex was still going strong in 1978, with a regulating agency that had yet to refuse one nuclear plant license.

Would uranium and plutonium be the fuels of the future? It certainly looked that way as the decade opened. But as the number of nuclear plants jumped from around 20 to nearly 80, with more under construction and planned, opposition spread. So did interest in alternatives to nuclear power. The 1970s would see a lot of solar-related experiments and increasing commercialization of alternative energy sources.

The following pages present just some of the major events from 1970-1978 that are important in the history of commercial atomic power in the U.S. For greater detail, consult resources at the end of chapter and in footnotes.

Towards a Nuclear Future
Between 1960 and 1970, energy use doubled in the U.S. The electric way was the clean, modern way. It seemed like the future was set. Advertising encouraged heavy electrical use. In 1969 alone, utilities spent $323.8 million on sales and advertising—and $41 million on research and development.[54] Utilities gave heavy electrical users promotional rates: the more energy used, the lower the price. For example, a resi-

dential TVA customer would pay 4¢ for the first 75 kilowatt hours used each month, but only 1¢ per kwh if more than 500 kwh were used during the month.[55]

Consumption patterns seemed to be set in a never-ending upwards spiral. Future production patterns were set too. Although in 1969 there were only 16 nukes licensed to operate in the U.S., 54 were under construction and 35 more had been ordered.

Meanwhile, the AEC was furious about new environmental laws and citizen-scientist intervention in plant licensing proceedings. At the time, nuclear plants were producing a mere 1% of the nation's electricity. Still, in 1971, an AEC spokesman predicted "power shortages" if the "constipated licensing machinery" involved in nuclear construction wasn't "unplugged."[56]

Radiation: Revelations
In 1969 the AEC's radiation-protection standards were publicly revealed to be so high as to cause thousands of cases of infant mortality and cancer. The controversy found the AEC attacking its own research scientists. The battle dates back to 1963 when Glenn Seaborg asked noted medical physicist and doctor John Gofman to study the effects of radiation released during the agency's atomic tests and peaceful programs on people.

> In 1963 we were asked by the Atomic Energy Commission to undertake long-range studies of the potential dangers for man and other species from a variety of so-called "peaceful uses of the atom." Nuclear electricity generation is one such atomic program. Naturally, we presumed that the Atomic Energy Commission seriously wanted to

Dr. John Gofman
(Credit: Lionel Delevingne)

know the truth concerning the magnitude of possible hazards. In fact, in assigning this study mission to us, Chairman Glenn Seaborg assured us that he wanted favorable or unfavorable findings made available to the public. "All we want is the truth," Chairman Seaborg said in 1963.

We have learned, to our great dismay, that these assurances were illusory. It is now clear to us that the Atomic Energy Commission had not contemplated seriously that the studies might reveal serious flaws and dangers in the "peaceful atom" programs. This kind of "truth" has proved to be quite unwelcome.[57]

After years of study, Gofman and his associate at the AEC's Lawrence Radiation Laboratory in Livermore, California, Dr. Arthur Tamplin, came out with their findings. In October 1969 they demanded a ten-fold reduction of the AEC's maximum permissible-radiation dose to the general population—from 170 millirads a year to 17 millirads annually. They said that "the hazard to this generation of humans from cancer and leukemia is TWENTY TIMES as great as had been thought previously. The hazard to all future generations in the form of genetic damage and deaths, had been *underestimated* even more seriously."[58] The scientists calculated that if everyone were exposed from birth to the "permissible" dose of 0.170 rads (assuming a 2% increase in cancer per additional rad of exposure), then **there could be an additional 32,000 cancer deaths each year, and from 150,000 to 1,500,000 extra genetic deaths per year.**[59]

Prior to the Gofman-Tamplin investigation, radiation hazard estimation was the exclusive domain of three groups: the National Council on Radiation Protection (NCRP), the International Commission on Radiological Protection (ICRP), and the Federal Radiation Council (FRC). The NCRP and ICRP were non-governmental organizations of scientists in the field of radiation-protection. They recommended radiation standards. The FRC was created to set official guidelines in 1959, to "offset concern about the fallout from weapons testing. The limits were established, however, with little experience and without accurate, well-developed statistical data."[60]

The Gofman-Tamplin findings were considered "heresy" by the AEC. Within months the responses came. The head of the NCRP completely rejected their conclusions. In a well-documented pattern of both petty and substantial harassment, the AEC had their staff "reassigned" and refused to pay them for days spent at meetings where they might be testifying about AEC laxity on the radiation-protection front. Meanwhile, other AEC staff were paid for attendance at meetings where they gave the correct "line" on radiation dangers—no problem.[61]

The Director of the FRC, Dr. Paul Tompkins, testified at Congressional hearings in Augusts 1970 that "the FRC guides must not be construed as an 'allowed' dose which could result in every person in the United States eventually being exposed up to the allowed level." In other words, the FRC doesn't want the U.S. population exposed to these limits even though they are "allowable." Testimony at the hearings showed that economics were a major FRC concern in arriving at guidelines. Said Tompkins: "The primary objective of the FRC is to make recommendations which represent a reasonable balance between biological risk and the impact on uranium mining."[62]

The Gofman-Tamplin hearings found support in the scientific community despite the AEC's campaign of harassment and "official denial."[63]

The controversy would not go away. In 1970 the National Academy of Sciences, at the request of the Secretary of Health, Education and Welfare, created the Advisory Committee of the Biological Effects of Ionizing Radiation (the BEIR Committee). It would investigate the Gofman-Tamplin data and evaluate existing AEC radiation standards.

The Committee released its report in 1972. It concluded that full exposure to the 170 millirem limit could cause from around 3,000 to 15,000 cancer deaths each year, with the "most likely" estimate being 6,000 death/year. Although the committee did not arrive at the same statistics as had Gofman and Tamplin, it agreed that current exposure standards were "unnecessarily high" and that radiation hazards had been seriously underestimated.[64] It is important to note that since their report *no change* had been made in the 170 millirem/year "allowable" limit.

By 1971 the AEC had tacitly admitted its error by proposing a hundredfold reduction in routine emission standards—5 millirem per person per year at the power plant boundary as opposed to the previous 5 rem standard. Emissions had to be kept "as low as practicable" (ALAP!).

But the ALAP standard created another controversy, since, by definition, "as low as practicable" implies that the role of the AEC was to determine not the "safest" level of emissions, but the lowest level of emissions that could be attained without causing excessive economic penalties for nuclear power producers.[65]

—Ralph Nader, 1975

There is no "end" to the radiation standard controversy. It continues today. Drs. Gofman and Tamplin left the AEC and have continued their work as independent researchers. The atomic establishment's rejection of data and findings that show the dangers of small amounts of radiation, of occupational exposure, and of past fallout continue to this day. "Dissident" scientists continue to evoke industry wrath and refutation—or attempts at it. (The attacks on Drs. Ernest Sternglass and Thomas Mancuso will be looked at in Chap. 4: Health Dangers.)

NEPA

The new National Environmental Policy Act went into effect on the first day of 1970. NEPA required the AEC to prepare an environmental impact statement (known as an "EIS") for nuclear plants before initial licensing. The statement would cover environmental effects of nuclear projects as well as possible alternative power sources and locations.

NEPA also created the Environmental Protection Agency (EPA). This agency would be responsible for establishing national pollution and radiation standards.

By the early 1970s, citizen intervenors with their scientific and legal experts were becoming ever more aggressive. Although victories were small and frustrations many, the interventions did manage to make plants somewhat safer, mitigate some of the worst environmental damage (through addition of cooling towers, for example), and did slow down the AEC's licensing process. According to the AEC, the average time for issuing construction permits had jumped from just over 10 months in 1967 to more than 20 in 1971. Delays were blamed on NEPA, the 1970 Water Quality Improvement Act, and of course the intervenors.[66]

It appeared that interventions might increase, not decrease, because of the new environmental legislation brought about by a new national consciousness of environmental problems. Before NEPA there was no basis in law for opposition to a nuclear plant because of environmental issues such as thermal pollution.

> Until 1970, the statutory basis for issuing a construction permit was the consideration of the "common defense and security" and the "health and safety of public." The AEC interpreted this language to mean that only the safety issue could be raised at the construction- or operating-license hearings.[67]

Now NEPA promised the opportunity for a more thorough environmental review—*if* the AEC would implement the law. The Calvert Cliffs case resulted in a landmark decision that supported and clarified NEPA as it related to atomic power plants.

Calvert Cliffs

The case involved the construction of twin 850-megawatt reactors by the Baltimore Gas and Electric Co. on a bank of the Chesapeake Bay about 30 miles from Washington, D.C. In 1969, a group of citizens who were mainly concerned with thermal pollution of the bay intervened at construction hearings. The AEC refused to consider the questions raised. The intervenors sued, claiming that NEPA required early consideration of this major environmental issue. The AEC said it had the right to limit consideration of nonradiological factors, like thermal pollution, to projects that had applied for a permit or license after 4 March 1971. This was a seemingly arbitrary date, fully 16 months after NEPA had theoretically gone into effect. The AEC's action would exempt the Calvert Cliffs plants and all others then under construction from the new law's requirements.

In July 1971 the U.S. Court of Appeals in D.C. decided in favor of the intervenors. Justice Wright outlined in some detail how the AEC should meet NEPA's requirements. In all, it upheld the intent of the Act:

> ...the very purpose of NEPA was to tell federal agencies that environmental protection is as much a part of their responsibility as is protection and promotion of the industries they regulate.[!] Whether or not the specter of a national power crisis is as real as the Commission apparently believes, it must not be used to create a blackout of environmental considerations.[68]

The court decision meant that 63 pending license applications involving 91 nuclear plants and 5 operating licenses were now open to environmental review. But the victory didn't prevent any plants from being built. About half-built at the time of the decision, the Calvert Cliff plants were completed in 1975 and 1977, two and three years behind schedule.

Just two days before the Calvert Cliffs decision, Glenn Seaborg resigned after ten years as AEC Chairman. In what one author has termed a "surprising move," Nixon appointed as his successor economist James Schlesinger, who had been assistant director of the Office of Management and Budget and had directed a nuclear-proliferation study at the RAND Corporation, the government's oldest think-tank. William O. Doub was appointed to a vacancy on the Commission. He had been on the President's Air Quality Advisory Board and chairman of the Maryland Public Service Commission when it tried to get jurisdiction over Calvert Cliffs plant siting. "These positions seemed to give him credentials acceptable to the environmentalists."[69]

> The Changing of the Guard at the AEC was exactly what it appeared to be: an effort to improve the image, reduce the agency's rather conspicuous credibility gap, and appease the environmentalist movement at the expense of the electrical industry, the gas industry, and the big oil companies that were running much of the energy establishment.[70]

One effect of these appointments was that the Calvert Cliffs Case was not appealed to the Supreme Court. In a speech to the nuclear industry shortly after his appointment. Schlesinger told them that from then on the AEC would act "as the referee of nuclear power, not its promoter."[71] But dramatic changes in AEC policy were not forthcoming, despite less of a pro-industry "line."

States Rights vs. the Atomic Establishment

Another important legal case that did make it to the Supreme Court was the 1971 *Northern States Power Company v. The State of Minnesota*. It upheld what is known as "federal pre-emption"—the government's right under the Atomic Energy Act of 1954 to regulate atomic energy without state interference.

The case began in 1968 as Minnesota tried to make the utility building a 640-megawatt plant in Monticello meet state radiation protection standards. Based on light-water reactor technology's capabilities, the state's requirements on radiation releases were 100 times more restrictive than the AEC's.

Members of the AEC, August 1972: Commissioners James Ramey, Clarence Larson, Dixy Lee Ray, William Doub, Chairman James Schlesinger. (Credit: J.E. Westcott, AEC, DOE-72-9772)

Northern States Power maintained that the state could not enact regulations more stringent than the AEC/government. The utility did admit that it could achieve state standards for its reactor, but said in court that it would be "impossible to comply fully" with the requirements. For to do so would delay construction for two years while safety-systems and filters were added, at a cost of $20 million in lost power production. The extra construction costs could be $9.5 million, and there were additional problems. It was a clear case of what chronicler Richard Lewis called the "*Cost vs. Radioactivity* issue."[72]

The case attracted a lot of attention because of the states-right issue. Eight other states and the Southern Governors' Conference joined Minnesota as "friends of the court" in the appeal. Although the state lost in both District and Supreme Courts, there were several positive results.

The conflict of radiation standards brought to light the fact that the AEC's standards were unreasonably lax. If plants were capable of releasing one-hundredth of the maximum radiation allowed by the AEC, then why not lower the federal limits?

Although Northern States won, they had already had to pay a price. In September 1970 the plant got its operating license from the AEC. The following April, Governor Wendell Anderson recommended to the state legislature "a moratorium on further construction of new nuclear power plants in Minnesota until such time as the Minnesota Pollution Control Agency (PCA) certifies that the new development can safely begin." The very next day the company wrote the state PCA that they would reduce emissions by 80% or more. The state had won a *de facto* victory. A new kind of nuclear power plant regulation had emerged—regulation by intervention of the citizens. Or, as utility men put it, by the "mob."[73]

The states right issue did not end there. Legislation was introduced in Congress to allow states to set more stringent standards than the AEC. It was defeated in 1972-73. Congressman Morris K. Udall (D. Ariz.) introduced similar legislation in 1977.

State action has continued to be effective in other areas concerning nuclear projects: land use and zoning, utility regulation, public health and safety, and the development of alternatives. Vermont was the first state to require the approval of its legislature for any new nuclear project (April '75). Since there are no plans for a second plant in Vermont, that law has not been challenged in the courts.[74]

The ECCS and Reactor Safety

Development of new reactor styles came faster than the research that would back it up. From 1967 to 1972, as world-wide orders for new giant 1000-Mw plants came into GE, Westinghouse and (to a lesser extent) Bechtel and Combustion Engineering, the federal light-water safety budget declined yearly—from about $31 million in 1967 to about $24 million five years later.[75] One rationale for the declining figure was that the government hoped to stimulate industry into doing its own safety research. It didn't work. Actually, federal funds needed for commercial light-water reactor safety research were going towards development of the contested Liquid Metal Fast Breeder Reactor, to be the "next generation" of power producers.

Key to reactor safety was the effectiveness of the emergency core cooling system, or ECCS. This safety system would flood a reactor core with water in case the reactor lost its primary coolant." Without adequate water in the core, the nuclear fuel could "melt down." (See pp. 112-113.)

In 1970, the AEC's six model ECCS tests in Idaho failed. The AEC's efforts to cover up the results failed too. Intervenors discovered what had happened. The results, among other things, gave them increasing reason to believe that the safety system would not work in case of accident. "Rather than rehash the ECCS issue at every licensing hearing, the AEC and intervenors prepared to have a showdown on the matter."[76]

The hearings opened in January 1978. Eighteen long months of testimony followed. The sum of the evidence revealed quite cleared that study and testing of the ECCS were inadequate. As a "last defense" before a fuel meltdown, the ECCS was very probably a dud. Internal correspondence and memoranda obtained by the Union of Concerned Scientists (who represented citizen intervenors in the hearings), revealed that top AEC officials thought so too.[77]

Regulatory Transformations
By the mid-70s, continuing revelations about the AEC forced a reorganization of the agency. In 1973, under threat of a Freedom of Information request filed by environmentalists David Comey and Friends of the Earth, the AEC released documents showing a cover-up of a 1964 reactor safety study. The study was an update of the 1957 WASH-740 report which had estimated that a "worst possible accident" could kill 3,400 people, injure 43,000, and cause $7 billion in property damage. The 1964 figures showed an increase in accident statistics: 45,000 people could die, 100,000 could be injured, with property damage of $17 billion or more! No wonder the AEC tried to hide the results. The internal documents had shown "a suppression of the 1964 update which was routine and repeated."[78]

Although ex-Commissioner Doub would tell a gathering of anti-nuclear activists in 1974 that: "The story about AEC secrecy...could perhaps not even have been written if we had not done such a complete turnaround on the policy of disclosure between 1971 and 1974," it was clear that the AEC-JCAE

atomic fiefdom was still working to promote nuclear power at all costs.[79] Further bad news for the AEC was the discovery of leaks in high-level waste storage tanks at the AEC's Hanford reservation in June 1973. The accidental leaks reflected poorly on the AEC/industry's ability to manage nuclear waste—even temporarily.

Since 1975, the AEC has been reorganized twice. The Energy Reorganization Act of 1974, effective 1 January 1975, split the promotional and regulatory functions of the agency. The promotional end—reactor development, military uses and research including non-nuclear energy development—were assigned to the newly formed Energy Research and Development Administration (ERDA). The licensing and regulatory functions were placed under the new Nuclear Regulatory Commission (NRC). Like the AEC, the NRC has five commissioners appointed by the President. The Atomic Safety and Licensing Board (ASLB) and the Atomic Safety and Licensing Appeal Board (ASLAB) were relocated to the NRC. The NRC would also control nuclear material safety and safeguards and do some assessment of commercial reactor safety.

Although the names changed, few of the faces did. Of ERDA's "new" staff, 84.3% were former AEC employees, mainly concentrated in the new agency's nuclear divisions.[80] Before ERDA went through another name-change, Ralph Nader would write:

There is serious question about ERDA's ability to develop decentralized, "low-technology" energy options such as solar energy or conservation—because of ERDA's major bias towards centralized, high-technology, and, particularly, nuclear, options. John M. Teem, ERDA assistant administrator for solar, geothermal, and advanced energy systems, resigned in January 1976 and later charged that the Ford administration was not giving solar energy the priority or support it deserved.[81]

Meanwhile, the powerful JCAE was under attack from all sides. Although in 1975 it succeeded in pushing through a ten-year extension of the Price-Anderson Act guaranteeing federal nuclear accident insurance, its days were numbered. Congress could no longer afford to ignore the Committee's blatant defense of the nuclear industry and the AEC. In 1975 the JCAE lost two important bills it backed. One came from the powerful Bechtel Company via the Ford administration. Their Nuclear Fuel Assurance Act would have provided $8 billion in federal guarantees to private companies building nuclear fuel enrichment facilities, like Bechtel. The other was a weak anti-proliferation bill, submitted by the JCAE to head off a stronger bill drafted by the House International Relations Committee.[82]

By the end of 1976, the most vehement supporters of nuclear power had all left the Committee. Nuke boosters Chet Holifield and Craig Hosmer retired in 1975, Senator John Pastore (D., R.I.) in 1976. In December 1976, the newly elected Democratic majority stripped the JCAE of its legislative powers. The next month they were assigned to five existing committees. The long period of JCAE hegemony in atomic affairs had ended.

The Department of Energy

On 4 August 1977 Jimmy Carter signed the Department of Energy Organization Act. The next day James R. Schlesinger was confirmed by the Senate as its first "Secretary of Energy." The DOE opened its doors on October 1 with a first-year budget of $10.4 billion and a staff of nearly 20,000 people inherited from the agencies now reorganized under the DOE. These included ERDA, the Federal Power Commission and programs from the Departments of Interior, Commerce, Housing and Urban Development and the Interstate Commerce Commission.[83]

Creation of the Cabinet-level Department was one part of the Carter energy program. Although the DOE would encourage the development of non-nuclear energy sources, a nuclear bias remained, reflected in budget priorities and staff selection. Although candidate Carter had termed nuclear power a "last resort," saying that they should be constructed underground— if at all—the new Carter energy plan still called for around 350 nuclear plants in the U.S. by the turn of the century.[84] Although this was down from the Nixon goal of 1,000, it offered little encouragement for the growing number of Americans who opposed any further nuclear construction.

Carter did please environmentalists in April 1977, when he announced that the U.S. would "defer indefinitely all civilian processing of spent nuclear fuel." The action was taken to "reduce the risk of nuclear weapons proliferation" through theft of nuclear materials.[85] Although it would slow down production of plutonium for future breeder reactors, the decision also meant that there would be more spent fuel to store. This would increase the pressure for a long-term solution to the nuclear garbage mess.

In October 1977, the administration announced a new plan whereby the government would take responsibility for all nuclear waste storage for a one-time storage fee. The proposal let utilities off the hook on the storage question. The unprofitable and difficult parts of the nuclear fuel cycle would be "nationalized," at taxpayer expense, while the utilities could profit from their "private" investments—nuclear plants.

By the late 70s, it was well-known to atomic power watchers—whose number was ever-increasing—that the atomic industry had failed to protect the public. Minor accidents at nuclear plants were common. The fire at Alabama's Browns Ferry reactors in March 1975 was yet another close call. Leftover "tailings" from uranium milling remained in piles at various locations in the Southwest. They polluted ground water there and more (see p. 102). New evidence showed that the NRC had underestimated the health effects of uranium mining by a factor of 100,000!

Although funds for the Clinch River breeder reactor long planned for Oak Ridge were vetoed by the President, enough money was restored by Congress to allow the program to limp along (along the pork barrel path). The breeder, though hotly contested, was still around.

The death of plutonium worker Karen Silkwood in November 1974 raised many questions. Was she killed because she knew about a plant cover-up of defective fuel rods? Was there even more going on at the Kerr-McGee plant in Oklahoma? In any case, her death at least made people more aware of the danger faced by nuclear workers on the job.

And the Chickens Come Home to Roost

The lies, the cover-ups, the billions of taxpayer dollars wasted in nuclear programs, the callousness and deceit of the atomic establishment, all resulted in the growth of a broad citizen movement opposed to continued development of commercial atomic power.

Early critics of the 1960s were now joined by more small groups of intervenors, as well as Ralph Nader, and new organizations like the Union of Concerned Scientists, the Consolidated National Intervenors, the Task Force on Nuclear Pollution, the Friends of the Earth and more.

In November 1976, voters in six western states defeated a variety of referenda on nuclear power and safeguards. Although the referenda were voted down—as was the California major safeguards referendum in June 1976—the issue was brought before the public as never before.

As people learned about nuclear power and legal action against plants failed to stop their construction, a new activist wing of the movement emerged. Although citizen opposition remained based on public education—informing others of nuclear power dangers—civil disobedience was adopted as a tactic as well. Non-violent direct action against nuclear plants began with Sam Lovejoy's tower-toppling. Group civil disobedience actions were organized by the New England-based Clamshell Alliance and other Alliances formed from 1977 on. (See pp. 393-400.)

Nuclear power was an international issue as well. Because other countries do not have similarly involved licensing procedures, public opposition took on more direct forms: petitions, demonstrations, finally site occupations, and a number of violent confrontations with police and national army troops. In other countries, such as the Philippines, no public opposition was tolerated at all. (See Sect. 4, The International Story)

The movement against nuclear power will be discussed in Sections 4 and 5. As we look at the stories of nuclear opponents in this country and others, we see a similar pattern of increased awareness, increased understanding, increased anger, increased action.

And the story is still unfolding...

Footnotes

1. Glenn T. Seaborg, William R. Corliss, *Man and Atom: Building a New World Through Nuclear Technology* (New York: E.P. Dutton & Co., 1971), p. 13.

2. Scientific research following Hahn and Strassman's January 1939 paper on neutron bombardment of uranium was intense. Within a year more than 100 scientific papers were published on atomic fission.

3. Otto Nathan and Heinz Norden, eds., *Einstein on Peace* (New York: Simon and Schuster, 1960). p. 295. Emigre physicists Enrico Fermi, Leo Szilard, Eugene P. Wigner, Victor F. Weisskopf and Edward Teller were especially concerned about reported German research: "Reports reached the United States that Germany had discontinued the export to all foreign countries of uranium ore from Czechoslovakia, which was now under German control, and that an entire section of the Kaiser-Wilhelm-Gesellschaft of Berlin was engaged in secret work involving atomic research directed toward the achievement of a nuclear chain reaction." (p. 289) Szilard was the main force behind the Einstein-FDR letter; Wigner and Teller accompanied him on visits to Einstein.

4. Roger Rapoport, *The Great American Bomb Machine* (New York: E.P. Dutton & Co., 1971). pp. 19-20. Also: Leslie R. Groves, *Now It Can Be Told: The Story of the Manhattan Project* (New York: Harper & Bros., 1962), pp. 230-233.

5. Rapoport, *op. cit.*, p. 20.

6. Stephane Groueff, *Manhattan Project* (Boston: Little, Brown & Co., 1967), p. xi.

7. *Ibid.*, p. 340.

8. *Ibid.*, p. 214.

9. Oppenheimer was a politically controversial figure due to his close contacts with Communist Party members during the 1930s. He continued to be active and influential in postwar atomic politics until 1953 when he was deemed a security risk. This may have also had something to do with the fact that he opposed development of the H-bomb. By 1954 he had lost his security clearances and was out of the atomic establishment. See Philip Stern's, *The Oppenheimer Case*, (New York: Harper & Row, 1969).

10. Groueff, *op. cit.*, pp. 251-258.

11. David R. Inglis, *Nuclear Energy—Its Physics and Its Social Challenge* (Reading Ma: Addison-Wesley Pub. Co., 1973), pp. 220-221.

12. The Franck Report was submitted to the Secretary of War on 11 June 1945 by a committee of seven scientists appointed by Arthur H. Compton, director of the Manhattan Project's Chicago lab. The report urged that the U.S. demonstrate the power of the new weapon by exploding it in an uninhabited area. See Inglis, *op. cit.* Summary, Franck Report, pp. 348-351. For information on the men and period from spring 1945 to August 1945 see Michael Amrine's *The Great Decision: The Secret History of the Atomic Bomb* (New York: G.P. Putnam's Sons, 1959).

13. *Bulletin of Atomic Scientists*, September 1977, p. 19.

14. Summary, Franck Report: "Nuclear bombs cannot possibly remain a 'secret weapon' at the exclusive disposal of this country for more than a few years...Unless an effective international control of nuclear explosives is instituted, a race for nuclear armaments is certain to ensue following the first revelation of our possession of nuclear weapons to the world...

"We believe that these considerations make the use of nuclear bombs for an early unannounced attack against Japan inadvisable. If the United States were to be the first to release this new means of indiscriminate destruction upon mankind, she would sacrifice public support throughout the world, precipitate the race for armaments, and prejudice the possibility of reaching an international agreement on the future control of such weapons.

"Much more favorable conditions for the eventual achievement of such an agreement could be created if nuclear bombs were first revealed to the world by a demonstration in an appropriately selected uninhabited area."
—Inglis, *op. cit.*, p. 350. The report was published *Decision*, P.R. Baker, ed. (New York: Holt, Rinehart and Winston, 1968); recommended by Inglis.

15. Gordon Dean, *Report on the Atom* (New York: Alfred A. Knopf, 1953), p. 11.

16. *Ibid.*, p. 10.

17. David E. Lilienthal, *Change, Hope, and the Bomb* (Princeton, NJ: Princeton University Press, 1963), pp.110-111.

18. An official history of the Manhattan Project was published in the fall of 1945. Henry DeWolf Smyth's *Atomic Energy for Military Purposes: the Official Report on the Development of the*

Atomic Bomb under the Auspices of the United States Government, 1940-1945 (Princeton, N.J.: Princeton Univ. Press, 1945). The book is a modified re-publication of the official report issued by the U.S. Corps of Engineers.

19. Dean, *op. cit.*, p. 18.

20. Richard S. Crutchfield, *Public Reaction to the Atomic Bomb and World Affairs* (Ithaca, NY: Cornell University, April 1947), pp. 95 and 2.

21. Ralph Nader and John Abbotts, *The Menace of Atomic Energy* (NY: W.W. Norton & Co., 1977), p. 276.

22. Dean, *op. cit.*, p. 21. The May-Johnson Bill came to symbolize military control: the McMahon—Douglas Bill became the symbol of civilian control, backed by the atomic scientists.

23. Atomic Energy Act of 1946, as quoted in Dean, *op. cit.*, p. 23.

24. Rapoport, *op. cit.*, p. 22.

25. Dean, *op. cit.*, p. 25.

26. Inglis, *op. cit.*, p. 222. Referenced was Philip Noel-Baker's *The Arms Race* (Oceana Publications, 1958). Wrote Inglis: "For several years American diplomacy stood on its laurels, having made this supposedly generous proposal. Meanwhile, the Russians went ahead and developed the A-bomb, which they first tested four years later, in 1949."

27. For an excellent brief rundown on Rocky Flats that describes repeated fires, contamination, see Rapoport, *op. cit.*, pp. 31-49.

28. Cultural Workers Collective, *Workbook on Nuclear Power* (Amherst, MA, 1977), p. 6.

29. J. Luntz, editor of *Nucleonics*. Quoted in *Our New Life with the Atom*, Robert and Leona Train Rienow (NY: Thomas Y. Crowell Co., 1959), p. 132.

30. Of 50,000 kilograms of uranium-235 earmarked for sale in 1956, only 5,000 kilos were pledged to underdeveloped nations; most went to developed Western powers (UK, W. Europe), and Japan. Rienow, *op. cit.*, p. 135.

31. Rienow, *op. cit.*, p. 133.

32. *Ibid.*, p. 132.

33. U.S. and Export-Import Bank loans are given to countries so that they can invest in U.S. nuclear plants. Often these loans have been preceeded by years of gifts of technical facilities, nuclear materials, training of nuclear technicians, etc. These were made available to Third World and non-Communist countries as part of federal Atoms for Peace programs.

34. "For legislation dealing with atomic energy...the JCAE acted as both legislative committee (that is, it introduced the bill) *and* conference committee. If bills were unfavorably amended in the House and Senate during floor debate, the JCAE could drop the amendment in conference. Invariably, the conference bill submitted to both houses for a final vote would be identical to the original bill submitted to the Congress by the JCAE." Ralph Nader and John Abbotts, *The Menace of Atomic Energy* (NY: Norton, 1977), pp. 275-6.

35. Mr. Benjamin Sigal, representing the CIO, expressed concern over monopoly development: "The people of the United States have already invested over $12 billion in the course of acquiring the technical and scientific knowledge concerning the production of atomic energy...If the proposed amendments are adopted, the know-how acquired in the course of that manufacture will be placed at the disposal of the few fortunate companies who have been or will be in a position to acquire access to all of this know-how. It requires no great insight to see that the present contractors who have been running AEC plants, or who have had contracts for experimentation and development, have a running start on the whole field. They have experienced personnel and the technical knowledge which will enable them to obtain control and determine the future industrial development of atomic energy." Cultural Workers, *op. cit.*, p. 7.

36. Arnold Kramish and Eugene M. Zuckert, *Atomic Energy for Your Business: Today's Key to Tomorrow's Profits* (NY: David McKay Co., Inc., 1956), p. 11.

37. From a report submitted 11 August 1958 by the UN Scientific Committee on the Effects of Atomic Radiation. The report showed some awareness of the dangers of radiation: "The committee concludes that all steps designed to minimize irradiation will act to the benefit of human health...Even the smallest amounts of radiation are liable to cause deleterious genetic, and perhaps also somatic, effects." *New York Times*, 11 August 1958. Quoted in Rienow, *op. cit.*, and footnote p. 191.

38. Sheldon Novick, *The Careless Atom*, (Boston, MA: Houghton Mifflin Co., 1969), p. 98.

39. See Ernest J. Sternglass' classic *Low Level Radiation* (NY: Ballantine Books, 1972).

40. Metzger, *op. cit.*, p. 85. See his Part III, The Turning Point: Atomic Fallout, pp. 79-113.

41. Ralph E. Lapp, *The New Force*, also *Atoms and People* (NY: Harper & Bros, 1953 and 1956 respectively); Daniel Lang, *Early Tales of the Atomic Age* (NY: Doubleday & Co., 1948); Norman Lansdell, *The Atom and the Energy Revolution* (NY: Philosophical Library, 1958); William L. Lawrence, *Men and Atoms* (NY: Simon and Schuster, 1959), also *Dawn Over Zero* (NY: Alfred A. Knopf, 1946).

42. Seaborg, *op. cit.*, p. 188.

43. Lilienthal, *op. cit.*, p. 110.

44. Cultural Workers Collective, *op. cit.*, p. 102.

45. *Ibid.*, p. 103.

46. Seaborg, *op. cit.*, p. 28.

47. Phillip Mullenbach, *Civilian Nuclear Power* (NY: Twentieth Century Fund, 1963), p. 140. Quoted in Novick, *op. cit.*, p. 32.

48. Novick, *op. cit.*, p. 33.

49. John G. Fuller, *We Almost Lost Detroit* (NY: Reader's Digest Press, 1975), p. 234.

50. *Ibid.*, p. 51.

51. *Ibid.*, p. 115.

52. Barry Commoner, *The Closing Circle*. See Chap. 3, "Nuclear Fire," pp. 45-62.

53. Cultural Workers Collective, *op. cit.*, p. 103.

54. Ralph Lapp, "The Nuclear Power Controversy—Safety," *The New Republic*, 23 January 1971, p. 18.

55. Richard S. Lewis, *The Nuclear Power Rebellion: Citizens vs. the Atomic Industrial Establishment* (NY: The Viking Press, 1972), p. 262.

56. Chet Holifield. From a speech given 11 May 1971 to the NY branch of the American Nuclear Society, quoted in Lewis, *op. cit.*, p. 261.

57. John Gofman and Arthur Tamplin, *Poisoned Power—The Case Against Nuclear Power Plants*, (Emmaus, PA, Rodale Press Inc., 1971), pp. 24-25.

58. *Ibid.*, p. 25.

59. *Ibid.*, p. 133.

60. Nader and Abbotts, *op. cit.*, p. 69.

61. *Ibid.*, pp. 69-75; Lewis, *op. cit.*, pp. 81-108.

62. Gofman and Tamplin, *op. cit.*, pp. 106-108.

63. Nader and Abbotts, *op. cit.*, p. 74.

64. *Ibid*, pp. 74-75.

63. Nader and Abbotts, *op. cit.*, p. 74. Scientists joining in criticism of the allowable radiation standards included Nobel laureates James Watson, co-discoverer of the DNA molecule; Harold Urey, chemist at the U/Calif; Linus Pauling, Stanford chemist, and George Wald, Harvard biologist.

64. *Ibid.*, pp. 74-75. National Academy of Sciences, National Research Council, *The Effects on Populations of Exposure to Low Levels of Ionizing Radiation* (Washington, D.C., November 1972), p. 2.

65. *Ibid.*, p. 75.

66. Lewis, *op. cit.*, p. 264.

67. *Ibid.*, pp. 259-260.

68. *Ibid.*, p. 284.

69. *Ibid.*, p. 286.

70. *Ibid.*, p. 287.

71. From a report by *Science*, Lewis, *op. cit.*, p. 291.

72. Lewis, *op. cit.*, p. 125. See his whole chapter on this and more, "The Intervenors," pp. 109-147.

73. *Ibid.*, pp. 133-135.

74. Nader and Abbotts, *op. cit.*, p. 341.

75. Fred C. Finlayson, "A View From the Outside," *Bulletin of the Atomic Scientists*, September 1975, vol. xxxi, no. 7, p. 21.

76. McKinley Olson, *Unacceptable Risk: The Nuclear Power Controversy* (Bantam Books, 1976), p. 80.

77. Daniel F. Ford and Henry W. Kendall, Union of Concerned Scientists, *An Assessment of the Emergency Core Cooling Systems Rulemaking Hearings* (UCS/Friends of the Earth, 1974) 4.2-4.4.

78. Nader and Abbotts, *op. cit.*, p. 118. Also *U.S. Atomic Energy Commission, WASH-740, Theoretical Possibilities and Consequences of Major Accidents in Large Nuclear Power Plants*, Washington, D.C., March 1957, p. viii.

79. From "Remarks of William O. Doub, Former Commissioner of the Atomic Energy Commission at Ralph Nader's 'Critical Mass 74' Meeting, Friday, November 15, 1974." Washington, D.C.

80. Nader and Abbotts, *op. cit.*, p. 278.

81. Les Gapay, "Solar-Energy Planning Is Being Slighted by Ford, Former.Chief of Program Says," *Wall Street Journal*, 26 February 1976. From Nader and Abbotts, p. 279.

82. Nader and Abbotts, *op. cit.*, pp. 288-290.

83. DOE *Information*, Weekly Announcements, vol. 1, no. 1, week ending 14 October 1977.

84. Carter said that he considered nuclear plants to be a "last resort" at campaign speech in Manchester, N.H., 4 August 1976. The October '77 estimates from the administration were: 110,000-120,000-Mw on line in 1985 and 380,000-Mw by 2000. At the time there were 47,000-Mw nuclear in U.S., 82,000-Mw worldwide. They anticipated construction permits between 1977-1990 to average 19 nukes/year.(!) From *Nucleonics Week*, vol. 18, no. 41, 13 October 1977.

85. DOE letter to utilities, 20 December 1977.

Chapter 2:

Atomic Power, Nuclear Plants

No Nukes

When the first NO NUKES bumper stickers appeared in early 1974, pedestrians and drivers seeing the bright blue and white bumper sticker often yelled to the driver of a stickered car: "What's a nuke?" We would roll down the window and yell back: "Nuclear power plant..."

"Nuke" has always been slang for nuclear weapons—"the bomb." One may recall General Curtis LeMay's advice to President Lyndon Johnson on how to win the Vietnam war—"Nuke 'em back to the Stone Age."

So, NO NUKES means no nuclear power—neither for war nor for domestic so-called peaceful uses.

NO NUKES does not distinguish between military and domestic uses of nuclear power because in the long run the dangers are the same. Nuclear plants were developed during World War II to create enough plutonium to make an atom bomb. From the translation of scientific equations into a primitive pile of graphite blocks beneath the University of Chicago stadium, to present-day 1000-megawatt GE reactors, the technology has been greatly refined and sophisticated. But the military basis remains: nuclear power plants are factories of potential bomb material.

The side-effects of nukes are the same for both bombs and power plants: thermal pollution, radiation, radioactive by-products—wastes that must be stored for thousands of years. Once disturbed, there is no "peaceful" atom.

What Is Atomic Power?

Atomic power refers to the energy that is released when atoms of matter are split. In 1905, Albert Einstein showed mathematically in his Theory of Relativity that matter could be changed into energy, that it has energy in it. The famous formula $E = mc^2$ showed how much energy could be released. The energy (E) from uranium (for example) would be equal to the mass or amount (m) of uranium, multiplied by the square (c^2) of the speed of light (186,324 miles per second).

Atomic power refers to the power of very specific atoms. Basically two elements are used: an isotope of uranium called uranium-235 and the man-made plutonium-239. The atoms of these materials are split for three reasons. The first is to produce an explosion—an atomic bomb. The second is to produce bomb grade materials in a nuclear production reactor. The third use is to produce heat, make steam, and generate electricity in a commericial nuclear power plant.

The technology based on nuclear, or atomic, power is tremendously complex. Yet its principles can and should be understood by the people who are supposedly being served by it and who must pay its costs.

Inside The Atom

Scientists consider atoms to be the basic building blocks of matter. The material things we are familiar with in everyday life like water, wood, glass, and steel, are all composed of clusters of atoms called molecules. Some molecules, such as water, contain just a few atoms. Others, like proteins, enzymes, the nucleic acids DNA and RNA, and some synthetic chemicals like polyvinylchloride, have as many as several hundred atoms.

An atom consists of an extremely dense nucleus surrounded by a swarm of electrons. The nucleus is composed of a certain number of positively charged protons and electrically neutral neutrons held together by a very strong nuclear force. For every proton there is a corresponding negatively charged electron, thus making the atom electrically neutral. Protons and neutrons have roughly equal mass but are 2,000 times heavier than the electron, and account for almost the total weight

of an atom. If the nucleus were the size of a marble 1 centimeter in diameter, then the electron would circle about the nucleus with a radius of about 1 kilometer.

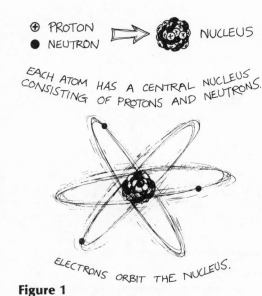

⊕ PROTON
● NEUTRON   ➡   NUCLEUS

EACH ATOM HAS A CENTRAL NUCLEUS CONSISTING OF PROTONS AND NEUTRONS.

ELECTRONS ORBIT THE NUCLEUS.

Figure 1

The chemical properties of an atom are determined by its number of electrons and protons. There are 104 different kinds of atoms, called elements. Each has a different number of protons in its nucleus. Helium, carbon, zinc, gold, thorium, uranium, neptunium and plutonium are all elements. The first 92 elements, from hydrogen to uranium, occur naturally. The remaining 12 have been created artifically.

What Is An Isotope?

While the nucleus of an element has a fixed number of protons, it can have different numbers of neutrons. Nuclei which have the same number of protons but a different number of neutrons are called isotopes. Uranium, with 92 protons, has several different isotopes. The most abundant of these is U-238 with 146 neutrons and U-235 with 143 neutrons. The isotope U-235 is valuable for use in atomic bombs and nuclear fuel but makes up only 0.7% of natural uranium.

What Is Fission?

Nuclear power plants derive their energy from the splitting—or fissioning— of the uranium isotope U-235. When a U-235 nucleus captures a neutron it becomes a highly unstable U-236 nucleus. The U-236 nucleus decays by flying apart into two large pieces, called fission products. Several neutrons and gamma rays are also released. This splitting process is called fission.

Figure 2: Fission

The fission products form part of the waste of the nuclear power and weapons industries. They are highly radioactive isotopes, some of the most lethal being strontium, iodine, and cesium. (For a discussion of radiation, see Health Dangers, pp. 72-95.)

What Is A Chain Reaction?

Each time a U-235 nucleus fissions, 2 or 3 neutrons are set free. These neutrons may be captured by other U-235 nuclei, causing *them* to fission. Each fissioning nucleus releases more neutrons, which are captured by more U-235 nuclei, and so on. This process is known as a chain reaction.

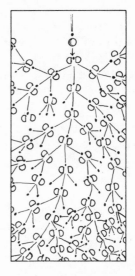

Figure 3:

Chain Reaction

If each fissioning U-235 nucleus causes on the average more than one additional U-235 nucleus to fission, an uncontrolled chain reaction takes place resulting in an atomic explosion. If, however, some of the neutrons are removed by a neutron absorbing material so that each fissioning U-235 nucleus causes only *one* other U-235 nucleus to fission, then the chain reaction is controlled. Nuclear power plants use controlled chain reactions.

The chain reaction may be stopped altogether by inserting neutron absorbing control rods into the reactor core. Even so, the reactor must be continuously cooled because of the enormous heat produced by the decaying fission products. In a 1000-megawatt reactor this heat amounts to approximately 100 megawatts.

What Is A Critical Mass?

In order to sustain an uncontrolled chain reaction a certain minimum amount of fissile material, called the critical mass, is required. For uranium, the critical mass is about 10 lb. of U-235, about the size of a grapefruit. An atomic bomb can be made by smashing two subcritical pieces of uranium together so that their total mass becomes critical.

In a nuclear power plant the concentration of U-235 is not large enough for a critical mass to exist if, for example, the core should melt. For a fast breeder reactor, however, the situation is not so clear.

Making Electricity...

The source of electricity which runs our electric lights and household appliances, and which forms the basis for a complex industrial society, remains a mystery and wonder to most of us. Yet the principles of electricity have remained constant since their development before the turn of the last century.

Electricity is produced by the rapid turning of a generator in which a coil of wire spins within a magnetic field, producing current. The generator is turned by a turbine, powered by water in hydroelectric plants or by high-pressure steam. In fossil-fueled plants, steam is made in boilers where water is heated by burning coal, oil, or gas.

Fossil-fueled Plant

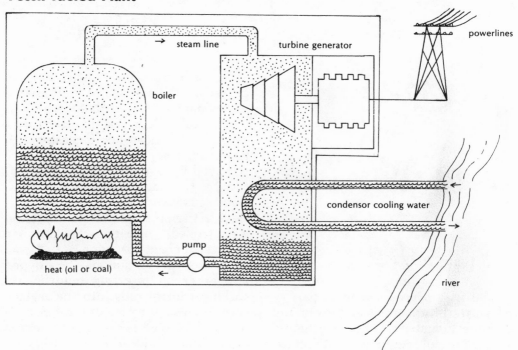

Figure 4: Fossil-fueled Plant—This is a schematic representation of a conventional fossil-fueled (thermal) generating plant. (Graphic: Susanna Natti)

Boiling Water Reactor

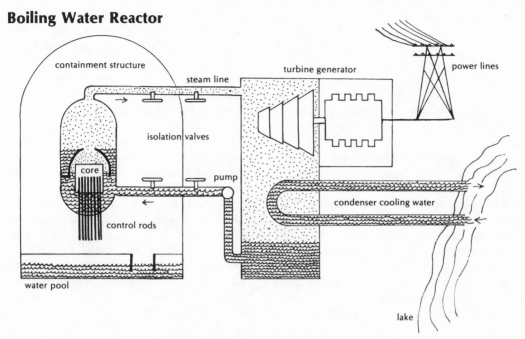

Figure 5: BWR—This is a schematic representation of a boiling water reactor nuclear power plant. (Graphic: Susanna Natti)

...With Nuclear Power

In a nuclear plant, steam is produced by the heat coming from the controlled chain reaction occurring inside the uranium fuel rods within the reactor core. Nukes are a very complex way to boil water!

A nuclear plant's reactor core is suspended inside a steel vessel with thick walls like a giant pot. Inside the core are the 12-foot-long fuel rods. The uranium fuel is in the form of ceramic pellets the size of a pencil eraser, encased in rods or tubes of zirconium-alloy metal "cladding."

No U.S. reactors use natural uranium for fuel, although it is used in Canadian and British reactors. Naturally occurring uranium contains very little (0.71%) of the fissionable isotope

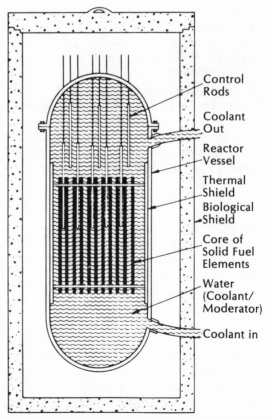

Figure 6: Reactor core (Source: Gofman and Tamplin, *Poisoned Power*, p. 39; kind permission of Rodale Press Inc., Emmaus, PA 18049.)

uranium-235. To make nuclear fuel, the percentage of U-235 in uranium must be increased to about 3% through an enrichment process. (See Fuel Cycle page 45.) The common reactor fuel is uranium dioxide (UO_2), with the uranium containing 1-3% U-235.

Inside the core the fission process is controlled in two ways. First, by the use of control rods. These regulating rods are inserted in the core among the fuel rods. They contain a material, such as boron or cadmium, that absorbs neutrons. When the control rods are withdrawn, a chain reaction will start as the neutrons from the split uranium nuclei quickly multiply. When a reactor is on, or "critical," the rods are adjusted up and down to maintain a desired level of power, or "a steady-state reaction rate." To shut the reactor down, the control rods are inserted completely into the assemblies. Inserted, they absorb excess neutrons, and the chain reaction stops. A quick shutdown by insertion of the control rods is called a "scram." The fission process (chain reaction) is immediately stopped when the reactor is scrammed. However, even after the chain reaction has been stopped, the reactor must be continuously cooled for a period of days because of the "after heat" generated by the hot radioactive fission products.

The second way the nuclear chain reaction inside a reactor is controlled is by the coolant, usually highly purified water, which surrounds the fuel rods and assemblies in the core. The coolant besides cooling the reactor also acts as a moderator. All U.S. reactors but one are "water moderated." The moderator slows down the neutrons and in the process makes fission of the fuel more complete. Neutrons are more likely to cause fission if slowed from their natural speed of 10,000 miles per second to about 1 mile per second.

Types of Reactors

During the late 1930s, European physicists like Enrico Fermi in Italy, Irene Curie and Frederic Joliot in France, and Otto Hahn, Lise Meitner and Fritz Strassman in Germany were experimenting with radioactive elements derived from the neutron bombardment of uranium. In January 1939, Lise Meitner and her nephew O.R. Frisch correctly interpreted an experiment done by Hahn and Strassman. They understood that neutron bombardment had actually caused a uranium nucleus to split, dividing it into two nuclei of roughly the same size. It was they who first proposed the name "fission" for the process and calculated that the process would release large amounts of energy as well as radioactive fission products.[1]

The first continuing, self-sustaining chain reaction occurred on 2 December 1942 as part of the U.S. government's Manhattan Project, which was charged with developing an atomic bomb.

Enrico Fermi and a team of international scientists, many of whom were refugees from Hitler's Europe, had constructed the first nuclear reactor in an improvised secret laboratory beneath the University of Chicago's stadium. There they built an "atomic pile," which was literally that—a stack of graphite blocks 19 feet high and 24½ feet on each side. Inside the graphite pile were rods of natural uranium and a few cadmium control rods. As scientists watched from a nearby balcony, their instruments measured the build-up of neutrons, moderated by the graphite blocks. As the cadmium rods were withdrawn, a chain reaction occurred and the first controlled nuclear reaction was finally achieved.

One radioactive by-product of the pile was a new heavy element they named **plutonium**. Plutonium-239 and

Figure 7: Fermi's Pile—Artist Gary Sheahan's painting depicting the moment when criticality was achieved, 2 December 1942, in the dank raquets court beneath the stands of Stagg Field at the University of Chicago. Present are 26 members of the team of scientists who assisted the late Enrico Fermi. (Painting by Gary Sheahan) DOE-62-6782

uranium-235 are the best elements with which to build a bomb. Because of its intense radioactivity, more concentrated than that of uranium, plutonium can be used for smaller bombs of greater power. Not found in nature, plutonium is created by the absorption of a fast neutron by U-238 (see figure 11). Fermi's first pile was the prototype of the large-scale reactors that operate for the military at Savannah River, S.C. and Hanford, Washington, producing this new potent fissionable element.

Thermal Reactors (Light Water)
Slow neutrons are called thermal neutrons. Reactors that use moderators, like water or graphite, to slow down the neutrons are called thermal reactors. There are two common types of thermal reactors: one is the pressurized water reactor (PWR), the other, the boiling water reactor (BWR). Both use ordinary water to slow down, or

moderate, the neutrons. And both are known as "light water" reactors to distinguish them from the Canadian "heavy water" or deuterium-moderated reactors (CANDUs). In PWRs and BWRs, the control rods and fuel assemblies in the cores are surrounded by water, which is heated to make the steam necessary to turn the turbine and generator.

The Pressurized Water Reactor—Made By Westinghouse
In this type of reactor, which was developed for the U.S. Navy's submarines, water is contained in the core under high pressure (2,250 pounds per square inch) to keep it from turning into steam. The water circulates at about 600° F. It carries the heat generated by the fuel rods to a heat exchanger, which contains water that quickly boils, turns to steam, and runs the turbine. Once through the turbine, this steam enters a condenser, another

Pressurized Water Reactor (PWR)

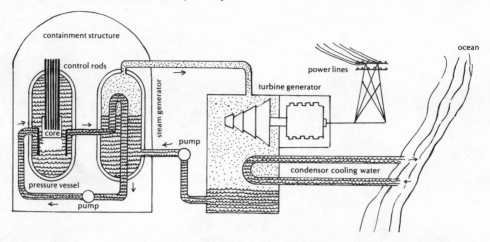

Figure 8: PWR—This is a schematic representation of a typical pressurized water reactor. (Graphic: Susanna Natti)

heat exchanger. This time the steam is cooled by river or ocean water pumped through the condenser, where the steam is cooled back to liquid form. After passing through the condenser, the cooled water returns to the first heat exchanger to be converted once again into steam. Meanwhile, the cooling water which was used in the condenser is returned, many degrees warmer, to the cooling water source— a river, lake, or ocean. In older plants the water was discharged directly into the river or body of water. Cooling towers are now required to first lower the temperature of the discharged water.

A PWR has three separate water cycles. Unless there are leaks in the first reactor core water system, the water in the other two systems should not be contaminated with radiation. But small leaks and some contamination seem to be inevitable.

The Boiling Water Reactor—Made by General Electric

There are only two water cycles in the BWR. The same water that moderates the reactor turns the turbine. Water enters the reactor core (pressurized to 1,000 pounds per square inch) and is turned to steam by the heat of the fuel rods. The steam is piped to the turbine, then through a condenser which cools it so that it can be returned to the reactor core. As in the PWR, the condenser uses river or ocean water, which is usually circulated through a cooling tower, to condense the steam.

Water in the reactor core becomes highly radioactive from contact with fissioning fuel due to small, unavoidable leaks in the fuel rod cladding. Since the steam that turns the turbine in a BWR is radioactive too, there must be no leaks anywhere else in the system. If the turbine or the condenser unit leak, radiation will be released into the air or cooling water. The water system of the PWR thus gives a little more protection to the cooling water than the BWR, as the steam that turns the

PWR turbine and enters the condenser has not been irradiated by direct contact with the reactor core.

Both the PWR and the BWR are fueled with enriched uranium. The first reactors that were built for commercial use in the U.S. were PWRs, such as those at Shippingport, Pennsylvania (1957) and Rowe, Massachusetts (1960). The first commercial BWR was the 200-megawatt Dresden I in Illinois, started up in 1959. Other old BWRs are small units at Big Rock Point (Charlevoix), Michigan, and the plant in Humbolt Bay, Eureka, California, which was finally shut down in 1977.

Reactor Cooling

American physicist and energy expert Amory Lovins has said that using nuclear power to boil water is like cutting butter with a chain saw. The analogy is a good one. Temperatures from the nuclear fuel reach 4,300° F! Obviously, a lot of heat is wasted.

The cores of light-water reactors are kept cool by the moderating water, which lowers the surface temperature of the fuel pellets to around 550° F.[2]

If the flow of cooling water is interrupted, the fuel can melt. The molten fuel would generate such tremendous temperatures and pressures that the containment vessel could not hold it. Melting through the reactor foundation, the molten mass could reach the ground or air, releasing tremendous amounts of deadly radiation.

A fuel meltdown was defined by the Atomic Energy Commission as the "worst possible accident" that could happen in a nuclear power plant. In 1974 the Union of Concerned Scientists described it in this way:

> Such an accident is surely possible in principle *and* practice. A broken pipe, a ruptured vessel, or other cause could see the reactor coolant lost and the core, left to heat under the drive of the intensely radioactive "ashes," subject to soaring temperatures, soon melting and collapsing, burning its way down through all man-made structure. Release of radioactivity in unacceptable amounts would be certain.[3]

Cooling Tower—Water for cooling enters at right, goes through reactor, enters cooling tower. Although cooled in this manner, the water is returned to its source warmer than it was at the beginning of the cycle. Note water vapor "plume." (Graphic: Susanna Natti)

The nuclear industry has called this accident the "China Syndrome," because the molten fuel could melt its way through the containment vessel and theoretically keep on going—all the way to China!

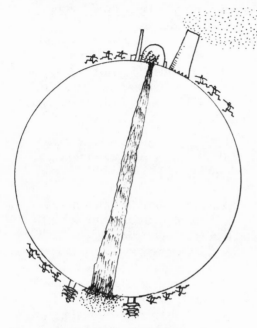

Figure 10: The China Syndrome

Other Atomic Fission Reactors

There are three other types of thermal or slow neutron reactors. One is an early type that uses natural uranium as a fuel and is moderated with carbon or graphite and cooled by air. This system is used in some British reactors and for manufacturing weapons-grade plutonium at Hanford, Washington.

A second type of natural uranium fueled reactor is moderated by heavy water (D_2O). The Savannah River South Carolina plant and some research reactors are of this type.

The Canadian atomic energy program developed the heavy-water type reactor because it could be fueled with natural uranium, avoiding the expensive and difficult uranium enrichment process. This type of reactor has been sold by Canada to European and other countries.

Gas-Cooled Reactors

There are several types of gas-cooled reactors. The best known is England's Calder Hall, opened in 1956 and officially the first "power reactor," although there were smaller ones operating in the U.S. and U.S.S.R. in 1954.[4] The Calder Hall and Windscale (Scotland) reactors use natural uranium fuel and a graphite moderator. They are cooled by carbon dioxide. Other types of high temperature gas-cooled reactors (HTGRs) are cooled by helium gas. Different variations have been tried with mixed success. The first U.S. HTGR was the Peach Bottom I near Philadelphia (1966). It was shut down in 1974 after Philadelphia Electric claimed the 40-megawatt plant was "too small to be of commercial value."[5] There are now two 1,065-megawatt BWRs at Peach Bottom.

The only U.S. helium-cooled HTGR now is the Fort St. Vrain nuclear plant located 40 miles north of Denver, Colorado. On 23 January 1978 it leaked radioactive gases from its cooling system. Roads near the plant were cordoned off and 200 workers were evacuated. The $1 billion plant was still in an experimental start-up period when the accident occurred.[6]

Other HTGRs scheduled for Delaware and Pennsylvania have been cancelled, and Gulf-General Atomics has announced that it will not be building any more reactors.

Research Reactors

There are 49 TRIGA MARK research reactors around the world, 14 at U.S. universities. This reactor type has a "pulsing feature" that can cause tremendous power surges every few minutes, raising its capacity from 250-kilowatts to 250-megawatts. Some of the teaching reactors are at urban universities (Cambridge's MIT, the University of California at Berkeley, etc.). Columbia University in New York City has been trying to fire one up since 1967, but the reactor start-up has been delayed by a long series of community protests and legal action. In April 1977, the New York City Board of Health vetoed Columbia's application to operate the reactor saying it would endanger the health and safety of students and local community. The university is appealing the decision.[7]

Laugh while you cry:

A sign on the University of Florida's research reactor building reads: "Please don't flush the toilet while the reactor is running." It seems that when the toilet is flushed, the water needed to cool the reactor drops, and it must be shut down to prevent over-heating. The problem? The reactor's secondary cooling system is supplied by the same water main that feeds the nearby toilet![8]

Floating Nukes

A unique solution to the problems of obtaining an adequate supply of cooling water for reactors—and overcoming local opposition to nuclear power—has been the scheme of floating nukes offshore. The nuclear plants would be mounted on huge platforms somewhat like offshore oil drilling rigs, and their cooling systems would be adapted to use sea water. Westinghouse and Tenneco planned to build a "nuclear island" three miles off the New Jersey coast; others were slated for the Florida coastline. The New Jersey plan has been indefinitely postponed because of its cost and shoreline opposition. The Florida one is also facing financial problems.

On To The Breeder

Don't ask me what a breeder reactor is: ask Dr. Schlesinger. But tell him not to tell you, because unless you are one of those Ph.D.'s, you wouldn't understand it either, but I do know that here we have the potentiality of a whole new breakthrough of power for peace...[9]

President Richard Nixon
Hanford, Washington
26 September 1971

Before the problems with thermal (or "slow") fission reactors had all been revealed, let alone solved, the Atomic Energy Commission was at work developing what is known as a liquid metal fast breeder reactor (LMFBR). This was to be the "next generation" of nuclear reactors and the solution to the problem of what to use for reactor fuel when uranium supplies eventually run out. Early AEC projections called for 400 fast breeders by the year 2000, and assumed that the reactors would be producing commercial electricity by the 1980s.

A "fast" reactor has a smaller core, fueled with a highly radioactive fissionable material such as mixed uranium and plutonium oxides (UO_2 and PuO_2). There is no moderator. Neutrons are not slowed—it is a "fast" reactor.

What makes this reactor a "breeder?" The breeder is commonly described in the press and industry as "a reactor that produces more fuel than it consumes." What that means is that breeders create plutonium over time. The new plutonium is "bred" by irradiation of U-238.

A breeder reactor's core is surrounded by a blanket of natural uranium containing U-238. Uranium-238 is a "fertile" material because it can be converted into a fissionable material—plutonium. Some of the neutrons resulting from the fission taking place in the core are absorbed by the U-238 in the blanket. This absorption process transforms some of the U-238 into plutonium (Pu-239). Theoretically the irradiated U-238 blanket would be removed and the plutonium separated chemically. The resulting plutonium would be used to fuel other reactors—or to make nuclear weapons.

Small in size, the breeder core generates tremendous heat. It requires a coolant that can withstand super-high temperatures. Although there has been research on a gas-cooled breeder,[10] the usual coolant is liquid sodium, which melts at 98° C. (208° F.) and boils at 880° C. (1616° F.). Although it has good heat transferring characteristics, liquid sodium is potentially very dangerous. It will explode and burn on contact with air or water.

Breeder reactors are the most controversial part of nuclear fission technology. They are expensive, dangerous and would require the production and shipping of large amounts of plutonium. Plutonium is the poisonous, cancer-causing material that is used in atomic bombs and nuclear weapons. Widespread use of breeder reactors would usher in what has been called "the plutonium economy."

But the nuclear industry needs breeders to ensure a future for nuclear power beyond this century. Light-water reactors use up only 66% (2/3) of the U-235 in the fuel. It was foreseen by the industry that when uranium resources were depleted—perhaps around the turn of the century—fast breeders would move "on line," using as fuel plutonium that had accumulated as a light-water reactor by-product. There would also be a lot of U-238 left over from the enrichment process.

Thus breeder reactors would use up the recovered uranium and plutonium from the first generation of nuclear reactors and "breed" more nuclear fuel by creating more plutonium over time. It was the "alchemists' dream." Except that the new product

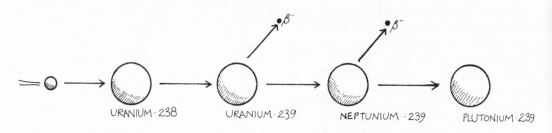

URANIUM · 238   URANIUM · 239   NEPTUNIUM · 239   PLUTONIUM · 239

Figure 11: Pu-239 Breeding—Plutonium-239 is created when U-238 captures a fast neutron (at left) producing U-239, which then undergoes two beta-decays to produce Pu-239. It takes 23.5 minutes for U-239 to turn into neptunium-239 and 2.3 days for Np-239 to become plutonium. (Graphic: Susanna Natti)

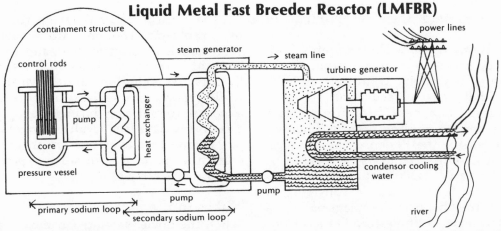

Liquid Metal Fast Breeder Reactor (LMFBR)

Figure 12: LMFBR—This is what the breeder looks like. The reactor core is cooled by liquid sodium. The super-heated sodium makes water boil, and that steam is used to drive a turbine generator. The steam is then cooled back to a liquid in a condenser with cooling water from a river, lake, or ocean, and is pumped back into the steam generator to be turned to steam again by the hot sodium. (Graphic: Susanna Natti)

created from the old would not be gold, but deadly plutonium.

But the breeder reactor has run into some big problems. (Further discussion of this issue is contained in the chapter on History and the section, The International Story.)

The Thorium Alternative

President Carter has suggested that the element thorium be used in fast breeders instead of plutonium and enriched uranium, as has been done in some Navy reactors. The Navy's Admiral Rickover is a leading proponent of the thorium breeder. In his view, thorium is much safer than uranium because it does not produce plutonium. Therefore, thorium nukes would not lead to bomb proliferation as much as uranium-fueled ones, where the fuel can be readily diverted for military uses. In the late 1960s, thorium was considered to be a possible future nuclear fuel, an economical one for the time when uranium supplies would run low.[11]

There are three basic fissionable materials: uranium-235, plutonium-239, and uranium-233. These can all be bomb material as well as heat sources. In addition, two materials are "fertile": uranium-238 and thorium. Being fertile, they can be converted into fissionable elements (plutonium-239 and uranium-233) when irradiated by neutrons.

Thorium is found in the ore material monazite, in amounts from 1-5%.[12] Thorium has been found in India. It is also found in granite deposits like New Hampshire's White Mountains. In December 1977, a thorium breeder demonstration core using the "proved technology" of the pressurized water system was put into operation in the early PWR at Shippingport, Pennsylvania.[13] Shippingport, the first commercial nuke in the U.S., is now owned by the Navy.

Is a thorium-U-233 breeder really any better than a plutonium-fueled breeder? If so, it's not that obvious. Although U-233 is less explosive than plutonium, it too is dangerously radioactive and can be used to make nuclear weapons. The proliferation problem would not be solved by introducing thorium into the "next round" of reactors.

Along with the United States, England, France, Germany, other European Community countries, and the U.S.S.R. have breeder reactor programs. The best functioning fast breeder may be the French "Phenix," named for the Phoenix, the mythical bird that rises from its own ashes. A commercial 1,200-megawatt "Super-Phenix" is now under construction near the Phenix in the village of Creys-Malville in southwestern France. Construction of this plant and the Kalkar breeder in northern Germany have been fought by anti-nuclear groups from every country in Europe. (See International Section.)

Nukes On And Under The Sea

Nuclear reactors were refined by the Navy, and naval nuclear research, development, and use continues to be extensive. Nuclear reactors serve as the propulsion means for at least 8 surface vessels (aircraft carriers and cruisers) and 108 submarines, including Fleet Ballistic Missile Submarines which carry Poseidon missiles with nuclear warheads.

The aircraft carriers have more than one reactor on board; the USS Enterprise has eight reactors. In 1977, there were twenty-nine more nuclear-propelled submarines and five large surface vessels under construction. Most are built either in Groton, Connecticut at Electric Boat, or in Newport News, Virginia.

Nuclear power provided the Navy with its big breakthrough in submarine development. The uranium-fueled reactors allowed the Nautilus and nuclear submarines that followed to stay underwater longer than ever possible before, as the ship did not have to surface frequently to refuel.

The nuclear Navy is facing some new problems. Demonstrators have been active at Electric Boat and the Trident submarine base in Kitsap County, Washington State. Meanwhile, reports have surfaced on worker exposure to radiation during early nuclear Navy days (see Health Dangers, p. 94), and cost overruns are threatening the completion of some expensive aircraft carriers.[13]

Nukes in the Sky

When the Soviet satellite Cosmos 954 fell to earth on 24 January 1978, most earthlings realized for the first time that there are flying nukes too.

The satellite that broke up over northern Canada carried a nuclear reactor containing about 100 pounds of the highly radioactive isotope uranium-235. Although the North American Air Defense Command and government officials knew that the satellite was falling from its orbit, the public was not told until the event occurred. The Soviet Union and 17 other countries were notified. A White House security advisor explained that: "Forewarning of the public could have led to widespread panic."[14]

Although the radiation damage—actual and potential—was naturally downplayed by the government, the news gave a hint of what the consequences would have been had the Cosmos come down over a major city. The first large fragment found was 3 inches wide, 10 inches long, and a mere ½-inch thick. Yet it gave off radiation at an intensity of more than 200 rads an hour—more than 40 times the dose allowed for a nuclear worker in one year, and 400 times the value presently recommended by many scientists![15]

The Cosmos satellite carried a fission reactor, which converted the heat of controlled fission into electricity.

The Cosmos fall was not the first. Two U.S. spacecraft carrying nuclear electric generators have made flaming re-entries into the earth's atmosphere. The first was a military navigation satellite in 1964, the other was the 1970 ill-fated Apollo 13 moon mission.

At the end of 1976 there were 836 satellites in orbit. A "couple of dozen" carry nuclear generators similar to the Cosmos 954's. The U.S. has launched a total of 28 spacecraft with nuclear power sources. The U.S.S.R. has launched at least 9 other reactor-powered satellites.[16]

On 30 January 1978, President Carter said he would "favor" an agreement with the Soviets to ban atomic reactors in earth-orbiting satellites.[17]

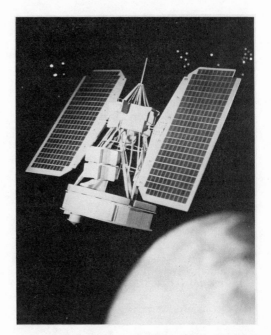

Figure 13: Nimbus-B Satellite—One of NASA's weather satellites, Nimbus-B has two radioisotope thermoelectric generators (atomic batteries) and solar cell paddles for power. (Credit: DOE-68-8292)

Soviets nor the U.S. government spokesman ever mentioned the fact that the total amount of biologically serious radioactivity released in the satellite crash to the world's air, water, food and milk equals that of the detonation of about 10 modern atomic weapons. Nor has any of them mentioned that animal studies at the University of Rochester carried out over a period of nearly 10 years showed that even the less toxic natural uranium, when released as fine oxide dust, was found to induce a startlingly high number of lung cancers seven to ten years after very low concentrations of this material were inhaled by dogs. —Dr. Ernest Sternglass, "Nuclear satellites: Government secrecy hides the potential for real disaster," *Boston Globe*, 19 February 1978.

Footnotes

1. David Dietz, *Atomic Science, Bombs and Power* (New York: Collier Books, 1962), p. 117.

2. McKinley C. Olson, *Unacceptable Risk: The Nuclear Power Controversy* (New York: Bantam Books, 1976), p. 30.

3. Union of Concerned Scientists, *An Assessment of the Emergency Core Cooling Systems Rulemaking Hearings* (San Francisco, CA: Friends of the Earth, 1974), p. 1.1.

4. John J. Berger, *Nuclear Power: The Unviable Option* (Palo Alto, Calif: Ramparts Press, 1976), pp.49-50.

5. Olson, *op. cit.*, p. 19.

6. *Washington Post*, 24 January 1978.

7. Report from Committee to End Radiological Hazards, 166 Second Ave., New York, N.Y. 10003, August 1977.

8. *Boston Globe*, 21 April 1977, p.16.

9. *Congressional Record*, 94th Congress, 30 July 1975.

10. Andrew W. Kramer, *Understanding the Nuclear Reactor* (Barrington, Ill: Technical Publishing Co., 1970), p. 80.

11. *Ibid.*, p. 82.

12. *Ibid.*, p. 91.

13. *Ibid.*, p. 81.

14. *New York Times*, 29 January 1978.

15. UPI, "Lethal Fragment of Satellite Found," *Boston Globe*, 3 February 1978. "Neither the

16. Robert Cooke, "Generator is common device in space," *Boston Globe*, 25 January 1978. Nuclear reactors are used in spy (reconnaissance) and eavesdropping satellites because they are less easily destroyed in space (by an enemy) than the larger, more fragile solar panel-powered models.   —Dr. Kosta M. Tsipis, physicist at MIT's Center for International Studies, from "How dangerous are those satellites?" *Boston Globe*, 29 January 1978.

17. Richard D. Lyons, "Carter Favors Ban on Atomic Reactors in Earth Satellites," *New York Times*, 31 January 1978.

Sources of Information

The following are valuable sources of information on nuclear energy:

PERIODICALS

• *Critical Mass Journal*
P.O. Box 1538
Washington, D.C. 20013
Monthly, $7.50/year or $13.50/2 years.

• *Not Man Apart*
Friends of the Earth
124 Spear St.
San Francisco, CA 94105
Biweekly, $10.00/year.

• *Nuclear Opponents*
Box 285
Allendale, NJ 07401
Monthly newsletter, $3.50/year.

•*The Power Line*
Environmental Action Foundation
724 Dupont Circle Building
Washington, D.C. 20036
Monthly, excellent on utility news; $15.00/year;
$7.50/year low-income.

• *People & Energy*
Citizens Energy Project
1413 K St., N.W.
Washington, D.C. 20005
Monthly; $10.00/year; $7.00/year low-income.

• *WIN* Magazine
503 Atlantic Ave./5th Fl.
Brooklyn, NY 11217
Biweekly; $15.00/year.

• *Nucleonics Week*
McGraw-Hill, Inc.
1221 Avenue of the Americas
New York, NY 10021
Great source of info, only $400 or so/year!

• *Nuclear News*
244 Ogden Avenue
Hinsdale, Illinois 60521
Official organ of American Nuclear Society;
around $40.00/year.

• *News Releases*
NRC: "News Releases," Office of Public
Affairs, Washington, D.C.   20005. DOE:
"Weekly Announcements," Office of Public
Affairs, Washington, D.C. 20005. Both free
from the NRC and DOE.

• *Nuclear Industry*
7101 Wisconsin Ave., N.W.
Washington, D.C. 20014
AIF monthly, with $60/year membership.

• *No Nuclear News*
Monthly newsclippings service
c/o Boston Clamshell Coalition
1151 Mass. Ave.,
Boston, MA 02138
$.50 each.

ORGANIZATIONS

• Atomic Industrial Forum (AIF)
7101 Wisconsin Ave, N.W.
Washington, D.C. 20014
Bibliography; general information; reports.

• Critical Mass Energy Project
P.O. Box 1538
Washington, D.C. 20013
Bibliography; publications.

• Committee for Nuclear Responsibility
MPOB Box 11207
San Francisco, CA 94101
Publication list.

• Environmental Action Foundation
1346 Connecticut Ave., N.W.
Washington, D.C. 20036
Utility resources; publications.

• Environmental Policy Center
317 Pennsylvania Ave., S.E.
Washington, D.C. 20003

• Friends of the Earth
124 Spear St.
San Francisco, CA 94105

• Mobilization for Survival
1213 Race Street
Rhiladelphia, PA 19107
The Mobilizer newletter; resources on nuclear
power/weapons.

• Nuclear Information and Resource Service
1536 16th St., N.W.   (NIRS)
Washington, D.C. 20005
Technical data; information referral; skills.

• Scientists Institute for Public Information
355 Lexington Ave.
New York, NY 10007

• Sierra Club
330 Pennsylvania Ave., S.E.
Washington, D.C. 20003

• Southwest Research and Information Center
P.O. Box 4524
Albuquerque, NM 87106

• Supporters of Silkwood (SOS)
317 Pennsylvania Ave., S.E.
Washington, D.C. 20003

• Task Force Against Nuclear Pollution
153 E St., S.E.
Washington, D.C. 20003

• Union of Concerned Scientists (UCS)
1025 15th St., N.W.
Washington, D.C. 20005
Publications list.

Also: Check National Regional Reports and
contact groups near you. Many groups have
newsletters and literature lists with up-to-date
sources of information on atomic and solar
energy.

Chapter 3:

The Nuclear Fuel Cycle

The nuclear power plant, complex as it is, is but one small part of the nuclear fuel cycle. The production of electricity by atomic power takes many steps.

The nuclear fuel cycle begins in the uranium mine and ends with the storage of wastes created by nuclear plants. The fuel cycle includes the following steps before fission can take place in a nuclear power plant:

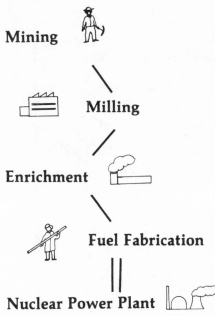

Mining

Milling

Enrichment

Fuel Fabrication

Nuclear Power Plant

These activities are known as the fuel cycle's "front end" because they occur before electricity can be generated in a nuke.

The rest of the nuclear fuel cycle occurs after the fuel is used in a reactor and is called the "back end." This part of the cycle includes:

Nuclear Reactor Wastes

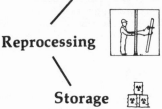

Reprocessing

Storage

Another crucial part of the fuel cycle is:

Transportation

In this section we will also look at other parts of the nuclear power picture, although these are not commonly included as part of the fuel cycle:

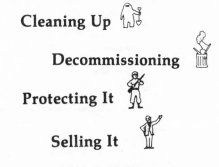

Cleaning Up

Decommissioning

Protecting It

Selling It

The nuclear fuel cycle is extremely expensive, energy-intensive, and remains to this day incomplete. Here we will follow the workings of the fuel cycle from front end to back end.*

THE FRONT END OF THE FUEL CYCLE

Mining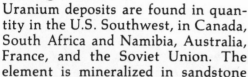

Uranium deposits are found in quantity in the U.S. Southwest, in Canada, South Africa and Namibia, Australia, France, and the Soviet Union. The element is mineralized in sandstone deposits and other rock formations. High-grade ores contain up to 3% uranium. These rich ores are beginning to be exhausted, and ore with 0.4% and less uranium is now being worked. Uranium ore is extracted from surface and underground mines.

As much as 90% of U.S. uranium resources are located on Native American reservations. Local tribes have been poorly paid for the use of their land and labor. Mining is also taking its toll on the health of the miners, many of whom suffer from cancer caused by the radioactive radon gas released during mining.

In Australia, miners' labor unions have organized to stop uranium mining because of its fundamentally antisocial uses.

---

*The health and safety dangers associated with each phase of the nuclear fuel cycle will be discussed in Chapter 5, Nuclear Safety Along the Fuel Cycle.

Potential Uranium Resources by Region
(Tons of $30 per pound U₃O₈)*

18,000
138,000
428,000
0
446,000
108,000
120,000
71,000
77,000
86,000
1,168,000
259,000
1,000

*Geological estimate   Source: ERDA

The New York Times/April 7, 1977

Geological areas of probable and speculative uranium reserves—The size of these reserves is a matter of controversy. A Ford Foundation report says there may be enough domestic uranium resources that plutonium-recycling and the breeder reactor will not be necessary—a view the Energy Research and Development Administration challenges. (See Victor McElheny, "U.S. Uranium Supply Figures Disputed," *New York Times*, 7 April 1977.)

Milling

Once extracted, raw uranium ore is crushed and ground to a sandy consistency at mills that are usually located near the mines. Sulfuric acid is used to extract the uranium, creating a mixture of uranium oxides, uranium-238 and -235, known as "yellowcake." Yellowcake contains 85% uranium oxides by weight and is the raw material of reactor fuel.

About four pounds of yellowcake can be extracted from an average ton of ore. This ratio has already dropped and will continue to do so as high-grade ores become ever more scarce.

What is left after milling the yellowcake are tons of waste materials known as tailings. These tailings contain radium, a radioactive element found with uranium, and radon gas decay products of radium—known as "radon daughters." Disposal of these wastes received a lot of attention when it became known that they had been indiscriminately used as fill material in communities near mines and mills, leaving homes and buildings with radioactive foundations. Piles of discarded tailings blow around and pollute runoff water with radioactive particles.

Oil companies have expanded into the nuclear business, from uranium mining to nuclear construction. In 1970, 17 oil companies controlled 55% of drilling, 48% of known low-cost uranium reserves and around 28% of uranium ore processing capacity.

Exxon, Kerr-McGee, Atlantic Richfield, Continental, Gulf, Getty, Standard of Ohio, and Sun Oil all have exploration or reserve uranium holdings. Six are involved in mining and milling.[1]

Enrichment

The concentration of fissile U-235 atoms is not great enough in yellowcake for it to serve as reactor fuel in light-water reactors. Enrichment plants use a process called gaseous diffusion to concentrate the uranium-235 to a level where it can be used for reactor fuel (3%) or, at a higher concentration (about 90%) for weapons use.

Atoms of U-235 pass just slightly more quickly through a thin porous membrane than do those of U-238. This difference is the basis of the gaseous diffusion technology.

The process begins with the conversion of the solid yellowcake into a gas, uranium hexafluoride (UF_6). The gas is very corrosive and explosive, requiring careful handling and special pipe and container materials. The gas is pumped and cooled on its way through a succession of diffusion chambers where it passes through special thin membranes of porous metal. The lighter U-235 diffuses slightly more quickly; the concentration of this isotope is increased in each cell by only about one part in a thousand.

The output of a gaseous diffusion plant is measured in "separative work units" which reflect the amount of energy used to enrich the uranium.

Uranium enrichment plants are the largest industrial plants in the world. They have been built in Britain, France, the U.S.S.R., and China. The three U.S. plants are in Oak Ridge, Tennessee (run by Union Carbide), Portsmouth, Ohio and Paducah, Kentucky (both run by Goodyear Aerospace). These plants were built for the military. Although owned by the government, they are operated by private industry under Department of Energy contracts. The three U.S. plants represent a total investment of $2.4 billion of taxpayer dollars. Costs of building a similar plant now would run to $3.5 billion.[2]

The plants are huge, taking up hundreds of acres each. They circulate

Oak Ridge TN Gaseous Diffusion Plant—Facility built in 1943 for the production of enriched uranium for the Manhattan Project of WW II. (Credit: F. Hoffman for U.S.AEC. (DOE-71-9189)

millions of gallons of cooling water daily and consume vast amounts of electricity to run the many pumps and condensers.

According to nuclear critic David Dinsmore Comey, the three enrichment plants consume about 3% of all the electricity produced in the U.S.!

This means, for a start, that the net amount of electricity produced by nuclear power in 1975 was not 8% but 5%.[3]

Fuel Fabrication

Turning the enriched uranium-hexafluoride into nuclear plant fuel is a complicated process as well. Since the uranium oxides are radioactive, most work is done by remote control.

At fuel fabrication plants the enriched uranium is solidified into small ceramic pellets, about the size of a pencil eraser. The pellets are loaded into thin metal fuel rods.

Once loaded, the rods are placed in fuel assemblies.

Fuel rod assembly
(Credit: Lionel Delevingne)

Each fuel assembly holds from 50 to 300 rods. A 575-megawatt PWR like the Connecticut Yankee plant contains 157 fuel assemblies in its core. Each assembly has 204 rods. The total weight of the fuel is 82.5 tons. In a typical giant 1,150-megawatt reactor the nuclear fuel would weigh 152.2 tons, with 64 rods in each of 732 assemblies.

The largest fuel conversion and fabrication plants in the world are the Westinghouse owned-and-operated plant in Columbia, South Carolina, and Exxon's plant at Richland, Washington.

The plutonium oxide fuel used in the experimental fast breeder reactors is even more difficult to handle than uranium oxide. Plutonium fuel rod fabrication is dangerous business, especially for workers in these fabrication facilities.

In the early 1970s there were four companies making plutonium fuel rods: Nuclear Fuel Service, Inc., Nuclear Ma-terials and Engineering Corp. (NU-MEC), Gulf United Nuclear Fuels, and the Kerr-McGee Corp. Three of the four plants are now shut down. Gulf United in Long Island quit the business after a December 1972 fire and explo-sion injured one worker and contamin-ated two others. At Kerr-McGee's Ci-marron, Oklahoma plant, 73 workers were contaminated with plutonium during a four-year period. Karen Silk-wood worked there and exposed the unsafe working conditions. (See p. 138 for her story.) The plant was shut down in December 1975. At present only the NUMEC plant near Pittsburgh is functioning.

At the Nuclear Power Plant

The fuel assemblies are transported, usually by truck or rail, to nuclear plants across the country. About once a year, barring special problems, the reactor core is opened for refueling and

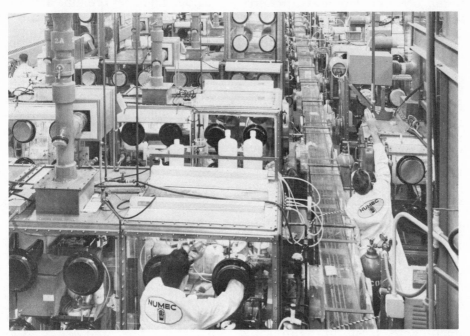

Fuel Fabrication—Glove-boxes in laboratory for research on plutonium fuel fabrication techniques. (Credit: Nuclear Materials and Equipment Corporation, DOE-64-7401)

the spent fuel rods are removed. Rods are considered "spent" when two-thirds of their fissionable U-235 atoms are gone. Each year about one-quarter of the core is removed and replaced with fresh fuel assemblies.

The used fuel rods are so "hot"—radioactive—that they must cool off in on-site storage pools from four to six months. All operations involving the core and used fuel must be done by remote control under water to prevent worker contamination.

THE "BACK END" OF THE FUEL CYCLE

Fuel Reprocessing— Theory and Practice—
What happens to the used fuel? For years, government and industry booklets and literature have been cheerfully telling us that everything is under control and that the fuel cycle marches on to reprocessing. However, the process is not so simple.

> The next stage of the fuel cycle is reprocessing to recover and separate the unused and very valuable fissionable material from the nuclear wastes. These reusable materials—up to 25 percent of the original fuel—are recovered and used again. Any remaining nuclear wastes are collected and prepared for safe storage.[4]

Each spent fuel rod contains about .6% plutonium and .8% usable uranium-235. Theoretically, 90% or more of the plutonium and uranium in spent commercial fuel can be recovered for future use. Nuclear economists once estimated that mixing reprocessing plant products with fresh uranium could save between 20% and 35% of the uranium used, stretching out uranium

supplies and cutting costs anywhere from 5% to 30%.[5]

Before 1966 all fuel reprocessing was done at the government-owned installations in Hanford, Washington and Savannah River, South Carolina, and at Idaho's National Reactor Testing Station. The first commercial reprocessing plant was built by Nuclear Fuel Services, Inc. in 1966 in New York State. By the 1970s there were to be three commercial plants operating: in West Valley, New York; General Electric's Mideast Fuel Recovery Plant in Morris, Illinois; and the Allied-General plant in Barnwell, South Carolina.

However, not one of these plants is operating at this time. The only plants now functioning anywhere in the West are the large French facility in La Hague and a small plant in Windscale, England. At these plants spent fuel rods from Japanese and European reactors arrive and are cut up into small pieces to remove the nuclear material inside. The fuel remains are then dissolved in nitric acid so that the "valuable fissionable material"—uranium and plutonium—can be removed to be used once again in other reactor fuel. As the spent fuel is intensely radioactive, all work is done by remote control behind heavy shielding.

> ...No reprocessing capability exists or is forecast.[6]
> ERDA, May 1977

What went wrong?

The West Valley Scandal
In 1963, Nelson Rockefeller, then governor, officially broke ground for the nation's first privately-owned nuclear fuel reprocessing facility at West Valley, New York, a rural area 33 miles south of Buffalo. The $32.5 million plant was built and operated by Nuclear Fuel Services (NFS), a subsidiary of W.R. Grace-Davison Chemical Company. Rockefeller said the operation

would "make a major contribution towards transforming the economy... of the entire state."[7]

The plant started up in 1966 and reprocessed about 625 metric tons of nuclear fuel during the six years it operated. Although the plant did reprocess waste fuel from civilian reactors here and abroad, more than 60% of all wastes processed came from government-owned reactors in Hanford, Washington. The plutonium recovered was used for nuclear weapons.

In 1969, Davison Chemical Company sold NFS to Getty Oil. The plant continued to operate at a financial loss and in 1972, reprocessing ceased. West Valley's other function—the storage of high and low-level nuclear wastes—continued until the spring of 1975.

West Valley is now closed, a silent symbol of the brash hopes of nuclear pioneer Rockefeller, among others.

Lots of things went wrong at West Valley. There were leaks of radioactivity and periodic radioactive emissions. The plant's laundryroom was contaminated several times, and on 11 June, 1968, the plant's lunchroom as well. Workers, their clothing, personal belongings, and land adjacent to the plant all became contaminated at different times. And the plant's practice of using young transient workers from the area's large pool of unemployed

people for particularly "hot" jobs—where they would receive their annual or quarterly radiation dose in minutes or hours and be sent home with a day's pay—undoubtedly condemned many innocent people to future cancers. As no or inadequate records were kept of the workers' health over time, it is not known just how many people have had cause to suffer from exposure to radiation at West Valley.

It is known that radiation was released from the plant into Cattaraugus Creek,* and there has been leaching of buried radioactive wastes into the creek, which feeds into Lake Erie, source of Buffalo's municipal drinking water.

> If the goal of low-level nuclear-waste disposal is 100 percent retention of the waste for the duration of its hazardous lifetime (300 to 1,000 years), then in 14 years West Valley has failed.[8]
>
> EPA Regional Administrator
> Gerald M. Hansler

In 1975, Getty Oil announced its decision to shut the plant down permanently. Changing regulatory requirements, the company said, would have called for an additional investment of $600 million—almost 20 times the plant's original cost—to make it acceptable.

The legacy of the West Valley plant is all too real.

Getty left behind 600,000 gallons of boiling high-level wastes contained in temporary underground tanks, and 2 million cubic feet of buried trash. A 1976 federal government study said that the West Valley site could have an intense earthquake on an average of

---

*In a report that has aroused much controversy, Dr. Ernest Sternglass, professor of radiology at the University of Pittsburgh Medical School, used federal statistics to show that infant mortality in Cattaraugus County rose 54% in the year after reprocessing began at West Valley. He attributed the rise to contamination of water and milk.

once every 750 years or so. Of course, high-level wastes such as those stored at West Valley will be dangerous for hundreds of thousands of years.

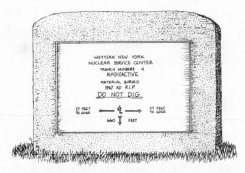

West Valley Waste Storage Marker—Drawing of a photo that appears in an EPA booklet, "Hazardous Wastes" (EPA/1975 SW-138), p. 13. (Credit: Susanna Natti)

Who will clean up? Who will pay?

The original contracts made between New York State and Nuclear Fuel Services and approved by Rockefeller gave the state final responsibility for the containment and disposal of wastes as well as decontamination and decommissioning of the plant. ERDA estimated that the costs of solidifying and storing the wastes alone could run as high as $500 million. Full decommissioning could cost as much as $1 billion; it's hard to know as no comparable facility has ever been decommissioned.

But the money won't come from Nuclear Fuel Services. Under the contracts, the company was required to put money aside in a reserve fund "for perpetual care and management of nuclear wastes." But there is now less than $4 million in the account. Meanwhile, New York State will pay between $2 and $3 million each year just to maintain the wastes as they are.

New York's Governor Carey has asked the federal government to help pay the costs left behind by NFS and has declared that he will not allow nuclear construction in the state until the waste question is resolved.[9] (But see what's happening in New York State, p. 258.)

The $65 Million White Elephant

General Electric's $65 million Midwest Fuel Recovery Plant in Morris, Illinois was abandoned in 1975 after six years of construction and a cost overrun of $28 million. The facility never processed any reactor wastes. Its supposedly simplified system of isotope recovery kept clogging and malfunctioning during tests. Rebuilding the plant would have taken another four years and an additional $90-130 million, with no promise of success. The facility is now being used to store spent fuel rods and is licensed to receive 750 tons of spent fuel.

Barnwell, South Carolina

Construction of the Barnwell Nuclear Fuel (reprocessing) Plant and waste storage facility began in 1971 at the Savannah River weapons complex on land made available by the Atomic Energy Commission. The original price tag was $100 million. The plant was a joint venture financed by Allied Chemical (Standard Oil), Gulf Oil, and Royal Dutch-Shell under the name Allied General Nuclear Services (AGNS). The plant would use reprocessing technology similar to West Valley's, but would be five times its size. By 1976 the cost had jumped to $250 million, with no end in sight.

AGNS then asked the federal government to take over the reprocessing end of the plant as it was not going to pay off economically for them. The government has responded with a $14 million grant to keep the plant "viable" until October 1978, when a decision on plutonium is supposed to be made.

The Barnwell reprocessing plant was scheduled to begin operating in 1975. Without the facility there is no commercial reprocessing in the U.S., and the back-up of spent fuel at nuclear plants across the country is reaching serious proportions. At many plants the storage pools for used fuel rods are filled to capacity. There is not even space in some to put in large sections of the core should an emergency require removal of a reactor's fuel assemblies.

Many utilities are requesting NRC permission to enlarge their nuke plant storage pools to compensate in a temporary way for the reprocessing roadblock. Barnwell occupies a crucial position in the fuel cycle. It's failure to operate may be one more factor leading to a moratorium on nuclear power.

Even without active fuel reprocessing, all is not well, or safe, in the Barnwell area. AGNS is going ahead with commercial licensing hearings for a nuclear dump, a "fuel receiving and storage station" (FRSS). The NRC is considering granting AGNS permission to open the dump, even though there are no plans for doing anything with the wastes at this time. The AGNS (locally known as "Agnes") plant is anticipating more than 500 shipments every year from power plants across the country.[10]

Transportation

Our roads, railways, and airways have been used for years to ship radioactive materials. Mines, enrichment plants, nukes, and storage dumps are spread across the country. This map shows a sample path of just one possible fuel cycle trip.

And nuclear materials frequently travel in and out of the country as well. Enriched uranium shipments are regularly exported to West Germany, where the material is converted to reactor

Nuclear Materials on the Highway
One route among many that crisscross the nation

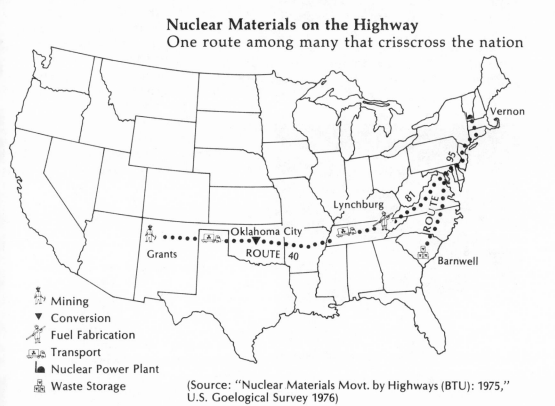

Mining
Conversion
Fuel Fabrication
Transport
Nuclear Power Plant
Waste Storage

(Source: "Nuclear Materials Movt. by Highways (BTU): 1975," U.S. Goelogical Survey 1976)

fuel and then resold for research reactors to the Netherlands, Sweden, Denmark, Austria, France, Japan, and even back to Canada.[11]

Fresh nuclear fuel does not pose as much of a threat to its handlers, shippers, and people living along the transportation routes as the super-hot wastes from spent fuel, which are extremely hazardous. But all nuclear material shipments run the risk of being hijacked or stolen by people or groups who might want to get hold of uranium or plutonium.

On the Road—The route most traveled by trucks with radioactive cargo is U.S. Interstate 80, which spans the country from San Francisco to the Hudson River. Highway I-95, the north-south route that goes from Maine to Florida, is probably number two. This route was used for the shipment of wastes from eastern reactors to Maxey Flats, Kentucky, and now sees trucks going on to Aiken and Barnwell in South Carolina.

NRC shipping regulations require some safeguards, but do not distinguish between shipments of radioactive materials traveling through rural or even empty desert areas and those going through narrow streets of congested cities with large populations.

In August 1975, the New York City Department of Health banned the shipment of radioactive material through the city's streets. Regular shipments of wastes from the Brookhaven National Laboratory on Long Island had been coming right across Manhattan, over the George Washington Bridge, and then south to Aiken for storage. The results of an accident in the middle of this city of 12 million people were judged to be too great, no matter how low the statistical probabilities of such an event.

In November 1977, the federal Department of Transportation held hearings on the ban and questioned its justification. Hundreds of people were on hand to support continuation of the ban.

Following the New York City transportation ban, the wastes were sent by regular passenger ferry to Connecticut and shipped on that state's roads. Shipments contained 14 uranium fuel elements each. There were no guards on the truck "because the amount of fuel would not be enough to make a bomb," said Brookhaven's vice-president, R. Christian Anderson.[12]

After a truck carrying low-level, solidified radioactive waste tore through a low bridge on a Connecticut highway in April 1976, Governor Ella Grasso asked for a complete review of rad-waste transport.[13]

In the Air—Nuclear materials are international big business. But there are dangers. In January 1976, New York City banned the shipping of uranium and plutonium—special nuclear materials (SNM)—from Kennedy International Airport. Following this ban, radioactive materials were diverted to O'Hare in Chicago, the world's busiest airport. Since August 1975, over two

Transporting Radioactive Wastes—
(Credit: Vermont Public Interest Research Group, Inc.—VPIRG—1976)

tons of SNM have been shipped on commercial jets through O'Hare. After a *Chicago Sun-Times* article revealed the extent of the shipments, people became concerned, and the O'Hare traffic was halted on 2 December 1977 by Chicago Mayor Michael Bilandic and the NRC, pending a safety study.

According to affidavits made public by the New York Public Interest Research Group in 1975, "between 2,000 and 46,000 lung cancers could develop from the crash of an airplane transporting plutonium under possible meteorological conditions."[14]

Waste Storage—
Where Does the Garbage Go?

Nearly all operations that produce or use nuclear materials generate radioactive waste. Most waste comes from the Energy Research and Development Administration's military reactors, commercial nuclear powerplants (spent fuel elements)* and Federal and commercial fuel cycle activities— mainly fuel fabrication and reprocessing facilities.

*Spent fuel has not yet been defined by the Nuclear Regulatory Commission as high level waste and may not be, because of its potential value as a source of fuel if reprocessed. This report will consider spent fuel as a "potential" high level waste.[15]

General Accounting Office
Report, 1977

Waste storage is one part of the fuel cycle that the nuclear establishment wishes would go away. In the heat of discovery and development of nuclear power during World War II, little thought was given to the final disposal of wastes. Scientists assumed that like

many new problems confronted during that time, waste disposal would also be solved. But the Achilles Heel of the nuclear industry is no small matter.

Radioactive wastes are a dangerous end to the fuel cycle. They are toxic. Once released into the environment, they contaminate land and water virtually "forever."

Radioactive isotopes in nuclear waste have different half-lives—the amount of time it takes for half of a given amount of radioactive material to decay. Some decay in a few hours. Others, like the common decay products of uranium-235, strontium-90, and cesium-137, last longer, with half lives of 12 and 30 years. It takes around 120 to 130 years before they can be considered harmless. Still others, like plutonium-239 take far more time. The half-life of plutonium is 24,300 years! After more than 24,000 years only half of a given amount of plutonium is gone. It takes about ten half-lives for radioactive material to become "harmless." So plutonium must be kept out of the environment for a quarter to a half million years if it is to decay completely. (See chart on p. 75 for an idea of just how much time that is.)

More than 50 radioactive particles are created in the fission process of nuclear plants. Here are some fission products:*

krypton-85	iodine-129
strontium-89	iodine-131
strontium-90	xenon-133
zirconium-95	cesium-137
niobium-95	barium-140
technetium-99	lanthanum-140
ruthenium-103	cerium-141
rhodium-103	cerium-144
ruthenium-106	praseodymium-143
rhodium-106	praseodymium-144
tellurium-129	promethium-147

---

*from Charles Fox, *Radioactive Wastes*, (Oak Ridge Tennessee: USAEC, 1969), p. 41.

At this time there is no agreed-upon safe way to isolate radioactive materials from the environment for thousands of years, a time span longer than human civilization. Nuclear storage facilities have had a hard time protecting wastes for even a decade.

There are currently 7 million cubic feet of radioactive waste from nuclear electric and weapon-making facilities. By the year 2,000, there will be more than 11 million cubic feet of waste.[16]

There are three categories of nuclear wastes, as well as the mining wastes (tailings) mentioned earlier.

Low-Level Waste

The Environmental Protection Agency (EPA) has estimated that by the year 2000, federal and commercial nuclear power together might generate up to 400 million cubic feet of low-level waste. These wastes include anything that has picked up radiation during any part of the fuel cycle. Also included are medical wastes contaminated by hospital use of radiation, as well as tools used in mining and gloves and uniforms of workers in enrichment and reprocessing plants. Another low-level waste is the radioactive plant cooling water. Highly contaminated cooling water is removed from the core, allowed to cool and evaporate while short-lived radioactive by-products decay, and is then mixed with cement and solidified in 55-gallon steel drums. The barrels are buried as low-level waste.

Low-level wastes have historically been handled with some abandon. Between 1946 and 1962, 47,500 55-gallon drums of radioactive waste from atomic weapons and research were dumped into the ocean near the Farallones Islands 35 miles west of San Francisco and off Cape Cod. An EPA oceanographer estimated that about 25% of the barrels had broken open and that low levels of radioactive waste had leaked out in an area where fish such as the deep sea sole and the commercially important sable fish were observed. However, only a few of the 28,800 barrels dumped into the Atlantic Ocean near the Maryland/Delaware border were found broken open.[17] The two dumping areas were licensed by the AEC for low-level waste disposal from 1946 until 1970.

There was also casual dumping of radioactive tools near a mining and milling operation in Beatty, Nevada, exposing people unnecessarily to radiation. People had entered the poorly-guarded dumping reservation to make off with seemingly new, abandoned tools. Several house foundations were poured using a radioactive cement mixer taken from the dumping area.

There are six major commercial burial sites for low-level nuke waste. One of these, the West Valley site, was closed in 1975 when it was finally revealed that the burial trenches were leaching into nearby creeks that feed Lake Erie.

Similar leaching of radioactive wastes from trenches where barrels, boxes, and cannisters full of waste are buried has been discovered at Maxey Flats near the Morehead, Kentucky disposal area. In the fall of 1977 the facility was closed because of the leaks, including one that was reportedly 14 years old.[18]

Intermediate—Level Waste

So-called intermediate wastes are liquids and materials contaminated with fission products, including uranium and plutonium. These wastes are not necessarily less dangerous than high-level wastes, but are less concentrated and do not contain spent fuel rods, although used fuel cladding is included.

About 75% of all U.S. nuclear waste is stored at ERDA's Hanford, Washington reservation. There intermediate level waste has been put into concrete covered trenches called "cribs," which let radioactive materials such as plutonium-239, cesium-137, strontium-90, and tritium (a radioactive form of hydrogen), percolate into the soil below. It is assumed they will stop long before reaching the desert-like reservation's water table far underground. There are evidently extensive amounts of plutonium buried at Hanford in this way.[19]

High-Level Waste

These wastes contain uranium-235 and plutonium-239. They are highly radioactive. They are dangerous in any form; they can be used to make an explosive weapon. A large nuclear power plant turns out this much waste.

Most radioactive wastes from the civilian nuclear program are still in the spent reactor fuel where they were created. As mentioned in the quote from the GAO report, the NRC has not yet defined spent fuel as high level waste because of its potential value as fuel if reprocessed. However, as no reprocessing is in the offing, the used fuel *is* a waste product, defined or not.

And the spent fuel is piling up at commercial reactor sites. Now about 3,000 metric tons of spent fuel are stored on-site. Without reprocessing going on, the amount could grow by an additional 17,000 metric tons over the next ten years. There will be a severe shortage of on-site storage capacity by 1985.

It has been widely believed that commercial nuclear power plant wastes were but a small part of radioactive wastes in this country, the bulk being

High-Level Waste

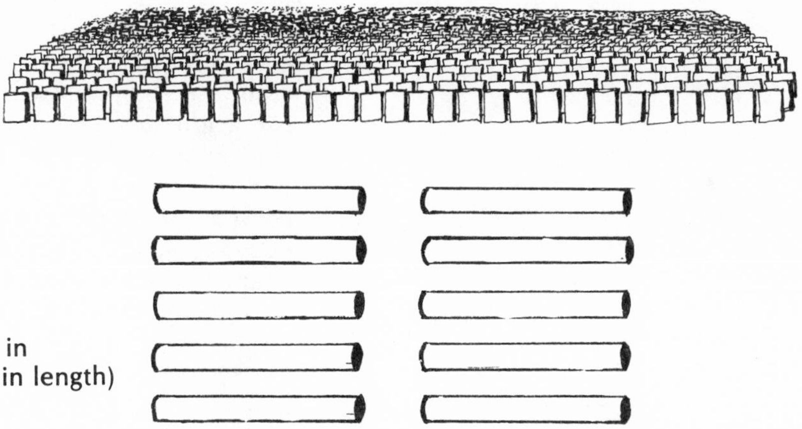

Liquid
9,000 gallons

Solid
10 canisters (1 ft. in
diameter x 10 ft. in length)

Volume of high-level waste from an average 1,000-megawatt nuke in one year of operation!

from nuclear weapons and submarine (military) sources. But a study published in the late summer of 1977 revealed that this is not so.

> Contrary to widespread belief, the accumulated inventory of fission products generated by the still small U.S. civilian nuclear power industry may already be comparable to that generated by U.S. military nuclear programs. Although the volumes of the military wastes are very large, they are on the average almost 100 times more dilute than projected commercial high-level wastes.[20]

Although most commercial wastes are still inside the spent fuel, they are growing at an alarming rate. As the graph below shows, the "civilian inventory" of wastes will continue to climb, unless the industry is cut back or shut down.

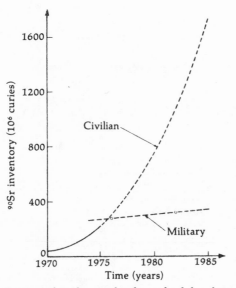

Estimated civilian and military high level waste inventories measured in terms of their ^{90}Sr content as function of time. (*Science*, 26 Aug. 1977)

Waste Storage Now

About 71 million gallons of high-level waste are now being stored "temporarily." Fifty million gallons are at the Hanford Reservation in Richland, Washington, 21 million gallons are at Savannah River in Aiken, South Carolina. Another 3 million are at the Idaho National Engineering Lab in Idaho Falls. These wastes are from the weapons program, leftovers following reprocessing of spent fuel from the DOE's production reactors which make uranium-235 and plutonium for nuclear weapons.

> Until the 1960s, little effort was made to develop technologies for the long term storage or "permanent" disposal of hazardous radioactive waste. The production of atomic weapons materials and development of commercial nuclear power-plants received the highest priority. Decisions as to the management of military waste were based on short term expediency rather than long term considerations.[21]   GAO report

The super hot liquid wastes are stored in concrete-encased carbon or stainless steel tanks (the former tanks for acidic acid, the latter for neutralized waste). The wastes generate such heat that they often boil, and must be cooled. Although the tanks are supposed to last for 50 years, the stress on them from hot, corrosive, and acidic wastes has caused far shorter tank life and a series of leaks.

By 1970, there had been 15 tank failures: 11 at Hanford and 4 less serious ones at Savannah River. The worst was discovered on 8 June 1973 at Hanford. The waste storage facility was then being run by ARCO (Atlantic Richfield Co.). Tank 10-6T, an old one

Radioactive Storage Sites: Where Are They?

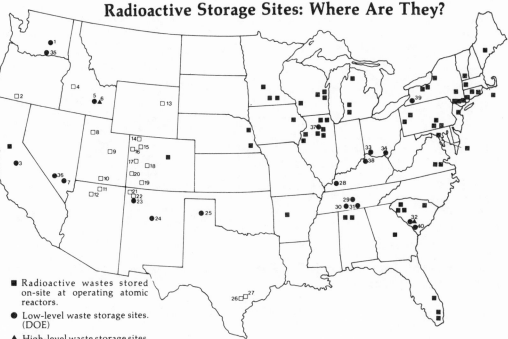

■ Radioactive wastes stored
  on-site at operating atomic
  reactors.

● Low-level waste storage sites.
  (DOE)

▲ High-level waste storage sites.
  (DOE)

□ Inactive uranium mill sites
  (uranium tailings).

1. Low-level wastes stored at
   Hanford, Washington
2. Inactive uranium mill site at
   Lakeview, Oregon
3. Low-level waste at Lawrence
   Livermore Lab, Livermore,
   California
4. Inactive uranium mill site at
   Lowman, Idaho
5/6. High and low-level wastes
   stored at Idaho National Engineering
7. Low-level wastes stored at
   the Nevada test site
8. Inactive uranium mill site at
   Salt Lake City, Utah
9. Inactive uranium mill site at
   Green River, Utah
10. Inactive uranium mill site at
    Mexican Hat, Utah
11. Inactive uranium mill site at
    Monument Valley, Arizona
12. Inactive uranium mill site at
    Tuba City, Arizona
13. Inactive uranium mill site at
    Converse County, Wy.
14. Inactive uranium mill site at
    Maybell, Colo.
15. Two inactive uranium mill
    sites at Rifle, Colo.

16. Inactive uranium mill site at
    Grand Junction, Colo.
17. Inactive uranium mill site at
    Naturita, Colo.
18. Inactive uranium mill site at
    Gunnison, Colo.
19. Inactive uranium mill site at
    Durango Colo.
20. Two inactive uranium mill
    sites at Slick Rock, Colo.
21. Inactive uranium mill site at
    Shiprock N.M.
22. Inactive uranium mill site at
    Ambrosia Lake N.M.
23. Low-level waste storage at
    Los Alamos Scientific Lab,
    Los Alamos, N.M.
24. Low-level waste storage at
    Sandia, N.M.
25. Low-level waste storage at
    PANTEX, Amarillo, Tex.
26. Inactive uranium mill site at
    Ray Point, Tex.
27. Inactive uranium mill site at
    Falls City, Tex.
28. Low-level waste storage at
    Paducah, Ky.
29. Low-level waste storage at
    Oak Ridge National Labora-
    tory, Oak Ridge, Tenn.
30. Low-level waste storage at
    Oak Ridge Gaseous Diffu-
    sion Plant, Oak Ridge, Tenn.

31. Low-level waste storage at
    Y-12, uranium enrichment
    building Oak Ridge, Tenn.
32. High and low-level waste
    storage at Savannah River
    Plant, Savannah River, Ga.
33. Low-level waste storage at
    Fernald, Ohio (Feed Mater-
    ials Plant)
34. Low-level waste storage at
    Portsmouth, Ohio
35. High level waste storage by
    DOE   at Richland Wash.
    and low-level commercial
    waste storage by the Nu-
    clear Engineering Co. at
    Richland, Washington
36. Low-level solid waste stor-
    age at Beatty, Nev. by
    Nuclear Engineering Co.
37. Low-level solid waste stor-
    age Sheffield, Ill. by Nuclear
    Engineering Co.
38. Low-level solid waste stor-
    age at Morehead Ky. by
    Nuclear Engineering Co.
39. Low-level solid waste stor-
    age at West Valley, N.Y. by
    Nuclear Fuel Services
40. Low-level solid waste stor-
    age at Barnwell S.C. by
    Chem-Nuclear Services, Inc.

(Source: *Critical Mass Journal*, 1976)

COOLED WASTE STORAGE TANK

Stress—Relieved Primary Liner 1,300,000 Gallons

Type III

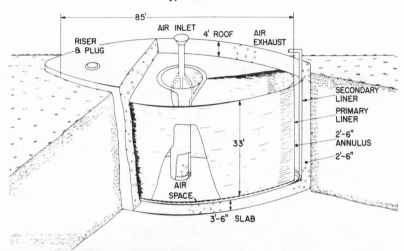

Current high-level waste tank similar to one that leaked in Hanford.
(DOE-72-9444)

built in 1944, had leaked from corrosion some 115,000 gallons of liquid high-level waste. A leak was finally discovered that was draining the tank by some 2500 gallons a day. It had leaked for 51 days. Experts say that methods for detecting leaks are crude, and there may be many small breaks that simply go unnoticed. Typically, poor records were kept on the tank. The 115,000 gallons contained 14,000 curies of strontium-90, 40,000 curies of cesium-137, and 4 curies of plutonium, with other fission products as well.

Between August 1958 and this June 1973, an estimated 422,000 gallons containing more than half a million curies seeped out of 15 other tanks, all of which have since been "retired." But the leak in 10-6T was something different. It was the largest single accidental release of radioactive waste in the Commission's history, and easily its most embarrassing incident since Project Baneberry, a weap-

ons test that went awry in Nevada in 1970, sending a puff of fallout all the way to the Canadian border.[22]

The AEC claimed that all the radiation would be contained underground and would pose no threat to the Columbia River, just 10 miles from the spill site. In fact, abnormally high levels of radioactivity have already been monitored in the river, its fish, plankton, and wildlife. These levels may be due more to direct discharge of wastes into the ground than to spills from the high-level waste storage tanks. But the contamination is there.

Some intermediate-level waste contaminated with plutonium is stored at Hanford in concrete-covered trenches called "cribs." A 1972 government report said that enough plutonium had collected in the soil of the Hanford cribs to "conceive of conditions which could result in a nuclear chain reaction," which could cause an explosion (such as what happened in the Soviet Union in 1958; see p. 156). Subsequently, the plutonium-contaminated soil was dug up for reprocessing and storage elsewhere.[23]

And Later—

Managing nuclear waste is less difficult than managing many other by-products of our industrial society. The technology to handle nuclear wastes is available today...The Federal Government is presently reviewing several permanent techniques for storing high-level waste. The most promising method is burial in deep salt deposits.
Northeast Utilities' pamphlet "The Way It Is" July 1975

Utility and government hopes for an easy solution to the waste mess have been repeatedly dashed. There have been many disposal methods investigated, from shooting the wastes into outer space (too expensive) to burial in rock formations, arctic ice, deep wells, and surface vaults. More than $1 billion has been spent in vain. A report called *The Nuclear Fuel Cycle* prepared by the Union of Concerned Scientists in 1974 reviewed the chancy nature of nuclear waste storage solutions.

Except for the storage of liquid wastes in tanks, for which experience from weapons production applies, all proposals for long term storage or disposal of high-level waste from the nuclear industry lie at the research and development stage. The proposals so far considered seriously by the AEC for the disposal of wastes are dubious in concept (caverns evacuated by nuclear weapons, depositing wastes in liquid form in rock caverns), not technically feasible (disposal in solar orbit), or

they are so dependent upon site specific geological characteristics that suitability cannot be determined *a priori* without expensive on-site investigation (disposal in bedded salt or under Antarctic ice.)

For awhile it looked like the Lyons, Kansas salt mines would be the solution...but they were full of holes from exploratory oil well drilling.

One such site, the salt beds at Lyons, Kansas, was studied carefully for several years in the 1960s and was finally judged unsuitable. The matter of manmade vaults at or near the surface for long-term storage (500 years) is equally uncertain. Their maintenance depends upon the existence of social and political institutions, the permanence of which cannot be guaranteed...[26]

Not much has changed since the UCS report was issued. But public and even official awareness of the problem has heightened. In July 1976, a court ruling on an appeal of the licensing of the Vermont Yankee nuclear plant suspended the granting of construction licenses for nukes from July until September 1976, when the NRC issued a report on the environmental impact of reprocessing and waste management parts of the fuel cycle for light-water reactors. The court ruling agreed with the New England Coalition on Nuclear Pollution, and maintained that those aspects of the fuel cycle had been inadequately covered in licensing hearings.

The NRC report, called the Bishop Report after one of its editors, chose the salt-bed disposal method as the most feasible. Here is what such a disposal area might look like.

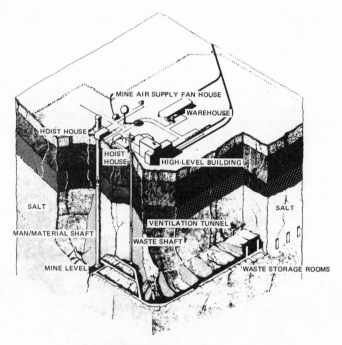

BEDDED SALT PILOT PLANT

(Credit: Oak Ridge Natl. Lab., DOE-74-10102)

In West Germany, intermediate and low-level wastes are stored in heavy barrels in abandoned salt mines (plans for high-level also), but indefinite future storage by this means may not work. Dr. Hannes Alfen, Nobel Laureate in physics, has said: "There is no doubt that the salt mines could be considered safe for any normal waste products. But because of the very large quantities of extremely poisonous substances, it is required that the repository should be absolutely free of leakage for a period of hundreds of thousands of years. No reasonable geologist can guarantee this, simply because the problem is one of which we have no experience."[25]

The GAO report summed up the desperate waste problem quite succinctly:

To safeguard present and future generations, locations must be found to isolate these wastes and their harmful environmental effects. A program must be developed for present and future waste disposal operations that will not create unwarranted public risk. Otherwise, nuclear power cannot continue to be a practical source of energy.[26]

Constipation at the Back End of the Fuel Cycle

In October 1977, President Carter announced that the federal government would take responsibility for storage of nuclear wastes for domestic utilities as well as other nations. The DOE promises a geological waste disposal facility or other storage place for spent fuel by 1985. But no state seems to want to house the wastes, and delays in this program have been constant in the past. Meanwhile, the nuclear industry is already running out of temporary storage place for spent fuel. With no return to commercial reprocessing in sight, the utilities are in a tight situation.

As of January 1977, utilities operating 36 of the 63 present nuclear reactors have notified the Commission (NRC) of their interest to increase storage capacities at their reactor pools by reducing the amount of space between stored fuel elements (compaction). The safety of such action has been questioned by the Natural Resources Defense Council. In response, the Commission has undertaken a generic environmetal impact statement of the storage of fuel elements. While the statement has not been completed, the Commission has allowed compaction on a case-by-case basis.[27]

As of January 1977, the NRC had approved compaction in 14 of the 36 reactors. There has been protest against this move as some people fear that compaction could increase chances of a critical mass being reached in the storage pool itself.

The waste storage situation is bad and appears to be growing worse. Certainly so for the utilities with nuclear plants, as the public becomes more aware of the dangers from the ever-growing stockpiles of wastes and demands action. Meanwhile, nobody wants the stuff in their "back yards," for obvious reasons! In 1977 the Minnesota legislature passed a bill prohibiting construction or operation of radioactive waste management facilities in the state. Minnesota, Montana, New Mexico, South Dakota, Vermont, and Louisiana have laws prohibiting the transportation of radioactive waste into the state for permanent storage unless authorized by the legislature.[28]

Cleaning Up

There is one very important aspect of the fuel cycle that is seldom mentioned by the nuclear industry, but accompanies all activities along the fuel cycle

Low-level Waste—By the year 2000, there will be enough low-level radioactive waste in this country to cover a four-lane highway one foot deep from coast to coast.[29](Credit: Susanna Natti)

path. That is the process of decontamination, or cleaning up the radiation that results from spills, leaks, and accidents.

Since the particulars vary according to the situation, here is a generalized picture of what decontamination involves.

Room/Factory Contamination—Following an accident in a nuclear facility where there is a release of radiation, the room or affected area may be sealed off temporarily to let the radiation level subside somewhat. Then shielded, heavily-dressed crews go in to clean up and decontaminate by washing walls, ceilings, and floors and removing radioactive objects. They clean with vacuum cleaners, soap, water, and detergent. Of course, their clothes and the results of the cleanup also have to be buried as radioactive waste...

If radiation levels are intense, workers can only spend a brief time in the area and must be replaced by "fresh teams" of workers who have not yet received their quarterly or annual maximum dose. Thus the dangers of exposure are the same during cleanup as during other nuclear related-work.

Land Contamination—This calls for "remedial measures" which can include "controlled plowing of contaminated areas, covering such areas with oils, plastics, or asphalt, or actual removal of upper layers of soil for controlled burial on the site or elsewhere."[30]

An example of the extent of cleanup involved is the case of the Rocky Flats nuclear weapons plant. There, in June 1976 "workers wearing protective jumpsuits and using respirators began...the year-long task of removing 400 cubic yards of radioactive dirt contaminated by plutonium." The ground had been contaminated eight years before "by plutonium-tainted oil seeping through corroded 55-gallon metal drums in a Rocky Flats storage field."[31] The contaminated area was room-sized. The dirt was shipped to Idaho for storage.

Air—Airborne radiation, whether from low-level normal plant emissions, high-level accident releases, or atomic bombs, is known as fallout. Cleanup of fallout begins once the radiation collects on the ground. If the amount is not concentrated enough to make land cleanup physically or economically possible, then the only way to decontaminate is on an individual basis, by washing all vegetables and avoiding dairy products. When the level of airborne radiation reaches a certain level (which varies in different places according to political and other winds), all dairy products in the affected area are withdrawn from sale. Milk is a most affected product, as cows pick up fallout from fields as they graze, and the contaminants are concentrated in the milk. For this reason, milk testing is done on a regular basis near nuclear plants.

People—For external contamination of skin and clothing, the radioactive particles on the body are washed off, and clothing is stored as low-level waste. Radioactive particles on the skin are washed off, depending on the severity of exposure, with simple soap and water or painful multiple scrubbings with detergent and bleach.

Protecting It: Fuel Cycle Safeguards

Uranium and Plutonium are valuable. There have been thefts and losses at every turn in the fuel path, and it is reasonably certain that a black market in plutonium exists.

In August 1977 it was revealed that more than 8,000 pounds of highly enriched uranium and plutonium were missing as of September 1976 from military weapons-related facilities. There have been hundreds of violations of stringent (on paper) security and accounting regulations at government nuclear installations over the past 20 years.[32]

Security has been lax at nuclear facilities. In 1972 a General Accounting Office investigation found many security violations at three plants housing enriched uranium and plutonium. They discovered holes in fences, broken locks on doors, and alarms either missing or unanswered.[33] The AEC moved to tighten security, and the NRC is still trying to do so. There have been numerous accounts of people entering commercial nuclear plant sites without detection, although new regulations should have tightened up access to the plants. In February 1977, the NRC issued new requirements for the physical protection of nuclear plants.

One of the most controversial was a requirement for physical "pat-down" searches of utility plant workers, an order now delayed until August 1978.

Protection of special nuclear materials (enriched uranium and plutonium) is expensive. In 1977 $31,352,000 of the ERDA budget went to nuclear materials security and safeguards, and the 1978 Congressional Conference authorization is up to $42,900,000.[34]

Guarding nuclear facilities raises civil liberties questions as well. A document prepared in 1975 for the NRC by Stanford University law professor John Barton surveyed potential threats to civil liberties in light of nuclear-related theft and terrorism. He said there would be a potential need for "a nationwide guard force, greater surveillance of dissenting political groups, area searches in the event of loss of materials, and creation of new barriers of secrecy around parts of the nuclear

Susanna Natti

program." The report anticipated wiretapping, detention, and harsh interrogation procedures "perhaps employing lie detectors or even torture."

In constitutional language, the most serious effects are on freedom of association and discussion (particularly on nuclear issues) and on privacy. It is clearance procedures and continuing surveillance of political dissidents which create the greatest dangers to association and discussion. Psychological testing of industry employees and the possible use of area searches following a nuclear loss create the greatest dangers to privacy.

Unless there are terrorist incidents which lead to wide-sweeping searches, the greatest dangers to civil liberties lie in continued or expanded government surveillance of dissidents. The need to prevent nuclear theft could be used as a persuasive justification for continuing these activities, even though the activities are now under political attack. Although the NRC would not itself conduct such surveillance, it must take into account the civil liberties impact of this surveillance and must ensure that domestic surveillance agencies do not overreact to the nuclear terrorist threat.[35]

Barton urged that the NRC keep "intrusive procedures such as clearance systems and psychological testing" to a minimum, and design safeguards "so that their routine operation does not violate the existing U.S. pattern of civil liberties."

This report was one of many studies contracted for by the NRC in a congressionally-requested inquiry on whether or not the NRC should establish an independent police force. The agency decided that such a force was not needed, but the head of the Department of Energy does have the power to call in U.S. military in case of a "nuclear emergency."[36]

Decommissioning: What Do You Do With A Used Nuke?

Probably the most ignored aspect of nuclear power has been what happens to nuclear plants when their 30-40 year life spans are over. Much like waste storage, decommissioning of reactors has been a problem to be solved at some "future time."

> If we can send a man to the moon, we can figure out how to cut up a defunct commercial nuclear reactor.
> Peter Erickson, NRC official
> *Wall St. Journal*
> 12 October 1977

When their operating lives are over, reactors remain intensely radioactive for years. Among the radioactive isotopes produced are long-lived ones such as nickel-63 (requiring 2,070 years to decay to safe levels) and carbon-14 (needing 65,000 years). Theoretically, if the used-up reactor were just closed, welded shut, and guarded—a process known as "mothballing"—the concrete of the containment vessel would be long since turned to dust before the reactor contents would be safe.

There are two methods proposed for decommissioning a nuke: mothballing and entombment (covering the reactor with concrete). Complete dismantling is tricky business, expensive, and dangerous to the workers involved. The walls of a used reactor are so highly radioactive that they must be cut up under water! The water blocks the intense radioactivity. Then the water-filled reactors can be cut up into pieces by remote-controlled welding arms, and the reactor pieces shipped away for burial. An experimental reactor at Elk River, Minnesota was dismantled at a cost of $6.2 million; the plant had cost about $6 million to build. That was a small reactor. No one knows exactly how one of the new 1000-plus-megawatt reactors could be dismantled, nor how much that would cost, but current estimates range from $31 million to $100 million. Presumably, the cost will be much higher later on when the late 1960 and 1970s reactors are ready for the trash-heap.

DOE has reported that it now has 300 obsolete nuclear facilities among the 1,500 existing. There will be 100 more by 1981. DOE estimated that the costs alone for decommissioning these facilities would run to $25 and $30 million annually for 100 years.[37]

But who will pay for decommissioning commercial nuclear reactors? These costs are not now figured in when utilities plan, and charge for, nuclear plant construction. No commercial reactor has ever been decommissioned, so accurate cost estimates are hard to make. But someone will have to pay: utility customers, now or in the future; state or federal taxpayers. In July 1977 several environmental groups petitioned the NRC to require utilities to establish a $13 million escrow account to cover decommissioning costs before allowing more reactor licenses.

Safe methods have yet to be developed to decommission accelerators, fuel fabrication facilities, enrichment plants, fuel reprocessing plants and uranium mills. Different isotopes will demand different methods for each of these. And the costs will continue to climb. Right now,

ERDA is figuring out how to dispose of 21 abandoned uranium mills in the West. The estimate for that job is $80 million. ERDA's decommissioning budget for fiscal years 1976 and 1977 totals only $15 million.[38]

Decommissioning is an expensive detail that utilities would rather not deal with. So it, like other nuclear-related problems, may be dumped in the laps of rate and tax-payers. Such seems to be the case in New York State where the dismantling of the Nuclear Fuel Service's West Valley Plant is estimated to cost from $500 to $600 million. Nuclear Fuel Services no longer exists as a company, and the radioactive mess sits in New York State hands. DOE has not been willing to get financially involved, and in fact can't afford to. Decommissioning is clearly one of nuclear power's "hidden costs."

Selling It: Nuclear Power Today and Tomorrow—A Good Neighbor*

Nuclear power certainly doesn't "sell itself." If it did, the millions of dollars spent by the industry in producing fancy pro-nuclear ads, booklets and literature, and the hosting of conferences and tours would be unnecessary. But their efforts are clearly needed, now more than ever.

Every utility has its public relations staff. Part of their job is to convince consumers that nuclear power is the best deal around. They do this by placing ads, by visiting classrooms with pro-nuke slide shows and films, and by inserting colorful reminders about nuclear efficiency inside monthly electric bills.

*Title of speech by A.P. Bray, Manager of Applications Engineering, Atomic Power Equipment Dept., General Electric, San Jose, California to Pennsylvania insurance department hearings on nuclear power plants, 16 August 1973.

Moreover, there are utility and industry associations that produce literature for "decision-makers" and that lobby state and federal governments. Three major associations are the Atomic Industrial Forum, the American Nuclear Society, and the Edison Electric Institute. The Atomic Industrial Forum (AIF) is the most active of the three in the public realm.

The AIF is a trade association of reportedly over 800 corporate members, all with vested interests in the nuclear industry. Of these members, some 56 are huge electric utilities. AIF headquarters were moved a year ago (1975) from New York to Washington, where members are supporting two lobbying groups with $300,000 budgets each. One of these lobbies, Americans for Energy Independence, claims to be unbiased, but its actions belie the pretense. Its membership, according to columnist Jack Anderson, reads like a nuclear Who's Who, with Dr. Dixie Lee Ray, former Atomic Energy Commission (AEC) Chairman; physicist Dr. Hans Bethe, so often quoted in news releases; and former AEC Commissioner James Ramey.[39]

With a budget of over a million dollars annually, the AIF produces slick, attractive propaganda.

In 1975 they stepped up their campaign of "Public Affairs and Information" by adopting a plan of action that included: visits by home-town newspapers and officials to nuclear plants; "news feature placement" or "ghost-writing" of pro-nuke articles "on behalf of distinguished experts"; offering expert testimony to local members; setting up an enlarged speakers' bureau to defend the controversial breeder reactor.

To counter the June 1976 California nuclear safeguards initiative and other anti-nuclear ballot questions and initiatives, the AIF set up a special task force. Its purpose was to "motivate and persuade the public to observe the positive values of nuclear energy and its safe use, and the alternate consequences if not used: i.e., the loss of jobs which the scarcity of energy would cause; the extreme social unrest which would result and the high cost to the taxpayers who still have jobs to support the unemployed; the very real and most serious threat to national security by foreign dominance caused by our basic reliance on foreign middle eastern oil which has no credible line of defense as a reliable source of energy to the United States, Europe and Japan." They decided to use economic scare tactics to counter what they saw as the "anti-nuclear, anti-growth, anti-technology forces (which) have sold fear."[40]

In late 1975 a journalist working for the AIF quit after the near disastrous fire at the Browns Ferry nuclear plant. He told staff members at Friends of the Earth: "I've gone from being skeptical about nuclear power to out and out opposition." He felt that the AIF leadership had false expectations about the anti-nuclear storm:

> I think that these guys live in a never-never land. It's like the Vietnam war. You keep hearing these guys say that there's light at the end of the tunnel. You hear them say this week in and week out and slapping each other on the back and not admitting that there's any problem.[41]

One Edison Electric Institute pro-nuclear gambit is a game for high school classes that has as its theme the siting of a nuclear plant. Students act out roles in a community discussion of

Susanna Natti

energy needs and environmental concerns, taking their cues from 32 role models provided in the game.

Conservation groups have charged that the game is pro-nuclear and reduces real questions and opposition to nuclear power to shallow stereotypes: the college physics teacher who is categorically against plant construction versus the thoughtful, reasoning pro-nuclear utility executive. These games have been sold by EEI to 40 utilities for $15 each. They are then distributed as a public relations gift to schools.

Early pro-nuke salespitches to the public stressed how clean, safe, and economic nuclear power was. During the campaigns against the state initiatives that put nuclear power before voters in various states, the importance of nuclear power as a source of energy for a growing economy and as a means for maintaining high employment was stressed. Now as the economic realities of nuclear power—its true costs—are becoming known and consumers are being hit with nuclear related rate increases, the pro-nuke argu-

ment is "bolstered" by threats of blackouts and electric power rationing if nukes being planned are not built. For example, Wilfred Uhl, senior vice-president of the Long Island Lighting Company (LILCO) predicted in August 1977 that if the two proposed nuclear plants were not built in Jamestown, Long Island: "each year the situation will grow worse and LILCO will have to resort to frequent brownouts and rotating blackouts of major segments of our system to keep demand matched to available supply." Suffolk County Executive John Klein had maintained that the utility has long overestimated future power demand for the area and replied that: "If anyone's figures were made up it was LILCO's, because they've been out of line for the past four years on their projections."[42] In January 1978, LILCO announced that the company was postponing Jamesport 1 and 2 for four years precisely because the plants wouldn't be needed sooner. LILCO admitted that its projections for electricity were "overstated."[43]

Footnotes:

1. Norman Medvin, *the Energy Cartel* (NY: Vintage Books, 1974), p. 34.

2. McKinley C. Olson, *Unacceptable Risk, The Nuclear Power Controversy* (NY: Bantam Books, 1976), p. 149.

3. *Ibid.* p. 150.

4. "The Way it Is" Information Bulletin, July 1975, Montague Nuclear Project Information Center, Turners Falls, MA.

5. *Wall Street Journal,* 15 July 1976.

6. "LWR Spent Fuel Disposition Capabilities," ERDA 77-25, 19 May 1977, p. 1.

7. Eleanor Blau, "Nuclear Waste Found Leaking At Site Upstate," *New York Times,* 10 February 1977.

8. Richard Severo, "Too Hot to Handle," *New York Times Magazine,* 10 April 1977, p. 15. Much of the information in this section comes from this article, with permission from, and thanks to, the author.

9. *Ibid.*

10. "Warning: You Live in a Radioactive Hazard Zone," Palmetto Alliance, Spring 1978.

11. Richard Pollock, "Flying the Friendly Skies at O'Hare," *Critical Mass Journal,* January 1978, p. 1.

12. Michael W. Millican (AP), "Nuclear Waste Route Fixed," *Greenfield Recorder,* 5 March 1976.

13. Elise Vider, "Nuclear Waste Load Hits Railroad Bridge," *Valley Advocate,* 24 April 1976.

14. Pollock, *op. cit.*

15. "Nuclear Energy's Dilemma: Disposing of Hazardous Radioactive Waste Safely," General Accounting Office, Report to the Congress, 9 September 1977, iii.

16. "Failure to Adequately Protect the American People from the Hazards of Radiation," GAO Draft Report, 1977, p. 41.

17. Fred Garretson, "Wierd Sea Life in Atomic Waste," *Oakland Tribune,* 12 September 1976.

18. *Critical Mass Journal,* vol. 3, no. 8, November 1977, p. 7.

19. Olson, *op. cit.,* p. 163.

20. Hartmut Krugmann, Frank von Hippel, "Radioactive Wastes: A Comparison of U.S. Military and Civilian Inventories," *Science,* 26 August 1977, vol. 197, no. 4306, p. 883.

21. "Nuclear Energy's Dilemma..." *op. cit.,* iv.

22. Robert Gillette, "Radiation Spill at Hanford: the Anatomy of an Accident," *Science,* vol. 181, August 1973, p. 728.

23. Olson, *op. cit.,* p. 164.

24. Thomas C. Hollocher, "Storage and Disposal of High Level Wastes," *The Nuclear Fuel Cycle,* Union of Concerned Scientists and Friends of the Earth, 1974, p. 21.

25. *Ibid.,* p. 9.

26. "Nuclear Energy's Dilemma..." *op. cit.,* i.

27. *Ibid.*

28. "Bulletin of Conference on Alternative State and Local Public Policies," January 1978.

29. Jeff Cox, "Nuclear Waste Recycling," *Environment Action Bulletin,* 29 May 1976.

30. *Environment News,* U.S. EPA, New England Regional Office, Boston, MA, January 1978, p. 9.

31. *New York Times,* 29 June 1976.

32. David Burnham, "8,000 Pounds of Atom Materials Unaccounted for by Plants in U.S.," *New York Times,* 5 August 1977.

33. Robert Gillette, "Nuclear Safeguards: Holes in the Fence," *Science,* 14 December 1973, vol. 182.

34. U.S. ERDA Fiscal Year 1978, Congressional Action Table, *Congressional Record,* 17 October 1977.

35. John H. Barton, "Intensified Nuclear Safeguards and Civil Liberties," 31 October 1975. (NRC Contract no. AT(49-24)-0190)

36. Senate Bill 826 (which established the DOE), Section 616.(a). From International Indian Treaty Council, 77 UN Plaza, Suite 10F, New York NY 10017.

37. *New York Times,* 28 October 1977.

38. William Greer, "What do you do with a Dead Nuke?" *Environmental Action,* 10 September 1977.

39. "The Inimitable AIF," News Letter no. 5, 8 July 1976, Gen. Cook (Ed.) Coalition for Safe Electric Power, Citizens for Clean Air and Water, 312 Park Bldg., 140 Public Square, Cleveland, OH 44114.

40. "AIF Declares War on Initiatives," *Not Man Apart,* Friends of the Earth, May 1976.

41. Jim Phillips, quoted in "Tales of Power: AIF Editor Leaves the 'Nuclear Never-Never Land,'" *Not Man Apart,* May 1976.

42. Iver Peterson, "Lilco Warns of Power Failures in 1980s Unless Jamesport Plants are Approved," *New York Times,* 17 August 1977.

43. Warren Liebold, "The Jamestown Nukes Lose One Round," *WIN Magazine,* 16 March 1978.

Chapter 4:

Health Dangers

The "time for decision" about nuclear power is quickly passing. Nukes exist. Stockpiles of nuclear waste are growing daily. The great debates that are now taking place in this country in the media, on television, and in classrooms and communities across America are twenty years late. Nuclear power is a reality today. It is finally a subject of debate because *people*, people all over the world and not governments, have forced the issue to light.

Motivating concerns behind the Great Nuclear Controversy are the issues of health and safety. The economics of nuclear power are increasingly disastrous (as you will see in Section 2) but this fact was not so clear when local communities and intervenor groups began to oppose nuclear construction in the 1960s.

These groups were alarmed by the potential for danger in nuclear power plants. And it was hard to get information from the government and the nuclear establishment on just how great the dangers were.

From the pioneering work of scientists like Drs. Alice Stewart, John Gofman, Arthur Tamplin, Ernest Stern-

glass and others came the revelations about the health and safety dangers inherent in nuclear technology. Now the information available is increasing all the time. And with it, public awareness of the many problems that go hand in hand with nuclear power development.

The health dangers of nuclear power are inseparable from environmental dangers. Human beings are not and cannot be separate from "the environment." It is our food, our water, our (dis)comfort, our work...Our health and livelihoods depend on its continued existence, unharmed. For we are all part of nature, of the ecosystem. Changes in air and water temperatures, pollution of land and water, will affect us too, now or in the long run.

Nuclear opponents are ecologists, concerned with the whole ecological system. We are fighting to protect our own lives and genes—and thus the lives and health of children and future generations—our communities, the land and agriculture, water supplies, and the health and genetic continuation of other animal species. Nuclear power poses dangers to us all.

*Graphic: Susanna Natti (after an original by Janet Kailin, Comm. for Nuclear Responsibility)

Why Are Nuclear Plants Dangerous?

• Radioactive poisons from used nuclear fuel can cause cancer, leukemia, birth defects, genetic damage, heart disease, premature aging, and general poor health.

• Every nuclear power plant releases some radioactive poisons to the environment.

• An accident could release enough radiation to kill thousands of people and contaminate cities, land, and water for decades.

• One of the poisons created—plutonium—is the raw material of atomic bombs. Theft of plutonium or enriched uranium could lead to nuclear disaster or cancer epidemics.

• The nuclear fuel cycle from the mining of uranium to waste storage endangers its workers and communities near nuclear facilities. Workers and their offspring are the ones who bear the brunt of the nuclear threat.

This chapter will examine the health dangers of nuclear power. We'll start with the most basic characteristic of atomic energy.

Radiation (A Brief History)

Radiation is the name given to the invisible atomic particles that are released by unstable, radioactive materials. While most of the world became aware of the intense, deadly nature of radiation only after atomic bombs were dropped by the United States on Hiroshima and Nagasaki in August 1945, the most obvious qualities of radiation were known before the turn of the century.

Prof. Wilhelm Roentgen discovered x-rays in 1895 in his laboratory in Bavaria. After discovering a force coming from a glass tube through which he was passing a current of electricity, Roentgen called it x-rays, since he could not determine at the time the cause and characteristics of the rays.

In early 1896 the discovery went public. Thomas Edison was meanwhile doing somewhat similar experiments and did more investigation of the nature of these mysterious rays. He showed his x-ray fluoroscope at a New York City electrical exposition in May 1896. People were amazed to see their internal organs and bones revealed when they stepped between the x-ray tube and a specially treated screen. (Fluoroscopes were widely used for a long time. In the 1950s they were even used in shoe stores to check the fit of children's shoes. The practice was finally stopped when the dangers of this unnecessary irradiation became known.)

Late in 1896, doctors and others were experimenting with the rays. There were no monitors of voltage or amps as today, and researchers learned of the dangers of exposure to these still relatively weak rays with their own health, and in some cases, with their lives.

In 1896 a U.S. designer of X-ray tubes named Elihu Thomson made the following observations which hold true today. He demonstrated that:

• X-rays could damage human tissue.

• The amount of damage was related to the amount of exposure.

• There was evidently a point beyond which exposure could not go without causing serious trouble.

• Several short exposures would have the same effect if made within a few days as the same dose given at one time. In other words, spreading the dose over a longer period of time would not necessarily reduce the damage caused.

• The intensity of the rays decreased as the square of the distance from the x-ray source.

• There was an incubation period—effects would not appear immediately.[1]

Despite Thomson's suggestions on x-ray protection, by 1922 it was estimated that 100 early radiologists had died from overexposure to radiation.[2]

Investigators Marie and Pierre Curie were exposed during their path-breaking experiments with radium. He died accidentally, but she died of cancer.

In 1934, Marie Curie's daughter Irene and her husband Frederic Joliot discovered radioactive isotopes. Common elements could be turned into radioisotopes, radioactive variants of elements, by bombardment from a radioactive, neutron-emitting source. Irene herself died of radiation-induced leukemia.

In 1934 Italian physicist Enrico Fermi reported that uranium could be bombarded with slowed neutrons, and new "transuranic" elements created.

The uranium atom was split by German chemists in December and January 1939. Quickly other physicists in Europe and the U.S. followed up on the pioneering experiments of Hahn, Strassman, Meitner, and Frisch. The discovery that the uranium atom could be split by neutron bombardment, releasing energy, led directly to the development of the atomic bomb under the team of Manhattan Project scientists.

Ionizing Radiation

When radioactive atoms decay, they give off one or more of four types of radiation: alpha particles, beta particles, x-rays and gamma rays, and neutrons. These rays and particles are called ionizing radiation because they cause the formation of ions, electrically charged particles, from particles which were previously neutral.

Ions are atoms that have lost one or more electrons due to radiation. Radiation causes ionization in tissue, disrupting and injuring the cellular atoms.

Ionizing radiation acts almost like a bullet. Shot through the body, it disrupts the complex web of cellular life processes.

> ...Disruptive actions of ionizing radiation can best be regarded simply as a massive, non-specific *disorganization* or injury of biological cells and tissues...[A] reasonable analogy would be the effect of jagged pieces of shrapnel passing through tissues.[3]
>
> Dr. John Gofman
> and Dr. Arthur Tamplin

Types of Ionizing Radiation

alpha particles—(symbolized by the Greek letter for a, $\propto$) are positively charged nuclei of helium atoms ejected by the nuclei of elements which are heavier than lead. If not blocked, alpha particles will travel about one millimeter in human tissue before stopping. They are high energy particles and can do a great deal of cell damage. But they can be stopped by a single piece of paper, a few inches of air, clothing, or skin layers of dead cells. The most dangerous effect comes when a radionuclide that gives off alpha particles is inhaled or ingested, lodging within the body and exposing nearby living cells to the ionizing radiation.

"Hot" particles are tiny dust-like particles of alpha-emitting substances, such as plutonium-239. Plutonium is "hot" because of its intense alpha emissions, which cause extensive cellular damage to tissue on which it is deposited. It rapidly kills the cells it is on, but might initiate a cancer in the cells nearby which are injured but not killed outright. Long-term studies are needed to understand just how sensitive the lungs are to this type of injury. Such studies have just begun.

beta particles (β)—are high speed electrons shot off from an unstable, radioactive atom. Faster than alpha particles, they can penetrate several centimeters in human tissue before being stopped. They can be stopped by thin metal sheets, a few feet of air, or thick cardboard. Passing through live tissue, beta particles rip electrons from atoms, leaving positively charged ions. The freed electrons in turn ionize other atoms.[4]

x-rays and gamma rays (γ)—are called photons. They are cousins to the ordinary light we see with, the difference being that they "pack a wallop" when they hit instead of gently touching. Strictly speaking, x-rays come from the electron cloud surrounding the nucleus, while gamma rays come from the nucleus. These photons travel in straight lines and are very penetrating. When they hit matter, they knock loose electrons causing ionization. They easily pass right through the body leaving a track of ionized particles behind.

neutrons (n)—are uncharged nuclear particles which can travel very great distances in air, tissue, or metal. They collide with hydrogen atoms, knocking them loose. These hydrogens now behave like small alpha particles. Neutron-emitting elements are man-made.

Nuclides or Isotopes

The fission fragments produced by the splitting of heavy atoms like uranium-235 and plutonium-239 are called nuclides or isotopes. Nuclides are variants of common elements but differ slightly from them in their atomic weights. Most nuclides are stable, having an even number of protons in their nucleus and electrons in orbit around it. But some nuclides are unstable and give off radiation. These are known as radioactive nuclides or radionuclides. For example, one radioactive nuclide of iodine is iodine-131. A radioactive variant of the element cesium is a radionuclide called cesium-137.

There are about 800 of these radionuclides or radioisotopes. A few are used in medical diagnosis and treatment. Iodine-131 is used for thyroid scans and polygrams. It is dangerous, and is sometimes used to deliberately destroy tissue (as in hyperthyroid treatment). In medical uses the risk *and* benefit are felt by the same person. There should be good cause before permitting this type of exposure.

Radionuclides have different half-lives. **A half-life is the length of time it takes for a radioactive substance to disintegrate to half of its original amount.** The decay continues at this fixed rate. When generated by nuclear power plants as the by-products of the fissioning of the uranium fuel, radionuclides are wastes and must be isolated from the environment.

Some Radioactive Nuclides in Nuclear Plant Wastes

Nuclide/Isotope	Half-Life	Type of Radiation
Cesium-137	30.2	Beta, Gamma
Cobalt-60	5.2 years	Beta, Gamma
Iodine-131	8.1 days	Beta, Gamma
Iron-59	45 days	Beta, Gamma
Krypton-85	10 years	Beta, Gamma
Strontium-90	28 years	Beta
Zinc-65	145 days	Beta, Gamma
Plutonium-239	24,300 years	Alpha

Lifetimes and Half Lives

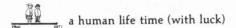 a human life time (with luck)

 since the Mayflower...

 since Rome fell...

 8,000 yrs.

25,000 yrs.

Half-lives of Plutonium and other isotopes—

praseodymium-144 (17 sec)	praseodymium-143 (13.8 da.)	ruthenium-106 (1 yr)
rhodium-106 (30 sec)	cerium-141 (32.5 da.)	promethium-147 (2.62 yr)
rhodium-103 (57 min)	niobium-95 (35 da.)	krypton-85 (9.4 yr)
lanthanum-140 (40 hr)	ruthenium-103 (39.8 da.)	strontium-90 (28 yr)
xenon-133 (5.3 da.)	strontium-89 (54 da.)	cesium-137 (33 yr)
iodine-131 (8 da.)	zirconium-95 (55 da.)	iodine-129 (1.7 yr × 10⁷)
barium-140 (12.8 da.)	cerium-144 (590 da.)	technetium-99 (210,000 yr)

For a rough estimate of storage time necessary to protect the environment, multiply the half-life by 20—here is the 500,000 year storage time needed for plutonium.

 500,000 years of storage represents 7,142 life-times   or 16,666 generations.

Plutonium

This radionuclide produced in nuclear reactors is one of the most toxic materials known. Because of its cancer-causing properties the "acceptable body dose" is less than one millionth of a gram, an invisible particle. Yet even a millionth of a gram can cause cancer 10 to 30 years after the particle is inhaled. Plutonium is absorbed from the lungs into the blood stream where it can cause liver cancer. It is also taken up in the skeleton, producing bone cancer and leukemia. There is evidence that it collects in the gonads—sex organs—at a concentration twice that of its point of entry into the lung. Infants are especially sensitive to the substance. In pregnant women, it also crosses the placenta into the embryo where it can kill developing cells and damage the fetus. This type of action is called Teratogenic and is like the action of the drug Thalidomide.

Plutonium is handled like iron in the body and is combined with the iron transporting protein and stored in the iron cells of the bone marrow and liver.

One pound of plutonium, if it could be deposited in the lungs of people throughout the world, would be enough to kill every man, woman and child on earth.[5]

About five tons of plutonium were dispersed in the atmosphere of the northern hemisphere during the superpowers' atomic bomb testing between 1953 and 1963. Much of it has fallen to the ground and into the ocean and is with us...and will continue to be for many thousands of years. The southern hemisphere has also been contaminated by U.S. and French atmospheric testing in the South Pacific.

Since around 13 pounds of plutonium is enough to make a Nagasaki-type atomic bomb, a large reactor can theoretically produce enough plutonium for many arsenals.

A single big water-moderated reactor, not primarily a breeder, makes enough plutonium for several hundred atomic bombs a year (at roughly half a gram per megawatt-day thermal).[6]

Background Radiation

Radiation that occurs naturally in soil and water, and cosmic radiation from outer space, are known as background radiation. For example, there is an appreciable amount of uranium in granite and other stone deposits, making some stone structures naturally radioactive.

Utilities that have "gone nuclear" and their public relations front organizations like the Atomic Industrial Forum, are quick to point out that nuclear plants are not the only source of ionizing radiation. They seem to take shelter in the fact that their plants emit less external radiation than already exists in an area as background, or natural, radiation. If you're already getting some, they say, a little bit more won't hurt.

Some radiation may be "natural," but that doesn't mean it's safe. Radiation from any source is dangerous, whether it be from bomb test fallout, the sun, a medical x-ray, a plane ride in the upper atmosphere (where there is less air to shield against cosmic rays), or a nuclear plant.

Much of the background radiation now being measured is from bomb testing and other man-made pollution. There is no safety involved in keeping pollution levels at 5% of background, while continuously increasing the background level!

Background radiation is something we have to live with and minimize if possible. It is not a safe, base or acceptable dose. If anyone tells you it is, tell

Sources of Radiation Exposure

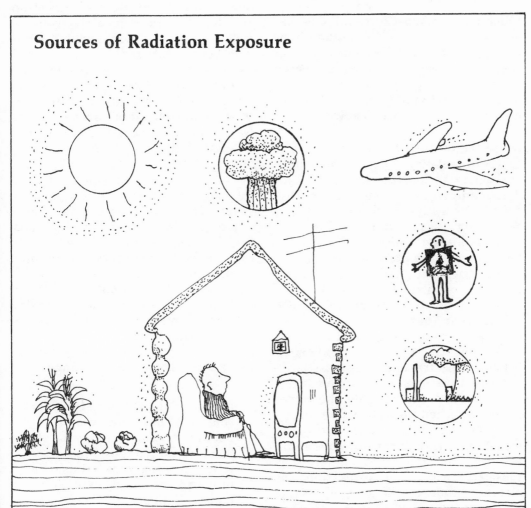

source	amount (millirems/year)	source	amount (millirems/year)
sun/cosmic radiation	90*	x-ray (chest)	50
food	25	nuclear plant	**
soil	11 (varies greatly)	TV, watches, misc.	1
stone building	35-50	fallout	5
coast-to-coast jet	5		

Federal official maximum for average population group: 170 millirems/year.

* Annual background radiation varies significantly. In the Monazite Sand area of Kerala, India, (100,000 people) the average exposure is 1,300 mr/year! In Denver the average is 180 mr/year. Cosmic radiation at sea level is 35-50 mr/year. U.S. average: 90 mr/year.

** Who knows? Official (AEC,AIF) estimates range from 0.01 mr/year to 10 mr/year. But Dr. Sadao Ichikawa's experiments with the Spiderwort plant show that while a nuclear plant's external gamma radiation detectors report an annual dose to the outside world of from 5-8 mr/year, the biological *absorbed dose* to life around a plant can be as much as 300 mr! (See pp. 85-87.) Monitoring of nuclear plants, facilities and transportation routes is so inadequate now, we do not really know just how much radiation we are exposed to from the nuclear power industry.

them about the people living in Kerala, India, where the background radiation is unusually high. A 1976 study indicates that the high levels of radiation there are associated with increased genetic damage, especially mental retardation and mongolism.[7] Most all genetic mutations are negative.

Measurement of Radiation

Doses of radiation are commonly measured in two units: the rad and the rem. The roentgen (R.), named for the discoverer of x-rays, is also used. These terms may seem confusing as they refer to doses of radiation that cannot be seen and have little weight or other characteristics to help in measuring and defining them.

A rad (radiation absorbed dose) is a measure of the energy that matter receives from ionizing radiation. Rem stands for "Roentgen equivalent man." When radioactive exposure to a source exterior to a person is involved, the two measures are roughly the same. However, when the radioactive source is within the body, in the lungs or ingested with food for example, rems will be about ten times higher than rads because a rem measures biological effects rather than energy present. Radiation exposure is commonly measured in millirads and millirems, units one-thousandth of one rad or rem.

These measurements are most easily understood by looking at the relative dangers of doses. There are several things that determine just how serious exposure to radiation is.

For alpha and beta radiation, internal exposure is much more dangerous than external, since skin and clothing serve as barriers. If alpha and beta-emitting radionuclides are inhaled or swallowed, they give off radiation inside the body and have far more chance to cause harm because they are in contact with living cells. Internal expo-

sure comes from breathing in radioactivity, drinking radioactive water or milk, and eating contaminated foods. The body treats radioactive materials as if they were ordinary chemicals, incorporating them into tissue and bones. Most frequently this affects the lungs, stomach, blood, thyroid, bones, liver, and sex organs. Radioactive particles that stay on the skin can cause skin cancer.

The federal government and nuclear industry have severely and consistently underestimated and played down the dangers of ionizing radiation. Even so, there have been constant reductions over the years in the amount of ionizing radiation considered "safe," a "tolerance level" below which there was thought to be no damage. The first tolerance levels were set before the turn of the century on the theory that if you couldn't see any damage right away, there was no danger.

In fact, in the 1950s and even in the early 1960s, it was still a pervasive opinion that some effects could be observed only when experimental animals or human bodies were exposed to higher than 25 rem radiation doses. This opinion was often misread, sometimes intentionally, [to mean] that the radiation doses lower than 25 rem are harmless. The truth was that enough and clear evidence was not available at that time concerning the effects of smaller doses of radiation. It has to be remembered that the famous Albert Schweitzer asked, "Who permitted them to permit?", when he heard that experts had determined *permissible* doses.[8]

Japanese radiologist,
Dr. Sadao Ichikawa

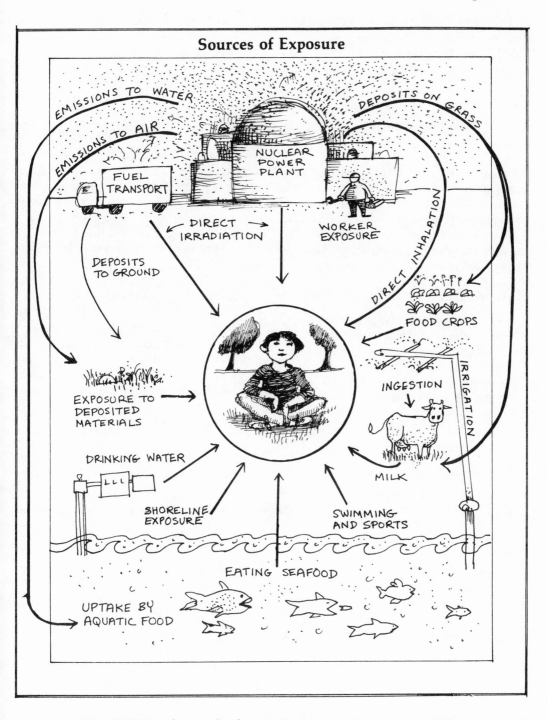

Sources of Exposure

(Source: U.S. NRC Regulatory Guide 4.2, Revision 1—Preparation of Environmental Reports for Nuclear Power Stations—January 1975. Graphic credit: Susanna Natti.)

Maximum Permissible Exposures Per Year For Workers—
("Adult Nuclear Personnel")

1910	100,000 millirems	(or 100 rems)
1934	30,000 millirems	(or 30 rems)
1948	15,000 millirems	(or 15 rems)
1958	5,000 millirems	(or 5 rems)

As you can see, the current maximum permissible exposure level for workers is one-twentieth of the 1910 maximum and has not been revised for 20 years. The current "dose guidelines" set by the Environmental Protection Agency are indicated in the chart below.

How Much Is Too Much?

All the evidence, both from experimental animals and from humans, leads us to expect that even the *smallest* quantities of ionizing radiation produce harm both to this generation of hu-

mans and future generations. Furthermore, it appears that progressively greater harm accrues in direct proportion to the amount of radiation received by the various body tissues and organs.[9]

Drs. Gofman and Tamplin

We are now facing a cancer epidemic. Today, one American in four will get some form of cancer in their lifetime. At a major conference of cancer researchers in 1976, the medical people attending agreed that a full 90% of present cancers are induced by chemicals added to our environment through food additives, insecticides and artificial fertilizers, industrial chemicals like PCB's and Kepone, dyes, and of course by radiation created by the nuclear power program, and the fallout still in circulation from above-ground weapons testing. Cigarette smoking is linked to the increases as well.[10]

CURRENT EPA DOSE GUIDELINES (PER YEAR)[11]

1 millirem	Expected average dose to U.S. citizens from nuclear power.
5 millirems	Expected average dose to "population" in nuclear plant impact area.
88 millirems	Average "natural" background radiation.
170 millirems	Established by the International Commission on Radiation Protection (ICRP) as recommended maximum average dose in addition to natural and medical.
500 millirems	Legal exposure limit for minors working in nuclear plants, and maximum for the general public.
5,000 millirems	Legal exposure limit for adult nuclear personnel, on a lifetime average.
12,000 millirems	Maximum permissible dose in special situations for adult nuclear personnel as long as their average for the years after the 18th birthday is not above 5,000 millirem.

According to Joshua Lederberg, Nobel prize-winner and professor of genetics at Stanford University, the present radiation standards in force now allow for a 10% increase in the mutation rate. He thinks that a 1% increase should be the maximum allowed for radiation and chemicals combined.[12] A 1968 Atomic Energy Commission report on "The Genetic Effects of Radiation" gave that agency's point of view:

A 10% increase in mutation rate, whatever it might mean in personal suffering and public expense, is not likely to threaten the human race with extinction, or even serious degradation... [It] is bearable if we can convince ourselves that the alternative of abandoning radiation technology altogether will cause still greater suffering.

If the number of those affected is increased, there would come a crucial point, or threshold, where the slack could no longer be taken up (by those not affected). The genetic load might increase to the point where the species as a whole would degenerate and fade toward extinction—a sort of "racial radiation sickness."

We are not near this threshold now, however, and can, therefore, as a species, absorb a moderate increase in mutation rate without danger of extinction.[13]

And here's a nice radiation fact offered to the public in a 1974 handout from the Vermont Yankee Nuclear Power Plant's Public Information Office:

Radiation In Perspective
...Indeed, each human body contains some radioactivity, and so when a boy hugs a girl, each is receiving nuclear radiation—in small quantities of course—from the other person. We hesitate to point this out, because some critics who are hysterical about radiation might well try to outlaw hugging.

The Health Effects of Radiation
Uranium = Thalidomide Forever
(Australian anti-nuclear slogan)

More may be known about radiation and its effects than is known about a lot of common chemical pollutants, but our knowledge is still very incomplete. Most information comes from observation of survivors of the Hiroshima and Nagasaki bombings, Pacific islanders who were contaminated during 1950s weapons testing, people treated with radiation therapy, and from animal experiments. The monitoring of people who have worked or are now working in jobs where they are exposed to radiation is totally inadequate.

Several key things are known:

• **There is no safe dose of radiation**. There is no proven "threshold" below which biological damage does not occur.

• **Radiation causes cancer, leukemia and genetic damage** which is sometimes seen as birth defects or chronic disease, but can go undetected for one or more generations. There are some 2,000 diseases caused by genetic mutation, diseases like cystic fibrosis and dwarfism. Dr. Helen Caldicott, pediatrician and specialist in cystic fibrosis and genetic diseases, describes the biological properties of radioactive waste:

All cells of the body have a central nucleus which contains genes, the basic inherited material which controls all our characteristics (colour of eyes and hair, size, facial characteristics, enzyme systems, etc.). Genes are changed by radioactive particles. Cells and genes which are actively dividing (as in fetuses, babies and young children) are most susceptible to the effects of radiation. If a gene which controls the rate of cell division is altered by radiation, the cell may divide in an uncontrolled fashion to produce cancer and leukemia. It may take from 15-30 years before cancer appears after the cell is exposed to radiation. If a gene in the sperm or egg is altered by a radioactive particle, the young may be born either with an inherited disease, or the baby may appear normal, but will transmit the damaged gene to future generations, to become manifest in later years.[14]

Radiation can also cause heart disease, sterility, premature aging, premature births and miscarriages.[15] Higher rates of suicide and violence among persons exposed to low-level radiation are found in reports from Hiroshima and Nagasaki as well as reports on uranium miners and in some radiation therapy studies.

• **Effects of exposure may be seen immediately** with high doses of 25 rads or more. Leukemia (cancer of the blood) has a latent period of between three to five years. The latent period is the time between exposure and clinical diagnosis of the disease. The effects of cancers aside from leukemia may not be seen for 10 to 20 or more years after exposure. This latent period makes it hard to pinpoint the exact cause of a cancer. Thus the industry can claim that there is no record of anyone having been killed by plutonium. Nonexistent or incomplete worker health records also aid in the cover-up. For the general population, it is impossible to know when we are being exposed to low-level radiation.

The detection of cancers and health problems caused by nuclear plant low-level radiation is made more difficult still by the fact that detailed statistics on the health situation in an area are not gathered *before* nukes are built. An area can have a rise in a very rare cancer, or even leukemia, and not even become aware of it because there is no way to compare the health picture of a region before and after a nuke begins operating.[16]

• **We are suffering now from weapons testing fallout**. According to an important study by Dr. Gofman, past weapons tests have put so much plutonium into the lungs of residents of the northern hemisphere that 116,000 people in the U.S., and about one million people in the entire northern hemisphere, "have been committed to plutonium-induced lung cancer."[17]

Some Characteristics of Radiation
Radioisotopes or nuclides, the particles that are created by nuclear fission, can harm the body in different ways. This is because different isotopes are attracted to different body organs or areas, according to their chemical make-up.

For example, the common fission product strontium-90 is chemically similar to calcium. Radioactive strontium has been put into our environment by atomic bomb testing, nuclear plants, and submarines. With a half-life of over 29 years, it is active—and dangerous—for hundreds of years. Airborne, strontium will settle on the land, where it enters the food chain. The main path of strontium is through cow's milk. Cows eat grass, the strontium on the grass becomes concentrated in the cow, and further concentrated in her milk. In the body, the radioactive strontium is absorbed like calcium. It concentrates in the skeleton, causing bone cancer. Deposited in the bone marrow, it destroys the mechanism for making the blood cells. It concentrates further in human breast milk. Children and babies—generally heavy milk drinkers—are especially vulnerable to this particular radioisotope.

Other fission products, like radioactive iodine-131 and -129, concentrate in the same way. These two collect not in the bones like strontium, but in the thyroid gland which attracts the iodine that is a necessary element for thyroid functioning and human health.

> Atmospheric releases of iodine-129 may result in its accumulation in the thyroid glands of persons living in the area surrounding the point of release. For radioiodines, the most significant pathway for exposure of man is generally the grass-cow-milk chain, particularly when milk is not diluted with uncontaminated supplies. Direct deposition on foliage is likely to be the most important route of contamination of edible herbage...Because of the long half-life of iodine-129,* plant uptake of this radionuclide from the soil should also be considered.[18]
>
> Environmental
> Protection Agency, 1974

The poster (next page) shows where other radionuclides collect in the body.

Low-Level Radiation—Exposed!

Several scientists have concerned themselves with the effects on human health of radiation at very low levels of exposure, similar to amounts that people living near nuclear power plants are exposed to.

The first study connecting "peacetime" radiation with health effects in children was done in 1958 by Dr. Alice Stewart of Oxford University. She interviewed mothers who had been x-rayed during pregnancy and found that those mothers who had been exposed to x-rays in the first trimester ran twice the risk of having their children develop leukemia before the age of ten as those who were not x-rayed.[19] According to Dr. Ernest Sternglass, another researcher of low-level radiation effects: "This pioneering study represents the first quantitative evidence that total doses comparable to those received from background radiation in one year can produce serious health effects..."[20]

Subsequent studies have confirmed Dr. Stewart's findings.[21] Although the fetus is at all times more sensitive to radiation and chemical pollutants than children or adults, the period of greatest sensitivity is during the first three months of development, when cells are dividing rapidly and the organs are forming. This is the period when people may be exposed unknowingly, as for example newly pregnant fuel cycle workers. The drug Thalidomide was the cause of gross deformities when taken during this crucial time in fetal development.

The first official connection made between low-level radiation and increased birth defects was in a survey requested by the Canadian Minister of Health for the Province of Alberta in March 1960. A comparison of birth defects in Alberta in 1959 and 1962 showed a rise of almost 78% in two years! The increase was largely attributed to Soviet bomb testing near the Artic Circle in 1958, followed by heavy rainfall in 1960 and 1961 which brought the fallout to the ground.[22]

Correlations between nuclear fallout and infant mortality were also made by Dr. Ernest Sternglass, professor of radiation physics at the University of Pittsburgh. Infant mortality, which had decreased in the U.S. during

---

*16 million years

IONIZING RADIATION

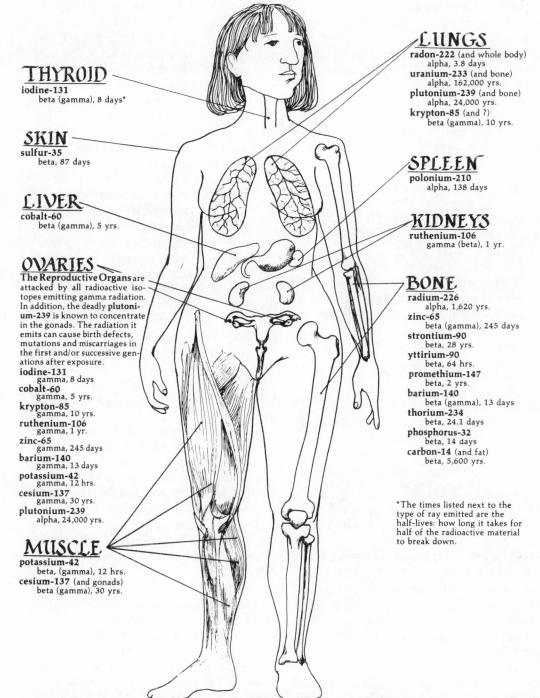

THYROID
iodine-131
    beta (gamma), 8 days*

SKIN
sulfur-35
    beta, 87 days

LIVER
cobalt-60
    beta (gamma), 5 yrs.

OVARIES
The Reproductive Organs are attacked by all radioactive isotopes emitting gamma radiation. In addition, the deadly **plutonium-239** is known to concentrate in the gonads. The radiation it emits can cause birth defects, mutations and miscarriages in the first and/or successive generations after exposure.
iodine-131
    gamma, 8 days
cobalt-60
    gamma, 5 yrs.
krypton-85
    gamma, 10 yrs.
ruthenium-106
    gamma, 1 yr.
zinc-65
    gamma, 245 days
barium-140
    gamma, 13 days
potassium-42
    gamma, 12 hrs.
cesium-137
    gamma, 30 yrs.
plutonium-239
    alpha, 24,000 yrs.

MUSCLE
potassium-42
    beta, (gamma), 12 hrs.
cesium-137 (and gonads)
    beta (gamma), 30 yrs.

LUNGS
radon-222 (and whole body)
    alpha, 3.8 days
uranium-233 (and bone)
    alpha, 162,000 yrs.
plutonium-239 (and bone)
    alpha, 24,000 yrs.
krypton-85 (and ?)
    beta (gamma), 10 yrs.

SPLEEN
polonium-210
    alpha, 138 days

KIDNEYS
ruthenium-106
    gamma (beta), 1 yr.

BONE
radium-226
    alpha, 1,620 yrs.
zinc-65
    beta (gamma), 245 days
strontium-90
    beta, 28 yrs.
yttirium-90
    beta, 64 hrs.
promethium-147
    beta, 2 yrs.
barium-140
    beta (gamma), 13 days
thorium-234
    beta, 24.1 days
phosphorus-32
    beta, 14 days
carbon-14 (and fat)
    beta, 5,600 yrs.

*The times listed next to the type of ray emitted are the half-lives: how long it takes for half of the radioactive material to break down.

the 1930s and 1940s due to better medical care, began to rise again in the 1950s. Sternglass and others attributed the rise to bomb testing fallout. After the tests stopped in 1963, infant mortality rates declined, only to rise once more. Sternglass saw a connection between the rise of infant mortality in certain areas and the presence of nuclear plants in the vicinity. The plants were releasing low levels of radioactivity, enough to cause a statistical increase in infant deaths. He published his findings in a book called *Low-Level Radiation* in 1971.

The nuclear industry and the Atomic Energy Commission raised a furor over his conclusions and challenged his statistics as well as his theories. He was subjected to bitter attacks from other scientists. In 1969 Drs. John Gofman and Arthur Tamplin, then working for the AEC, were asked to review Sternglass' claim that 400,000 infant deaths in the U.S. resulted from Nevada bomb tests in the 1950s. Tamplin found that Sternglass' estimates were too high, but that about 4,000 infants had died as a result of the tests.[23] Dr. Sternglass' statistics have been questioned then and since. Dr. David R. Inglis, an eminent physicist from Manhattan Project days to the present, summed up his conclusions on the "Sternglass Affair" in 1972, by saying that "despite...reservations, the collection of cases that Sternglass presents would seem to indicate that there is a relationship between fallout and infant mortality of the general nature he suggests."[24]

Dr. Sternglass has kept up his work. In a report released in the fall of 1977, he examined the amount of strontium-90 in milk supplies near two nuclear plants in Connecticut. Sternglass found that children are receiving annual doses of Sr-90 to their bones that are up to 241% (in 1976) of the natural background strontium radiation. Mean-

while, the utility (Northeast Utilities) contends in its environmental statements that any Sr-90 around is from fallout. But Sternglass found more Sr-90 around the Connecticut plants and in other areas which receive milk from the nuclear neighborhood than in other areas. If NU's fallout theory was right, all areas would tend to have the same high Sr-90 counts.

Sternglass also found an excessive infant mortality rate after the 1970 start-up of the Millstone I nuclear plant (Haddam Neck, Connecticut), in both Rhode Island (close to the plant to the east) and in Connecticut, as compared to New Hampshire. In 1975, overall cancer death rates in Connecticut were highest in three towns within 30 miles of the Millstone I plant.[25]

The Sternglass findings should stimulate intensive research into possible health effects in the vicinities of every nuclear plant in the U.S. Instead, we find that health effect studies are being hindered rather than helped by the federal government. In the meantime, the efforts of dedicated individuals around the world go on, as they work to expose the real dangers of nuclear radiation to the unsuspecting public. One such researcher is Sadao Ichikawa, who helped develop a unique means of proving that nuclear plants do emit dangerous amounts of radiation.

The Spiderwort Strategy: Experiment Shows Nuclear Plants' Radiation Can Cause Mutations—

Prof. Sadao Ichikawa, a radiation geneticist at the Department of Agriculture, Kyoto University in Japan, has developed a simple experiment that can be repeated with similar results. It uses a small flower to test for genetic changes near nuclear power plants. He has found mutations that seem to be caused by nuclear plant emissions.

Ichikawa and biology teacher Moto-yuki Nagata, planted a common flower native to North America at different points around a nuclear power plant. The flower was the spiderwort (*Tradescantia*). The experiments went on during 1974 and 1975 at the Hamaoka Nuclear Power Plant of the Chubu Electric Power Company in Hamaoka, Shizuoka Prefecture, a plant with two GE boiling water reactors. One reactor was of 540-megawatt capacity, the other was still under construction at the end of 1976.

For two years the pair examined the stamen hairs of the spiderwort for any sign of mutation in the plant. The scientists chose this plant because mutations in the spiderwort are easy to spot. The petals, stamen filaments and stamen hairs of the type of spiderwort used (clone KU7 of *Tradescantia ohiensis*) are normally blue. The color is determined by a dominant gene. There is a recessive gene that produces the color pink. When the dominant gene mutates or is deleted from a cell, the recessive pink color appears in any new cells.

They found that:

If such mutations or deletions of the dominant gene occur during the development of the stamen hairs, we can observe sectors of a single or two or more contiguous pink cells in the matured stamen hairs.[26]

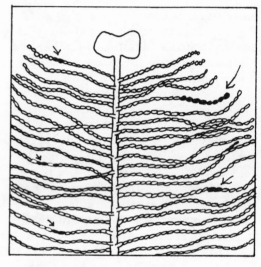

Stamen Hairs
(Graphic: Susanna Natti)

From July through October 1974, they examined 640,000 stamen hairs or 17,600,000 stamen-hair cells and had detected 2,778 pink mutations from their sample. After analyzing the frequency of mutations separately for the ten points where spiderworts had been placed and making comparative calculations, they discovered that there were in fact statistically high mutation rates. The increase in mutations was most conspicuous at one location close to the plant and at several sites down-wind. The periods of increases in mutations corresponded with reactor operating periods. Similar results were obtained in 1975 and 1976, and the study continued in 1977 with an ever-larger number of teachers spending their

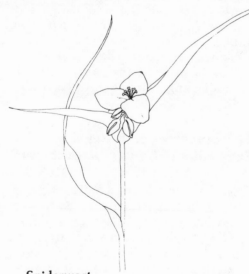

Spiderwort
Tradescantia ohiensis
(Graphic: Susanna Natti)

early mornings collecting small flowers from the spiderworts placed around the nuke.

Before concluding that the increase in mutations in the spiderwort was due to radiation from the nuclear plant, the researchers examined other environmental factors that might have caused the changes—pesticides, car exhaust, atmospheric fallout, etc. But the only connection they could find was with wind direction.

How much radiation was coming from the nuclear plant at Hamaoka? The company had publicly guaranteed a level of less than 5 millirem increase per year. And the power company was telling the public that there was no detected increase at all. But Prof. Ichikawa analyzed the data collected by the Health Institute of Shizuoka Prefecture and the Chubu Electric Power Co. which had been doing continuous radiation monitoring around the plant. He found that the radiation levels had quite obviously increased in 1974 and 1975 by as much as 7.5% and 8.7% in those years—these figures being the averages for readings over widely distributed points. But because of the type of dosimeters used in the monitoring, these increases were only for gamma radiation. The monitoring devices were measuring the external gamma-ray dose for living organisms. But the spiderworts were showing the absorbed dose.

When radioactive nuclei attach to plants or animals or are incorporated into their tissues, absorbed radiation dose, especially of beta rays, becomes very much higher. Thus, the magnitude of increase of the dose absorbed by biological tissues due to concentration of a radioactive nuclide is very much greater than the concentration factor of the nuclide.

Therefore, the increase of environmental radiation level monitored represents only a part, probably a minor part, of the actual additionally absorbed dose (external and internal) in living organisms. In fact, **the increases of pink mutations detected in the spiderwort stamen hairs corresponded to that induced with at least 300 millirems.**[27] (emphasis added)

The spiderwort experiment shows the important biological aspects of radiation exposure: attachment, incorporation, and concentration.* The spiderwort experiment has demonstrated the extent of genetic damage from biological concentration of low levels of radiation in living plant tissue.

Since the first spiderwort experiments in Hamaoka, other researchers have planted the flower around six more Japanese nuclear plants. Similarly, significant mutation frequencies were found. Activists from other countries are interested in repeating the spiderwort experiments.

The lovely flowers of spiderwort, which are honest enough to show the radiation effects within only one or two weeks, are continuously sending *stop signals* to nuclear power by changing their color from *safe* blue to *dangerous* pink, in place of human beings in which the effects of low-level radiation should be observed several decades later.[28]

Prof. Ichikawa and European anti-nuclear activist Petra Karin Kelly have named this "non-violent movement armed with the tiny flowers" the **spiderwort strategy**...

---

* One plant waste that is discharged in small amounts is iodine-131. It is known that iodine-131 is concentrated from air into plant tissues with an extremely high concentration factor of 3.5 to 10 millions.

Protection From Low-Level Radiation: What You Can Do

The health dangers of low-level radiation are best eliminated by removing the source of the problem—nuclear weapons and all nuclear facilities. But while we work to stop nuclear power, there are some measures that we can take to protect ourselves.

The basic rule of good health applies to radiation also: prevention is the best medicine. Although nuclear plants pose awesome radiological dangers, radiation from medical sources is generally the major source of exposure to radiation for most of us. And medical x-rays should be taken with the greatest precautions.

> **X-rays kill between 1,800 and 14,000 Americans every year and cause between 600 and 14,000 serious illnesses and disabilities.**[29]

Eminent health physicist Karl Z. Morgan estimates that the use of medical x-rays, which is from two to ten times higher in the U.S. than in other industrialized countries, could be "easily" reduced by 90% through using better techniques and equipment, operated by trained personnel.[30] One obvious step we can take is to avoid x-rays whenever possible, including dental x-rays which are often considered routine. These x-rays give a relatively high dose because they are of low penetration, and are well absorbed by local tissue structures.

Fluoroscope examinations may be even more dangerous than x-rays, as doctors tend to leave the machine on longer. There seems to be a connection between long examinations and children's subsequent leukemias.[31]

The x-ray-like procedure of screening for breast cancer called mammography has also been revealed to be dangerous. In February 1978, before a House subcommittee on health and environment, Dr. Irwin Bross predicted that "the worst breast cancer epidemic in medical history" involving a quarter of a million American women, will break out in 15-20 years as a result of the methods used to screen for the disease. Dr. Arthur C. Upton, director of the National Cancer Institute, has admitted that the use of mass x-ray screenings for breast cancer detection will kill women. One study showed that 22 women would die from the screenings for every 116 lives saved.[32] What price are we willing to pay for possible detection of cancer?

Diet is an important factor in maintaining human health *and* protecting ourselves from the effects of low-level radiation. Radiation concentrates as it is taken up in the food chain: when fish eat large amounts of plankton that have been contaminated with radioactive particles, the radiation is concentrated in the flesh of the fish. When small fish are eaten by larger ones, the concentration effect continues. Thus a small emission of radiation into the air or water can lead to sizeable doses to humans and other animals.

Cows graze on open pasture in many areas. When there is airborne contamination it settles on the land. Cows will eat the radiation along with grass; it becomes concentrated in their milk. The radioactive isotope of strontium—strontium-90—is a key element

of fallout and low-level radiation. It becomes concentrated in cow's milk. Strontium-90 resembles calcium in its chemical structure. It is taken up by our teeth and bones. There are federal (EPA) standards that set allowable levels for strontium-90 in milk, but they are high. Although milk samples are taken in the vicinity of nuclear plants, these may not always reflect the true amount of contamination, as samples from different farms are blended for testing purposes. Any milk that might be contaminated should be avoided. After the Chinese bomb test in October 1976, some states ordered dairy products off the shelves and farmers were told to keep their cows inside. In states where these warnings were not made, there was a significant increase in infant mortality.[33]

Wheat also picks up strontium-90, second only to milk and dairy products. The Robert A. Taft Sanitary Engineering Center of the Public Health Service in Cincinnatti estimates that we receive 89.6% of our daily intake of strontium-90 from the food we eat: 50.5% from dairy products and 39.1% from other foods, such as wheat and vegetables.[34] Radioactive dust can be largely removed from vegetables by thorough washing, advice that was given to people over the radio by the Connecticut Department of Public Health following contamination from the Chinese bomb test. It is a good practice at any time.

Cesium-137, another common reactor by-product, is found at especially high levels in meat. If cows are producing radioactive milk, their meat is also radioactive. Animals vary in their uptake of radioactivity—pigs are six times as vulnerable as cows.[35] A diet low in meat and high in organically grown grains would offer some protection against the effects of this contaminant.

Low-level radiation seems to remove basic minerals from the body, causing mineral deficiencies that give a variety of symptoms, from constant fatigue, headaches, and numbness in hands and feet to boils and loss of appetite. An extra supplement of foods containing these essential minerals—including calcium—may be a good way to prevent or lessen the effects of fallout and low-level radiation. Here is a summary that health writer Linda Clark has made of protective foods and supplements:

Foods
—leafy green vegetables
—smooth skinned fruits and vegetables
—protein to build body resistance and energy
—seeds and sprouted seeds; sunflower seeds
—liver or desiccated liver tablets or powder
—oils, vegetable, cod liver and others
—brewers yeast

Supplements
—vitamin C
—vitamin B complex
—vitamin B6
—bone marrow (can be combined with bone meal in tablets)
—calcium
—magnesium
—natural iodine
—kelp tablets or other sources of all minerals
—lecithin
—pectin (fruits, sunflower seeds or other products)[36]

Another preventative measure is to stop—or not start—cigarette smoking. It is well known that cigarettes are a major factor in lung cancer, but they also amplify the effects of low-level radiation.

Worker Safety— Worker Contamination

More than one million American workers face on-the-job exposure to ionizing radiation.[37] About 85,000 workers may be exposed to radiation in the nuclear industry. Around 10,000 have worked in factories where plutonium is present.[38] These Americans and their offspring bear the brunt of the radiation dangers of nuclear power. As workers, they are allowed to receive far more radiation from the nuclear fuel cycle than the public at large. This exposure is in addition to their exposure from medical and general sources.

When we are told that nuclear power exposes "members of the public" to minuscule amounts of radiation, we must be aware that **legally, nuclear** personnel are not a part of the "public." By definition "any person inside the boundary of the plant is no longer a member of the population."[39]

Workers are allowed to receive much more radiation than "the public."

As the chart below shows, workers can receive 5,000 millirems of radiation each year, while the limit for the general public stands at 500 millirems from non-medical sources, and the legal average is 170 millirems. But the 5,000 millirems are only the beginning. This compilation of radiation exposures to workers in the nuclear industry prepared by citizen-activist Gertrude Dixon of Wisconsin shows that higher levels of exposure have taken place.

Radiation Dosages to Workers

Millirems/year	Categories
5,000	Legal personnel limit. This or more was received by 201 workers in the production of nuclear power in 1974 (only 4 of whom were reported "overexposed").
6,000	Estimated life-time "natural" dose. This or more received by 92 workers in 1974.
6,760	**Average** dose to workers at the West Valley Reprocessing Plant in 1971. The worker exposure limits did not apply to a reprocessing plant. Plant is now closed.
7,150	**Average** dose to workers at the West Valley Reprocessing Plant in 1972.
12,000	Legal personnel limit for one year by "quarters" (3,000 mrms is a "permissible" workers exposure in any calendar quarter, average of 5 rad per year over age 18. The total lifetime dose cannot exceed 5 rads (N-18) where N is age.
25,000—EVACUATE!!	Exposure level at which evacuation of populations would take place.
50,000	"Accumulated" dose needed to double genetic defects. This or more is the legal accumulated dose for workers over 27 years of age.[40]

Worker exposure levels have been coming down since the early days of nuclear power, and most higher exposures eliminated. There are, however, growing numbers of workers exposed around the 1 rad level—and this is serious. Dr. Irwin Bross has challenged the currently permitted radiation levels for workers on the basis of his research that shows significant genetic damage at exposures near 1 rad (1,000 millirad).

The true dirtiness of nuclear power really shows when we look behind the clean, white facade to see how the nuclear industry goes about its business. Could radiation exposures to workers be lowered? Probably, but accidents do happen in any factory, and nuclear-related ones are no exception, as we will see on examination of the different aspects of the fuel cycle. And accidents aside, safety procedures take time and training. Protective devices are expensive and can malfunction anyway. Nuclear plants cannot be built at a cost that makes "economic sense" without these high levels of worker exposure. It's part of the price we are forced to pay...unless we insist otherwise.

In Japan, the *hibakusha* ("the bombed ones"), people exposed to atomic bomb fallout and their children, are shunned as marriage partners by people who fear the defective genes they may carry. In an important essay, H.W. Ibser, professor of physics at the University of California, asks: "Would nuclear industry workers be avoided as marriage partners as the *hibakusha* have been in Japan?"[41] A nuclear worker over 27 years of age is legally allowed to accumulate the 50,000 millirems that would double the genetic risks to his/her progeny.

Criticisms of the current exposure limits include recommendations that they be lowered by a factor of 40 to 50 (Dr. Karl Z. Morgan) or by as much as 100,000 (the Natural Resources Defense Council). Dr. Jeanne Stellman, presidential assistant for health and safety of the Oil, Chemical, and Atomic Workers Union has said:

> I am very greatly concerned about the health and safety of our workers. Unfortunately, the area of atomic health is more political than scientific. We have been fighting a losing battle to obtain compensation for exposed workers who have developed leukemia or other forms of cancer...The effects on our members are devasting.[42]

The Truth Will Out...

In October 1974, reporter Robert Gillette wrote an article in *Science* magazine about the use of "transient workers." They are the people hired to do jobs that are too "hot" for regular nuclear plant workers—jobs that often expose the temporary worker to a full quarterly or yearly dose of radiation in less than a day—sometimes less than an hour. Gillette pointed out that the NRC "has long condoned the use of virtually untrained supplemental or 'transient' workers in potentially hazardous radiation jobs, as long as they received some instruction in safety procedures and close supervision."[43] Here's the story of the use of part-time workers in a dangerous situation:

> At Indian Point I, a reactor owned by Consolidated Edison, New York City's electric utility company. About 1,500 men were used to locate, make welding repairs to, and cover with insulation six four-and-one-half-inch hot-water pipes, parts of the plant's steam generator system. Men worked in radiation fields of up to 15 rems per hour. Even

using the maximum lead shielding possible, the welding was done in a 6-rems-per-hour radiation field, allowing only about fifteen minutes of actual work per man...[S]upervisors find, not surprisingly, that under such conditions work is done with extremely low efficiency and many errors. Supervision is accomplished largely by means of closed-circuit television.

Almost every union welder in the New York-Westchester area was used on the Indian Point job, after which more were imported. The repair took six months and cost almost $2 million.[44]

As records on the health histories of transient workers are generally not kept, there are no studies which can show the extent of damage done to part-time nuclear industry workers. But this does not mean that there are no effects, and a pattern of genetic damage may yet appear in areas where there are nuclear facilities employing many local part-time workers.

For full-time workers, studies are finally beginning to reveal the hazards of nuclear employment. In 1975, data on workers at Oak Ridge, Tennessee, Savannah River, South Carolina and Hanford, Washington were examined. The data was based on autopsies of 30 plutonium workers. Two researchers found a comparatively high rate of cancer deaths in the group as well as evidence of plutonium contamination in all, although at levels below established government limits. Based on this small sample of 30 workers, the rate of cancer (11 out of 30) was twice the rate generally found among white males.[45]

The Mancuso Study

In June 1965, Dr. Thomas F. Mancuso became the principal researcher in a major project to determine the "biological effects, if any, of low level ionizing radiation among workers employed in atomic energy facilities."[46] The study was funded first by the AEC, then ERDA, and has now been terminated by the Department of Energy (DOE). After 12 years of funding and $5.2 million in government grants, the DOE has removed Dr. Mancuso from the study. Why? Perhaps they do not like the preliminary results of this massive health study.

The study examined the death certificates of 3,520 workers who died between 1944 and 1972.

So far, the project has shown that very small amounts of ionizing radiation—amounts at and below approved levels for workers—have caused cancers in workers at the Hanford, Washington plants and nuclear facilities.

The study shows that there is a definite relationship between low level ionizing radiation and the development of cancer.

Data from the Hanford study have shown that sensitivity to the cancer-induction effects of radiation is at a low ebb between 25 and 45 years of age. At younger and older ages there is a cancer hazard associated with low level radiation which affects bone marrow cancers more than other neoplasms and cancers of the pancreas and lung more than other solid tumors.[47]

The study indicates that there is 6-7% cancer mortality rate associated with radiation at the Hanford nuclear facility. The dose required to double a person's normal chances of contracting cancer is less than half of the legal dose allowed for nuclear workers.[48]

The history of the study itself has been attracting as much attention as the findings. And for good reason.

In the summer of 1974, Dr. Sam Milham of the Washington State Health Department began a review of occupational causes of death in the state, a study independent of Mancuso's. From his preliminary data, he found that "one of the things that popped out was too much cancer in Hanford workers."[49]

Milham got in touch with Mancuso, and set about publishing his own findings. "I went over and talked to the AEC people in Hanford and they sort of said they'd be a lot happier if I didn't publish right then; you know, there was a lot of anti-nuclear feeling around."[50] Finally the paper was published in 1976 by the National Institute of Occupational Safety and Health, an agency independent of the AEC/ERDA.

After the Milham data became known in AEC circles in 1974, Mancuso was urged by the agency to publish his own data, which at that time had negative cancer findings. He refused, on the ground that not enough time had elapsed for true statistical findings. "In essence," he wrote when his report was published in the summer of 1977, "if the latent period for the development of the cancer among the workers occurs at an interval of 30 years after initial exposure, then any statistical analysis prior to that period of years, would provide a false negative effect because a sufficient number of years had not elapsed to produce that effect."[51] And so he refused to publish prematurely, to avoid a misleading report containing "false negative findings."

As if to prove his point, positive findings did appear in the final year of the study. In the last year of the project, and after years of negative data, an independent statistical analysis and evaluation by Dr. Alice Stewart and George Kneale found "positive findings" of a "definite relationship between low levels of ionizing radiation and the development of bone marrow cancers."[52] Meanwhile, ERDA decided to remove Dr. Mancuso from the study and transfer the entire project to the Oak Ridge Associated Universities and Battelle Pacific Northwest Lab. Since Oak Ridge Nuclear Laboratory is owned and operated by Union Carbide, an obvious conflict of interest is involved here. The Battelle Lab handles DOE research, but has never before conducted a health research project like Mancuso's.

As of 31 July 1977, Mancuso's funding was cut. ERDA (now DOE) gave as reasons Mancuso's refusal to publish his data when they asked him to (prematurely) and his upcoming retirement. However, at age 62, Mancuso has another 8 years before the Unisity of Pittsburgh requires him to retire.

The removal of Dr. Mancuso from the study and the transfer of data to Oak Ridge is an obvious attempt to scuttle this enormous and important research effort. It turns an independent study into an "in-house" project, where results can be closely monitored by the government's nuclear program people at Oak Ridge. According to Dr. Milham the move is "like the fox watching the chicken coop."[53]

In the spring of 1978, Dr. Mancuso was fighting to retain his study and seeking private funding to continue his data evaluation. But his study is not the only one on health effects of low levels of ionizing radiation that has had its funding cut.

Dr. Irwin Bross of the Roswell Park Memorial Research Institute recently lost his funding from the National Cancer Institute for publishing findings from the Tri-State Leukemia Data under a study called *A Program of Biometric Research and Cancer Epidemiology*.

The study involved 13 million people, who were followed for three years, and their verified exposure to diagnostic x-rays. The study shows significant genetic damage and large increases in leukemia for both children and adults receiving diagnostic x-rays. Dr. Bross has written several important works on the genetic effects of low-level radiation and has taken strong public stands against nuclear power and the hazards of x-rays.[54] Dr. Rosalie Bertell, a researcher with Dr. Bross, has published papers on the aging effect of exposure in adults. She also has spoken out publicly against the current permissible radiation levels. Their strong stands may well be reasons for the cut in funding and the termination of this important project.

According to Mancuso's study, the amounts of low-level radiation that workers were told were safe—5 rems per year and less—have in fact caused a considerable number of deaths. In addition, both the Hanford study and the Tri-State study have similar estimates of the doubling dose of exposure for leukemia—the amount of radiation exposure that will double the person's chances of getting leukemia. Their estimates are that the amount is much lower than the level now used by government and industry to predict deaths. Both studies are at *low* levels of exposure (around 1 rad). Present standards are based on studies at *high* levels of exposure (above 50 rad).

What will these findings mean for the nuclear industry? According to David Burnham, reporter for the *New York Times*, the effects could be two-fold:

> One serious question is whether additional radiation shielding that might be required to prevent cancer would be so costly that it would adversely affect the economic viability of gener-

ating electric power with nuclear reactors.

> A second question, not limited to employees, is whether the Mancuso-Stewart findings will require a major increase in the official Government estimates of the deaths that would be caused among the public in the event of a major reactor accident.[55]

Mancuso's data so far has shown that workers are already suffering from amounts of radiation that they were told would have no effect. It is clear proof that small amounts of radiation can cause cancer *and* that workers are the "peaceful atom's" first victims. At Congressional hearings on the Mancuso study in February 1977, Dr. Edward Radford, chairman of the National Academy of Sciences Advisory Committee on the Biological Effects of Ionizing Radiation (BEIR), said that workplace exposure limits to low level ionizing radiation are 10 times too high and can lead to a 100% greater chance of the worker developing cancer over a 40 year period.[56]

Proof and More Proof...

Recently there have been two other reports of cancer deaths among workers who were exposed to amounts considered to be safe, occupational exposures. In New Hampshire, a young hematologist has begun to study former workers at the Portsmouth Naval Shipyard, where two of the country's first nuclear-powered submarines, the *Nautilus* and the *Tullabee*, were overhauled in the late 1950s and early 1960s. "The problem is this is a very big job for one person," said Dr. Thomas Najarian in December 1977. "There may be as many as 20,000 people who worked with radiation during those years. All I can do is open the door and get someone interested in starting the study."[57] Najarian became aware of the shipyard exposure question when he treated a retired nuclear welder who had worked with three other nuclear welders on the *Nautilus* in Akron, Ohio, twenty years ago. His patient now has hairy cell leukemia and says that the other three men "died at an early age."[58]

Meanwhile, a former soldier's compensation claim, contending that his leukemia resulted from his presence at a 1957 Nevada bomb test, has led to a study by the National Center for Disease Control in Atlanta of other veterans present at the test. If enough other cancer and leukemia victims are located, it would indicate that levels of atomic radiation previously considered safe have in fact caused unnecessary cancers and deaths. The implications are enormous. It has been estimated that about 300,000 people were exposed to radiation at bomb test sites.[59]

Nevada Proving Ground—Army troops observing the detonation of an atomic bomb, Fall, 1951, by the Department of Defense. (Credit: U.S. AEC, DOE-55-4605)

Footnotes

1. Jack Schubert, Ralph E. Lapp, *Radiation: What it is and How it Affects You.* (New York: Compass Books Edition, Viking Press, Inc., 1958), p. 17.

2. *Ibid.*, p. 18.

3. John W. Gofman, Arthur R. Tamplin, *Poisoned Power.* (Emmaus, Pa.: Rodale Press Inc., 1971), pp. 64-65.

4. *Ibid.*, p. 64.

5. Helen Caldicott, "Nuclear Power Hazards" (leaflet).

6. David R. Inglis, *Nuclear Energy: Its Physics and Its Social Challenge.* (Reading, Ma: Addison-Wesley Publishing Co., Inc., 1973), p. 159.

7. "Down's Syndrome and related abnormalities in an area of high background radiation in Coastal Kerala," *Nature*, vol. 262, July 1976, pp. 60-61. Mentioned in Rodale's *Environment Action Bulletin*, vol. 7, no. 22, 30 October 1976.

8. Sadao Ichikawa, "The Spiderwort Strategy" from a 12 page report, 1977, p. 2.

9. Gofman and Tamplin, *op. cit.*, pp. 92-93.

10. Nuclear chemist Edward Martell hypothesizes that radioactivity in tobacco is the real reason behind the increase of lung cancer in smokers. The culprit may be polonium, a radioactive alpha-emitter found in tobacco. See: Edward A Martell, "Radioactivity of Tobacco Trichomes and Insoluble Cigarette Smoke Particles," *Nature*, 249, 17 May 1974, pp. 215-217,

and "Radioactive Smoke Particles: New Link to Lung Cancer?" *NCAR Quarterly* (Boulder, Colo. National Center for Atmospheric Research, May/August 1974).—Ralph Nader and John Abbotts, *The Menace of Atomic Energy*, (New York: W.W. Norton & Co., 1977,) pp. 78-79.

11. Gertrude Dixon, "Personnel Radiation Exposure in the Nuclear Power Industry," 8 March 1976, p. 3.

12. Gofman and Tamplin, *op. cit.*, pp. 76-77.

13. "The Genetic Effects of Radiation," U.S. AEC, Division of Technical Information, September 1968, pp. 44-45. Reprinted in *ECO*, Stockholm Conference Atomic Reactor Safety Hearings, Washington, D.C., 21 August 1972. Friends of the Earth.

14. Caldicott, *op. cit.*

15. Rosalie Bertell, "X-Ray Exposure and Premature Aging" in *Journal of Surgical Oncology*, 9:379-391, 1977.

16. Cancer deaths would be noticed in a region, but not cancer incidence, which is more frequent. Thus it would take longer to see a possible increase in actual cancer cases. Chronic diseases and earlier occurrences of disease are not detected. (Dr. Rosalie Bertell)

17. John Gofman, "Estimated Production of Human Lung Cancers by Plutonium from Worldwide Fallout." Committee for Nuclear Responsibility Report 1975-2, summary of conclusions, 10 July 1975.

18. "Environmental Radiation Dose Commitment: An Application to the Nuclear Power Industry." U.S. EPA Office of Radiation Programs, February 1974. (From a leaflet by LAND Educational Associates Foundation, Inc.. Stevens Point, WI 54481), p. D-6.

19. A. Stewart, J. Webb, and D. Hewitt, "A Survey of Childhood Malignancies" in British Medical Journal, 1: 1495, 1958. Referenced: Ernest J. Sternglass "Radioactivity" in Environmental Chemistry, J. O'M. Bockris, ed. (New York: Plenum Press, 1977), p. 494.

20. Ibid., p. 494.

21. Two follow-up studies were done with large numbers of children who were x-rayed in utero: B. MacMahon, "Prenatal X-Ray Exposure and Childhood Cancer" in Journal of National Cancer Institute, 28: 1173, 1962. This study was based on hospital records of some 800,000 children born in New York and New England. A follow-up study by Dr. Stewart was based on 10 million children born in England and Wales between 1943 and 1965: A. Stewart and G.W. Kneale, "Radiation Dose Effects in Relation to Obstetric X-Rays and Childhood Cancers" in Lancet, 1: 1185, 1970.

22. L.J. leVann, "Congenital Abnormalities in Children Born in Alberta During 1961" in Canadian Medical Association Journal, 89: 120, 1963.

23. John J. Berger, Nuclear Power—The Unviable Option. (Palo Alto, Ca: Ramparts Press, 1976), p. 79.

24. McKinley C. Olson, Unacceptable Risk: The Nuclear Power Controversy, (New York: Bantam Books, 1976), p. 100. The analysis of Sternglass' work can be found in Dr. David R. Inglis and Dr. A. R. Hoffman's "Radiation and Infants" in Bulletin of Atomic Scientists (September 1972). Sternglass' points are in his "Infant Mortality and Nuclear Tests" in Bulletin of Atomic Scientists, April 1969. See also A. Nilsson and G. Walinder: "Strontium-90 Dosages and Infant Mortality" in Bulletin of Atomic Scientists, May 1970.

25. Ernest J. Sternglass, "Strontium-90 Levels in the Milk and Diet Near Connecticut Nuclear Power Plants," draft of report to Congressman D. J. Dodd of Connecticut, 27 October 1977. Table of Cancer Mortality Rates in Ct. and New England Before and After Start-Up of the Millsone Nuclear Plant in Waterford, Ct. (Source: Connecticut Health Dept., Registration Reports; U.S. Monthly Vital Statistics Reports.)

26. Sadao Ichikawa, "Nuclear Power Plant Suspected to Increase Mutations". Revised report by Motoyuki Nagata, Shizuo Oki, and Sadao Ichikawa (Laboratory of Genetics, Faculty of Agriculture, Kyoto University, Kyoto 606 Japan.)

27. Ibid.

28. Ichikawa, "The Spiderwort Strategy." p. 12.

29. Rodale's Environmental Action Bulletin, 30 October 1976, vol. 7, no. 22, p. 2.

30. Karl Z. Morgan, "Reducing Medical Exposure to Ionizing Radiation" in American Industrial Hygiene Assoc. Journal, May 1975, p. 359. For tips on ways to limit or control your exposure to medical x-rays, see Priscilla W. Laws' "Medical and Dental X-Rays, A Consumer's Guide to Avoiding Unnecessary Radiation Exposure," available for $3.00 from Public Citizen, Health Research Group, 2000 P. St., N.W., Washington D.C. 20036.

31. Joel Griffiths and Richard Ballantine, Silent Slaughter. Quoted in Linda Clark, Are You Radioactive? (Greenwich, Conn: The Devin-Adair Co., 1973).

32. Valley Advocate, Amherst, Ma., 8 March 1978.

33. Debbie Galant, "The Effects of Gamma Rays" in Environmental Action, 3 December 1977, p. 12. "Infant mortality rose an average of 17% in 4 of the 6 states with the heaviest fallout from the nuclear tests, according to Sternglass. In the other two, Rhode Island and Massachusetts, where pregnant mothers drank milk from cows placed on stored (uncontaminated) feed or milk imported from states with no fallout, the mortality rate actually fell during that period."

34. Prevention Magazine, October 1970, pp. 126-7.

35. National Academy of Sciences: "The Effects on Populations of Exposure to Low Levels of Ionizing Radiation." Report of the Advisory Committee on the Biological Effects of Ionizing Radiation, November 1972. From Gertrude Dixon's "Statement to the Radiation Protection Council, Wisconsin Department of Health, Concerning Radiation Monitoring." 3 January 1975, p. 5.

36. Linda Clark, Secrets of Health and Beauty, (Old Greenwich, Conn: Devin-Adair, 1969), quoted in Are you Radioactive?, p. 88. Strontium-90 resembles calcium, and is taken up by our teeth and bones. One way to counter this contamination is to take extra calcium as a food supplement. The sodium alginate in brown kelp seaweed has a chemical structure that bonds with calcium—or strontium-90—and helps the isotope be eliminated from the body, instead of collecting permanently. Powdered kelp is available at most health food stores. It can be added to many foods as a tasty seasoning.

37. EPA copy of draft report by GAO: "Failure to Adequately Protect the American People from the Hazards of Radiation," Fall 1977, p. ii.

38. David Burnham, "Rise in Cancer Death Rate Tied in Study to Plutonium," *New York Times*, 6 June 1976, p. 42.

39. Dr. John Gofman, "Alice in Blunderland," Committee for Nuclear Responsibility Report 1975-3, October 1975. Quoted from Gertrude A. Dixon's "Personnel Radiation Exposure. in the Nuclear Power Industry," a paper presented to the state of Wisconsin Assembly Committee on Commerce and Consumer Affairs, 8 March 1976.

40. "Personnel Radiation Exposure in the Nuclear Power Industry: A Preliminary Study of Standards and Risks," Gertrude A. Dixon, Research Director, League Against Nuclear Dangers, Inc. (LAND), March 1976, p. i.

41. Dr. H.W. Ibser, "The Nuclear Energy Game: Genetic Roulette" *The Progressive*, January 1976, p. 8.

42. From a letter by Jeanne M. Stellman, Ph.D., presidential assistant for Health and Safety, Oil, Chemical and Atomic Workers International Union, Denver, Colorado, 1 March 1974 to Dr. Gerald Drake. Quoted in Dixon's paper, *op. cit.* p. 15.

43. Robert Gillette, "Transient Nuclear Workers: A Special Case for Standards" in *Science*, 11 October 1974. In February 1978, the NRC finally moved to tighten up regulations concerning exposure to transient workers. Realizing that workers might accumulate more than their allowable dose by working at several facilities, the NRC is proposing additional regulations requiring employers to "have continued knowledge of occupational doses to their workers from sources not under the licensee's control." Thus the entire exposure history of a worker would be known by the employer. ("Licensees would have to obtain information from a prospective employee on doses already received during the calendar quarter in which the individual is hired, if there is a chance that the employee may exceed 25 percent of the limits.") According to the NRC, "Inspections, investigations and reports showing more frequent radiation doses to transient workers prompted the NRC to propose the rule changes." U.S. Nuclear Regulatory Commission *News Releases*. 7 February 1978.

44. *Ibid.*

45. David Burnham, *op. cit.*

46. Thomas F. Mancuso, M.D. "Study of the Lifetime Health and Mortality Experience of Employees of ERDA Contractors," Final Report no. 13, 30 September 1977. Department of Industrial Environmental Health Sciences, Graduate School of Public Health, University of Pittsburgh. Prepared for U.S. ERDA, p. 1.

47. *Ibid.*, p. 4.

48. Letter to environmentalists and concerned citizens from Bob Alvarez, Environmental Policy Center, 317 Penn. Ave., S.E., Washington, D.C. 20003, 22 November 1977.

49. William Hines, "Cancer Risk in Nuclear Plants? Government hushes up alarming study," *Chicago Sun-Times*, 13 November 1977.

50. *Ibid.*

51. Mancuso Study, *op. cit.* p. 2.

52. *Ibid.*

53. Hines, *op. cit.*

54. EPC (Alvarez) letter, *op. cit.*

55. David Burnham, "Study of Atom Workers' Deaths Raises Questions About Radiation," *New York Times*, 25 October 1976.

56. *Washington Post*, 10 February 1977.

57. Bob Stevenson, "Did Radiation Threaten Life at Shipyard? 'Scary Data' Leads to Study," in *Foster's* Daily Democrat, Dover, N.H., 8 December 1977.

58. *Ibid.*

59. Preliminary findings of the Center for Disease Control show a rate of leukemia among the groups of soldiers who participated in the 1957 "Smoky" blast in Yucca Flats, Nevada, **25 times greater** than for the general population.—Testimony of Dr. Glenn Caldwell, Center for Disease Control, before the House Interstate and Foreign Commerce Subcommittee on Health and the Environment, 23 January 1978. (From Statement of Robert Alvaez, Environmental Policy Center, before the House Covernment Operations Subcommittee on the Environment, Energy and Natural Resources—Concerning Federal Radiation Health and Safety Responsibilities—13 July 1978.)

Resources (See also p. 132)

Bross, Irwin D. J. et. al.
• *A Program of Biometric Research and Cancer Epidemiology*, National Cancer Institute Grant No. CA11531.
• "Leukemia from Low-Level Radiation," *New England Journal of Medicine*, 287:107-110, 20 July 1972.
• "Screening Random Asymptomatic Women Under 50 by Annual Mammographies: Does it Make Sense?" *Journal of Surgical Oncology*, 8:437-445, 1976.
•"Genetic Damage From Diagnostic Radiation," *Journal of the American Medical Association*, vol. 237, no. 22, 30 May 1977.
• Proceedings of a Congressional Seminar on Federal Ionizing Radiation Standards, House Interior Committee, 4 May 1976. Reprinted by Environmental Policy Institute, 317 Pennsylvania Ave. S.E., Washington, D.C. 20003.

Materials on the health and safety aspects of nuclear power are extensive. Books listed below are of basic importance. The ones that are starred (*) should be on your local libraries shelves. (If they're not, ask that they be ordered.) There are hundreds of articles on nuclear power health and safety with more appearing all the time. For current information, check the periodicals listed at the end of this section, as well as major newspapers. Scientific studies can be found by consulting the indexes of professional journals, such as *Health Physics*. Here we can only identify a few landmark studies.

Books mentioned previously contain valuable information about health and safety issues. The following are expecially concerned with these issues:

BOOKS—Health

• *Poisoned Power: The Case Against Nuclear Power Plants.* John W. Gofman and Arthur Tamplin. Rodale Press Inc. Emmaus, Pa. 18049. June 1971.

• *Low-Level Radiation.* Ernest J. Sternglass. Ballantine Books. New York, 1972.

• *The Nuclear Fuel Cycle.* Union of Concerned Scientists. Friends of the Earth for the UCS. 1974.

• *Radiation Protection: A Guide for Scientists and Physicians.* Joseph Shapiro. Harvard U. Press, Cambridge, MA, 1972.

• *Ionizing Radiation and Life.* Victor Arena. C.V. Mosby Co. St Louis. 1971. (SBN: 8016-0278-5)

• *Are You Radioactive?* Linda Clark. Pyramid Books. 1974.

• *Work is Dangerous to Your Health.* Jeanne M. Stellman, Susan M. Daum. Vintage Books, New York. 1973. (Chapter Six).

Safety

• *We Almost Lost Detroit.* John Fuller. Reader's Digest Press. 1975

• *The Accident Hazards of Nuclear Power Plants.* Richard E. Webb. Univ. of Mass. Press. 1976.

General ·

• *Environmental Pollution.* Laurent Hodges. Holt, Rinehart & Winston. 1977. 2nd Edition.

• *Electric Power Plants in the Coastal Zone: Environmental Issues.* John Clark and Willard Brownell, 1973. $5.00. from the American Littoral Society, Highlands, NJ 07732.

• Daniel F. Ford and Henry W. Kendall, *An Assessment of the Emergency Core Cooling Systems Rulemaking Hearings,* Friends of the Earth for UCS, 1974, $4.95.

ARTICLES & STUDIES—Health

• "An Epidemiologist Takes a Look at Radiation Risks." Dr. Alice Stewart, U.S. Dept. of Health, Education and Welfare, Public Health Service, Food and Drug Administration. (Available from Superintendent of Documents, U.S.

GPO, Washington, D.C. $1.25 #1715-00045).

• "Radiation Dose Effects in Relation to Obstetric X-rays and Childhood Cancer." A. Stewart and G.W. Kneale, *Lancet,* 6 June 1970, pp. 1185-1187.

• "Radiation and the War on Cancer." Senator Mike Gravel in *Congressional Record,* vol. 118, no. 6, 25 January 1972, pp. E403-414 (Good review of dangers; bibliography.)

• "Radiation Doses and Effects in a Nuclear Power Economy: Myths vs. Realities," John W. Gofman. April 1976. CNR Report 1976-2. (Available from the Committee for Nuclear Responsibility, MPOB Box 11207, San Francisco, CA 94101.)

• "The Cancer and Leukemia Consequences of Medical X-Rays," John W. Gofman. An *Osteopathic Annals* Reprint, (New York: Insight Publishing Co., 150 East 58th St., New York, NY 10022), November 1975.

• "The Cancer Hazard From Inhaled Plutonium," Dr. John W. Gofman, May 1975, CNR Report 1975-1.

• "Estimated Production of Human Lung Cancers by Plutonium From Worldwide Fallout," Dr. John Gofman, July 1975. CNR Report 1975-2.

• "Epidemiologic Studies of Carcinogenesis by Ionizing Radiation," Dr. John Gofman, Dr. Arthur Tamplin, July 1971. (This paper summarizes the work which set off the radiation controversy in 1969 over the "permissible dose.")

• "The Fission-Product Equivalence Between Nuclear Reactors and Nuclear Weapons," Dr. John Gofman. May 1971. (These calculations were the source of the recognition that a 1,000 megawatt nuclear power plant produces as much radioactivity every year as 1,000 Hiroshima atom-bombs). Available from CNR.

• "Strontium-90 Levels in the Milk and Diet Near Connecticut Nuclear Power Plants," Ernest J. Sternglass, Professor of Radiological Physics, Dept. of Radiology, University of Pittsburgh, Pittsburgh, PA 15261, 27 October 1977.

• "Summary of Recent Laboratory Evidence Indicating an Unexpectedly Large Biological Effect of Low Doses of Radiation Given Over Long Periods of Times," E.J. Sternglass, Univ. of Pittsburgh, Pittsburgh, PA.

• "Recent Evidence of Increased Mortality Rates Associated with Nuclear Fallout and Radioactive Waste Discharges from Nuclear Reactors," E.J. Sternglass, Univ. of Pittsburgh, 17 March 1975.

• "The Effects on Populations of Exposure to Low Levels of Ionizing Radiation," Report of the Advisory Committee on the Biological Effects of Ionizing Radiations. (BEIR Report) National Academy of Sciences. National Research Council, Washington, D.C., November 1972.

Chapter 5:

Safety Along The Fuel Cycle

"No Record of Deaths..."*

"In the history of commercial nuclear reactors there is no record of even one death caused to the general public."

This is the public relations statement with which we must deal, and it tells us quite a lot about the philosophy espoused by the utility companies and the proponents of nuclear energy.

Just a superficial reading of this statement tells us that really "death" is the only thing worth counting as a health hazard. It does not matter if radiation pollution causes a whole host of chronic debilitating diseases which undermine the quality of life and deplete financial savings. Then again, on second reading, it is not even death that is important, but the *record* of death. If no records of such events are kept, one need not even be con-

cerned about deaths. Then again, on third reading, it seems that only nuclear generators count. This might be construed to mean that pollution of the environment by release of radon gas at mines and tailing piles is not important, and that the industry is not really responsible for the transportation of radioactive material, or the disposal of the waste. Now that we begin to really look at this statement, we see that the whole military operation is excluded by the term "commercial." It is incredible that such a statement should be foisted on the American public!

The health dangers of nuclear power are directly tied to the question of nuclear safety. No one would argue that nukes are not *potentially* dangerous. Any building that contains as much radiation as 1,000 or more Hiroshima-type bombs deserves careful watching.

*A speech given by Sr. Rosalie Bertell at a rally against nuclear reactors on Long Island, 16 September 1977.

There are grave dangers to our health and safety associated with each part of the nuclear fuel cycle. To understand the stakes involved in nuclear development, we will follow the uranium cycle from mining through power production and transportation to storage, paralleling the discussion in chapter 3 (the Fuel Cycle), which gave a brief run-down on what takes place at each stage in the cycle.

Mining

The main danger posed by mining is worker exposure to radioactivity in the form of uranium by-products known as "radon daughters." These are nuclides with short lives that are the decay products of radon-222, a radioactive gas formed from the natural decay of radium found along with uranium-238, the main type of uranium in natural ore.

It was known from the late 1500s on that certain types of miners in Austria, Czechoslovakia, and Germany suffered and died from a fatal lung disease they called "Mountain Sickness." These were radium or "pitchblende" miners. They suffered for generations before the actual cause of their illness—radiation—was determined in the 1920s.

In the mines, workers inhale radon and its "daughters," which are often attached to water droplets or dust. The alpha radiation emitted by the nuclides causes most of the lung damage. Approximately 30% of premature deaths in uranium miners is due to lung cancer.[1] Studies show that the number of lung cancers in miners is highest where there are large concentrations of radon daughters in the mines, where miners have worked for ten years or more, and when the miners are moderate to heavy cigarette smokers. Although both smoking and non-smoking miners have higher cancer rates than the general population, the rate of cancer among uranium miners is ten times higher for smokers than for non-smokers.[2]

Large scale mining of uranium for atomic weapons began in the Southwestern U.S. in 1946 following passage of the Atomic Energy Act, and continued through about 1968 when the existence of adequate stockpiles of uranium led to a reduction of mining activities. During this period, and especially from 1946-1960, some 6,000 underground miners were significantly and needlessly exposed to radioactive gases present in the air of uranium mines.[3]

It was found that from 1946-1960, 4,000 uranium miners who were studied had received an average occupational exposure of 700-1000 rad to their lungs. Maximum exposures are believed to have been as high as 10,000 rad! The average exposures were lowered in the 1960s, when radon control programs were finally instituted.

From 1950 through 1974 the health of some 3,400 uranium miners was followed. It was estimated that as of 1971, the excess of lung cancer deaths among the total group of about 6,000 miners must be on the order of 100-200. "Predictions of 600-1,100 excess lung cancer deaths due to irradiation have been made for this group."[4]

In 1957 the U.S. Public Health Service published results of surveys made in U.S. mines on amounts of radon daughters present. They predicted "a significant mortality from lung cancer among the miners."[5] By 1965, two American studies had finally shown "conclusively" what had been known for decades: that there was a cause-effect relationship between airborne radiation in uranium mines and respiratory cancer.

Open Pit Uranium Mine—Grants, New Mexico, location of the largest uranium mine in the U.S. Since mining rates are often greater than mill capacity, some ore is stockpiled (note the irregular dump). The spiral dump is waste. (Credit: U.S. AEC, DOE-68-8465)

What did the Atomic Energy Commission do about this problem? There has never been a technological impasse to improving mine safety. With adequate mine ventilation, the radon daughters can be removed in large enough quantities to protect miners— a measure known and practiced in Europe by the 1940s.

The AEC failed to regulate uranium mine practice and to protect the health of miners because of a peculiar interpretation of the Atomic Energy Act. The Act was interpreted *by the AEC itself* not to include uranium mining but, at the same time, to apply to all other aspects of uranium processing and use.[6]

It was clearly within the scope and legal rights of the AEC to regulate mining as part of the nuclear fuel cycle.

They chose not to do so. As a result, it was not until the early 1960s that there were effective radon control programs. Only in 1967 did the Federal Radiation Council apply nationwide a uniform standard of acceptable levels of radon daughters.

It was estimated that by 1974 more than 230 miners' deaths were related to radiation exposure.[7] And "the estimates are that another 1,000 may die of exposure they have already had, even if they stop uranium mining now."[8] It is clear that miners and former miners will continue to die from past exposure.

Milling

The waste product from milling of uranium ore is a gray, sandy material called tailings. Piles of tailings lie discarded around uranium mills. In 1971 there were more than 90 million tons of radioactive sand found at some 30 mills in nine western states: New Mexico, Wyoming, Colorado, Utah, Arizona, Oregon, Washington, South Dakota, and Texas.[9]

When uranium is extracted from mined ore, radium and its associated radon daughters remain in the tailings. The tailings are dangerous in any form. The radioactivity from abandoned piles enters the water table as rains leach the radium into surface and ground water.

In the summer of 1975, the Washington-based Public Interest Research Group urged the NRC and EPA to notify 200 New Mexico uranium mine and mill workers and their families "that their drinking water contains high concentrations of radium and other radioactive substances."[10] Drinking water was being contaminated from the improper treatment of waste water by mining and milling companies, including the Kerr-McGee Nuclear Corporation, United Nuclear Corporation, Homestake Partners and the Anaconda Company.

In addition, tailings pose a health threat when they are used as fill. This has happened in several communities around mills. The most well-known example is the town of Grand Junction, Colorado. There the seemingly harmless mine tailings were used in the construction of 5,000 homes. No one warned construction companies or homeowners of the danger until the houses were built—with radioactive cellars and foundations. The Colorado State Department of Health calculated "that the lungs of the occupants in 10 per cent of those 5,000 houses are known to have been exposed to the equivalent of more than 553 chest x-rays per year."[11] The people are stuck: they cannot afford to rebuild their homes and will have an understandably hard time selling them. Homes in

other milltowns in Colorado were also built on mine tailings.

The Atomic Energy Commission took no responsibility for the tailings; their safe disposal was not part of mill licensing requirements. Meanwhile roads, golf courses, homes, and even schools in Colorado were built using the mine wastes.

In the fall of 1977, Congressman Clifford Allen (Tenn.) charged that the NRC's Atomic Safety and Licensing Boards had "grossly underestimated" poisonous radioactive emissions, specifically from the mining and milling phases of the nuclear fuel cycle. Clifford cited an NRC memorandum prepared by Dr. Walter H. Jordan, for many years the Assistant Director of the Oak Ridge National Laboratory. Jordan said in his memo that the emission of radon-222 into the atmosphere and environment from mining and milling was 100,000 times greater than had previously been figured. The report concluded:

> Since the radon continues to seep from the tailings pile for a very long time, the total dose to people over all future generations could become very large. Deaths in future generations due to cancer and genetic effects resulting from the radon from the uranium required to fuel a single reactor for one year can run into hundreds.[12]

After studying the report, Rep. Allen concluded that: "If the number of nuclear plants continues to increase to many hundreds, or even a thousand, then the deaths to future generations from cancer and genetic effects would multiply in geometric progression to hundreds of millions of people who would die..."[13] Allen said at a press conference that a nuclear moratorium should be considered because of the error cited in Jordan's report.

Fuel Enrichment

Fuel enrichment facilities receive uranium yellowcake or uranium hexafluoride gas and enrich this material to a level where there is enough uranium-235 to sustain a chain reaction. The enrichment of reactor fuel is generally up to around 3% U-235. For weapons, the level of enrichment is closer to 90%. Since this is the first place on the fuel cycle where uranium-235 exists in any degree of purity, there are the twin dangers of radioactive exposure to workers and theft of the enriched uranium.

In 1965 a now-closed enrichment facility in Apollo, Pennsylvania was unable to account for 381.6 pounds of enriched uranium.[14] A recent article by Howard Kohn and Barbara Newman in *Rolling Stone* charges that enriched uranium from the Apollo plant, and other facilities in Europe as well, was stolen by agents of the Israeli government, and that the stolen material was used to make nuclear weapons.[15]

As of September 1976 nuclear facilities in the U.S. could not account for more than 8,000 pounds of plutonium and highly enriched uranium. These "special nuclear materials" (SNM) now fall into the "materials unaccounted for" or MUF category. (MUF was recently redefined by the NRC and is now "inventory difference" or ID. MUF had a negative tone to it!) The nuclear materials are lost ("trapped in machinery") or else diverted, stolen or sold.[16] The nuclear cat has been out of the bag for some time.

Fuel Fabrication

The main dangers at the fuel fabrication stage of the fuel cycle are worker exposure, release of radioactivity to the environment, and theft of enriched uranium, the raw material of nuclear fuel. At fuel fabrication facilities, fuel rods are loaded with pellets of enriched uranium or plutonium (for the experimental fast breeder reactor program). Since there is a lot of enriched uranium in such a facility, it is here that the fuel cycle is most susceptible to organized theft of fissionable material.

Worker Safety—In 1974 Robert Gillette reported on his investigation of commercial plutonium processors. He concluded that:

> The safety record compiled by the three main commercial processors (Kerr-McGee, NUMEC, and Nuclear Fuel Services) is subject to differing interpretations, but from a review of inspection reports made public by the AEC, it is hard to see that any of them is quite in command of the technology.[17]

At the Kerr-McGee plant in Oklahoma which made mixed plutonium-uranium fuel rods, at least 87 workers were exposed to excessive levels of plutonium.[18]

The Babcock & Wilcox NUMEC plant near Leechburg, Pennsylvania which also produced mixed oxide fuel for the Fast Flux Test Facility (which tests breeder reactor fuel) at Hanford, Washington, has overexposed at least 45 plutonium workers.[19]

And the Gulf United Nuclear Fuels plutonium fabrication plant near Buffalo, New York, was shut down after an explosion and fire in December 1972.[20]

There are numerous cases of worker exposure at this point in the fuel cycle.[21] But if one case can sum up the true dangers of nuclear power—including fuel fabrication—from the workers' point of view, it is the story of Karen Silkwood, an employee at the Kerr-McGee fuel fabrication plant in Cimarron, Oklahoma.

The Karen Silkwood Story*

The time was 7:30 p.m. on 13 November 1974. Karen Silkwood was driving her car to a meeting with a health expert for the Oil, Chemical, and Atomic Workers International Union (OCAW) and a *New York Times* reporter. On the seat beside her lay a manila folder stuffed with documents taken from the plant where she worked. For the previous six weeks she had been on a special assignment for the OCAW, investigating allegations that the plant was violating AEC regulations and jeopardizing the health of its workers.

Suddenly her car, a lightweight Honda Civic-Hatchback, swerved off the road, hit a concrete abuttment, lurched through the air, and came to rest in a muddy culvert. Silkwood died instantly.

The Oklahoma highway patrol ruled that she had fallen asleep and drifted to her death. But there was substantial evidence that the crash had not been an accident. A private investigator hired by the OCAW found telltale dents in the Honda's bumper and fender indicating that another vehicle had forced her off the road. And the manila folder of documents had mysteriously disappeared.

No one has ever found the folder and no one knows for sure what documents were inside. But they almost certainly had to do with the issue of safety at the Kerr-McGee's plutonium plant 20 miles outside Oklahoma City. The plant was built in 1970 primarily to make plutonium-filled fuel rods, about six feet long and pencil-thin, for the AEC's fast-breeder program. The nuclear industry's thinking at that time called for phasing out conventional reactors and replacing them with fast-breeder reactors, so named because they generate more plutonium

*prepared by Howard Kohn

than they burn.

When Silkwood went to work at the plant as a lab analyst in 1972, she believed in the nuclear promise as much as the AEC. But after her co-workers began describing how they were frequently exposed to airborne plutonium she developed doubts. Plutonium is a fiercely toxic substance— one millionth of a gram has caused cancer in animals—and it cannot be retrieved once it escapes into the air.

By fall 1974 Kerr-McGee had been obliged to report 73 contamination incidents to the AEC, including one that involved Silkwood, and workers claimed that dozens of other incidents went unreported. In one incident, a plant employee was emptying a bag of plutonium wastes when a fire erupted, shooting the radioactive dust in the air. Seven workers breathed in the dust, but Kerr-McGee waited a day before calling the physician and four days later the seven had still not been tested for plutonium in their lungs.

Silkwood, who had just been elected to her local union's governing board, became a clearinghouse for other workers' complaints. What she learned was that the plant had become a menace both to the workers and the Oklahoma public. One problem was that the plant's safety officer had been rushed onto the job as part of a strike-breaking tactic and lacked experience.

On 26 September 1974, Silkwood and the two other local union officials explained the situation at OCAW headquarters in Washington, D.C. but, lacking proof, the OCAW could do little. So Silkwood volunteered to return to the plant and work undercover while she collected documentation.

Then the car crash cut short her detective work. The FBI and a congressional subcommittee entered the case but both abandoned it without resolving the questions raised by her investigation and death. Two years later, however, a lawsuit was filed against Kerr-McGee on behalf of Silkwood's estate in a final attempt to find some answers.

The lawsuit is due largely to the efforts of Kitty Tucker and Sara Nelson, members of the National Organization of Women, who formed an ad hoc group called Supporters of Silkwood (SOS). The SOS pressured Congress to get involved and, when that investigation aborted, Tucker and Nelson—with the blessing of Silkwood's parents—arranged to have the suit filed.

In turn, the suit helped motivate two former plant department heads, Jim Smith and Jerry Cooper, to come forward in the fall of 1977 and corroborate most of Silkwood's original allegations. According to Smith and Cooper, the plant operation was often dangerously sloppy and in conflict with AEC guidelines. Leaking pipes and defective equipment regularly contaminated workers with plutonium, and the company sometimes ordered them to continue working while leaks went unrepaired for days.

Kerr-McGee also allegedly shipped plutonium waste in unsafe containers that sometimes spilled on the plant grounds and may have been responsible for contaminating a public area in Kentucky where the waste was buried. Acid that had been mixed with the plutonium waste would eat through the containers, the two men said, and in one instance an entire truck became so radioactive that it had to be dismantled and buried.

Smith and Cooper later gave depositions so their testimony could become part of the lawsuit. And, at this writing, a half-dozen other former Kerr-McGee employees have agreed to provide further corroboration when the case goes to trial.

Kerr-McGee has filed motions to have the suit dismissed on technical grounds. But if the judge allows a courtroom showdown, it seems clear that Silkwood will be posthumously vindicated.

Nuclear Power Plants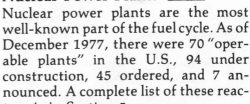

Nuclear power plants are the most well-known part of the fuel cycle. As of December 1977, there were 70 "operable plants" in the U.S., 94 under construction, 45 ordered, and 7 announced. A complete list of these reactors is in Section 5.

Nuclear plants are potentially dangerous for many reasons. There may be mistakes made during construction that can lead to later problems. Replacement parts may be defective. Back-up systems may break down during an emergency. Valves and hardware in the maze of mechanical fittings that surround the reactor are prone to failure. These are all weak points in the technology that can cause accidents.

And of course there is the human element. The best machine is only as good as its operator, and in a nuke, a wrong move at a crucial moment can lead to catastrophe.

Another danger comes from below. A number of nuclear plants are sited on or near earthquake faults or areas of potential seismic activity. Seismic questions were neglected or suppressed during the licensing hearings of many nukes.

A major environmental problem created by nuclear plants is thermal pollution—the heating of water that can destroy the delicate balance in the ecological systems of lakes, rivers, and oceans. Thermal pollution is caused when water that is heated from its use as plant coolant is returned to a natural body of water.

The best evidence of dangers in nuclear reactors comes from two sources: the reactors themselves (dramatically shown as accidents and "incidents"), and people who have worked for a long time within the nuclear establishment.

First we will look at the safety record set by reactors themselves.

Across is a small section of a computer print-out of "abnormal occurrences" (AO) for 1973. This page details some of the 39 AOs reported at the Vermont Yankee nuclear plant on the Connecticut River in Vernon, Vermont. This plant has had a particularly bad operating record. During one 19 month period of operations it was shut down 17 times. Its record makes it one of the 10 worst nukes in the country.

Some of the AOs are examples of small component failures. Others, as the last listed seem more ominous. It tells of "an apparent detonation" in the off-gas system which led to "radioactive releases," which were, however, "within allowable limits." Note that the *amount* of radiation released was not given, just the fact that the releases were "legal."

The detailed listing of AOs from nukes nationwide was getting staggeringly long when the definition of an AO was conveniently changed by the Energy Reorganization Act of 1974. The new definition of AOs, now known as "reportable occurrences," was very strict, limiting the list only to cases where there was proven potential of radioactive release, catastrophic accident, etc. In the first five months of 1973 alone, there were about 850 AOs reported to the AEC from 30 reactors. Under the new definition, only 6 "incidents" were reported in the first six months of 1975!

In the "Summary of Abnormal Occurrences Reported to the AEC During 1973," there was a total of 850 "events" listed. Of these, the AEC graded 55% (461 events) of the total "insignificant,"

43% (371 events) "potentially significant," and 2% (18 events) "directly significant." The report says that "over half of the reported events had no direct or potential safety significance." What it didn't say was that 45% *were* potentially significant or worse. GE's boiling water reactors fared the worst. Of the directly significant events, 77.7% were reported in GE reactors.

The 1973 AO roster gives a good indication of what goes wrong in a reactor. Component failure led to 51% of the AOs (442 events), while personal error was the stated cause of 15% (132 events). Other causes were design errors, external causes, defective procedures, and "unspecified reasons."

In 1973, the Browns Ferry reactor in Alabama led the list in number of events reported, with 65. This is interesting because it was that reactor's first year of operation. Two years later it would be the scene of one of the worst nuclear accidents to happen in the U.S. (See p. 120.)

Some reactor accidents—or near-accidents—seem almost absurd until you realize that "some day these problems may result in a nuclear accident which renders several states of this Nation uninhabitable." (Senator Mike Gravel of Alaska.) In March 1972, Sen. Gravel read this one into the Congressional Record:

From *ROE 69-10* [ROE means reactor operating experiences, an AEC regular report] we learn that, during a routine check at a power reactor, abnormal radioactivity was observed in the building water distribution. The presence of radioactivity was confirmed in the plant drinking fountains. The contamination was found to have arisen from an inappropriate cross-connect between a 3,000-gallon radioactive waste tank and the water

MAR 26, 1974   ACR ANNUAL REPORT FOR 1973   PAGE 136

FACILITY/ SYSTEM/ COMPONENT/ CAUSE CODE	DOCKET NO.	EVENT DATE/ REPORT DATE/ REPORT TYPE	EVENT DESCRIPTION/ CAUSE DESCRIPTION
VERMONT YANKEE-1 EMERGENCY CORE COOLING SYSTEM SENSORS, PRESSURE COMPONENT FAILURE	050-0271	071173 071973 30 DAY	A BARTON MICROSWITCH INSTALLED IN DPIS-2-129 B FAILED TO ACTUATE AT THE REQUIRED SET POINT OF 1 .5 PSID. AO-73-21. THE MICROSWITCH ARM WAS MECHANICALLY BOUND AND FAILED TO DROP AT THE SET POINT.
VERMONT YANKEE-1 PERS. PROT. RAD. MONITORNG SYS RADIATION MONITORS PERSONNEL ERROR	050-0271	073073 073173 10 DAY	FCUR RADIATION MONITORS WERE NOT SOURCE CALIBRATED AT THREE MONTH INTERV AL SPECIFIED IN TECH SPEC. REPORT AO-73-22. SOURCE CALIBRATION WAS NOT COMPLETED PER SURVEILLANCE TESTING SCHEDULE.
VERMONT YANKEE-1 PERS. PROT. RAD. MONITORNG SYS ELECTRONIC FUNCTION UNITS COMPONENT FAILURE	050-0271	080273 080373 30 DAY	AREA GAMMA MONITOR ON THE PERIMETER FENCE BECAME INOPERABLE POWER SUPPLY FAILED
VERMONT YANKEE-1 CONTAINMENT SYSTEMS PIPES, PIPE FITTINGS DESIGN ERROR	050-0271	081673 082273 30 DAY	INSTRUMENT LINES MONITORING SUPPRESSION CHAMBER PRESSURE WERE INCORRECTL Y TUBED TO DIFFERENTIAL PRESSURE SENSORS WHICH OPERATE PRESSURE SUPPRESS ION CHAMBER-REACTOR BLDG VACUUM BREAKERS. TECH SPEC VIOLATION SECTION 3. 7.A.3.A. LINE CORRECTIONS WERE MADE AND ALL SIMILAR PLANT SENSORS WERE I NSPECTED. AO-73-24 INSTALLATION DRAWINGS WERE IN ERROR FOR THESE SENSORS. DRAWINGS WERE CO RRECTED.
VERMONT YANKEE-1 OFFGAS SYSTEM OTHER OR NOT KNOWN COMPONENT FAILURE	050-0271	090373 091173 10 DAY	DURING OPERATION, AN APPARENT DETONATION IN OFF-GAS SYSTEM FRACTURED AIR EJECTOR RUPTURE DISC. OFF-GAS SYSTEM THEN VENTED TO BLDG. SECURED BLDG VENTILATION SYSTEM AND SHUTDOWN REACTOR. RADIOACTIVE GASEOUS RELEASES WE RE WITHIN TS VALVES. (AO-73-26.) CAUSE OF RUPTURE DISC BURSTING IS UNDER INVESTIGATION. SYSTEMS WERE REP: IRED AND TESTED PRIOR TO RETURN TO OPERATION
VERMONT YANKEE-1 OFFGAS SYSTEM OTHER OR NOT KNOWN COMPONENT FAILURE	050-0271	090973 091773 10 DAY	DURING OPERATION, AN APPARENT DETONATION IN OFF-GAS SYSTEM FRACTURED THE AIR EJECTOR RUPTURE DISC. RADIOACTIVE RELEASES WERE WITHIN ALLOWABLE LI MITS. EXTENSIVE INVESTIGATION DID NOT IDENTIFY POSITIVE DETONATION SOURC E. PRIOR TO STARTUP, NEW OPERATIONS PROCEDURE AND CONTINOUS AIR PURGE WE RE USED. RECURRENT EVENT. NO EXACT CAUSE IDENTIFIED. NO ELECTRICAL STORMS IN AREA. EXTENSIVE INVE TIGATION DID NOT IDENTIFY SOURCE. ISSUED NEW EMERGENCY OPS PROCEDURE AN INTRODUCED CONTINUOUS AIR PURGE TO SYSTEM.

system. The report concludes: "The coupling of a contaminated system with a potable water system is considered poor practice in general."[22]

The AEC always was a master of bureaucratic understatement—especially when explaining away nuclear dangers!

In January 1974, Ralph Nader spoke before the Joint Committee on Atomic Energy about a secret AEC study on nuclear plant safety (an October 1973 AEC internal document, "Task Force Report: Study of Reactor Licensing Process"). The report detailed "major deficiencies in AEC regulatory practices," and showed that plant licensing reviews had overlooked many problems in nukes that have "real safety significance."[23] Nader listed some of these problems. Here is one example:

> Steam pressure reduction systems at various Westinghouse nuclear power plants were improperly designed, the Task Force concludes. In one case, a rupture injured seven plant personnel; in another case, rupture injured eight plant personnel; in a third case, two were killed. The tragedies were the result of basic design deficiencies by Westinghouse, the Task Force concluded.[24]

Communities near nuclear plants are familiar with the incidents that happen periodically at their local nukes. Accidental spills of radioactive water into rivers, "small" releases of radiation into the atmosphere, unplanned shut-downs that mean costly replacement fuel for utility and rate-payer alike, these have become all too frequent events in plant operations.

For many people, the "proof of the pudding" came when people inside the nuclear establishment left because they could no longer be part of such an unsafe industry. Several important resignations in 1974 and 1976 brought home to many the reality of nuclear plant danger. Now the people behind the reactors were speaking out, verifying the dangers for which long lists of abnormal occurrences had been mute testimony.

Resignations—Cracks In The Nuclear Establishment

In September 1974, reactor safety expert Carl J. Hocevar resigned from the AEC and went to work for the Union of Concerned Scientists, a group which has made devestating critiques of nuclear safety and safeguards. He said upon resigning:

> (Despite) the soothing reassurances that the AEC gives to the uninformed, misled public, unresolved questions about nuclear power safety are so grave that the United States should consider a complete halt to nuclear power plant construction while we see if these serious questions can, somehow, be resolved.[25]

On the same day that Hocevar's resignation hit the papers, the AEC ordered 60-day shutdowns for 21 of the 50 U.S. nukes in operation to check for leaks in their cooling pipes.

On 2 February 1976, three scientists in management positions resigned from General Electric's nuclear research center in San Jose, California. Two weeks later, in introducing their technical testimony on reactor safety deficiencies, the three said in a joint statement:

> We resigned our jobs to commit ourselves totally to the education of the public on all aspects

and dangers of nuclear power as we have learned them over our many years of experience in the industry.

The nation is continually assured by the industry, the power plant owners, and the NRC that nuclear power plants are designed to be very safe....But "actual" performance doesn't meet "theoretical" projections.[25]

In their long testimony in a packed JCAE hearing room, the three scientists—GE's own—went through a long list of factors that indicate what makes nuclear power unsafe. Their testimony is too detailed to summarize, but here is an outline of the deficiencies they found in their years in the industry:

Nuclear Power—Deficiencies in Many Areas Combine to Make It Unsafe—

A. Design Defects
  1. Flow-induced vibration in the core
    a. Sparger Failure
    b. Local Power Range Monitor (LPRM) Failure
    c. Effectiveness of Core Spray
    d. End of Cycle SCRAM Reactivity Effect
  2. Control Rod
    a. Control Rod Life
    b. Rod Drop Accident and Patches
  3. Pressure Vessel Integrity
    a. Nozzle Break Between Vessel Wall and Biological Shield
    b. Pressure Vessel Pedestrian Acceleration
    c. Structural Integrity of Pedestel Concrete
  4. Containment
    a. Mark I Pressure Suppression Containment
    b. Mark II Containment
    c. Mark III Containment
    d. Primary Containment Fatigue Life
    e. Erosion of Design Margins
    f. Corrosion Allowance in material Thickness
    g. Containment Electrical Penetration Seals
    h. Wetwell/Drywell Vacuum Breakers
    i. Summary—Primary Containment of BWR's and PWR's
  5. Miscellaneous Components
    a. Valves—All Types
    b. Heat Exchangers
    c. Main Condensors
    d. Valve and Pump Seals
    e. Inspection Techniques
  6. Material Failures
  7. Fuel Storage Facilities
    a. New Fuel
    b. Spent Fuel Storage
B. Reliability Calculations
C. Redundancy v. Diversity
D. Political, Economic, and Technological Pressures on the NRC and Utilities Prevent the NRC from Effectively Regulating Nuclear Power in the Interest of Public Health and Safety

After discussing all of the points above and giving examples of design deficiencies and resulting component failures, the trio went on to criticize the NRC's quality assurance program requirements as "inadequate" and the NRC's also inadequate regulation of product qualification. I have included this obscure-to-the-average-citizen listing of reactor problems to show the depth and breadth of the scientists' criticisms—and of the problems themselves. The "GE Three" as they came to be known, concluded by telling the Joint Committee that:

...the point we want to emphasize to this Committee, is that the *cumulative* effect of all design defects and deficiencies in the design, construction and operation of nuclear power plants *makes a nuclear power plant accident, in our opinion, a certain event.* The only question is when, and where.

They made 15 specific recommendations, including the evaluation and study of many of the problems they had raised in their testimony. A thorough reading of their statement is a quick course on the internal weaknesses of nuclear plants given by people who know what they are talking about.

The former GE nuclear engineers were not the only ones testifying that day on the dangers of nuclear power. Another "nuclear drop-out" added his voice in opposition to nuclear power. He was Robert D. Pollard, who had resigned several days before from the NRC where he had worked for six and one-half years as a technical intern, reactor engineer, and finally project manager. He began by saying:

As a result of my work at the Commission, I believe that the separation of the Atomic Energy Commission into two agencies has not resolved the conflict between promotion and regulation of commercial nuclear power plants. Because I found that the pressures to maintain schedules and to defer resolution of known safety problems frequently prevailed over reactor safety, I decided I had to resign. I could no longer, in conscience, participate in a process which so effectively evades the single legislative mandate given to the NRC—protection of the public health and safety.[27]

At the time of his resignation, Pollard was project manager for the NRC review of Consolidated Edison's Indian Point II nuclear plant, 26 miles north of Manhattan on the Hudson River. Pollard claimed that the plant was "an accident waiting to happen." He said that the NRC "suppresses the existence of unresolved safety questions and fails to resolve these problems prior to allowing reactors to operate."[28]

There are any number of examples of these safety problems to choose from—and they all need to be evaluated. In addition to the generic safety problems affecting many plants, there are specific problems affecting both old and new plants now operating and under construction: vital circuit breakers which cannot be tested adequately anywhere in the world; emergency systems under construction for which not even computer analyses, much less experimental data, are available; unknown earthquake magnitudes that may be greater than plant design limits; construction permits issued without adequate technical basis; a one-of-a-kind reactor with a multitude of unique problems; and several operating reactors which have serious, known safety deficiencies which have been given legal exemptions from the regulations. There certainly is no shortage of problems to be explored.[29]

Nuclear Plant Safety

This is being advertised as a no-risk business and that's not true. We don't know that reactors are unsafe, but we're concerned about their being as safe as the manufacturers would like you to believe. Maybe it's time the AEC told the public that if people want to turn the lights on they are going to have to expect to lose a reactor now and then, and possibly suffer great dislocations and property losses as well.[30]

A senior reactor safety engineer
National Reactor Testing
Station, Idaho Falls, Idaho

What Would An Accident Mean?

What would a severe accident at a nuclear power plant mean? In 1956 the Atomic Energy Commission commissioned a report from the Brookhaven National Laboratory on Long Island to determine the possible effects of a major nuclear accident. The report came out in March 1957. It was called "Theoretical Possibilities and Consequences of Major Accidents in Large Nuclear Power Plants," but is commonly known as the "Brookhaven Report" or by its code name of WASH-740.

The study dealt with three types of accidents that could happen in a 200-megawatt nuclear reactor about one-sixth the size of the giant 1000+ megawatt nukes now being built. The theoretical accident took place at a plant 30 miles from a city. (The Indian Point reactors are only 26 miles from New York City.)

The report concluded that a "runaway" incident, where 50% of the reactor core's radiation escaped (the AEC's "maximum credible accident") could **result in 3,400 deaths and 43,000 injuries, property damage of as much as $7 billion, and contamination of a land area the size of the state of Maryland.** People could be killed at distances of up to 15 miles away from the plant, and injured at distances of about 45 miles.[31]

Neither the AEC nor U.S. utilities and reactor manufacturers were very happy with the Brookhaven results. The report suggested that the potential damage would be too much for a utility to stand. Still, the figures did not cause them to hesitate in developing their nuclear programs. Rather, the study made clear to them the need for some kind of liability protection, insurance for nuclear plants in case of a devastating and expensive accident. In 1957, to encourage utilities to "go nuclear," the Price-Anderson Act was passed by Congress. It set up a joint utility-federal insurance pool to cover reactor accident costs, since no private insurance company was willing to be responsible for the huge payments that a catastrophic accident would require. A cut-off limit on payments was set at $560 million per accident. (For more on the Price-Anderson Act, see p. 10.)

If the nuclear establishment cringed at the Brookhaven findings, they certainly weren't about to publicize the even more distressing conclusions of a report issued in July 1957 by the Engineering Research Institute of the University of Michigan at Ann Arbor. The report was called "Possible Effects on the Surrounding Population of an Assumed Release of Fission Products into the Atmosphere from a 300Mw Nuclear Reactor Located at Lagoona Beach in Monroe, Michigan." Lagoona Beach was the site of the infamous Enrico Fermi breeder reactor, which experienced a partial fuel meltdown in 1965 (see p. 118). The report said that given a maximum radioactive release, 133,000 people would receive a high dose of radiation (450 rads) and half of them would die. As many as 181,000 people could receive 150 rads, enough to prove fatal in many cases. These findings were much higher than those of WASH-740.

The study was marked "classified" and quickly buried by the AEC.

In 1964, the AEC commissioned an up-dating of the WASH-740 report. But the results were so shocking that the agency refused to issue the report and even denied its existence. Finally the update was brought to light in 1973, when Chicago attorney Mike Cherry threatened to sue the AEC under the Freedom of Information Act. What did the AEC want to hide? These conclusions: **a worst possible accident could kill 45,000 people, injure 100,000 and do $17 billion worth of damage (in 1965 dollars). Radiation could contaminate land downwind from the accident, an area the size of Pennsylvania.** No wonder the AEC was reluctant to let the public know the facts.[32]

The Safety Research Rip-Off

During the early 1970s, the major safety issue in the U.S. was the effectiveness of the emergency core cooling system, or ECCS. It is the main safety back-up system in a reactor. Its quick flooding of an overheated reactor core would be the last mechanical protection from the fuel meltdown that was the "maximum credible accident" on which the Brookhaven studies were based.

Numerous articles from this period show that the AEC was reluctant to admit its concerns about the ECCS, even those of its own staff.[33] The Union of Concerned Scientists made a thorough critique of the ECCS, showing that it is of doubtful usefulness in an emergency when it would have about 28 seconds to flood the reactor core with water before the core reached uncontrollable temperatures.

In 1970, the Atomic Energy Commission hired the Aerojet Nuclear Company to run a series of tests of the emergency core cooling system. They used a 9-inch model reactor core. All the tests failed. The next year, Aerojet Nuclear reported that it was "beyond the scope of currently used techniques and...some areas of present engineering knowledge" to predict what might occur in a loss-of-coolant accident. The results of the tests were not released to the public until nuclear critics found out about them and forced their disclosure.[34]

In January 1972, the AEC held public hearings on the ECCS. After the hearings, the Union of Concerned Scientists, acting as the technical arm of the Consolidated National Intervenors who represented 60 concerned citizens' groups from around the country, concluded that:

> There is a major controversy on ECCS effectiveness and LOCA analysis model capabilitites between the scientists from the AEC's own ECCS research centers and the AEC's Regulatory Staff management; after a superficial review of ECCS in the spring of 1971, the AEC Regulatory Staff sided with the industry against the AEC's own safety experts to set technically indefensible ECCS acceptance criteria that would not interfere with nuclear power plant licensing...

> Margins of safety in loss-of-coolant accidents, once thought adequate, are now shown to have dwindled, in some cases to zero. Accordingly, protection to the public health and safety cannot in this situation be assured.[35]

And they revealed an internal memorandum in which Milton Shaw, then Director of the AEC's Division of Reactor Development and Technology, admitted to the General Manager of the AEC, R.E. Hollingsworth, that the ECCS was of dubious effectiveness:

Although test information is available on the response of simulated fuel pin bundles to a range of emergency coolant flow conditions, *no assurance is yet available* that emergency coolant can be delivered at the rates intended and in the time period prior to clad and subsequent fuel melting due to decay heat generation.[36]

At the same time that the ECCS controversy was going on, crucial nuclear safety research was being delayed, cut back, or otherwise stalled by poor management and lack of funds. In 1963 the AEC started construction of a nuclear reactor at the Idaho Falls testing station that would be used for "loss-of-fluid" testing. Loss-of-fluid occurs when the piping bringing the cooling water into a core breaks. The LOFT (loss-of-fluid test) reactor was supposed to be finished in 1966, at a cost of $18 million. The project was extremely important. Only by understanding exactly what happens in a reactor that has suffered a ruptured pipe could scientists see how to compensate for this type of accident, how adequate the back-up systems were, etc. By 1972 the project was 80% completed, but six years behind schedule and with construction costs of $35 million.[37] The test reactor finally went critical for the first time on 5 February 1978. Its first nuclear experiment is scheduled for late spring 1978.[38] But by now, scores of nuclear plants have been built without the research experience this reactor could have provided. And its test results will be of even less importance because the loss-of-fluid test that was to show ECCS effectiveness in such an accident will not be performed. Why? The reactor is now too great an investment for it to be (possibly) destroyed!

As if to prove its lack of commitment to safety research, the AEC canceled a half-completed fuel rod test at the Oak Ridge National Lab in 1971. The experiments were also important for testing the effectiveness of the ECCS.[39]

Another testing facility, the Power Burst Facility at the Idaho reservation, was finally completed in 1972, four years late and with a 100% ($8 million) cost overrun. The reactor tests nuclear fuel "under stress" to better understand fuel-related accidents.

During this period, the AEC's Division of Reactor Development and Technology was evidently diverting much of the funding needed for the light-water-reactor safety program into research on the plutonium-fueled fast breeder.[40] Thus new, large 1000+-megawatt reactors were being built all over the country without benefit of basic research into some of the most crucial components of nuclear plants.

How Likely Is a Nuclear Accident?

In the fall of 1977, Carter's Federal Energy Administration head, Jack O'Leary, told people assembled at Ralph Nader's Public Citizen Forum in Washington, D.C. that "between now and the year 2000 there would be a serious core meltdown of a nuclear reactor." But with "proper siting," O'Leary added, he thought such accidents "could" be contained"...[41]

Since the AEC could not take comfort in its own commissioned studies nor in the unsuccessful tests of the ECCS, the agency's case for nuclear safety became based on probability—a numbers game. The theory was that reactors were safe because the probability or *chance* of an accident was so low. The AEC sought statistics to back up this claim, and in 1972, James Schlesinger, then AEC Chairman, charged Massachusetts Institute of Technology (MIT) engineering professor Norman C. Rasmussen with preparation of a mathematical assessment of nuclear reactor risks. The report took two years and $3 million to complete. It came out in late 1974, just as the AEC was split into the NRC and ERDA. The massive report was called the "Reactor Safety Study (An Assessment of Accident Risks in U.S. Commercial Nuclear Power Plants)," shortened to RSS, WASH-1400, or just the "Rasmussen Report." Most of the study was done at AEC headquarters by people from that agency, the national laboratories, private labs, and universities. It was definitely not an "independent" analysis. The AEC clearly saw it as a "last chance" to calm the troubled waters of reactor safety.

The Rasmussen Report

Although the Rasmussen Report was pleasing to the AEC and the atomic industry, its conclusions have been pretty well demolished by a large number of independent analyses and critiques.

Basically, the study came up with figures to delight all close neighbors to nuclear plants—if only they could believe! After examining the ways core meltdowns can happen, and determining the likelihood of these accidents occurring, the report conclusively states that:

> From the viewpoint of a person living in the general vicinity of a reactor, the likelihood of being killed in any one year in a reactor accident is one chance in 300,000,000 and the likelihood of being injured in any one year in a reactor accident is one chance in 150,000,000.[42]

The probability of 1,000 or more fatalities from a reactor accident was one in a million years, the same as for 1,000 people being killed from a meteorite shower. Compared to driving cars, and dangers from falls, fires, electrocution, and lightning, the risks of living within 20 miles of a nuclear plant were deemed to be "negligible."

One of the interesting aspects of the Rasmussen study was that it de-emphasized the danger of a core meltdown. The report statistically found that the "most likely core melt accident" would not cause any deaths or injuries, but could have property costs of around $100,000, mostly costs of evacuation. That figure does not cover costs of repairing a damaged plant, which could run far higher. The report concluded that the oft-challenged ECCS would work, lessening the effects of a core meltdown and preventing catastrophe.

The study found that this most-likely core melt would occur on the average of once every 17,000 years per plant. If there were 100 plants operating, it could be expected in one of those every 170 years. But if there were 1,000 reactors, the probability of such an accident would be one every 17 years!

The study found that the chances of a major nuclear accident causing a thousand or more injuries was very remote—one in a million years or more. And should the improbable happen, the results would not be as severe as most of those estimated by the 1957 or the 1965 Brookhaven reports. The new maximum consequences of an accident: 3,300 fatalities, 45,000 "early illnesses," and more than 1,500 latent fatal cancers that might appear decades after the accident. The area of radiation effects—and evacuation—would be much smaller: 290 square miles. And property damage would "only" amount to $14 billion or more.

As soon as the report was released—in draft form in August 1974, the critiques started coming in.

The Environmental Protection Agency (EPA) said that the study's estimates of the health effects of nuclear accidents was ten times too low. The Union of Concerned Scientists said that the figures for deaths and injuries were actually sixteen times too low. And the American Physical Society, in a study on light-water reactor safety sponsored by the AEC and the National Science Foundation, concluded that the numbers given by WASH-1400 for long-term latent cancers and genetic defects for a particular accident were underestimated by a factor of 50![43]

What Wasn't Studied...

Nuclear power presents dangers to communities, individuals, and nations in different ways. These were not touched upon by the Rasmussen study. It was a "Reactor Safety" study only. Moreover, the group had determined that the core melting was the most important nuclear accident and the only one worth analyzing.

What wasn't covered under the area of risks?

The most obvious omission was the entire nuclear fuel cycle. Without mines, mills, enrichment facilities, transportation, and waste storage there could be no functioning nuclear plants. Yet these were not examined.

Another unexamined source of risk was human error. That intangible factor so important in a nuclear plant—where sloppiness, a wrong move at a crucial time, or a correct decision made too slowly can all mean the difference between normal operation and catastrophe—was completely bypassed.

Thirdly, reactors other than the two main types used commercially were not mentioned, including the floating nuke, which would present special risks beyond those of a conventional reactor, and the breeder reactor.

The Union of Concerned Scientists and the Sierra Club noted another omission in their preliminary joint review of the RSS—the possibility of sabotage to a reactor. WASH-1400 does not estimate the probability of sabotage, nor discuss its prevention.

Means and Methods

A major criticism of the Rasmussen report involves its methodology—the way that accident possibilities were figured out and probabilities assigned. The study uses "fault tree and event tree reliability techniques," which were developed by the space program. They are computer techniques developed over time by the Department of Defense and NASA (National Aeronautics and Space Administration). They are used when comparing the effectiveness of different systems, but cannot in themselves provide definitive numerical answers to questions raised in any one system. This is the point made by Dr. William Bryan, a mechanical engineer from the University of California and the National Institute for Applied Research. On 1 February 1974, he testified before a California State Subcommittee on State Energy Policy. He explained the proper use of fault tree analysis:

> A fault tree analysis is where you start with some problem that can occur, some system malfunction, then you start tiering your analysis much like an organizational chart. You start with a box at the top that says you're going to have a loss-of-coolant accident. You then tier it down to the six or so things that can cause a loss-of-coolant accident, and then for each one

of those six things, you analyze the things that could cause each of those six, and you just keep tiering down until you're down to the nuts and bolts of the system.

The problem in building a fault tree and getting a number out of the fault tree analysis is obvious. You have this huge tree of possible failure mechanisms that all interact and all lead into other events for which you have no quantifiable data. The only possible way to quantify each one of these boxes is to have a failure rate for each one...You just have to have the failure rate for every point in the analysis, and there just does not exist that type of information. So you end up doing the same thing we've always done. Where you can get failure rates, you use them. Where there are industrial failure rates, use them...where there is no industrial failure rate, you go back to some qualitative method or some guessing game.

If you're consistent in the use of these numbers in the fault tree, when you get done you can certainly compare one design against another and say this design is better than the other, if you used a common data base. (But) only for comparison. The absolute value of the number is totally meaningless. *There is just no way that the number can mean anything in terms of the real-world probability of failure.*[44]

And yet the Rasmussen report gave its computer data as *the* definitive statement on accident possibilities and the reliability of nuclear reactors.

Since there are so many decisions to be made with numbers at every stage

in fault tree analysis, the system is "very subject to manipulation," according to Dr. Bryan. His own conclusions were "that, in general, the AEC is up to ten years behind the times as far as implementing aerospace reliability and safety techniques is concerned, *and as a substitute for good analysis, is pushing phony reliability and safety numbers to assure us of just the opposite...*"[45]

Dr. Bryan's conclusion was echoed in all the major critiques of the report.

Amory Lovins was another scientist who criticized the study's methodology:

According to Lovins, the frequency of real-life reactor accidents absolutely refutes the hypothetical probabilities computed by the Rasmussen group. Lovins found that, "The RSS data and methodology yield absurd results when used to predict the likelihood of major multiple failures *which have actually occurred.*" Applying the Rasmussen techniques to one particular sequence of failures in boiling water reactors, the techniques imply that the failures would occur only once in many billions of reactor-years. "Yet," wrote Lovins, *"at least fifteen such accidents have already occurred in the USA."*[46]

In May 1976, Keith Miller, a professor of mathematics at the University of California, Berkeley, and a consultant to the NRC's Advanced Code Review Group, wrote a letter to Stan Fabic at the NRC criticizing from a first-hand perspective that agency's use of computer techniques. He said: "It seems to me that the extraordinary degree to which NRC and the nuclear industry place reliance on computer simulation of complex phenomena is one of the weakest links in nuclear reactor safety..." Although his letter was mainly about ECCS failure, he ended by saying:

...I am surrounded here by the noise and the fury of the nuclear debate and am appalled at the level of misunderstanding on nuclear safety which is being spread. It is hard to stand idly by while being told in the press or media by noted and supposedly knowledgeable scientists, and straight from the executive summary of the NRC's own prestigious Reactor Safety Study, WASH-1400, that I am more likely to be killed by a falling meteor than by a nuclear accident. It is evident to me that those within the NRC concerned with the realities of nuclear safety research have not been speaking up forcefully enough within the organization. It would be a great pity if a study begun to help pinpoint the areas of greatest safety research need should turn out to result in complacency and the denial of system improvements which are vitally needed. I think that WASH-1400 will come to be viewed as a severe blow to the scientific credibility of the NRC. There exist already devastating criticisms of its methodology, conclusions, and misleading summary—couched now in polite technical jargon, but sure to be picked up and translated into more accessible language.[47]

As Herbert Dennenberg, once commissioner of insurance for the state of Pennsylvania, has said:

The probability of anyone believing the Rasmussen Report is one in a million!

The NRC review of WASH-1400 is continuing. Meanwhile, Norman Rasmussen was named to the Board of Directors of Northeast Utilities, a major private nuclear utility in New England. He is supposed to represent "the consumer" on the board. Although the Rasmussen report has been roundly criticized from many angles, it continues to be the gospel quoted by nuclear proponents. But many people feel that the NRC cannot run an unbiased independent study of nuclear power. Its interests are too deeply tied to the continuation of nuclear power to allow any meaningful criticism to come to light.

Nuclear Power Plant Accidents

If there has not yet been a catastrophic nuclear plant accident, there have been several close calls—too close for anyone's comfort. There have been hundreds of potential accidents, which were caught in time. Here is a list of major nuclear "incidents," examples of the most serious nuclear-related accidents. Although several happened at reactors outside the U.S., they are important milestones in the reactor hazard story.

2 December 1952. Site: the NRX experimental test reactor in Chalk River, Ontario, about 200 miles northwest of Ottawa. A combination of human error and control rod jamming led to a partial fuel meltdown and the release of more than a million gallons of radioactive water inside the reactor. It took six months to decontaminate the site.

November 1955. Site: the EBR-1 experimental enriched uranium-235-fueled breeder reactor in Idaho Falls at the AEC reactor testing station in Idaho. During tests the reactor went out of control. Nearly half of the core melted; luckily it did not turn into a critical mass, which probably would have led to an explosion. The accident was caused by misshapen fuel rods and was not brought under control because of human error. A reactor operator hit the wrong button to trip control rods, causing a short delay during which the reactor went out of control.

7 October 1957. Site: the Windscale Pile No. 1 reactor on the edge of the Irish Sea on the English coast. A fire in the graphite-moderated reactor came close to causing an explosion. Water eventually was used to cool the reactor, but there were sizeable releases of radioactive iodine and other fission products. Milk from a 200 mile area containing up to six times the permitted level of iodine-131 was confiscated and dumped into the Irish Sea. The reactor was permanently shut down.

23 May 1958. Site: the NRU experimental uranium-238-fueled reactor at Chalk River, Canada, near the NRX that was the scene of an accident in 1952 (No. 1). A defective fuel rod was improperly removed following a sequence of technical and mechanical errors. Tremendous amounts of radiation were released. No one was injured and no radioactivity reached the environment, but the clean-up was a long and painful process.

3 January 1961. Site: the SL-1, a small test reactor in Idaho Falls. The SL-1 was one of 17 experimental reactors on the AEC's Idaho testing ground that covered 892 square miles. The reactor had not been functioning well and was shut down temporarily for inspection and maintenance work. On the night of 3 January, three men were reassembling the control rod drives to prepare for the reactor's start-up. Somehow the reactor went out of control, perhaps from too-rapid lifting of a crucial control rod. All three men were killed, one impaled by part of a

control rod on the ceiling of the reactor building. After months of dismantling and examination it was still not clear just what had gone wrong. There is a good description of the accident aftermath in John Fuller's *We Almost Lost Detroit* and in the very interesting three-part film *The SL-1 Accident* (available free of charge from DOE's film library).

5 October 1966. Site: the Enrico Fermi fast breeder reactor about 30 miles from Detroit, Michigan. The first commercial breeder reactor was the scene of a partial fuel meltdown during start-up operations. A metal plate at the base of the reactor had worked loose and blocked the flow of coolant to the reactor core. Several fuel assemblies partially melted, an "incredible" accident. An explosion of the core was possible but luckily didn't take place. It took a year and a half to discover the cause of the accident. An (anonymous) engineer at the Fermi project told John Fuller: "Let's face it, we almost lost Detroit." His statement became the title of Fuller's book, which should be read for its dramatic account of this expensive and potentially dangerous white elephant on Lagoona Beach. After several attempts to put the reactor back into operation (and after a sodium coolant explosion), Detroit Edison finally decided to call a halt to the Fermi saga. When the AEC refused a license-extension in August 1972, the plant was closed for good. (Meanwhile, the AEC has decided to build a new breeder reactor near Oak Ridge—the infamous Clinch River project.)

5 June 1970. Site: Commonwealth Edison's Dresden II Nuclear Power Plant in Morris, Illinois. The reactor went out of control for two hours after a meter gave a false signal and a monitor "got its pen stuck." Radioactive iodine was released into the

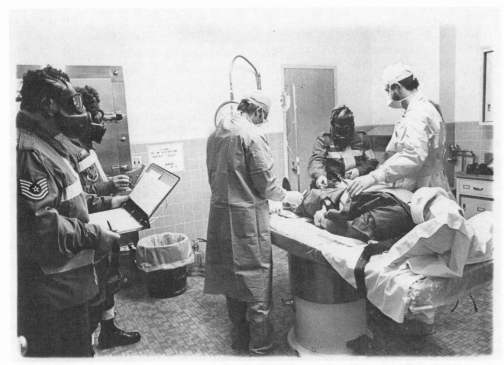

Treatment of a "radiated person"—Noble Hospital, Westfield, MA during Disaster Preparedness drill, Westover Air Force Base, 1976. (Credit: Lionel Delevingne)

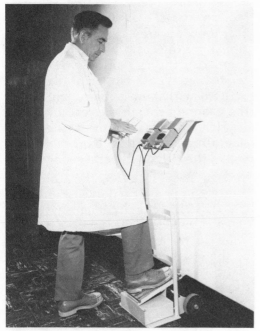

Employee checking hands and feet for alpha radiation contamination—He's using a portable hand and foot counter. (Credit: DOE-74-10409)

Sample containers for rad-waste—(Credit: Idaho Operations Office, DOE-66-7856)

containment vessel at 100 times the permissible concentration. After the accident the plant was closed for repairs, during which time it was discovered that there were problems with the emergency core cooling system. The AEC's journal *Nuclear Safety* made this closing comment in its report of the accident:

> It is unfortunate that procedural, mechanical and control inadequacies can be recognized only upon the occurrence of some incident that puts them to a real test.[48]

19 November 1971. Site: the Northern States Power Company's Monticello, Minnesota reactor. All of the reactor's waste storage space was filled, and the company began spilling radioactive water into the Mississippi River. By November 21 about 50,000 gallons of wastes had been dumped into the river, and some were sucked into the domestic water intake for St. Paul before its gates could be closed.[49]

During the year ending 30 June 1974, the AEC found a total of 3,333 safety violations at the 1,288 nuclear facilities it inspected. Ninety-eight of these posed a threat of radiation exposure to the public or to workers. The AEC imposed punishments for only eight of these violations.[50]

22 March 1975. Site: the Browns Ferry Nuclear Power Plant near Decatur, Alabama. An electrician using a candle to search for air leaks in the cable-spreading room started a fire that burned for seven hours and destroyed 1,600 control cables, many connected to safety devices, including the emergency core cooling system for Unit 1 of the twin nuke. Investigations blamed the fire on faulty equipment design, and a Senate investigation revealed that final reactor design had been approved even though it did not meet regulatory requirements. The plant came close to a meltdown. Total cost of the accident was at least $150 million.

6 June 1975. Site: Commonwealth Edison Company's Zion Nuclear Power Plant, Illinois. Fifteen thousand gallons of radioactive water leaked into the reactor containment building at the Zion plant. (Zion has had the highest rate and number of abnormal occurrences of any nuclear plant in the U.S.)[51]

Mid-July 1976: Site: Vermont Yankee Nuclear Power Plant, Vernon, Vermont. Eighty-three thousand gallons of water contaminated with radioactive tritium were spilled into the Connecticut River. This was the second of three similar spills, this one caused by a faulty valve.

The Earthquake Factor

Since nuclear plants require tremendous amounts of water, they are often built in coastal areas. In California, the San Andreas and related fault areas run along the coast; all the plants sited there run the risk of an earthquake-related accident. No plant has been built to withstand a major shifting of the ground beneath the reactor vessel.

Here are some instances where consideration of seismic danger has affected the siting or operating of nukes.

Bodega Bay—In 1958, the California utility company, Pacific Gas and Electric (PG&E), bought land on Bodega Head, a beautiful peninsula about 60 miles north of San Francisco. It was to be the site of a 340-megawatt nuclear plant. But the site was just a few thousand feet from the San Andreas fault, which caused the great 1906 San Francisco earthquake and has continued to be active, with frequent tremors and signs of more action to come. Area residents actively opposed the plant because of the obvious earthquake potential. The AEC did not share their alarm and gave initial approval to the site even though it was too close to the fault to comply with their own regulations. Later the agency began to express doubts, probably because of citizen opposition. In October 1964, after six years of "bitter struggle," PG&E announced that it would give up the Bodega Head site. But the hole for the reactor had been dug and remains a mute testimony to the utilities lack of caution. [52]

Other California problems—California's PG&E has continued to have siting problems:
• In January 1973 they withdrew their application to the AEC for two reactors in Mendecino county because the site was within the San Andreas earthquake fault zone. This time the AEC told the utility they could not approve the site.[53]
• PG&E's relatively small (65-megawatt) Humbolt reactor opened in 1963 in Eureka, northern California. It was built directly on top of a small but potentially active fault. Local geologists alerted the NRC in 1976 and the plant was finally closed down.
• After PG&E built the large Diablo Canyon nuclear plants on the coast near San Luis Obisbo, it was discovered that they were several hundred feet from the Hosgri fault. Citizen groups are opposing the plant's opening on this seismic issue, among others.
• The other large nuclear complex on the California coast, the San Onofre plant near San Clemente built by the Southern California Edison Company and San Diego Gas and Electric Company in 1968 (unit 2 scheduled to open in 1981) sits dangerously close to the San Andreas fault.

And in the East—Two major seismic problems have also been identified.

• Hearings were held in the spring of 1976 on whether earthquake faults in the Hudson area could damage the Indian Point nuclear plants 26 miles north of New York City.
• In November 1976, the NRC fined the Virginia Electric and Power Company (VEPCO) $32,500 for "material false statements" made by the utility and its geological consultants about an earthquake fault at the site of VEPCO's North Anna nuclear plants in Louisa County, Virginia.[54] In the fall of 1977 it was revealed that the NRC's own hearing board, hoping to ensure licensing, had withheld information on the extent of danger from the "faulty" site.

Thermal Pollution
Nuclear plants require tremendous amounts of cooling water. According to a 1971 article in *Scientific American*, power plants in that year used 10% of the total U.S. streamflow for cooling! That figure includes all power plants, but the article pointed out that nukes require 50% more cooling water than fossil fuel plants of equal size. There is a lot of heat being wasted, as heated cooling water gets dumped into our oceans, rivers, lakes, and streams. **The waste heat from power generated today would be more than enough to heat every home in the U.S.** Instead, the waste heat is released into the air and waters, posing environmental problems.[55]

Not enough study has been done on the effects of thermal pollution. Probably our knowledge will be gained when it is too late to reverse the changes that the waste heat has caused. Utilities are more interested in seeing if lobsters and shellfish can be made to grow faster in cages near plant effluent, than in assessing the changes to the biosphere over time from their plants' pollution.

One aspect of thermal pollution is well known. Fish kills have happened at several coastal and major riverside nuclear plants. Fish kills can occur for several reasons. One cause is a change in water temperature. Some species of fish are attracted to warmer temperatures, but are very sensitive to changes in water from hot to cold. Large schools of fish may cluster around the outflow pipes of reactors and swim in the warmed water. Suddenly the reactor is shut down, whether for repairs, refueling, or for some "unscheduled" reason. The fish are exposed to the colder waters. Thousands can die from this "thermal shock." In January 1972, 250,000 menhaden were killed at the Oyster Creek, New Jersey nuclear plant. The fish had been attracted to the warm effluent and did not migrate south as usual. When the plant shut down that month, water temperatures dropped from around 54° to 34° F. in four days.

The discharges from this plant also caused another problem—a shipworm epidemic. When hot water was dumped into Oyster Creek, the area became a perfect breeding ground for "shipworms," which grow to two feet in length and thrive on wood, such as piers. The plant owner, the Jersey Central Power and Light Company, was forced to buy four marinas for $2 million just to tear the piers down, as they were ruined by the shipworms. In December 1974, the AEC ruled that the plant had changed the creek's ecology through its thermal discharges, allowing the shipworms to breed. And they still are...[56]

Reprocessing

Currently there is no commercial reprocessing of reactor wastes going on in the U.S., and none planned at this time. There are commercial reprocessing facilities in Great Britain (Windscale), France (La Hague), Japan (Tokai-Mura), and presumably in the Soviet Union and China. The dangers were revealed in this country during a short and bitter experience with Getty's West Valley reprocessing plant in New York State.

Spent fuel, shipped to reprocessing facilities for the extraction of valuable plutonium and the unburned uranium (for re-use as nuclear fuel), is extremely radioactive. Dr. Helen Caldicott has given a graphic example of its power (she heard it from ex-GE engineer, Greg Minor!). She says that if a single freshly removed spent fuel rod were placed on the ground, a motorcyclist driving past the rod at 90 miles an hour would be killed from exposure to its radiation!

Workers in a reprocessing plant are the ones who must face exposure to this deadly radiation—and especially the people who do necessary plant repair and maintenance work in areas of radioactive contamination.

Other dangers come from the wastes that are the by-products of reprocessing.

West Valley gave us all the proof we needed in order to know just how dangerous this part of the fuel cycle can be. Wastes from the plant contaminated local streams as well as the ground around the plant. Infant mortality rates rose in the surrounding county. And workers, especially part-time "transient" workers hired for the very "hot" jobs, received high doses of radiation. (For a more complete discussion of the West Valley Scandal, see pp. 50-52.)

We can also learn much from the experience of the La Hague plant, on the French coast of Normandy. There employees have to work in areas that have accidently become contaminated, making their jobs far more dangerous and cumbersome. The plant has been closed off and on because of industrial accidents. In the fall of 1975 the workers went on strike, protesting the government's plan to turn the plant's ownership over to private industry. The union members feared that this change of management would mean still further lowering of safety standards and even more dangerous working conditions. One of their actions was a dramatic march down the streets of Cherbourg dressed in their protective working gear: white suits, cloth booties, rubber gloves with taped wrists, and gas masks under several layers of protective headgear. The union subsequently won its point about ownership, but working conditions remain a major problem.[57]

Besides the dangers to workers, communities, and water supplies near reprocessing plants, there is another big problem—the possibility of theft or diversion of plutonium for use as bomb material. Reprocessing is the one part of the fuel cycle where bomb grade materials are collected in great volume. A country with a reprocessing plant has a nuclear weapons capability.

Transportation

Transportation is one of the weakest links in a generally weak nuclear-safeguards program. Trucks carrying radioactive wastes are usually driven by only one person. Radio contact with security forces is minimal. There is the danger of an accident, or of something happening to the driver. And all nuclear material shipments, whether moved by land or air, may be targets for hijackers.

Air transport of nuclear materials was banned from New York City's Kennedy International Airport in January 1976. Dr. Leonard R. Solon, director of the City's Bureau of Radiation Control and a strong supporter of the ban, explained that "We were concerned about accidents, sabotage and terrorist attacks. We did not want to increase the number of targets of opportunity for terrorists and crazies in our city."[58]

The nuclear industry talks at great length about the safety of shipping nuclear materials. They list the impressive endurance tests that truck and rail shipping casks undergo, including drops of thirty feet onto a

Locomotive Cask Test—DOE-run test to test strength of a nuclear fuel shipping cask. The 28-ton cask remained intact as a locomotive crashed into it at 82 mph. (Credit: DOE-77-11212)

The "Paducah Tiger"—Ten-ton cylinders are used to transport gaseous diffusion plant enriched uranium hexafluoride. Transport is by rail as well as by truck. (Credit: Union Carbide, DOE-74-10318)

concrete surface and eight hour submersion in water. Here is a typical defense of current shipping practices in a handsome Atomic Industrial Forum Public Affairs and Information booklet called "Managing Nuclear Wastes:"

> Now let's look at the record. There have been hundreds of thousands of shipments of radioactive materials between 1949 and 1970, many of which consisted of high-level spent fuel casks. In 20 years, there was a total of 26 shipping accidents in which some radiation was released outside the shipping vehicle. None of these resulted in overexposure or injury to the public and, perhaps more important, none of them involved a modern shipping cask used for high-level radioactive wastes or spent fuel.[59]

But the NRC relies upon cask manufacturers to test the safety of their product; and some tests are done on scale models rather than the real casks.[60]

Accidents do happen, however. Here is the story of the worst highway accident to date. The nuclear material involved was the processed ore known as yellowcake. It was not being shipped in the heavy casks, but rather in simple steel barrels. This is what happened:

> A tractor-trailer carrying 50 steel drums of uranium oxide overturned in Southeastern Colorado (in early October, 1977), spilling 15,000 pounds of the radioactive substance.

> According to federal officials it was the largest spill of this type ever recorded. The material, known as "yellowcake," is a fine powder used in the processing of nuclear fuel.

Paul B. Smith, the Environmental Protection Agency's Denver radiation expert, said that if the spill had occurred in a major urban area it could have posed a major health hazard. Minute amounts of yellowcake dust will cause lesions of the kidneys and liver when inhaled.

Exxon Corp., which manufactures the material, rushed a crew of workers equipped with respirators and special clothing to the area to begin clean-up operations. They estimated the yellowcake had contaminated an area greater than 5,000 square feet. Before they arrived, over 25 policemen were examined for contamination after working at the accident site...the yellowcake is shipped in ordinary industrial containers. More than 2 million tons of the toxic material have passed along the same route, which includes downtown Denver, this year.[61]

Communities Take Action

In 1975 and 1977, some town meetings in western Massachusetts, Vermont, and New Hampshire voted on whether or not to ban the transportation of radioactive materials through their towns. Although no town on a major waste transport route passed the ban, the issue of transportation dangers became widely known and talked about. A Vermont Public Interest Research Group study on the issue warned:

> More than 600 shipments of radioactive materials each year will travel over Vermont highways if currently proposed power generation facilities are built,

...But here's how it's often transported! (Credit: Vermont Public Interest Research Group, Inc.—VPIRG—1976)

and, using U.S. Atomic Energy Commission and Vermont Highway Department statistics, VPIRG anticipates that a truckload of radioactive materials can be expected to be involved in some type of accident at least once every four years somewhere in the state.

Once every 7.5 years there will be an accident involving a truckload of highly radioactive spent fuel if all these facilities are built.[62]

Airport Bans

When shipments of radioactive materials were banned from Kennedy Airport in 1976, much of the traffic was diverted to Chicago's O'Hare Airport, the nation's busiest. Two tons of the material went through O'Hare from August 1975 until December 1977— and enough weapons-grade material to make 50 to 100 homemade atomic bombs.[63]

> On February 8, 1977 NRC inspectors detected at least two security lapses when the largest shipment ever to go through O'Hare was sitting on the ground awaiting a Lufthansa flight bound for Frankfurt, Germany. About 1,700 pounds of highly enriched uranium— enough to produce several Hiroshima-sized bombs was at the site.[64]

This material was being shipped out in a commercial, passenger airline—one that has been a major target of terrorist threats and hijackings. In late November 1977, the *Chicago Sun-Times* did a story on the shipments, which were finally banned a week later.

Waste Storage/Disposal

Radioactive wastes are real—and deadly. Disposal of radioactive waste is the major problem now facing the nuclear industry in the U.S.

> Radioactive wastes being highly toxic can damage or destroy living cells, causing cancer and possibly death depending on the quantity and length of time individuals are exposed to them. Some radioactive wastes will remain hazardous for hundreds of thousands of years. Decisions on what to do with the wastes will affect the lives of generations to come.[65]
>
> General Accounting
> Office Report

Radioactive wastes are dangerous when they enter the environment. They contaminate land and water and cause cancer and a wide range of health problems in people and other animals who are exposed.

Radioactive wastes are dangerous when improperly stored. The temporary storage of used fuel rods on site has posed one serious problem. Compaction of spent fuel rods in reactor storage pools can be dangerous, for if rods are placed too closely together, a critical mass can possibly be formed.

At every waste storage facility, there is already a long history of leaks and spills. In a 1976 report prepared by Mason Willrich for ERDA, the storage of radioactive waste at nine locations in the U.S. was called a "major health hazard."[66]

Leaks

Some 18 leaks at the Hanford storage facility in Richland, Washington, releasing 430,000 gallons of high-level wastes over 20 years, show the real dangers of present storage methods.

Waste by Rail—From Upton, Long Island NY, to Oak Ridge TN, these ten-ton "vaults" are transported by truck and by rail for permanent burial. (Credit: Brookhaven National Laboratory, DOE-63-6996)

Trenches for Wastes—Containers are buried in trenches 12 feet deep and covered with earth. Burial depth is above water table level in a geological formation of Conasauga shale. (Credit: DOE-66-7764)

At Maxey Flats storage area near Morehead, Kentucky, radioactive materials seeped from their burial spots into nearby streams. Leaks have also happened at the West Valley dumps in New York State and at the Oak Ridge reservation in Tennessee.[67]

In February 1976, the EPA published a report by G. Lewis Meyer that described the leaching of plutonium (Pu), with its half-life of 24,300 years, from Maxey Flats: "According to many technical references, Pu normally does not move through the soil and subsurface more than a few centimeters, yet at Maxey Flats, it has been detected tens and hundreds of meters from the trenches. The burial site was expected to retain the buried Pu for its hazardous lifetime, but plutonium has migrated from the site in less than ten years."[68]

Radioactive waste also leaks out from functioning nuclear power plants.

Columbia University geologists have found accumulations of cesium-137 and cobalt-60 from the Indian Point nuclear plants in sediment from New York City's harbor, some 26 miles downriver from the plants.[69]

Says Gus Speth of the Council on Environmental Quality:

> Perhaps the waste problem is manageable in theory; perhaps not. I hope it is. But many things that are theoretically doable never get done. Certainly the sorry history of radioactive waste management in this country to date provides no basis for confidence that things will work out.[70]

The Council recommended that use of nuclear power not be increased until a solution is found to the waste problem.

Soviet Waste Accident— The Kyshtym disaster

A serious accident involving nuclear plant wastes has already happened. In November 1976, a *New York Times* story told of a report by a Soviet biochemist, Dr. Zhores A. Medvedev, now living in Britain. He had written a story in the British *New Scientist* about an explosion of stored radioactive wastes that had killed hundreds of people, contaminated thousands of people and rivers and a large land area. According to the report, an atomic waste dump in the Ural Mountains exploded without warning in March 1958. Clouds of radiation were blown hundreds of miles and many villages were affected.[71]

More than a year later, the Critical Mass Energy Project used the Freedom of Information Act to get more information on the accident from CIA files. The CIA knew of the accident all along. Ralph Nader surmised that the information had not been released because of "the reluctance of the CIA to highlight a nuclear accident in the USSR that could cause concern among people living near nuclear facilities in the United States."[72]

According to the heavily censored documents, the accident happened in the small rural town of Kyshtym, 43 miles from the industrial city of Chelyabinsk. The explosion wrecked part of a nuclear plant there, presumably a weapons center. One document said that people in the region "grew hysterical with fear, with the incidence of unknown 'mysterious' diseases breaking out."[73] Victims at a local hospital were seen with skin "sloughing off" their faces, hands, and other exposed parts of their bodies, a horrible symptom of radiation sickness first seen at Hiroshima. The area where the accident happened is now a wasteland.

Drivers are warned not to stop as they pass through. Villages lie burned and abandoned.

Nuclear Wastes and Proliferation

It has long been maintained by the international nuclear industry that bombs cannot be made from reactor waste. But at the October 1977 meeting of the International Agency for Atomic Energy (IAEA) in Vienna, ERDA representatives dropped their own bombshell, announcing that crude and "dirty" (high in fallout) but "effective" bombs could be made from commercial reactor waste! They revealed that:

> **In a 1974 experiment, AEC scientists were able to make an atomic bomb from commercial reactor wastes.[74]**

Some Questions and Answers About Nuclear Health and Safety...

Can Nuclear Plants Explode?—The nuclear industry and utilities always calm our fears of an accident by assuring the public that light water reactors "can't explode like a bomb," and are therefore safe. But...

• It's really the release of radiation that is dangerous, and that can happen when there are leaks, spills, or explosions of other types, such as in the cooling system.

• Steam or chemical explosions might occur if a reactor could not be cooled immediately during a loss-of-coolant accident. A strong steam explosion in the core could have the same effect as if the core had itself reached an uncontrolled critical mass and exploded.

• A breeder reactor could possibly explode, if coolant was lost in the core. There is enough plutonium in a breeder reactor's fuel for hundreds of critical masses. If there was a core meltdown, the fuel rods might come together in a critical mass. This was feared during the Fermi fuel meltdown in 1965.[75]

Doesn't Burning Coal Create Radiation Too?—The comparison between the amount of radiation produced by coal and by nukes is another weapon in the nuclear industry's meager public (mis)information arsenal. They say that coal plants produce as much radiation as nukes. Is this so?

• Coal-burning plants do emit radioactive gases and heavy metals, such as lead and cadmium, which are dangerous when inhaled or swallowed. Coal itself contains small amounts of uranium and thorium. Radioactive releases from the stack of a coal-fired plant include radioactive isotopes created by U-238, U-235, thorium, and radon.

Radon also creates radioactive gases (the radon daughters) in the mines. These are a danger in mines, but are not a problem when mines are adequately vented, as is also necessary in uranium mines.

• Scrubbers, the cleaning devices that remove pollutants from coal smokestacks, are also very good at removing radiation—between 90% and 95% effective. Of course, coal does have very real health and safety problems. Miners in unsafe mines are potential victims of black-lung disease, lung cancer, methane gas explosions, and cave-ins... The ash that is the waste product of burning coal is very acidic and can pollute storage and burial areas.

But at this time, the danger of radiation is much greater from a nuclear plant than a coal-fired one.

The comparison between nuclear and coal-fired generators sometimes focuses only on emissions from the stack, which of course focuses on the "worst" part of the coal cycle and a minimal part of the nuclear cycle. The argument uses real figures of death and injury in the coal cycle (inflated by numerous violations of health and safety laws) as a contrast to euphemistic projections for nuclear. There is also a time distortion: coal health effects are more immediate, while nuclear effects extend over hundreds of thousands of years and many generations. It is like "paying now" or "charging to future generations." Effects of coal burning can be reduced substantially by enforcement of safety and anti-pollution measures, and new methods of burning.[76]

Dr. Rosalie Bertell

Footnotes

1. Samuel S. Epstein, "The Political and Economic Basis of Cancer" in *Technology Review* (July/August 1976), p. 36.

2. Arell S. Schurgin and Thomas C. Hollocher, "Lung Cancer Among Uranium Mine Workers" in *The Nuclear Fuel Cycle*, Union of Concerned Scientists, Friends of the Earth Energy Papers; 2, 1974, p. 133.

3. *Ibid.*, p. 117.

4. *Ibid.*, p. 117.

5. *Ibid.*, p. 129.

6. *Ibid.*, note, p. 140.

7. V.E. Archer, J.D. Gillam, and J.K. Wagoner, "Respiratory Disease Mortality Among Uranium Miners" in *Annals N.Y. Academy of Science*, p. 271.

8. John Gofman, "Alice in Blunderland," Committee for Nuclear Responsibility Report 1975-3, October 1975.

9. H. Peter Metzger, "Dear Sir: Your House is Built on Radioactive Uranium Waste," *New York Times Magazine*, 31 October 1971.

10. Public Interest Research Group (PIRG) Press Release, "PIRG Urges Federal Action to Warn New Mexico Uranium Workers of Radioactive Drinking Water," 17 August 1975.

11. Metzger, *op cit.*

12. Written statement by Rep. Clifford Allen, 29 November 1977, quoting NRC report of 21 September 1977. Here is Dr. Jordan's finding of the error in full: (from Memorandum for James R. Yore, Chairman, Atomic Safety and Licensing Board Panel. From Walter H. Jordan, ASLBP, Subject: Errors in 10 CFR 51.20, Table S-3.)

"One section of the table deals with radiological effluents. The quantity of radioactivity discharged is given in curies for each important nuclide and is stated as being the total amount emitted 'per annual fuel requirement or reference reactor year.' For example, the maximum quantity of Kr-85 that might be released to the atmosphere as a consequence of operating a reference reactor (1000 MWe, 80% capacity factor) for one year would be 400,000 curies and would be released from the plant that reprocesses the fuel. The table includes 1.1×10^7 curies of high-level wastes (to be buried at a Federal Repository) that would be generated for each reference reactor year (RRY) of operation. With one exception the figures given do indeed conservatively state the total amount of radioactivity that would be released as gas, liquid, or solid as a consequence of operating a reference power reactor for one year or alternatively as a consequence of mining and milling the quantity of uranium required to fuel such a plant for one year, the so-called annual fuel requirement (AFR).

"The one important exception has to do with the quantity of Rn-222 where the figure given is '74.5 curies. Principally from milling operations and excludes contribution from mining.' This figure is in error. The correct value would be some 100,000 times greater! The technical basis for my conclusion will be discussed in a later section, but is based on the fact that a mill tailings pile continues to emit radon for thousands of years."

13. Saundra Ivey, "Most Radon Deaths Said Unrelated to Processing," in *The Tennessean*, 26 November 1977.

14. David Burnham, "House Aid Tells of Suspicion U.S. Uranium Was Stolen 10 Years Ago," *New York Times*, 9 August 1977.

15. Howard Kohn and Barbara Newman, "How Israel Got the Bomb," *Rolling Stone*, no. 253, 12 January 1977.

16. David Burnham, "8,000 Pounds of Atom Materials Unaccounted For by Plants in U.S." in *New York Times*, 5 August 1977.

17. Robert Gillette, "Plutonium (I): Questions of Health in a New Industry" in *Science*, 20 September 1974.

18. Testimony of John Abbotts, Public Interest Research Group (PIRG) on Chapter IV-D, Section 1.1, Status of Mixed Oxide Fuel Fabrication Industry, (pp. IV-D-7—IV-D-9), p. 2.

19. *Ibid.*, p. 3.

20. *Ibid.*

21. There are accounts reported in daily newspapers and magazines that are too numerous to cite.

22. Senator Mike Gravel (Alaska) in the *Congressional Record*, 22 March 1972.

23. Statement by Ralph Nader before the JCAE, 28 January 1974, p. 4. (From PIRG, Washington, D.C.)

24. *Ibid.*, p. 5.

25. Carl J. Hocevar, quoted in Berger, *Nuclear Power*, p. 58.

26. Testimony of Dale G. Bridenbaugh, Richard B. Hubbard and Gregory C. Minor before the JCAE, 18 February 1976. This testimony is available from the UCS (Resource Section) or in Peter Faulkner (ed.), *The Silent Bomb*, (New York: Vintage Books, 1977).

27. Testimony of Robert D. Pollard before the JCAE, 18 February 1976, from Faulkner, *op. cit.*, Appendix B, *The Silent Bomb*.

28. David Burnham, "U.S. Panel Releases Reports that Critics Say Show Failure To Act on Safety Before Licensing Atom Reactors," *New York Times*, 13 February 1976.

29. Pollard testimony, *op. cit.*

30. Robert Gillette, "Nuclear Safety (I): The Roots of Dissent," *Science*, September 1972, p. 771.

31. "Theoretical Possibilities and Consequences of Major Accidents in the Large Nuclear Power Plants," WASH-740, Atomic Energy Commission, 22 March 1957.

32. McKinley Olson, *Unacceptable Risk: The Nuclear Power Controversy* (New York: Bantam Books, 1976) p. 22.

33. See Daniel Ford and Henry Kendall, "Nuclear Safety," *Environment* magazine, vol. 14, no. 7, September 1972. Also Berger, *op. cit.*, pp. 56-60 and Gillette, *op. cit.*

34. Olson, *op. cit.*, p. 32.

35. Daniel F. Ford and Henry W. Kendall, Union of Concerned Scientists, *An Assessment of the Emergency Core Cooling Systems Rulemaking Hearings* (Friends of the Earth, 1974), p. 14.

36. *Ibid.*

37. Robert Gillette, "Nuclear Safety (II): The Years of Delay," *Science*, 8 September 1972.

38. U.S. Nuclear Regulatory Commission, *News Release*, vol. 4, no. 6, 7 February 1978.

39. Gillette, *op. cit.*

40. Robert Gillette, "Nuclear Safety (III): Critics Charge Conflicts of Interest," *Science*, 15 September 1972, vol. 177.

41. *The Power Line*, November 1977, vol. 3, no. 4, p. 6.

42. "Reactor Safety Study (Draft) An Assessment of Accident Risks in U.S. Commercial Nuclear Power Plants." Summary Report (Washington, D.C., AEC, August 1974).

43. Carl J. Hocevar, Union of Concerned Scientists, "Report to the American Physical Society by the Study Group on Light Water Reactor Safety," American Physical Society, 28 April 1975. From Carl J. Hocevar, Union of Concerned Scientists, "Nuclear Reactor Licensing: A Critique of the Computer Safety Prediction Methods," August 1975, p. 3.

44. Dr. William Bryan, quoted in "Nothing Can Possibly Go Wrong, go wrong, go wrong...," *Not Man Apart*, Friends of the Earth, mid-May 1974, pp. 1/10.

45. *Ibid.*, p.1. "Another item that casts serious doubts on the credibility of the unrealistically low failure rates in the WASH 1400 report is the fact that the AEC Regulatory Group found 98 critical safety problems during fiscal year 1973-74 routine power plant inspections. By the AEC's own definition, these 98 violations 'posed a health threat in that they *caused* or were *likely to cause* radiation exposures to employees or the public in excess of permitted limits.' The tremendous differences in these assessments from those presented in WASH 1400 illustrate how much the final answer can be manipulated through different assumptions, techniques, and data to provide any answer the analyst desires." From: William M. Bryan, "Comments on the AEC WASH 1400 Report Reactor Safety Study," 11 October 1974, p. 12.)
"The risk projections rest on a very small experience base. Studies based on the design of just two light water cooled nuclear power plants were applied to 44 others now on line in the United States and extrapolated to cover the 100 or so which will be on line by 1980." (From: Samuel H. Day, Jr. "Scant Cause for Reassurances," Editorial, *The Bulletin of Atomic Scientists*, October 1974.)

46. Amory Lovins, "Nuclear Power, Technical Bases for Ethical Concern," (London: Friends of the Earth Ltd., March 1975). Quoted from Berger, *op. cit.*, p. 66.

47. Letter from Prof. Keith Miller, consultant, Advanced Code Review Group to Stan Fabic of NRC (Washington, D.C., 7 May 1976).

48. "Dresden II Incident of June 5, 1970," *Nuclear Safety*, September-October 1971. Quoted by Senator Gravel in *Congressional Record*, 22 March 1972 (S4499).

49. From "Record on Nuclear Safety," Saskatchewan Coalition Against Nuclear Development.

50. *Ibid.*

51. "The 10 Most Dangerous Nuclear Plants," *The Elements*, February 1977.

52. McKinley Olson, *op. cit.*, pp. 6-7.

53. John Abbotts and Margaret McCarthy, "What's Wrong with the Atomic Industry?", 55 Case Studies of Basic Nuclear Problems (Washington, D.C., PIRG, July 1977).

54. *Ibid.*

55. Earl Cook, "The Flow of Energy in an Industrial Society," *Scientific American*, September 1971, p. 142. This entire issue was devoted to "Energy and Power" and is full of interesting information.

56. Abbotts and McCarthy, *op. cit.*, p. 18.

57. The union, CFDT, commissioned a film that tells the workers' story in a very interesting and powerful way. It is called *Sentenced to Success (Condamnes a Reussir)* and is available for rental or purchase in an English version through Green Mountain Post Films, Box 177, Montague, Mass. 01351.

58. Richard Pollock, "Flying the Friendly Skies at O'Hare," *Critical Mass Journal*, January 1978, vol. 3, no. 10, pp. 1/10.

59. Dr. Jerry Grey, Managing Nuclear Wastes (Atomic Industrial Forum, April 1974) pp. 9-10.

60. Jack Anderson, *New York Post*, 6 December 1975.

61. *WIN* Magazine (Nukes Bureau), 20 October 1977, pp. 17-18.

62. Vermont Public Interest Research Group (VPIRG), "Radwaste on the Roadway: The Transportation of Radioactive Materials in Vermont," February 1977, p. 2.

63. Pollock, *op. cit.*

64. *Ibid.*, p. 10.

65. General Accounting Office, Report to Congress, "Nuclear Energy's Dilemma: Disposing of Hazardous Radioactive Waste Safely," 9 September 1977, p. i.

66. David Burnham, "Radioactive Waste at the Nation's Nine Storage Centers is Called Major Health Hazard," *New York Times*, 8 September 1976.

67. George Laycock, "Some say it will kill you; if I die I guess I'll know," *Audubon*, November 1976.

68. *Ibid.*

69. "Radioactive Waste Builds up in Hudson," *New York Times*, 18 October 1976, p. 58.

70. "A Smaller Tomorrow: Adjusting to the New Limits on Nuclear Power," remarks by Gus Speth, member, Council on Environmental Quality, before the ALI-ABA Conference on Atomic Energy Licensing and Regulation, Washington, D.C., 29 September 1977.

71. "Exiled Soviet Scientist Says that an Explosion of Nuclear Wastes in 1958 Killed Hundreds," *New York Times*, 7 November 1976, p. 18.

72. Richard Pollock, "Soviets Experience Nuclear Accident," in *Critical Mass Journal*, January 1978, vol. 3, no. 10, p. 9.

73. *Ibid.*

74. (IAEA - bomb from commercial wastes)

75. *ECO*, Friends of the Earth newpaper of the Stockholm Conference, nuclear industry meetings, 9 November 1973. See also Richard Webb's *The Accident Hazards of Nuclear Power Plants* (Amherst, Mass: University of Mass. Press 1976).

76. From a personal letter by Sr. Rosalie Bertell to the author.

Resources—Health and Safety (cont.)

• "Hazards of Nuclear Fission Power and the Choice of Alternatives," John T. Edsall, M.D. *Environmental Conservation*, vol. 1, no. 1, Spring 1974.

"X-Ray Exposure and Premature Aging," Rosalie Bertell, Ph.D., *Journal of Surgical Oncology*, 9:379-391, (1977). (Available from Sr. Rosalie Bertell, Roswell Park Memorial Institute, 666 Elms St., Buffalo, NY 14263).

• "Nuclear Power and Public Health," Rosalie Bertell, Roswell Park Memorial Institute, Buffalo, N.Y.

• "Radiation Effects Underestimated," Skip Laitner, *Critical Mass Journal*, vol.II, no. 2, May 1976.

• Testimony on Behalf of Public Interest Research Group, Sidney N. Wolfe, M.D., Director, 4 March 1977. (All PIRG materials available from: Public Interest Research Group, P.O. Box 19312, Washington, D.C. 20036).

• "Suggested Reduction of Permissible Exposure to Plutonium and other Transuranium Elements," Dr. Karl Z. Morgan, *American Industrial Hygiene Association Journal*, August 1975, pp. 567-575.

• "Medical and Dental X-Rays, A Consumer's Guide to Avoiding Unnecessary Radiation Exposure," Priscilla W. Laws. (Available from Public Citizen, Health Research Group, 200 P. St., N.W., Washington, D.C. 20036, $3.00).

• "Surprising Findings About Plutonium Dangers to Man Reported at the International Atomic Energy Agency Meeting in San Francisco, Calif., 17-21 November 1975." Summary by John C. Cobb, Public Interest Research Group, Washington, D.C. 20036.

• "Radioactive Man: A Plutonium Casualty," Robert Wallace, *Rolling Stone*, 19 May 1977. (Michael Olveda, a worker contaminated at Rocky Flats, undergoes experimental decontamination operation called "lung lavage.")

• "Blast Endangers 8 at Nuclear Complex," *New York Times*, 31 August 1976, p. 1,12. Also: "Riddled by Isotopes," *Newsweek*, 21 March 1977, p. 49. (On the Hanford, Washington glove box explosion.)

• "Principles and Practices for Keeping Occupational Radiation Exposures at Medical Institutions as Low as Reasonably Achievable," Draft, December 1977. Office of Standards Development. U.S. Nuclear Regulatory Commission. NUREG-0267. (Reflects growing concern, finally, for medical-related overexposure.)

Safety

• "The Nuclear Power Controversy: Safety," Ralph E. Lapp, *The New Republic*, 23 January 1971.

• "Nuclear Safety I: The Roots of Dissent," Robert Gillette, *Science*, 1 September 1972.

• "Nuclear Safety (II): The Years of Delay," Robert Gillette, *Science*, 8 September 1972.

• "Nuclear Safety (III): Critics Charge Conflicts of Interest," Robert Gillette, *Science*, 15 September 1972.

• "Nuclear Safety (IV): Barriers to Communication," Robert Gillette, *Science*, 22 September 1972.

• "Sources of Radiation and Their Control," Merril Eisenbud. Prepared for the Department of Interior and Atomic Industrial Forum Seminar on the Engineering Aspects of Siting and Operating Power Plants, Washington, D.C., 13-14 February 1973.

• "Approaches to Population Protection in the Case of Nuclear Accidents," U.S. EPA, Office of Radiation Programs, November 1974. EPA, Washington, D.C. 20460

• "Testimony of Dale G. Bridenbaugh, Richard B. Hubbard, Gregory C. Minor Before the Joint Committee on Atomic Energy," 18 February 1976, Washington, D.C. Reprinted by the Union of Concerned Scientists, Cambridge, Mass.

• "What's Wrong With the Atomic Industry?" John Abbotts, Margaret McCarthy, PIRG, Washington, D.C. (55 Case Studies).

• "The Hot River Valley," McKinley C. Olson, *The Nation*, 3 August 1974. (Nuclear concentration and dangers on the Susquehanna River.)

• "The 10 Most Dangerous Nuclear Plants," *The Elements*, February 1977.

• "The Burning Question of Browns Ferry," James Nathan Miller, *Reader's Digest*, April 1976. (Reprints available.)

• "Nine Reactors Sited on or Near Calif. Quake

Zones," Phyllis Gapen, *Critical Mass Journal*, vol. II, no. 2, May 1976.

Evacuation

• "Run for the Hills," Robert H. Holden, *Sunday Plain Dealer*, Cleveland, OH. 13 November 1977.
• "Evacuation Plans: The Achilles' Heel of the Nuclear Industry," Ron Lanoue, Public Citizen, 1975. 133 C St. S.E., Washington, D.C. 20003. (Important study on evacuation law, how to obtain and understand plan of plant near you.)
• "Nuclear Evacuation Planning: Blueprint for Chaos," Mass PIRG Report, 6 July 1977. (Mass. Public Interest Research Group, 233 N. Pleasant St., Amherst, MA 01002.

See also sources mentioned in footnotes.

Resources—BOOKS

• David Rittenhouse Inglis, *Nuclear Energy: its physics and its social challenge.* Addison-Wesley Publishing Co. Inc., 1973. 395 pp. $4.95
• Matthew Gaines, *Atomic Energy: Knowledge Through Color.* Bantam Books, 1973 (from Grosset and Dunlap 1970). 159 pp. $1.45.
• McKinley A. Olsen, *Unacceptable Risk: The Nuclear Power Controversy*, Bantam Books, 1976. 285 pp. $2.25.
• John J. Berger, *Nuclear Power—The Unviable Option*, Ramparts Press 1976. $4.50. 384 pp.
• Walter G. Patterson, *Nuclear Power*, Penguin Books Ltd., Great Britain 1976. 304 pp. $3.50.

PAMPHLETS

• Denis Hayes, "Nuclear Power: The Fifth Horseman," Worldwatch Paper 6, May 1976. 68 pp. $2.00. Worldwatch Institute, 1776 Masachusetts Ave. N.W. Wash., D.C. 20036.
• Drs. George Wald and Elise Jerard, "The Case for the People, by the People, In a Time of Technological Tyranny," Independent Phi Beta Kappa Environmental Study Group, 115 Central Park West, New York, N.Y. 10023. 68 pp. $2.50.
• William H. Millerd, "Nuclear Energy: The Morality of Our National Policy," Center for Science in the Public Interest CSPI Energy Series V. 67 pp. $4.00.
• "Nuclear Power," A Science for the People Pamphlet. (Box 4161, Berkeley, Ca. 94704). $0.25.

Fuel Cycle

• Union of Concerned Scientists, *The Nuclear Fuel Cycle*, Friends of the Earth for the UCS 1974. 205 pp. $4.95.
• Daniel F. Ford and Henry W. Kendall, *An Assessment of the Emergency Core Cooling Systems Rulemaking Hearings*, Friends of the Earth for UCS 1974, $4.95.

FROM OUR FILES

• McKinley C. Olson, "Nuclear Fuel: The Hot Shuffle," *The Progressive*, April, 1975.
• Richard Burt, "Carter Calls for an International Nuclear Fuel Bank," *New York Times*, Oct. 20, 1977.
• Statement by John Abbotts, Public Interest Research Group, Before the Nuclear Regulatory Commission Hearing on Nuclear Energy Center, June 1975. (Avail. from PIRG, P.O. Box 19312, Washington, D.C. 20036. Overview of issues relating to nuclear "parks." 12 pp. $.50

Barnwell

• "Nuclear Energy and the Reprocessing Experiment," Environmentalists, Inc., 1339 Sinkler Road, Columbia, S.C. 29206. October 1976. $.40 for the 12 page booklet.
• "Some Important Unexamined Questions Concerning the Barnwell Nuclear Fuel Reprocessing Plant," Dr. John Gofman, Testimony Before the Nuclear Study Committee of the Legislature of the State of South Carolina, Columbia, S.C., January 7, 1972. 25 pp. $1.00 from Committee for Nuclear Responsibility, MPOB Box 11207, San Francisco, CA 94101.

West Valley

• U.S General Accounting Office, "Issues Related to the Closing of the Nuclear Fuel Services, Inc. Reprocessing Plant at West Valley, N.Y.," Report to the Conservation, Energy, and Natural Resources Subcommittee, House Committee on Government Operations. By the Comptroller General of the United States. March 8, 1977. (EMD-77-27) 34 pp.

Transportation

• *Managing Nuclear Wastes*, Atomic Industrial Forum, "Shipping of Wastes," pp. 8-10. April 1974.
• Vermont Public Interest Research Group, "Radwaste on the Roadway; the Transportation of Radioactive Materials in Vermont." 15 pp. February, 1977. $1.00.
• Dr. Karl Z. Morgan, "Appropriateness of Regulations for Air Shipments of Radioactive Materials." Georgia Institute of Technology, Atlanta 1974.
• "Everything You Always Wanted to Know About Shipping High-Level Nuclear Wastes" (ERHQ-0002), 50 pp. $.65. Available from the Superintendent of Documents, U.S. Government Printing Office, Washington, D.C. (For further information contact: Transportation Branch: Division of Environmental Control Technology, ERDA, Wash. D.C. 20545.)
• U.S. Nuclear Regulatory Commission, Office of Standards Development, "Final Environmental Statement on the Transportation of Radioactive Material by Air and Other Modes." NUREG-0170, vol. 1. October 1977 Draft.

• Todd R. La Porte, "Nuclear Waste: Increasing Scale and Sociopolitical Impacts," *Science,* vol. 201, 7 July 1978, pp. 22-28.

• William L. Rankin and Stanley M. Nealey, "Attitudes of the public about nuclear waste." *Nuclear News,* June 1978, pp. 112-117.

• Gary Dau and Robert Williams, "Secure Storage of Radioactive Waste," EPRI Journal, July-August 1976, pp. 6-14.

• Bernard L. Cohen, "The Disposal of Radioactive Wastes from Fission Reactors," *Scientific American,* June 1977, vol. 236, no. 6, pp. 21-31.

• J.C. Malero, "High-Level Nuclear Waste Management in the United States: A Time for Decisions, "Nuclear Safety," vol. 19, no. 3, May-June 1978, pp. 356-364.

• Major Unresolved Issues Preventing a Timely Resolution to Radioactive Waste Disposal," General Accounting Of ice, EMD-78-94, 13 July 1978, 10 pp.

• "Storage of U.S. Spent Power Reactor Fuel," Draft Environmental Impact Statement. Department of Energy, August 1978. (DOE/EIS-0015-D)

Protecting It...Safeguards

• U.S. Nuclear Regulatory Commission, "Requirements for the Physical Protection of Nuclear Power Reactors," Chapter 1-NRC, Part 50-Licensing of Production and Utilization Facilities; Part 73—Physical Protection of Plants and Materials. February 18, 1977.

• NRC, (10CFR Part 11, 50 and 70), Special Nuclear Material: Authority for Access to or control. *Federal Register,* vol. 42, no. 52, March 17, 1977.

• ERDA, "Fact Sheet: ERDA Response Capability to Nuclear Threats, *Weekly Announcements* (Information from ERDA, Washington, D.C. 20545) vol. 3, no. 23. Week ending June 10, 1977.

• Richard T. Kennedy, U. S. Nuclear Regulatory Commissioner, "Safeguards—A Regulatory View," (Speech before the Institute of Nuclear Materials Management, Wash., D.C. June 29. 1977. *News Releases.* U.S NRC, Office of Public Affairs (Washington D.C. 20555.) Week ending July 27, 1977, vol. 1, no. 26.

Half a million people have signed the Task Force's Clean Energy Petition. Pass it around! Names are sent to your Congresspeople.

A CLEAN ENERGY PETITION

I petition my representatives in government to sponsor and actively support legislation to: (1) foster wide use of solar — including wind — power NOW, and (2) phase out operation of nuclear power plants as quickly as possible.

Sign here	Name printed here		Date
Your permanent street address	City	State	Zip

No Nukes Dictionary

A

abnormal occurrence—Now "reportable occurrence." Nuclear Regulatory Commission (NRC) euphemism for accident.[From 1 January 1972 to 30 May 1973 alone, there were approximately 850 abnormal occurrences reported to the AEC from 30 reactors. The definition of "abnormal occurrence" was changed by the Energy Reorganization Act of 1974. Now "reportable occurrences" are limited to accidents with very specific dangerous characteristics. Under the new definition, only six incidents were reported in the first six months of 1975!]

absorption—The process whereby radiation is stopped and reduced in intensity as it passes through matter. Lead is a good absorber of x-rays.

accelerator—A device for increasing the energy and velocity of charged electrons and protons through an application of electrical and/or magnetic forces. Commonly called an atom-smasher.

actinides—Heavy elements that result from the disintegration of radioactive materials. Actinides produced by fission of reactor fuel are: actinium (Ac), thorium (Th), protactinium (Pa), uranium (U), neptunium (Np), plutonium (Pu), americium (Am), curium (Cm) plus several others. These must be stored as radioactive wastes.

activation—Neutron absorption making a substance radioactive.

active—Common term meaning radioactive.

activity—Refers to the radiating power of a radioactive substance; may be given in terms of atoms disintegrating per second.

acute exposure—Short-term irradiation that may endanger health.

Advisory Committee on Reactor Safeguards (ACRS)—A Nuclear Regulatory Commission committee responsible for the assessment of safety of reactors to be licensed in the U.S.

afterheat—Heat produced from the continual decay of radioactive materials.

alpha—Name given to one type of radiation: others are beta, gamma and neutrons. See **alpha particle**.

alpha-emitter—A particle which is characterized by its alpha radiation. Plutonium-239 is an alpha-emitter.

alpha particle—A positively charged particle of two neutrons and two protons, the nucleus of a helium atom, which is emitted by certain radioactive material. A dangerous carcinogen when inhaled or ingested.

American Nuclear Society (ANS)—A private professional-membership organization established to promote nuclear technology.

americium—A white radioactive element, an actinide, that is used as a radiation source in research and an ionizing agent in smoke detectors.

Argonne National Laboratory—A laboratory in Argonne, near Chicago, Illinois, one of several created by the AEC after the wartime Manhattan Project. Affiliated with Argonne Universities Association, Associated Colleges of the Chicago Area, Associated Colleges of the Midwest and Central States Universities. Does various government research projects aside from nuclear-related work.

atom—A unit of matter, the smallest unit of an element, consisting of a dense central, positively charged nucleus surrounded by a system of electrons. The structure is usually indivisible by chemical reactions and is electrically neutral.

atomic bomb—An explosive weapon of great destructive power whose energy comes from the fissioning of the heavy radioactive elements uranium and plutonium.

Atomic Bomb Casualty Commission—The U.S. organization in post-war Japan studying victims of Hiroshima and Nagasaki.

atomic cloud—A cloud of gases, smoke, and dust plus radioactive elements that results from an atomic bomb explosion.

atomic energy—The energy released from an atomic nucleus in fission or fusion.

Atomic Energy Act—Passed by Congress in 1946, it set up the Atomic Energy Commission (AEC) and the Joint Committee on Atomic Energy (JCAE), both since abolished (1974, 1976).

Atomic Energy Commission (AEC)—The federal agency created by the Atomic Energy

Act of 1946, responsible for both promotion and regulation of nuclear power. The duties and staff were divided in 1974 by the Energy Reorganization Act into the NRC and ERDA (now part of the DOE).

Atomic Industrial Forum (AIF)—A private membership organization that promotes nuclear power. With its $1 million-plus annual budget from utilities and nuclear manufacturing firms, the AIF lobbies Congress, distributes pro-nuclear press stories, arranges press tours, etc.

atomic nucleus—The core of an atom, composed of protons and neutrons.

atomic number—The number of protons in an atomic nucleus.

Atomic Safety and Licensing Board (ASLB)—An NRC board, usually of three people, which conducts hearings on license applications for every U.S. nuclear plant.

atomic wastes—Radioactive solids and gases and contaminated liquids produced by the splitting of uranium fuel. Generally classed as high, intermediate, or low-level waste dependent on curie per liter count. [There are now more than 7 million cubic feet of radioactive waste from nuclear electric and weapons-making facilities.]

B

back-fitting—Also **retrofitting**. Altering an existing nuclear power plant to meet new requirements.

background radiation—Radiation coming from outer space (cosmic) and commonplace materials found on earth. Also called **natural radiation.**

beta—A type of radiation.

beta-emitter—A radioactive element that is characterized by its beta radiation.

beta particle—A high energy electron emitted by decay in a radioactive nucleus. Can cause skin burns and, when ingested, cancer.

binding energy—The energy that holds together the component neutrons and protons of a nucleus.

biological dose—A dose of radiation absorbed in biological matter measured in **rems.**

blowdown—What happens where there is a break in a reactor's primary cooling system, and it loses all the water it once contained; when the coolant is purged under controlled conditions.

body burden—The amount of radioactive material present in the body of a human or other animal at any given time.

boiling water reactor (BWR)—The type of nuclear reactor in which water is converted to steam in the reactor vessel. Made by General Electric.

bone seeker—A radioactive isotope that tends to accumulate in the bones, such as strontium-90.

boron—chemical element; powerful absorber of neutrons sometimes used in reactor control rods.

breeder—A reactor which creates more fissile nuclei than it uses. Types of breeders include: the liquid metal fast breeder reactor (LMFBR), molten salt breeder reactor, and thorium breeder reactor.

breeding—The process of creating new fissile material. In a breeder reactor radioactive plutonium is created by the neutron bombardment of U-238.

British Thermal Unit (Btu)—The amount of energy needed to raise the temperature of one pound of water by one degree Fahrenheit. [150 million Btu's heats the average home for a year. 100 million Btu's runs the average car for a year. One 42-gallon barrel of oil equals 5.8 million Btu's. One cubic foot of natural gas equals 1,031 Btu's. U.S. consumption in 1973 equaled 75 quadrillion (7.5×10^{16}) Btu's, or the equivalent of 35 million barrels of oil.]

C

Calvert Cliffs Case—A landmark 1971 Federal Appeals Court Case that forced the AEC to comply with the National Environmental Policy Act of 1969 which requires that all ecological effects of a nuke be con-considered in an environmental impact statement.

Canadian Deuterium Uranium Reactor (CANDU)—Canadian heavy-water reactor type that uses natural uranium as a fuel source; produces twice as much plutonium as a light-water reactor.

carcinogen—A cancer-causing substance.

cave—Also **hot cell**. A room with heavily shielded walls where highly radioactive materials are handled by remote control.

cesium-137—A biologically hazardous beta-emitting fission product. It has a half-life of 30 years and concentrates in muscle tissue.

chain reaction—A nuclear reaction that is self-sustaining.

China Syndrome or **China Effect**—Name given by scientists and engineers to a possible consequence of a reactor fuel **meltdown**. The fuel would become a molten mass of intensely radioactive material that could burn through the reactor vessel and containment building, continuing into the earth to...China?

cladding—The alloy fuel rod sheath intended to prevent leaks of the radioactive fuel into the cooling water within the reactor vessel. Made of a zirconium alloy. See **zircaloy**.

closed cycle cooling—A nuclear plant cooling system where water is "recycled" from steam generators to cooling towers back to the generators. The temperature of the heated cooling water is brought down in cooling towers. This system is an improvement over the biologically dangerous, once-through cooling of early reactors.

closed cycle reactor system—A design system in which the primary heat of the fission reaction is transferred outside the reactor core for useful work, such as driving a turbine.

comment period—The period of time allowed by the NRC for public comment before putting a new regulation into effect.

common-mode failure—When the failure of one component in a nuclear plant leads to the failure of other identical "redundant" or "back-up" devices, causing a more serious accident.

compaction—A type of spent-fuel storage where the amount of space between fuel rod assemblies in on-site storage pools is reduced to allow for more capacity. A measure being taken by utilities for storage of spent fuel pending some solution to the lack of reprocessing facilities.

construction permit—A permit recommended by the ASLB and granted by the NRC to a utility for construction of a nuclear power plant.

containment vessel—The large concrete and steel shell around a reactor whose purpose is to contain any radioactivity that might escape from the reactor itself.

control rod—A rod of a material that absorbs neutrons, used to control the power of a nuclear reactor. Control rods are usually raised from the core to start a chain reaction and lowered, or "fully inserted," into the core to halt fissioning.

coolant—A liquid (water, molten sodium) or gas (carbon dioxide, helium, air) circulated through a reactor core to remove heat generated in the core.

cooling pond—A deep tank of water at nuclear plant sites into which irradiated fuel or faulty fuel elements are placed until ready to ship for reprocessing or disposal.

cooling tower—A massive structure, often a parabolic tower, used to cool water in a nuclear plant's closed cycle cooling system.

core—The "heart" of a reactor containing the fuel and moderator in which the fission reaction occurs and heat is produced.

cosmic ray—A stream of ionizing radiation of extraterrestrial origin, chiefly of protons, alpha particles, and other atomic nuclei but including some high energy photons and electrons. A "natural" source of radiation.

critical mass—The smallest mass or amount of a fissionable material that will sustain a nuclear chain reaction.

criticality—The state of a nuclear reactor when it achieves a self-sustaining chain reaction.

crud—Particulate impurities deposited inside nuclear plant circulating water systems.

curie—A unit of radioactivity giving off 37 billion (3.7×10^{10}) disintegrations per second, the radioactivity of one gram of radium. Named after Marie and Pierre Curie, the discoverers of radium.

cyclotron—A device for accelerating nuclear particles to high energy.

D

daughter product—A decay product of a radioactive nucleus.

decay—Gradual disintegration of radioactive material over time. See **half-life.**

decay heat—Heat generated by the fission process which cannot be shut off.

decontamination—Removal of unwanted radioactivity from surfaces, equipment, or people.

degraded fuel—Faulty fuel rods that have leaked into the reactor coolant.

densification—The compaction of fuel inside the cladding leading to hot spots within the fuel rods.

Department of Energy (DOE)—Energy agency opened in October 1977, includes Federal Energy Administration (FEA) and Energy Research and Development Administration (ERDA).

derating—The restriction of the power output of a nuclear power plant to less than the design capacity, a measure usually taken to improve its margin of safety.

design basis accident (DBA)—A computerized hypothetical accident that nukes are designed to withstand. DBA's do not include accidents caused by human error or "acts of God."

deuterium (H-2)—Also **heavy hydrogen**. From *duo*, or "two," deuterium is a heavy version of ordinary hydrogen (H_1). It's nucleus contains the one proton of hydrogen and an additional neutron. See **fusion**.

direct-cycle reactor system—A nuclear power system in which the coolant or other heat transfer fluid travels from the core directly to the turbines, as in a boiling water reactor.

discharge pipes—Pipes through which cooling water is returned to the environment after cooling the reactor water in a once-through cooling system.

dismantling—The complete removal of a defunct nuke, an expensive process (current estimates run up to $100 million), requiring the complete removal of all reactor parts, which remain highly radioactive.

diversion—The theft of nuclear material, especially enriched or weapons-grade uranium or plutonium.

dose—The amount of energy absorbed in a unit of mass or an organ or individual from irradiation.

dosimeter—A device that measures daily radiation exposure to workers in nuclear power plants and other atomic facilities.

doubling dose—The radiation dose which will cause a doubling of the occurrence of a particular disease in a given population.

drywell—The concrete containment around the reactor pressure vessel of a boiling water reactor.

E

effluent—Liquid discharge from a nuke.

electron—A negatively charged atomic particle, lighter than a proton or neutron.

embrittlement—Increased brittleness of fuel rods caused by certain conditions inside the reactor.

emergency core cooling system (ECCS)—A safety system designed to immediately flood the reactor core with water following a loss-of-coolant-accident (LOCA).

energy release—ERDA terminology for explosion.

Energy Research and Development Administration (ERDA)—One of the two agencies created when the AEC was divided in 1974. ERDA controlled the energy research budget and the development and handling of nuclear weapons. As of October 1977, part of the Department of Energy (DOE).

enriched—Uranium in which the proportion of fissile U-235 has been artificially increased above the 0.7% level found in natural uranium.

enrichment—The process of making enriched uranium, commonly by the gaseous diffusion process.

Enrico Fermi Breeder Reactor—First commercial breeder reactor near Detroit which suffered a partial meltdown in 1966 and is now decommissioned.

entombment—The encasing of a worn-out reactor in concrete. Process requires long-term monitoring to detect and prevent radiation leaks.

Environmental Impact Statement (EIS)—An evaluation prepared by the NRC of the environmental impact of construction and operation of a plant, its costs, benefits and alternatives. Required by the National Environmental Policy Act (NEPA) prior to plant licensing hearings.

Environmental Protection Agency (EPA)—A federal agency created in 1970 as part of implementation of NEPA. The EPA is responsible for setting and enforcing pollution and radiation standards in the U.S.

erg—A measure of energy equal to that required for an electron to ionize about 20 billion atoms of air.

excited—Having an increase of energy.

exposure—Being exposed to radiation.

extraterrestrial disposal—The scheme of rocketing radioactive garbage into high orbit or to the sun.

F

fallout—Airborne radioactive fission debris which descends to the surface of the earth. Created by above-ground nuclear explosions.

fast neutron—A high-energy neutron resulting from atomic fission.

Fast Flux Test Facility—A sodium-cooled experimental breeder reactor under construction at Hanford, Washington. Designed to test fuel rods for the breeder program.

Federal Radiation Council (FRC)—This now-defunct council set radiation standards and guidelines until that function passed to the EPA in 1970.

fertile—Materials such as U-238 and thorium that can become fissionable through neutron absorption.

film badge—A film packet used for estimating radiation exposure to workers in atomic and related facilities.

Final Safety Analysis Report (FSAR)—The final report submitted by the applicant prior to receiving an operating license for a nuke. The report details all safety systems and control measures to be used in the project.

fissile—Any material capable of undergoing fission.

fission—The splitting of a nucleus into two lighter fragments, accompanied by the release of energy and generally one or more neutrons. Fission can occur either spontaneously or as the consequence of absorption of a neutron.

fission products—The nuclei formed by the fission of a heavy elements plus the nuclides that are formed as a result of their radioactive decay. Some fission products decay rapidly, others exist as nuclear waste for centuries.

fissionable material—Reactor fuel or fissile elements: uranium-235, uranium-233, and plutonium-239.

flux—The moving cloud of neutron particles in the reactor core.

fuel—Material containing fissile nuclei fabricated into a form that can be used in a reactor core.

fuel assembly—A unit made up of many long fuel rods which can be inserted into or removed from the reactor core by remote control. Also known as a fuel bundle.

fuel cycle—The path of nuclear power that begins at the mine and ends with waste storage.

fuel fabrication—The part of the fuel cycle where uranium oxide is made into fuel pellets and loaded into fuel rods.

fuel pellets—Uranium dioxide or other nuclear fuel, in powdered form, that has been ground and pressed into pellets that fit into the fuel assembly rods.

fuel reprocessing—The process of taking highly radioactive spent fuel and chemically breaking it down to extract the remaining fissionable material.

fuel rating—The power output per unit mass of fuel, measured as kilowatts per kilogram of uranium.

fuel rod—A single tube of cladding filled with uranium fuel pellets.

fusion—The fusing of two or more atoms into a single atom with the simultaneous release of energy—the opposite of fission. The most common fusion reaction is the combining of two heavy hydrogen atoms to form a helium atom.

G

gamma ray—High energy, short wavelength, electromagnetic radiation emitted by a nucleus with great penetrating power.

gas centrifuge—A method of isotope separation in which heavier U-238 nuclei are separated from lighter U-235 nuclei by the centrifuging of uranium hexaflouride gas.

gas-cooled reactor—A nuke in which gas, such as helium, is used as the coolant.

gaseous diffusion—The common but cumbersome method of isotope concentration in which uranium-235 and -238 molecules in a hexaflouride gas are diffused through thousands of porous metallic membranes, slowly allowing accumulation of lighter U-235. A process used in the part of the nuclear fuel cycle known as **enrichment**.

gaseous wastes—Radioactive gases such as iodine-131, xenon-131, and krypton-85, created by nuclear fission.

genetic defects—Radiation effects that can be transferred from parent to child, or any damage in the genetic material, chromosomes, of sex cells.

GESMO—A 1976 NRC report on the possible use of recycled plutonium as a reactor fuel ("Final Generic Environmental

Statement on the Use of Recycle Plutonium in Mixed Oxide Fuel in Light Water Cooled Reactors" NUREG-0002).

gigawatt—One billion watts; used when describing electrical generating capacity.

glove box—A sealed box in which workers handle radioactive materials without exposure (hopefully!) because hands are protected by heavy gloves.

graphite—Black compacted crystalline carbon used as a moderator and reflector in some types of reactor cores.

ground zero—The point directly below the center of a nuclear explosion.

H

half-life—The time it takes for half of any radioactive substance to disintegrate. Half-lives range from a second to millions of years.

heat exchanger—A device that transfers heat from one fluid, liquid or gas, to another.

heat sink—Anything that absorbs waste heat from reactors. Usually a body of water and surrounding atmosphere.

heavy hydrogen—See **deuterium (H$_2$)**.

heavy-water—Deuterium oxide. Water containing more than the natural proportion of heavy hydrogen atoms to ordinary hydrogen atoms.

heavy-water reactor—A reactor that uses heavy water as a moderator because it slows down neutrons effectively and has a low neutron absorption rate.

helium—A light chemically inert gas used as a coolant in high temperature gas-cooled reactors.

hex—Short for uranium hexaflouride. The gas used in the uranium enrichment process.

high-level—Pertaining to the intensity of radioactive waste with medium to long half-lives.

hot—Highly radioactive.

hot cell—See **cave**.

hot spot—A part of the fuel rod surface that has become overheated.

hydrogen—The lightest element; number 1 in the Periodic Table of Elements.

hydrogen bomb—A nuclear bomb that produces its destructive power largely from atomic fusion.

hypothetical core disassembly accident—AEC-NRC terminology for an accident in a breeder reactor that could melt the plutonium fuel in such a way that a nuclear explosion might occur, blowing up the reactor ("core disassembly").

I

implosion—When a material has its volume suddenly reduced by compression. It becomes supercritical, producing a sudden release of energy. The principle employed in detonation of plutonium H-bomb.

indirect-cycle reactor system—A cooling system in which the primary heat is transformed to a secondary system which then drives a turbine, as in a pressurized water reactor (PWR).

intake pipes—The pipes through which cooling water is taken into the reactor.

intermediate heat exchanger—A system in a sodium-cooled reactor in which the hot radioactive primary sodium coolant transfers heat to a secondary nonradioactive sodium coolant.

International Atomic Energy Agency (IAEA)—An international body set up in Vienna in 1957 to control safety and proliferation of nuclear materials world-wide.

International Commission on Radiological Protection (ICRP)—Created in 1925 to make recommendations for radiation tolerances for all nations.

intervenor—The legal designation of a participant other than NRC officials or utility representatives in an NRC licensing hearing.

intervention—The process by which citizens or groups are allowed to participate in nuclear power plant licensing hearings.

inventory difference (ID)—See **material unaccounted for**.

iodine-131—An extremely hazardous fission product which tends to accumulate in the thyroid gland. It has a radioactive half-life of 8 days.

ion—An atom, molecule, or elementary particle that has lost or gained one or more electrons, therefore taking on an electrical charge. A positive ion has lost one or more electrons; a negative ion has gained one or more electrons.

ionization—The process of adding or removing electrons so as to form ions. Ionization can be caused by high temperatures, electrical discharges, or nuclear radiation.

ionizing radiation—alpha, beta, or gamma radiation, which, when passing through matter can ionize it. Ionizing radiation can cause cell damage as it passes through tissue.

irradiated—Having been exposed to or treated with radiation.

irradiated fuel—Nuclear fuel that has been bombarded with neutrons.

isotope—A radioactive variant of a common element with a different atomic weight but similar characteristics. Isotopes are created by the fission process. Also known as **(radio)nuclides**.

isotope separation—The process of separating isotopes from one another by gaseous diffusion, electromagnetic separation or use of a centrifuge. One step in the uranium enrichment process.

J

Joint Committee on Atomic Energy (JCAE)—A joint Congressional Committee of nine senators and nine representatives that was given wide powers over nuclear development by the Atomic Energy Act of 1946. The JCAE was dissolved in 1976, its authority spread out among various House and Senate committees.

K

kilowatt—One thousand watts. See **watt**.

kilowatt hour—A unit of energy equal to one kilowatt for one hour. Monthly utility bills charge by the kilowatt hour.

kinetic energy—Energy created by motion.

krypton—The chemically inert radioactive gas, krypton-85, is created by nuclear fission and is a nuclear plant waste. It has a half-life of ten years. Accumulates in fatty tissue.

L

laser—A device that converts incident electromagnetic radiation of mixed frequencies to one or more discrete frequencies of highly amplified radiation.

laser enrichment—The separation of uranium-238 and -235 to create material enriched in U-235, by exciting one isotope with a laser. A potential short-cut to uranium enrichment which could increase proliferation of fissile material.

latent period—The amount of time that elapses between exposure and the first sign of radiation damage.

leakage—The escape of neutrons from a reactor core.

leukemia—Cancer of the blood distinguished by overproduction of white blood cells. Children are especially vulnerable to the disease, which has a latent period of around five years.

light-water reactor (LWR)—A reactor type that uses ordinary water instead of heavy water, includes the boiling water reactor (BWR) and the pressurized water reactor (PWR).

liquid metal fast breeder reactor (LMFBR)—A reactor fueled by plutonium or a uranium-plutonium oxide mixture that uses liquid sodium as its coolant. It creates additional plutonium through irradiation of a U-238 shield.

long-lived radiation—Radiation that remains active anywhere from 100 to 240,000 years.

loss-of-coolant-accident (LOCA)—One of the most feared nuclear plant accidents, in which cooling water would be lost from the primary cooling system as a result of a pipe rupture or blockage. A LOCA could lead to the overheating of the core and a meltdown.

loss-of-fluid test (LOFT)—A test in which the effectiveness of the emergency core cooling system (ECCS) is studied. The ECCS is the cooling water back-up system. In six tests of a model cooling circuit, the system failed to function adequately.

low-level—Refers to radioactivity of low intensity.

M

Manhattan Project—Code name for the World War II government project that built the first atomic bombs.

mass—The amount of matter or substance in a body.

material unaccounted for (MUF)—Missing fissile material. A 1977 GAO audit found that more than 8,000 pounds of plutonium and highly enriched uranium were missing from U.S. nuclear facilities. In 1978 the NRC changed the term to "inventory difference" or ID "to get away from the idea that any inventory difference is a mistake." (*Power Line*, Jan. 1978) (They don't want anyone to know they've "muffed" it!)

maximum credible accident—The most serious nuclear plant accident a computer has been able to anticipate based on equipment failure, human error, or other problems.

maximum credible threat—NRC definition of security risk to facilities handling **special nuclear materials**. Until early 1977 the maximum threat was seen as a theft conspiracy involving one employee and three outsiders armed with legally obtainable rifles and pistols. In February 1977 the possible threat was redefined to include a conspiracy of two or more "insiders" and an outside terrorist group armed with automatic rifles, plastic explosives and recoilless cannons. Nuclear facility safeguards are now supposedly geared to this new definition.

maximum hypothetical accident—The worst conceivable accident. The reactor core would blow up (in NRC terminology: "experience a rapid disassembly") and cause widespread contamination ("breach the containment vessel releasing radioactivity to the environment"). The NRC refuses to recognize this accident possibility, saying it just can't happen. Referred to as a Class 9 accident.

maximum permissible dose (MPD)—Also known as "maximum allowable dose." Standard set by the NRC for worker and personnel exposure to ionizing radiation. Atomic industry workers can receive as much as 5 rems per year. The EPA has set the maximum dose levels for the public at 0.025 rem per year, down from a previous 0.5 rem.

maximum permissible level (MPL)—The amount of radiation allowed by the NRC in a nuclear plant or facility. A false guide of "safe radiation exposure" as there is no proof that any level of radiation is safe.

megaton—The energy of a nuclear explosion that is equal to one million tons of TNT.

megawatt—One million watts of electrical generating capacity.

meltdown—Melting of the fuel in the reactor core due to a rapid, uncontrolled increase in core temperature which would cause the fuel cladding and rod assemblies to liquify or melt.

millirem (mr)—One-thousandth of a **rem**.

mixed oxide—Reactor fuel in which the fissile nuclei of plutonium-239 are mixed with natural or reprocessed uranium in a proportion that would equal, in radioactive

potential, enriched uranium. Developed for breeders, proposed for LWRs.

moderator—A material, such as ordinary water, heavy water or graphite whose nuclei are of predominantly low atomic weight. Used in a reactor to slow down high velocity neutrons, increasing the chance of their absorption by fissionable material.

molecule—A group of atoms held together by chemical forces.

monitor—A radiation detector used to determine radiation levels.

moratorium—A legislative halt to nuclear construction for a given amount of time.

mothballing—Cheapest way to close up defunct, irradiated reactors: weld the reactor vessel shut and guard the plant—forever.

Murphy's Law—If something can go wrong, it will! [A law not adequately respected by the NRC in its risk/accident calculations.]

mutation—A sudden variation, the offspring differing from its parents in one or more heritable characteristics due to changes within the chromosomes or genes.

N

National Council of Radiation Protection and Measurements—A group of physicians and scientists established by Congress in 1929 to set national radiation standards. Their duties were taken over by the EPA in 1970.

National Environmental Policy Act (NEPA)—A 1969 federal law requiring the AEC (now NRC) to prepare an environmental impact statement on each proposed nuclear plant before it can be given a construction permit.

national laboratories—Science labs sponsored by the federal government. Argonne, Ill., Oak Ridge, Tenn., and Brookhaven, N.Y., are sites of several of the largest laboratories that do research for the NRC. There are 14 main laboratories.

National Reactor Testing Station (NRTS)—A facility in Idaho, part of the National Engineering Laboratory: used to conduct tests and safety research experiments under contract from ERDA (now DOE).

natural radiation—See **background radiation**.

natural uranium—Uranium as it occurs in nature. Only about 0.7% of natural uranium is the radioactive U-235; the rest is the stable but fertile U-238.

neutrino—A sub-atomic particle which has only spin, without mass, or electric charge, named by Enrico Fermi. (*Neutrino* is Italian for "little neutron.")

neutron—An uncharged particle in the nucleus of every atom heavier than hydrogen. A free neutron is unstable. With a half-life of 13 minutes it will decay into a proton, electron, and neutrino. Ejected at high energy during fission, neutrons sustain a nuclear reactor's chain reaction.

non-destruct testing—Pre-testing of equipment with x-rays or ultrasonics to detect flaws or structural damage.

Nonproliferation Treaty (NPT)—Signed in March 1970 by 42 nations, the treaty is supposed to control the spread of nuclear weaponry and technology.

nuclear—Involving a nucleus specifically, or relating to nuclear energy generally.

nuclear energy—Energy produced by a nuclear reaction: fission or fusion.

nuclear explosive—A bomb using fission or fusion of atomic nuclei for its power source.

nuclear physics—Scientific study of forces, reactions and internal structures of atomic nuclei.

nuclear power plant—Any generating plant that uses nuclear energy as its power source. Nuclear-fueled electrical power generating stations.

nuclear reaction—A reaction involving a change in the atomic nucleus: fission or fusion.

nuclear reactor—A device in which a fission chain reaction is initiated and maintained, and (hopefully) controlled.

Nuclear Regulatory Commission (NRC)—Created in 1974 when the functions of the Atomic Energy Commission were divided. The NRC has responsibility for licensing and regulating nuclear power plants in the U.S. and Puerto Rico.

nucleus—The positively charged center of an atom, composed of protons and neutrons and containing most of the atom's mass.

nuclide—Any atom that exists for a measureable length of time. A nuclide can be identified by its atomic weight, atomic number, and energy state.

nuke—A nuclear power plant or nuclear weapon (noun). "To nuke" (verb) has been used to mean "attack with nuclear weapons."

O

Oak Ridge National Laboratory—An atomic research center in Tennessee operated for the NRC by Union Carbide Corporation.

off-gas—Radioactive gases that are routinely released into the atmosphere from a reactor, usually through a filtered stack.

once-through cooling—The nuclear plant cooling system that takes cooling water from a river, lake, or ocean and returns the water, heated from its use as coolant, directly to the body of water. Creates thermal pollution.

operating license—Granted by the NRC; required of a utility before a nuclear plant can start up.

over pressure—Transient pressure above normal atmospheric pressure caused by a shock wave following a nuclear explosion.

P

photon—A "packet" of energy, with no mass, which travels at the speed of light. Photons range from very low energies (such as heat and light) to moderate energy (ultraviolet and x-rays) to high energy (gamma rays).

pile—An experimental device used to produce a controlled, sustained chain reaction. The first atomic pile was built in 1942 in Chicago by Enrico Fermi and a team of Manhattan Project scientists.

pipeline inventory—The total amount of fissile material involved with one reactor, including material in the core and cooling pond, as well as at a reprocessing plant, in fuel fabrication, and as waste in transit.

Plowshare—The former AEC's plan to use nuclear explosives for "peaceful purposes."

plutonium (Pu-239)—A heavy, highly toxic, radioactive metallic element, man-made, used as breeder reactor fuel and for atomic weapons. Highly carcinogenic.

power burst facility—A reactor built by NRTS to subject nuclear fuel to conditions of abnormal stress in order to study the behavior of fuel rods under these conditions.

power cooling mismatch accident (PCMA)—An accident in which uneven cooling of the core causes fuel rods to overheat and melt.

power density—Refers to the heat output per unit of volume in the reactor core, measured in kilowatts per litre.

power excursion accident (PEA)—An unpredictable accident caused by faulty fuel rods or fuel densification which could lead to uncontrollable power surges to the point of criticality.

power reactor—A reactor designated for commercial electrical purposes as distinguished from reactors used for research or production of weapons material.

Preliminary Safety Analysis Report (PSAR)—A report submitted to the NRC by a utility applying for a construction permit detailing safety systems and quality control in a proposed nuke.

pressure supression pool—A circular tunnel at the bottom of the drywell in a BWR, filled half-way with water to condense steam from the reactor cooling system if needed.

pressure vessel—A large, strong-walled container of welded steel that houses the core of most types of reactors, plus other internal reactor parts as the moderator, reflector, thermal shield, and control rods.

pressurized water reactor (PWR)—A reactor in which the heat from the core is transferred to a heat exchanger under constant pressure to achieve a high water temperature without boiling the water. A secondary circuit produces the steam for the generators.

Price-Anderson Act—An act of Congress first passed in 1957 and since renewed that limits the liability of reactor owners to $100 million in the event of an accident and that provides for limited federal indemnity.

production reactor—A reactor designed to produce large amounts of plutonium-239 or uranium-235 for weapons use by neutron irradiation.

proprietary information—Information that the NRC deems confidential trade secrets.

proton—An elementary particle with a single positive electrical charge that is a part of all nuclei.

R

rad—A measure of exposure to radiation, the absorbed dose. See **rem.**

rad waste—Industry lingo for "radioactive waste."

radiation—the emission of neutrons, alpha particles, beta or gamma rays from a radioactive source. See **ionizing radiation.**

radiation accidents—Accidents involving the spread of radioactive material or exposure of people to radiation.

radiation monitoring—The determination of the amount of radioactivity present in a region. May be performed continuously (such as in a reactor exhaust gas "smoke" stack) or periodically (such as monthly air or water samples collected by the State).

radiation protection guide—The EPA guide which determines what radiation doses should not be exceeded. Formerly referred to as **maximum permissible level (MPL).**

radiation sickness—Illness induced by exposure to ionizing radiation, ranging in severity from nausea to death.

radiation source—Any man-made source of radiation used in such things as radiography, chemotherapy, or even wristwatches.

radiation standards—Exposure standards for permissible radiation concentrations, rules for safe handling and transportation, and regulations for control of radiation exposure.

radiation therapy—Any form of disease treatment that uses radiation; commonly known as radiotherapy.

radiation threshold—The level of exposure below which it is assumed that no damage takes place. Doctors and scientists have challenged the assumption that such a threshold exists.

radioactive contamination—The presence of unwanted, harmful radioactive matter; exposure to ionizing radiation.

radioactive waste—The radioactive products resulting from fission, such as Pu-239, Sr-90, I-131, Ce-137, and many, many more. See **atomic wastes.**

radioactivity—The spontaneous decay of an unstable atomic nucleus accompanied by the emission of ionizing radiation.

radiogenic—Certain types of diseases caused by radiation.

radiology—The science that uses all forms of ionizing radiation in the diagnosis and treatment of disease.

radionuclide—See **isotope.**

radium—An intensely radioactive metallic alpha-emitter, found in nature. Element 88, with a half-life of 1600 years.

radon—An alpha-emitting radioactive gas given off by radium, also present during the mining of uranium.

radon daughters—The four radioactive short-lived decay products of radon: polonium-218, lead-214, bismuth-214, and polonium-214, all metals.

rapid disassembly—Term used by the nuclear industry to mean explosion.

reactor—An assembly of nuclear fuel which can sustain a controlled chain reaction based on nuclear fission.

recycling—The re-use of fissionable material in irradiated fuel, recovered through reprocessing.

refueling—Replacing the fuel assemblies after they are exhausted or "spent."

rem—The abbreviation of "Roentgen Equivalent Man." The unit measuring an absorbed dose of ionizing radiation in biological matter.

reportable occurrence—See **abnormal occurrence.**

reprocessing—The mechanical and chemical treatment of spent reactor fuel to remove all useable fissile material.

research reactor—A reactor that supplies neutrons or other ionizing radiation primarily for experimental purposes. A popular model is the TRIGA MARK reactor, designed by General Dynamics (now the Gulf Oil subsidiary General Atomic).

residence time—The time during which radioactive material remains in the atmosphere after a nuclear explosion.

roentgen—The unit of exposure to gamma or x-rays named after William Conrad Roentgen, who discovered x-rays in Munich, Germany in 1895.

retrofitting—See **back-fitting**. Also: rebuilding a structure to carry solar energy equipment.

rule making hearing—A hearing by a regulatory body to gather information and revise regulations for general application.

runaway—An accidental, uncontrollable nuclear chain reaction.

S

safeguards—Protection measures to prevent the theft of nuclear material.

Safety Analysis Report (SAR)—Report concerning the safety of a proposed nuke. Required from applicant by NRC prior to issuance of a license.

scram—the sudden shutdown of the fission reaction in a reactor usually by remote control insertion of the control rods.

separative work unit—A measure of energy; term used in the uranium enrichment process.

shielding—A wall of absorbing material surrounding a source of radiation to reduce radiation intensity and protect personnel, equipment, or experiments from radiation injury.

shock wave—A tremendous pressure pulse in the air, water, or earth following a nuclear explosion.

shut-down—Stopping a nuclear chain reaction, usually by insertion of control rods.

somatic effects—Health effects from direct exposure to radiation, as distinguished from genetic effects. Also known as "physiological effects."

Special Nuclear Materials (SNM)—Fissile material capable of being used for nuclear weapons; uranium-235 and plutonium-239.

specific activity—The amount of radioactivity per unit mass.

spent fuel—Reactor fuel that is depleted to the extent that it can no longer sustain a chain reaction.

steam generator—A boiler in which hot coolant from a reactor raises steam to turn a turbine generator.

strontium—A biologically hazardous beta-emitter, particularly strontium-90, which causes bone cancer. Strontium-90 is produced in approximately 5.7% of all U-235 fissions.

sub-critical—A reactor core insufficiently supplied with neutrons and unable to sustain a nuclear reaction.

T

tailings—A fine grey sand that is left over from the milling of uranium ore. Contains radium which emits radon.

thermal efficiency—The measure of the efficiency with which a generating plant converts thermal energy to electrical energy.

thermal pollution—Heat discharged into the environment. Approximately two-thirds of the heat created in a nuclear plant is presently thus discharged.

thermonuclear bomb—Also "device." A hydrogen bomb.

thermonuclear reaction—A reaction in which two or more light nuclei are fused together through high temperatures, causing a sudden release of energy.

thorium—A fertile radioactive element that can be transmuted to fissionable U-233 by neutron irradiation. Element 90. Suggested replacement for plutonium in breeder reactor fuel.

torus—A doughnut-shaped suppression chamber located at the base of a reactor. The chamber, half-filled with around 500,000 gallons of water, is designed to shield and surround the reactor in case of accident.

transient—A change of conditions, in temperature or pressure, within a nuclear reactor.

tritium—A radioactive nuclear by-product, also known as H_3, from *tri* or "three," a heavy version of ordinary hydrogen (H_1). Produced in heavy-water moderated reactors.

U

uranium (u)—Element 92; a heavy metallic, slightly radioactive element. As found in nature it is a mixture of the isotopes uranium-235 (0.7%) and uranium-238 (99.3%). U-235 and the artificially produced U-233 are fissile. Uranium-238 is fertile.

uranium hexaflouride (UF₆)—The gas made from yellowcake which is used in the gaseous diffusion process of uranium enrichment.

V

vitrification—The fusing of high-level waste into glass-like solids, prior to long-term storage.

W

WASH-740—The AEC "Brookhaven" study: "Theoretical Possibilities and Consequences of Major Accidents in Nuclear Power Plants." It was estimated that, although the chances of a worst-case accident happening were small, the consequences could be 3,400 deaths, 43,000 injuries, and property damage of $7 billion. A 1964 up-date, which was suppressed, took into account current larger reactors and increased the toll to 27,000

deaths, $17 billion in damages, and contamination of an area the size of Pennsylvania.

WASH-1400—A 1974 AEC Reactor Safety Report: "An Assessment of Accident Risks in U.S. commercial Nuclear Power Plants." This study was headed by Prof. Norman. Rasmussen of the Massachusetts Institute of Technology and is also known as the "Rasmussen Report." The study took three years and cost $4 million. Its high estimates of reactor safety have been widely challenged.

waste—Equipment and materials which are radioactive and of no further use. After 20 years of effort, no safe long-term waste disposal method has been found to work.

watt—The product of the voltage (volts) times the amperes (amps) in an electrical circuit. An ampere is the measure of the current, or flowing electrical charge, in a circuit. A voltage of 1 volt and a current of 1 amp applied to a circuit for one hour would use one watt-hour of electrical energy. A kilowatt-hour (kwh) is 1,000 watt-hours. (From: *Kilowatt Counter*, Alternative Sources of Energy, Inc., 1975. P. 4)

X

x-ray—A penetrating form of electromagnetic radiation emitted when a metal target is bombarded with high speed electrons. X-rays can cause cancer, and are an over-used and abused medical practice.

Y

yellowcake—A solid material of mixed uranium oxides produced from uranium ore by the extraction process in uranium milling. Raw material of nuclear fuel.

yield—The total energy released in a nuclear explosion. Usually expressed in equivalent tons of TNT.

Z

zircaloy—An alloy of zirconium used as nuclear fuel cladding because it tends not to absorb neutrons.

—Prepared by Peter Natti and Anna Gyorgy

BEYOND OIL

"The United States might run out of oil someday. But there will always be an EXXON."

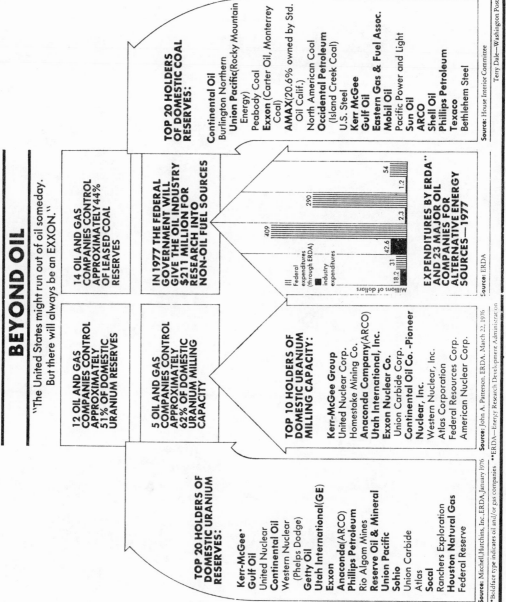

12 OIL AND GAS COMPANIES CONTROL APPROXIMATELY 51% OF DOMESTIC URANIUM RESERVES

14 OIL AND GAS COMPANIES CONTROL APPROXIMATELY 44% OF LEASED COAL RESERVES

5 OIL AND GAS COMPANIES CONTROL APPROXIMATELY 62% OF DOMESTIC URANIUM MILLING CAPACITY

IN 1977 THE FEDERAL GOVERNMENT WILL GIVE THE OIL INDUSTRY $211 MILLION FOR RESEARCH INTO NON-OIL FUEL SOURCES

TOP 20 HOLDERS OF DOMESTIC URANIUM RESERVES:

Kerr-McGee *
Gulf Oil
United Nuclear
Continental Oil
Western Nuclear (Phelps Dodge)
Getty Oil
Utah International (GE)
Exxon
Anaconda (ARCO)
Phillips Petroleum
Rio Algom Mines
Reserve Oil & Mineral
Union Pacific
Sohio
Union Carbide
Atlas
Socal
Ranchers Exploration
Houston Natural Gas
Federal Reserve

Source: Mitchell, Hutchins, Inc., ERDA, January 1976
* Boldface type indicates oil and/or gas companies

TOP 10 HOLDERS OF DOMESTIC URANIUM MILLING CAPACITY:

Kerr-McGee Group
United Nuclear Corp.
Homestake Mining Co.
Anaconda Company (ARCO)
Utah International, Inc.
Exxon Nuclear Co.
Union Carbide Corp.
Continental Oil Co. -Pioneer Nuclear, Inc.
Western Nuclear, Inc.
Atlas Corporation
Federal Resources Corp.
American Nuclear Corp.

Source: John A. Patterson, ERDA, March 22, 1976

EXPENDITURES BY ERDA AND 23 MAJOR OIL COMPANIES FOR ALTERNATIVE ENERGY SOURCES—1977**

Millions of dollars

Federal expenditures (through ERDA)
industry expenditures

Source: ERDA

** ERDA—Energy Research Development Administration

TOP 20 HOLDERS OF DOMESTIC COAL RESERVES:

Continental Oil
Burlington Northern
Union Pacific (Rocky Mountain Energy)
Peabody Coal
Exxon (Carter Oil, Monterrey Coal)
AMAX (20.6% owned by Std. Oil Calif.)
North American Coal
Occidental Petroleum (Island Creek Coal)
U.S. Steel
Kerr McGee
Gulf Oil
Eastern Gas & Fuel Assoc.
Mobil Oil
Pacific Power and Light
Sun Oil
ARCO
Shell Oil
Phillips Petroleum
Texaco
Bethlehem Steel

Source: House Interior Committee

Terry Dale—Washington Post

By Terry Dale—The Washington Post

Illustration reprinted with permission of the *Washington Post*

SECTION 2: THE ECONOMICS
OF NUCLEAR POWER

Chapter 1:

The Nuclear Power
Power Structure

There are many different kinds of power. Not all are obtainable at the flip of a switch. The corporations that produce and deliver energy to the people of the United States are part of a system of concentrated *economic power*. Control over the nation's energy economy increasingly lies in relatively few hands. These hands wield more and more political clout.

Decisions concerning nuclear power in the U.S. have had an enormous impact on the lives of everyone in this country as well as in many other countries. Yet these decisions have been made by a small part of the population—a minority of corporate executives with whom most people have little in common. The economic control they exercise takes many different forms.

When a few corporations control a large share of the market for the goods they produce, it is easy for them to cooperate in raising prices. If members of one company's board of directors sit on another company's board, spirited competition between the two companies is unlikely. If a bank provides

extensive capital (in the form of loans) to a company, that company may be discouraged from competing unnecessarily with the bank's other clients. When corporate executives donate money to finance political campaigns and when government officials retire and accept lucrative jobs in industry, the government cannot act as a watchdog over private interests.

This chapter is a guide to the nuclear power power structure and it documents all of these forms of control. Step by step, from uranium reserves to power plant construction, we name the corporations which profit from nuclear power. We also provide some clues to the question of how and why they brought us to where we are today.

It Started With Oil...

Much has been written about monopolistic tendencies within the oil industry, especially since the oil crisis of 1973. Robert Engler's *The Politics of Oil* (MacMillan, 1961) and John M. Blair's *The Control of Oil* (Vintage, 1976) provide a graphic account of the causes and consequences of monopolistic control. Now it is becoming increasingly clear that the monopolistic structure of the oil industry is being reflected and paralleled within the nuclear power industry. Moreover, as shown in Box 1, the giant oil companies are prime movers behind this trend towards monopoly. With considerable aid from the government, the companies are moving their nuclear building blocks into position to solidify their future role as all-energy companies. As one energy reporter recently wrote, "The United States may run out of oil someday, but there will always be an Exxon."[1]

A striking example of this new round of concentration is the case of Utah International, recently merged with General Electric. Utah is a major mining company. It has a petroleum and gas subsidiary (or branch firm) and important coal and iron ore holdings. It is also the seventh largest domestic uranium reserve holder and the third

largest miller of uranium ore. It is no accident that the General Electric Company is the top manufacturer of nuclear steam supply systems (nuclear reactor equipment), and the seventh most profitable corporation in the country. Summing up the sale, the *Washington Post* noted that now "one corporation has the skeleton for the ultimate in all-energy production—from the mines to the power plants."[2]

The Uranium Monopoly

How concentrated is the nuclear industry? To answer that question we should begin at step one: ownership of uranium reserves. Armed with vast amounts of available capital (profits) generated by the 1973 energy crisis, the oil companies "moved to acquire uranium acreage in the 1970s, and now own more reserves than the mining companies."[3] But oil company involvement began at an earlier date.

Petroleum interests established an

"Let me read you the recipe: Start out with a little monopoly and then..."

early foothold in the atomic industry. During the search and drilling for oil and gas after World War II, deposits of uranium were found. For a time, in the late 60s, there was an oversupply of uranium. When the Defense Department found it had all the uranium it

13 of the top 20 corporate sources of uranium are oil and gas companies.

needed and the power-plant industry had not taken up the slack, many producers were unable to sell their uranium and went out of business. Major oil firms were among those producers who could afford "to wait."[4]

Today, thirteen of the top twenty corporate holders of domestic uranium are oil and gas companies. Twelve of these firms control 51% of the market. Major producers include the leader Kerr-McGee, with 21% of the nations's known reserves, and Gulf Oil, with about 12%. Three other oil companies trail after: Continental Oil, Getty Oil, and Exxon. Together these five companies' share of "unknown" reserves—58%—has been estimated to be even greater than "known" reserves.[5]

Oil company control and ownership of nuclear fuel and its processing has had a decided effect on uranium prices.

Box 2—Top 20 Corporate Holders of Domestic Uranium Reserves (January 1976)

company	reserves (thous. of tons)	% of total US res.
Kerr-McGee	145.0	21.0
Gulf Oil	80.0	11.6
United Nuclear	40.0	5.8
Continental Oil	25.0	3.6
Western Nuclear (Phelps Dodge)	22.5	3.3
Getty Oil	20.0	2.9
Utah International (General Electric)	17.5	2.5
Exxon	17.5	2.5
Anaconda	15.0	2.2
Phillips Petroleum	12.5	1.8
Rio Algom Mines	9.0	1.3
Reserve Oil & Mineral	5.5	.8
Union Pacific	5.0	.7
Sohio	5.0	.7
Union Carbide	4.0	.6
Pioneer Corp.	4.0	.6
Atlas	3.0	.4
Socal	3.0	.4
Ranchers Exploration	3.0	.4
Houston Natural Gas	1.5	.2
Federal Reserve	1.5	.2
American Nuclear	1.0	.1
Total U.S. reserves	690.0	100.0
4 - Firm total	290.0	42.0
Oil companies	324.0	47.0

(source: U.S. Senate, Committee on Energy and Natural Resources "Petroleum Industry Involvement in Alternative Sources of Energy." U.S. Gov't Printing Office: 1977.)

In October 1977, Senator Edward Kennedy and the Senate Anti-trust and Monopoly Subcommittee held hearings on a horizontal divestiture bill. The bill would have required the oil companies to "divest" (or sell) holdings in alternative sources of energy, like uranium and coal. During the hearings, a Wyoming prospector whose firm stakes claims for major oil companies criticized his clients for registering phony claims and slowing down production in order to raise prices. "They tie up vast amounts of uranium acreage," John W. MacGuire testified, "and have been unwilling to allocate the financial resources necessary for full and timely development... they grab and withhold from competition as much acreage as possible by whatever means possible." MacGuire went on to point out that with their "power of manipulation," **the oil companies had no incentive to develop sources of energy cheaper than oil until they reach a comparable market price.**[6]

In 1973, the oil industry managed to shift some of the blame for increased oil prices on the "Arab embargo" and the exhaustion of domestic oil supplies. However, the oil giants were unable to find a scapegoat for uranium price increases. In 1972, the price of uranium was about $6/pound. Five years later, the price had increased to $42/pound, and it is expected to rise even further. Within the nuclear industry, the existence of a uranium cartel was general knowledge.[7] After Westinghouse filed a multi-million dollar lawsuit against cartel members, the international oligopoly became a matter of public record. Gulf Oil was the most prominent U.S. member of the club, whose members secretly set worldwide uranium prices and policed their respective national markets.[8]

Gulf initially attempted to shift the

Box 3—Principal Members of the of the Uranium Producers Club*

U.S.A.—
Gulf Oil Corp. (Pittsburgh, Pa.)
Englehard Minerals and Chemicals Corp. (Delaware)
Rio Algom Corp. (Delaware)

Canada—
Rio Algom Mines, Ltd.
Gulf Minerals Canada, Ltd.
Uranerz Canada, Ltd.
Noranda Mines, Ltd.
Denison Mines, Ltd.

Britain—
Rio Tinto Zinc Corp.
RTZ Services, Ltd.

France—
Uranex

West Germany—
Urangesellschaft G.m.b.H.

South Africa—
Nuclear Fuels Corp.

blame to its wholly-owned Canadian subsidiary by claiming that the Canadian government forced its participation in club activities. But the company's defense was very shaky, especially after explicit cartel memoranda (leaked by Australian environmentalists) found their way into Westinghouse's legal brief. In Congressional hearings during June 1977, Rep. Albert Gore sarcastically characterized the company as "some kind of corporate Patty Hearst, forced to act against [its] will...only afterwards did [it] develop an enthusiasm for the task."[9] **Gulf's chairman of the board was forced to admit that the company had participated in price-fixing, and that such actions brought about an increase in world and domestic uranium prices.**

*as named in lawsuits by Westinghouse Electric Corporation and Tennessee Valley Authority

Modern alchemists go to work.

It would be a mistake to see Gulf Oil as the sole villain in this melodrama. Westinghouse has had its own share of price-fixing scandals.[10] The point is that the concentration of economic power makes it possible and profitable for corporations to raise prices. Indeed, such behavior is considered quite natural. "Like most corporations," the *New York Times* editorialized, "Gulf seeks maximum profits. In 1972 one of its divisions had the opportunity to obtain them by joining a uranium cartel formed by the governments of Canada, Australia, and South Africa, and supported by France."[11]

Milling and Processing

Oil firms also dominate the next stage of the nuclear fuel cycle—the milling and processing of uranium ore. Eight firms control about 88% of the nation's uranium milling capacity. Five of them are oil companies, and they control 41% of the total national capacity. Led again by Kerr-McGee, this group includes United Nuclear Corporation, Anaconda (subsidiary of Atlantic-Richfield/ARCO), Utah International (subsidiary of General Electric), and Exxon Nuclear. Only two firms con-vert uranium ore into a fuel concentrate. Again the market is dominated by Kerr-McGee, accompanied by Allis-Chalmers. In 1977, however, Westinghouse announced its intention to join Farmland Industries in constructing a conversion plant at Farmland's Florida site.[12]

About ten private factories make enriched fuel into pellets and then fuel elements. All of these plants are linked with either one of the big four reactor manufacturers (discussed later) or major uranium-owning oil companies.

Enrichment

Following milling, uranium "yellow-cake" must be enriched before it is used for nuclear fuel. (See pp. 45-70, Fuel Cycle) The first enrichment facilities were built by the government for military purposes and their services were made available to civilian customers. Three government-owned but privately-operated plants service the domestic nuclear industry. The federal government briefly considered the possibility of turning the facilities—and the industry—over to private firms. The nuclear industry's terms proved too demanding, however, and political opposition forced the government to continue its enrichment role. Moreover, in early 1978, President Carter announced plans for a massive expansion of government enrichment facilities.[13]

There are interesting lessons to be learned, however, from the negotiations which took place over the question of private ownership of these enrichment facilities. Bechtel Corporation* suggested a joint venture with Goodyear, Williams, Union Carbide,

*See "The Bechtel File" by Mark Dowie, *Mother Jones*, Sept/Oct 1978, p. 28

Box 4—Top U.S. Uranium Millers (1976)

company	milling capacity (tons of ore per day)	Percent of total U.S. capacity
Kerr-McGee group	7,000	24.6
United Nuclear Corp.- Homestake Mining Co.	3,500	12.3
Anaconda Co.	3,000	10.5
Utah International, Inc.	3,000	10.5
Exxon Nuclear Co.	3,000	10.5
Union Carbide Corp.	2,500	8.8
Continental Oil Co.- Pioneer Nuclear, Inc.	1,700	6.2
Western Nuclear, Inc.	1,200	4.2
Atlas Corp.	1,000	3.5
Federal Resources Corp.- American Nuclear Corp.	950	3.3
Rio Algom Mines, Ltd.	700	2.5
Cotter Corp.	450	1.6
Dawn Mining Co.	400	1.4
Atlantic Richfield Co.	—	(*)
Uranium Recovery Corp.	—	(*)
Wyoming Minerals (Westinghouse)	—	(*)
U.S.total	23,450	
Top 4	16,500	58.0
Top 8	24,950	87.7
Oil firms	11,750	41.3

(source: U.S. Senate, Committee on Energy and Natural Resources, "Petroleum involvement in Alternative Sources of Energy". U.S. Gov't. Printing Office: 1977)

* less than 1%.

and Westinghouse to be called Uranium Enrichment Associates. The plans were to build a new enrichment plant in Dothan, Alabama with federal loan guarantees. The Ford Administration introduced legislation to the Congress that would provide $8 billion in such subsidies.[14]

Shortly before the bill was introduced the revolving door between government and industry began spin-ning. Former Treasury Secretary George Schultz became Bechtel's president. Former Secretary of Health, Education and Welfare, Casper Weinberger, joined Bechtel's executive ranks. And Richard Hollingsworth, a former general manager of the Atomic Energy Commission left government service for Bechtel.[15] Interpersonal contacts of this nature may facilitate the flow of subsidies from

"...and don't forget to take out the garbage."   *Bonnie Acker*

government to business. They may also reassure private corporations that continued federal control over some portions of the fuel cycle is in their long term interests.

Reprocessing and Waste Storage

The federal government recently assumed complete responsibility for the two most problematic parts of the fuel cycle—fuel reprocessing and radioactive waste storage. Thus, private industry has been absolved of responsibility for the adverse effects of low-level radiation leaks associated with waste storage. (See Health Dangers, pp. 71-98). It has also been relieved of a financial burden which taxpayers have assumed, most of us unknowingly.[16] (See the next chapter on Dollars and Cents of Nuclear Power.)

Nuclear Hardware

If the federal government succeeds in smoothing out the difficulties of later stages of the fuel cycle, the enormous potential for profits in reactor equipment (nuclear hardware) will be greatly enhanced by lack of competition in the industry. Four companies are in control, but as Box 5 indicates, three other firms have tried or are attempting to also become "vendors."

Today's top two, the General Electric Company and Westinghouse Electric Corporation, control an astonishing 68% of the market. Their only real competitors, Babcock and Wilcox, and Combustion Engineering, have to be content with the remaining 32%. General Atomic (a joint venture between Gulf Oil and Royal Dutch/Shell) dropped out of the market in 1976. (One utility executive was quoted by the *Wall Street Journal* as saying that

"General Atomic's reactor makes the Edsel look like a penny ante poker game."[17]) Allis-Chalmers (with their European counterparts Siemens/Kraftwerk Union) and Newport News Industrial (Tenneco) are apparently developing their first domestic contracts.

The vendors' market has always been the most visible of sectors within the nuclear industry. General Electric and Westinghouse make news daily. Reactors require an "exotic" technology, as well as huge amounts of capital. Companies that want a stake in the nuclear future must make a considerable investment just to enter the market, or even simply to stay in the game. Even Wall Street has been shaken by the magnitude of the sums involved.

From February to September 1977, three of the nation's industrial powers staged a spectacular stock market battle for control of the Babcock and Wilcox Company, number three manu-facturer of steam generating equipment, sold to both nuclear and coal utilities. Babcock and Wilcox also has lucrative contracts with the nuclear Navy and a highly profitable tubular products line offered to utilities. The company originally tried to fight off a takeover by United Technologies, a maker of gas turbines for electrical energy and aircraft engines. After much maneuvering, however, Babcock and Wilcox succumbed to merger with the J. Ray McDermott Company, which is involved with offshore construction and engineering, especially for oil and gas production. It was an exceedingly hostile takeover, often characterised by the press as "open, corporate warfare."[18] "The biggest guns in legal takeovers were hired by both sides," raved the New York Times.[19]

At one point, Babcock's chairman wrote a letter to United Technologies directors. "...It seems to us that the timing of your offer is related to the

Box 5A—Principal Nuclear Reactor "Vendors"

The Big Four	ranking '77	net profits
Westinghouse Electric	47	271.3
General Electric Company	6	1,088.2
Combustion Engineering, Inc.	313	67.2
Babcock & Wilcox Co.	76	191.5

(source 5A: *Electrical World*, "1978 Nuclear Plant Survey," 15 January 1978)

(source 5B: John Vinocer, "Outlook Bleak for Makers of Atomic Reactors," *New York Times*, 21 September 1977, p. 50)

Box 5B—Orders for New Nukes
Where Orders Went (1953-1977)

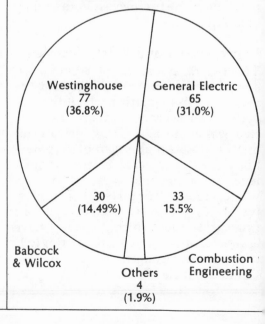

Westinghouse 77 (36.8%)

General Electric 65 (31.0%)

30 (14.49%)

33 15.5%

Babcock & Wilcox

Others 4 (1.9%)

Combustion Engineering

imminent development of a national energy policy," wrote George P. Zipf. "We cannot avoid suspicion of anticipatory piracy...This period of energy resources peril makes this a particularly inappropriate time to consider linking two of the largest American enterprises competing in the energy equipment field."[20]

The U.S. Justice Department felt remarkably similar. Filing the "biggest anti-trust challenge in many years," the government moved to block United Technologies' $510 million takeover on the grounds that such a merger would substantially reduce competition and further concentrate the boiler manufacturing industry.[21] After McDermott's offer succeeded, the New York Stock Exchange began its own investigation into the sale, citing the sharp decline in the price of McDermott's stock immediately before United capitulated. (Some believed the decline resulted from the selling of McDermott's stock by Technologies' backers.)*

As a result of what Chairman Zipf had called "corporate buccaneering," control over Babcock and Wilcox shifted to another "all-energy" company. Stock brokers and business analysts admired Babcock's future, tied to the energy crisis with a foot in both nuclear and coal fields.

---

*
In February of 1978, just as the McDermott and Babcock and Wilcox boards were setting the final merger agreement to paper, some indication of McDermott's corporate style surfaced in the press. Calling Gulf Oil's problems to mind, the McDermott company was charged in federal court on seven counts of racketeering, fraud, and unlawful campaign contributions, and later ordered to pay fines and forfeit profits totaling $1 million. Additional and perhaps more threatening charges of foreign payoffs and domestic price-fixing followed.

Profits in Hardware

Suppliers of nuclear hardware have not yet reaped large profits. Specific and up-to-date figures are almost impossible to find outside of industry boardrooms, but estimates by business journals suggest that nuclear business in 1976 accounted for a mere 3% of General Electric's total revenues and about 8% of Westinghouse's less-diversified operations.[22] Financial analysts also observe that since 1975 the vendors' profits wilted under the pressure of the economic recession and the growth of citizen opposition to nuclear power across the nation.

Bonnie Acker

However, large firms can afford to gamble, to forego immediate gratification (profits) in order to ensure a profitable future. For example, the first generation of nuclear power plants, called "turnkey" plants, were built under "fixed-price" contracts. By selling this early set of reactors at artificially low prices, the manufacturers hoped to lure utilities into the nuclear "bargain." As a result, General Electric lost about $200 million in the late 1960s. Using similar contracts, Westinghouse has cut itself off from profits in the steam turbine business until 1979.[23] Westinghouse's vulnerability to the uranium cartel, discussed earlier, grew out of its eagerness to guarantee low cost fuel to its customers. Other reactor vendors, such as Combustion Engineering, have promoted similarly risky "sweetening" schemes to garner a larger share of the market.[24]

Thus, the potential for future profits is still enormous. As of July 1977, a total of 101,000 Mw of nuclear generating capacity were either pending construction or had been publicly announced.[25] At an estimated cost of $3 billion per 2 unit 1,500-megawatt plant, this planned investment adds up to $102 billion: less than the enormous sums predicted only two years ago, but quite impressive nonetheless.

Survival Strategy

Meanwhile, the nuclear market is "temporarily" sagging and depressed. How are these giant firms able or willing to absorb their losses and remain in the game? In the first place, companies have reactor backlogs that can maintain the industry into the 1980s. Joseph Rengel, a Westinghouse executive, estimated that his company is good for "five or six years," GE for four, Babcock and Wilcox and Combustion Engineering for one each in unfilled orders.[26]

The companies may also sell overseas. Vendors have met with considerable success in selling their products to regimes in countries where citizen opposition is unlikely. Orders for the past two years have come to GE and Westinghouse from South Africa, Brazil, Iran, and South Korea (Combustion Engineering and Babcock & Wilcox have never won foreign contracts).[27] Recent reports on Westinghouse's activities in the Philippines suggest that successful international nuclear salesmanship may include considerable bribes paid to foreign officials, similar in scope to payoffs during the Lockheed incident in Japan. Evidence indicates that Westinghouse was able to greatly overprice its nuclear project sold to the Marcos government, secured in part by loans from the U.S. Export-Import Bank (and managed by executives from institutions like Citicorp International and Manufacturers Hanover Trust, Ltd.).[28]

Finally, vendors have tried to adjust to a down market by increasing their lobbying and public relations efforts. The much-imitated General Electric reshuffled its executives in 1977, adding another layer of top men to "focus on growing external problems,"[29] like the government's development of a national energy plan, and the political issues being raised by an aroused citizenry. Many nuclear firms have also created reactor consultant service teams, offering their technicians' and engineers' expertise to troubled utilities. Such teams may supervise an ongoing construction project, devise a "mitigation" plan to convince local communities to accept nuclear power plants, or act as an experienced buffer between the utilities and various federal and state agencies charged with overseeing aspects of domestic nuclear development.

Profits in Construction

The profits that are made from the sale of reactors and components are just the tip of the iceberg. The greater the role of electricity in the nation's energy picture, and particularly the greater the role of nuclear-generated electricity, the more Stone & Webster, Raytheon's United Engineers and Constructors, Halliburton's Brown and Root Division, Enserch's Ebasco Services, Fluor's Daniel International, Sargent and Lundy, and the unquestionably dominant Bechtel Corporation stand to prosper. They are, in the words of a New York brokerage researcher, "enormous cash machines—destined to become the core portfolio [read moneymakers] of the 1980s."[30]

By combining the number of contracts let for both engineering and construction, we find that seven firms control almost the entire market—99.9%.[31] The top three companies do 75% of the total business, and the Bechtel Corporation by itself holds 40% of all contracts to private firms. Even the government has been alarmed by levels of economic concentration in the industry. Ebasco Services, the number four constructor and number five engineering firm, used to belong to Halliburton, which also owns Brown and Root—number six in both areas. The Justice Department forced Halliburton to sell Ebasco, which it did in 1976.

Utilities and Banks

So far, we have focused on the concentration of direct economic control over market shares. There is additional evidence which helps us understand the wide scope of economic and politi-

---

Box 6—Principal Nuclear Engineering and Construction Firms and their Market Share

company (owner)*	ranking 1978**	net profits ($000,000)	market share ('77)
1. Bechtel Corporation, San Francisco, Ca. (Bechtel Group of Companies, S.F., Ca.)	(privately-held		
2. Stone & Webster Engineering, Boston, Ma. (Stone & Webster, Inc., N.Y., N.Y.)	information not available)		24.0%
3. United Engineers & Constructors, Philadelphia (Raytheon Co., Lexington, Ma.)	175	113.2	10.5%
4. Ebasco Services, Inc., New York, N.Y. (Enserch Corp., Dallas, Tx.)	283	74.1	8.9%
5. Daniel International, Greenville, S.C. (Fluor Corp., L.A., Ca.)	278	75.5	6.2%
6. Brown & Root, Inc., Houston, Tx. (Halliburton Co., Dallas, Tx.)	35	355.1	6.2%
7. Offshore Power Systems, Inc. (Westinghouse Electric Corp., Pittsburgh, Pa.)	47	271.3	3.8%
Top 3 ··············			74.8%
Top 7 ··············			99.9%

(source: Electrical World, "1978 Nuclear Plant Survey," 15 January 1978 and Energy Research Group, U/Mass, Amherst, Ma.)

*when different from company
**Forbes Profits 500

Box 7—The Ten Most Nuclear Utilities

utility	Forbes Profits 500/ranking '78	net profits ($000,000)
1. Tennessee Valley Authority	(govt. utility)*	.....
2. Commonwealth Edison (Chicago)	57	246.8
3. Duke Power (Charlotte)	75	192.3
4. Philadelphia Electric	92	173.4
5. Public Service Electric & Gas (Newark)	66	214.2
6. Carolina Power & Light (Raleigh)	153	121.0
7. Virginia Electric & Power (Richmond)	78	189.8
8. Washington Public Power Supply System	*	.....
9. Northeast Utilities (Berlin, Ct.)	259	81.7
10. Consolidated Edison (New York)	39	323.6

(source: Energy Research Group on the Political Economy of Nuclear Power; *Electrical World*, 15 January 1978, "Nuclear Plant Survey")
*information unavailable

cal power vested in corporate hands. Stock ownership, control of stock voting rights, interlocking directorates between boards of directors, and the power to allocate and manage the large sums of capital crucial to energy investments, are central to the nuclear power power structure.

Many journalists, academics, and even Congressional committees have sketched the primary and secondary interlocks between energy corporations, utilities, banks, major insurance companies, mutual funds, foundations, and industry pressure groups.* While a few of their more specific findings sometimes become out-of-date, the researchers' general conclusions re-

---

*Current and valuable examples include: James Ridgeway's *The Last Play*, John Berger's chapter "Atomic Power Plays," in *Nuclear Power: The Unviable Option*, Norman Medvin's *The Energy Cartel*, John M. Blair's already mentioned *The Control of Oil*, and Richard Morgan and Sandra Jerebel's *How to Challenge Your Local Electric Utility: A Citizen's Guide to the Power Industry* (Environmental Action Foundation, 1974).

main the same and are just as disturbing.

Utilities, engineering and construction companies, reactor manufacturing firms, and mining subsidiaries are all linked through the financial institutions which profit by making them huge loans. Over three-fourths of the electricity generated in the U.S. is produced by privately-owned utilities operated to make a profit for their investors. There are about two hundred of these investor-owned utilities (called IOUs), but many are actually owned by larger holding companies. American Electric Power Company, Middle South Utilities, and the New England Electric System are examples of this concentration of economic power into regional holding companies.

Bank loans cement the holding companies together. Major banks are usually among the top stockholders in utilities and, as might be expected, banks are heavily represented on the utilities' boards of directors.

One congressional study entitled "Disclosure of Corporate Ownership "

A report released by a Senate subcommittee in 1978 indicates that bank influence has grown even stronger.[33] The rapid growth of pension funds managed by banks has increased the top investment banks' voting power in utilities as well as other corporations.[34]

Institutional Investors

Banks are always joined by other "institutional" investors on "top ten" stockholders' lists. Utilities have been heavily invested in by stock brokerages (investment firms) and their non-

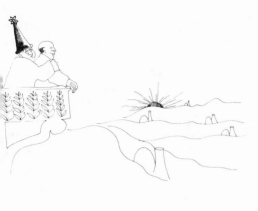

"All this could be yours..."

documents that at least half the stock of ninety-nine major investor-owned utilities were owned by their ten largest stockholders. In most cases banks were the principal stockholders.[32] Box 8 below charts the report's conclusion, listing the ten largest bank stockholders and the number of corporate pseudonyms (nominees used by the utilities to mask bank stockholders. Chase Manhattan,* MorganGuaranty Trust, and Manufactures Hanover Trust were among the ten largest stockholders for at least thirty different IOUs. Virginia Electric and Power, for example, (in the middle of our scale for most nuclear utilities), has Morgan Guaranty, Manufacturers Hanover, and Chase as its third, fourth, and sixth largest stockholders.

---

*   According to Peter Collier and David Horowitz, authors of *The Rockefellers: An American Dynasty* (NY: New American Library, 1976), prime banker David Rockefeller was involved in Chase's early decision to form one of the first atomic energy divisions in American banking, while his brothers Laurence and Nelson invested in and promoted nuclear energy development from their respective positions in business and in the Eisenhower administration.

Box 8—Major Banks' Stockholding in Public Utilities

bank	# of utils.*	# of nominees**
1. Chase Manhattan	42	4
2. Morgan Guaranty Trust	41	13
3. Manufacturers Hanover Trust	31	5
4. First National City Bank	29	8
5. State Street Bank &Trust (Boston)	21	8
6. Bankers Trust of New York	20	8
7. New England Merchants National	19	6
8. Bank of New York	15	7

(source: U.S. Senate, Committee on Government Operations "Disclosure of Corporate Ownership," March 1974)

---

*number of utilities of which the bank is among the top ten stockholders
**number of nominees, or dummy corporations, used by each bank

public clients, as well as by major insurance companies. These exercise significant influence over utility companies' decisions. In Connecticut's Northeast Utilities, for example, the largest stockholder is Cede & Co., a brokerage house "nominee" (or agent), while Hartford insurance companies (led by Travelers Insurance) own about one third of Northeast Utilities' outstanding stock, or slightly less than the share held by major New York banks.[35]

In addition, universities and colleges may be important stockholders. The most nuclear investor-owned utility, Commonwealth Edison of Chicago, is owned in part by the following colleges and universities: California, Illinois, Iowa, Kansas, Michigan, North Carolina, Oregon, Texas, Virginia, Wisconsin, California Institute of Technology, Harvard, Massachusetts Institute of Technology, Northwestern Pomona, Rochester Institute of Technology, Rutgers, and Williams.[36] Though the shares owned by individual schools may be small, they nonetheless create something of a community of interest between the ivory tower and the nuclear reactor.

Interlocking Directorates

Interlocking directorates are everywhere, and almost anyone can discover new ones with companies' latest annual reports and a copy of *Standard & Poor's Register of Directors and Executives* (available at most libraries). There are many primary and secondary interlocking directorates between utilities, banks, reactor vendors, insurance companies, universities, oil companies, and all other sectors of the "atomic-industrial complex." Recently one writer uncovered thirty-six interlocks between forty-nine of the largest banks and utilities.[37] The Senate

"Disclosure" report noted in turn that two of those banks, Chase Manhattan and Morgan Guaranty Trust, were interlocked with General Electric. Until very recently, Kerr-McGee was linked to GE, and Gulf to Westinghouse. Equitable Life Assurance Society of America was linked to United Nuclear and Combustion Engineering, which were both linked to Rockfeller Brothers, Inc., connected with Chase Manhattan Bank and the Exxon Corporation.

The special character of these corporate relationships can probably be better understood by "personalizing" the interlocks—and by naming names. J. Paul Austin, for example, is one of the select group of American business leaders "with the President's ear" on matters of national concern.[38] Austin is president of the Coca-Cola Company of Atlanta, and is also a director of **General Electric** (reactor manufacturer and uranium reserve holder) and of **Morgan Guaranty Trust** (major investment bank, principal stockholder and voter in many utilities and nuclear corporations). A colleague of Austin's on the Morgan board is George P. Schultz, former Nixon cabinet official and currently president of the **Bechtel Corporation** (largest nuclear engineering and construction company). Henry Howard Henley, a fellow director on the General Electric board, is also a director of **Manufacturers Hanover Trust** (another principal banking and investment firm with utility stocks, etc.). Conversation during the bank's directors' meeting is likely to turn occasionally to the subject of nuclear power because alongside Henley are George P. Zipf, president of **Babcock and Wilcox** (number 4 reactor vendor) and George B. Munroe, chairman of the board of **Phelps Dodge Corporation** (uranium reserve owner and miller). Furthermore, the president of Manufacturers Hanover, John F. McGillicuddy, sits on the board of directors at **Westinghouse Electric** (reactor vendor). We could continue tracing the nuclear family's roots, but perhaps the point has been made.

In Conclusion...

The major corporate and banking interests which dominate the nuclear power industry have played and will continue to play a central role in determining the country's choice of energy technology. The large corporations are not part of any "conspiracy" to promote nuclear power. If they could reap large profits by investing in non-nuclear technologies, they might jump at the chance. In fact, many corporations are already moving rapidly into the solar field.

However, nuclear power appears more profitable at the present time because it requires enormous investments—which means that the industry will never be a competitive one. Continued expansion of nuclear power could virtually guarantee high profit margins for many large U.S. corporations. But there are a number of economic and political obstacles to such expansion—obstacles that can only be overcome by federal subsidy and support.

Prepared by Don Michak

Footnotes

1. William Greider, "Oil Industry Stakes Out Role for the Future," *Washington Post*, 22 May 1977, p. 1.

2. *Ibid.*

3. James P. Meagher, "Uranium Seminar, There's Money to be Made, but Not Right Away," *Barron's*, 12 September 1977, p. 5.

4. F.M. Scheer, testimony before the Subcommittee on Energy, Joint Economic Committee, US Congress, *Horizontal Integration of the Energy Industry*, 19 November, 8 December, 1975.

5. Meagher, *op. cit.*

6. Carole Shifrin, "Energy Resources Withheld?" *Washington Post*, 4 October 1977, p. 5, and "House Uranium Hearing Told of Abuses That Tied Up US Exploration Acreage," *Wall Street Journal*, 14 October 1977, p. 16.

7. Richard Karp, "Uranium Short Sale," *Barron's*, 17 October 1977, p.5.

8. Tim Metz and Byron E. Calame, "Gulf Oil Now Faces New Heat Over Role in Uranium Schemes," *Wall Street Journal*, 25 April 1977, p. 1.

9. David Burnham, "Gulf Aides Admit Cartel Increased Price of Uranium," *New York Times*, 17 June 1977, p. 1-, and William Greider, "Gulf: Uranium Cartel Raised US Prices," *Washington Post*, 17 June 1977, p. 1.

10. "Uranium Cartel: Litigation Tangle Follows Price Rise," *Washington Post*, 8 May 1977.

11. "Gulf, Cartels, and Corporate Citizenship" (editorial), *New York Times*, 18 June 1977.

12. Press Release: Westinghouse Electric

13. "Portsmouth, Ohio, Is Chosen By US For Uranium Plant," *Wall Street Journal*, 12 July 1977, p. 2.

14. Johnathan Kwitney, "Enriching Venture: How One Company Got Ahead in Billion Dollar Race to Build Nuclear Fuel Plants," *Wall Street Journal*, 25 November 1976, p. 1.

15. "Room at the Top for Ex-Cabinet Men," *Business Week*, 1 September 1975, pp. 19-20.

16. Steven Rather, "US Sees No Permanent Disposal of Nuclear Waste Before 1988," *New York Times*, 16 March 1978, p. D3.

17. William M. Carley, "General Atomic's Gas Plant Ends in Fiscal Debacle," *Wall Street Journal*, 25 February 1976, p. 1.

18. Robert Metz, "Babcock & Wilcox: A Battle That Shook Wall Street Notions," *New York Times*, 19 September 1977.

19. Robert J. Cole, "Antitrust Division Comes to the Aid of Babcock & Wilcox," *New York Times* 10 July 1977, p. 13.

20. Jerry Flint, "Babcock is Fighting United Technologies on Plan for Tender," *New York Times*, 5 April 1977.

21. Robert J. Cole, "US Acts to Bar Takeover of Babcock by Technology," *New York Times*, 6 July 1977, p. 39.

22. "The Opposites: GE Grows While Westinghouse Shrinks," *Business Week*, 31 January 1977. January 1977.

23. "Westinghouse Greed Alleged by Gulf Oil,"

New York Times, 2 December 1977, p. D9.

24. "The Opposites," *op. cit.*, pp. 60-66; "Westinghouse Electric, can you be sure it is a lawsuit?" *Financial World*, 15 February 1977, p. 21; and John Papamarcos, "Westinghouse is best prepared to meet increased growth in nuclear power demand, says Kirby," *Power Engineering*, May 1977, pp.59-61.

25. *Monthly Energy Review*, July 1977.

26. Tim Metz, "Firms that Make Nuclear Power Plants Expect Slump in New Orders to Continue," *Wall Street Journal*, 30 November 1977, p. 27.

27. "Nuclear Man at Bay, Opposition to Nuclear Power Plants Draws on Strong Emotions In Democracies, So It Is Dictatorships Which are Building Them Fast," *Economist*, 19 March 1977, pp. 12-13; see also: Anthony J. Parisi, "U.S. Reactor Makers Recovery in Doubt After Four Year Market Dip," *New York Times*, 7 March 1978, p. 47.

28. Fox Butterfield, "Marcos, Facing Criticism, May End $1 Billion Westinghouse Contract," *New York Times*, 14 January 1978, p. 1/6; Barry Kramer, "Marcos Sets Review of Philippines Award for Nuclear Plant Westinghouse Builds," *Wall Street Journal*, 16 January 1978, p. 10; and "Westinghouse Defends Philippines Role; Marcos Orders Takeover of Disini Firms," *Wall Street Journal*, 17 January 1978, p. 20.

29. "GE's new billion-dollar small business," *Business Week*, 19 December 1977, p. 78.

30. Chris Welles, "The Market's Next Superstars," *Financial World*, 1 October 1977, pp. 13-17.

31. Figures from "1978 Nuclear Power Plant Survey," plants listed as complete or under construction in *Electrical World*, 15 January 1978.

32. "Disclosure of Corporate Ownership," US Senate, Committee on Government Relations (US Printing Office, 1974).

33. US Senate Subcommittee on Reports, Accounting and Management (US) Govt. Printing Office, 1977).

34. Barbara Ehrenreich, "Who Owns America?" *Seven Days*, 24 February 1978, p. 29.

35. "Disclosure of Corporate Ownership," *op. cit.*

36. "The 53 Colleges and Universities Whose Common Stock Holdings in Energy Corporations Are Tabulated Below," introduced into the *Congressional Record*, 28 December 1970, pp. 43722-43735, by Senator Lee Metcalf.

37. John J. Berger, *Nuclear Power: The Unviable Option* (New York: Dell, 1977).

38. Louis M. Kohlmeier, "The Big Businessmen Who Have Jimmy Carter's Ear," *New York Times*, 5 February 1978, p. F1/11.

Resources

"The point, however, is to change it."

Corporations are extremely powerful, but many people know very little about them. Unfortunately, the media have generally not helped us to understand the power vested in these modern capitalist institutions. Much of what has been reported describes the current corporate decision-makers as either conspiratorial or omnipotent. Neither is true.

At its best, power structure research can be like a good movie, documenting the process of decision-making by corporate executives as well as other groups within our country's power elite. It is research which can show exactly how certain decisions made by others affect our lives, and it can identify just who is making the decisions. Most important of all, power structure research can help activists select the critical issues and target the vulnerable decision-makers in their daily efforts to reshape modern capitalist society into a real democratic alternative.

The "Nuclear Power Power Structure" is only the beginning of a full-scale documentary of corporate decision-making within the nuclear industry. It is but a snapshot of relatively recent events. It is up to you to uncover the actual processes, the real men (as the nuclear industry is almost exclusively a male fraternity, of power, and the economic and social links between them. Here is a list of basic resources which will help you get started:

An introduction to Power Structure Research—

• C. Wright Mills, *The Power Elite*, (New York: Oxford Univ. Press, 1956).
• G. William Domhoff, "New Directions in Power Structure Research," a special issue of *The Insurgent Sociologist*, (Vol. 5, #3, Spring 1975; $3.00 from Insurgent Sociologist, Dept. of Sociology, University of Oregon, Eugene, Oregon 97403.

"How to" books, guides to actual research—

• *NACLA Research Methodology Guide*, by the North American Congress on Latin America, Inc., 1970. ($1.00, NACLA, P.O. Box 57, Cathedral Park Station, NY 10025 or P.O. Box 226 Berkeley, CA 94701).
• *Open the Books: How to Research a Corporation*, by Community Press Features, Urban Planning Aid, Inc., 1974. ($1.50, Urban Planning Aid, Inc., 120 Boylston St., Boston, MA).
• *Corporate Action Guide*, by the Corporate Action Project, 1974. ($2.50 Corporate Action Project, 1500 Farragut St. N.W., Washington, D.C. 20011).

Standard Reference Sources Available in Most Libraries—(check current year)

- *Standard and Poor's Registers of Corporations, Directors, and Executives.*
- *Dun & Bradstreet Million Dollar Directory* (and D&B's *Middle Market Directory*).
- *Moody's Industrial Manual* or *Standard Corporation Descriptions.*
- *Who's Who in America.*
- annual survey issues of *Fortune's* 500 industrials and *Forbes* Profits 500. (May)

Government reports—

- "Disclosure of Corporate Ownership," Senate Committee on Government Operations, Subcommittees on Intergovernmental Relations, and Budgeting, Management, and Expenditures, 1974.
- "Voting Rights in Major Corporations," Senate Committee on Government Affairs, Subcommittee of Accounting, Management, and Reports, 1978.
- "Interlocking directorates report," Senate Committee on Government Affairs, Subcommittee on Accounting, Management, and Reports, 1978.

Information on current corporate practices, proxy campaigns by investors—

- Investor Responsibility Research Center, 1522 L St., N.W., Washington, D.C. 20005.
- Interfaith Center on Corporate Responsibility, 475 Riverside Drive, N.Y., NY.
- The companies' annual reports (send to the company's main office, address listed in Moody's manuals).

Activists have used power structure research in many ways over the past decade. Anti-war organizers exposed "university complicity" with the war in Vietnam by uncovering the many links between major universities and "the military-industrial complex." Low-income and tenants' rights organizations have used power structure study to discover the real owners of their neighborhoods, and the actual developers and decision-makers laying waste to their communities. Since 1977, three campaigns have been mounted utilizing power structure research which can suggest similar campaigns to stop nuclear power.

The first involves universities as stockholders in corporations doing business in South Africa. Across the country, many students have organized actions designed to pressure their college and university trustees to divest their institutions of South African stock. Some colleges, like Hampshire College, sold their stock immediately. Others submitted resolutions to the corporations' directors. Haverford College demanded an end to Motorola's sales of radio and electronic equipment to South Africa's police and military. Bryn Mawr College required

an end to Kodak's photography equipment business in the country. The University of Minnesota filed resolutions with a dozen companies raising the South African question directly with the companies in which it invests. (...Many churches also traced down South African connections by examining interlocks between corporations. The United Church of Christ, being a stockholder of First National Boston Corporation, found itself a stockholder in South Africa through the Corporation's principal subsidiary, First National Bank of Boston. It also discovered seven other stockholder links, among them Citicorp, Manufacturers Hanover, Continental Illinois, Texaco, Standard Oil of California, Mobil...)

Another kind of effort has been mounted by over 20 religious groups which have formed Infact, or the Infant Formula Action Coalition. Together, the groups have brought proxy battles and other pressures on American Home Products Corporation and other producers of infant formula, directly challenging the companies' marketing and promotional practices in the Third World.

The last example concerns a very exciting development in applied power structure research. Seven unions and the Amalgamated Clothing and Textile Workers Union have taken on the J.P. Stevens Company in an attempt to force the latter into obeying labor union law. The unions have exploited their critical role as institutional investors by threatening to withdraw pension fund deposits from corporations linked with Stevens. In what the *Wall Street Journal* referred to as "resorting to terrorizing businessmen who do business with Stevens," the unions forced two directors—one from Manufacturers Hanover and another from Avon Products, Inc.—from the Stevens board of directors.

Chapter 2:

The Dollars and Cents of Nuclear Power

Introduction

The large corporations of the nuclear power industry have made their choice. They have invested a great deal of money in nuclear power in the hope of high profits, and they are using their vast economic power in an attempt to ensure that these hopes are realized. In the late 1960s it looked as if these corporations would be successful, but they have suffered a series of setbacks which now threaten to stop nuclear's advance altogether.

The problems confronting the nuclear plan are substantial. Utilities have encountered financial difficulties which inhibit their ability to build nuclear plants. The simple costs of nuclear power have risen dramatically despite large federal subsidies, and the economic uncertainties facing its implementation have grown.

The nuclear corporations have not given up yet. Their proposed solution is in the best tradition of big U.S. corporations faced with disaster: use the federal government to cut risks. They want continued federal subsidies, continued federal responsibility for critical parts of the fuel cycle, and new federal action to guarantee future profits. Taxpayers will pick up the bill, and everyone will bear the risks.

THE UTILITIES

Utilities are in a key position with respect to the introduction of nuclear energy. It is the utilities' choices between alternative power plants that ultimately determine whether any more electricity will be produced by nuclear generating stations. Although many factors influencing the utilities are beyond their control, it remains a fact that the choices lie with them.

Nuclear manufacturers push nuclear power for the simple reason that it is good for profits. For the utilities the case is not as clear. Recently, utilities have not been buying nuclear reactors. However, many of them continue to lobby for nuclear power even while cutting back on their orders for plants. A combination of political and economic factors has made the choice of a nuclear plant non-economical, and this combination of factors has dictated that what finally happens with respect to nuclear power will be settled by political forces. In order to understand the dramatic ups and downs in nuclear fortunes since the mid sixties, we will take a closer look at utilities.

The 1960s

The sixties were a boom for the economy in general and for the electrical utility industry in particular. Demand for electricity was expanding at a steady rate of about 7% a year, and investors were eager to supply the capital for new nuclear plants.[1] They were eager for two reasons. First, utilities regularly paid high dividends on their stocks. Second, utilities were growing and gave no indication of ever stopping. As a result, the price of their stock grew steadily. Since dividends and increases in stock price are the two components of return to a stockholder, investors were happy to provide new capital by buying utility stocks. In addition, steady growth in total revenues

meant that **retained earnings** grew and provided another source of capital for investment. Internally generated funds, which include retained earnings, supplied over half of utilities' capital needs during the sixties.[2]

There was another positive aspect to this period for the utilities. Costs of producing electricity continued a long decline. As more power was produced, prices to the consumer remained constant or even fell.

During this period **regulatory lag** worked in the utilities' favor. In other words, regulatory commissions were slow to cut rates in response to cost declines. As a result utilities were receiving money for expenses they didn't have to pay.

Capital Intensive Growth

For all these reasons, easy access to capital and declining costs of pro-

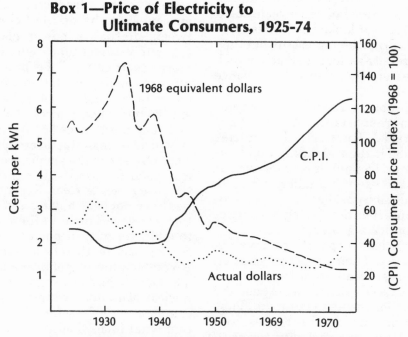

Box 1—Price of Electricity to Ultimate Consumers, 1925-74

Source: U.S. Federal Power Commission, *1970 National Power Survey* (Washington: U.S. Government Printing Office, 1971), p. I-19-2; and Standard and Poor, *Industry Surveys: Utilities-Electric* (New York: Standard and Poor, 1975), p. U-12.

duction, growth was the optimal strategy for utilities. They advertised heavily to expand demand through use of electric appliances and all electric homes, and they built new plants to meet that demand. The growth was self-sustaining. Declining electricity prices plus advertising stimulated demand. Growth created expectations of continued growth which were essential to investors in stock, and the growth in earnings and profits maintained the good financial position of utilities in general. These conditions created a bias toward capital intensive growth by these regulated utilities.

As regulated monopolies, utilities are allowed a rate of profit which is set by the regulatory commissions. It is not a rate of profit on all their costs, however. It is a rate of profit on their capital or "rate base." This rate base consists principally of plant and equipment like the buildings, boilers, and reactors which are required for generating power. The regulatory commission approves a rate structure which will allow the company to pay for such expenses as maintenance and fuel, and to earn the allowed rate of profit on its capital.[3]

This arrangement creates a bias towards capital intensity in the following way. When a particular item is included in a utility's rate base, the utility can recover that amount *plus* its rate of profit on it. If the item is not included in the rate base, the utility can recover only the amount spent. As a result, when a utility has a choice it will attempt to include as many of its costs as possible in the rate base in order to maximize its total profit.

It is this desire to maximize the size of the rate base—and thereby to maximize profits—which affects a utility's choice between a coal plant and a nuclear plant. There is a clear difference between the cost structure of a coal-fired plant and a nuclear-powered

one. For coal plants, fuel accounts for a much higher percentage of cost, while for nukes, a much higher percentage is capital cost. Fuel costs are not included in the rate base while capital costs *are*. From the point of view of management in the late sixties, investment in a nuclear plant was clearly more attractive than investment in an equivalent coal plant. Since a nuclear plant meant more capital invested and a larger rate base, it meant a larger total amount of profits. These larger profits meant greater **retained earnings** for reinvestment by management and further growth. They also meant high dividends for stockholders, which in turn made it easier to borrow additional funds to finance growth.

Capital intensive investment by utilities was also in the direct interest of banks and insurance companies, the largest investors in these stocks. They could earn a higher rate of profit on utility stocks than on alternatives and so were eager to buy more. Capital intensive investment also meant a larger total amount of stock sold and dividends paid out. For banks it meant a larger supply of highly profitable investments. Thus, bias towards capital intensive production and nuclear power in the late sixties derived directly from managements' decisions to maximize profits, and indirectly from profit-maximizing banks and insurance companies.

Nuclear power was on the rise. Between 1965 and 1977 the generating capacity of nuclear plants, which reflects plants ordered in the late sixties and before, grew from 926 Mw to 47,000 Mw, or from an insignificant proportion of the nation's net generating capacity to about 9%.[4] The 1970 annual forecast of the pro-nuclear trade journal *Electrical World* predicted that nuclear's share would grow to about 45% by 1985.[5] Cheap capital and high demand for electricity combined

In the 1960s utilities were rushing to buy nukes. In the 1970s they wanted to order more but many couldn't afford to.

to make nuclear power an attractive option for profit-maximizing utilities and their stockholders.

The 1970s
This nuclear euphoria didn't last long. The fortunes of the utilities worsened dramatically in the early 1970s along with the rest of the economy. The underlying problems of inflation and recession meant financial strain for the utilities. The weakened utilities could not continue to invest at the levels to which they were accustomed.

A major part of the problem confronting utilities was simply rising costs. These had their origins both in the increased cost of fuel resulting from the oil embargo and the overall inflation, which meant increased costs of materials, equipment, and labor. New plants of all kinds were larger and more expensive to operate.

The effect was to reverse the long-term decline in the cost of producing a unit of electricity and to end the stable or declining prices that electricity users enjoyed during the 1960s. These rising prices combined with the general recession to produce a dramatic decline in

Box 2—The soaring cost of power

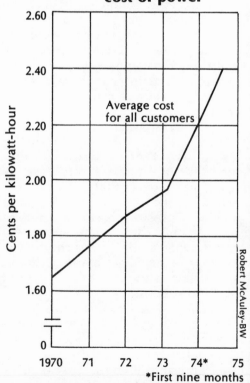

Average cost for all customers

*First nine months

(Source: *Business Week*, 20 January 1975)
Data: Edison Electric Institute BW est.

the demand for electricity. The annual rate of demand growth dropped to zero in 1974 from its usual 7%. Industry projections now are for a long-run rate of only about 3½-4% per year.[6]

Capital Crunch

The slowdown in earnings that followed the decline in demand-growth brought about financial deterioration through several mechanisms. First, it meant that stock dividends fell. Con Ed's failure to pay its quarterly dividend in April 1974 for the first time since 1885 was a dramatic blow to those who, like most investors, had associated utility stocks with high dividends. Con Ed's failure was symptomatic of utility problems in general and

meant closer scrutiny from investors of all utility stocks. As *Fortune* magazine put it, "No private utility escaped the force of that blow, for it destroyed the notion that utility dividends were inviolate."[7] Second, the decline in the long-run growth rate of demand signalled that utilites' earnings would not continue to grow at their old pace. Therefore, utility stock prices were not expected to continue their steady growth. Both of the elements that had made utility stocks so attractive in the sixties disappeared in the seventies.

Investors lost interest in utility stocks. Utility stock prices fell precipitously in late 1974 and early 1975. Stock sales became difficult. Utilities had to sell more stocks to raise any

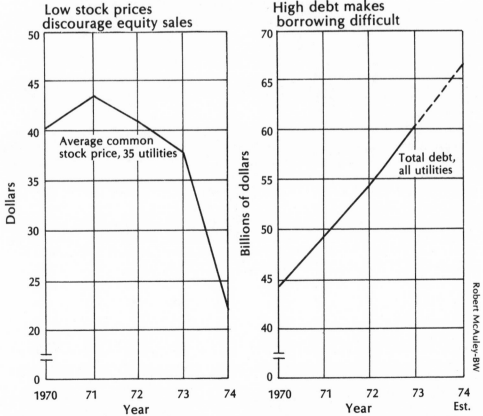

Box 3—Why utilities find it tough to raise funds

Low stock prices discourage equity sales

High debt makes borrowing difficult

Average common stock price, 35 utilities

Dollars

Total debt, all utilities

Billions of dollars

Robert McAuley-BW

Year

Year

Est.

Data: Standard & Poors Corp.   Data: Federal Power Commission, BW est.

(Source: *Business Week*, 20 January 1975)

Box 4—New nuclear power reactor orders are down sharply

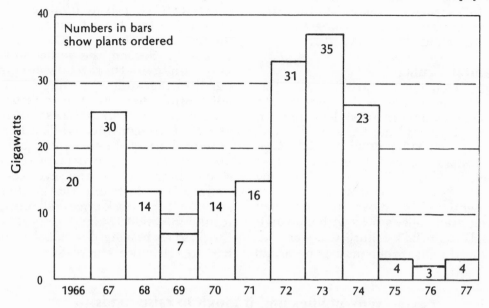

Source: Energy Research and Development Administration

given amount of capital. Because of the low price, these sales lowered the value of stock already outstanding.[8] To make matters worse, the drop in earnings and associated financial statistics led to a drop in the ratings given to utility bonds by investors' services like *Moody's*. In 1974 Moody's downgraded the bond rating of 38 electric utility companies and upgraded none.[9] Every cut in the rating meant an increase in the rate of interest that utilities paid on new debt. The decline in earnings also hurt internally-generated funds. The share of total capital needs generated internally fell to less than one quarter, and the amount of debt grew at the same time that the cost of debt was rising.[10]

As a result, it became very expensive to raise new capital. Just when many utilities had committed themselves to large construction projects, they were no longer able to afford them. In many cases they also no longer needed the added capacity. Where capacity was still needed, fossil fuel plants were easier for utilities to finance when capital was expensive precisely because they were less capital intensive. In order to meet the capital requirements of a nuclear plant, rate increases were required, while for fossil plants a substantial portion of the cost could be passed on to the customer via the already-established fuel adjustment clause.

The response from utilities was a

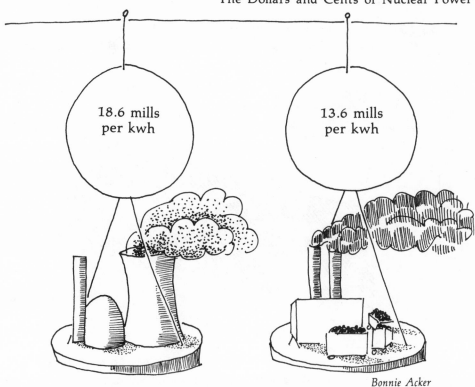

18.6 mills
per kwh

13.6 mills
per kwh

Bonnie Acker

drastic scaling down of all construction projects. Nuclear was especially hard hit. In 1974 about 170,000 Mw out of a planned 360,000 Mw of new plants were cancelled or delayed. Nuclear plants accounted for almost two-thirds of the cancellations.[11] Orders for nuclear plants fell from a peak of 35 in 1973 to 3 in 1976 and 4 in 1977.[12] *Electrical World* was forced to admit in 1977 that "almost all future nuclear additions have been rescheduled."[13] The magic cycle of growth and cheap capital had been broken, and at least some of the pro-nuclear bias went with it.

COSTS: NUKES VERSUS COAL

Nuclear power was originally heralded as an ultra cheap source of energy. In 1968, Arthur D. Little, Inc., an influential consulting firm, estimated that a 1000 megawatt pressurized water reactor could deliver electricity at .4¢ to .5¢ (4 to 5 tenths of a cent, or "mills")

per kilowatt hour. Even though the actual costs of operating such plants skyrocketed, Arthur D. Little continued to underestimate the rates of increase. In a study of electricity generation alternatives for New England in 1975, the firm estimated the costs of nuclear power to be at least 27% below those of coal.[14]

Even relatively recent estimates of the cost of nuclear power have varied widely. In 1975, *Electrical World* reported that the average cost of electricity from nuclear plants was 36% greater than the average cost of electricity from coal plants, or, 18.6 mills per kwh compared to 13.6.[15] The most recent *Electrical World* cost survey credits nuclear with a slight cost advantage.[16] It is difficult to obtain comprehensive data. Estimates of costs vary dramatically according to the sample of plants chosen and the assumptions made concerning the measurement of plant performance.

Box 5—Nuclear Cost Overruns

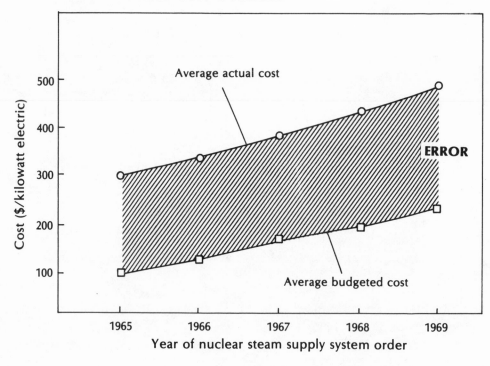

(Source: Bupp, et al., *Technology Review*, February 1975)

Gross misestimation of reactor costs has troubled the nuclear industry. The bottom line represents estimated costs of a reactor ordered in a given year, and the top line the actual costs ordered or expected (1973 dollars).

Estimates of the cost per kilowatt for every method of electricity generation have risen substantially in the last two years.[17] The most important elements in the overall cost increases for nuclear power are the rising cost of construction and operation, and low capacity factors.

Construction

The actual construction of a plant, including the cost of financing construction is termed the capital cost. It has always been recognized that nukes have higher capital costs than coal plants, but in general, estimates of

nuclear plant cost have proved too low by a factor of between two and three.[18]

Typically, Northeast Utilities' Millstone Point Two plant, originally budgeted at $186 million, had cost $418 million when finally completed. Specific cost overruns for selected nuclear plants are shown in Box 6.

Underestimates were, in part, the result of unanticipated inflation and increased labor costs. However, expensive delays due to the inability of components' manufacturers to deliver equipment on schedule contributed substantially to increases.[19] New safety requirements for reactor design and location (the result, in part, of

Bonnie Acker

"So you think your 1,000-Mw model will come in cheaper than coal? Great!"

"It'll cost 50% more than the original estimate! Are you kidding?"

pressure by concerned citizens groups) also led to unanticipated costs.

The costs of coal-fired generating plants have also increased, although not as rapidly as those of nuclear units. New federal requirements for the removal of sulfur dioxide by stack scrubbers add about 15% to the capital cost of coal plants.

Still, energy consultant Charles Komanoff, in testimony before the House Subcommittee on the Environment, Energy, and Natural Resources, estimated that the capital costs of a 600 megawatt coal-fired generator, with scrubber, would average $950 per kilowatt hour in 1985, while the capital costs of a twin 1,150-megawatt nuclear unit would average 26% more, or $1,200 per kilowatt hour.[20]

Box 6—Cost Overruns, Selected Nuclear Power Plants

company	plant	year finished	original estimate (M of $)	final cost (M of $)	cost overrun (%)
Baltimore Gas & Electric	Calvert Cliffs	1975	272	429	58
Carolina Power & Light	Brunswick 2	1975	200	382	91
Georgia Power	Hatch	1975	111	276	149
Indiana & Michigan Electric	Cook 1	1975	300	539	80
Northeast Utilities	Millstone Point 2	1975	186	418	125
Portland General Electric	Trojan	1975	235	465	98
Tennessee Valley Power Authority	Browns Ferry 1&2	1974-5	247	513	168

(source:*Nuclear Industry*, based on NRC "Operating Units Status Report" Gray Book of October 1977)

Capacity Factors and Reliability

The high capital cost of nuclear power plants is proving to be a substantial barrier to their construction. Factors which increase the capital burden of nuclear generation inevitably tip the scale in favor of coal. The typically poor performance and low reliabilty of nuclear generators have had just this effect. Capital costs, unlike fuel costs, must be paid for whether or not a plant is operating at its design capacity. If a plant is generating below its design capacity or is shut down for any reason, then the capital cost per kilowatt actually generated rises correspondingly.

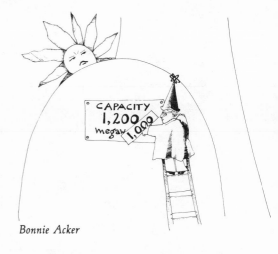

Bonnie Acker

Early in 1974 economist David Comey found a serious bias in Atomic Energy Commission estimates of the relative costs of coal and nuclear. AEC estimates assumed that both nuclear and coal plants operated at 80% of their design capacity. Yet Comey showed that nuclear power plants had not been able to generate much more than half the electricity they were designed to produce. When the AEC projections were adjusted to conform to these actual capacity factors, nuclear-generated power proved to be far more expensive than had been expected.

Comey went on to show that for operating plants over 100-megawatts the total cumulative capacity factor through 31 December 1975 was only 54.9%.[21] This discrepancy is important because a nuclear plant with an actual capacity factor of 55% produces electricity at a cost 22-29% higher than if it performed at the industry's projected capacity factor of 70-75%.[22] Coal has a much better record. The cumulative capacity of all coal plants between 1964 and 1974 was 68.9%[23]

Shortly after Comey's testimony appeared, the NRC took steps to improve nuclear capacity. They redefined the term "nuclear capacity" to refer to a plant's average output relative to its net output "during the most restrictive seasonal condition for condensor cooling efficiency." The gist of this technical jargon is that the design capacity is no longer to be used as a basis for comparison with actual performance. Instead, a smaller number (the "net output...") based on a reactor's worst period for net output during the year, is being used. The result is simply to raise the number reported as the capacity factor. Comey compared this new criterion to "computing a golfer's handicap solely on the score s/he got during a New Year's Day blizzard while hung over."[24] In some cases, the design capacity itself was revised downward!

Even using the NRC's "generous" definition of capacity, the nuclear power plant performance record has worsened since 1972. The cumulative average capacity factor from 1972 through the first seven months of 1977 was only 60%. Yet the same statistical publication which provides this data, the Department of Energy's *Monthly Energy Review*, continues to provide cost estimates for nuclear plants based on the assumption that plants will operate at 65% capacity. Box 8 offers a plant by plant breakdown of actual plant capacity performance.

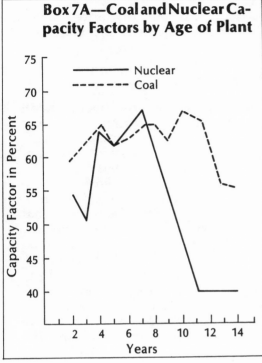

Box 7A—Coal and Nuclear Capacity Factors by Age of Plant

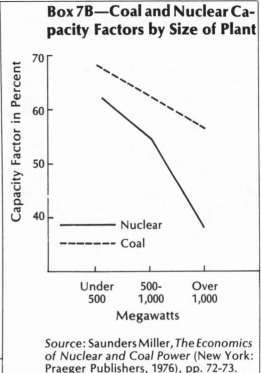

Box 7B—Coal and Nuclear Capacity Factors by Size of Plant

Source: Saunders Miller, *The Economics of Nuclear and Coal Power* (New York: Praeger Publishers, 1976), pp. 72-73.

Operation

Low reliability has been a more subtle but still serious problem for nuclear technology. The problem is related to the relatively large size of modern nuclear plants. Nuclear plants tend to be most economical when built in the 1,000 to 1,200-megawatt size range. The preferred size range for coal plants is 600 to 800-megawatts. It is ob-viously necessary to have more reserve generating capacity to accomodate the shutdown of a 1,200-megawatt plant than the shutdown of an 800-mega-watt one. Additionally, the smaller coal plants are individually more reliable. That is, they need to be shut down less often than the larger nukes. **The net result is that three coal plants with installed capacity of 1,800 Mw are the**

Box 8—Actual Plant Capacity Performance (Sample Plants)

plant	utility	ultimate net megawatt	cumulative capacity factor
Arkansas One 1	Arkansas P & L	850	61.8%
Beaver Valley	Duquesne Light	852	31.2%
Big Rock Point	Consumers Power	72	55.2%
Browns Ferry	TVA	1,065	35.5%
Browns Ferry 2	TVA	1,065	31.9%
Browns Ferry 3	TVA	1,065	72.5%
Brunswick 1	Carolina P & L	821	40.6%

(source: *Nuclear Industry*, based on NRC "Operating Units Status Report" Gray Book of October 1977)

equivalent in reliability of two nuclear units with a total capacity of 2,300 Mw.[25]

The low reliability of nuclear generators significantly increases the cost of their operation. Reactor malfunctions are not small problems. Because of radioactive hazards, the cost of repairs or service to nuclear plants can be enormous. Work that would be trivial in other circumstances can take a great deal of time. Quite often, when utilities are forced to shut down their nuclear plants they must buy electricity from other utilities at premium rates. These costs of poor reliability, which are unique to nuclear plants, are highly variable and difficult to predict.

The major variable cost of nuclear reactor operation is that of fuel. Principally, because of the exceptionally high heat content of uranium, the direct cost of fuel is now responsible for only about 13% of the cost of nuclear power. The price of coal accounts for about 37% of the cost of coal-fired electricity.[26] For this reason, fuel price excalation has less impact on the cost of nuclear electricity. However, the cost of uranium has been and continues to be subject to unexpected price rises.

Nuclear fuel cost will be more significant in the future. In the late 1960s most expectations were that uranium prices would remain near $4 per pound. Those days are long gone, in large part because of price-fixing by the uranium cartel.[27] Bids for 1980 uranium ore are already near $52 per pound.[28] Moreover, experience has shown that nuclear fuel produces much less electricity per pound than was originally projected. Charles Komanoff argues that by 1985 nuclear fuel costs will approximate 1.1¢ per kwh. Coal fuel costs will range from 2.7¢ per kwh in New England to .99¢ in the best coal mine territory.[29] In short, nuclear fuel may be slightly cheaper

than coal but the price difference won't be sufficient to compensate for the difference in capital costs.

Komanoff summarizes the coal-nuke tradeoff as follows:

No utility executive with an accurate perception of the costs of nuclear power and a sincere desire to minimize customer costs (with the possible exception of utilities in New England) would propose ordering a new nuclear plant. I believe that electricity from new nuclear plants will cost 22% more on average, than electricity from new coal plants with scrubbers, with the disadvantage of nuclear to coal costs ranging from 1% in the Northeast to 49% in the Mountain States and the Pacific Northwest.[30]

Federal Subsidies

Estimates of the simple costs of nuclear power don't tell the whole story. Taxpayers have made enormous contributions to the nuclear power industry

Bonnie Acker

Taxpayers provided the funds.

through a number of direct and indirect subsidies. Many of these subsidies, such as the government guarantees which diminish investment risk, cannot be measured. Others can be roughly quantified through an analysis of government budgets.

The Research and Development Subsidy

Taxpayers provided the funds for the extensive research and development required to apply nuclear technology to electricity generation. The Investor Responsibility Research Center has estimated that by January 1975, about $5 billion had been provided by the federal government for the development of civilian nuclear power.[31]

Research and development related to civilian nuclear power has consistently consumed between 30% and 40% of the total budget of these agencies. Research and development on non-nuclear sources was not funded until 1974. Since then, they have been granted only 15% of the budget. The relative lack of change in the distribution of expenditures between 1977 and 1978 is striking, especially in view of Carter's supposed emphasis on a new energy policy.

One way to get a perspective on the size of current subsidies of civilian nuclear power is to compare them to other areas of government spending. Such budget comparisons reveal seriously misplaced priorities. The most troublesome aspect of the use of coal for fuel lies in the deplorable working conditions of United States coal miners. However, the entire budget of the Mining Enforcement and Safety Administration of the Department of the Interior, the federal agency responsible for mining safety, is set at only $106 million for 1978, about one tenth of the subsidy for uranium enrichment alone.[32] The entire Occupational Safety and Health Administration was granted only $130 million in 1977, less than one-half the money spent on nuclear fuel cycle research and development.[33]

Another way to look at the effect of subsidies is to calculate the extent to which they allow nuclear-generated electricity to appear cheaper than it really is. In 1976, 192 billion kwh were generated by nuclear power plants.[34] **Total research expenditures on civilian nuclear plants in that year were $1.3 billion.[35] Had consumers paid that cost rather than taxpayers each kwh would have increased in price by 7 mills** (tenths of a cent).

The Insurance Subsidy

The nuclear industry would never have gotten off the ground without the passage of the Price-Anderson Act. This piece of legislation simultaneously limited the industry's liability for nuclear accidents and arranged for the federal government (again, the taxpayers) to share the costs. The Price-Anderson Act limits utility liability to $560 million, of which $100 million is insured by the federal government. This amount, $560 million, is less than 11% of the potential damage from a major nuclear accident. The NRC has recently conceded that a major nuclear accident could cause $40.5 billion in total damages. Former Pennsylvania insurance commissioner Herbert Denenberg has calculated that if insurance companies were willing to cover the risk, the premium required to insure a nuclear plant against such levels of damage would be about $23.5 million a year (a figure approximately equivalent to the entire current costs of plant operation and maintenance). If this subsidy were eliminated, the price of nuclear-generated electricity could rise as much as 3.8 mills per kwh.[36] The Price-Anderson Act was found unconstitutional in U.S. District Court. In the suit Duke Power Co. argued that,

Bonnie Acker

"And furthermore, in case of a nuclear accident, don't worry. We've got more than enough insurance to cover you all."

"without protection of the liability limit, investors would be unwilling to risk money in a power company, because of the possibility that claims from a nuclear accident could bankrupt them."[37] However, the Supreme Court unanimously overturned the lower court and upheld the constitutionality of the law.

The Enrichment Subsidy

Before uranium is ready to be packed into the fuel rods used in nuclear reactors, it must be highly enriched. Uranium enrichment facilities were first developed by the U.S. government for military purposes. Until late 1977, in part because their construction costs had been paid by the military, government enrichment plants offered their services to private customers at one-half to one-third the cost a commercial plant would have charged. The subsidy to enrichment has probably reduced the cost of nuclear-generated electricity by 4%, about 1 mill per kwh.[38]

President Carter recently approved an appropriation for the construction by the Department of Energy of a new gaseous centrifuge enrichment facility. Construction costs are estimated at $4.5 billion in 1978 dollars.[39] For the first time, the government will be allowed to charge a "fair market price." While it is unclear whether price increases will completely cover the cost of enrichment, there can be no doubt that the cost of nuclear power will rise.

The True Cost

The typical delivered residential rate for nuclear generated electricity was 4¢ per kwh in 1976. A conservative appraisal of the true cost, including the subsidies estimated above, is about 5¢ per kwh.

Actual rate	4.0¢
Enrichment	.1¢
Research and development	.7¢
Insurance	.4¢
per kwh	5.2¢

Expressed in pennies, it may not sound like much. Read it, instead, as a 25% increase in the monthly electric bill for customers of nuclear-powered electric utilities. Such an increase in price actually charged would have made and still could make alternative energy strategies look considerably more attractive. **By providing subsidies to the nuclear fuel cycle, the U.S. government is in fact choosing nuclear power over alternative methods of meeting our energy needs.**

RISK AND UNCERTAINTY

There is more to the economics of nuclear power than its simple costs, whether they are paid by utilities or taxpayers. Uncertainty or risk is a major consideration for companies making investment decisions. They are interested not only in their rate of profit if all goes well but also in the likelihood that everything *will* go well.

It just doesn't make sense for a utility to invest in nuclear power if it can't be sure that there will be adequate uranium supplies, or that it will be shut down for lack of waste storage facilities, or that the final costs of the power generated will be close to what is predicted when construction begins.

The uncertainties facing utilities fall into two basic categories. The first category includes problems surrounding the fuel cycle: the adequacy of domestic uranium reserves, bottlenecks in uranium reprocessing, and the lack of a long-run solution to the waste problem. The second category includes the problems involved in actually building and operating nuclear reactors: licensing and siting problems and escalating construction costs.

Fuel Supplies

Coal exists in the U.S. in amounts sufficient to meet projected demands for several hundred years: the adequacy of domestic uranium supplies, on the other hand, is questionable. A 1000-megawatt light water reactor requires about 6,000 tons of uranium

Bonnie Acker

during its thirty year projected life span. Estimates of known *probable* reserves total about 1.5 million tons, while total *potential* reserves are estimated at 3.5 million tons.[40] Now that the breeder reactor and commercial reprocessing have been delayed, U.S. nuclear-generating capacity could be restricted to 250,000 Mw if the estimate of probable reserves is accurate. Currently, plants with some 213,000 Mw of capacity are either operating, under constructing, or planned. In terms of uranium supply, this means that these probable reserves will be used up by plants now operating or now in the planning stages. In the words of *Monthly Energy Review*, "exhaustion of the prudent resource planning base could occur early in the next century."[41]

Overseas sources of uranium are more extensive. However, they are neither secure nor dependable. Even from the formation of a cartel by mining interests, export of uranium is a controversial political issue in many countries. The Australian labor movement successfully blocked uranium export for a period on the grounds that uranium use poses a threat to world health and safety. Uranium curtailment policies in Australia and Canada brought U.S. imports down to 4,408 tons in 1975, from 33,000 tons in 1974.[42] Australia, under a conservative government, recently lifted its ban on those uranium exports which had been guaranteed by contracts signed prior to the ban. There is no guarantee that a future labor government would not reimpose the ban.

Reprocessing

Little of the potential heat value of a reactor's fuel supply is actually consumed before the fuel becomes so contaminated with reaction products that fission becomes inefficient and the fuel rod must be removed. From the beginning of the atomic era proponents of nuclear power have predicted that fuel supplies could be made to last almost indefinitely by extracting, or reprocessing, the unconsumed uranium in used fuel. There now seems little chance that such hopes will be realized.

The history of the fuel reprocessing industry is replete with financial disasters. In West Valley, New York, a subsidiary of the Getty Oil Company, Nuclear Fuel Services, convinced the state of New York to join it in a commercial reprocessing venture. (Considerable pressure for the plant came from the avidly pro-nuclear Governor Nelson Rockefeller.) The plant proved both dangerous and unprofitable; it was shut down after a few years. The only problem was that a lot of radioactive waste was left over, and proper disposal of it could cost up to $660 million. Luckily for the company, their contract allowed them to leave the task and expense of cleaning up to New York State.[43] (For more on this story see pp. 50-52.)

A second reprocessing failure occurred when the General Electric Company, after spending $64 million, discovered that its Morris, Illinois plant would not work. *Science* magazine reported that GE had met its "technological Waterloo" and would not spend the additional $90 million or so required to make the facility viable.[44]

Still another, even larger, reprocessing plant is producing nothing but problems. Allis-Chalmers and General Atomic (a joint venture of Gulf Oil and Royal Dutch Shell) initially scheduled completion of their new Barnwell, South Carolina facility for 1974, and then 1978. The company spent $250 million only to find that expensive new safety measures would be required. In view of other technical uncertainties

Bonnie Acker

"You've brought us this far. You can't back down now."

the companies have been reluctant to invest more funds. They have petitioned the government for money to complete the plant. A manager explained that "finishing the plant alone would not be prudent management of stockholder's funds because of the difficulties involved in disposing of high-level radioactive wastes."[45]

Waste Storage
Technical and political problems in the storage of radioactive wastes persist. Many scientists believe that no genuinely safe method of storage is feasible. Serious leaks have already occurred in storage areas at Hanford, Washington, West Valley, New York, and Maxey Flats, Kentucky. Even temporary storage areas are in short supply. The nuclear power industry has openly acknowledged that it will run out of temporary spent fuel storage capacity by 1985.[46]

It is not clear that a satisfactory solution to the waste storage problem exists, nor is it clear how much any attempted solution will cost. Recent studies prepared by DOE indicate that costs of post-reactor services (services necessary once material leaves the reactor) for commercial nuclear

power plants have been underestimated. These studies argue that wastes must be solidified and encased in stainless steel before they are stored in "geologically safe" areas. Total costs of post-reactor services could range between 1.43 and 1.71 mills per kwh—more than three times the cost projected by the Atomic Energy Commission in 1974. [47]

Decommissioning
A nuclear power plant which has outlived its usefulness is the largest radioactive waste of all. Most industry estimates of the cost of completely dismantling nuclear plants fall between 10% and 15% of the cost of construction (in constant dollars). The lack of experience with decommissioning casts some doubts on the accuracy of these estimates. In at least one case, the cost of decommissioning actually equalled the cost of construction.[48] No private utilities have set ˋaside the capital required to decommission any plants. As Tom Wicker has pointed out, "In effect, future taxpayers will have to pay for current industry profits and relatively low consumer rates."[49]

Licensing and Construction
It is a standard complaint of utilities and nuclear supply industries that the licensing procedure for nuclear plants is inadequate. They argue that it takes too long (10 to 12 years) and that the exact length of time can't be predicted. Every increase in the time period of construction becomes an increase in the capital costs because of interest charges on borrowed capital and because inflation increases the cost of components and construction. Consequently, when a utility begins a nuclear plant, it can't reliably predict its final cost. *Electrical World* calls these cost increases "an almost indeterminable figure."[50]

In addition, utilities can't be certain when they begin construction that 10 to 12 years later they'll end up with a functioning power plant. Plants have been stopped and shut down for design faults, siting errors, and inadequate waste disposal plans. As safer technology is adopted, plants already in operation frequently have to be shut down so that the latest design can be built in (retrofitting).

Much of the difficulty in determining the costs of nuclear power has political roots. Many of these costs depend on a regulatory process which continues to be subject to political pressure. For example, the licensing procedure has a major influence on the length of the construction period and, therefore, on the capital cost of nuclear plants. Intervenors in the licensing process, as another instance, have successfully delayed the construction of nukes. Opponents of nuclear power won a legal victory in 1971 (Calvert Cliffs decision) when they made filing of a detailed environmental impact statement a requirement for new construction. Pressure brought on the AEC led to new regulations in 1971 which restricted radiation emissions to a level "as low as practicable." Citizen resistance has forced rejection of a variety of faulty waste disposal plants. The state of California has passed a law prohibiting the construction of new plants until an adequate waste storage plan is provided.[51]

Who Bears the Risks?
And Who Pays the Bills?

Much of the battle over nuclear power can be interpreted as a battle over who will bear the *real* costs* of nuclear power. When reactor manufacturers were forced by the AEC decision to build reactors which released less radiation, the price of reactors—and thus nuclear-generated electricity—went up. Instead of local residents bearing a non-monetary cost, the increased risk of cancer, utilities were forced to bear the cost of a safer reactor. When utilities are forced to take environmental impacts into account, the improvements save lives but cut profits.

When costs are rising, new construction means that rates must be raised to cover them. Each project requires another increase in the rates charged to consumers. Nuclear plants require the highest rate increases (of all utilities) because more of their costs end up in the rate base and consumers must pay that cost *plus* a profit. It is these basic facts that have changed the balance of political power for utilities.

No one-shot rate hike can restore the dynamic underlying conditions of the sixties. At that time the managements of utilities were largely independent of outside pressures. Regulators' role was restricted to the routine acceptance of new, lower-cost plants and to the determination of exact timing of rate cuts. Now that new construction requires rate increases, regulators are under more and more pressure from consumers to keep electric bills from skyrocketing. In states across the country consumer and anti-nuclear groups are successfully organizing against the rate increases necessary to finance nukes.[52] As a result, regulators themselves have become more critical about new projects. *Electrical World* calls them "an emerging breed of regulators brought up in an era in which the electric utility's every decision must be questioned."[53]

Summary

The simple costs of nuclear power have been rising dramatically. High costs of construction combined with low capacity factors and poor reliability have wiped out the cost advantage that nuclear once enjoyed.

*real costs include the uncalculated health and safety effects

Bonnie Acker

Nuclear power is running into trouble.

The true cost of nuclear is substantially higher than the simple cost. The cost competitiveness of nuclear depends on federal subsidies that ultimately come out of taxpayers' pockets. If these subsidies were removed, the cost of nuclear would increase by 25%.

Utilities' difficulties in raising capital combined with rising construction and operating costs have made it increasingly hard for them to build capital intensive nuclear power plants. In addition, political pressures on regulatory commissions have prevented the utilities from getting the huge rate increases that they need in order to build more nukes.

These cost and financing problems have slowed the purchase of nuclear plants. And increasing uncertainty about how high future costs will go has brought new construction to a virtual standstill. This uncertainty includes the cost of waste disposal as well as the final design and cost of reactors themselves.

Much of the uncertainty derives from political opposition which has already forced the industry to pay some costs which it wants the public to bear. The nuclear industry can't be sure that it won't have to pay even more of the costs in the future. The public's opposition to paying both simple costs and subsidies and to bearing the uncalculated health and safety risks of nuclear power could force the industry to pay all the real costs of nuclear development. This would destroy nuclear's current artificial cost competitiveness and mean an end to its economic viability.

The final outcome is far from clear, but what is certain is that it won't be settled by simple economic forces alone. The costs of nuclear development are high. The revival of profitable nuclear power depends on shifting these costs and risks to the public. In the end, growing public resistance to bearing these costs and risks could stop nuclear's advance.

Prepared by Joseph Bowring

Footnotes

1. Denis M. Slavich and Charles W. Snyder, "Meeting the Financial Needs of the Nuclear Power Industry," Nuclear Engineering International, March 1975.

2. David L. Scott, *Financing the Growth of Electric Utilities* (New York: Praeger Publishers, 1976).

3. Saunders Miller, *The Economics of Nuclear and Coal Power* (New York: Praeger Publishers, 1976).

4. "1978 Nuclear Plant Survey," Electrical World, 15 January 1978.

5. "21st Annual Electrical Industry Forecast," *Electrical World*, 15 September 1972.

6. "28th Annual Electrical Industry Forecast," *Electrical World*, 15 September 1977.

7. Carol J. Loomis, "For the Utilities It's a Fight for Survival," *Fortune*, March 1975, p. 184.

8. David A. West, "Adjusting Rates to Cost of Capital," *Public Utilities Fortnightly*, 15 September 1977, p. 20.

9. Roscoe C. Born, "Power Plan," *Barron's*, 21 November 1977, p. 10.

10. Jerome S. Katzin, "Effects of Inflation and Recession on Nuclear Project Financing In the U.S.A.," Nuclear Engineering International, March 1975, p. 185.

11. "Utilities: Weak Point in the Energy Future," *Business Week*, 20 January 1975.

12. "1978 Nuclear Plant Survey," *op. cit.*

13. "Nuclear Survey: Market Still Depressed," *Electrical World*, 15 January 1977.

14. Ron Lanoue, *Nuclear Plants: The More They Build, the More You Pay,* Center for Responsive Law, 1976, p. 33.

15. *Ibid.*

16. "20th Steam Station Survey," *Electrical World*.

17. *Ibid.*

18. Irwin C. Bupp, Jean Claude Derian, Marie Paule Donsimon, Robert Treitel, "Economics of Nuclear Power," *Technology Review*, February 1975.

19. Marc Messing, "Reasons for Delay in Power Plant Licensing and Construction," Environmental Policy Institute, September 1977.

20. Charles Komanoff, "Nuclear Power is More Expensive Than Coal," *Environmental Review*, December 1977.

21. David D. Comey, "Nuclear Power Plant Reliability: the 1973-4 Record," *Not Man Apart*, April 1975.

22. Lanoue, *op. cit.*, p. 35.

23. Komanoff, *op. cit.*

24. Comey, *op. cit.* A more detailed account of the capacity factor issue may be found in "Nuclear Plant Performance/Update: Data through Dec. 31, 1976" by Charles Komanoff and Nancy A. Bower of Komanoff Energy Associates, 1977, Council on Economic Priorities, 84 Fifth Ave., N.Y., N.Y. 10011. They point out that 18 of the 48 commercial nuclear plants which they analyzed actually reduced their *design* capacity factors. They perform a statistical analysis of capacity trends, taking into account the negative impact of increased nuclear plant size on capacity factor. They derive projections of 49% capacity for pressurized water reactors (PWR's) and 44% for boiling water reactors (BWR's) of 1150 Mw—the typical size of new planned nuclear units.

25. Komanoff, *op. cit.*

26. "20th Steam Station Survey," *op. cit.*

27. See discussion in previous chapter on the nuclear power power structure.

28. Komanoff, *op. cit.*

29. *Ibid.*

30. *Ibid.*

31. John Abbott, Ralph Nader, *The Menace of Nuclear Power*, p. 228.

32. U.S. Government Budget, Gov't Printing Office, Washington D.C., 1977.

33. *Ibid.*

34. *Monthly Energy Review*, June 1977.

35. Box 6 shows how this figure was derived.

36. Abbott and Nader, *op. cit.*, p. 229.

37. *Electrical World*, 1 May 1977.

38. Abbott and Nader, *op. cit.*, p. 227.

39. *Monthly Energy Review*, September 1977.

40. Saunders Miller, *op. cit.*

41. *Monthly Energy Review*, May 1977.

42. *Monthly Energy Review*, July 1976.

43. Richard Beer, Peter Biskind, "West Valley: The Tombstone of Nuclear Power," *Seven Days*, 28 March 1977.

44. Robert Gillette, "Nuclear Fuel Reprocessing: GE's Balky Plant Poses Shortage," *Science*, 30 August 1974.

45. Harvey Wasserman, "The Barnwell Bomb: Reprocessing Nuclear Disaster," *Seven Days*, 28 March 1977.

46. Tom Wicker, "Nuclear Power," *New York Times*, 22 September 1977.

47. *Monthly Energy Review*, November 1976.

48. *Demolition Age*, December 1977.

49. Tom Wicker, *op. cit.*

50. 28th Annual Electrical Industry Forecast, *Electrical World*, 15 September 1977, p. 56.

51. Bupp et al., *op. cit.*

52. Harvey Wasserman, "People Against Power," *The Progressive*, April 1978.

53. "The Management Report: Who is Managing Electric Utilities?," *Electrical World*, 15 July 1977.

GLOSSARY

bond — A company issues bonds as a way of borrowing funds. They are a promise to repay the face value at a future time plus a certain rate of interest.

bond rating — Since early 1900s bonds have been assigned quality ratings by companies like Moody's which reflect the riskiness of the bond or the likelihood that the bond will not be paid back with full interest.

capacity factor — The power actually generated by a plant as a percentage of its designed capacity to generate power.

Con Ed — Consolidated Edison is one of the largest privately owned utilities in the U.S. It serves N.Y.C. and surrounding areas.

design capacity — The amount of power that a power plant is designed to produce in a year if everything works properly.

earnings — The total revenue of a company in a year.

profits — The total earnings minus costs of production. Profits are divided into parts for utilities: dividends, which are distributed to stockholders and retained earnings, which the company keeps for reinvestment.

retained earnings — see profits

Chapter 3:

The Economic Impact of Nuclear Power

Jobs

Two hundred years ago, a Frenchman named Pierre Bastiat wrote a satire entitled "Petition of the Candlemakers" in which he proposed "blocking sunlight from all houses and buildings in order to increase employment among candlemakers, which would, in turn, stimulate employment in whaling, match making, wick production and other industries—to the immense benefit of all the classes of the realm." Although their scheme is just as irrational, proponents of nuclear power are not being funny when they claim that increased development of nuclear power is the best route to economic growth and increased employment.

Anti-nuclear activists are often accused of blocking progress and of condemning people to freeze in the dark. There is no substance to this accusation. An investment of several billion dollars in a nuclear power plant can offer economic growth and jobs. **However, an investment of comparable size in conservation, industrial cogeneration, or solar technology promises a greater stimulus to economic growth and far more employment as well.**

The value of non-nuclear alternatives would be more widely recognized if policy makers had taken the trouble to look closely at the issue of jobs. In recent hearing before the Joint Economic Subcommittee, Senator Kennedy summarized the problem:

> ...it became clear that in writing the National Energy Plan the Department of Energy did not calculate the employment impact of its decisions except by consulting one macroeconomic model. The department still does not have this capacity. It has not worked closely with the Department of Labor. *Because of subsidies to energy and capital we have consistently disadvantaged labor and reduced the number of jobs available. Because of subsidies to utilities, solar energy is at a disadvantage.* Nonetheless solar hot water heating and improved housing construction would create 3 times as many jobs in

189

Long Island and 4 times in California, according to the testimony of our witnesses. Conservation is the best job creator of all, outperforming all other energy measures by a margin of 3 to 1.[1]

Energy and Unemployment

Energy and labor are substitutes for each other in the production process. Industries that utilize large amounts of one tend to utilize small amounts of the other. For example, the agricultural and manufacturing sectors of the economy are heavy energy consumers, but they account for a shrinking proportion of the labor force. In fact, while the labor force as a whole grew by almost 9,000,000 persons between 1970 and 1976, the number of people employed in agriculture and manufacturing actually declined.[2] Machines were doing the work, and fewer workers were needed to produce more goods. Most of the expansion of employment took place in the services and in wholesale and retail trade.

Capitalist manufacturing firms have replaced workers with energy-intensive machines for two main reasons. First, machines can't go on strike, complain about working conditions, or demand benefits and pay increases. Secondly, machines are often less expensive than labor—especially unionized labor. Decades of federal subsidies and tax policies have artificially lowered the price of electricity and sped up this process of substituting capital for labor.

Automation can eliminate some tedious jobs and increase productivity. It is often associated with higher rates of hourly pay for those who remain employed. If investment in new machines creates new jobs, automation may not increase overall unemployment. However, automation often displaces trained and experienced workers, who often can't find other jobs. In

Bonnie Acker

They would have us believe that no nukes means no jobs.

Electricity is a substitute for labor.
Bonnie Acker

the process, it places an additional burden on taxpayers who finance unemployment compensation and welfare.

A well-planned decrease in energy consumption in the U.S. would not threaten jobs. In fact, it might well retard the pace of energy-intensive automation without hindering economic growth. According to the 1976 Ford Foundation Energy Policy Project, a move to slow growth of energy consumption from its historical 3.4% increase per year to 1.9% would increase employment an extra 1.5%. Because labor is a substitute for energy, the Energy Policy Project projected that employment would rise an extra 3.3% by the year 2000 if a zero energy growth policy were to be adopted.[3]

In the past, energy consumption and gross national product have grown at similar rates. However, there is no necessary relationship between the two. West Germany and Sweden, with standards of living comparable to that of the U.S., consume about half as much energy per capita. **Almost 40% of U.S. energy production is wasted.** An increase in the efficiency of energy use could contribute enormously to economic growth. For instance, if U.S. energy inefficiency were reduced, U.S. products would be more cost competitive with foreign goods. Billions of dollars now slated for investments in energy would find more productive uses. Expansion of decentralized energy technologies would increase the self-sufficiency of the U.S. and diminish the destructive impact of such economically disastrous events as oil embargoes and central power station blackouts.

Electricity and Jobs

Money invested in electricity-generation creates fewer jobs than money invested in almost anything else. Much of the money spent on building a generating plant pays for the materials and equipment which go into it. Most of these materials and equipment are themselves produced in industries, such as steel, where the number of jobs per unit of capital is relatively low. Economists term this type of investment "capital intensive." Electricity generation is one of the most capital intensive of all industries. At $105,000 per job, the capital investment per employee in public utilities is second only to that of the petroleum industry. In contrast, the average manufacturing job can be created with an investment of $19,500, and jobs in services, for $9,500.

It's not surprising, then, that the electric utility industry has failed to provide many jobs. From 1961-1973 the industry increased its kilowatt output by 130% and its revenues by 260%.

thousand dollars spent on the average basket of goods for personal consumption buys a labor input of 8 jobs (8 person-years went into it), while the same dollar amount of electricity contains a labor input of only 4 jobs.

If conservation of electricity is achieved through public education and "positive" incentives, consumers will have more money to spend on job-creating purchases. The resulting decrease in the need for new power plants would lead to new jobs in other industries. Conservation measures which decrease electric bills, such as reductions in lighting use, create jobs indirectly. However, if conservation is imposed by price increases which lead to higher electric bills, consumers will have less money to spend on other things, and fewer jobs will be created.

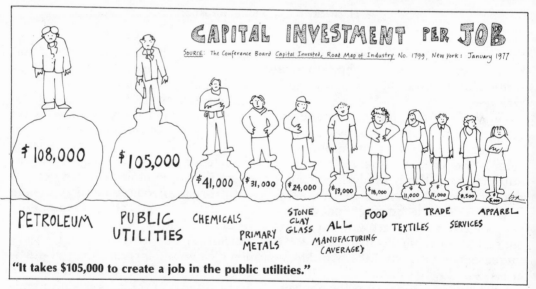

CAPITAL INVESTMENT PER JOB

SOURCE: The Conference Board Capital Invested, Road Map of Industry No. 1799, New York: January 1977

$108,000 — PETROLEUM
$105,000 — PUBLIC UTILITIES
$41,000 — CHEMICALS
$31,000 — PRIMARY METALS
$24,000 — STONE CLAY GLASS
$19,000 — ALL MANUFACTURING (AVERAGE)
$18,000 — FOOD
$11,000 — TEXTILES
$11,000 — TRADE
$9,500 — SERVICES
$5,000 — APPAREL

"It takes $105,000 to create a job in the public utilities."

Construction expenditures rose about 340%. But employment in the industry increased only 21%.[4]

If conservation could reduce their electric bills, consumers would spend their money on other items. Almost anything else that they might choose to buy would support more jobs than purchases of electricity. One hundred

A Few Jobs Versus Many Jobs
Nuclear power provides fewer jobs than does any alternative investment in the energy area. Even coal plants, which are capital intensive relative to other alternatives, offer considerably more employment than nuclear plants. Although it takes a larger amount of labor to construct a nuke, over the 30

Sending people down the primrose path.

Bonnie Acker

year life of both plants, a coal plant provides about 30% more employment: 28,500 person-years versus 22,000 person-years for the nuclear plant.[5] New technologies for wood combustion are even more labor intensive.

Solar space and hot water heating, photovoltaic solar-electricity cells, and conservation are all economically viable methods of providing energy. All of these methods rate far higher in job potential than centralized electric generating utility plants, be they nuclear or coal. **According to a number of estimates, solar technologies would provide, at the very least, 2 more jobs per unit of energy produced than would nuclear power.**[6] Alternatives may provide as much as 5 times the number of jobs. Likewise, a comprehensive conservation program would create far more jobs than would be created by building new power plants to generate an equivalent amount of electricity.[7]

Several state and federal agencies have enthusiastically studied the job impact of specific investments in solar heat and conservation.

According to the Massachusetts Energy Policy Office, $480 million invested in fitting half the buildings in the state for solar hot water heating would create 32,000 jobs.[8] If such a plan were implemented, the equivalent of 9.5 million megawatt hours of electricity a year would be saved. Contrast this solar investment to the proposed Montague, Massachusetts nuke which, at an initial cost of $3.4 billion, would produce 13.5 million megawatts a year (at 65% capacity)—less than half the number of jobs, at 5 times the cost per unit of energy supplied.

A Senate Commerce Subcommittee Staff Proposal sent to President Carter shows that a $1.65 billion investment in conservation, using public service workers, would create 100,470 new jobs and save over 2,000 million gallons of oil per year.[9] Again, this makes far better economic sense than a $3.4 billion investment in a nuclear power plant which would create, at most, 11,000 jobs and save the equivalent of only 28 million gallons of oil.

As William Winpisinger, the president of the International Association of Machinists and Aerospace Workers has noted:

Credit: Syd Harris

William Winpisinger

...[we] have a tremendous opportunity to dovetail the development of the new energy sources such as solar, cogeneration, biomass, small hydro, and wind with a national manpower policy and full employment program.

...Probably no other program could be designed to better serve the national interest and the people's interest than achieving full employment through the development of alternate energy sources...of all sources solar power must be the people's power.[10]

Good Jobs Or Bad

Radiation is part of the job; if you don't want to work with it, don't work at all.
(Portsmouth Naval Shipyard occupational health officer to a worried worker.)

It's not only the number of jobs that should count, but also the quality of work. The extreme risks to worker health and safety posed by nuclear development have been presented in the previous section.

Recent epidemiological studies have begun to reveal the tragic consequences of occupational exposure to radiation hazards. In an examination of over 100,000 death certificates, including 1,752 from Portsmouth Naval Shipyard workers, Dr. Thomas Najarian recently made a horrifying discovery. While national mortality from cancer was 18% and that of shipyard workers was 21%, fully 38% of shipyard workers who worked on nuclear-related projects (with a risk of radiation exposure), died of cancer.[11] An analysis of mortality records of workers from the AEC's (now DOE) Hanford Reservation also indicates increased incidence of cancer.[12] As the chief steward of the Portsmouth Metal Trades Council characterized the situation, "Production comes first, safety second."[13]

Nuclear construction has also seen hazardous conditions of a more prosaic nature, perhaps because most plants are now contracted by large firms whose labor management practices are not the best. In at least one case, workers became so alienated and angry about their working conditions that they engaged in sabotage, welding obstructions inside pipes.[14] In response to organized workers' demands for good pay and safe working conditions, the industry has begun a major "open-shop" campaign. **Forty-three nuclear and coal plants are currently being constructed without union protection for workers.**[15]

Meanwhile, unions such as the Oil, Chemical and Atomic Workers are zeroing in on the safety issue. Union president A.F. Grospiron recently stated:

"Radiation deaths? Not a single documented case."

Bonnie Acker

we will not accept the proposition that worker health and the natural environment must be further degraded in order to provide more energy....If an energy source is found to be inherently unsafe or highly destructive of the natural environment, then that energy source must be abandoned.[16]

Jobs For Whom?

DOE has estimated that the current total employment in nuclear fission electric activities is about 80,000 people: mostly engineers, mathematicians, physical and earth scientists, technicians, welders, plus "all other employees." Nuclear energy development utilizes far fewer nonprofessionals per scientist or technician than does solar energy; for nuclear the ratio of nonprofessionals to scientists or technicians is about 2:1; for solar, it is 9:1.[17]

A recent Federal Energy Administration report stressed **that employment associated with energy conservation techniques is local, low to moderately skilled, and concentrated in or near urbanized areas which are experiencing the most acute unemployment problems.**[18] In contrast, centralized energy production complexes usually have to bring in highly skilled labor from outside the construction area.

Some groups representing minorities have taken a strong position on this issue. As Mandine Cooper, the Deputy Director of the National Urban League's Washington bureau, recently said,

...we look upon conservation as a key initial step in a successful energy policy...The needs of poor people and workers must be taken into the equation rather than left as an afterthought. We can no longer afford to divert

Bonnie Acker

"Sure, there are a few jobs for welders and electricians, but go and see how many of us are down there."

solar, electrical workers, for instance, may see expansion of centralized electrical generating capacity as advantageous. Unfortunately, many of the workers having the most to gain from alternative technologies are unemployed or not well represented by unions. It is difficult for these workers to bring political pressures to bear upon energy decisions.

Even so, a number of unions are in the forefront of the fight for conservation and alternative energy. These unions are working hard to educate the public on the merits of non-nuclear energy strategies.

For example:

The Laborer, a journal of the Laborer's International Union, (AFL-CIO) wrote that jobs for its members in the solar energy field could well mount into the hundreds of thousands.[20]

The International Association of Machinists and Aerospace Workers (IAM) Grand Lodge Convention in Florida passed the following resolution in 1976: "An all out federally sponsored program to convert home water and space heating to solar would not only decrease America's dependence on foreign oil, but create millions of needed jobs for construction workers, machinists, metal workers, and other industrial workers."[21]

Sheet Metal Workers president Carlough has pointed out that, "Even figured conservatively, energy saving modification work and an expanded solar energy could put all unemployed sheet metal workers back to work."[22]

our capital into energy sources without demonstrated employment benefit.[19]

Alternative Technology and the Trade Union Movement

The potential for jobs in conservation and alternative energy is enormous. However, because of a general lack of initiative in instituting full-scale programs, relatively few jobs have been created. Unless advocates of non-nuclear energy can begin to make concrete proposals and to actively redirect investments toward job-creating programs, their claims will seem like pie in the sky to someone who needs a job right away.

It is understandable that construction workers look enthusiastically upon the enormous quantities of material and labor that go into nuclear plant construction. Given the current lack of jobs in cogeneration, conservation, and

Bonnie Acker

"Those guys don't know what's good for me—I mean them."

It is extremely important that anti-nuclear activists work with unions to promote credible alternatives to nuclear power.

No One Should Freeze in the Dark

A non-nuclear future promises more jobs and better jobs. The direct employment which would result from investment in conservation and solar far exceeds what nuclear power can provide. A decrease in the rate of growth of electricity consumption would increase the demand for goods and services, indirectly increasing the number of jobs available.

It would be a mistake, however, to assume that the widespread adoption of conservation and alternative technologies alone would eliminate unemployment. If U.S. firms follow their profit-maximizing logic, they might manufacture solar collectors and home insulation in low-wage Third World countries.

Unemployment is part of a political business cycle which takes place independently of trends in technology and energy use. Energy consumption increased steadily in the U.S. until 1974, but unemployment has followed the ups and down of the business cycle.

Even if a substantial number of jobs are created, unemployment will remain an integral part of the U.S. economy until the political battle for full employment is won. In a capitalist economy, unless workers can be threatened with the loss of their jobs and livelihood, they tend to make wage demands which put pressure on profits. When profits get pinched, investment slows down and workers are laid off. Unemployment goes up, wage demands diminish, and real wages decline. The conditions for profitability are then reestablished and the cycle can begin all over again.[23]

The enormous job potential in conservation and alternative technologies highlights the contradictions—and the waste of human resources—inherent in the business cycle. When there are so many things that need to be done to provide safe and reliable sources of energy, should anyone who desires a job be denied one? Can it be inflationary to put people to work saving or supplying much-needed energy? The money which is now spent subsidizing the expansion of electricity production should go to create an energy conservation job corps, or to bring solar power into homes of many U.S. citizens. **The demand for full employment should play an integral part in the fight against nuclear power. No one should have to "freeze in the dark."**

"Buy now and get one free gift, folks."
Bonnie Acker

Consequences for Local Communities

In a 1977 referendum the people of Seabrook, New Hampshire and surrounding towns voted 51% to 49% against the siting of a nuclear power plant in their community. Their decision carried no weight before the federal and state agencies which actually had the power to block construction. The towns responded by voting, in March of 1978, to deny the builders of the plant access to town water supplies. In the same month, the people of Wasco, California voted 2 to 1 against what would have been the world's largest nuclear project, a $5 billion installation which would feed electricity to Los Angeles. Once a relatively non-controversial issue, the economic and environmental impact of a nuclear power plant upon its host community is rapidly becoming a focus of political controversy.

Most utilities attempt to win local support for the installation of nuclear power plants by arguing that they offer extraordinary rewards to the host community. Advocates of nuclear plant construction often claim that local residents can expect long-term relief from property taxes, many employment opportunities from the building of a plant, and additional indirect employment in commerce and services. In short, people who live in a community where a nuclear plant has been proposed are frequently led to expect that the plant will bring economic prosperity to their area. It's only fair to say that sometimes this expectation is borne out.

The local effects of nuclear plant construction are not as simple as they first appear, however, and many communities have seen their expectations tarnished by unforeseen complications. Simply by virtue of its size, a nuclear plant can have an enormous impact on a non-industrial rural area, generating extreme changes in the tax structure, school attendance, the real estate market, and other aspects of life.[24] Often unevenly distributed, such effects can cause real hardship for local residents, for many of whom there may be little or no compensation.[25]

Misleading Projections

Although the law requires that "socioeconomic impacts" be considered by the appropriate regulatory bodies prior to the granting of a construction permit for a nuclear power station,[26] most utilities and regulatory agencies have paid little attention to this requirement. Utilities have often submitted assessments so deficient as to be grossly misleading.[27] Generally limited to a few pages, these "evaluations" commonly present the benefits of construction with unjustified optimism and utterly fail to recognize significant costs. Treating possible problems as trivial or unquantifiable, utilities compare the costs and benefits of their projects and conclude that the benefits greatly exceed the costs.[28]

Skeptics who take the trouble to examine any particular siting situation will develop a very different picture of the socioeconomic costs of a nuke. In doing so they can learn a great deal from the growing body of literature on socioeconomic impacts and from experienced groups of intervenors, which have often developed written critiques

Bonnie Acker

of utilities' projections. A case in point is the Massachusetts Energy Facilities Siting Council's critique of Northeast Utilities' socioeconomic impact report for the Montague nuclear station.

Islands of Wealth

It is easy to see how the increase in tax base provided by nuclear plants can make it possible to increase municipal spending. For instance, the value of the proposed Montague nuclear station is more than twice the total value of the county's existing tax base. The New Jersey township of Lower Alloways had total revenues from taxes approaching $50,000 in 1970, but in 1975, thanks to the nuclear station under construction, enjoyed revenues that amounted to well over $5 million (some $2,500 for each child, woman, and man.)[29] The town of Vernon, Vermont used its increased tax revenues to build

a municipal swimming pool. Wiscasset, Maine built new primary and secondary schools, a health center, a public works garage, improved the sewage system, installed sidewalks, purchased new vehicles, and made numerous other improvements. It became the envy of its neighbors.[30]

In states which allow host communities to retain all of the tax revenues from nuclear facilities, plant sites are often "islands of wealth surrounded by poorer neighbors."[31]

Such windfall wealth has not gone unnoticed. As Alice Shurcliff, regional economist at M.I.T. observes, "There is pressure everywhere, perhaps stimulated by the extreme situations created by the siting of nuclear power plants in small communities, to equalize the capacity of local governments to fund public services in general, and schools in particular. These ongoing changes

Bonnie Acker

"Too bad you don't have a nuke in your town."

make it difficult to predict future tax benefits."[32] Recent court decisions and legislative action in California, Massachusetts, Oregon, Wisconsin and other states support the trend toward adopting uniform property taxes or equalizing transfer payments from tax-rich areas to tax-poor ones.

Such revenue-balancing schemes can reduce or eliminate local tax benefits from nuclear plants. Pennsylvania taxes utilities on a state-wide basis and distributes the proceeds to cities and townships in proportion to their own tax collections. In 1975 Philadelphia was granted about $5.6 million from utility taxation, while Peachbottom, the site of two nuclear plants, received only $643.[33] In 1975 the state of Maine, following precedents in other states, decided that the unusual revenues at Wiscasset should be shared by the entire state in order to equalize funding for education. Until a recent state-wide referendum reversed this decision, Wiscasset forwarded to the state $289,000 per month, receiving in return only $250,000 per year to pay the bill for its grand new facilities.[34]

Dissociation of Costs and Benefits

If significant tax revenues can be expected, it is essential to answer the questions, "Where will the costs and benefits flow?" and "When will the costs and benefits come to bear?"[35]

Cost-benefit analyses which only consider costs and benefits over large regions or long periods can be very misleading. The problems of inequitable or untimely distribution of costs and benefits are so common that planners have developed terms for them: "spatial and temporal dissociation of costs."[36]

Typically, several towns near a reactor site have to bear costs of increased road traffic and new residents, etc., while only the town in which the plant is actually located derives taxes from it.

The case of the proposed Montague nuke illustrates this inequity. Cities and towns are empowered to tax property in Massachusetts. Counties and other regional bodies cannot. If the state does not pre-empt taxation, the town of Montague alone could receive tax revenues from the plant. Meanwhile, Montague's neighbors would actually lose money.

For instance, Montague's partners in the regional education district would have to pay more for its services. In Massachusetts, regional education facilities are funded jointly by the district and the state. The state awards funds to districts in inverse proportion to their wealth. The district's share is then contributed by its 18 member towns on a per capita basis. If the valuation of the district triples, the state will reduce its funding. The district will then have to come up with the balance. For every town in this poor county but Montague any additional bill could be a real hardship.[37]

"Dissociation over time" usually occurs when a community must make substantial investments in planning and public services for construction-related growth years before a facility's assessed value supports comparable amounts of money from taxes. This might mean paying for the construction of new roads, sewage facilities, and schools for workers' children—all needed before the plant is operating.

Communities compelled to pay heavy dissociated costs may be forced to borrow beyond their capacity. They may then have to raise taxes to such high levels that long-time residents must move or sell their property.[38] Clearly, hardships can occur even for communities which expect long-term tax advantages.

Tax Write-offs

It is important to note that a number of exemptions often reduce the tax revenues from power plants. Many states routinely exempt industrial machinery from the property tax in order to encourage job development; some even exempt nuclear fuel. In addition, recent federal legislation permits utilities to deduct from their tax bills many costs incurred to reduce damage to the environment. When broadly construed, such privileges can be quite significant. Boston Edison Co., for example, writes off fully one-third the value of its Pilgrim Nuclear Station to the environmental protection exemption alone.[39] **It cannot be overemphasized that residents of any community for which a nuclear station is planned should not take the utility's estimates of tax benefits at face-value.**

Disruptive Growth

Ironically, even those towns which are fortunate enough to gain great tax advantages can experience problems stemming directly from their excess of riches. Certainly, in most cases an expansion of the tax base per se is advantageous to a town, enabling it to provide better services or to lower the tax rate. However, there can be severe complications for many residents.

In remote rural areas, power plant construction may lead to a scenario reminiscent of the fable of Midas' touch.[40] When construction workers and their paychecks bring new demands and sudden wealth to a relatively poor region, dramatic changes in housing, commerce, and services occur. Property values and rents rise, businesses expand, and public services, previously limited, become hopelessly inadequate. In a few years construction is complete, and the many construction workers are replaced by a few operating personnel. Soon there

"Yes, we can give you an exact estimate." *Bonnie Acker*

isn't enough money to support the newly expanded businesses, and they fold. Such economic disruption can initiate a local depression.

Even communities located close to major urban centers can suffer the ill effects of disruptive growth.

Plymouth, Massachusetts and Waterford, Connecticut both lowered their tax rates and improved services when nuclear plants were built within their borders. New tax wealth led to important but very different changes in the characters of these two towns.[41]

Plymouth, not anticipating the problems in store, failed to enact restrictions on development. Real estate and construction interests, especially large firms based in nearby Boston, moved in quickly to take advantage of the opportunity. Housing developments were thrown up, and the population grew. Plymouth's planning and public services were quite inadequate to cope with the rapid growth in population—as much as 11% per year, for several years.[42] Within a short time, townspeople, without the means for satisfactory local control, saw their rural town transformed into a surburban strip.

Even areas which are fortunate in having able and energetic planners can still experience subtle but substantial costs. Waterford, fortunate enough to have stringent zoning regulations before the plant was built, saw its tax benefits attract an influx of immigrants eager to build expensive houses where their tax rates would be lowest. Land values shot up, and with them, housing costs. The town became "an affluent enclave with little room for young couples, the elderly, and the less affluent."[43]

By some measures, both Plymouth and Waterford were better off after the construction of the nuclear plants. But residents who valued Plymouth's quiet rural aspect, or who were young,

Economic disruption can initiate a local depression.

old, or poor in Waterford might disagree.

Many adverse impacts represent conflict of interests within the towns, with the balance of power seriously disturbed by plant construction. No report on the economic and human consequences of plant construction is complete without an investigation of its effects on *all* sectors of the local population.

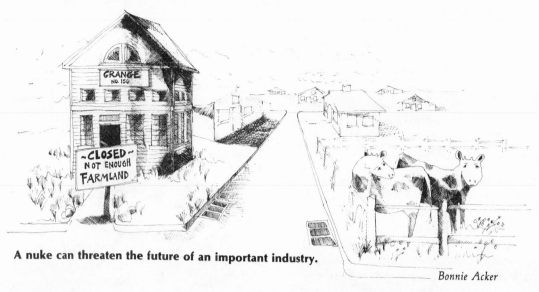

A nuke can threaten the future of an important industry.

Bonnie Acker

Mitigation

In response to criticisms and interventions from planners and state siting agencies, and in the face of increasing local resistance to nuclear sitings, utilities have begun to offer compensation for some disruptive fiscal side-effects with so-called mitigation plans. A plan frequently cited as a model is a contract between Skagit County, Washington and Puget Sound Power and Light Company whereby the utility agreed to prepay taxes in amounts sufficient to support the increased fire, police, and educational needs of the construction period.[44]

Such mitigation plans can be a substantial help to affected communities, but there are many important impacts for which such mitigation is difficult or impossible. For example, a nuclear power plant can threaten the future of an important local industry. The cooling tunnels of the Seabrook plant will cause changes in the ocean environment harmful to local shellfish and fishing industries. (Their early construction phase already has.) The proposed Wasco, California plant was voted down by citizens because they feared its demands on their precious supply of irrigation water would be too great. The proposed Montague plant

COOLING
TUNNEL

"The neighborhood's shot."

would pre-empt one of the few prime sites for industrial development in a chronically underemployed county.

The conflict and uncertainty associated with the siting process may itself prove a liability. Many years can elapse between a utility's announcement of its intention to build and the actual start of construction. Business-investment decisions—and regional planning—are often stalled for long periods until the uncertainties are resolved.

Local Jobs

Utilities have gone to great lengths to convince the public that nuclear construction offers tremendous job potential. The discussion, earlier in this chapter, of the national employment picture demonstrates just how faulty this claim is. Similarly, faulty claims have characterized estimates of local jobs.

Although the amount of employment required for construction of a nuclear station seems large, perhaps 11,000 person-years for a 1,150-megawatt plant, it offers little indication of just how many jobs will be available to to local workers.[45] Although nuclear-construction employment is spread out over a ten-year period, there are relatively few jobs at the beginning and end of this period. Instead, there is a pulse of very high employment in the middle years.[46] Different skills are required at each stage of construction.[47] The net effect is that the average term of employment is only a couple of years.

Nuclear plant construction requires a high proportion of skilled workers, like steamfitters and electricians. If the employment needs of the plant aren't met by skills and union workers available from the area, the workforce will be brought in from other areas, and the local unemployment rate may be largely unaffected.[48] A case in point is Plymouth, Massachusetts, where the unemployment rate actually remained *much higher* than the county and state averages throughout the construction of the Pilgrim nuclear station (6.2%, local, compared to 4.3%, county, and 3.8%, state, in 1970.)[49]

Most nuclear plants are now built by giant international contracting firms, Bechtel, Brown and Root, etc.[50] These firms have developed their own traveling teams of skilled personnel to perform much of the specialized work. They may or may not subcontract locally.[51] Even operating stations offer few long-term jobs. A typical two-unit plant employs only 128-130 persons.[52] Many of these workers with special skills will come from outside the region.

The prospects for indirect employment, supplying goods and services, are not much better.

In order to reduce transmission costs, most nuclear plants are built relatively close to the loads they serve. Eighty-five percent of the plants now proposed are or will be within 60 miles of a metropolitan center.[53] Few workers will move their families for such short-term jobs.[54] Most workers building these plants can be expected to commute from residences within the metropolitan areas.[55] To the extent that the workforce does not move into the immediate vicinity of the site, the demands upon public services will be reduced, but so will the potential contribution to the rural economy.[56] Most paychecks, and similarly most construction purchases, will flow to the urban regions.

Citing such factors as those discussed above, several studies have concluded that nuclear construction typically offers few jobs to local people.[57]

Environmental and Political Impacts

Indirectly acknowledging the hazards that nuclear reactors pose, Nuclear

Regulatory Commission guidelines now require that plants be sited away from major population centers.[58] As a political columnist for the trade journal *Nucleonics* has commented, "...**rural sites are desirable because of atmospheric dispersion, ease of evacuation, and the fewer people living in the area means there are fewer people to intervene in public hearings** (sic)."[59] The industry is well aware that rural areas rarely have the professional expertise or experience to anticipate adverse impacts of nuclear development or to act effectively in their own behalf.

plant or during transporation. Although these risks are potentially quantifiable in monetary terms, their real significance is in human pain and suffering.

There are suggestions that infringement of local civil liberties may become a problem. Already, Georgia Power and Light has admitted maintaining extensive security files on utility activists in its area.[61] As existing or special security forces are charged with protecting nuclear materials and installations, they are likely to command extraordinary powers.

"This is the spot."
Bonnie Acker

Environmental and political impacts, while substantial, are often so subtle that they are not anticipated by inexperienced people.

Some scientists have argued that residents in the vicinity of a "normally operating" reactor suffer some increased incidence of cancer, and possibly of genetic damage.[60] The risks to health are increased by accidental releases of radioactive material at the

Further problems will probably be seen once it's time to dismantle each plant. Some experts estimate that dismantling plants will cost nearly as much as constructing them.[63] Since most nuclear utilities have made no provisions for funding decommissioning, it is not unlikely that many communities will have to live with the plants permanently. "Mothballed" plants will be conspicuous health hazards and will require constant surveilance. There will be no tax revenues from defunct nukes.

Public perception of the risks of nuclear power is growing; the fact is that nuke plants are recognized as detracting from the quality of life. In addition to the many social and political problems caused by nuclear power, changing attitudes will also affect property values. The day will come when people will no more choose to live near a nuke plant than they would choose to eat DDT or breathe asbestos.

Summary

The socioeconomic impact issue is becoming increasingly important in the overall evaluation of nuclear power, and especially so in siting decisions.[64]

Neither utilities nor regulators are anxious to build nuclear plants in the face of local resistance. Vigorous local opposition highlights many of the problems that they would prefer to gloss over. Public recognition of these problems will turn the utility industry's "technical considerations" into the political issues they should be.

A nuclear utility may make promises of jobs and taxes, but a community has no guarantee that they will be fulfilled. The many economic uncertainties that plague the industry could impose considerable instability on a small community. The many risks to health and safety associated with reactor operation could have devastating consequences. Whatever the future holds, residents of a community sacrifice a substantial measure of control over their own lives in a gamble they can ill afford.

Prepared by Nancy Folbre, Tom Harris

No one "should freeze in the dark!"

Footnotes

1. Opening Statement by Senator Edward M. Kennedy, Subcommittee on Energy, Joint Economic Committee, "Creating Jobs through Energy Policy," press release, 16 March 1978.

2. *Statistical Abstract of the U.S.*, (Washington, D.C., U.S. Dept. of Commerce, U.S. Census, 1977).

3. *A Time to Choose: America's Energy Future*, Ford Foundation Energy Policy Project (Cambridge, Ma: Ballinger Publishing Co., 1974).

4. Edison Electric Institute, 1973, cited in Schipper, *Energy Conservation: Its Nature, Hidden Benefits, and Hidden Barriers* (Berkeley: Lawrence Berkeley Lab. and U. of Calif. at Berkeley, 1 June 1975).

5. Ron Lanoue, *Nuclear Power Plants: The More They Build, The More You Pay* (New York: Center for the Study of Responsive Law, 1976). Wash.

6. Skip Laitner, "The Impact of Solar and Conservation Technologies Upon Labor Demand," paper presented to the Conference on Energy Efficiency, Washington, D.C. 20-21 May 1976.

7. Gail Daneker, Richard Grossman, *Jobs and Energy* (Washington, D.C.: Environmentalists for Full Employment, 1977), pp. 9, 10.

8. *Ibid.*, p. 14.

9. *Ibid.*, p. 10.

10. Testimony by William W. Winpisinger, in national president, International Association of Machinists and Aerospace Workers, before the Subcommittee on Energy, Joint Economic Committee, 16 March 1978.

11. "Cancer from Nuclear Sub Work," *Clamshell Alliance News*, March/April, 1978. See also "The Danger of Radiation at Portsmouth Shipyard," *Boston Globe*, 19 February 1978, p. 1.

12. Richard Pollock, "Uncovering Nuclear Cancer," in *In These Times*, 22-28 March 1978.

13. *Clamshell Alliance News, op. cit.*

14. William Boly, "Inside Trojan: Building a Nuclear Lemon," *Oregon Times*, January 1975.

15. "San Francisco: Critical Reactions at High Flux" in *Nuclear News*, January 1978, p. 37.

16. Testimony by A.F. Grospiron, President, Oil, Chemical and Atomic Workers, before Subcommittee on Energy, 16 March 1978.

17. Daneker and Grossman, *op. cit.*, p. 15.

18. *Ibid.*, p. 10.

19. Testimony by Mandine Cooper, Deputy Director, National Urban League's Washington Bureau, before Subcommittee on Energy, 16 March 1978.

20. Daneker and Grossman, *op. cit.*, p. 14.

21. *Ibid.*

22. *Ibid.*

23. James Crotty, Ray Boddy, "The Political Business Cycle," in *Review of Radical Political Economy*, Summer 1974. Another good source on unemployment is *U.S. Capitalism in Crisis*, published by the Economics Education Project of the Union for Radical Political Economics, January 1978. 41 Union Square West, Rm 901, New York, N.Y. 10003.

24. *State and Local Planning Procedures Dealing with Social and Economic Impacts from Nuclear Power Plants*, Battelle Memorial Institute, Human Affairs Research Centers, prepared for NRC, January 1977.

25. Elizabeth Peele, "Social Effects of Nuclear Power Plants," in *Social Impact Assessment*, C.P. Wolf, ed. (Milwaukee, Wisconsin: Environmental Research and Design Association Conference, December 1974), pp. 116-119.

26. National Environmental Policy Act, *Calvert Cliffs Coordinating Committee vs. AEC*, 449 F 2nd 1109, 1128 (D.C. cir. 1971).

27. Massachusetts Energy Facilities Siting Council, the Commonwealth of Massachusetts, *EFSC Staff Review and Findings: Northeast Nuclear Energy Company's Socioeconomic Impact Analysis of the Proposed Montague Nuclear Station* (Boston, December 1977), p. 41.

28. *Ibid.*, p. 44.

29. *Ibid.*, p. 41.

30. Alice W. Shurcliff, "The Local Economic Impact of Nuclear Power" in *Technology Review*, January 1977, p. 46.

31. "Socioeconomic Impacts: Nuclear Power Station Siting," Policy Research Associates for NRC, June 1977, p. 115.

32. Shurcliff, *op. cit.*, p. 45.

33. "Socioeconomic Impacts," *op. cit.*, p. 115.

34. Shurcliff, *op. cit.*, p. 46.

35. *EFSC Staff Review and Findings, op. cit.*, p. 53.

36. *State and Local Planning Procedures, op. cit.*

37. Conversation with Fred Muehl, county planner, Franklin County, Ma., February 1978.

38. "Elma Caught Up in Boom—Paying Price of Progress," *Seattle Post-Intelligencer*, 19 June 1977.

39. D.J. Bjornstad, *Fiscal Impacts Associated with Power Reactor Siting: A Paired Case Study* (Oak Ridge, Tennessee: Oak Ridge National Laboratory, February 1977), p. 10. This is a book-length report; should you want it, request ORNL/NUREG/TM-86.

40. *Rapid Growth from Energy Projects*, (Washington D.C.: U.S. Departments of Housing and Urban Development Office of Community Planning and Development, March 1976).

41. Harbridge House, Inc., *The Social and Economic Impact of a Nuclear Power Plant Upon Montague, Mas-*

sachusetts and the Surrounding Area, Boston, Mass., November 1974.

42. Bjornstad, *op. cit.,* p. 43.

43. M. Knight, "A Connecticut Town Discovers its Nuclear Plant is a Mixed Blessing," *New York Times,* 22 May 1973.

44. Board of County Commissioners, Skagit County, Wisconsin, "Resolution no. 6279" with Exhibits A, B, C, and D.

45. *Environmental Report for the Montague Nuclear Power Station,* Northeast Nuclear Energy Co., March 1975.

46. *Ibid.,* Supplement 7, 4.1.1.2.

47. *Evaluation of Power Facilities: A Reviewers Handbook,* Berkshire County Planning Commission, Pittsfield, 1974, 175.

48. "Socioeconomic Impact," *op. cit.,* pp. 71-72.

49. Shurcliff, *op. cit.,* p. 42.

50. "1978 Nuclear Power Plant Survey," *Electrical World,* 15 January 1978.

51. Shurcliff, *op. cit.,* p. 43.

52. *EFSC Staff Review and Findings, op. cit.,* p. 8.

53. "Socioeconomic Impacts," *op. cit.,* p. 43.

54. *Ibid.,* pp. 59-60.

55. *Ibid.,* pp. 67-77.

56. *Ibid.,* p. 65.

57. *Evaluation of Power Facilities, op. cit.,* p. 175; Shurcliff, *op. cit.,* p. 42.

58. Title 10, Code of Federal Regulations, Part 100.

59. James Hanchett, "Letter from Washington," *Nucleonics,* May 1967.

60. Ernest J. Sternglass, "Strontium-90 Levels in the Milk and Diet Near Conneticut Nuclear Power Plants," draft of report to Congressman D.J. Dodd of Connecticut, 27 October 1977.

61. Tom Baxter, "Georgia Power Has Files on Foes," *Atlanta Journal,* 9 September 1977, p. 1.

62. Ralph Nader and John Abbotts, *The Menace of Atomic Energy* (New York: W.W. Norton, 1977), pp. 140-141.

63. "The Management Report," *Electrical World,* 15 July 1977, 1 and 5 August 1977; Frank Clemente, letter in *Nuclear News,* February 1976.

Resources

• Gail Daneker and Richard Grossman, *Jobs and Energy,* Environmentalists for Full Employment, Washington, D.C., 1977. (Available from EFFE, Room 300, 1785 Massachusetts Ave. N.W., Washington, D.C.   20036. Contributions to EFFE are tax deductible). A well written, readable analysis of the job implications of nuclear power versus alternatives, this pamphlet is one of the best resources around—a must for organizers.

• Harvey Wasserman, "Unionizing Ecotopia," *Mother Jones,* June 1978, pp. 31-38. This article provides a good political analysis of the way in which conflicts between environmentalists and trade union are built into our economic system. It also explains why and how these conflicts can be overcome.

• "Winpisinger," *In These Times,* 17-23 May 1978. This article contains an inspiring speech on energy and unemployment made by William Winpisinger, President of the Machinists and Aerospace Workers. *In These Times* is an independent socialist newspaper, published 50 times a year. Subscription: 1509 N. Milwaukee Ave., Chicago, ILL 60622: $17.50/year.

• The best short summary of the local socioeconomic impacts of nuclear power plants is Alice W. Shurcliff's "The Local Economic Impact of Nuclear Power," *Technology Review,* January 1977.

• The most comprehensive treatment of the issue from a pro-nuclear point of view is *Socioeconomic Impacts: Nuclear Power Station Siting,* prepared for the U.S. Nuclear Regulatory Commission, NUREG-0150, June 1977. Write to your congressperson for a copy of this report.

• An excellent critique of optimistic generalizations often made by nuclear power proponents can be found in the specific case study of the proposed Montague nuclear power plant by the Massachusetts Energy Facilities Siting Council, entitled *Staff Review and Findings: Northeast Nuclear Energy Co.'s Socioeconomic Analysis of the Proposed Montague Nuclear Station* December 1977.

Chapter 4:

In the Political Arena

Nuclear Momentum

It would be a mistake to think that all of the economic problems with nuclear power will stop the continued or even increased use of nuclear powered generating stations. Continued reliance on central power station generated electricity in the absence of a major conservation effort leaves utilities with nuclear as a major option for meeting power needs. Industry is pressing hard for a favorable resolution of nuclear troubles and the Carter Administration is making firm moves towards establishing such a resolution.

Right now the nuclear industry is surviving. With a lead time of 10 to 12 years for nuclear and about 6 years for coal plants, new capacity for the next few years is more or less fixed. Although only 69 reactors are now operable, commitments have been made for an additional 147. Of these, 98 are expected to be in operation by 1985. This means that installed nuclear capacity would more than double, from a present capacity of around 50,000 Mw to a projected 111,000 Mw. This increase would make nuclear's share of electrical generating capacity more than 20%.[1]

Much of the downturn in nuclear orders since 1974 has been the result of a recession in combination with a shift to a lower long run rate of demand for electric power. This has left utilities with substantial over-capacity after their large building programs of the late sixties. So, despite construction cutbacks in the 70s their capacity to generate power has remained adequate. In fact, utility excess capacity at peak demand reached record highs in 1975 and 1976, when it measured 34.4% and 34.5% as compared to the 18 to 20% considered safe by the industry.[2]

This situation can't last forever. Even with demand growing at its new lower rate, new generating capacity of some type is going to be required. Utilities are going to have to begin planning construction of that new capacity soon. It seems generally agreed by spokesmen for the nuclear industry that what happens in the next five years will determine the future of nuclear power. Utilities will have to decide during this period whether they will use nuclear plants to meet at least part of projected electricity demand. **A** spokesman for General Electric, the leading nuclear manufacturer, has said that by the early 1980s there will either be signs that the market is returning strongly or there will be no market at all.[3]

It is also generally agreed in the industry that the key to guaranteeing that this critical period will restore rather than destroy the market is the reduction of uncertainty about the costs and future of nuclear. The sources of this uncertainty have been described above (Sec. 2, Chapt. 2); the most important point is that their solution lies in the political arena. The main factors affecting the uncertainty about the costs of nuclear derive from the questionable solutions to the problems of waste disposal and possible design and site changes. The uncertainty for utilities in planning new capacity derives mainly from their problems in raising enough capital at reasonable prices.

These problems can only be resolved politically. There is no purely technical solution because nuclear power cannot be made riskless. The decision about whether underground "permanent" waste storage is acceptable is a social decision. The decision that current reactor designs are adequate is a social decision. The decision that the impact of a nuclear plant on a particular community is unacceptable is a social decision. The actual nature of this political decision-making process is still being determined. Nuclear opponents are trying to ensure that the decision-making process involves the people who will be affected. If industry has its way the decision will be made by those who stand to reap the profits from nuclear power, or by those who are sensitive to industry pressure.

Focus on Washington

The federal government is going to have a significant impact on the final fate of nuclear power. The sudden jump in oil prices and the "energy crisis" of the early seventies made it clear that energy supplies would no longer take care of themselves. Since that time, national administrations have recognized that the federal government must play a role in energy planning that is beyond the capacities of any particular industry.

This planning does not take place in a vacuum, of course. A major constraint on available options is the structure of the economy. Under capitalism the control of production rests in the hands of a minority who make decisions about production with the primary goal of maximizing profits. This has several clear implications in the case of the utility industry. Privately owned (or investor owned) utilities provide the bulk of the nation's electrical power. For them, large central power station production is the most profitable way to generate this power. This is the case for two reasons.

First, utilities maximize their profits by maximizing the amount of assets used in power production. Since utilities are guaranteed a fixed rate of profit on their assets, any increase in their assets means an increase in their total profits.

The second reason is control. Centralized generation means that utilities control power production. Decentralized generation in any form including solar, wind or hydro can be established, owned and operated by the individuals and communities that need them. These methods of generation constitute a threat to control by huge utilities or utility-holding companies and thus a threat to the profits that result from such control.

The result is that if national energy planning is not to disrupt the current structure of the utility industry, energy options are relatively limited. Oil imports must be cut in order to reduce U.S. vulnerability to a new embargo and to ease pressure on the dollar in international financial markets. Carter's plan for cutting oil consumption focuses on industrial users of oil. The primary substitute for oil specified in the plan is electricity.

The Carter Plan

Carter's energy plan calls for a substantial increase in electrification. Under the plan 53% of the energy supplied between now and 1985 will be in the form of electricity as compared to its current contribution of only 28%. It will be produced with coal and nuclear plants which are, with oil and natural gas, the only currently viable technologies for central station power generation. In other words, if electric power production is to continue to grow and if power is to continue to be produced by central power stations under the control of privately owned utilities, then the only options are coal and nuclear. From the planner's perspective, there are just too many problems with coal to permit sole reliance on it. For these reasons Carter's plan contains a clear commitment to nuclear energy.[4]

The energy plan initially called for a jump in nuclear's share of electricity production from 9% in 1975 to 25% in 1985. Although the 1985 date may have to be pushed forward a few years, the goal is clear.

The actual implementation of the nuclear alternative will be facilitated by measures to deal with three key areas of nuclear's current troubles: siting and licensing procedures, waste disposal, and utility regulation.

The Siting Bill

The nuclear plant siting bill or the Nuclear Regulatory Reform Act is designed to speed up the licensing and construction of nuclear power plants. It is designed to remove what are, from the utilities' point of view, the critical

uncertainties surrounding the actual implementation of decisions to build nuclear plants. As such it is an absolutely essential part of Carter's plan to ensure the acceptance of nuclear power. When the final draft of the bill was presented to Congress in March 1978, Energy Secretary Schlesinger promised that the bill would cut licensing and construction time from its current 12 years to 6½ years.[5]

The bill's provisions include the establishment of standardized designs for reactors, early site approval, joint construction permits and operating licenses, and limited work authorizations.

Nuclear proponents would have us believe that the length of the licensing and building time is the result of excessive regulation and irrational opponents. The Carter administration represents the bill as simple streamlining. In fact the bill simply ignores substantial outstanding safety issues and bypasses most citizen involvement in the process. Although such involvement is already constrained and has only limited success in actually stopping nuclear plants, interventions in the hearing process have had an impact by forcing real improvements in safety and design.

A **standardized reactor design** is one which has been approved in general and which can then be used as the design for any particular plant without additional hearings. The question is whether it is really possible to have a safe reactor design with current levels of technology.

The current practice of the NRC is to concentrate on specific plant licensings. This focus on specific plants has meant that "generic" safety issues, ones which affect more than one plant, receive less attention. As Robert Pollard noted when he resigned from the NRC in 1976, the "pervasive attitude in the NRC (is) that our most important job is to get the licenses out as quickly as possible and to keep the plants running as long as possible."[6]

There are currently over 200 generic safety issues before the NRC which are not being actively considered. These generic issues are generally not considered unless some unusual event like the Browns Ferry fire forces the NRC's attention. Typically, consideration of these problems means delays in ongoing construction as well as the shut-down of currently operating plants for retrofitting.[7]

The Carter bill's proposal for standardized designs contains no mention of these generic problems and there is no evidence that proposed standardized designs will incorporate solutions to them. However, there is evidence that standardization will mean that serious safety problems represented by outstanding generic problems will be ignored. A former chairman of the NRC (1976-77), Marcus Rowden, contends that the NRC and industry "have made major progress in standardizing design."[8]

Industry spokesmen are even more clear. George L. Gleason, Executive Vice President and General Counsel of the American Nuclear Energy Council put it this way in his recent testimony before Congress. "The basic problem is that for standardization to work there must be acceptance by the NRC of the fact that Lightwater reactors represent a mature technology. It requires a recognition that the current level of technology is safe, economical and environmentally sound."[9]

Standardized designs are not going to make nuclear power plants safe. Repeated design changes forced by intervenors have demonstrated that industry's interest is cost minimization and not maximum safety. Safety costs money and every increase in costs makes nuclear less economically viable. Standardized designs remove the power of local regulators and concerned citizens to assess nuclear reactor safety for themselves. They are, finally, an attempt to permit construction of reactors without continuing interventions and resultant expensive design changes.

Currently, the construction permits for a nuke must be approved for operation in a second set of public hearings. The granting of **limited work authorizations** without hearings means that construction can begin without any public input. Once construction begins and resources are committed, the pressure on regulators for approval increases significantly.

Combining the operating license approval with construction approval removes a step with demonstrated importance in catching serious safety and construction problems.[10]

Early site approval without construction data or plans will create "site banks" which can be drawn on without further hearings. This reduces incentive of local people to get involved in the process. Without knowledge of a utility's plans, objecting to sites could be a waste of time. Early approval will simply make it easier to get sites approved without close scrutiny.

Waste Disposal

Carter has also advanced a proposal on waste disposal, the other major problem plaguing the future of nuclear power. Under the proposal the federal government will take all nuclear wastes and store them in yet to be determined sites. The utilities would pay a one time storage fee. The Department of Energy has estimated that the fee will raise the cost of nuclear generated electricity about 4-5%. They argue that this fee amounts to charging the utilities a price that will cover the real costs of storage. But the true cost can only be underestimated. The plan does not allow the government to retrieve any cost overruns from the utilities. So the difference, which could be enormous, will be paid by taxpayers.[11]

The plan also promises permanent waste storage. Temporary storage will be provided until a permanent solution is found. After 30 years of failures which have included radiation leaks at government and privately managed storage sites, this seems unlikely. Five months after the original plan promised permanent facilities by 1985, the DOE announced that a solution is impossible before 1988. In the same five month period the estimated cost doubled from 2.5% of the cost of nuclear generated electricity to 4-5%.[12] In addition resistance has already begun to proposed permanent sites in 36 states. James L. Larocca, New York Commissioner of Energy said, "I doubt very much if the Federal Government will find acceptance for that proposition anywhere in the United States, least of all in the State of New York."[13]

These proposals all have something in common. In each case the costs and uncertainties of nuclear power are removed from privately owned utilities and reactor manufacturers and transferred to the public. The risks are not miraculously disappearing. They are simply being transferred to the public. The risks to utilities and to reactor manufacturers were not created by regulators or by opponents of nuclear power. Extreme risks to health and safety are an inherent feature of nuclear power. Opponents and regulators have forced the industry to take at least partial account of these risks. They have forced the industry to deal with problems they didn't want to deal with. The Carter proposals are intended to limit the impact of opposition and to ensure that the nuclear industry will not have to pay the real costs of nuclear power.

Utility Regulation

A plan to overhaul the utility regulatory process was an important part of Carter's original bill. Although it was transformed into guidelines for voluntary compliance after frantic last minute lobbying by utilities from across the country, we probably haven't seen the last of it. *Electric World* said "the betting in Washington is that the issue, though stayed, is not dead."[14] The proposal provides an idea of what a comprehensive plan to solve the utilities' financial problems might look like.

The essence of the problem now facing utilities is how to ensure that they will be able to pay their costs and still earn their maximum allowed rate of profit. Rising costs of generating power are a problem for utilities only because they can't be guaranteed that their rates will be raised enough to cover them. The "new breed of regulator," under political pressure from consumers, has been reluctant to grant utility requests for rate hikes. These requested rate hikes would have gone a long way towards relieving the financial pressures on utilities which restricted new construction plans. Profits would have improved and construction of new plants been made more likely.

The Carter proposal would solve the utilities' problem by simply requiring the regulatory commission to charge rates that covered the cost plus profit of the most recent addition to capacity.[15] Massive rate hikes paid by consumers would inevitably result from its introduction. If a utility built a nuclear plant it would be guaranteed that its costs would be covered and that it would earn its profit. The bill would have removed a critical bottleneck in the acceptance of nuclear power.[16]

Other Solutions

There have been a variety of locally oriented proposals which attempt to do much the same thing for utilities. Provisions for CWIP or "Construction Work in Progress" have been passed or proposed in a number of states where nuclear plants are being built. CWIP means that plants would be included in the rate base while still under construction. Consumers would pay higher rates which would yield a profit to investors on capital not yet being used to produce power. Right now, without CWIP, consumers pay rates which yield a profit only on assets actually being used to generate electricity. **With CWIP, consumers are forced to contribute funds which utilities can't raise in other ways to build plants. Consumers are being forced to become investors. They are being forced to guarantee that a rate of profit will be earned on the plant even before it is built. Once again consumers are being forced to bear the risk of nuclear plants, in this case a financial risk.**

A recently proposed plan in New York State embodies another solution to utility cash problems. The seven private utilities in the state have proposed forming a consortium or group, called Empire State Power Resources Inc. (ESPRI) to take over the construction and operation of all new private power plants. The key ingredient in the proposal is a clause which gives the consortium the authority to pass construction costs on to consumers automatically. In combination with the existing fuel adjustment clause, this would give private utilities the right to pass all cost increases on to consumers. Most importantly this pass through would take place automatically and without regulatory hearings or consumer input.[17]

The effect of each of these plans is the same. Quite simply that terrible problem spot for utilities, how to get big rate increases to finance new plants would be solved. In each case there is an automatic pass through of utility costs to consumers. Consumers will be denied the right to a voice in rate hearings. Consumers will be forced to become investors in power plants and consumers will be forced to bear the financial risks in the hopes of getting electricity which investors now bear in the hopes of making a profit.

The plans would remove a critical barrier to the building of new nuclear plants. An almost certain result would be that private utilities would step up construction plans. George P. McNamee, president of First Albany Corporation, an investment banking house with a speciality in utilities, put it quite succinctly in reference to the New York State Plan. "ESPRI is an entity that will exist solely to build power plants. You can fairly assume that if it passes, more power plants will be built. Perhaps more than we need."[18]

Who's Pushing Who?

Those with a stake in the gains to be reaped from nuclear power understand that the battle will be won or lost in the political arena. They are not waiting for Carter to do what is in their best interests. In fact industry fears the power of anti-nuclear activists within the administration as well as those who bring pressure from the outside. Industry tactics reflect their understanding. General Electric's "warning" to Schlesinger in 1977 is only one highly visible example. Spokesmen for all the major reactor manufacturers have stated that "Washington is the key to turning things around for the nuclear industry." Most of the companies now support an intensive high-level lobbying effort. They provide the financial backing for the Atomic Industrial Forum (AIF), the American Nuclear Energy Council (ANEC) and the American Nuclear Society, to name the largest. These are in order, the industry's trade association, its lobbying arm and its professional association. These groups are all engaged in steady lobbying of Congress in support of pro-nuclear legislation.

In addition, some very large companies like GE and Westinghouse engage in independent lobbying. Westinghouse alone employs an impressive list of influential people to plead its case. They include former United States Ambassador to the International Atomic Energy Agency Dwight Porter; former United States Representative from Ohio, Orval Hansen; and former Massachusetts Governor, Endicott Peabody.

Not all of the nuclear industry's efforts are expended on influencing the higher levels of government. The industry has mounted well-financed campaigns to defeat local referenda on the nuclear question. In 1976 initiatives to restrict nuclear power appeared on the ballet in seven states. Instate and out-of-state utilities, nuclear suppliers and other corporations with a stake in nuclear power invested huge sums of money to defeat them.[19] These companies recognized that nuclear power could be slowed down by a political decision and they acted to influence that decision.

Let's Negotiate
The attempt to negotiate with the opposition represents another trend in industry efforts to ensure the acceptance of their aims.

The American Arbitration Association (AAA) has been awarded a grant by the Dept. of the Interior to find ways of resolving "Major energy-environmental disputes." Their goal is to streamline the process of settling environmental conflicts and avoid courtroom litigation through substituting arbitration, mediation and other procedures. Explicit targets of the new methods are conflicts over uranium mining and nuclear plant siting. The AAA will prepare a handbook as a help to "identify, manage and resolve" these disputes.[20]

Those who want to speed up the process of nuclear licensing are unanimous in calling for "less formal" public participation. Carter's licensing bill would require only legislative-style hearings for environmental challenges in place of current courtroom proceedings.

A news feature in an engineering trade journal put the matter in perspective. "If industry is smart it won't ignore (problems with nuclear power). Instead it will join forces, as many have suggested, with moderates on the other side of the nuclear fence who are more critical of nuclear power than they are arbitrarily against it. Together they probably would be able to reduce the risks to manageable levels."[21]

The objective of the move towards negotiation and arbitration is to cut the time and cost now involved in disputes over nuclear power as well as other environmental issues. Arbitration is being introduced explicitly as a means of expediting the introduction of nuclear power. It is designed to remove the nuclear issue from the adversary environment of the courtroom where nuclear opponents have clear legal options and place it in the less formal setting of arbitration where agreement by "moderates" is possible. It is designed to split "moderates" from the ranks of nuclear opponents. The problem with the process of arbitration is that it assumes the existence of some acceptable middle ground between those who are pushing for nuclear power and those who oppose it.

Summary
The nuclear industry is not dead. Their profits are still adequate and their lobbyists work overtime. In fact, if the Carter's plan is successful, the production of nukes could return to the levels of the early 1970s. **The licensing bill and the waste proposal are attempts to**

"solve" the problems of nuclear power by declaring them solved.

Reactor design faults and the lack of any forseeable solution to the waste problem will be ignored so the plants can be built quickly. Public involvement will be limited.

CWIP and other financial schemes will be pushed so that utilities can proceed to order nuclear plants with adequate cash and without interference from consumers who pay the bills.

All is not lost, however. Opposition to nuclear power continues to grow. States are refusing to accept nuclear power plants without adequate waste storage, and they are refusing to store nuclear waste under Carter's "waste management" plan. Consumers are resisting the rate increases and financial ploys required for nuclear construction.

These proposals by Carter and the nuclear industry must pass if the promise of huge profits from nukes is to be realized. They are designed to reduce the uncertainties facing the nuclear industry. Successful opposition to them will help stop nuclear power.

Prepared by Joseph Bowring

Footnotes

1. *Quarterly Report: Energy Information*, Report to Congress, First Quarter 1978, July 1978. DOE/EIA-008/1 (78).

2. Statistical Abstract of the United States 1977, Govt. Printing Office, Washington, D.C.

3. "Commercial Viability: A Complex Issue," *Nuclear News*, February 1978, pp. 55-60.

4. The National Energy Plan, Executive Office of the President, April 1977.

5. *New York Times*, 18 May 1978.

6. Robert Pollard, Letter to Chairman William A. Anders, NRC, 6 February 1976.

7. John Abbotts, PIRG, Summary Statement Before the Subcommittee on Energy and Power, House Committee on Interstate and Foreign Commerce, 9 February 1978.

8. Marcus Rowden, "Licensing of Nuclear Power Plants," AEI Journal on Govt. and Society, January/February 1978, pp. 40-56.

9. George L. Gleason, American Nuclear Energy Council, Statement to House Committee on Interior and Insular Affairs, Subcommittee on Energy and Environment, 15 February 1978.

10. Abbott, *op. cit.*, p. 21.

11. *New York Times*, 16 March 1978.

12. *Ibid.*

13. *Ibid.* "So far, 11 states have barred a nuclear waste repository within their borders, and 15 more are considering such bans, according to the Nuclear Regulatory Commission." Douglas Martin, "Atom Waste Stirs Debate; 11 States Already Bar the Dumps," *Wall St. Journal*, 29 August 1978.

14. "Washington Comment," *Electrical World*, 1 January 1978.

15. The National Energy Plan, *op. cit.*

16. The bill was opposed by a coalition of regulators and utility officials primarily because it deprived them of their independence in important areas of responsibility. They were resisting a bid to centralize authority over utilities in the federal government. Further, the Carter administration made no attempt to persuade utilities that its bill would aid their cause. In fact, the bill had already passed the House before utilities really learned about it. However their subsequent successful organizing ensured its defeat in the Senate and was instrumental in reducing the final bill to a voluntary measure.

17. *New York Times*, 9 April 1978.

18. Dick Kirstchen, "Nuclear Lobbying," *National Journal*, 18 February 1978, pp. 261-4.

19. The case of the 8 June 1976 California iniative illustrates what happened. By the end May, opponents had received over $2.3 million in contributions. The money came from utilities and corporations. California's three largest utilities donated a total of $510,000. They were joined by more than thirty out-of-state utilities which included Carolina Power and Light, New England Electric System, Baltimore Gas and Electric and Consolidated Edison of New York. Bechtel Corp. gave $230,000, G.E. and Westinghouse gave a total of $240,000 and Combustion Engineering gave $35,000. The Bank of America, Atlantic Richfield, G.M., U.S. Steel, Kaiser Industries and Bethlehem Steel chipped in $25,000 apiece. The list goes on but the point is clear. *Business Week*, 7 June 1976, p. 36. *ENR*, 20 May 1976, p. 42.

20. *Public Utilities Fortnightly*, 5 January 1978, p. 5.

21. Anderson, *op. cit.*

COMMENT:

The Politics of Nuclear Power

'WE'RE GOING TO BLOW UP YOUR YARD . . . INTERESTS OF SCIENCE, AND ALL THAT . . . DON'T HAVE TIME TO TALK RIGHT NOW . . . CONGRATULATIONS . . . '

Nuclear power is an issue that touches many aspects of life. It harms the environment. It harms our health and that of future generations. It touches our pocketbooks as we pay the costs of nuclear power, both as ratepayers and as taxpayers.

The use of commercial nuclear brings up two very fundamental political questions. First—should any government or industry have the power to make decisions that can be so costly to so many? Second—should so many material resources, so much brain power, human time and energy by diverted into this energy source at the expense of other urgent social needs?

Nuclear power has not been a major public issue so far in the U.S. for several basic reasons. Its harmful ef-

fects are not immediately recognized. Its workings are veiled in mysterious technical language. And it is mostly controlled and regulated out of public view.

The Invisible Issue
Radiation can't be seen, and the effects of low-level radiation exposure can't be felt immediately. Atomic power does not leave a calling card. There are a lot of carcinogens loose in our environment—how can anyone prove the connection? Although the connection can be shown statistically, if no one looks for these patterns they won't be found.

Another reason that nuclear power has been an "invisible issue" is that nukes are located either on military reservations where privacy for the nuke-builders is assured, or in rural areas. Sites are chosen with an eye towards avoiding possible opposition.

Nuclear power development has been further removed from public view by the atomic establishment's consistent suppression of evidence that might expose problems. Scientists within the AEC have been harassed and forced out when their views did not meet the "party line." Expert advice that goes against the nuclear establishment's grain is ignored; contradictory reports are permanently "shelved."

> It has now become clear that the continuing expansion of the nuclear program to its present size has depended, in substantial measure, on misrepresentation and manipulation of information—much of it safety-related. Research into nuclear safety has been diverted or distorted, and the results of the research concealed or inaccurately reported on a disturbingly large number of occasions.[1]

AEC suppression of dissent is well-documented. Most universities and private research centers depend to some degree on government grants. The federal government's pro-nuclear, no-questions-asked bias of the past 30 years has had a chilling effect on the scientific and academic climate in the U.S.

The public is reputedly very impressed and influenced by scientists. But scientists are not independent, interest- or value-free. For example, in February 1975, 32 "notable scientists" signed a "Scientists Statement on Energy Policy" that supported the government's position of continued nuclear development. The statement did not let on that fully two-thirds of the emminent scientists had personal ties with big business—for example as con-

sultants to GE, General Dynamics, Gulf General Atomic and other corporations heavily involved in building nuclear reactors. More than half the men were actually on the boards of directors of major U.S. corporations, including energy giants like Exxon that are heavily involved in nuclear power and uranium.[2]

Speaking of scientific integrity, Dr. John Gofman had this story to tell:

> For some strange reason, biologists have enjoyed an aura of respectability. There is a group of people one could trust.

> The AEC funded some twenty laboratories for twenty years at a rate of 50 to 90 million dollars per year to study the hazards of ionizing radiation. In that entire period there were probably fewer than 10 pages of studies from that whole effort which even mentioned...possibilities of deaths from cancer from peaceful uses of the atom. When Tamplin and I started to calculate deaths (a task *we* interpreted as our assigned mission) from radiation, the entire AEC, particularly its prominent staff biologists, began to suffer from widespread internal hemorrhages. The garbage with which they endeavored to stem the flow of their bleeding was a sight to behold. So much for how much you can trust the biologists.[3]

Why do scientists go along with the charade that nuclear power is a reasonable and reasonably safe energy source? Number one, says Dr. Gofman is job security. Under tremendous social and peer pressure, people have great ability to rationalize away their own responsibility in any situation.

The atomic establishment is a real "boys club." The revolving door between the nuclear industry and the regulatory agency is well-traveled. And the regulators stand behind their industry, protecting it from outside challenges. For example, after the June 1976 California Nuclear Safeguards Initiative went down to defeat, the General Accounting Office revealed that ERDA had carried on an intensive information program "in an attempt to influence Californians to vote against the referendum."[4] The man who spearheaded the anti-safeguards effort as head of ERDA's San Francisco office, Robert D. Thorne, was then chosen by Schlesinger to run DOE's energy research program. His nomination was confirmed over environmentalist objections. So it goes.

Nuclear power's privileged position of invisibility is changing. Nuclear power is finally becoming a national topic of discussion—and there's a lot to talk about. Nuclear power cuts across divisions of sex, age, race, class, country of origin, religion, and ideology....In some way everyone is affected.

But some are affected more than others. Native Americans, for example. About 55% of U.S. uranium supply is on native lands, on the Navaho and Laguna Pueblo reservations in northwestern New Mexico and on the Spokane Indian reservation in Washington State. Indian people are directly affected by the front end of the fuel cycle: uranium exploration, mining and milling.[5]

Nuclear workers are also especially affected. They and their families, along with the soldiers exposed during atmospheric testing and part-time workers and close nuclear neighbors, have been unnecessarily exposed to radiation. It is important that the jobs of the 140,000 or more workers in nuclear industries be replaced with safer and more productive work.

Why Oppose Nuclear Power?

There are so many dimensions to the nuclear issue that objections to commercial atomic development fall across many political points of view. There are reasons for everyone to oppose nuclear power. Different arguments are compelling to different people.

For example, there are what might be called "conservative" arguments against nuclear power, based on unanswered questions of national security. A typical 1000-Mw nuke contains 1,000 times the radiation of one Hiroshima-type bomb. Although the industry claims that nukes are built to withstand the direct hit of a 747 jumbo jet, no answer is given about the effect of a missile attack. An enemy nation could bomb a nuclear plant and break the containment vessel releasing deadly radiation that could destroy a whole city. So much for national security,

Related to this argument is the terrorism angle. Plutonium and enriched uranium travel our roads and highways every day. Tons of the stuff have already been stolen, and more undoubtedly will be. Already Boston has had an atomic bomb hoax that had the nuke squad (known as NEST—the DOE's Nuclear Emergency Research Team) out in force. In 1976 a Princeton senior produced a blueprint for a model bomb costing under $2,000 that could be built by almost anyone with the motivation and a physics background.[6]

Another rather conservative argument is the insurance problem. In case of an accident, forget it! Present levels of compensation (under the Price-Anderson Act) would return only pennies on the dollar. More probably, a major accident would be termed a national disaster, and taxpayers would foot the bill.

Recent polls have shown that the

aspect of nuclear power most disturbing to most U.S. residents is the waste situation, the fact that no guaranteed long-term method of storage of radioactive waste exists. Related to this is the problem of the transportation of wastes.

Environmentalists are especially concerned about concentration of radiation in the ecosystem and in people as part of it. Thermal pollution is a big worry too.

Religous groups question the moral and ethical implications of nuclear power. In October 1975 the National Council of Churches came out against the fast breeder and a plutonium economy. Many people are opposed to nuclear power on explicitly moral grounds. They question the right of any group of people to condemn others to death—even if the deaths may happen long after and to unknown people.

Then there is the civil liberties issue. What kind of society do we want to live in? Nuclear power is such a dangerous technology that it requires special methods of social control. All aspects of the fuel cycle must be monitored and guarded, including the guards themselves. No security precaution is too great. Since the dangers of nuclear power go on and on—given plutonium's half-life of 24,000 years— the security needed for a safe nuclear powered economy must be guaranteed for centuries to come. But how can a stable future be guaranteed—forever? The prospect seems made to order for an authoritarian system, depending for its survival on what Dr. Alvin Weinberg, former head of the Oak Ridge National Laboratories, has called a "military priesthood."[7]

Each country now has its own AEC that sets standards or, in some cases, actually monitors or operates reactors. Perhaps this

will be sufficient forever. Yet no government has lasted continuously for 1000 years; only the Catholic Church has survived more of less continuously for 2000 years or so. Our commitment to nuclear energy is assumed to last in perpetuity— can we think of a national entity that possesses the resiliency to remain alive for even a single half-life of plutonium-239? A *permanent* cadre of experts that will retain its continuity over immensely long times hardly seems feasible if the cadre is a national body.[8]

The dangers of nuclear power call for tighter national security measures. People who might be a threat to the existing social institutions must be monitored. We already know that antinuclear activitists are suspect in this regard. Phones are tapped, organizations are infiltrated...it's a now familiar pattern. This heightened "security" is why nuclear opponents in Europe have adopted as one common slogan, "Atom State equals Police State." Is this the society we really want?

A Feminist Perspective

Women, as child bearers, are very much affected by the genetic threat that a radiation-filled society represents. Women are still the main "caretakers" in society, caring for the home, the sick and children. We are the ones who are caring for the people who suffer from "permissible" and "tolerable" levels of radiation.

Commercial use of nuclear power is a clear development of a male and wardominated society. It was a wartime discovery, adopted for peacetime uses as a money-maker and a cover for a continued military program. There were other alternatives at the time. Nuclear power was not the only choice. Solar energy, wind power, alcohol fuels, these are not new energy sources. They were known, and even tried to some small extent. But scientific development became screwed as priorities were determined by desires for profit and power. It's time for a change, away from atomic domination and deadly garbage that can't be taken "out."

Natural energy sources—the renewable ones that nature provides—offer us the chance to live in harmony with nature. Why should matter be split creating poisons, when by living in harmony with the biosphere we can get all the energy we need?

To discover is not to mass produce. Nuclear power was commercialized without regard for its implications for human health. The technological achievements thus far are staggering. It's not easy to contain invisible deadly poisons, and what has been done is impressive—technologically. But it's not necessary in the first place. Why do it? The answer, of course, is profit and control.

Natural energy sources, as we will see in the next section, offer us the opportunity for greater community and individual control over the energy we need and use. Their use also reflects a greater respect and understanding for our natural surroundings.

Nuclear power elicits reactions in people that its proponents have labeled "emotional." But angry arguments are made for good reason. To many people, the atomic establishment's callous disregard for human—and all beings—health and genetic future is intolerable. From the inside, of course, nuclear power is "business as usual." Opposition to it is suspect and dangerous and must be put down (if not refuted) at all costs.

Dr. Gofman has suggested that there be a new series of Nuremberg-type trials to place responsibility on those who have led the country—and the world—onto the nuclear path. This would be a good start to a period of intense educational activity and debate. We call for such a period to accompany an immediate moratorium on new nuclear construction and a phase-out of existing nuclear capacity. Let's do it before an accident shuts down the nuclear industry. Let's make sure that the people control energy policy so that this doesn't happen again. For it may happen in the years to come than an administration will reach the wise conclusion that nuclear power "must go." The industry could then be subsidized for losses incurred in closing down, be paid to go into centralized solar technology, and the book closed with "no regrets,"—and no changes.

Part of the national debate needed in this country should address the creation of new social structures that will allow for scientific development with citizen awareness, understanding and control. Atomic energy was sold to the public for private profit and political prestige, with the full facts consistently concealed. The people involved in bringing us nuclear power should now be forced to take responsibility for their acts. Until new structures for approving technological development are created, similar criminal "mistakes" are inevitable.

The real political lesson of the nuclear debacle is that technology is not neutral and that no major steps that affect everyone should be taken without the full knowledge and approval of the people.

Footnotes

1. Daniel F Ford and Henry W. Kendall, "Nuclear Misinformation," *Environment*, vol. 17, no. 5, July/August 1975, p. 17. The examples they gave centered around the AEC's safety studies involving loss-of-coolant accidents, the AEC's

reluctance to implement NEPA, their "charade-like" licensing procedures, and the attempted suppression of the 1964-65 WASH-740 update. AEC Chairman Glenn Seaborg reportedly said about the report: "We didn't want to publish it because we thought it would be misunderstood by the public." —*Ibid.*, p. 27. (From *New York Times*, 10 November 1974.)

2. Letter from Charles Schwartz, professor of Physics, Univ. of California, *Science for the People*, May 1975.

3. John W. Gofman, "A Sane Solution to the Energy Problem," 24 September 1977, Committee for Nuclear Responsibility, Main P.O.B. 11207, San Francisco CA 94101.

4. David Burnham, "U.S. Move to Sway California Nuclear Vote Disclosed," *New York Times*, 16 January 1978.

5. National Indian Youth Council, Inc. 201 Hermosa N.E., Albuquerque NM 87108, September 1978.

6. G. Wayne Miller, "Could Someone Blow up Boston?" *Boston Sunday Globe*, 10 September 1978.

7. Gus Speth, Arthur Tamplin, Thomas Cochran, "Plutonium Recycle or Civil Liberties? We Can't Have Both," *Environmental Action*, 7 December 1974.

8. *Ibid.*

SECTION 3: SOME ALTERNATIVES

Chapter 1:

Conservation

Conservation doesn't mean making do with less. It means doing more with the same amount—improving the efficiency of energy use. Enormous and unnecessary energy waste is built into our economic system because our industrial processes, building practices, and consumption habits were formed during periods when energy was cheap. It will take time, money, and political struggle to eliminate this waste, but the benefits will be enormous. Comprehensive, well planned energy conservation programs will generate new sources of employment, save consumers money, and benefit the environment. In short, *conservation offers an alternative form of economic growth*, not a substitute for it.

Energy conservation is practical *now*. It can meet our energy needs for the space of time necessary to research and develop renewable energy sources. The U.S. could meet all its new energy needs for the next 25 years simply by turning its waste energy to productive uses.[1] Scientists Mark Ross and Robert Williams have shown that,

using only commercially viable technologies, the standard of living in the U.S. in 1973 could have been provided with about 40% less energy.[2]

Big business and government have operated under the assumption that continued expansion of energy use is necessary for economic growth and well being.

> Conservation opponents claim a correlation between cutbacks in energy use and economic stagnation. If this were so, one would expect greater per capita energy use to be associated with a higher standard of living. International comparisons prove this assumption false. Some countries are able to achieve a higher level of income while using much less energy than ours.[3]

Sweden and West Germany maintain a standard of living comparable to that of the U.S. on less than 60% as much energy per capita. Japan uses even less. Only one country—Luxembourg—uses more. (See Box 1)

225

Box 1: U.S./World
Comparison: Energy
and Gross National Product (GNP)

country	per capita energy consumption as % of U.S.
Argentina	14
Bulgaria	31
Canada	83
Colombia	6
Cuba	1
Germany, DR (est.)	52
India	2
Japan	24
Luxembourg	142
Sweden	53
U.S.	100
U.S.S.R. (est.)	39
United Kingdom	48

(source: *Transitions: Toward a New Energy Policy*, Oregon Energy Office) —1968

There are people who believe that energy conservation in the U.S. will take place "automatically" as energy prices rise—that the "free market" can allocate energy efficiently. The fact is, however, there is no such thing as a free market in energy. Large oligopolistic firms and international cartels control our energy economy (see discussion in the Nuclear Power Power Structure). In a competitive economy, price increases usually lead to an increase in supply. In a monopolistic economy, however, high prices may just increase the profits, the power, and the influence of a few companies. Profit maximization doesn't always lead to rational or efficient energy planning.

Price increases are not necessarily effective in increasing the efficiency of energy use. What's more, they have a tremendously unequal impact. When fuel supplies are expensive, the wealthy can buy as much as they want. Many poor and working people are inevitably deprived. Energy use by families that earn less than $8,000 a year is almost entirely for essentials. Households with an average income of $24,500 utilize over two and a half times as much energy as those which average $2,500 (see Box 2).

The real discrepancy, however, comes in indirect consumption of energy—the energy that goes into construction, recreation, and all consumer goods. If all those areas of difference in energy use could be calculated, the difference in energy use between rich and poor would be even greater.[4] To conserve energy, the affluent can certainly be asked to tighten their belts. However, the poor should not be penalized for using energy while affluent consumers or business corporations squander finite energy resources.

Energy conservation is not a technical problem. It is a social problem and a political issue. It is impossible to understand the sources of energy waste without analyzing the institutional context in which energy decisions are made. It will be difficult to change our current patterns of energy use unless there is widespread public support and participation. Energy conservation efforts should be designed to dovetail—rather than conflict with—other social goals.

Box 2: Average BTU's per Household*
By Average Income Class (direct use)

	$2500	$8000	$14000	$24500
Natural Gas	118	129	142	174
Electricity	55	81	108	124
Gasoline	34	85	153	180
Total	207	295	403	478

* millions

(source: *The Energy Consumers*, Dorothy K. Newman, Dawn Day—Ford Foundation 1975, p. 90)

Electricity and Utilities

Of all sectors of the economy, electric utilities have the greatest potential for saving energy. In 1973 they consumed 16% of the total energy budget (Box 3). They are the most rapidly growing consumer of energy among the five major categories of energy users.

The following discussion focuses on possibilities for conservation which go beyond obvious changes in personal behavior, such as turning out the lights or turning down the thermostat. It shows, sector by sector, how energy conservation could be implemented. Because electricity generation consumes so much fuel and creates so many environmental problems, we must not be mislead to think that additional generating capacity is necessary to meet our electricity needs—because it is not. The first sections of this chapter will focus specifically on electricity conservation, while later parts will deal briefly with energy conservation as a general issue.

Between 1960 and 1970, while consumption of fossil fuels grew by 51%, the use of electricity grew by 104%.[5] Current projections indicate continued growth. A 1975 Federal Energy Administration report, for sake of comparison, suggested that electricity consumption will grow at 5.5% per year while total energy consumption will grow at only 2.8%.[6]

Increasing the role of electricity will only decrease the efficiency of fossil fuel utilization. For every unit of energy delivered to the home, 3.3 units of energy must be consumed in fuel at the power plant. It takes 10,500 BTU's to produce a kilowatt in a generating plant. But a kilowatt of electricity in the home provides only 3,412 BTU's of heat.[7] In other words, *two thirds of the potential energy is cast off as waste heat.*

Rather than building new electrical generating capacity, utilities could concentrate on producing electricity more efficiently. Better management could provide part of the solution.

Load Management—The demand for electricity varies considerably over the day, month and year. On a hot and humid summer day, peak power use can exceed twice the minimum demand on the same day. In 1974, an average of less than half of the existing electric generating capacity was utilized, yet twice this average capacity had to be available to meet peak demands.[8]

The implications of electric power produced on such a schedule are profound. A utility usually plans its generating plant construction to meet its highest, or peak, demand. By distributing peak demand more evenly, existing generating capacity would be made much more efficient, and the need for new plants would be considerably reduced.

Such redistribution of demand to reduce peaks and troughs—what in company terms is called "load management"—can be achieved in many ways. Like telephone calls, electricity can be priced according to the time of day it is used. For large users this creates a healthy incentive to use electricity at off-peak times. Innovations in electric rate structures have been placed into effect or are the subject of official study and experimentation in all but 4 states in the U.S. Time-of-day rates have been adopted in 18 states and are being used experimentally in 21 others.[9] Where time-of-day rates have been adopted, industrial firms consuming large amounts of electricity have a significant incentive to reduce their electrical overhead by "load scheduling" at the factory level. This need not be achieved by instituting "graveyard" or all night work shifts, but by staggering shifts to avoid peak periods of residential use.

Peak demand can also be reduced by simple modification in the delivery system—i.e., creating a mechanism that switches off nonessential loads during periods of high demand. The California Energy Commission suggested installation of such control switches on air conditioners. During peak load periods, 70-80% of customers would be subject to periodic reduction in the use of these appliances—no more than 13-15 minutes each half hour for an air conditioner.[10] Involuntary cutoffs like these could easily be misused; they should always be planned in the context of a broader rate policy which ensures a "lifeline" of electricity to everyone, especially to the disabled, low-income, and elderly.

If electrical energy were generated during times of low demand (at night, for instance) and stored for later use at times of high demand, the capacity of the power system would be increased. One method now in use is pumped-storage, where water is pumped uphill using electricity generated during off-peak hours, and is stored in a reservoir. During peak hours, when additional electricity is needed, the water is released from the reservoir and used to generate electricity. But pumped storage has many problems. It is not very energy efficient, and there are few sites where it is environmentally desirable and economically practical to build a large reservoir.

Some more attractive alternatives to pumped-storage are now being developed. Compressed air storage is one possibility. High temperature storage batteries, electro-magnets made of superconductors and flywheels are other options being researched.[11]

Still another option is "storage" of electricity in the home. Peak demands during hot weather might be reduced by using electricity to chill water in a storage tank at night. This chilled water can then be used to cool air the next day. The practicality of this system has been demonstrated by Wisconsin Electric Power Co. in three experimental homes.[12]

Electricity and Industry

Industry consumes 33% of energy used in the U.S. and more electricity than any other sector (see Box 3). Utilities have long offered electricity to industrial users at far lower prices than those individual customers pay. Discounts for large energy users have ranged from 15-35%.[13] These rate structures not only encourage waste, they also discourage manufacturers from generating their own electricity with waste heat expended in the manufacturing process.

Cogeneration—Many industries use steam in their manufacturing processes. Most steam is produced by burning oil or natural gas. But industrial establishments can produce electricity along with the steam. This process is known as "cogeneration"—the combined production of heat and power. The Mass. Governor's Commission on Cogeneration has estimated that the process "can typically save 30% of the fuel that would otherwise

Box 3: U.S. Direct Energy Use Comparison by Sector—1973		
sector	U.S. million BTU per capita	% total energy
Household	50.8	14.7
Commercial	38.3	11.1
Industrial	114.9	33.3
Transportation	85.5	24.8
Electric Utilities	55.1	16.0
Total	**344.6**	**99.9**

(source: U.S. data from *Energy Facts*, p. 46. Hydroelectricity input adjusted to 3413 BTU per kwh)

be needed to produce given amounts of heat and electricity independently."[14] When a factory can provide its own electricity there are additional savings because no electricity is lost in long distance transmission.

A study by energy consultants at Thermo-Electron Corporation shows that by 1985 electricity amounting to more than 40% of today's U.S. consumption could be produced with gas turbines as a co-product of process steam generation at industrial sites.[15] No new technology would be required. West German industry already produces 18% of that country's electricity by cogeneration.[16] Specific studies of many U.S. industries have already laid the engineering groundwork for cogeneration.[17]

Senator Hart (D-Indiana) testified at a 1977 DOE conference that if cogeneration were promoted over the next decade, consumers' utility bills could be lowered 15% and air pollution reduced by 50%.[18]

Electricity in Homes and Businesses

North American families and businesses alike tend to be careless about electricity consumption, partly because of habits formed when electricity was cheap. We also don't really know how much power we are using until the end of the month. If dollars and cents (rather than kilowatt hours) could be read from a meter that was placed in a very visible place, we would all be more likely to notice steadily mounting electricity bills. Tests conducted by Princeton's Center for Environmental Studies found that homeowners provided with daily feedback

on energy consumption cut their electric bills by 10%.[19]

One of the most significant areas of electricity waste is in excessive lighting of stores, schools, public buildings, and businesses. The Illuminating Engineering Society of America has increased lighting standards by 250% since 1950—in the form of recommendations for architects.[20] A number of studies have shown that these recommended levels are both impractical and unnecessary. Lighting systems need flexibility—the potential to provide a great deal of light when needed, rather than the uniformly high levels characteristic of most commercial buildings. For efficiency, desk lamps are far superior to ceiling lights. More realistic lighting standards could reduce lighting loads by as much as 50%.[21]

If reduced lighting needs were met by fluorescent lights rather than the common incandescent bulbs, the use of electricity could be cut even further, to 25% of existing levels.[22] (The incandescent bulb is extremely inefficient, putting out only 17.4 units of light per watt of electricity compared to 50 units for fluorescent tubes.) Fluorescent lamps produce less heat as well, an advantage in warm climates where heat from light bulbs account for much of the air conditioning load in office buildings.

Electric Heat—Electric heat is wasteful and expensive, and is seldom included in houses built at the owner's initiative and to the owner's specifications. However, incentives offered to large developers by electric utilities led to the doubling of the number of all-electric houses placed on the market between 1967 and 1971. Even after the 1973 energy crisis, the number of electrically heated homes continued to increase. In 1975 there were 714,000 new electrically-heated residential units; in 1976 there were 910,000.[23]

The only encouraging news is that many of these electric homes use heat pumps instead of electric resistance heat and electrically-run air conditioners. The heat pump is an ingenious device that uses the evaporation and condensation of a fluid to heat as well as to cool—like an air conditioner that can operate in reverse. Heat pumps are efficient in areas where air temperatures do not often go below 20° F. In mild climates heat pumps need far less electricity to operate than conventional heating and cooling systems. According to one energy expert, heat pumps save at least 30% of total energy and 20-30% of the total costs of using electric resistance heat. Heat pumps can also be easily adapted to work in conjunction with solar heat. In 1972, heat pumps comprised only 5.8% of the total number of air conditioning units sold; by 1977 the figure had jumped to 19.3%.[24]

Electricity and Appliances—Most electric appliances found in the home could be redesigned to use electricity much more efficiently. Water heater, refrigerators, and air conditioners, in particular, consume significant amounts of energy (see Box 4).

U.S. Residential Direct Energy Comparison, 1973

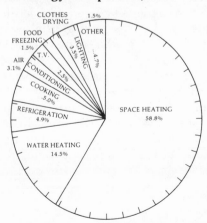

One recent innovation which promises considerable savings on consumption of electricity for hot-water heating is the heat exchanger, a device which "captures" exhaust heat that otherwise would be lost to the environment and recycles it into productive use. By attaching a heat exchanger to their air conditioning units and using the exhaust heat to provide hot water, Florida homeowners have experienced savings in their electricity bills of over 30% per month. The initial investment in a heat exchanger was recovered in a single year. Heat exchangers not only increase the efficiency of air conditioning, but are easily adaptable to use with heat pumps. Residential use alone, it has been estimated, would save Floridians 5.5 billion kilowatt hours each year.[25]

Efficient appliances often have a higher initial cost, turning away consumers who have no convenient way of calculating the actual total cost over the appliance's lifetime. Most people have no way of knowing that a refrigerator costing several hundred dollars can actually use thousands of dollars of electricity over its lifetime, far more than a seemingly more expensive model.

For instance, the least efficient air conditioner on the market consumes 2.6 times as much electricity per unit of cooling as the most efficient one. The least efficient machine costs less to buy, but costs more to operate. If in 1970 all the air conditioners used had been the most efficient models, over 15 billion kilowatt hours of electricity would have been saved.[26]

The National Energy Plan set voluntary targets for 1980 to increase central air conditioning efficiency by 25% with a 47% improvement in refrigeration.[27] The U.S. Department of Commerce is also planning a small experimental program to label home appliances with information including life-cycle costs and energy efficiency.

The California Energy Commission has proposed stiff rules to lower the energy consumption of refrigerators, freezers, and air conditioners. At the time the proposal was made, only one manufacturer was producing appliances that met the standards. **The Commission claims that ten years after the new rules go into effect, enough energy will have been saved to eliminate the need for three large nuclear power plants.**[28]

Fossil Fuels and Industry

Dramatic increases in the price of oil and shortages of natural gas have come as quite a shock to industries which previously considered the cost of energy to be relatively unimportant. Following the price hikes, a number of possibilities for more efficient energy use suddenly became apparent. Some took the form of more careful management. Simple straightforward steps like adjusting combustion equipment and controlling plant ventilation have yielded fuel savings of over 10%.[29] Dow Chemical, Dupont, and AT&T among others have publicized internal energy management programs to decrease energy consumption still further.

There are three principal uses for industrial fuels. Just over 45% is used to produce steam. Direct combustion heating accounts for an additional 29%, and 25% is used for motors, lighting, and electrolysis.[30] The potential of reducing energy needed for direct heating is particularly great. Better insulation of heat-treating furnaces nationwide could save 30,000 barrels of oil a day. In many industrial heat furnaces, 50% or more of the energy used goes up the chimney. Heat recovery equipment could save approximately 450,000

barrels of oil a day.[31] In certain direct heating operations, more than 30% of total fuel consumption could be eliminated.

Aluminum refining presently consumes huge amounts of electricity. Innovations in the refining process are expected to reduce energy needs by almost one-third. The greatest opportunities for energy savings lie with recycling aluminum, a process that requires only 5% as much energy as the original manufacturing.[32] In paper manufacturing, the adoption of the best available technologies could reduce fuel demands by 50%. The use of wood wastes as fuel could slash the industry's demand for fossil fuels to 25% of current levels.[33]

Firms are increasingly coming to realize that some types of investment in conservation may actually be profitable. Investments to save energy are far more effective than investments in new electric generating capacity. A *Business Week* article points out that "New electric power plants range anywhere from $45 billion per quadrillion BTU's for coal to $90 billion for nuclear. By contrast, an investment in capital equipment to save the equivalent amount of energy often costs less than $1.5 billion per quad of energy each year and is sometimes zero."[34]

Fossil Fuels in Homes and Businesses

Residential and commercial buildings use 32% of the U.S. energy budget. According to the American Institute of Architects, much of the energy used is wasted: between 25-50% in older buildings and from 50-80% in newer ones.[35]

The National Bureau of Standards has estimated that improvements in insulation and construction can reduce the energy now consumed in heating and air conditioning by 40-50%.[36]

It's interesting that older buildings, even though they tend to be less well insulated, are more energy efficient than most new ones. One reason is that in the days before air-conditioning builders paid a lot of attention to natural currents and air flow to ensure that cooling breezes would circulate in homes and other buildings. Walls were usually thick to protect against the elements as well as to retain cool air in summer. Now it is standard for office buildings and many urban apartment houses to have "climate controlled" air circulation systems totally dependent on internal air-conditioning and heating units. Windows are often built so that they can't be opened. In addition, office buildings have excessive lighting. In some areas heat from lighting alone accounts for as much as 60% of the air-conditioning load in office buildings.[37] Excessive lighting and airconditioning are two reasons why the World Trade Center towers in New York City consume as much electricity as a city of 100,000 people. The tower builders got a 99-year contract from Con Edison for cheap, bulk-rate electricity. Without it the project would have been too costly.

Space Heating—Space heating and cooling account for about 33% of the U.S. energy pie.

Dramatic reduction in energy use can be achieved through better design of new buildings. The Pennsylvania Power and Light Company's experimental low energy house would reduce energy use by as much as two-thirds compared to ordinary homes. Here the California Energy Commission has taken the lead. By 1985, its new building performance standards will have saved 15 billion kilowatt hours of electricity and 100 billion cubic feet of natural gas—a $760 million saving in utility costs for building operators.[38]

Although meaningful for the future, the contribution that new houses can make is still limited. The stock of housing in the U.S. is so large that the number of new homes built in a year is just 1-2% of the total.[39] For this reason, retrofitting—the installation of energy-conserving devices on existing buildings—will be particularly important. "If all homes in 1975 had the 'economic optimum' amount of insulation," say scientists Hirst and Moyers, "energy consumption for residential heating would have been reduced 42%."[40]

Easy improvements include plugging leaks in existing buildings with insulation and weatherstripping, and installing storm windows and storm doors. In 1975 only 46% of U.S. homes had storm windows and doors, and only 74% had any form of attic insulation.[41] Every building must be examined carefully to see where heat is being lost and how conservation efforts can best pay off. From improving furnace maintenance to fixing cracks in windows and doors, conservation efforts begin at home; added up, they can have a tremendous cumulative effect on total energy use and householders' energy bills.

Conservation Creates Jobs
(DOE-78-11347)

Food Production

In our highly mechanized agricultural system, it takes an amazing 2,000 trillion calories of fuel to provide about 252 trillion calories of food.[42] Energy is used not only for machinery, but also for irrigation and the production of chemical fertilizers. Many of these uses of energy have alleviated part of the drudgery and risk of commercial farming. But others have been thoughtlessly promoted by agribusiness firms that had an eye only for profitable sales. In some cases, new mechanical innovations (such as the tomato harvester) were developed with taxpayer money for the explicit purpose of breaking the power of farmworkers unions.[43]

A reasonable program to conserve energy in agriculture could develop ways of integrating new innovations with good employment policies—instead of pitting farmworkers against machines. Agricultural equipment should be redesigned to meet rigorous safety standards as well as to save energy. Chemical fertilizers can be supplemented by organic wastes. Chemical pesticides would only be used as part of an integrated pest control program which includes nonchemical, biological methods.

Agriculture itself accounts for a very small part of the total energy that goes into U.S. food production: 18%. (See Box 5) If overrefining, overprocessing, and overpackaging were eliminated in food processing, much energy could be saved.

Transportation

Transportation consumed 29% of all the energy used in the U.S. in 1977. If indirect consumption is also counted—manufacturing, highway and parking garage construction, and so on—then the automobile alone used almost 21% of that 29%.[44] The possibilities for

Box 5: Energy Use in U.S. Food Production	
activity	% of total use
Food Processing	33%
Households	30%
Agriculture	18%
Wholesale & Retail Trade	16%
Transportation	3%

(source: Dennis Hayes, *The Case for Conservation,* p. 17)

restructuring our inefficient modes of transportation are tremendous.

The federal government has played a major role in influencing transportation options:

> In 1956, under intense lobbying from the automobile and construction industries, Congress created the Highway Trust Fund. Nourished by taxes on gasoline and auto parts, the Fund has contributed over $100 billion to interstate and local highway construction. No such funds existed for public transportation networks, and states got a clear message from the federal government: "Build highways and we'll pay 90% of the cost; build public transit and you're on your own."[45]

Highway construction continues to receive about $7 billion a year—relative to $1 billion a year on mass transit. If the automobile were to decrease in importance, many major corporations would lose their growth potential. Yet it is becoming increasingly clear that what is good for General Motors is not necessarily good for the country. In fact, General Motors played a central role in shutting down the efficient electric trolley systems which once served many major U.S. cities. Along with Firestone Tire, they bought out

**U.S. Transportation
Direct Energy Comparison**

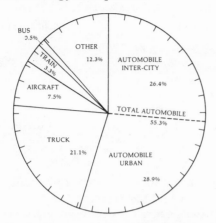

BUS
2.5%

OTHER
12.3%

TRAIN
3.3%

AIRCRAFT
7.5%

AUTOMOBILE
INTER-CITY

26.4%

TOTAL AUTOMOBILE
55.3%

TRUCK
21.1%

AUTOMOBILE
URBAN

28.9%

the companies and converted them to buses, ensuring a profitable market for their own products.[46]

Trains and buses are far more energy efficient than trucks, cars, or planes, but these comprise the smallest slices in the transportation energy pie (see Box 6). Over 70% of all employed household heads commuting by car say public transport is not readily available either at home, at work, or both.[47] Energy conservation in the transportation sector should include subsidies to

mass transit (to the same degree as highways, if not more) and an overhaul of the nation's railroads for high speed passenger service and more efficient freight hauling.

In 1971, 55% of all gas used by cars went for urban trips of one mile or less.[48] More efficient town planning could cut down on wasteful and pollution-producing short trips by integrating stores with housing, connecting work places with public transportation routes, developing bicycle paths and pleasant urban walkways. Many Americans would enjoy the opportunity to combine exercise with shopping and commuting.

There is room for improvement in all existing forms of transportation, including automobiles (see Box 7). Just filling up more seats makes an enormous difference. The simple "technical fix" of increasing auto mileage to 30-35 miles per gallon cuts a car's energy needs in half. However, continued dependence on the automobile will probably bring gas rationing and price increases in its wake.[49]

**Box 7: Actual and Minimum Possible
Energy Use Per Passenger Mile, by Transportation Mode, 1970**

mode	Actual BTU's/ passenger mile	% seats used	Possible BTU's/ passenger mile	% seats used
Intercity:				
Bus	1600	46%	740	100%
Railroad	2900	37%	1100	100%
Automobile	3400	48%	1600	100%
Airplane	8400	49%	4100	100%
Urban:				
Automobile	3800	20%	760	100%
Public Transit	8100	28%	2300	100%

(Source: Newman and Day, p. 78. See fn 4.)

Obstacles

If energy conservation is really so simple, why can't we just "sit back and let it happen?" Unfortunately, there are a number of obstacles to conservation built into our economic system. The utility industry itself has exerted considerable influence against conservation. Historically, growth has been linked to profitability for utilities. Although the escalating costs of the last few years have reversed this association, utilities still tend to see growth as the main avenue to higher profits.[50] Utility representatives continue to make pronouncements that conservation cannot make a significant contribution to the nation's electric power needs.[51] Most utilities have instituted conservation programs begrudgingly, in response to pressure from citizens' groups or the courts. While the industry has organized a National Energy Watch to promote conservation, it has been less than enthusiastic in the pursuit of its modest conservation goals.

The federal government has taken a similarly ambivalent stand. The National Energy Plan calls for a reduction in the annual growth of energy demand from 2.5% to 1.8% and a reduction in the annual growth of electrical demand from 5.2% to 4.5%.[52] Such figures represent a token endorsement of conservation, not a full commitment. Many of the energy conservation measures suggested by the current administration rely upon increased taxes on gasoline and oil. Such taxes will definitely decrease the demand for energy, but they will also impose significant hardships on the unemployed as well as average working people. While the new bill calls for income tax deductions for homeowner's investments in such items as insulation and storm windows, these are trivial compared to the investment tax credits and accelerated depreciation allowances which may cover as much as 40% of the cost of a large power plant facility. Federally funded research into conservation has been minimal. In 1977 the DOE allocated a mere 4.6% of its budget to conservation research.[53]

Theoretically, private businesses should be quick to seize opportunities to cut costs through conservation. However, on the average, energy is a small part of industry's costs—only 10%. Many firms lack the capital necessary to make new investments, and many have large investments in buildings and machinery which they will be reluctant to write off, no matter how inefficient. In addition, electricity is made available to firms at a price based upon the average cost of generating electricity, despite the fact that the costs of electricity from new plants are considerably higher. Even though an investment in conservation could provide more energy at a lower cost than an investment in new generating capacity, utilities' pricing policies continue to make it more expensive for a firm to invest in conservation.[54]

A rapid increase in the efficiency of energy use in the U.S. will not happen until we can mobilize the resources necessary for extensive research, education, and implementation. Increases in the price of energy and electricity have imposed hardships on many, but have not motivated an adequate response from either industry or the average consumer. Most people simply don't have the experience necessary to calculate the *real costs* of lack of insulation or inefficient appliances. People who are aware may not have the money available to invest in conservation—even if it is deductible from their income tax. Landlords have no incentive to invest in insulation or storm doors if their tenants are the ones who pay the oil and electric bills.

A tenant would be foolish to invest money in a house when (s)he could be forced to leave.

Possibilities for Action

Initiative for effective conservation programs can be channeled into programs which are being developed on the state level. The Energy Policy and Conservation Act of 1975 authorized a three year, $150 million federal grants-in-aid program to assist states in developing and carrying out their energy conservation plans. By early April 1977, all 50 states had prepared state energy conservation plans.[55] Various policies of the California Energy Commission, discussed earlier in this chapter, are a case in point. Colorado is planning to develop a statewide bikeway program as well as institute staggered work hours and a four day work week (possibly) in metropolitan areas. Massachusetts added strict energy conservation requirements to the state building code for all new construction after fall 1977. Maine's plan included public education programs, energy audits for buildings, workshops for business and industry, and a proposal to institute a load management study with the state's public utility company. In New York, Gov. Carey has suggested a requirement that a seller furnish a home buyer with both a copy of the previous year's fuel bills and an assessment of the building's energy efficiency.[56]

A number of successful programs have been developed on the municipal level. The city of Seattle, Washington commissioned a study of alternatives for its municipal electric company, ranging from an all-electric local economy to zero-electric sales growth by 1990. Seattle citizens learned that a full-scale conservation program in that city would eliminate the need for 840 megawatts of electric capacity.[57]

The town of Winona, Minnesota devised a comprehensive conservation plan with the University of Minnesota that would make the town energy self-sufficient by the year 2000. The plan called for conservation measures, use of solar, wind, and other alternate energy sources, and "the gradual evolution of a more labor-intensive, less energy-consumptive economy."[58]

Davis, California, with a population of 34,000, has launched a far-reaching program of energy conservation that includes extensive bike lanes, town-wide recycling, and a building code geared to solar construction and retrofitting. Since 1973, the town's electrical consumption has dropped 10%, and its goal for 1985 is a 50% cut.[59]

A more immediate approach was taken by the city of Los Angeles when it faced severe fuel shortages during the 1973-74 oil embargo. The mayor and city council drew up an ordinance designed to cut electrical consumption in two phases. First, residential consumers were to cut their use by 10% and commercial users by 20% for a specific period of time that corresponded to the previous year. Under Phase Two, residential use was restricted by 12%, industrial use by 16%, and commercial use by 33%. The penalty for excess use was a surcharge of 50% on the entire bill for the first period violation, and cutoff for subsequent violations.

The regulations were tough and the fines were high, but they didn't prove too difficult to meet. People's response to the ordinance was remarkably positive. Instead of the expected 12% reduction in Phase One, use fell by more than 17% in the first two months. A Rand Corporation study showed that most establishments maintained the reductions they first made during the period the ordinance was in effect—both for economic reasons and because they could operate satisfactorily with less electricity.[59]

Local efforts have just begun to scratch the surface of the possibilities for energy conservation. One thing is clear though—conservation programs can and should take place on the grass-roots level. They can't simply be imposed from above in the form of price increases, or left up to reluctant electric utilities. Innovative programs need to be designed to provide good jobs and to win the support and participation of working people. The longer it takes to make serious conservation programs a reality, the harder it will be to forge a non-nuclear future.

Prepared by Nancy Folbre, Anna Gyorgy

Footnotes

1. Denis Hayes, *Energy: The Case for Conservation*, Worldwatch Paper #4, January 1976, p. 7.

2. Marc H. Ross, Robert H. Williams, "The Potential for Fuel Conservation," *Technological Review*, February 1977, p. 55.

3. Nancy Jacobs, "Conservation: The Untapped Option," *The Power Line*, January 1972, vol. 2, no. 7, p. 4.

4. Dorthy K. Newman, Dawn Day, *The American Energy Consumer*, Report to the Energy Policy Project of the Ford Foundation. (Cambridge, Ma: Ballinger Publishing Co., 1975), p. 90.

5. Roger F. Naill, George A. Backus, "Evaluating the National Energy Plan," *Technology Review*, July/August, 1977, p. 52.

6. *Ibid.*

7. Project Independence, *Energy Conservation in the Manufacturing Sector, 1954-1990*, Federal Energy Administration Task Force Report, p. 3.

8. Jacobs, *op. cit.*, p. 4.

9. *Air Conditioning, Heating and Refrigeration News*, 20 March 1978.

10. *Ibid.* 20 March 1978.

11. Arthur L. Robinson, "Energy Storage: Using Electricity More Efficiently," in *Energy Use, Conservation, and Supply*, Phillip H. Adelson, ed., American Association for the Advancement of Science, 1974.

12. *Air Conditioning, Heating, and Refrigeration News*, 25 July 1977.

13. Jacobs, *op. cit.*, p. 4.

14. Daniel Yergin, "An overlooked source of energy," *Boston Globe*, 18 September 1978. "Today, we have two independent energy systems. One produces electricity at central power stations and ships it over wires to homes and factories. The other produces steam at factory sites for industrial processes. The amount of energy wasted in having these two systems separate has been estimated as equivalent to 7 million barrels a day of oil—which in turn is about the level of U.S. oil imports per day."

15. Elias P. Gyftopoulos, "Energy Conservation and a Healthy Economy," *Technology Review*, June 1977, p. 32.

16. *Ibid.*

17. G.N. Hatsopoulos, R.W. Sant, Elias P. Gyftopoulos, T.F.Widmer, "Capital Investment to Save Energy," *Harvard Business Review*, March-April 1978.

18. Proceedings of the Energy Research and Development Administration Conference on Cogeneration and Integrated Energy Utility Systems, Washington, D.C., 3 June 1977.

19. *Air Conditioning, Heating, and Refrigeration News*, 6 March 1977.

20. Lloyd J. Dumas, *The Conservation Response*, (Lexington, MA: D.C. Heath and Co., 1976), p. 90.

21. *Ibid.*, p. 94.

22. *Ibid.*, p. 100.

23. *Air Conditioning, Heating, and Refrigeration News*, 27 June 1977.

24. *Ibid.*, 5 December 1977.

25. *Ibid.*, 25 July 1977.

26. Lee Schipper, "Toward More Productive Energy Utilization," paper prepared for U.S. Energy Research and Development Administration, Energy and Environment Division, Lawrence Berkeley Laboratory, University of California.

27. *Air Conditioning, Heating, and Refrigeration News*, 20 February 1978.

28. "A Regulatory Shock for Appliance Makers," *Business Week*, 26 July 1977, p. 46.

29. Charles A. Berg, "Conservation in Industry," in Adelson, *op. cit.*, p. 27.

30. Hayes, *op. cit.*

31. Berg, *op. cit.*, p. 29.

32. Hayes, *op. cit.*

33. *Ibid.*

34. "Will Energy Conservation Throttle Economic Growth?" *Business Week*, 25 April 1977, p. 73.

35. Jacobs, *op. cit.*, p. 5.

36. Dumas, *op. cit.*, p. 100.

37. Schipper, *op. cit.*

38. *Air Conditioning, Heating, and Refrigeration News*, 18 July 1977.

39. Newman, Day, *op. cit.*, p. 45.

40. Eric Hirst, John C. Moyers, "Efficiency of Energy Use in the U.S." in Adelson, *op. cit.*, p. 18.

41. U.S. House of Representatives, Committee on Ways and Means, statements submitted on Administrations' Energy Proposals, June 9, 1977.

42. Albert J. Fritsch, Linda W. Dujack, Douglas A. Jimerson, "Energy Used in Production, Processing, Delivery, and Marketing of Selected Food Items," in *Energy and Food*, Center for Science in the Public Interest, C.S.P.I. Energy Services, VI, 1975, p. 1.

43. "Growers Prefer Machines to UFW Members," *Dollars and Sense*, March 1978.

44. Hayes, *ibid.*, p. 26.

45. "Mass Transit—Not for the Masses," *Dollars and Sense*, November 1975.

46. *Ibid.*

47. Newman and Day, *op. cit.*, p. 78.

48. Dumas, *op. cit.*, p. 107.

49. Carter Henderson, "The Inevitability of Petroleum Rationing in the United States," A Princeton Center for Alternative Futures, Inc., Occasional Paper, April 1978.

50. W.R.Z. Willey, "Energy Conservation, Capacity Expansion, and Investment Finance: The Case of Pacific Gas and Electric Company," Environmental Defense Fund Prepared Testimony (Amended Application nos. 55510).

51. See summary of speech by Karl H. Rudolph, Chairman of Edison Electric Institute, in *Air Conditioning, Heating, and Refrigeration News*, 20 March 1978.

52. Naill and Backus, *op. cit.*, p. 52.

53. Ralph Nader and John Abbotts, *The Menace of Atomic Energy* (New York: W.W. Norton and Co., 1977), p. 279.

54. Hatsopoulos, et. al., *op. cit.*, p. 39.

55. Ken Bossong, "Grassroots Energy Planning," Center for Science in the Public Interest, 1757 S Street, N.W., Washington, D.C. 20009.

56. *Ibid.*

57. *Ibid.*

58. Jacobs, *op. cit.*, p. 6.

59. James Ridgeway, "A City's Energy Saving," *New York Times*, 12 January 1978.

60. J.P. Acton, M.H. Gransbord, P.J. Weinschrott, *Electricity Conservation Measures in the Commercial Sector: The Los Angeles Experience*, Rand Report, R-1592-FEA, September 1974.

Resources—Conservation

- *A Time to Choose*, Ford Foundation Energy Policy Project, (Cambridge, MA: Ballinger, 1974).
- *Reader's Digest Complete Do-It Yourself Manual* (Pleasantville, NY: The Reader's Digest Association), 600 pp. 1973, $16.95.
- Floyd Hockok, *Home Improvements For Conservation and Solar Energy*, (St. Petersburg, FL 33743), 1977. (paper $6.80, cloth $16.00)
- *Guide to Energy Conservation in Public Buildings*, Ontario Ministry of Energy. (416) 965-3246.
- Roger Peters, *Techniques of Community Energy Conservation*, Consumer Interest Study Group, Consumer and Corporate Affairs, 15th floor, Zone 4, Phase 1 Place du Portege, Hull, Quebec k1AOCG
- *Questions and Answers About Energy Conservation in Schools*, Education Facilities Laboratories Inc. 850 3rd Ave., New York, NY 10022.
- *Ideas and Activities for Teaching Energy Conservation, Grades 7 - 12*, University of Tenn. Environment Center, 1977, 225 pp. Free from Tenn. Energy Authority, Suite 250, Capitol Hill Bldg., Nashville, TN 37219.
- Citizens' Energy Project, 1413 K Street, N.W. Washington, D.C. 20005: *The Contrasumers* (actions for home and community), 195 pp., 1975, $3.50; "Industrial Energy Conservation," 10 pp., 1978, $.85; "Energy Conservation— What You Can Do," 11 pp., 1978, $.90.

See also sources mentioned in footnotes.

Chapter 2:

Recycling

The U.S., with 7% of the world's population, consumes 35% of the world's resources and generates more than half of its garbage! Recent national figures estimate that each person in this country generates an average of 3.2 pounds of trash a day. Of this, 25% is glass and another 25% includes paper products and newspaper.

The U.S. is drowning in trash. Landfill sites are becoming harder to find. Taxes for municipal garbage service are going up. In fact, the average cost for collecting and disposing of solid waste runs $24-30 a ton—a figure that the Environmental Protection Agency says is twice the cost of garbage service eight years ago. This is only one of the hidden costs of trash. Other include the price we pay for highway clean-up and litter control.

Solid waste became a real problem with the introduction of disposable packaging. Back in the days preceeding the double-strength sack at the supermarket, pre-packaged cuts of meat and produce, or the six ounce cup of yogurt,

folks went to the store with their own cloth bags and filled them with merchandise right off the shelf or out of the barrel. Many areas of the world still operate this way. Beer and soft drinks are produced and bottled by local concerns using returnable, refillable bottles; milk is delivered by the local dairy in returnable, refillable bottles. In much of the world, plastics just don't exist. In the U.S., plastics are the up-and-coming source of packaging for just about anything you can name, from margarine to soda.

In 1971, packaging used 47% of the U.S. paper production, 14% of aluminum production, 75% of glass, 8% of steel, and 29% of plastic production.[1]

While a plastic container is lighter, less breakable, and possibly stronger than its paper, glass, or metal counterpart, it also stands out in another way: it's very difficult to reuse and nearly impossible to recycle. It usually winds up getting thrown "away."

About twenty years ago, recycling was a word heard only in certain industries. Papermills, steel factories and glass factories have always taken everything left over from a production run, as well as all the not-quite perfect items, and reused them. For the consumer as well, the standard word was "reuse." Soda and milk bottles were returned to be refilled. Containers were made to last and serve several different functions. People kept them and used them around the house.

Until the mid-60s, returnable bottles were the rule, not the exception. The rise of no-deposit/no-return bottles and aluminum cans came hand-in-hand with the increasing role of large, monopolistic firms in the beverage industry. Anxious to cut labor costs, and armed with enormous advertising budgets, they used the one-way throwaways to up prices and cut the bother and labor involved in handling returnable bottles.

In the 1950s there were 300 breweries in the U.S.; now there are under 100. Soft drink bottles are down from 5,200 in 1947 to 2,300 in 1970. Besides the loss of jobs and locally-run businesses, the trend toward ever-increasing concentration in the beverage industry and the use of throwaways has meant an extra several million tons of reusable materials thrown away by consumers annually and 224 trillion BTUs of energy wasted in additional production and transportation.[2]

There have been two nationwide responses to this expensive waste. One is the setting up of local recycling centers, the other, statewide and national efforts for bottle bills that would bring back the refillable bottle by law.

Why Recycle?

People are recycling because it is an immediate, short-term response to the waste now occurring in this country.

People who save their bottles, newspapers, cans, and other items return them to recycling centers. From the centers, materials go to manufacturers who either reuse them or sell them in bulk elsewhere.

The aluminum recycling process saves 95% of the energy it takes to smelt new aluminum from virgin materials.

Old newspapers can be recycled into new newsprint and paperboard for packaging. Newsprint is now being chemically treated and used as building insulation.

There are undoubtedly numerous additional uses for recycled materials that could be developed.

Along with volunteer programs, recycling can be instituted at the town level. Local Boards of Health are generally given total jurisdiction over solid waste. They can simply dictate: no glass goes in the dump; no newspapers will be picked up with regular household trash, etc.—thereby forcing people to recycle. The standard participation that can be expected from a voluntary separation program is 25%. Towns that have imposed mandatory recycling have participation rates of about 75%, with lower disposal costs.

Bottle Bills

Although recycling programs keep some glass and cans out of dumps and off the roadsides, they are basically an inefficient and only partial solution to the problem—at least for glass and aluminum cans. Increasingly, people are seeing the wisdom and necessity of banning aluminum cans and requiring returnable, refillable bottles. A 1975 public opinion poll found that 73% of those surveyed favored bottle bills.[3]

A national deposit system would save the equivalent of 81,000 barrels of oil per day, and as much electricity as the combined use of NYC and Chicago![4]

A uniform bottle bill could reduce steel consumption by 1.5 million tons per year, and aluminum (an intensive user of electricity) by 400,000 tons annually. Industrial air pollution would be down by 750 million to 1.2 billion pounds (of yuck) annually, and 140-210 million pounds of wastes would be kept out of our waterways.[5]

With all this wonderful savings and the majority of Americans seemingly in favor, why don't we have a national bottle bill? The answer of course is that there are powerful and rich economic forces that would be hurt—like the container industry. According to beer magnate William Coors, the industry has spent $20 million on fighting bottle bills. In Dade County, Florida, where a bill was rejected 132,000 to 98,000, industry outspent citizen groups $180,000 to $1,742.

Manufacturers may have the bucks on their side, but they certainly don't have the facts. They claim, for instance, that jobs will be lost. And in some cases they will be. EPA Deputy Administrator Barbara Blum estimates that between 4,900 and 10,400 jobs might be lost nationally in the glass container production industry, and between 14,200 and 22,000 in metal can manufacturing. But these losses would be offset by the 80,000 to 100,000 new jobs that would be created, mainly in the distribution and retail sectors of the economy.[7]

(Credit: *Environmental Action*, 1978)

As of spring 1978, five states had passed bottle bills—Oregon, Maine, Michigan, Vermont, and Connecticut. Although Carter's energy plan did not mention a bottle bill, there has been a lot of pressure building for national legislation. It makes sense. There have been bottle bills before every state legislature in the country. Probably there will be national action after a few more states adopt the bill, to avoid the confusion of having different regulations in every state. All this work to get back to where we used to be!

The Other 94%

If throwaway bottles and cans make up 6% of the nation's garbage, what do we do about the rest?[8] There's step-by-step approach that begins long before the trash containers. It starts at the point of purchase with the question, "Do I really want/need that?" The next question is, "Do I really want/need it in that particular container/package?" And then, "Is this same type of product available in a reusable container, or one that's easily recyclable?" If every consumer asked these questions before making any purchase, our solid waste problems could be reduced by about one-third.

Excess packaging wastes materials and energy. It should be kept to the absolutely necessary minimum by law. In the meantime, every kitchen, pantry, or back porch can be turned into a miniature recycling collection center, with separate containers for recyclable items, and a general "away" for the stuff that can't be recycled or reused. (Already) a small industry has been created to produce stacking bins specifically designed to handle recyclable material and save space in the kitchen.

Paper should be recycled, in towns and at business establishments that are heavy users—like the federal government!

In countries of the world with fewer raw materials to waste and systems oriented towards conservation and against profit, recycling is complete. In China, almost everything is returned when broken or "used up" to area redemption centers, where all materials are recycled or reused in some way.

However, in the U.S. one new solution to the waste problem is "resource recovery" incineration.

This massive closed system burns everything and uses the heat to spin turbines to generate steam or electricity—thereby "recovering the resources" of the trash. At this writing, there are about 15 such plants in operation throughout the country, all in major metropolitan areas. An equal number is planned for the near future.

There are several major drawbacks to these incinerators. First, they are costly to construct. Second, they require massive diets of trash to operate at economic efficiency. A large plant, capable of handling 1,000 tons of trash per day, costs about $50 million; a relatively small unit that handles 100 tons per day costs about $2 million. In addition to cost, there are numerous operational kinks that keep operating costs—and, as a result, disposal costs—higher than anticipated.

These systems may have some valid role in solid waste programs, especially in large cities. But to institutionalize trash as an energy resource in itself would be a sham. Far more energy is used in excess packaging than can be recovered by burning!

The more we as individuals do to cut down on the trash generated; the more local communities do to encourage or legislate recycling and reuse; the more preventative measures we take before containers become garbage; the more incentives we demand for manufacturers to use recycled materials— the more energy we'll save and the more tax increases we'll avoids. Corporations should also take some responsibility for cleaning up the trashy end of the energy use picture.

—Special thanks to Bob Rottenberg for assistance in preparing this chapter.

1. *American City*, February 1975. From "Packaging and the Consumer," Arcata Community Recycling Center, Arcata, CA.

2. "Things Go Better for Coke," Debbie Galant, *Environmental Action*, 11 March 1978, pp. 4, 7-8.

3. U.S. Environmental Protection Agency, *Environment News*, New England Regional Office, Boston, MA, March 1978, p. 5.

4. *Environmental Action*, 8 April 1978, p. 13. Also write for "Bottles & Sense," Environmental Action Foundation, 724 Dupont Circle Bldg., Washington D.C. 20036 and New York State Bottle Bill, $1.50 from New Yorker for Returnable Containers, Inc. 211 E. 53rd St. N.Y. 10022. The Environmental Action Foundation has been lobbying for a national bottle bill since 1972 and have helped coordinate local campaigns. Contact them to get in touch with efforts in your state.

5. EPA, *op. cit.*, p. 5.

6. *People & Energy*, January 1978, p. 5.

7. EPA, *op. cit.*, p. 5. See also Gondy Rao, "An Economic Analysis of Energy and Employment Effects of Deposit Regulations of Non-Returnable Beverage Containers in Michigan," Planning and Economic Research Division, MI Public Service Comission. Available from PIRGIM, 615 E. Michigan Ave., Lansing, 48933; Taylor H. Bingham et al., "Energy and Economic Impacts of Mandatory Deposits," FEA (DOE).

8. EPA, *op. cit.*, p. 13.

Resources
Environmental Action Foundation, Dupont Circle Bldg., Suite 724, Washington, D.C. 20036. Available from EAF: "Bottles & Sense" (1976) "Resource Recovery: Truth & Consequences" (1977), "Garbage Guide," among others.

"Fourth Report to Congress: Resource Recovery and Waste Reduction" U.S. Environmental Protection Agency, 1977.

"Recycle: In Search of New Policies for Resource Recovery," League of Women Voters, Washington D.C. 1972.

"Resource Recovery: The State of Technology," U.S. Govt. Printing Office, 1973.

Chapter 3:
Coal

Although coal supplies in this country are evidently adequate for several centuries to come at present levels of use, King Coal should be considered a transitional fuel at best. Right now half of the electricity used in the U.S. is produced by burning coal. It will obviously play a significant role in the years and decades to come, no matter how soon other alternatives are introduced. But it should be used to provide energy during the transition from a fossil to a renewable-energy based future.

Why should coal be phased out? Why is it not the answer to U.S. energy needs? We will review the major social and environmental problems of coal use.

Coal mining is dangerous business for workers. Surface strip mining is environmentally disastrous. And finally, coal combustion is dangerous, a major source of air and thermal pollution.

The Workers' View

Coal mining is still, despite numerous health and safety advances in the last 10 years, the most dangerous job around. On average, the coal industry kills one worker every two working days and in general, a coal miner is eight times more likely to die on the job than an average private sector worker.[1]

However, this outright squandering of life is only the tip of the iceberg. Accident rates are twice as high as the private sector average and every year 63 of every thousand workers are disabled. Finally, there is the "silent killer," pneumoconiosis, better known as "black lung." It is a respiratory disease caused by inhaling microscopic coal dust particles in underground mines. It is a painful and debilitating disease, terminal in many cases. In 1969, after years of needless deaths from black lung and coal mine disasters, workers and public pressure finally forced Congress to enact a comprehensive mine safety law. Although enforcement of the law over the last ten years has been inconsistent at best, it has helped to bring about safer conditions in the mines. But despite dust limitations and more stringent safety standards imposed by this law, new cases of black lung continue and mining accidents are still all too frequent.

If coal mining is to play a constructive role in a U.S. energy future, both these safety and health dangers must be removed through better ventilation of underground mines, more effective personal pollution control equipment, greater safety controls, and good, free, and prompt medical treatment for those already affected.

Workers in eastern underground mines have a strong cultural and union tradition. Western strip-mining operations are for the most part not unionized. (Credit: FEA, DOE-77-11184)

The Lack of Health and Safety in the Mines[2]

	1947	1961	1969	1976
Production (million tons)	631	403	561	665
Employment (thousands)	419	150	125	216
Deaths (per thousand workers)	1.14*	1.83	1.62	0.65
Non-fatal disabling injuries (per thousand workers)	63.5*	66.0	79.3	

Note: Figures refer to all bituminous coal mining, union and non-union, surface and underground combined. * means 1949 figures (1947 injury data not available).

(Sources: National Coal Association, *Coal Data 1976* and *Coal Facts 1974-75*; Bureau of Labor Statistics.)

The Environmental View—Land

Although strip mining is considerably safer and less damaging to workers' health than mining underground, it is environmentally the most destructive method of coal extraction. The environmental impacts of surface mining— removing the soil "overburden" to expose a seam below—are easily seen by visiting an unreclaimed strip mine. There are thousands in Appalachia alone. In 1960, 32% of total coal production came from surface mines. In 1976, the figure had jumped to 56%.[3]

Following strip mining, mineral sulfides (called pyrites) in the soil combine with moisture to form sulfuric acid. This mixes with the runoff from denuded hillsides, pouring into rivers and lakes where it kills aquatic life forms and chokes the rivers, creating floods and tremendous property damage.

In the past, states were either unwilling to regulate strip mining or ineffective in their efforts. A national effort pressured Congress to come up

Strip mining is environmentally destructive.
(Credit: DOE-76-10955)

with standards for the mining and reclamation of surface coal mines.

In 1977, President Carter signed the Federal Strip Mine Control and Reclamation Act, which sets down the guidelines intended to make sure that the coal operator will return the strip mined land to a condition similar to or better than before mining took place. Whether or not such reclamation can really succeed and be economically feasible for the companies involved remains to be seen.

The Environmental View—Air

Coal combustion is a primary source of air pollution and has specific and predictable effects on public health. The sulfur, nitrogen, ash, and certain trace elements found in coal are all released in varying amounts during burning. Without pollution control equipment, the pollutants escape into the air—and eventually into people's lungs, eyes, etc. The fallout of these pollutants is a real problem too, for they can be carried downwind for hundreds of miles before settling to the ground.

Some, but not all, of coal's pollutants can be controlled or removed with the use of mechanical devices either before, during, or after combustion. Particulate matter above micron size (a micron is one-millionth of a meter), can be trapped between a series of plates called "electrostatic precipitators." In this process, one plate emits an electric charge to the particle. The opposite plate draws the charged particle and traps it until the plates are cleaned. The submicron particles can be trapped in fabric filters. Like huge vacuum cleaners, these "baghouses" are very effective. But even so, the very smallest, and perhaps the most dangerous, particles can still escape into the atmosphere.

The process of washing coal can remove much of the ash that forms the particulates. It is an effective means of reducing the load the control equipment has to carry. Sulfur dioxide, on the other hand, is difficult and expensive to control. Utility companies have relied upon low sulfur coal, coal washing, or coal blending (mixing very low sulfur coal with higher sulfur coals) to achieve the SO_2 emissions standards set by the EPA. For power plants in air quality control regions with stricter standards than can be achieved with low sulfur coal, mechanical "scrubbers" are used. These SO_2 removal scrubbers drench the stack gas with a spray of limestone dissolved in water. The limestone absorbs the SO_2. But then the contaminated limestone sludge has to be disposed of properly.

Scrubbers currently cost between $40 and $130 per kilowatt. Estimates of costs in the 1980s range from $75 to $220 per kilowatt. The Federal Power Commission estimates costs will be around $100 per kilowatt.[4] In addition to removing sulfur dioxide pollution, scrubbers also trap a significant amount of particulates during the process.

A 1974 EPA report concluded that scrubber desulfurization units were reliable and effective, although many utilities complain about their costs.[5] However, in the long run it is far cheaper to use eastern coal that is higher in sulfur with a scrubber, than to ship east western coal that may be lower in sulfur.

A recent improvement in coal combustion technology may provide an effective and economically viable solution to sulfur dioxide and nitrogen dioxide pollution. Atmospheric fluidized-bed coal combustion boilers eliminate these pollutants from coal burning. Fluidized-bed coal combustion boilers appear to have considerable potential as small decentralized boilers for industrial and commercial residential use because they are small and relatively simple to operate. The spent bed material is more stable than the wet limestone sludge produced by scrubbers, and may find use in manufacture of low-grade building material and roadbed fill. The Department of Energy is continuing tests on a 30-megawatt fluidized bed boiler in Rivesville, West Virginia. It is smaller than conventional boilers of comparable steam generating capacity.

Another coal technology currently of interest is coal gasification. This is a coal cleaning technique that has been used for generations. The gas is a by-product of coke, which is used in steel-making, and was used to light street lamps in the 1920s. It has not been an attractive coal utilization technology since natural gas became widely available. But with diminished supplies of natural gas and Congressional efforts to ban the use of oil and gas for industrial and electric utility boilers, there is a renewed attention being paid to coal gasification.

Thermal Pollution

The environmental problem that is common to all energy-producing processes involving combustion is thermal pollution. Although not immediately threatening to our health, it is very definitely a danger. The main problem comes from production of carbon dioxide, and more CO_2 is produced by coal combustion than by burning either oil or gas.[6]

Buildup of CO_2 in the atmosphere raises the earth's temperature by slowing down the escape of heat into space. This buildup causes what is known as the "greenhouse effect." Increased temperatures could mean polar ice-cap melting, alter weather patterns and bring on extensive disruptions in land use and agriculture. **Thermal pollution alone may be reason enough to end all fossil fuel burning.**

Fluidized Bed Furnace
(Credit: ORNL Drawing, DOE-75-10760)

Coal Power

In addition to environmental and health considerations, coal use is also undesireable because it means large centralized power stations that are highly capital intensive. Coal as a resource is increasingly controlled by large corporate interests. As with other energy resources, ownership of coal has become increasingly concentrated. A 1973 United Mine Workers study found that more than 60% of U.S. coal sales were controlled by 13 new major outside interests—corporations like Kennecott Copper, General Dynamics, and the omnipresent energy companies—Gulf Oil, Occidental Petroleum, Standard Oil and so on.[7] Coal use clearly does not offer workers, their unions, or consumers enough control or decision-making in its appropriation or use.

Renewed interest in coal came following the 1973-74 oil embargo and the consequent increase in oil prices. Carter's energy plan calls for increased coal dependence. One aspect of the plan would have utilities convert from oil and gas-fired electrical generating units to coal-fired ones. No major oil and natural gas burning units (over 2-3 megawatts in size) would be allowed. Critics of this part of the plan say that this is happening anyway, as market forces cause utilities to turn away from the more expensive and less dependable fuels.

Before considering coal as an immediate alternative for nuclear power, there are several things that come first. We must see how energy is used and question that use. Real needs must of course be met, but much of our energy is squandered on unnecessary goods and planned inefficiency and obsolescence. Secondly, we must practice conservation to make sure that the electricity we do need is used at peak efficiency. Finally, we must demand the safest, cleanest coal possible, even though it means lower profits for the coal industry.

With proper mine safety and miners' rights, with adequate pollution controls and with a strict program of land restoration, coal can continue to serve as an interim source of energy. But hopefully it will be phased out by the less damaging renewable energy alternatives we will consider next.

Footnotes:

1. "Behind the Hard-Fought Coal Strike," *Dollars and Sense*, no. 36, April 1978.

2. This graph was exerpted from a larger graph found in *ibid*.

3. Dan Marschall, "Big Changes in Big Coal," *In These Times*, 15-21 March 1978.

4. From information prepared by John McCormick, August 1978, Environmental Policy Center, 317 Pennsylvania Ave., S.E., Washington, D.C. 20003.

5. *Ibid*.

6. Denis Hayes, *The Solar Energy Timetable*, (World Watch Paper 19), April 1978, p. 6.

7. Marschall, *op. cit.*, p. 4.

Resources

United Mine Workers' (UMW) Journal
900 15th St. N.W., Washington, D.C. 20005
The official mineworkers publication with news from the coalfields. Subscription: $5 per year.

Special thanks to John McCormick for assistance in the preparation of this chapter.

Resources—General

• Farrington Daniels, *Direct Use of the Sun's Energy*, (New York: Ballantine, 1974).

• Wilson Clark, *Energy for Survival*, (Garden City, N.Y.: Anchor Press/Doubleday, 1974).

• Hazel Henderson, *Creating Alternative Futures: The End of Economics*, (New York: Berkley-Windover Book, 1978). $4.95 plus $.50 handling from: Berkley Mail Sales, Department BW, 200 Madison Ave., 15th floor, New York, NY 10016.

• David Dickson, *The Politics of Alternative Technology; A Revolutionary Call for Political Change*, (New York: Universe Books, 1975). $3.95 from Universe, 381 Park Ave. South, New York, NY 10016.

• *Rainbook: Resources for Appropriate Technology*, de Moil, Lane - Editors of *Rain Magazine*, (New York: Schocken Books, $7.95. Order from: Schocken Books, 200 Madison Ave., New York, NY 10016).

• Richard G. Stein, *Architecture and Energy*, (Garden City, N.Y.: Anchor Press, 1977), cloth $12.95.

• *Introduction to Appropriate Technology*, R.J. Congdon, ed., (Emmaus, PA: Rodale Press), 1977, paper $7.95 from Rodale, Organic Park, Emmaus, PA 18049.

• *Producing Your Own Power; How to Make Nature's Energy Sources Work for You*, Carol Hupping Stoner, ed., (Emmaus, PA: Rodale Press), 1974, $8.95.

•*Starting Your Own Energy Business*, Institute for Local Self-Reliance, 1717 18th St., N.W., Washington, D.C. 20009, 50 pp. 1978, $4.00. Also from the Institute: "Energy Self-Reliance," 16 pp., $1.00; "Kilowatt Counter: A Consumer's guide to energy concepts," 36 pp. $2.00; "Garbage in America: A guide to low-technology recycling programs across America," 35 pp. $2.00; "Appropriate Technology and Community Economic Development: An overview of an increasingly important issue," 10 pp. $1.00.

• *1977 Solar Age Catalogue*, Editors of *Solar Age*, 230 pp., $8.50 from Solar Bookshop, Total Environmental Action, (TEA), Inc., Church Hill, Harrisville, NH 03450.

• Bill Yanda and Rick Fisher, *The Food and Heat Producing Greenhouse*, 161 pp., $6.00 from TEA.

Passive Solar Energy

• "Passive Solar Buildings Soak Up Sun," 1978, Citizens' Energy Project, 1413 K St., N.W., Washington, D.C. 20005, $.65. Also from CEP: "Homeowner's Guide to Passive Solar," 1978, $.55.

Solar Energy

• Bruce Anderson, *The Solar Home Book*, 304 pp., $8.50 from TEA. Also: *Solar Energy and Shelter*

Design, 1973, 150 pp., $7.00 from TEA.

• "Solar Energy and the Poor," 1977, $.45 from Citizens' Energy Project. Also: "Solar Plans List," 1978, $.70; *Solar Compendium*, 1978, $6.00.

• Anita Gunn, *A Citizen's Handbook on Solar Energy*, Public Interest Research Group, 1976. 2000 P St., N.W., Washington, D.C. 20036.

• *Connecticut Solar Handbook*, Conn. Citizens Action Group, Box 6, Hartford, CT 06106.

Wind Power

• Douglas Coonley, *Design With Wind*,1974. 140 pp., $8.00 from TEA. Also: *An Introduction to the Use of Wind*, 1975, 22 pp., $2.00 from TEA.

• Henry Clews, *Electric Power From the Wind*, Solar Wind, P.O. Box 7, East Holden, Maine 04429, 42 pp., $2.00.

• "Wind Energy—Big Companies Blow It," 1977, $.50 from Citizens' Energy Project.

• Frank Eldridge, *Wind Machines*, (Washington, D.C.: U.S. Government Printing Office, 1976).

• *AWEA Newsletter*, a quarterly publication of the American Wind Energy Association, 54468 CR 31 Bristol, Indiana 46507. Subscriptions part of yearly membership fee; non-members $10.00/year. For non-members: *Wind Technology Journal*, $15.00/year.

Intermediate and Appropriate Technology

• International Scholarly Book Services, Inc. P.O. Box 555, Forest Grove, OR 97116. (Intermediate technology bibliography, books, inexpensive and practical; A.T. for developing countries.)

• **META Publications** P.O. Box 128, Marblemount, WA 98267. (Books, pamphlets and plans for A.T. and related topics.)

Other

• From Citizens Energy Project: "Water Power: Problems & Promises," 1977, $.95. "Bioconversion," 1978, $.80. "Gasohol," 1978, $1.05. "Solar Satellites or How to Make Solar Energy Centralized, Expensive and Environmentally Unsound," Report no. 40, $.65. "Geothermal Energy Resources," 1978, $.85.

See also sources mentioned in footnotes.

Chapter 4:

Energy Sources:
Now and For the Future

We have seen that conservation is the most attractive and immediate way to lessen our need for the energy that nuclear plants provide. Recycling of basic materials will help too. Coal will continue to provide energy, although its environmental, health, and other social costs must be eliminated.

But we still need sources of energy to replace oil and nuclear power.

It is no longer enough for safe energy advocates to answer that the alternative to nuclear power is "solar energy." Almost everyone agrees! For the vast promise of natural energy sources has begun to capture public imagination and interest. Unlike a few short years ago, people are realizing the enormous potential benefits of living with natural energy systems.

What we need to know now is how to do it: which sources to develop first, where they will be most successful, and how they will affect our lives. There is no doubt that enough energy is available to meet both people's and industry's needs without using fossil fuels or atomic power. But the when and how of using solar power is an intensely political question.

To evaluate the alternatives to nuclear power we need some basic understanding of the choices before us. Given a steady and welcome proliferation of materials on alternative energy (see Resource Section at end of chapter), our purpose here will be to see briefly just what energy sources are available, their major benefits, and attendant problems.

It Starts With the Sun

No energy source on earth exceeds the power of the sun. Its energy comes to us free day after day. It has been estimated that on a clear June day "the sunshine falling on New York City is equivalent to the energy produced by all power plants in the world at peak performance."[1]

249

Figure 1: Solar school—Solar collector panels mounted on the roof of an elementary school in Atlanta, Georgia are shown during construction. The system is expected to supply more than 60% of the year-round heating and cooling for the 32,000-square-foot building. (Credit: Frank Hoffman) DOE-75-10805

The main problem with using the energy in sunlight—manifest in the form of heat—is collecting, concentrating, and storing it, since it arrives in dispersed form during daylight hours. Proof that such concentration is possible is no farther away than a small magnifying glass which, when used to focus the sunlight that touches it, can heat wood to the point of combustion. Lately the world has been introduced to the concept of solar collectors, like the rooftop panels increasingly used for home and commercial space-heating and hot water.

Actually, fabricated solar collectors are puny in comparison to the earth's natural collectors: rivers and their watersheds, the winds, the surface of the oceans, and plant life—*all* plant life.

Although hard at first to accept, a tree is actually a stick of solar energy. Plants absorb sunlight and use it directly to produce growth and develop their own stored energy. Ancient

swamps locked in the solar energy of vast amounts of biomass* material. Slowly compressed and concentrated over millions of years, the plant material was transformed into underground deposits of coal, oil, and gas. Energy from biomass is also released through decomposition and burning, or indirectly, by fermentation, producing alcohol.

The hydroelectric potential of a river is another measure of the power of the sun. Rivers begin as rain. More accurately, they begin as water vapor suspended in the sky, lifted there by the sun's heat; eventually it falls and is collected and concentrated by watersheds into the streams and rivers that can power turbines.

The winds are even more direct expressions of solar power. They result from the differences in heating of the various climatic zones on the earth's surface, or from the temperature fluctuations tied to clouding and rain in the evapotranspiration cycle. Winds not only translate heat energy differentials into forceful motion of air, but also do the crucial job of preserving the global heat balance—collecting heat reflected by the land and water surfaces, shaking it out of vegetation, returning as much to space each day as the earth has received.

Finally, there are the oceans and other large bodies of water. These collect solar energy as heat in their upper levels and remain cool or cold below. The power of the oceans is also manifest in their waves and tides.

A great variety of engineering systems are harvesting the energy stored in these natural collectors. When these systems are taken together with the collectors devised by people, from simple roof panels to the photovoltaic cells

---

*Biomass is a term describing all organic material, alive or dead, that can be used as fuel or converted to fuel.

that turn sunlight directly into electricity, it becomes perfectly clear that the means exist to provide—naturally—all the energy that the whole of humankind will ever need.

Practical applications of solar energy production abound. And yet we know that current technology is in the "dark ages" compared to the advances that will be made when the creative, scientific, technical, and finally, financial resources of this country are dedicated to the effort. Experimentation with solar technology is still just beginning. Glamorous and exciting scientific careers have for too long been identified with high energy physics and the nuclear and space programs. Meanwhile, much of solar know-how has come from backyard inventors and small companies. That picture is changing now, but should be remembered as we review the existing alternative technologies.

"LOW"
TECHNOLOGY APPLICATIONS

Passive Solar

Passive solar means designing, siting, and building structures so that the buildings themselves function as solar collectors. It is the easiest, cheapest, and most practical way to use the sun's energy. Although it is mostly limited to new construction, occasionally old buildings can be converted to passive— by the addition of a solar greenhouse, for instance.

Here a builder talks about passive solar energy methods.

...It is a mistake to assume that solar energy is a new concept. Through the ages architects have carefully used the sun and the surroundings to temper the climate within enclosed spaces. It is only in recent years that buildings have been designed to shut the occupants off from local climatic conditions. With proper siting, a house should avail itself of natural heat flow and discourage heat thieves. By building into the southern slope of a hill, or building earth berms along the north side, a house is protected from winter cold. Since there is very little heat gained from the north, and a great deal lost, it should be closed off as much as possible... Evergreen woods or windscreens to the north keep out fierce winter winds. Deciduous trees to the south allow the sun to penetrate during the cold winter months, but shade the house during the summer when they are in full leaf. The house should be oriented to the south and the east whenever possible. It should take advantage of early morning sunlight and midday warmth and avoid westerly extremes and northerly breezes.

Solar Heat—Once a house is situated to best advantage, it is an easy matter to get heat from the sun by putting the windows in the right place. On a clear winter's day on Martha's Vineyard, approximately 1600 BTUs (British thermal units) will pass through each square foot of south-facing glass. One BTU is the quantity of heat required to raise the temperature of one pound of water by one fahrenheit degree. This means that on a cold, clear day each square foot of glass admits enough heat to raise five quarts of well water (at 52°) to the boiling point. By building into the south wall of a building as much glass as possible, one can gather substantial quantities of heat.

Here we have the beginnings of one of the most efficient solar heating systems. It is called passive solar heating because it uses no mechanical contrivances to transfer and distribute the heat...* Bringing heat directly from the sun and funneling it into the house, which can itself act as both collector and storage, eliminates transmission losses, mechanical difficulties, and expense.

Once inside the house, heat from the sun warms the air, the objects in the room, and the superstructure. But as the inside temperature rises, the heat tends to flow back through the walls, windows, and roof to the cooler climate outside, since heat always flows in a direction that will equalize temperatures. As evening comes, input from the sun slows down, the air outside grows cooler and cooler, and the heat inside works harder and harder to escape...

Heat finds many ways to escape from houses, especially from the large south windows that function as collectors and from other windows throughout the house. Once the sun goes down, and on cool cloudy days, heat passes easily through the glass, which has very little resistance to heat flow. To tilt the balance, and to make the heat we've gained work to serve our needs, we must cover the windows at night and on cloudy days when we are away from the house. Insulated shutters that close tightly over the windows will substantially reduce heat losses. Whatever the night insulation devised by the homebuilder—insulated shutters, roll-down insulated cloth, pop-in sheets of polystyrene foam, or any one of a host of other solutions—it must fit tightly so as to minimize drafts between window and insulator. Drapes are ineffective because they hang away from the window, allowing cold air currents to develop. One problem with night insulation is that people are not used to the daily ritual of opening up the house in the morning and closing it down at night. It should not be hard to adapt to this, for it is a good common-sense method for regulating environmental comfort, much the same as putting on and taking off clothing.[2]

—John Abrams
Solar Energy, A Gentle Resource

Inside-Outside Company's passive solar home in Sunderland MA. (Credit: Lionel Delevingne)

---

*When pumps, blowers, or any mechanical devices are added to help distribute heat or for any other reason, the system is known as a "hybrid" or "hybrid-passive" one—i.e., passive solar with some mechanical parts.

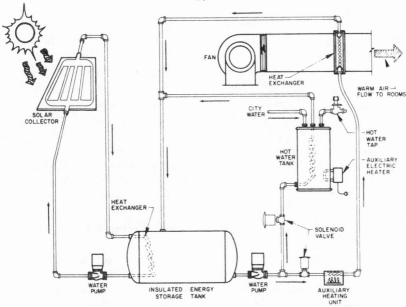

FAN

HEAT EXCHANGER

WARM AIR → FLOW TO ROOMS

SOLAR COLLECTOR

CITY WATER

HOT WATER TAP

HOT WATER TANK

AUXILIARY ELECTRIC HEATER

HEAT EXCHANGER

SOLENOID VALVE

WATER PUMP

INSULATED ENERGY STORAGE TANK

WATER PUMP

AUXILIARY HEATING UNIT

Figure 3: Schematic diagram of a solar heating and hot water system—from a DOE publication, "Solar Energy for Space Heating & Hot Water," Division of Solar Energy, May 1976

Other principles of passive solar heating involve thermal mass—the use of walls and floors of thick masonry, brick, or stone—to hold heat during the day and release it at night, the use of massive central fireplaces, tanks of water and indoor ponds as direct thermal storage mediums, and ventilation systems that pull cool air through the house to prevent overheating. Slightly more involved passive methods include attached greenhouses and the vertical glass-covered concrete wall collectors known as Trombe Walls after Dr Felix Trombe, the French professor who pioneered their development.

Collecting the Sun

The most commonly known of the solar processes is the low-temperature photothermal (LTP) conversion system that operates with collector panels mounted on roofs, walls, or ground surfaces adjacent to buildings. In this system, circulating air or water (or other appropriate "operating fluid"), insulated but exposed to sunlight as it passes through these panels, absorbs solar heat to the level of about 140° F (hotter than the average washwater or bath). The liquid or air then passes to a storage area, an insulated water tank, or for air, a pile of rocks or other heat-holding material. The heat is then distributed from the storage area by conventional systems to living space and water supplies. In areas of intense heat and sunlight, such as the U.S. Southwest, the system can operate at higher temperatures that enable it to power heat-exchanger equipment for air conditioning as well.

Technology for LTP energy conversion is well developed and increasingly economical, although it is still mainly a high-income level investment. Passive solar building techniques run less than one-third the cost of active systems. And passive solar is built-in and does not require the maintenance of active systems. Still, active and passive systems share some similar advantages—independence and increased control for the user, technological simplicity, and comprehensibility. Collectors can be made of scrap, inexpensive, and easily available materials. But for new construction, architechture utilitizing passive solar and conservation should be a prerequisite.

Solar collectors can provide the low-grade temperatures that are now produced at the cost of one-third of the world's energy budget. Solar heating and cooling can play a big role in industry as well as at home. Low temperature heat under 100° C can be achieved with elementary solar technologies. For higher temperatures solar can be used to pre-heat, saving valuable fossil fuels.[3]

Solar Hot Water

The simplest task to accomplish directly with solar power is heating water, and solar water heaters are being utilized in many countries. More than two million have been sold in Japan, and tens of thousands are in use in Israel. In the remote reaches of Australia, where fuels are expensive, solar water heaters are required by law on all new buildings. Until replaced by cheap natural gas, solar water heaters were much used in California and in Florida; Miami alone had about 50,000 in the early 1950s. Since 1973, interest in solar water heaters has rekindled in many parts of the world. In poorer countries, cheap hot water can make a significant contribution to public well-being: hot water for dish-washing and bathing can reduce the burden of infectious diseases, and clothes washed with hot water and soap outlast clothes beaten clean on rocks at a river's edge.[4]

Jobs

As for employment, the 1974 "Project Independence Report" of the Federal Energy Administration (now part of DOE) estimated that full implementation of LTP and related solar technologies could yield 3-4 million jobs by the year 2000.[5] And these would be jobs that provide usable, constructive skills: building construction, plumbing, welding, etc. The employment potential of many solar technologies is tremendous. Rebuilding communities for greater self-sufficiency could end unemployment.

Government encouragement of advances in LTP installation includes advice to individuals anywhere in the U.S. on the economic cost-benefit ratio of installing such equipment in their particular weather zone. Numerous catalogs also exist that advertise LTP equipment in all its varieties.

Harnessing the Winds

With reasonable energy conservation efforts and windpower, there doesn't need to be a single additional water-sucking, land-gobbling, waste-making, life-threatening nuclear power plant built in the Great Plains Region![6]
—Bill Ward, founder of
non-profit Windustries
Topeka, Kansas

At various locations around the world, winds like the Trades and the Westerlies (the latter in the northern hemisphere) provide moving volumes of air with sufficient predictability and velocity to sustain large-scale electrical generation, or high-volume production of hydrogen gas and related fuels. The technology to use those volumes of air for such purposes is available, and has been for some time.

A 1.25-megawatt windmill generator was demonstrated between 1941

Figure 4: Rede—An "egg beater" windmill developed with aerospace technology. (Credit: Lionel Delevingne)

and 1945 atop Grandpa's Knob, a hilltop in central Vermont. It was decommissioned when other modes of generation offered lower-cost power.[7] A 200-kilowatt generator operated for 20 years in Denmark without incident, adding to a whole network of smaller wind generators now in their fifth and sixth decades of trouble-free service (although the system has been de-emphasized in favor of imported hydroelectric and nuclear power from neighboring Sweden).[8]

Denmark now boasts the largest windmill ever built. The giant three-bladed 2-megawatt Tvind mill, built cooperatively at low cost by students and faculty at the Tvind school, was completed in November 1977. The mill cost about $660,000. Teachers contributed their salaries, and much labor was donated. There was no government funding. (By contrast, DOE has awarded Boeing a $10,000,000 contract to build a 2.5-megawatt wind-turbine in Boone, North Carolina by 1980.) The Tvind mill is expected to provide all the school's energy needs—electricity and heat—and still have some surplus juice to sell to the local power company.[9]

By now, technological advances in metallurgy, generator, and airfoil design make 2-megawatt wind generator units feasible and—compared with the costs of nuclear and fossil-fuel plant installation—economical as well. Linked in series and operating at full capacity with winds of about 20 mph, groups of these generators can be used to supply baseload power in large and constant quantities. But what happens when the winds don't blow?

The answer to slack winds is storage, but not storage of electricity itself. What would be stored is another form of energy. A variety of systems have been designed to accomplish this, including flywheels which store momentum, compressed air, and the most generally favored option, production and storage of hydrogen gas. In this approach, a small portion of the wind generator's electrical output is passed through water, inducing the process of electrolysis, which breaks water into hydrogen and oxygen. The hydrogen gas is then liquified or compressed and stored. When winds drop off, the hydrogen is passed through fuel cells and converted back into electricity—a process used on NASA spacecraft. Alternatively, the hydrogen can be used directly as a fuel, or chemically treated to form methanol (a motor fuel much cleaner than gasoline), ammonia, or fertilizer.

Potential siting areas for major wind installations in the U.S. include the Gulf and Alaskan coasts, areas of the Great Plains and the Great Lakes, and oil and nuclear-dependent New England where the Westerlies swoop down on the Atlantic coastal shelf and accelerate in passage away from land. Researchers at the University of Massachusetts (UMass) have designed a system of framework-mounted wind generators—some frames afloat, some anchored in the seabed—in three lines roughly parallel and many miles apart, stepping east from Cape Cod into Georges Bank, the rich fishing area northeast of Boston.

With hydrogen storage facilities either undersea or ashore, estimated output of current from this 41,000 generator system (each generator rated at 2-megawatt capacity) would be 360 million megawatt hours per year—as much as 70 nuclear stations of 1,000. The total is more than enough to meet the total electrical power needs of New England, which have been estimated in the 243-million Mw/h range for the 1990s (an estimate postulated prior to recent steep rises in energy costs).[10]

According to Prof. Heronemus, who helped formulate the plan, initial output of power from such an installation could begin in as little as four years "from scratch." The sale price of the electricity generated is predicted to be competitive at 3¢ per kwh. That figure, like all energy prices, is subject to post-1977 inflation in capital, construction, labor, and equipment costs. But unlike dominant energy modes, there is no fuel cost nor fuel-cost inflation.

In addition to massive, regional service installations, wind generator systems allow for decentralized power planning and production. There are already small-scale machines available for individual homes and small industries, and DOE development grants have been assigned for "advanced" 8-kilowatt home and 40-kilowatt farm or business models to be completed by about 1980. Individual utility installa-

Figure 5: Dr. Heronemus with a model of his offshore wind station, June 1977. (Credit: Lionel Delevingne)

tions are also possible. Cuttyhunk Island, Massachusetts, has a privately financed 200-kilowatt windmill, and Clayton, New Mexico has a 200-kilowatt DOE-backed facility.[11] Hydrogen gas production at central large-scale installations would enable pipeline distribution to local converter stations, which could be managed locally.

Federal government estimates of wind-power potential for meeting national energy needs run as high as 23% by the year 2000 and are probably conservative. One study says a minimum of 250,000 new jobs could be created in the process.[12] Yet as recently as the mid-70s, total government funding for research and development of wind power was below a million dollars. That has changed now, but not by the necessary factor of increase. The 1979 DOE budget includes $41 million for wind energy, while giving $462 million for fast-breeder reactor research and construction. While an offshore test installation has been proposed, the first serious steps toward large-scale wind power generation have yet to be taken.

Hydroelectric Power

In the 1920s, hydroelectric plants produced one-third of U.S. electrical generating capacity. Today they provide about 13% and much of that comes from pumped-storage facilities at large hydro and nuke projects.[13]

The most significant future gain from hydroelectric sources here will come from the renovation of multitudes of small abandoned hydro stations and installation of turbines at "low head"* dams that have never been tapped for electricity. When fossil fuels were cheap, many dams and plants were retired as poor investments. "From 1961 to 1970, dams totalling 230,747 kilowatts of capacity were retired; from 1970 to 1976 the retired capacity totalled 146,944,"[14]

Low head dams do not impound significant amounts of the rivers they block. In some instances, particularly on small streams, they cannot provide year round base-load power. When in summer the stream dries up, the electricity dries up too. But the consumption patterns and economics of electric power enable these low head facilities to be used quite efficiently to cut the expense of high cost daily or seasonal peak-load power that is now provided by costly on-line reserve stations, pumped-storage hydroelectric operations, and instant-on facilities with gas or diesel generators. Small-scale hydro is clean, non polluting, and inherently decentralized. Power can be used where it is produced, or be fed into a transmission grid.

In New England, the number of untapped low head dams is high—an estimated 9,000—with many dating from early industrial days. Here the year's highest non-urban peak loads are in the winter heating months—coinciding neatly with available stream flow. The savings in fuel and money to be gained from applying the unused low head capacity to the peak need are substantial. The town of Springfield, Vermont, anticipates a savings to municipal and residential accounts of up to one-third from a peak-power hydroelectric system based on the town's multiple low head factory dams on the Black River.[15]

A brief 1977 study of small-scale hydro potential requested by President Carter of the Army Corps of Engineers gave an estimate of its possibilities.

> The Corps concluded that new hydro power at existing small dams could provide 26,600 megawatts with a potential yield of 84.7 billion kilowatt hours annually. They counted 49,500 dams in the U.S., most of which fall in the low head category. In addition, expanding or rehabilitating existing dams (both large and small) could yield an additional capacity of 21,000 megawatts.[16]

Not all potential sites can be used: there are environmental problems in some cases, possible interference with recreational and other uses elsewhere. And hydro has high "front end" installation costs.

Although small-scale hydro has been bypassed for many years in the U.S. in favor of nuclear power and centralized thermal plants, its promise has not been ignored elsewhere. New bulb turbines developed and used in Europe and the USSR have increased efficiency and reduced installation costs. Water

* "head" refers to the height beneath the dam.

power is inherently a good deal because the fuel is available, dependable (given climate and flow changes), and free. There is no thermal or chemical pollution. Efficiency is high—up to 94%—and hydroelectric systems have longer lives than conventional thermal plants. Although building a hydroelectric plant "from scratch" can cost up to $2,000 per kw, most hydro systems have lower operating costs and an expected life two to three times longer than conventional thermal plants.[17]

Biomass

Of all the energy alternatives to nuclear power, biomass is the oldest, the least spectacular, but the most widely applicable. There are few places where biological materials like animal wastes, crop residues, and weed vegetation are not available, and only slightly fewer where some form of fuel-base biomass material cannot be purposefully grown.

> Four major processes exist to convert biomass to energy. Wood, garbage and others can be burned directly; most organic matter can be fermented to produce alcohol; sewage and manure can be converted to methane in digesters which are tanks that provide a comfortable environment for anaerobic bacteria that convert sludge to gas; and organic matter can be pyrolized, a process which is analogous to methane digestion but happens with extremely high temperatures instead of bacteria. Methane digestion and fermentation are highly efficient and produce no waste heat, but digestion is somewhat slow and unpredictable. Pyrolysis produces gas at high temperatures, oils at low temperatures,

but is expensive, and produces waste heat and materials.[18]

A fully developed biomass energy system could go a long way towards meeting U.S. energy needs for heating and cooking, and could also provide electricity if necessary.[19] Such a system could produce all the motor fuel we need. Three basic components of a biomass system will be described here: local "digesters" converting wastes to biogas, distilleries for "brewing" alcohol fuels, and wood energy.

Methane Digestion—In a methane or biogas plant, organic material is "digested" by bacteria in the absence of oxygen (anaerobic digestion takes place). This natural process produces methane (biogas, CH_4), an odorless, colorless gas similar to natural gas. Experiments show that a pound of dry organic solids can produce 3 to 5 feet of gas containing 55% methane. Production plants have been built for digestion of animal manure (especially at feedlots) as well as municipal sewage sludge—a good way to keep it out of rivers and landfills. Anaerobic decay is going on all around us. Methane produced by anaerobic decay in a Los Angeles landfill dump is now being tapped for energy! The EPA has estimated that such digestion occurs spontaneously in 13,000-20,000 landfills across the country.[20]

Some advantages of this system? Its byproducts include large amounts of fertilizer. Extensive biomass development would also create large numbers of jobs. And a transmission system for biogas/methane is already in place. Dr. Barry Commoner points out that natural gas pipelines could gradually be filled with methane produced at decentralized plants across the country. Thus, unlike other large-scale solar systems, a new infra-structure would not be necessary to get the "power to the people." Methane could act as a natural energy "bridge" between current energy technologies and future ones.

Decentralized biomass systems also work well in heavily agricultural societies without national energy transmission systems. China has 2 million biogas systems and India is constructing many thousands yearly.[21]

There are many significant sources of biomass fuel—stock materials in the U.S. that would not compete for arable farmland. One might be the water hyacinth, a plant that chokes our own southern rivers and warm-climate streams all over the world. There has been Navy and university interest in cultivating kelp seaweed off the California coast and in the south Atlantic, although there seem to be problems with this idea. It would require new and energy-intensive technology, and the environmental impact is not yet understood. The scale and large amounts of capital required for giant off-shore kelp farms makes this application of biomass most attractive to big companies—not the case with other less complex biomass schemes.[22]

Alcohol Fuels—

Coal and oil are going up and are strictly limited in quantity. We can take coal out of a mine but we can never put it back. We can draw oil from subterranean reservoirs but we can never refill them again. The world's annual consumption has become so enormous that we are now actually within measurable distance of the end of the supply. What shall we do when we have no more coal or oil? We can make alcohol—a beautifully clean and efficient fuel—from sawdust, the waste products of our mills...from cornstalks, and in fact from any vegetable matter capable of fermentation. Our growing crops and even weeds can be used. The waste products of our farms are available for this purpose, and even the garbage from our cities.[23]

Alexander Graham Bell,
February 1917

Alcohol fuels offer a reasonably priced and less-polluting alternative to gasoline. Known about for years, alcohol was used extensively during World War II petroleum shortages in Europe. Two types of alcohol can be used. Methyl alcohol, made from non-farm products like wood and coal, is less expensive than the ethyl alcohol that can be distilled from farm crops like wheat and corn, as well as various wastes.

Natural alcohol fuels can be added to gasoline in amounts up to 10% with no engine modifications necessary. "In an Illinois Department of Agriculture experiment, gasohol containing 10% alcohol from corn stalks was sold to motorists with great success."[24]

Although this biomass substitute for petroleum was not even mentioned in Carter's original energy plan and will receive $15.3 million for research in the '79 DOE budget (as opposed to $609.4 million for coal research, $73.7 million for petroleum and $30.0 million for gas research), interest outside of Washington is high. Some midwestern farmers see it as a solution for surplus and damaged or inferior grain crops. Producing their own fuel would also give farmers a greater degree of self-sufficiency.

All in all there seems to be a good future for biomass alcohol, given its use of low quality grain surpluses, its production of protein-rich cattle feed as a byproduct (two-thirds of a bushel of mash produced for each bushel of wheat used), its low pollution level, and given the increased self-sufficiency it would offer farmers, its users, and the country as a whole.

Given the availability of resources and the simplicity of biomass technology, it is not surprising that numerous and varied approaches are under way to tap its potential.

Wood—Wood, burning as it does without dangerous pollutants and leaving ashes useful in fertilizers, seems to be leading in biomass use. This is especially true in New England where many rural homes now heat with woodstoves and use fuel oil furnaces as backups.

Technologies for extracting energy from wood in commercial applications include direct burning to generate steam heat or electricity, pyrolizing wood, a costly process which extracts gas and oil from wood at very high temperatures, and fermenting methanol from wood, which can be used as automotive fuel, or as a source of industrial process steam.

The Eugene (OR) Water and Electric Board was the first municipal utility to burn wood in a steam-electric plant, in 1941. The 33.8 Mw plant provides 1/6 the electricity to 175,000 people, as well as steam heat to a 2 sq. mile area [that includes] a large cannery and a 16-acre greenhouse complex. The plant saves almost $2 million in fuel costs over oil; it generates less than 1/25 as much pollution as the burners it replaced, and it has helped to solve the local residue disposal problem.[25]

A 1977 New England Federal Regional Council report found that if we used only unmerchantable trees and logging residues, and "if the present volume of growing stock were to be maintained as a minimum amount desired in New England, over 44 billion cubic feet of wood could be used as a resource between now and the year 2000. This is equivalent in energy to about 540 million tons of coal or 2.3 billion barrels of oil. Stated another way, this represents the total power output of 10 nuclear plants operating from now until the year 2000."[26]

A study by the Maine Wood Fuel Corporation says that wood in that state could replace all the oil now used to generate electricity at a savings of $200 million a year, while producing 1,800 jobs and 10,000 jobs indirectly. In Vermont, the Governor's Task Force on Wood found that wood could supply 25% of that state's energy while providing jobs for 3,500 and grossing $63 million.[27]

In Burlington, Vermont, a 50-megawatt municipally-owned power plant is getting set to burn wood chips for fuel.* Improved chipping machines and gasification procedures are the basis for a planned installation of up to 40 generating stations of 30 Mw each in dispersed forest sites in Maine. Here the proximity to fuel trees would ease problems of transportation of logs that work against the economics and ecological desirability of wood burning in some instances.[28]

Wood could generate 100% of electricity needed in the states of Washington, Oregon, and California. The Department of Forestry in Sacramento

---

*In Oregon, a recently patented wood pelletization process known as Woodex is turning out 100 tons per day of a uniformly-sized fuel capable of direct substitution for coal. The process can use anything from sawdust and mill scraps to tree leaves and peanut shells. And east-coast franchise for this system is planned in the Carolinas. (from *People and Energy*, vol. IV, no. 5, May 1978, p. 6)

Figure 6: Log-splitter—As New Englanders use more wood, new woodsplitters are being developed. This one can split a large log in seconds. (Credit: Lionel Delevingne)

reports that the wood "wastes" (bark, limbs and chunks) left after logging in the state's 42 million acres of forest and woodlands could produce the electrical power equivalent to four giant nuclear plants (of Rancho Seco size) at less than half the cost."

As with other solar energy systems, the economic development and employment potentials of biomass energy conversion are large when compared with fossil and nuclear modes. The California Forestry report found that new wood burning, steam-generating facilities cost less than half the price of a nuclear plant, but slightly more than oil and gas burning plants. Converting present fossil-fueled plants to wood costs much less than building new plants. Compared to nukes, wood burning plants create far less waste heat (thermal pollution), use a low-cost, renewable fuel, and could employ nine times as many workers. Above all, they eliminate the risk of catastrophic and slow radiation contamination and the necessary storage of dangerous wastes.[29]

However, wood will never be a complete answer to the energy crisis, even in heavily forested New England. Massive wood utilization could leave forest floors with inadequate fertilization from normal decay, and the

amount of wood required would imply a highly centralized management and control structure. Big stations need the wood equivalent of 5,000 acres a year clear-cut. Giant trucks would have to be entering with wood constantly to "fuel the fires."

Thermal pollution is another problem. When wood is burned to make electricity, two-thirds of its potential energy is lost in conversion. Wood may turn out to be most useful in small decentralized plants based on forest thinning, maintenance, and paper pulpwood production, as well as for home heating fuel in rural (and even suburban!) areas.

The 1979 federal energy budget calls for $27 million for biomass research and development, compared to $905 million for nuclear-related R & D.

"HIGH" TECHNOLOGY APPLICATIONS

Solar

There are some very fancy, complex, and "sophisticated" ways of using solar energy to produce power. Most of the high technology approaches are after electricity from the sun.

Photovoltaic Cells—"Solar cells," of all the solar-electric technologies, have the greatest potential for low-cost environmentally-safe, decentralized electrical power production.

The crystalline devices of silicon or cadmium composition have been used since 1954 to provide power for space satellites. They are the only means thus far evolved for direct conversion of sunlight to electricity. The sun appears and, without any mechanical, thermodynamic intermediary devices, current begins to flow through the wires. Moreover, true decentralization of power production would be possible; the current can flow from either individual, scattered rooftop emplacements or from more centralized large-scale photovoltaic stations, or both. But since electricity is lost in transmission, photovoltaics would allow for the closest possible (so far) connection between the sun and the lightbulb.

Cell production technology is still underdeveloped, and major problems in the present generation of photovoltaic cells must be overcome. Their efficiency must increase (commercially available units convert about 12% of received sunlight to electricity) while production costs—presently around $11 per peak watt, down from $200 in 1959—must continue to fall. Also, before power cells can be a base-load resource, a good storage system for dark-hour electricity will have to be added, meaning that some form of mechanical or thermodynamic connective apparatus will be needed for fullest use. And although the cells have passed the 20-year mark in durability testing, only more time will tell whether their productive life can match the 50-year mark established by wind and hydroelectric machinery.

Breakthroughs are happening. Researchers have predicted that the combination of improved technology offering efficiencies of up to 30% and mass production techniques are likely to bring the cells within reach of competitive pricing (5¢ per kwh) by 1985, and push through to a possible 1¢ per kwh early in the next century.

At such prices, the spread of photovoltaic cells might be very rapid indeed. If so, the results could be dramatic. Even at a 10% efficiency rate, an array of photovoltaic cells covering the roofs of only 20% of the nation's buildings (an aggregate area of 360 square miles) would provide almost all the electricity now consumed in the U.S. Beyond that, the possibility may exist for combined installation of photovoltaic cells and LTP collector systems that would

French bumpersticker

utilize the 70% or more of sunlight not converted by the cells to produce space heat and hot water, thereby greatly cutting down on decentralized fuel requirements. The FEA's "Project Independence" report estimated that even a low level of development of photovoltaic systems could yield over three million jobs by century's end.[30]

Storage requirements for decentralized emplacement have no easy solution within view of present day technology. Only large-scale photovoltaic installations similar to solar farms can spare the power, space, and cost to produce hydrogen or run huge flywheels or operate pumped-storage hydroelectric facilities to provide current during hours of darkness.

On the other hand, centralized installation of photovoltaic cells in areas of high-intensity sunlight—including floating arrays at sea—is as possible as HTP collector solar farms.

High-Temperature Photothermal (HTP) Conversion—This system collects more sunlight and concentrates it far more than in the LTP collector approach. Enough heat is created to produce steam to operate turbine generators. The two primary design approaches to the HTP process are the solar farm and the "power tower."

The Solar Farm—This concept would place horizontal collectors over vast areas of land in the southwestern U.S., or similar desert locations around the world. Heat would be accumulated in a collector fluid such as molten salt, which would reach and hold temperatures up to 1000° F, sufficient to produce the high-energy steam required for large generators. Daily exposure to the sun would cause the collector fluid to heat enough so that power generation could continue during some hours of darkness. A storage system, perhaps a hydrogen exchange, would provide the necessary additional continuity.

Figure 7: Power Tower—Concentrated sunlight from 1775 mirror facets is shown striking the steel target mounted 114 feet up on the 200-foot-high "power tower" at U.S. DOE's Solar Thermal Test Facility at Sandia Lab causing molten steel to drip from the target. In the first major focusing test of 71 heliostat arrays, a 2 x 3-foot hole was burned in the ¼-inch thick steel plate in less than two minutes. (Credit: Sandia Lab) DOE-77-11219

As with the OTEC system of national-capacity size (see p. 264), power could be distributed throughout the country from such centralized facilities either in the form of hydrogen gas for local conversion to current, or as electricity itself.

The environmental impacts of the extensive shading caused by solar farms is not known, but proponents claim that it would be far less than the amount of land that would be strip-mined for a coal-burning plant of similar size. Aden and Marjorie Meinel, developers of the solar farm concept, say it would take no more land than a nuclear plant (including a nuke's safety "exclusion zone").[31]

The "Power Tower"—This approach, now in moderate-sized experimental form in at least two locations, uses mirrors near ground level to focus and reflect sunlight onto a boiler placed in their midst on a column up to 1,500 feet high. Elevation of the boiler enables mirrors to face upwards, thus catching and reflecting the maximum amount of falling sunlight. The boiler can heat water directly for steam, or hold a sodium-based fluid for circulation of heat to generators on the ground. A test prototype backed by the DOE involves a 40-acre mirror field and 200-kilowatt tower in New Mexico. There are plans for a 10-megawatt power plant in Barstow, California to operate by 1980.[32]

Costs of the power tower concept are estimated to be competitive with fossil fuel systems, and testing the next few years will determine whether that is true. Their use will be limited to zones of bright, constant sunlight, but in those areas their potential output is significant; towers of a size sufficient to supply the electricity needs of small cities are within range of designs now being tested.

One big problem with both of these HTP processes is that they use water: in both the production of steam and hydrogen gas. Surface water is scarce by definition in desert areas, and in the southwestern U.S. subsurface water is being depleted at an alarming rate due to the demands of an expanding population and farmland irrigation. Whether or not this limits the applicability of HTP systems at all size levels remains to be seen, but at present it seems to be a significant factor in considering truly large-scale solar farm or power tower installation.

The solar farm and power tower concepts offer large centralized sources of power. What are the drawbacks of large power plants built far from the communities and industries they service? Although building big may involve some economies of scale, there are large-scale inefficiencies as well. Big plants usually produce electricity for urban centers that may be many miles from the facility. The electricity is sent over transmission lines. It is generally agreed that power lines are unsightly, but, of more consequence, they take up a lot of land area and can endanger those living and working near them.[33] Large electric grids (series of power lines transmitting electricity) are also inefficient as electricity is lost in transit along the wires. For example, of the four environmentally disastrous coal-burning plants at Four Corners near Grants, New Mexico, the equivalent of the total output of one is lost on route to Los Angeles, where the power is used.

Large centralized stations do not generally serve their host communities; rural areas are often sacrificed to meet gluttonous urban power demands. And centralization causes insecurity and expense; a number of units must be standing by should the giant station fail. If this large idle capacity is not available, then a power failure at the large plant could be a disaster. These problems, as well as the lack of local control over power production, are inherent qualities of big centralized plants whether they are solar powered or not.

Ocean Thermal Energy Conversion (OTEC)

The year-round fall of sunshine on southern seas lifts surface water temperatures—in the Gulf of Mexico, for instance—into the 70's (° F), while deep subsurface waters remain in the 40's (° F). The stored solar energy in this surface layer is recoverable precisely because the waters beneath it are so cold.

The method of recovery is simple in conception. A fluid that boils at a low temperature—ammonia is currently most favored—is sealed in a closed-cycle heat exchanger. One chamber is bathed by warm surface water, which causes the ammonia to vaporize and expand. It escapes with sufficient speed and force to turn a turbine before passing on to a cooling chamber for condensation. Here, cold water sucked from deep below chills the vapor causing it to liquify. The ammonia is then returned to the first chamber for heating. This closed (ammonia) cycle produces power by making use of the great differences in temperature found in some parts of the ocean.

As with windpower system designs, the Civil Engineering Department of the University of Massachusetts (U/ Mass at Amherst) has been a leader in OTEC design. Study teams at Carnegie-Mellon University in Pittsburgh and at the TRW Corporation's research center in California have also been involved in conceptual work. Power plant designs and siting proposed by these various groups differ somewhat, but

Figure 8: Ocean Thermal Energy Conversion (OTEC)—An artist's conception of a structure proposed by Lockheed's Ocean Systems division for an OTEC system. The structure is a platform with crew quarters and maintenance facilities. Attached around the outside are turbine-generators and pumps. It is 250 ft. in diameter and 1600 ft. long and weighs about 300,000 tons. The concept is designed to send 160 million watts of power ashore to distribution networks—enough power to fulfill the needs of a city with 100,000 residents. (Credit: Lockheed Missiles & Space Co.) DOE-77-10735

there is basic agreement that the resource involved is both accessible and vast.

The UMass prototype—guided by Prof. Heronemus, with his long navel engineering background in submersible hull design—makes use of an added oceanic feature to enhance the OTEC system; the massive Gulfstream current. UMass designers propose the anchoring of as many as 8,000 semi-submerged or surface-floating OTEC units spaced apart in a fifteen-mile wide, 550-mile-long stretch of the Gulfstream between Key Sombrero, Florida and Charleston, South Carolina. Built to withstand full-force hurricanes as well as the constant pressure of the current, each of these generator stations, about 100-feet-wide by 900-feet-long, would produce some 400 megawatts of electricity. Collectively, they would generate enough electric current for the entire country. The current could then be distributed nationwide through a new breed of super-cooled, low-loss transmission cables. (Heronemus suggests that these might be placed along the interstate highway system's rights-of-way.) Alternatively, the current could be converted in whole or part to hydrogen or into methanol motor fuel through interaction with the seawater and its components. Those energy products could be shipped or piped around the country or the world.

The main function of the Gulfstream in the UMass design is to bring each power plant a constant fresh supply of both warm and cold water. Any installation of such size in a less mobile sea would tend to homogenize the temperature differences of the thermal layers, adversely affecting the ecosystem.

According to its authors, the U/Mass plan could be implemented in a decade from scratch. But the federal research and development budget for OTEC ($33 million in 1979 DOE budget) seems better keyed to results in the 21st century.

Federal hesitancy is supported in a May 1978 report by the Office of Technology Assessment that found that: "Although no scientific breakthroughs are needed to build an OTEC plant, no OTEC plant has been fully designed because of technical problems involved with the heat exchangers, the cold water pipe, the working fluid, the ocean platform, and the underwater transmission lines from plants which would generate electricity."[34]

More Power From the Sea

OTEC is not the only possible way to tap the immense energy of the ever-moving sea. Other ideas of mechanically harnessing the power potential of ocean waves include compressed air pillows and rocking float platforms. Wave power would be a naturally decentralized energy source for coastal areas and is being investigated in Great Britain.

Harnessing the power of the tides is possible at a few sites in North America. Wherever the total rise approaches 20 feet per tide, and there are a number of such locations in the world, it is possible to build impoundment dams and catch pools enabling operation of hydroelectric generators.

A demonstration tidal power facility has been built on the north Pacific coast of Russia, and a 240-megawatt station is operating with acceptable success in the French Rance River estuary. So far, there are no other significant tidal power installations.

In the U.S. and Canada, plans to harness the potential of the Bay of Fundy—where tides averaging 30-35 feet on the Canadian shore are the highest in the world—have for years risen and fallen like the tides themselves.[35] The main problem seems to be the cost and—for the U.S.—the fact that Canada simply doesn't need the electricity. But attempts in recent years to locate supertanker-fed oil refineries at Machiasport and Eastport, Maine, has highlighted both the clean power potential of the tides there and the rising costs of fossils fuels that make the "harvesting" of tides economically more attractive.

Geothermal Power

The earth's core is hot. At the base of the "continental crust," the outer 30-50 miles (50-80 km) of the earth beneath the continents, the range of tem-

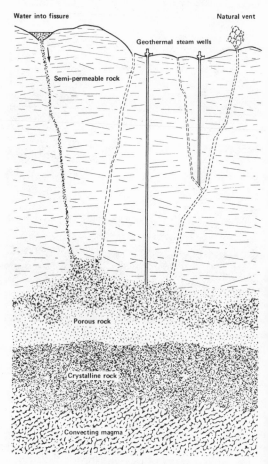

Figure 9: Geothermal site—Heat from the magma moves by convection to a layer of porous rock containing water. Deep in the ground and under high pressure, the water remains liquid; as it rises in a natural vent, it expands, boils, and produces steam. A well can tap the vent or the porous layer. (Source: William W. Eaton, "Geothermal Energy," DOE publication, 1975, p. 5.)

peratures is from 200°-1000° C (400°-1800° F). At the earth's molten center temperatures may range from 3500°-4500° C (6000°-8000° F). This virtually inexhaustible heat is the result of long-lived radioactive materials.[36]

In some locations around the world, the molten rock or "magma" of the earth's center has pushed close to the surface, and we find active volcanoes. In other areas where underground heat encounters underground water, close-to-surface manifestations of geo-thermal power take the form of steam geysers like "Old Faithful" in Yellow-stone National Park, or more gently as hot springs. For many years people have taken advantage of these emis-sions for heat, hot water, and even electricity.

Some geothermal wells yield a com-bination of steam and hot water under pressure. These are known as "wet steam" fields. Major fields of this type have been found in Mexico, the Salton Sea-Imperial Valley area of California, the Yellowstone region of Wyoming, and in Japan, New Zealand, the Philip-pines, Indonesia, Taiwan, and Turkey.

The Salton Sea-Imperial Valley region is a good example of a

Figure 10: Geothermal well—Located in Hawaii, the Nero Geothermal Well is the hottest in the U.S. at 356° C. It is free of the large quantities of dangerous disolved solids and gases that are sometimes present in geothermal outflow. (Credit: DOE-77-11254)

potentially enormous source of geothermal energy in a wet-steam field that, if developed, could provide very important economic benefits for that sec-tion of the country. This active geothermal area covers approx-imately 1,000 square kilometers (400 square miles), and tem-peratures of 300° C (570° F) have been verified at depths of only 1,500 meters (5,000 feet).[37]

There are examples of use of geo-thermal power, both for direct heating of homes and hot water and for elec-trical production from turbines turned by steam. Underground steam heat has been used for residential heating in Boise, Idaho since 1890. In the 1930s, Iceland's capital city Reykjavik estab-lished a geothermal system that pro-vides heat and hot water to 90% of its homes. As far back as 1913, geother-mal steam has operated power plants in Larderello, Italy. Production there in 1975 was up to 365 megawatts from 13 plants. More recent developments closer to home include a 400-mega-watt-geothermal steam plant in a gey-ser-rich area of northern California which produces current at about half the cost of a nuclear generator. Its final planned capacity is as much as 1,200 megawatts.

There is quite a geothermal poten-tial for the U.S., with active areas near hot springs throughout the western U.S. and in large basins under the Gulf Coast. But there are environmental problems associated with geothermal energy that, along with the general lack of research in this field, may slow development.

Problems associated with tapping geothermal energy resources include noise considerations, safe disposal of toxic and saline liquid wastes involved with some hot water fields, dangerous gases that can be released, subsurface water contamination, and waste heat thermal pollution. One consideration is that the withdrawal of large volumes of liquid from underground can cause land subsidence, or sinking, that can endanger nearby structures and water sources. This land subsidence has already occurred in a geothermal field in New Zealand and is irreversible. Another important question is whether reinjection of used water too near fault lines causes earthquakes.

If these problems can be overcome, geothermal energy may provide a substantial amount of energy, either as heat or electricity, in areas where such resources exist:

> With regard to power generation, estimates of installed geothermal electrical capacity in the U.S. by 1985 range from a conservative 500 megawatts, assuming only technology presently available or under development, to a potential 20,000-30,000 megawatts, based on an energetic and successful research and development program by both industry and the Federal Government. If this potential could be realized, it would represent about 3% of the total electrical generating capacity of the country projected for 1985.[38]

As for economic costs, experience in other countries has shown that the use of geothermal heat in agriculture, industry, and home heating is less expensive than any other means, including hydroelectric power. And, "with the development of multi-purpose geothermal plants for several combined end products, such as electricity, hot water uses, de-salination, and mineral production, the economic benefits can be expected to be correspondingly greater than for single purpose facilities.

"SUPER—HIGH" TECHNOLOGY

There are two technologies so far that qualify under this heading. One is an application of solar power, the other of atomic energy. The latter, fusion energy, has been a research and development project for two decades. The other is the solar satellite power station, a scheme whose popularity in some quarters has recently risen dramatically.

Neither of these possible power sources meets the criteria of a truly ecological society—that power production be decentralized, accessible, understandable, and available for local control. However, both are being considered as possible alternative sources of power for the 21st century. And so we need to understand their appeal, possibilities, and problems.

Solar Satellite Power Stations

> For those still naive enough to believe that no one can own the sun or that solar energy is inherently decentralized, environmentally benign, and technically simple, solar satellites should be sufficient to dispel such lingering myths.[39]

There is one central-system solar proposal that "rises above" storage requirements. It's the so-called solar satellite. This scheme calls for a series of satellites in synchronous orbit around the earth at an altitude of some 22,000 miles, spaced apart in order to "see" the sun at all hours. A satellite would hold some 14 billion solar cells. Big enough to produce from 5,000-10,000 megawatts of electricity each (as much as 5-10 conventional large central power stations), they would transmit it 24 hours a day via a microwave beam to the earth below.

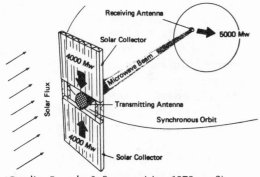

Receiving Antenna

Solar Collector

5000 Mw

4000 Mw

Microwave Beam

Solar Flux

Transmitting Antenna

Synchronous Orbit

4000 Mw

Solar Collector

(Credit: *People & Energy*, May 1978, p. 3)

"...the technical complexity of the entire proposition suggests another problem area—namely that of control and centralization by large industrial concerns." (Citizens' Energy Project Report - see Resources)

In April 1978 two federal House Science and Technology Subcommittees approved a $25 million authorization for development of SSPS and determination of its economic and environmental impacts. The costs of a development program could reach $60 billion. A full 100 satellite system could come to $800 billion! The program represents an astronomical financial commitment, and an environmental one as well.

The idea was first presented in 1968 by Dr. Peter Glaser of the Arthur D. Little consulting firm in Cambridge, Mass. At the time, people thought he was crazy...Now the idea has new appeal, especially to NASA and the aerospace industry, as it offers a reason for continued space development—and a beginning to the "industrialization of space." One idea is to have the power satellites built in space, perhaps using the space shuttle and a space station as bases. It has even been suggested that materials for building the satellites be mined from the moon in order to conserve the vast amounts of fuel needed just to place the building materials for the satellites and construction facilities in orbit.

In theory the station would be fairly simple. Moving panels would carry the photovoltaic cells. The cells would generate electricity from the constant sunlight and send it back to earth as a beam of microwave radiation. The beam would be targeted on huge receiving antennae, called rectennas, that could cover around 35 square miles. The satellites would receive and transmit energy almost continuously, moving to avoid the earth's shadow.

If the program is ever implemented, it would call for a long-term commitment of billions of dollars in industry-contracts for hardware. It therefore came as little surprise when a coalition of the concerned companies recently formed a non-profit corporation called the Sunsat Energy Council to "educate" federal decision-makers about the benefits of solar satellites. Its members include Grumman Aerospace, Westinghouse, G.E., Boeing, Lockheed, Martin Marietta, McDonnell Douglas, RCA, Southern California Edison, Arthur D. Little, Universities Space Research, and MIT, among others.[40]

The objections to the solar satellite are fairly obvious. Besides the fact that the project would use tremendous amounts of capital and provide few jobs, the environmental effects of the microwave radiation should give all pause to consider. A few books (Paul Brodeur's *The Zapping of America* and

Louise Young's classic *Power Over People*) have presented the dangers from such radiation. It is becoming known that microwaves do genetic and physiological damage, cause cataracts and central nervous system disorders. And what would be the effects on birds and aircraft and other things that happened to get in the beam's path? What would happen if the beam slipped "off-target," either by accident (mechanical or personnel error) or by design, moved off course by an enemy rocket or satellite?

The single dissenting vote to the subcommittee bill was cast by Rep. Richard Ottinger (D. N.Y.), who termed the project a "perversion of the potential of solar energy." Warning of the program's "huge cost," the creation of "vested interests" and "unanswered environmental and safety questions," he said that solar energy should be used and collected "here on earth."[41]

Fusion*

Fusion energy is considered to be one "high-tech" alternative energy source for the future. It would produce electric power through the coalescence, or fusing together, of atomic nuclei. If successful, the process would release great amounts of heat to, once again, boil water to produce steam to run turbines to generate electricity.

A fusion reaction is the opposite of a fission reaction in which a single nucleus splits into two smaller nuclei.[42] In fission the released energy comes from a repulsion between the two positively charged smaller nuclei that pushes them apart at great speeds. In a fusion reaction, energy is released when two nuclei join to form a larger but more stable nucleus. When such a fusion reaction occurs, energy is released as the protons and neutrons making up the two smaller nuclei

*Prepared by Sam Lovejoy, Montague, Ma., and by Peter Lichtner, Physicist, Univ. of Md.

"settle down" into a new and more stable configuration which "weighs" less than the sum of the initial nuclei. The energy of the so-called A-bomb comes from fission, whereas the "thermo-nuclear" or H-bomb gets its incredible energy from fusion.[43]

Two examples of simple fusion reactions of interest for fusion reactors are the coalescence of two deuterium nuclei and the coalescence of a deuterium and tritium nucleus. The latter reaction is the least demanding technically for a practical fusion device because more energy is released. The extra neutron carries away most of it which is eventually turned into heat to produce electricity. Other more complicated fusion reactions "power" our sun and the stars.

In order to bring two nuclei close together so that they may fuse they must be moving fast enough to overcome the repulsive "coulomb force" holding them apart. This requires energy. Unlike a fission reaction, a fusion reaction is not self-starting. A self-sustaining fusion reaction requires temperatures upwards of 100 million degrees centigrade—10 times the temperature at the center of the sun! At these temperatures all matter exists in a state called a plasma—a hot gas of positively charged nuclei and negatively charged electrons.

There are two different approaches now being investigated for the attainment of a practical fusion reactor.[44] One problem is to successfully confine the plasma. Material walls won't work, not because the plasma would necessarily melt them, but because there would be too great an energy loss as the plasma particles bounced off the walls. A sustained reaction would be impossible. Two basic methods are now being investigated. One is magnetic confinement or the "magnetic bottle" method, which uses strong magnetic fields to hold the plasma together.[45]

Inertial confinement is used, for example, in laser fusion. Here a small pellet of fusion fuel is compressed by high intensity light rays.

There are three basic designs of the magnetic bottle containment: tokamaks, magnetic mirrors, and so-called theta-pinches. Currently the tokamak is the main hope for obtaining fusion. Although invented in the U.S.S.R. in the early 1960s, it was first taken seriously in the U.S. in 1969. It is distinguished by its toroidal, or doughnut shaped, reactor vessel. The most recent success of the tokamak was achieved in July 1978, when a team of scientists at Princeton's plasma physics laboratory headed by Dr. Melvin B. Gottlieb, reached temperatures of 60 million degrees centigrade for a 20th of a second.[46] Previously the record temperature was only 26 million degrees, not enough to sustain a reaction, which requires at least 44 million degrees. To produce a net gain in energy will require 100 million degrees sustained for at least one full second, which is still a long way off. Present estimates are that fusion generation of electricity cannot happen until 2005, and only after another $15 billion is added to the $2 billion already spent.

Inertial confinement has offered a new and second major avenue of research.[47] Here the idea is to virtually instantaneously compress small pellets of fusion fuel to densities 10 thousand times higher than normal matter densities by symmetrically irradiating them with super-powerful lasers, relativistic electron beams or heavy-ion beams (heavy-ions are heavy nuclei such as oxygen or uranium nuclei). Critical problems include developing the requisite lasers and particle-beam generators and the design of pellets for high power output. An added complication is the international military interest in laser and particle-beam weapons as well as the possible relevance of inertial confinement to fusion bombs. **This new, extremely lethal and vicious "1984" weapons field makes this area of fusion research essentially a Pentagon project, and many aspects of it are highly classified.**[48]

There are a number of fundamental difficulties in making fusion an economically viable energy source.[49] Once the plasma is confined there is still the problem of retrieving useful heat energy. This is to be done with a huge blanket at least one meter thick surrounding the plasma, designed to stop the high energy neutrons produced by the fusion reaction thus creating heat which can then be used to boil water. Because heat is only retrievable outside of the plasma and not throughout its volume, as is the case in a fission reactor, there is a limit on the physical size of a fusion reactor of a fixed power output.[50] This is because there is a limit on the amount of energy flow known materials can withstand. The surface area of the material around the plasma must be large enough so that the amount of energy per square meter passing through the surface is less than the damaging point of the material. The smallest fusion reactors would probably be quite large, implying big initial capital costs.

The lifetime of the blanket is expected to be between 2 and 10 years because of radiation damage due to the high intensity neutron bombardment. Developing suitable materials is one of the most critical problems involved in successful commercial fusion reactor. Furthermore, repair will be extremely cumbersome and difficult because material in the reactor will become highly radioactive.

And there will be radioactive waste! Tons of it would be produced annually due to neutron activation of the reactor materials. There is also the problem of containing tritium, a beta- emitter with a half-life of 12.3 years that diffuses easily through almost all metals. A fusion reactor will contain far more tritium than a fission one. Its containment presents unsolved technological problems both during normal plant operation and as a result of so-called "postulated" accidents.[51]

As already mentioned the "dirty" deuterium-tritium reaction appears the most feasible for obtaining a controlled fusion reaction rather than the "clean" deuterium-deuterium reaction. It has been used in all experimental fusion devices to date. Deuterium is in plentiful supply in the oceans and is cheap to extract.[52] Tritium, however, is nearly nonexistent in nature. It will be produced by neutron bombardment of lithium within the reactor. Thus lithium is the limiting fuel. But the real limiting factor might be the availibility of materials. Recycling will be difficult if not impossible due to radioactive contamination.

Even if the dream of a self-sustaining fusion reactor fails to be realized, that might not mean the end of fusion power. For a new monstrosity is looming on the horizon—the "hybrid" or fusion-fission reactor presently being pursued in the U.S.S.R.[53]

The hybrid is a compromise fusion device, in that it is not necessary for the fusion reaction to be self-sustaining. This makes it much easier to achieve. Here fusion is used as a source of fast neutrons rather energy. **Its neutrons convert a blanket of uranium-238 wrapped around the plasma into plutonium for use as fuel in light-water reactors. A hybrid reactor would supposedly produce 3000 kg of plutonium per year! Some scientists fear that such a plant might appear so attractive that the search for a truly self-sus-**

taining fusion reactor might be prematurely abandoned.

Research into fusion energy is going on at all major U.S. nuclear research centers—Princeton, San Diego, Oak Ridge, Livermore and Los Alamos. The U.S.S.R., England, France, West Germany and Japan have already heavily invested in fusion.

Among the avid proponents of fusion energy is the ultra-rightwing U.S. Labor Party (USLP) or National Caucus of Labor Committees (NCLC) headed by Lyn Marcus, (also known as Lyndon LaRouche). In 1974 the USLP/NCLC founded the Fusion Energy Foundation (FEF), its think-tank on fusion energy. FEF publishes two journals: The *International Journal of Fusion Energy*, a professional looking technical journal on fusion, and *Fusion Magazine*, a monthly. *Fusion* has carried such enlightening articles as, "There is no Cancer Epidemic" by Dr. Richard Pollak, which purports to demonstrate that the "...scare stories about carcinogens from the environmentalists have more to do with their prejudices against industrial society than with scientific facts."[54]

(In the spring of 1977 the USLP was involved in gathering information for the New Hampshire State Police to target the Clamshell Alliance as a "cover for terrorist activity.")

In Conclusion
There appears to be a wide variety of alternative sources of power available for use now and in the years and decades to come. The most dependable involve technologies already known—ones that will undoubtedly become more efficient and cost-effective over time —which can be used to tap the power potentials of the sun, wind, water and earth.

These alternatives have diverse applications. It would seem that a combination of systems could meet the different needs for power that exist. Passive solar obviously makes a lot of sense for new construction. Small-scale hydro will only be useful in areas with as yet untapped rivers (although it has also been suggested that small turbines be put in western irrigation systems that carry large loads of water at certain periods). The wind can provide electricity in many areas, and solar cells promise a future of completely decentralized solar electricity.

Our energy future does not depend on "choosing" one of these technologies. Instead we must understand their attributes and drawbacks and develop a flexible energy plan for the future based on multiple use. We have to learn which technologies are appropriate for what needs. "Appropriate technology"or "AT" is a term that is being heard more and more these days. What does it mean? Bruce Anderson, a solar builder, architect, writer and editor of *Solar Age* magazine defines it this way:

Appropriate technology embodies many beneficial features. (1) It makes efficient use of energy and other resources, and in other ways enhances environmental quality; (2) it is light on capital use and particularly conducive to small-business participation; (3) it depends as much as possible on, and seeks to dignify, human labor; (4) it uses local materials and labor; (5) it is simple to install, operate, and maintain; (6) the technology serves people rather than dominates them—it is responsive to human needs; (7) it emphasizes technologies conducive to decentralized control (individual, collective, community) and de-

mocratic decision-making; (8) it results in durable recyclàble systems and/or products, and offers low life-cycle costs to the user.[55]

What this means, among other things, is that just because a particular method of producing energy is solar-powered, it is not necessarily "appropriate." What we must ask is: Whom does it serve; who controls it; and what are its costs in social, environmental, and financial terms. As we approach and begin to enter the solar age—and enter we must—let us not be fooled into thinking that solar technology is inherently smaller scale and therefore "better." Solar systems can be very high-technology stuff. They can be complex, centralized, expensive—and unnecessary.

If our goal is to meet our energy needs, we would be wise to first examine these needs. We need to conserve, recycle, and demand goods that will last. We don't need wasteful planned obsolescence. We should question the squandering of vast amounts of energy on the production of weapons. It would be a sad state of affairs if we traded nuclear plants for other, equally dangerous, expensive and centralized technological systems—the solar satellite or fusion power for example.

As we enter a new era, it is appropriate to question the standards by which the new energy sources will be developed. Will it be for maximum profit, for private enterprise, including investor owned utilities? Or will the solar age have values and goals besides profit: things like the quality of life, health and safety, creation of good jobs, maximization of public and local control. As we will see in the next chapter—Going Solar—choosing the appropriate alternatives is not an economic problem but a political and social one.

Prepared by Anna Gyorgy, Steve Turner

Footnotes

1. "The Use of Solar Energy for Space Heating and Hot Water," Report of the Mass. Energy Policy Office, April 1976, p. 7.

2. John Abrams, "Solar Energy: A Gentle Resource," *Island*, vol. 1, 1977. Vineyard Haven, MA 02568.

3. Denis Hayes, *Rays of Hope: The Transition to a Post-Petroleum World* (NY: W.W. Norton & Co., 1977), pp. 160, 162.

4. Denis Hayes, *Energy: The Solar Prospect*, World Watch Paper 11, March 1977, p. 14.

5. Environmentalists for Full Employment, *Jobs & Energy*, Spring 1977, Washington, D.C. 20005

6. *People & Energy*, June 1978.

7. David R. Inglis, "A Tale of Two Energies," Committee for Nuclear Responsibility, Report 1976-1. p. 1.

8. Gary Soucie, *Audubon*, 76:81-8. May 1974.

9. The Tvind Schools are a "freestanding community" of about 1,000 people located in West Jutland about 10 km from the North Sea coast. Contact: Energikontor, Tvindskolerne, Tvind, 6990 Ulfborg, Denmark. —Lee Johnson and Marshall Merriam, "Small Groups, Big Windmills," *Wind Power Digest*, Winter 1977/78, pp. 30-31. See also: WISE (World International Service on Energy), no. 1, May 1978.

10. Steve Turner, conversation with Prof. Heronemus, June 1977.

11. "Just off the southern coast of Massachusetts, the island of Cuttyhunk now receives half of its electricity from a 200-kw, Americanized version of the Danish Gedser mill (*Rain*, April 1977, pp. 12-14), which cost only $280,000. Its federally-funded equivalent, the 200-kw NASA-DOE Mod OA wind-turbine, sitting on neighboring Block Island, R.I., was given to a private utility after costing $3,000,000!"— Johnson and Merriam, *op. cit.*, p. 30.

12. Environmentalists for Full Employment, *op. cit.*, p. 13.

13. At pumped storage facilities off-peak power is used to pump water up into elevated reservoirs. The water can then be released to run turbines during peak periods.—Helene S. Kassler, "Power From the Streams," *Solar Age* Magazine, July 1978, p. 16. Pumped storage is an inefficient way to make electricity. About two units of power are needed to pump up water that then produces 1 unit on its return down through the turbines.

14. Kassler, *op. cit.*, p. 16.

15. Springfielders estimate a combined savings from municipalization and the switch to hydro of at least 30%. —Steve Turner, "Power to the People," (*New England Magazine, Boston Globe*, 9 July 1978.)

16. Kassler, *op. cit.*, p. 17. See also: U.S. Army Corps of Engineers, *Estimate of National Hydroelectric Power Potential at Existing Dams*, July 1977. Ruben S. Brown and Alvin S. Goodman, "Small Hydropower—Promise and Reality in New York State and the Northeast," N.Y. State Energy Research and Development Authority, Agency Building No. 2, Empire State Plaza, Albany, NY 12223.

17. Kassel, *op. cit.*, p. 17. The People's Republic of China had more than 60,000 small hydro plants in 1975. See Vaclav Smil, "Intermediate Technology in China," *Bulletin of the Atomic Scientists*, February 1977.

18. David Holzman, "Biomass Fuel: Fermenting Self-Sufficiency," *People & Energy*, February 1978, p. 10.

19. NASA predicts that bioconversion could produce 30 quads of energy by the year 2000. See "Deriving Liquid and Gas Fuels from Waste or Grown Organics," NASA Technical Note D-8156, Lewis Research Center, Cleveland, OH 44135.

20. David Holzman, *op. cit.*, p. 10. Other information in this paragraph from "FACTSHEET 2. Fuels From Wastes/Bioconversion," John M. Fowler. National Science Teachers Association, produced under contract with ERDA (now DOE), "facts those of the authors." Bibliography. Copies of 19 energy factsheets can be ordered from: Oak Ridge, TN 37830. See also for basic information on how it works/doing it and bibliography: "Methane Digesters," New Alchemy Institute Newsletter no. 3, 1973. Box 432, Woods Hole, MA 02543.

21. Hayes, *op. cit.*, p. 195. In India, 25,000 biogas (gobar) plants were sold in 1976 alone.

22. A joint study team of Navy and Calif. Institute of Tech. scientists began experiments in 1976 on undersea culturing of fast-growing kelp, aiming at an eventual "farm" of 100,000 acres with a daily harvest sufficient to produce "43 million cubic feet of synthetic methane gas, as well as great quantities of crop fertilizers and silage...enough fuel energy and nutrients for crops and animal fodder to sustain a city of at least half a million people." *New York Times*, 31 July 1976.

23. *People & Energy*, March 1978, p. 18.

24. *People & Energy*, February 1978, p. 11. The article also says: "The governor of Hawaii wants to create a program of mandatory blending of alcohol and gas in that state. Under the

plan, alcohol would come from the currently depressed sugar cane industry and be distilled in the now idle Seagrams rum plant...Cars have run on 100% alcohol in New Zealand and other places, and Stanley Barber of Arkansas has invented a device which allows a car to switch between gas and alcohol at the flick of a switch and can be installed for $300 (Barber's address is c/o SB Construction Co., 8 Boston Sq., P.O. Box 6156, South Station, Fort Smith, AR). The Southwest Alabama Farmers Cooperative (SWAFCO), a group of 100 low income black farmers is now producing 40 gallons per day of alcohol, which they are blending with gas for use in farm vehicles. They are using grain contaminated with alfatozin, which is useless for food production." Also: Hal Bernton, "Alcohol Fuels: A Major Source of Power Only a Few Years from Here," Rodale's *Environment Action Bulletin* (no longer publishing), 29 October 1977.

25. *People & Energy,* vol. iv, no. 5, May 1978, p. 6.

26. "The Potential of Wood as an Energy Resource in New England," New England Federal Regional Council, September 1977. Available from NEFRC, Rm. E-431, JFK Bldg., Boston, MA 02203. The Federal Regional Council is an interagency, intergovernmental coordinating group. Its chair is FEA Regional Administrator and it includes 11 grant making federal agencies.

27. *People & Energy*, May 1978, p. 5.

28. *Ibid.*

29. Calif. Dept. of Forestry, Sacramento. *People & Energy*, May 1978, p. 5.

30. Material here from Denis Hayes, *Energy: The Solar Prospect, op. cit.*, p. 22. "Increased production is of paramount importance in lowering the prices of photovoltaics. In an 18-month period of 1975-76, U.S. purchases of photovoltaic cells for earth-bound purposes doubled and the average price per cell dropped by about 50% Price reductions of from 10 to 30% for each doubling of output have been common in the electrical components industries, and photovoltaic production should prove no exception to the rule."—p. 27. The cells now cost about $11 per peak watt, down from $21 in 1977. DOE's goal is to reduce the price to 50¢ per peak watt by 1986.—"Consumer Briefing Summary," Office of Consumer Affairs, DOE, 30 March 1978, p. 9.

31. Hayes, *Rays of Hope*, p. 164.

32. *Ibid.*

33. See Paul Brodeur, *The Zapping of America*, (New York: W.W. Norton and Co., Inc., 1977); and Louis Young, *Power Over People*, (New York: Oxford University Press, 1973).

34. From Office of Technology Assessment News Release, 7 June 1978. See "Renewable Ocean Energy Sources, Part 1: Ocean Thermal Energy Conversion." May 1978. OTA, Washington, D.C. 20510. Gov't Printing Office. GPO-052-003-0053-1. $2.50.

35. John Chappell, Jr., "Oil Refinery Threatens Tidal Power Resource," 1977, (with thanks).

36. Material for this discussion from: William W. Eaton, *Geothermal Energy*, U.S. ERDA (now DOE), 1975, pp. 3-4, 13-14, 32, 34-36.

37. *Ibid.*, p. 6.

38. *Ibid.*, p. 36.

39. *People & Energy*, May 1978, p. 3.
Energy, May 1978, p. 3.

40. *People & Energy*, May 1978, p. 3.

41. Solar Energy Intelligence Report, 1 May 1978, p. 124.

42. For a brief but lucid introduction into the physics of fusion reactors and their problems see David J. Rose and Michael Frietag, *Technology Review* 79, no. 2, 1976, p. 21.

43. Actually the most powerful nuclear weapons are fission-fusion-fission devices which work as follows: A plutonium trigger sets off a fusion reaction producing high energy neutrons which in turn cause a blanket of uranium-238 surrounding the fusion reaction to fission. The energy produced is divided roughly 50-50 between the fusion reaction and the fission of the uranium blanket.

44. An excellent comparison of the various approaches to fusion from a technological, environmental and economical point of view can be found in John P. Holdren, *Science* 200, 1978, p. 168. See also: Rose and Frietag, *op. cit.*

45. Magnetic confinement operates on the principle that charged particles moving in a magnetic field have the property of spiralling along the magnetic field lines. It's then just a matter of building the magnets properly so that the field lines stay within the confines of the reactor vessel. But in practice the magnetic bottle concept yields only partial confinement. It is still an open question whether it will really work for a commercial power reactor. One major technical difficulty is that the magnets must be superconducting if there is to be any hope of a net energy gain. This requires keeping their temperature close to absolute zero while the nearby plasma is a swirling inferno of millions of degrees!

46. William D. Metz, *Science* 201, 1978, p. 792. A brief description of tokamaks, magnetic mirrors and theta-pinches can be found in Rose and Frietag, *op. cit.*

47. Holdren, *op. cit.*, and Rose and Frietag, *op. cit.*

48. Holdren, *op. cit.*, gives several references to the weapons connection.

49. A good review of the problems of fusion can be found in: David Holzman, *People and Energy*, no. 7 and 8 , 1978. (Citizen's Energy Project, 1413 K St., N.W., Washington, D.C. 20005)

50. W.E. Parkins, *Science* 199, 1978, p. 1403.

51. Robert Cowen, *Technology Review* 79, no. 5, 1978, p. 8.

52. See Holdren, *op. cit.*

53. *Ibid.* and Cowen, *op. cit.*

54. For a detailed account of the USLP/NCLC see *NCLC: Brownshirts of the Seventies*, by the Terrorist Information Project, now the Repression Information Project, July 1976, and *The Public Eye* 1, no. 1, Fall 1977, by the same organization. See also: Deborah Shapley, *Science* 190, 1978, p.

55. Bruce Anderson, "Appropriately, Hard Choices Ahead," *Solar Age*, July 1978, p. 2.

Sources of Information—Alternatives

There are extensive resources now available on alternative energy sources and appropriate technology. Please contact the following for their magazines/catalogues/publications lists:

● **Alternative Sources of Energy**
Route 1, Box 36B, Minong, Wisconsin 54859. Quarterly magazine ($5.00/4 issues); *Spectrum*, an alternate technology equipment directory; lending library.

● **Citizens' Energy Project**
1413 K. St., N.W., Washington, D.C. 20005. *People and Energy*, $10.00/year; $7.00/year low-income. Bulk subscriptions available.

● **Environmental Action Reprint Service (EARS)**, 2239 East Colfax, Denver, Colo. 80206. Literature, books, teaching materials on all aspects of alternative energy; also buttons and bumperstickers.

● **Friends of the Earth**
124 Spear St., San Francisco CA 94105. Complete energy bibliography for $3.50; Amory Lovins' books; general ecology books and resources.

● **new roots,** Notes on Appropriate Technology and community Self-Reliance for the N.E. P.O. Box 459, Amherst, MA 01002. Monthly subscription: $8.00/year; $6.00/year low income. (Send checks to: Universtiy of Massachusetts/new roots).

● **Rain**
2270 N.W. Irving, Portland, OR 97210. Appropriate Technology/alternate energy magazine, $10.00/year.

● **Solar Energy Digest** (monthly newsletter on large and small-scale solar technologies). P.O. Box 19776, San Diego, CA 92117. $27.00/year.

● **Solar Energy Intelligence Report**, (weekly industry, government-oriented solar news). Business Publishers, Inc., P.O. Box 1067, Silver Spring, MD 20910. $90.00/year.

● **Solar Lobby**
1028 Connecticut Ave., N.W., Washington, D.C. 20036. *Sun Times*, monthly publication, $15.00/year.

● **Total Environmental Action (TEA)**
Church Hill, Harrisville, NH 03450. Catalogue of solar books. *Solar Age* Magazine: $20.00/year, $32.00/2 years. "*Solar Age* is the one magazine devoted to full coverage of all aspects of solar energy and the industry which will make it all happen."

● **U.S. Department of Energy**
National Technical Information Center, P.O. Box 62, Oak Ridge, TN 37830.

● **U.S. Dept. of Housing and Urban Develop. (HUD),** National Solar Heating and Cooling Information Center, Box 1607, Rockville, MD 20850. (For free booklet and other information call 800-523-2929).

Chapter 5:

Going Solar

The Only Way to Go

Our energy future depends on the renewable sources of power generally known as "solar." These include wind, hydroelectric, biomass, and ocean energy. They are the only energy resources we know of that are dependable, non-polluting, renewable. We have examined the problems with nuclear energy and the environmental and social costs of greatly increased coal use. A plutonium society, a world heated by unceasing thermal pollution—these are not what we want for ourselves or for future generations.

Life could not exist without solar energy. The sun makes our food grow. From the basic biological processes like photosynthesis to sailing and even clothes drying—we count on the natural energy of the sun and wind. Across the globe, about one-fifth of all energy used now comes from wind and water power, biomass and direct sunlight.[1] But this is only a beginning.

Says 1978 Sun Day coordinator, energy researcher and writer Denis Hayes:

A major energy transition of some kind is inevitable. For rich lands and poor alike, the energy patterns of the past are not prologue to the future. The oil-based societies of the industrial world cannot be sustained and cannot be replicated; their spindly foundations, anchored in the shifting sands of the Middle East, have begun to erode. Until recently most poor countries looked forward to entry into the oil era with its airplanes, diesel tractors, and ubiquitous automobiles. However, the fivefold increase in oil prices since 1973 virtually guarantees that the Third World will never derive most of its energy from petroleum. Both worlds thus face an awesome discontinuity in the production and the use of energy.[2]

In the last chapter we looked at some energy alternatives for now and the future. We have seen that energy conservation is a crucial first step towards a non-nuclear future. We know there is a great potential in wind power, biomass and solar energy. But conservation must be practiced in all parts of the economy, and solar tech-

Many small steps are now being taken towards a solar future. Many more steps—even leaps and bounds—must follow. The different moves have political as well as practical significance.

How we go solar and *when* are decisions that will largely determine what kind of world we and our grandchildren will live in. The political implications of a solar-based economy are great. Solar energy is a dispersed, diffuse, decentralized and internationally-shared resource. As such, it is a poten-

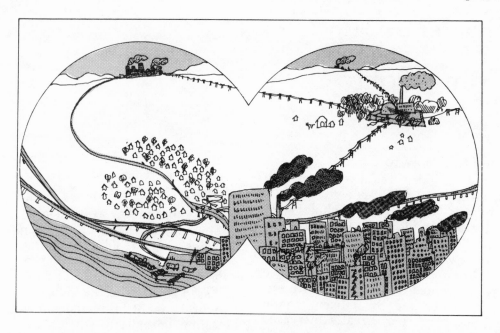

nologies must be mass-produced and put in place. How will we make the transition from the Fossil/Atomic to the Solar Age?

So far there are several timetables suggested and a few mechanisms. More and more, the political scene will have to focus on ecological issues, energy first and foremost. The existing economy depends on staggering oil imports, which have as related problems, inflation, weakening of the dollar worldwide, high-priced imports, and insecurity.

tial challenge to a basic pattern that has arisen in energy production in this century.

Centralization — Decentralization

Most of our electricity is produced in large, centralized power plants, increasingly coal-burning or nuclear ones, built according to utilities' needs for convenience and profitability. Electricity is generated and sent out over transmission lines for regional distribution. There are some very real problems with this system, beyond the reality that the fossil fuels and uranium needed for large plants cannot be replaced. Other problems are related to the fact that the plants are centralized.

Solar technologies threaten this traditional and increasing centralization of power. Sun, wind and biomass energy are essentially "democratic" energy sources. They can be used with relative simplicity almost everywhere. A rooftop solar hot water heater gives a feeling of "energy independence." Taken as a whole, the prospect

ecological damage.[3] When generation is highly centralized, electricity must travel long distances. Much is lost in transmission along the powerline wires. At the four massive coal-burning plants in Grants, New Mexico, the power equivalent of one plant's output is lost as the electricity journeys to its destination, Los Angeles.

As far as dependability goes, centralized generating facilities have their drawbacks too. Every large 1000-Mw plant must have backup generating

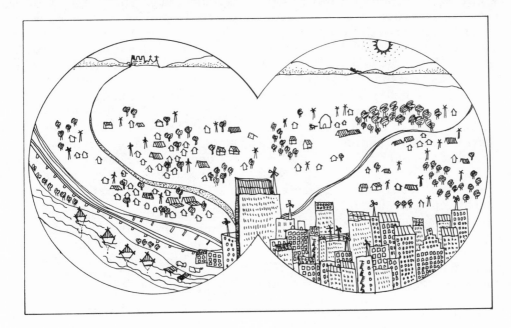

of the solarization of modern society is a crucial challenge to the existing pattern of power production, distribution, and control. At the heart of the challenge is the difference between centralized and decentralized power production, and who controls energy.

Some of the problems of centralization are technical ones. When primary fuels (oil, gas, coal) are burned to generate electricity, fully two-thirds of the potential energy is lost in the conversion. This energy is released as thermal pollution, with its ensuing

capacity available when the large plant is being refueled (nuclear plants) or is shut down for any reason. The pattern of building giant plants means that utilities need to have a large amount of reserve capacity standing idle, ready to be activated should the primary plant go out of service, or they must purchase expensive replacement power elsewhere. Smaller base-load units would allow for much more flexibility in management. Less reserve capacity would be needed. And blackouts and brownouts would be much less likely to happen. If they did, their effects would scarcely be felt. With our electricity supplied by a web of small power facilities we would not have risked the chaos that arose when Con Ed's Indian Point nuke had to shut down on a hot July evening in 1977. We are told by utilities and their "experts" that we will have blackouts and brownouts if nukes are not built soon. Actually, the nuclear option is the one that will cause the greatest insecurity and problems.

Then there are the social and political effects of centralized power generation. The reduction of crucial electric power sources to a relatively few giant installations, each representing enormous outlays of capital, gives the owning utilities (and their banker backers) a great deal of political power. In most parts of the U.S. investor-owned utilities have imposed massive, centralized patterns of electrical production while the public can only pay the costs.[4]

At Four Corners in the Southwest where the four coal-burning plants are located, centralization of electrical production has created a "colonial" pattern. The power is not produced where it is needed. Rather, the plants are placed where the fuel is to save coal transportation costs. The people who lose are the inhabitants of the Southwest, and they lose in terms of land (Native American), water resources, air quality, and social and economic disruption.

This pattern of centralized large plants, of concentrated power, removes people from the realities of energy production. We need only demand and consume; somewhere else others pay for it environmentally and physically. On the other hand, decentralized closer-to-home power generation makes us aware of the ways energy is produced.

Decentralization would mean that L.A.'s power needs, for example, would have to be met with energy resources found in the area: sun and wind, sea, geothermal, and biomass energy. Citizens and companies in L.A. might actually find that they could trim their needs if they had to bear all the environmental and social costs of energy consumption.

Renewable energy alternatives offer great flexibility and an opportunity to return control of energy supply to the public from the individual homeowner on up. Much of solar technology is simple. Maintenance is easy and people really can "do it themselves." People have the opportunity to take more control over this aspect of their lives.

Of course, decentralization does not mean that everyone will *have* to take personal responsibility for her/his power needs (although we *can*!). Decentralization of energy production would be based on community needs for energy as well as personal ones. Available local resources would meet those needs first.

> Unlike conventional energy technologies there would probably not be any single "best way" to exploit solar energy all over the world or even around the United States...most collected forms of solar energy are not easily transported over long distances, and different regions are endowed with quite different solar energy resources and mixes of energy demands.[5]

Although the sun's energy falls very democratically on the earth, solar technologies are not all simple and decentralized. As we have seen in the previous chapter, some of the solar applications are large-scale and centralized, developed to "plug into the grid"—fit into the existing system of power distribution. The solar farm and power tower concepts, OTEC, and of course the solar satellite, are all centralized means of electrical generation. To advocates of decentralization they are costly and unnecessary. Other systems can use natural energy in a more diversified and flexible way closer to home.

Hard and Soft Paths

> Two main policy paths for the rich countries are now rapidly diverging, and we must jump for one or the other. The first is high-energy, nuclear, centralized, and electric. The second is lower-energy, fission-free, decentralized, less electrified, softer-technology, based on energy income.[6]
>
> —Amory Lovins, 1975

Amory Lovins, U.S. physicist and Friends of the Earth (FOE) representative in Britain, has been very influential in defining the goals and some of the means of the Solar Age transition. In a landmark essay, "Energy Strategies, The Road Not Taken?," first appearing in late 1976, Lovins contrasted the present "path" of energy policy with an alternative one based on natural, renewable sources of energy. He called the choices the "hard" and "soft" paths towards the future.

The hard path is one of "centralized high technologies"—or more of same... It features giant nuclear and coal plants, oil and gas pipelines, coal gasification, extraction of oil from mountain shale, offshore oil exploitation. It is what David Brower (FOE International) calls "Strength Through Exhaustion."

The soft path is the solar/natural energy alternative. Lovins uses facts and figures to show that **by the year 2025, this country could meet fully 100% of its energy needs from essentially "benign" energy sources.** The soft path starts with comprehensive energy conservation. Necessary energy would then come from a mix of decentralized technologies. Solar energy would heat homes and water. Photovoltaic cells, small hydroelectric plants, and community windmills would generate electricity. Biogas plants would produce cooking gas; distilleries would make liquid fuels. Industrial process heat could be derived from solar, wood, and other biomass sources. Energy sources would be matched in scale, quality, and location to the end-use needs. That means that "high-grade" electricity produced at high temperatures in Washington State would never be used for a "low-grade" end-use like warming a room in San Francisco.[7] According to Lovins, electricity should be used only where really required. Although only 8% of our energy needs are best met by electricity, 13% of U.S. end-use needs are now met electrically.[8]

The vision of an energy future based on renewable, clean sources was held by others before Lovins, but he assembled a wide range of existing data to prove that such a future was indeed possible. In fact, he says it holds the only possible hope for the future, that it must get underway soon, and that both paths can't be followed at once. Because of limits on the capital available for energy production, the two directions are mutually exclusive.

Lovins has presented his pro-alternatives thesis to such diverse groups as the boards of directors of major banks and the Clamshell Alliance. Others have sounded warnings against the nuclear future. He is advising decision-makers on how they can change and even benefit by doing so. For this, he has come under vicious attack from pro-nuclear critics.[9]

From another viewpoint, Australian writer Brian Martin presents a "friendly critique" of Lovins' work. For although welcoming Lovins' technical expertise and even sharing his vision of the decentralized "soft energy future," Martin questions the political assumptions of Lovins' analysis. Lovins maintains that the two paths—hard and soft—cannot be followed at the same time. Martin disagrees, seeing the existing power structure capable of accepting soft energy choices within the current political/economic framework. One example would be adoption of mass transit systems, which, "through their rate structures, routing, and differing qualities of service maintain inequality as well as [leave] decision-making about the system to the planning experts." Another example would be producing solar units in a traditional centralized manner to sell in the existing marketplace.

As we have seen, solar energy technologies are not inherently decentralized or available for local, democratic control. Martin suggests that those technologies will be adopted that are least threatening to the status quo of economic control and production.

> My basic conclusion is that a slow transition to a combination of hard and soft technologies is possible, in which the soft components are introduced in such a way as to maintain private control over production, maintain economic inequality, and maintain lack of local control over the design of society.[10]

He asks that we "look at the *political and economic implications* of any energy strategy, not just whether it is hard or soft." Critical of Lovins' orientation towards "decison-makers," Martin advocates organizing for political change in order to make other alternatives possible.

A Timetable for the Future

Despite utility projections of future growth in electrical use, some analysts say that with conservation and increased efficiency, U.S. energy needs cannot only be cut in half, but that by 2025 this country could achieve a near-100% solar energy budget. Here are two projections of how energy could be supplied.

Amory Lovins' "Alternative Illustrative Future for U.S. Gross Primary Energy Use" (Fig. 1) shows fossil fuels completely phased out by 2025.[11]

Denis Hayes' "Proposed World Energy Production Timetable" (Fig. 2) includes limited reliance on fossil fuels.[12]

Hayes' timetable is presented in an April 1978 Worldwatch Institute paper that describes—source by source—a possible transition to "world solar energy."[13] (Hayes is probably the U.S. alternative energy strategist most concerned with Third World adoption of alternative, renewable energy sources.)[14] He sees a staged progress towards increasing reliance on active and passive solar heating, biomass fuels, and hydroelectric, wind power, and solar electric energy that can increase more than tenfold from 1980 to 2025.[15]

What no one seems to have an answer for is what political changes will be necessary and will be made so that industries that profit from nuclear and fossil development, the agencies with a vested interest in them (their regulators), government, and society as a whole will switch the needed resources and commitments toward renewable energy sources. Will bankers, senators and DOE bureaucrats someday soon become "convinced" of the righteousness and necessity of the solar path? Or will it take a new political movement of people demanding a reorientation of energy production towards real human and ecological

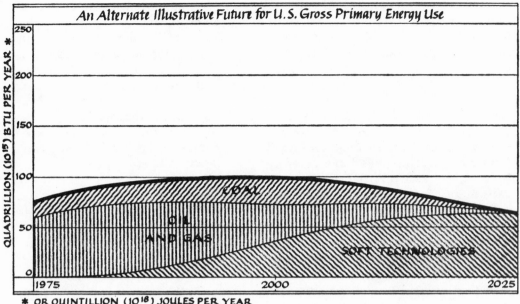

An Alternate Illustrative Future for U.S. Gross Primary Energy Use

* OR QUINTILLION (10^{18}) JOULES PER YEAR

Proposed World Energy Production Timetable, 1980-2025*

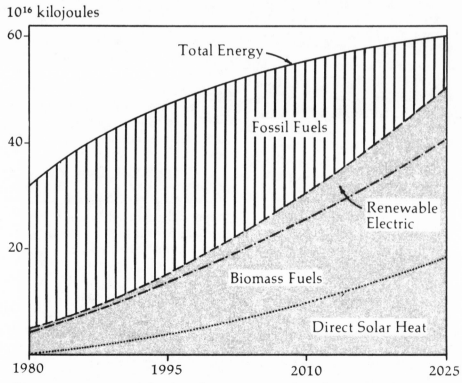

10^{16} kilojoules

*Energy sources supplying less than 1 percent of total are omitted.

needs, urban reconstruction, full employment, local control? To get some idea of how it will happen, let's look at how it *is* happening. For there is interest and increasing amounts of action on the "solar front."

Getting There: The Big Boys

Although early pioneers in solar energy were mainly individuals and small firms, large companies have recently become interested. With the industrial capabilities for mass production and distribution of new products, they are in a position to capitalize relatively quickly on the interest in solar energy.

In the spring of 1976, the newsletter *People & Energy* surveyed solar energy patents and found that an increasing number of them were being acquired by major U.S. corporations in the oil, aerospace, and automotive industries. Of 47 patents assigned since the mid-60s, 30 went to big corporations. Companies acquiring solar heat patents included Mobil Oil, GE, General Motors, Martin Marietta, Dupont, Boeing, and United Aircraft.

Solar electricity production by photovoltaic cells is big business too. Companies developing solar cells include GE, Westinghouse and Bell Telephone. The traditional energy companies are involved too. Gulf Oil and Exxon have extensive research programs in the field and Mobil Oil has taken over Tyco Labs, an important developer of solar cell production.[16]

The federal government does no research on its own. As with nuclear research and development, public funds for solar R & D go to private companies. Who is profiting from the government's solar programs (as token as they have been)? In 1975, Federal Energy Administration official Don Craven's report to the Senate Select Committee on Small Business included the information that:

of almost ten million dollars awarded for solar energy in 1974, $8.7 million (or 89%) went to large private corporations, with the remaining $1.1 million going to small businesses or businesses of unknown size. FEA contrasted this finding with the fact that of the 39 companies producing flat plate collectors in 1974, only seven were identifiable as large companies. The *People & Energy* survey (1976) indicated that the 1974 FEA results are still valid and that there is a continued preference by both the Energy Research & Development Administration (now part of DOE) and the National Science Foundation for large corporate research and development.[17]

G.E. (with Westinghouse the major nuclear reactor manufacturer in the U.S.) was the largest single ERDA contractor for the year ending July 1976, with more than $19 million in contracts.[18] Boeing was chosen to build and test "the largest wind turbine ever constructed" with ERDA funding.[19] Westinghouse and the Lockheed Missles and Space Company got DOE contracts totaling over $4 million to design OTEC systems.[20]

The FEA statement said that small companies have a hard time competing for federal funds because of the red tape and paperwork involved. It's also well known that the DOE looks favorably upon large companies with their large grant requests. The deck is stacked in favor of the big boys, from industry-agency management sharing (using the infamous "revolving door" through which executives pass between industry and agency), to the organization of grant-giving. For under the present system there is much less paperwork involved for DOE staff in one large grant than in numerous small grants awarded to modest firms and groups just getting off the ground or expanding.

Although large energy corporations are getting involved with solar, they have not been particularly optomistic about it. In 1974 both G.E. and Westinghouse carried out federally-funded studies on the possibilities of solar energy. They found that surprisingly low percentages (1.6 and 3.04 respectively) of national energy requirements could be met with solar systems by the year 2000. (Could these major nuclear reactor manufacturers be hoping that solar energy will only come into the picture when all their nuclear plants have lived out their full "lifetimes?") A year later the National Science Foundation estimated that solar energy could contribute almost 4% by 1985 alone.[21] And that can be considered a low estimate.

Getting There: Legislation
Recent years have witnessed increased testimony on solar energy and appropriate technology on Washington's Capital Hill. Solar-related legislation is popular.[22] Many bills subsidize homeowners, veterans, and businesses in their purchases of solar equipment through federal loan guarantees and tax credits. Conservation efforts are similarly suggested, along with guidelines on energy conservation and solar energy design for construction and renovation of federal and federally-assisted buildings.[23]

The availability of credit and loans is a crucial factor in people's decision to add or build with solar hardware. DOE itself has reported that a decrease in interest rates for loans from 13-18% to 7-8% would dramatically affect the solar heating market.[24]

By 1978 thirty states had tax credits for solar equipment. These bills are intended to stimulate the consumer market for solar equipment. Although they are doing this to some extent, so far they have not helped rural areas or the urban poor or the 44 million people who rent their homes. Property tax abatements and state sales tax exemptions benefit those who have the funds to buy solar equipment in the first place—generally white middle and upper income homeowners.

Following opposition from black and other community leaders to tax-abating legislation in San Francisco, the reform-minded Conference on Alternative State and Local Public Policies started a committee to draft "new environmentally responsive legislation that also addresses the needs of low-income, moderate-income, working-class, and minority communities."[25]

Getting There: State Action
Limited as it is so far, legislation on the state level does seem to offer broad opportunities for solar energy adaptation. At this point, state action toward the solar future is being led by California, where a combination of factors has advanced the solar transition program.

California—the Soft Path? California, with the world's eighth largest economy, is the world's ninth largest energy user.[26] A 1977 DOE-commissioned study evaluated "soft energy path" options for the state. Assuming both population and economic growth, the first part of the study ("Distributed Energy Systems in California's Future: Interim Report"), found that by the year 2025 California could become almost completely energy self-sufficient. Energy would be produced by renewable, indigenous sources: solar heat and solar industrial cogeneration, bio-mass from land and water, wind, hy-dropower and geothermal, along with extensive conservation.

Although large land requirements might be necessary for certain solar systems, the report found that "the environmental impacts of certain of the 'soft' technologies would prove markedly smaller than those of virtu-ally all of the traditional 'hard' technol-ogies, as well as smaller than those of the more centralized technologies for harnessing renewables."[27] The study will continue evaluating the transi-tional steps required to get the state onto a renewable energy path.

Also released in 1978 was a Califor-nia Public Policy Center study on the jobs that a solar-oriented economy could provide for the state. It found that the feasible uses for solar water and space heating alone in the state be-tween 1983 and 1990 could generate more than 376,000 jobs, $41.2 billion in increased personal income, $51.1 billion in gross state produce and $19.8 billion in tax savings.[28]

Since the 1976 initiative on nuclear safeguards, awareness of nuclear po-wer dangers and interest in safe alter-natives have been high in the state. Gov. Jerry Brown is an outspoken advocate of alternative energy sources, and current state programs reflect a far more ambitious move toward pre-paring for the next century than do those of the national government.

Brown has proposed that 1.6 mil-lion homes in the state be outfitted with solar components by 1985. The Carter Energy Plan calls for only 1.3 million nationwide. California homeowners who buy solar heating or cooling sys-tems get a 55% tax credit, the highest in the country. The state wind pro-gram includes 200 generators along the coast and in the mountains, and Brown has pledged to double geother-mal production in the state by 1981.[29] It remains to be seen if the current "tax revolt" will lessen state spending on alternative technology.

The California Campaign for Eco-nomic Democracy (CED), which evol-ved from Tom Hayden's 1976 Senate race, introduced "SolarCal," a proposal of energy bills that would lead to "maximum feasible solarization" of the state by 1990 by solarizing every possi-ble structure in the state by then. Bills in the solar package seek to "avoid corporate control of solar energy. One proposal prohibits investment in the solar industry by major energy corpor-ations and restricts any company to a maximum of 10 percent of the solar market."[30] Other bills seek to strength-en small business competition through state loan programs. Several bills re-late to financing; one calls for utility low-interest loans for solar systems. The CED has organized a grass-roots pressure campaign of support for the SolarCal bills.

The California Energy Commission tries to work through local govern-ment to implement conservation and solar construction. A year-long project began in February 1978 to "develop the information and technical assistance mechanisms needed to help California building inspectors, planning officials, and elected officials to deal with solar technologies."[31] The program includes workshops and manuals for building inspectors on solar installations.

The California programs are help-ing to meet some of the barriers to solar development that were spelled out in a 1976 report "The Use of Solar Energy for Space Heating and Hot Water," prepared by the Mass. Energy Policy Office. The barriers described then were: the traditional fragmenta-tion of the construction industry; the uncertain economics of solar; tax disin-centives (somewhat alleviated since this report was issued); lack of information; building regulations; market risks; financing; insurance, lack of skilled tradespeople.[32]

A program begun in Vermont in 1976 should go far in helping solve some of these problems at the local level. A state statute provided for "substantially expanded opportunities for citizen involvement in community energy development."[33] The law empowers towns to appoint an energy coordinator to guide development of local energy projects. These can range from involving school students in assessments of the town's local power sources, organizing insulation purchasing coops, and researching local zoning ordinances that might impair alternative energy hardware, to organizing carpools and bikeways. By mid-summer of 1978, more than 45 towns had energy coordinators.[34]

Getting There: Community Action

Federal grants, big business interest and state programs are only part of the solar wave that is building in the U.S. and elsewhere. Experiments with solar technology are being carried on in communities across the country. Local papers report on ingenious home and hot water heating systems and other solar projects put together by area residents. Many small businesses have started up, based on one or several alternative technolgies.

Some federal programs help local towns too. In the Northeast, federally-funded community action agencies have been using DOE and Community Service Agency (CSA) funds to winterize low-income homes.[35]

A Citizens' Energy Project study gives examples of more than 100 community energy programs involving conservation and alternatives sources of energy. They range from Mountain View, California's drilling of wells in sanitary landfills to recover methane, to Colorado's 200-member San Luis (Valley) Solar Energy Association building its own solar system out of scrap materials.

In another case, Palo Alto's "city-owned utility is working with local residents to design plans and financial mechanisms for a proposal to construct a neighborhood solar utility." Individual homes will be retrofitted with solar collectors, as will a carport, to be constructed at a local medical center's parking lot. The proposal is to mount solar panels on the carport and distribute solar-heated water to the block of residents involved.[37]

In several experimental "whole systems" centers, like the New Alchemy Institute in Massachusetts, Prince Edward Island, Canada, and Costa Rica, and the Farallones Institute in California, groups have been working on low-cost, widely applicable approaches to self-sufficiency, in food as well as energy. Their experimental homes feature greenhouses for passive solar heat collection as well as year-round food production, ponds for heat storage and fish raising.[38] Both groups have encouraged interest in new ways of living and building more ecologically, with greater self-sufficiency.

An Urban Experiment—One important low-income application of alternative technologies is being demonstrated in New York City's Lower East Side, where several old tenement buildings are topped with solar panals. The panels on the remodeled building at 519 East 11th St. supply much of the building's hot water. Extra-heavy insulation installed by the tenants has cut the heating bill.

> On an investment of $11,000 for the insulation (which will pay off very fast) and $15,000

for the water heater (which will take longer), the building has cut its fuel bill by $4,000 a year.[39]

In December 1976, the building's rooftop windmill started feeding electricity into Con Ed's massive system, making the project the first urban wind power system in the nation.[40]

The 11th St. project, and others like it in the Bronx and Brooklyn, are small symbols of hope for future urban reconstruction. Tenants organized and bought the building themselves under a "sweat equity" program. They used their own labor to restore it while paying a long-term low-interest city loan. The group also received a small grant from the federal CSA to finance the solar installations and to produce educational materials on the project. They had to overcome many obstacles in dealing with both city and federal governments.

> ...the skeptics and the critics are being proved wrong. Slowly the work that we are doing in 519, as that of the Renigades in East Harlem and of other community groups, is beginning to prove that people taking over abandoned buildings is not a vague idea, a dream, but a reality—something which works. More than that, it is the only solution to the endless process of abandonment and demolition.[41]

As the Eleventh St. Movement says: "The high cost of housing, energy, and jobs are the critical problems confronting urban survival." They have shown that solar energy can be a key to a future national reconstruction that will put people to work at meaningful jobs that can cut the cost of energy too.

Jobs From the Sun

Most proponents of the large, complex energy systems concede that the systems they are promoting expose the public to a variety of dangers. But, they contend, there is absolutely no other way to meet the nation's energy needs, to provide for a strong economy, and to create sufficient numbers of jobs.

We disagree. Developing solar technology and increasing the efficiency of our energy use are both steps toward a prosperous and sustained economy. In fact, these policies yield more jobs and a more stable economy than does our present energy policy. It does so with less pollution, less disease, less social disruption, and less interference with community, labor-union, and individual rights.[42]

It is simply not true that across the board "energy creates jobs." In fact, the increased use of energy has led to increased unemployment as power-hungry machines replace human workers. Worker "productivity" is actually a measure of automation. As an industry is automated, energy is substituted for labor and (unless the work day or week is shortened) jobs are lost. People in manufacturing industries have been put out of work by this substitution of energy for labor. Then, as rate and taxpayers, they have had to subsidize the building of new giant plants—and the nuclear fuel cycle—that serve the expanded needs of automated industry.[43]

On the other hand, it has been shown that "a given amount of capital would produce two to four times as many jobs if invested in solar energy rather than electricity generation."[44]

"And now watch what happens when I plug this thing in!" (*Forum Europa*, no. 3/4, '76.)

Solar energy creates jobs, while electrical energy growth is actually stealing them. But being against increased electrical growth does not mean that certain jobs should not be automated. As Denis Hayes puts it: "Saving energy should not be used as an excuse to resurrect dreary, unrewarding forms of manual labor...but where human skill, intelligence, or craftsmanship have been replaced by automation, they should again be given reign."[45]

Investment in solar energy has several immediate benefits; it saves energy by using the sun and conserving heat; it creates employment; it lessens the need for expensive, dangerous new generating plants and imported oil.

The job opportunities created by solar use would cover many fields, but would be particularly concentrated in construction and manufacturing. The construction fields of plumbing, carpentry, roofing and ductwork would require manpower specializing in solar energy systems. Building architects and engineers familiar with solar technology would be needed for solar construction as well. The demand for solar products creates work for solar product designers, factory workers and sales people. Servicing and maintenance of solar equipment would become a necessary new trade. The increased local income that would result from solar energy use would create many other jobs as well, since demand for all goods and services would be increased.

If 50 percent of all buildings used solar energy by 1995, at least for hot water use, 600 million gallons of oil (or equivalent gas or electricity) could be saved yearly, retaining $480 million in the state, resulting in

32,000 jobs. Although these figures are hypothetical, they reflect the type of benefits that are probable should solar energy use begin now.[46]

—Mass. Energy
Policy Office, 1976

For these reasons, the Sheetmetal Workers, the United Auto Workers, and other union locals and spokespersons are on record in support of increased solar energy development. In 1978 a new national coalition formed of labor, community, and public interest groups. One of the Citizen/Labor Energy Coalition's purposes is to "encourage the creation of jobs through safe energy development."[47]

Strategies for Change

We decided to put a man on the moon in ten years. We didn't have the slightest idea how to do it then, and we did it in nine years. We already have the answers on how to use solar energy, so if we would make the decision to do it, we could do it much better, much quicker, much easier. When people ask me how soon will solar energy become widespread I always tell them "that's up to you!" We can decide to put it to work ten years from now, or we can wait another fifty years. But I'm not sure we can wait another fifty years...in my opinion we have a responsibility to future generations.[48]

—Dr. Erich Farber, solar pioneer

This quote brings up several interesting points. Farber suggests a program of solar development similar to the commitment made to put a man on the moon. However, political realities make this possibility remote at present. A solar commitment must compete with the thirty-year-old Atomic commitment which has had government support similar to the space program. It is unlikely that nuclear power will be shelved in favor of solar energy without a lot of changes in the "powers that be."

Farber is certainly right that we have the information and knowledge needed to begin. People are already using solar energy and practicing energy conservation, its soft path "twin." If the government is not ready to make a full commitment to solar energy because of its priorities and many conflicts of interest in the nuclear camp, how can people force the change?

The answers are already being given and will grow in strength and number. Citizens and communities are organizing and acting, responding to the challenge of entering the future now instead of later. What are some of these answers, these moves that together may make a realistic strategy for change?

The changes are taking place at the grass roots level, where people live. They start with a new awareness of energy and ecology, of the possibilities for energy and dollar savings, of the creativity and pleasure of living with nature instead of dominating it. Some of this consciousness has come by way of information sharing at numerous alternative energy fairs and activities that took place around the May 3rd 1978 Sun Day celebration. Word of mouth works too, as people share their new knowledge. This consciousness can only grow as people in suburbs, small towns and rural areas see people "going solar" and start doing it themselves, and as urban residents consider the advantages of better mass transit, urban bikeways, carpooling, urban greenhouses and insulation programs.

As homeowners and small business-people investigate the advantages of building or retrofitting with solar construction and equipment, they create a consumer demand for these products and services. This demand gives solar businesses the opportunity to gear up for greater mass production. As a result, costs fall. Of course one of the nice things about solar energy is that there are lots of ways to take advantage of it. Passive solar elements, solar collectors and hot water systems can be built and installed at low cost with simple and/or recycled materials.

Consumers can also lobby their legislators for the kinds of tax-breaks, loan programs, and sales tax exemptions that make commercial solar equipment more affordable.

Amory Lovins suggests another financial arrangment. He would like utilities to make loans to consumers for home insulation or other fuel-saving investment, using capital they might otherwise raise and spend for new generating facilities. The consumers would pay off the loans in their utility bills "at or below the rate at which the fuel-saving investment is expected to save them money."[49]

Capital transfers under this system would benefit both consumers and utilities. Consumers could heat their houses more cheaply than if they had not installed heat-saving or solar devices, yet without having to pay extra for the improvement. Second, insulation and solar heat would largely protect consumers from future rate hikes. Third, the fuel-saving investment would make the very costly new plants unnecessary, and would save the utility money and fuels by using present capacity more effi-

ciently; these things all help to avoid rate hikes in the first place.[50]

This idea would serve to justify the continued existence of large, investor-owned utilities. Another possibility is that utilities would themselves distribute—lease or sell—solar systems and insulation to rate-payers. Opponents of such utility programs cite higher consumer costs, market monopolization, and suppression of (perhaps cheaper) technologies. Most importantly, there are better alternative ways to commercialize solar.

Existing municipal entities like water departments could install solar technologies, as is being done in California. City governments can create solar co-ops to buy large amounts of solar hardware and pass the savings on to local consumers. Already more than 800 community action programs have solar commercialization projects. These could be expanded.

Other possibilities for solar commercialization involve leasing programs instituted by manufacturers themselves, or perhaps by groups of builders/construction companies.[51]

Meanwhile, some people are opposing outside corporate control of energy by turning to locally controlled power production and distribution. Public power as such has not been a great rallying cry. People are suspicious of large, bureaucrat-swollen federal ("public") agencies. But in communities across the country, ratepayers are seeing that municipal control over generating facilities and distribution systems is a way to get more efficient and cheaper administration free from stockholder profit dividends, and of introducing alternative energy technologies.

Public power is not a new thing in

the U.S. There are more than 3,000 public power systems in the country supplying electricity to one American in four.[52] Some of the existing systems are being asked to be more responsive to citizen wishes. For example, the Seattle Department of Lighting, a municipally-owned utility, agreed to do a study of need for a planned nuclear plant. The study showed that conservation programs alone would eliminate need for the facility. Plans for the nuke were dropped.[53]

The Environmental Action Foundation's well-known book *Taking Charge: A New Look at Public Power* is one of the best sources of information on this option for greater community control of power production and distribution. In communities in New York State, Vermont and elsewhere, citizens are looking toward public power as a means of increased control—and lower utility bills. In recent years towns like Massena, New York and Springfield, Vermont have voted to take over electric power franchises from private utilities.

Public utilities can borrow money at lower rates than private ones. This is one reason why they can help in the transition to small-scale decentralized sources of energy. Although communities wanting to "cut loose" from large IOUs are faced with a lot of hard work and problems, it is a trend that will probably continue and grow. For it offers a concrete way to change things locally—to oppose nuclear construction and encourage alternative methods of power generation. There is no reason why locally controlled utilities could not themselves help people pay for and install heat-saving devices, sell insulation wholesale, etc.

What can people do to help make the transition to the Solar Age? Demand that it happen and help make it happen. Meet with your legislators,

your neighbors and friends. Join a local energy group or help start one. Use your vote for progressive energy related measures on the local, regional, state-wide and national levels. Local community energy committees already formed in several states are a good way to begin a decentralized approach to energy planning.

The keys to the Solar Age are the ecological principles of diversity and decentralization. The place to begin is in communities across the country and world. One suggestion is that Community Energy Commissions be established, another variation on the energy committee, that are "responsible for developing a comprehensive plan for solar conversion of the neighborhoods, urban, rural and small town, that would integrate individual decisions such as rooftop solar collectors, with community resources, such as windmills, small hydropower plants..."[54] The Energy Commissions could apply for federal loans to fund local projects. Commissioners would be elected and have a good technical staff. In suggesting these locally based commissions, the independent socialist weekly newspaper *In These Times* wrote:

> The new solar technology, if it is to be used to construct a more democratic, equitable and stable economy, requires new institutions that depart from both the rule and ruin of corporate capitalism and from many of the commonplace assumptions of traditional socialist thought. The political issues are paramount; they cannot be swept aside in the rush for more photovoltaic cells and solar hot water heaters.[55]

It has been said many times by many people that the transition from nuclear and fossil-fueled energy to safe, renewable alternatives is a political problem, not a technical one. Hopefully, in this book we have showed once more that this is so. The physical tools to generate the power we need are available. The main problems we face as we enter the 1980s and the next century are—who will control energy and for what purposes?

If we are to turn from power for private profit and unplanned and unnecessary industrial growth and automation, to power for people and an ecologically sound world, we have to begin now. There are things that we as individuals can do, and other changes that we must work towards as part of a broader community. The new tools we need are political ones. We must develop them, before it is too late.

Footnotes

1. Denis Hayes, *Energy: The Solar Prospect*, (Worldwatch Paper 11), March 1977, p. 5. This is one of an excellent series of papers on energy. This one adapted from Hayes' book *Rays of Hope: The Transition to a Post-Petroleum World*.

2. *Ibid.*, pp. 5-6.

3. Denis Hayes, *The Solar Energy Timetable*, (Worldwatch Paper 19), April 1978, p. 6-7. Thermal pollution has two bad effects: It heats the water and air, and when combustion is involved, releases great amounts of CO_2 (carbon dioxide). Even slight changes of temperature in aquatic ecologies affects their residents causing death and ruining natural habitats. Heat pollution affects local climates. CO_2 (coal makes most) raises the earth's temperature by slowing down the escape of heat into space. "This CO_2 greenhouse effect was a matter of speculation as recently as five years ago, but most meteorologists now agree that it is a matter of concern...Although there is disagreement over just how soon major changes in the earth's climate could result from the buildup of CO_2 that has already begun, many knowledgeable observers feel dire consequences are possible before 2025." (p. 7). See also: William W. Kellogg, "Is Mankind Warming the Earth?," *Bulletin of the Atomic Scientists*, February 1978.

4. For a good description of how private utilities have risen to power, see *The Electric War*, p.

113-146, Sheldon Novick, (San Francisco, CA: Sierra Club Books, 1976). For run-down on how consumers pay for utility decisions, expenses, see *How to Challenge Your Local Utility*, Environmental Action Foundation.

5. Frank von Hippel, Robert H. Williams, "Toward a Solar Civilization," *Bulletin of Atomic Scientists*, October 1977, p. 15, 56.

6. Amory Lovins, "Nonnuclear Futures," Introduction to Lovins' and John Price's book, *Nonnuclear Futures: The Case for an Ethical Energy Strategy*. (Friends. of the Earth, Ballingers Publishing Co., 1975). This quote from reprint of article in FOE newsletter *Not Man Apart*.

7. Amory B. Lovins, *Soft Energy Paths* (Cambridge, MA: Friends of the Earth and Ballinger Publishing Co., p. 1977), p. 25.

8. "People do not want electricity or oil, nor such economic abstractions as "residential services," but rather comfortable rooms, light, vehicular motion, food, tables, and other real things. Such end-use needs can be classified by the physical nature of the task to be done. In the United States today, about 58 percent of all energy at the point of end use is required as heat, split roughly 23-35 between temperatures above and below the boiling point of water... Another 38 percent of all U.S. end use energy provides mechanical motion: 31 percent in vehicles, 3 percent in pipelines, 4 percent in industrial electric motors. The rest, a mere 4 percent of delivered energy, represents *all* lighting, electronics, telecommunications, electrometallurgy, electrochemistry, arc welding, electric motors in home appliances and in railways, and in similar end uses that now *require* electricity...Some 8 percent of all U.S. energy end use, then, and similarly little abroad, requires electricity for purposes other than low temperature heating and cooling." Yet 29% of U.S. fossil fuels are used to produce the electricity that meet 13% of all U.S. end-use needs. Lovins, *ibid.*, p. 39.

9. *Soft vs Hard Energy Paths: 10 Critical Essays on Amory Lovins' "Energy Strategy: The Road Not Taken?"*, Charles B. Yulish, ed., 229 Seventh Ave., New York, N.Y. 10011. 1977.

10. Brian Martin, "Soft Energy, Hard Politics," *Chain Reaction* (Friends of the Earth, Australia), no. 3(2), 1977. (51, Nicholson St., Carlton, Victoria, 3053, Australia. $1.00.)

11. *Alternative Long-Range Energy Strategies*, Joint Hearing before the Select Committee on Small Business and Committee on Interior and Insular Affairs, U.S. Senate, 9 December 1976, p. 159. (Also in Lovins' *Soft Energy Paths*, and the *Foreign Affairs* article: "Energy Strategy: The Road Not Taken?")

12. Hayes, *The Solar Energy Timetable, op. cit.*, p. 12.

13. Denis Hayes, *The Solar Energy Timetable*, pp. 13-14.

14. Denis Hayes, *Energy for Development: Third World Options*, Worldwatch Paper 15, December 1977.

15. *Ibid.*, p. 13. A good review of alternative energy sources follows. See also, *Rays of Hope: The Transition to a Post-Petroleum World* (NY: W.W. Norton & Co., 1977), pp. 153-203.

16. *People & Energy*, vol. II, no. 5, May 1976, p. 1. Published by Citizens' Energy Project 1413 K St. N.W., Washington, D.C. 20005. The *P & E* survey used the Small Business Administration definition of a large firm as one which employs more than 500 persons.

17. *Ibid.*

18. Joe Conason, "Putting a Meter on the Sun: Big Business Takes Over Solar," *The Real Paper*, Boston, MA, 7 May 1977, p. 20.

19. ERDA's Division of Solar Energy: Solar Energy Research & Development Report, 16 August 1977.

20. DOE Information, Weekly Announcement, Office of Public Affairs, vol. 2, no. 9, week ending 3 March 1978.

21. *People & Energy, op. cit.* A 1978 study by the Council on Environmental Quality (CEQ), *Progress and Promise*, concludes that solar technologies could provide one-fourth of all U.S. energy needs by the year 2000, *Sun Day Times*, May 1978. Sun Day/Solar Action, 1028 Conn. Ave., N.W., Washington D.C. 20036. Obviously, there are great variations in predictions, depending on amount of conservation called for, etc.

22. See "A Compendium of Alternative Energy Legislation—1977-78," *The Elements*.

23. S. 672 Solar Energy Govt. Building Act.

24. Paul D. Maycock, Chief Economic Analysis and Industrial Liaison, Division of Solar Energy, ERDA, "Solar Energy: The Outlook for Widespread Commercialization of Solar Heating and Cooling," 3 April 1976, p. 23.

25. Lee Webb "Preventing a Solar Backlash," *National Conference Newsletter*, Conference on Alternative State and Local Public Policies, p. 15. 1901 Que St. N.W., Washington D.C. 20009.

26. "DOE Explores Soft Path Energy Options for California by Year 2025," *Professional Engineer*, May 1978, p. 28.

27. "Distributed Energy Systems in California's Future: Interim Report Volumes I and II," HCP/P7405-01,2, March 1978, U.S. DOE, Washington D.C. 20545. 646 pages.

28. Fred Branfman, *Jobs From the Sun*, California Public Policy Center, Los Angeles, CA. $6.50 single copies; $10 for institutions.

29. Richard Pollock, "Jerry Brown vs. Jimmy Carter: Taking Different Paths to the Future," *Critical Mass Journal*, May 1978, p. 10.

30. Chuck Sherman, "California's SolarCal Program Takes Shape," *In These Times*, 3-9 May 1978, p. 15.

31. Peggy Niland, head of solar technology transfer and training at the California Energy Commission, Sacramento, "Hand in Hand: The Credit and the Codes," *Solar Age*, June 1978, p. 31. "Local government is the place to achieve energy conservation, not the state or federal level."

32. "The Use of Solar Energy for Space Heating and Hot Water," Massachusetts Energy Policy Office, Henry Lee, Director, April'76, pp 57-60.

33. "Vermont Town Energy Coordinators" report available from Citizens' Energy Project (see note no. 16).

34. Send for a 28-page report: "A Citizen Guide to Community Development," Vermont Tomorrow, 5 State St., Montpelier, VT, 05602, $1.

35. Write to Citizens' Energy Project for an overview of sources of federal funding for local energy projects.

36. "Local Energy Action Program Survey," CEP.

37. Ken Bossong, "Solar News Update," *People & Energy*, March 1978, p. 17.

38. The Farallones Institute has two centers, both "working demonstrations of how alternative technologies may be effectively utilized in urban and rural settings." The Institute sponsors workshops and has a publications list. Contact: The Rural Center, 15290 Coleman Valley Road, Occidental, CA 95464, or The Integral Urban House, 1516 Fifth St., Berkeley CA 94710. *Book of the New Alchemists*, Nancy Jack Todd, ed., E.P. Dutton, 201 Park Ave So., New York, NY 10003, 1977. $6.95. The Canadian Film Board has done a film of the New Alchemists. "Challenge for Change," National Film Board of Canada, Box 6100, Montreal, Quebec, Canada.

39. *New York*, 31 May 1976, p. 33.

40. Con Ed was not pleased. In May 1977 the New York State Public Service Commission ruled that the utility had to buy any excess power from the apartment cooperative's windmill. Con Ed had tried to disconnect service to the building because the wind generator, which was hooked into the company's power line, caused the customers' electric meter to run backwards!

41. From "Save the Lower East Side," The Eleventh St. Movement. See also, "Windmill Power for City People: A Documentation of the First Urban Wind Energy System," Energy Task

Force, NYC. CSA Pamphlet 6143-8, September 1977. $3.00 from the U.S. Govt. Printing Office, Washington D.C. 20402. To contact the Eleventh St. Movement: Michael Freedberg, 519 E. 11th St., N.Y., NY, (212) 473-9590, or Robert Nazario, Adopt-A-Building, (212) 677-8700. "The 11th St. Movement is part of the neighborhood Loisaida Environmental Action Coalition, which is spreading technologies like Solar and Wind Power throughout the Lower East Side. They are also working to develop energy efficient means of food production like organic gardens and agriculture systems that can be applied in the inner city. Such efforts are notable for their recognition that alternative technologies applied in a decentralized manner not only provide safe efficient, low cost source of energy and food but also provide much needed employment for residents of the local community. The Lower East Side sees the projects as potentially providing a material base for a more self-reliant community, no longer dependent on centralized Federal programs and policies."—Dan Chodorkoff, Goddard College, Plainfield, VT 05667. The Goddard College Institute for Social Ecology has worked with Lower East Side residents. The Institute has a program of courses that address the physical and political aspects of the Solar Age. (Send for information.)

42. Richard Grossman, "Energy and Jobs," *SUN: A Handbook for the Solar Decade*, Stephen Lyons, ed. (San Francisco: Friends of the Earth, 1978), p. 69. See also: Grossman and Daneker, *Jobs and Energy*, 1977, and "Jobs and Energy Update," Spring 1978: Environmentalists for Full Employment, 1101 Vermont Ave. NW, Washington, D.C. 20005, (202) 347-5590.

43. See Denis Hayes, *Rays of Hope*, pp. 146-148; Grossman, *op. cit. (SUN)*, pp. 71-75.

44. Barry Commoner, "How Solar Power Creates Jobs," *Solidarity*, 3 April 1978. *Solidarity* is the official publication of the International Union, United Automobile, Aerospace and Agricultural Implement Workers of America. Yearly subscriptions are $.60 for members, $1.00 for non-members, 8000 E. Jefferson Ave., Detroit MI, 48214.

45. Hayes, *op. cit.*, p. 148.

46. "The Use of Solar Energy for Space Heating and Hot Water," *op. cit.*, p. 56.

47. "Trade Unionists have an especially high stake in the kind of energy policy which this nation develops. Energy use, or mis-use, can have a significant impact on jobs."—Mike Olszanski, Environmental Chairman, Local 1010 United Steelworkers of America. On June 17, the Steelworkers (Illinois-Indiana District 31) passed a resolution opposing construction

for a site adjacent to a Bethlehem steel plant with 8,300 workers, and the Indiana Dunes National Lakeshore.—From the Bailly Alliance News, vol. 1, no. 1, August 1978, P.O. Box 847, Chesterton, Indiana 46304.

48. "Erich Farber: A pioneer talks about directions," *Solar Age*, January 1976, reprint, p. 1. Farber has worked for more than 20 years at the University of Florida. He is now research professor of mechanical engineering and director of the Solar Energy and Energy Conversion Laboratory.

49. Amory Lovins, "How to Finance the Energy Transition," *Not Man Apart* (FOE), mid-September-October, 1978, p. 8.

50. *Ibid.*

51. See "The Case Against Utility Involvement in Solar/Insulation Programs—1978." $.70 for a ten-page analysis from *People & Energy*, c/o Citizens Energy Project, 1413 K St. N.W., Washington D.C. 20005, 8th floor, (202) 393-6700.

52. Morgan, Riesenber, Troutman, *Taking Charge: A New Look At Public Power*. Environmental Action Foundation, 1976, p. 14. $2.50 single copy.

53. *Energy 1990*, Seattle City and Light, Office of Environmental Affairs, 1015 Third Ave., Seattle WA 98104. Summary and Overview— $8.

54. *In These Times*, 3-9 May 1978.

55. *Ibid.*

Resources

From Citizens' Energy Project, 1413 K St., N.W., Washington, D.C. 20005:

- Solar Energy: One Way to Citizen Control, 1976, 124 pages, $4.00.
- Survey of Local Energy Development Programs, 1976, 70¢.
- Vermont Energy Coordinators, 25¢.
- Federal Energy Funding, $1.00.
- Some Organizing Strategies That Are Doable—More or Less, 50¢.
- Jobs and Solar Energy—A Preliminary Annotation of Resources, 60¢.

SECTION 4: THE INTERNATIONAL STORY

Chapter 1:

Nukes Around the World

Since the first atomic bomb was dropped on Hiroshima, more than 600 reactors have been built around the globe. By 1980, 52 countries are expected to have reactors. Atomic power has become a big, multinational business: 15 countries now produce some form of nuclear technology.

Associated with the emergence of this world-wide nuclear industry are many frightening developments. In 1974, India used waste materials from one of its West-supplied reactors to set off a "peaceful nuclear explosion." The bomb, which exploded at the peak of Indira Gandhi's dictatorship, proved once and for all that the proliferation of atomic reactors is inseparable from that of nuclear weapons. For reactors produce plutonium which can be isolated by spent fuel rod reprocessing. Besides being a lethal carcinogen, even in minute amounts, plutonium is the raw material of atom bombs.

Nothing threatens world peace more severely than the spread of nuclear weapons around the world. And the proliferation of nuclear weapons is inextricably related to the spread of nuclear power plant technology. The "business" of nuclear plant export thus has major social and political meaning. As we will see, the U.S. has been responsible for the widespread adoption of nuclear technology. Unless the trend is reversed—and soon—the world will pay for this country's past actions.

Nuclear Power—
Global Big Business

Just as the domestic market is controlled by a few large firms in the U.S., so the world market is dominated by a few countries. First among these is the U.S. For 25 years this country, through its two leading nuclear industries, has been the major exporter of nuclear technology. By 1973, G.E. and Westinghouse accounted for 90% or more of the world's nuclear trade.[1] Internationally, all light-water reactor business traces its roots back to the two firms.

In the early days of atomic energy, the British made a strong entry with their gas-cooled reactor. Theirs was the first nuclear plant built in Japan. With it the British hoped for a strong share of future world reactor trade.

The U.S. was slower to develop commercial nuclear plants. Information on atomic power was a closely guarded government secret. Then the U.S.S.R. exploded its first atomic bomb in 1949. In the following years the veil of top-secrecy was lifted.[2] Within a little more than a decade, the U.S. light-water reactor models came to dominate the world market—a dominance which began in Europe.

The way for G.E. and Westinghouse's entry into European—and subsequently world—markets was paved by U.S. foreign policies initiated by the Eisenhower administration. The story is an involved one. Basically the "Atoms for Peace" program that began in 1953, bolstered by bilateral agreements with the individual countries, provided for the export of U.S. technology, research, enriched uranium and finance capital. The U.S. offered a nuclear package that Europe could not refuse and with which the British could not compete.

In 1957 the six countries of the European Economic Community (EEC; Common Market) signed the EURATOM (European Atomic Energy Community) Treaty, providing for joint development of commercial atomic power. EURATOM became the vehicle for the wholesale adoption of U.S. nuclear technology in Europe.[3]

By the 1970s the picture of U.S. domination had changed. Through profitable licensing agreements, the U.S. firms gradually allowed French, German, Japanese and other overseas companies into the reactor manufacturing club. G.E. and Westinghouse generally kept substantial shares in their related companies. Thus in the mid-70s, Westinghouse maintained a 45% share* in France's Framatome. West Germany's Kraftwerk Union (KWU) had licenses from both G.E. and Westinghouse. Even the Canadian industry which sells a heavy water reactor substantially different from the U.S. model, has nonetheless relied significantly on U.S. manufacturing and capital.

---

*now 15%

Westinghouse World-Wide
subsidiary companies:
ACEC — Belgium
WENESE — Italy
licenses and agreements with:
FRAMATOME — France
MITSUBISHI — Japan
KRAFTWERK UNION — F.R.G.
SIEMEN — Fed. Rep. Germany
total number of Westinghouse reactors sold: 112

General Electric World-Wide
subsidiary companies:
GETSCO — Switzerland
G.E. of U.K. — United Kingdom
Canadian G.E. — Canada
licenses and agreements with:
TOSHIBA — Japan
HITACHI — Japan
KRAFTWERK UNION — F.R.G.
ASEA — Sweden
total number of G.E. reactors sold: 56

(Source: Center for Development Policy)

The International Fuel Cycle

Uranium is found in many countries. Mining and milling have been carried on in most of them.

Uranium

Substantial supplies of uranium ore have been located in:

Australia	Canada
France	Gabon
Niger	South Africa
U.S.	U.S.S.R.

Other parts of the fuel cycle have also long been developed abroad. The Canadians and British were wartime atomic partners and emerged in 1945 with significant scientific know-how. The U.S.S.R.'s A-bomb explosion in 1949 showed that they had industrialized the enrichment process needed to isolate fissionable uranium, and probably had reprocessing techniques as well. By 1960, France and the U.K. had both enrichment and reprocessing, although nowhere near the commercial capacity of the U.S., which established a virtual monopoly on commercial enrichment.

Enrichment is an expensive and complex technology, not easily accomplished without a sophisticated industrial base. Enrichment makes reactor and bomb-grade U-235 from milled uranium ore (see p. 47).

Enrichment

Countries with uranium enrichment facilities of varying sizes (all government run):

France*	FRG (W. Ger.)
Japan	Netherlands
South Africa	U.K.*
U.S.*	China*
U.S.S.R.*	

*Commercial Capacity

(Source: Albert Wohlstetter, "Moving Toward Life in a Nuclear Armed Crowd?" *Pan Heuristics*, Los Angeles, April 1976. Also, "U.S. Nuclear Export Policy," *Atomic Industrial Forum*, 21 July 1976)

Reprocessing plants, on the other hand, are comparatively cheap and simple. In these, fissile uranium and plutonium are separated from spent reactor fuel rods.

Other nations competed for U.S. nuclear research and technology and then for their own commercial capacity. Given the extent that nuclear know-how was shared by the U.S. from 1953 on, U.S. and U.S.S.R. monopolization of the basic fuel cycle processes—enrichment and reprocessing—was impossible.[4]

Reprocessing

Countries with nuclear fuel reprocessing facilities of varying sizes (all government run):

Argentina	Belgium*
France*	FRG (W. Ger.)
India*	Italy
Japan*	Spain
Taiwan	U.K.*
U.S.*	China*
U.S.S.R.*	

*Commercial scale

(Source: Albert Wohlstetter, *op. cit.*)

The U.S. and Fuel Supply

U.S. policies undertaken in 1974 spurred the spread of enrichment and especially reprocessing world-wide, at the same time that this country, mainly through the efforts of Henry Kissinger, was seeking accord among suppliers for more effective safeguards to prevent the military use of reprocessed plutonium.

The U.S. government owns about 95% of non-Communist world enrichment capacity. Foreign governments have always contracted with the AEC/ERDA for enriched uranium. In 1974, the agency suddenly closed its order books for uranium fuel enrichment services.

The AEC/ERDA took the action as one of several ways to encourage private enterprise's entrance into the enrichment business. It constituted a government slow-down in providing world enrichment services. The government was also stockpiling uranium far in excess of current needs. With less enriched uranium available on the world market, prices rose. Through these policies the U.S. created an artificial shortage of enrichment capacity. With enrichment facilities fully booked, some foreign customers were given preferential treatment, but no additional orders were allowed.[5]

In essence, the policy was another part of a Nixon-Ford effort to lay the groundwork for a private fuel cycle industry. By jacking up the price, they hoped private industry would be lured into the trade. Proposed legislation—the Nuclear Fuel Assurance Act—would give $8 billion in federal guarantees as a subsidy for private firms building their own enrichment facilities.[6]

But the bill did not pass and private firms did not get into independent enrichment. Instead, the government action encouraged foreign development of enrichment and international competition for assured nuclear suppliers.[7]

The government made future sales of enriched fuel to new foreign customers conditional upon the development of a domestic spent fuel and plutonium reprocessing industry, one which has never gotten off the ground.[8]

Meanwhile, foreign reactor owners found themselves without a reliable source of enriched fuel. Small wonder they began to look for their own sources. Indeed, pressure from the U.S. manipulations led directly to the 1975 deal in which West Germany agreed to sell the complete fuel cycle technology—including enrichment and reprocessing—to Brazil.

Proliferation

If the U.S. embarked upon the programs advanced by the Nuclear Regulatory Commission and the Atomic Energy Agency, by 1990, forty-six countries would have the capability to generate about 15,010 Kg. of plutonium, enough to make 3,000 bombs. Diversion or theft of enough plutonium to make one five kilogram bomb would require only .033 percent of their total projected production.[9]

Developing nations have become increasingly interested in having atomic power plants. Their interests were whetted by U.S. technical aid coming with bilateral agreements. By 1958, the AEC had agreements involving nuclear trade and cooperation with 43 countries.[10]

Some Current U.S. Bilateral Agreements for Cooperation in the Civilian Use of Atomic Energy (effective date and termination date):

Argentina—1969-1999, Brazil—1972-2002, Columbia—1963-1977, India—1963-1993, Indonesia—1960-1980, Iran—1959-1979, Ireland—1958-1978, Philippines—1968-1998, S. Korea—1973-2002, Portugal—1974-2014, S. Africa—1957-2007, Spain—1974-2014, Taiwan—1972-2014, Turkey—1955-1981, Venezuela—1960-1980, S. Vietnam—1959-1979*.

*Cut short by the Vietnamese victory in 1975.

(Source: John Gofman and Egan O'-Connor. "Atom-Bomb Proliferation: Business Wave of the Future," 1976.)

Under the agreements, the U.S. spread research reactors around the world and brought thousands of foreign students to study nuclear physics and engineering at U.S. universities and nuclear facilities. Since 1955, nearly 13,500 foreign nationals have been trained. By 1977 more than 1,367 Indians had been trained and 700 Taiwanese. Iranian students are among those studying here now.[11]

These students and the governments that send them are quite aware that weapons-grade plutonium can be separated from irradiated nuclear fuel. It's also clear that some countries that sign cooperation agreements are interested in U.S. exports so they can have "the Bomb."

Under these agreements, the United States exported research reactors with nuclear fuel and training to Argentina, Brazil, Taiwan, Iran, Korea, Pakistan, Israel, and Spain—all now thought to be interested in having nuclear weapons.[12]

Many reactor buyers are strong regional powers with local rivalries and imperial ambitions. Argentina and Brazil, Iran, Iraq, South Africa, South Korea and Taiwan all have military aspirations as do India, Pakistan, the Philippines and a long list of nuke-oriented dictatorships which read, as one commentator put it, "like a Who's Who from Amnesty International."[13]

Bombs for Everyone

On January 19, 1976, David E. Lilienthal, who was the first Chairman of the U.S. Atomic Energy Commission, publicly advocated an immediate, unilateral U.S. embargo on the export of nuclear reactors and other nuclear technology. He said:

"Many private citizens of this country would be shocked and indignant if they realized the extent to which the U.S. has been putting into the hands of our own commercial interests and of foreign countries quantities of bomb material...We have been shipping this stuff all over the world in great quantities for years...I'm glad I'm not a young man, and I'm sorry for my grandchildren."[14]

The average commercial reactor sold today produces around 500 pounds of plutonium each year. The bomb that destroyed Nagasaki was made with 10 pounds of plutonium—one fiftieth of the yearly output. It was in part to keep the deadly material under control that the International Atomic Energy Agency (IAEA) was formed in 1956 under U.N. auspices with headquarters in Vienna, Austria. But the bilateral agreements that the U.S. entered into in the early 1950s avoided the IAEA. Only with the non-proliferation treaty in 1970 did the agency take on the full inspection role intended for it.[15]

All in all, the IAEA mandate is shaky. It is ill-funded—the 1976 safeguards budget was $6.4 million—and can claim only around 90 inspectors with 315 nuclear facilities to monitor.[16] Perhaps most significantly, the organization has no "teeth." Even if discrepancies in inventories of fissionable materials show up, there is no way to force compliance or punish violators.

United States support for the IAEA has helped substantially to spread nuclear technology, in spite of the supposed safeguards. Although the IAEA was conceived by President Eisenhower as a repository of all the world's nuclear weapon material in order to reduce pressure for proliferation, most of its budget and activities since 1958 have gone to promote nuclear activities; its safeguard function is understaffed and underfunded.[17]

Nuclear Power Around The World

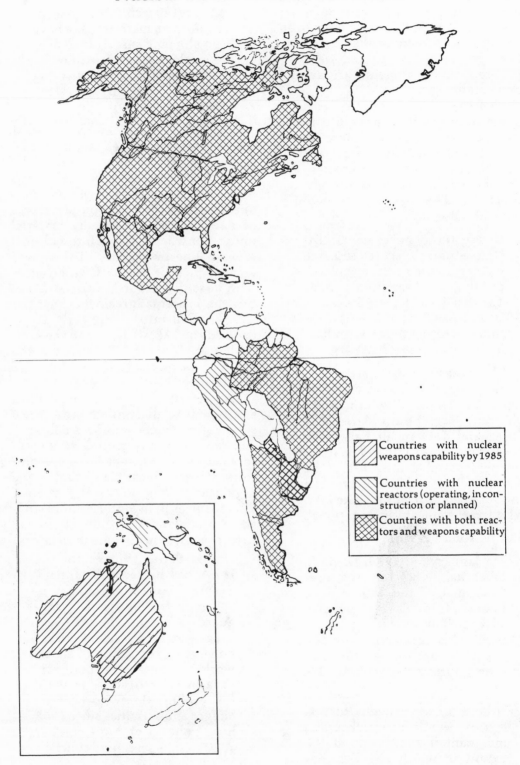

Countries with nuclear weapons capability by 1985

Countries with nuclear reactors (operating, in construction or planned)

Countries with both reactors and weapons capability

(Credit: Daniel Keller, Green Mountain
Post Films, and Mike Prendergast.)

Who's Got the Bomb?

Countries that have exploded an atomic bomb or "device":

France
U.S. A-bomb (1945), H-bomb (1952)
U.S.S.R. A-bomb (1949), H-bomb (1952)
U.K. A-bomb (1945), H-bomb (1957)
France A-bomb (1960), H-bomb (1968)
China A-bomb (1964), H-bomb (1967)
India A-bomb (1974)

Countries with nuclear weapons capability:

Australia	Belgium
Canada	Taiwan
Israel[18]	Italy
Japan	South Africa
FRG (W Ger.)	

Countries capable of making a bomb within 5 years unaided, or less if aided:

Argentina	Brazil
Chile	Czechoslovakia
Denmark	GDR (E. Ger.)
Egypt	Greece
Iran	Mexico
Netherlands	New Zealand
Norway	Pakistan
Portugal	S. Korea
Spain	Sweden
Switzerland	Turkey
Yugoslavia	

(Source: Richard Wilson, "How to have nuclear power without weapons proliferation," *Bulletin of the Atomic Scientists*, November 1977, p. 41. Dates of 1st bomb tests/use: David R. Inglis, *Nuclear Energy—Its Physics and Its Social Challenge*, p. 156.)

As of now, the U.S., U.S.S.R., France, China, India and Israel possess nuclear weapons. But thanks to the proliferation of atomic reactors, about 30 countries have plutonium that could be used in bombs. Half of them have refused to sign the 1970 International Treaty on Non-Proliferation of Nuclear Weapons, thus exempting them from even the limited oversight of the IAEA.[19]

The non-proliferation treaty (NPT) was promoted by the major nuclear powers to prevent further spread of atomic weapons. But it promotes what many small nations feel is an unfair double standard.

In signing the NPT, a buyer nation must agree to reject nuclear weapons or weapons material from any source. It also agrees to open its facilities to IAEA inspection. In return, the signees receive help in developing commercial nuclear power plants.

Nations already possessing nuclear weapons are required to refrain from selling weapons technology and materials. But unlike the requirements for nations without nuclear weapons, "Bomb" nations do not have to open their doors to the IAEA. Small wonder the treaty has been viewed with suspicion by importers of nuclear power.

The treaty, which first started taking shape in 1968, has not been signed by China, India or Israel, nor by two dozen non-weapons states including Brazil, Egypt and Iran.

Organizing for Safeguards

Nuclear technology exporters held their first major meetings in 1975 after India exploded a bomb made with nuclear materials from imported Canadian technology. At the insistance of Henry Kissinger, the largest atomic exporters—the U.S., U.S.S.R., U.K., France, West Germany (F.R.G.), Canada and Japan—met in great secrecy to discuss controlling the misuse of "peaceful" atomic technology and materials. In 1976 the group expanded its membership to include Belgium, Sweden, East Germany (G.D.R.), the Netherlands, Italy, Poland and Switzerland.

Together the exporters produced a set of guidelines that regulated the use of waste materials. Safeguards consisted mainly of promises extracted from buyers that nuclear materials would only be used for peaceful purposes. With no enforcement mechanism to back up the guidelines, and with a potential export market totalling some $25 billion over the next five years, fears that some nations will drop or bend the sellers' guidelines rather than lose sales are amply justified.

During this period, the U.S. was concerned about foreign sales of reprocessing facilities. France was negotiating to sell to Iran, South Korea and Pakistan, and West Germany was negotiating with Brazil. Still the U.S. continued to promote the export of nuclear power reactors. And it continued to supply enriched uranium fuel under existing contracts—even to countries that had refused to sign the non-proliferation treaty.[20]

The U.S. finally pressured South Korea to drop its request of reprocessing technology from France. And Secretary of State Kissinger offered the Shah of Iran $10 billion in sophisticated "conventional" weapons to sidetrack his interest in the Bomb.[21]

**International Suppliers
of Nuclear Technology**

1950s: France*   U.K.
    U.S.*   U.S.S.R.*
1960s: The 4 above plus:
    Canada*   FRG (W. Ger.)*
1970s: The 6 above plus:
    GDR(E. Ger.)   Italy*
    Japan*   Netherlands*
    Poland   Sweden*
    Switzerland

*Current reactor exporters

(Source: David Binder, "15 Major Nuclear Nations Will Discuss Ways to Curb Spread of the Ability to Make Atomic Weapons")
New York Times, 9 November 1976)

Implications of Import

Aside from the Bomb problem which increases instability and threatens health and safety world-wide, there is a long list of economic and other reasons why a nuke can be deadly for a developing country. Atomic energy—promised as a cheap, dependable source of power—is in reality a financial and political trap.

First, a reactor (average price now $1 billion) swallows up a huge amount of capital, diverting it from pressing needs—roads, schools, agricultural, health and housing projects. Thus far developing nations have committed $36,604,468,000 for 59 nuclear reactors. "In many developing countries, the cost of a single small reactor exceeds the value of all annual exports."[22] Because the buyers cannot raise this amount of capital themselves, the money often comes from government and private banks in the vendor countries. For example, the U.S. government's Export-Import Bank has given $7,909,195,000 loans and guarantees for nuclear exports, averaging 50% of the sales cost of each reactor financed. Export-Import Bank subsidies amounted to $6,318,861,000 for Westinghouse and $1,590,334,000 for G.E.[23] Loans for foreign reactor sales are really just subsidies to the domestic nuclear industry, with taxpayers and the Third World footing the bill. According to Rep. Clarence Long, "without Export-Import Bank financing, very few, (if any) nuclear power plants would be exported, probably none to the less-developed countries."[24]

Purchasing a nuclear plant in turn leaves the developing nation with a huge foreign debt. To pay it off the country must export labor resources, often at a profound disadvantage.

Although the IAEA has forecast that at least 293,000-Mw and as much as 437,000-Mw of nuclear capacity will be built in the developing world by the year 2000, nuclear power is ill-fitted to Third World energy needs.[25] Most developing countries are essentially agricultural, with dispersed rural populations and little if any need for centralized power supplies. In addition, most LDCs (less developed countries) have neither the necessary grid systems nor the back-up generating capacity to support a nuke. A 600-Mw reactor needs transmission lines capable of carrying at least 9200-Mw. Yet only India, Brazil, Mexico and Argentina in all the Third World have grids greater than 5000-Mw. A 600-Mw plant requires from 6000-10,000-Mw of installed back-up capacity. Only five Third World countries can provide this important security for even one small reactor.[26]

In order to pay their nuclear debt, the LDCs must not only install a bigger grid system (imported), but must also host export industries capable of generating the needed foreign exchange. The industries are often precisely those which need large supplies of electricity, and which take people off the land to serve as cheap labor in factories, exacerbating already severe urban problems. This situation is epitomized in the Philippines, where electricity from the proposed Bataan reactor (a Westinghouse 620-Mw PWR) is slated to serve two U.S. military bases and a U.S. dominated free trade zone, where 70% of all products are exported and 70% of all businesses are foreign-owned (many of them runaway shops) and tax-free.[27]

In other words, the chief function of the nukes in the long run is to power industries which serve the vendor nations while they undercut the traditional economies of those countries which have bought them. Nuclear plants are instruments of economic

colonization. Virtually every LDC that buys one will become dependent on foreign technicians, foreign fuel and foreign waste management technology to keep it going. Even Japan can't as yet control its own nuclear industry. And if the horrendous performance record there is any indication of what can be expected from exported reactors world-wide, the benefits will be sparse indeed.

Third World Energy Choices

Nuclear power is hardly the only energy option for Third World countries. Since they generally have rural populations, their energy needs now are decentralized and can be met with conservation and energy efficiency improvements and small-scale renewable energy alternatives. Early development of renewables could provide energy sources for future growth. In his *Energy for Development: Third World Options*, Denis Hayes concludes that:

> Tomorrow, both the industrial and the agrarian world are likely to turn to solar resources—sunlight, wind, hydro-power, and biomass—for their commercial energy. The Third World, however, has an advantage in that it can take a shortcut past the fossil fuel cul-de-sac. While the industrial world has 90 percent of its capital stock invested in buildings and equipment that are ill-suited to a solar transition, the Third World can undergo rapid economic growth with a clearer vision of its ultimate goal.[28]

One big stumbling block to such a transition is the pressure put on LDCs by First World vendors. Solar technology is not an option offered by either G.E. or Westinghouse, Framatome, etc. As long as nuclear power is good business abroad, companies will continue to push reactors. Since the repressive regimes of many developing powers see atomic weapons as an available ticket to world-power status, influence and military might, worldwide nuclear trade is not likely to end in the near future. Nor is it likely to end as long as every vendor can say "if we don't sell it someone else will." Rather, current proliferation problems will escalate and the export vendors will continue getting rich at the expense of the Third World.

Runaway Reactors[29]

> Westinghouse Electric Corporation...is apparently trying to sell to developing countries defective technology that it can no longer market successfully in the U.S.[30]

Overseas sales continue to represent a desparately needed "out" for First World vendors who are being met with mounting opposition and falling sales at home.

> Having watched their markets in the industrial world disappear in recent years, with deferrals and cancellations greatly outnumbering new reactor orders and with many industrial countries cutting their official forecasts for nuclear growth by two-thirds, the nuclear industry has eagerly turned to Third World markets to hawk its wares.[31]

For the nuclear industry, LDCs offer a new frontier where reactors can be built with easy public financing, where health and safety regulations are loose and enforcement rare, where public opposition is not permitted and where weak and corrupt regimes offer easy sales.

Both U.S. and European manufacturers have responded to inflation and delay at home by competing fiercely for sales in third [world] markets, especially in developing countries with authoritarian regimes that need not worry about public opposition to siting of nuclear power plants.[32]

Who Has Sold Nukes Where?

In the 1960s and early 1970s, G.E. and Westinghouse had firm grips on the international nuclear plant trade. German and French manufacturers switched from domestic designs to U.S. light-water reactor models under franchise and other agreements. In recent years, however, the U.S. has lost much of its hold. While from 1968 to 1972 G.E. and Westinghouse controlled virtually the entire market, their shares have fallen drastically in recent years. In 1977, the firms reported zero export sales.

What happened to turn the established pattern of U.S. market control around? G.E. and Westinghouse blame the controversy that accompanied the Nuclear Non-Proliferation Act before it was signed in the spring of 1978 and foreign competition for their losses. Now that the Act has been passed, industry fears that its regulatory red-tape will hinder foreign sales even more than the confusion preceeding the bill's passage.[33]

This bill, key to the Carter program to curb proliferation, bans U.S. export of enrichment and reprocessing technology, and places uranium fuel exports under special licensing arrangements. The part of the law that has had the most destabilizing effect internationally was the cancellation and forced renegotiation of all nuclear contracts and treaties. European customers were given just 30 days to agree

EXPORT ORDERS/MARKET SHARES
World—

EXPORT ORDERS/MARKET SHARES
Western Vendors Only—

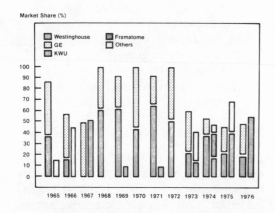

By Year of Announcement

By Year of Announcement

(Source: *Nuclear Exports From the United States*, Westinghouse Electric Corporation, April 1977, pp. 4-5.)

to renegotiation. Carter leaned on the French and West Germans heavily, hoping that they too would submit to U.S. guidelines on the production and sale of plutonium and enriched uranium producing facilities.

Under President Carter, U.S. nuclear policy has become profoundly schizophrenic.

On the one hand, the President has moved to curtail the spread of reprocessing and enrichment facilities. The steps are the first of their kind, and represent a landmark change in official U.S. consciousness about the proliferation of nuclear weapons around the globe.

But at the same time, official government institutions continue to aid in the sale of reactors overseas. While U.S. firms continue to hype the alleged benefits of nuclear power, sales are facilitated by the U.S. Export-Import Bank, a branch of the government. When push came to shove over the sale of uranium to India, Carter allowed the material to go overseas—demonstra-

ting his indecisive position on nuclear proliferation.

Furthermore, while the government professes to have its hands tied about the "independent decisions" of various Third World nations to buy reactors, the fact is that the U.S. has considerable leverage with many of these countries. We know from painful experience that many of the worst dictatorships on the planet would not be able to stand without overt and covert U.S. support. Many of those same regimes are now pursuing the nuclear path, for all the worst reasons.

There are, in short, many levers the Carter administration could use against both exporting companies and importing nations to halt the flow of nuclear power reactors.

Of late the industry and its apologists have proliferated a new line of their own—"if we don't sell them, someone else will," with the implication that the "someone else" will be less responsible than the U.S.

Western Vendor Export Sales

Vendor/ Home Country	Country of Reactor Sale	Prior to 1971 MWe-Plt	1971 MWe-Plt	1972 MWe-Plt	1973 MWe-Plt	1974 MWe-Plt	1975 MWe-Plt	1976 MWe-Plt
Framatome/ France	Iran					1850 2		
	Belguim					1800 2		
	South Africa							1844 2
BBR/ West Germany	Luxembourg					1290 1		
Atomenergo– Export/USSR	Bulgaria	1620 4						
	Czechoslovakia	760 2		760 2				
	Finland	420 1	420 1					1000 1
	East Germany	1680 5				880 2		
	Hungary			880 2				
	Rumania					440 1		
	Poland						440 1	
KWU/ West Germany	Argentina	319 1						
	Austria		692 1					
	Netherlands	447 1						
	Switzerland				920 1			
	Iran					2480 2		
	Brazil						2480 2	
	Spain						1000 1	
ASEA-Atom/ Sweden	Finland				660 1	660 1		
Canadian GE/ Canada	Pakistan	125 1						
AECL/ Canada	India	404 2						
	Korea				629 1			
	Argentina				600 1			
Group Const. Francais/France	Spain	486 1						
U.K. · Gen. Elec. Co./U.K.	Japan	157 1						
Nuclear Power Group/U.K.	Italy	200 1						
General Electric U.S.A.	Germany	252 2						
	Italy	990 2			982 1	982 1		
	Japan	1550 4	2134 2					
	India	380 2						
	Netherlands	53 1						
	Spain	440 1			930 1		1880 2	1000 1
	Switzerland	1231 2		942 1		1140 1		
	Taiwan	1208 2		1902 2				
	Mexico			654 1	654 1			
Westinghouse + WNE/USA	Belgium	1661 4				2012 2		
	Brazil		626 1					
	France	309 1						
	Japan	2222 3	1122 1					
	Italy	261 1			952 1		952 1	
	Korea	564 1					605 1	
	Spain	153 1	2706 3	2706 3			2000 2	
	Sweden	822 1	900 1	900 1				
	Switzerland	700 2						
	Taiwan					1800 2		
	Yugoslavia				615 1			
	Philippines							620 1

By 1978, the U.S. had sold 67 reactors abroad. Westinghouse sold 38, GE sold 29. The German Kraftwerk Union (KWU) sold 14; Framatome sold 6. (*New York Times*, 7 March 1978.)

But someone must start somewhere. The U.S. took the lead in spreading control of nuclear technology around the planet; it must now assume responsibility in getting it under a modicum of control, even if that means cutting back on enormously profitable reactor sales.

For the sum of U.S. policies has been to *promote* rather than curtail the spread of enrichment and reprocessing technology. Faced with a nation willing to sell reactors but unwilling to allow for independent fuel cycle technology, the nations that have bought the reactors are now, naturally enough, looking elsewhere to find guarantees of their fuel supply. As German commentator Michael Lucas puts it: "U.S. uranium blackmail...will accelerate the efforts of the Federal Republic (of Germany) to secure other sources in order, as much as possible, to achieve uranium and plutonium independence from the United States."[35] The law has also caused the German government to push for faster construction of a uranium enrichment plant at Gronau and a fuel reprocessing and waste storage facility at Gorleben (see German report, p. 351). France also has objected to the U.S. ultimatum on uranium contract renegotiation.

A more frightening counteroffensive from France came on April 18, 1978 with announcements in the press that French scientists are developing a French neutron bomb. The news is clearly intended to give the United States notice that France and the European Community will not stand by and be blackmailed with the political, economic and military arm of uranium and nuclear technology. The French announcement is also a chilling example of the political impossibility of separating peaceful and wardirected nuclear cooperation and competition.[36]

Plutonium Politics

The first U.S. reactors were designed and built to produce materials with which to make the Bomb. The Bomb was then produced, and used.

Can the U.S. now turn around and piously instruct the rest of the world not to follow the same path?

As long as U.S. corporations are willing to sell reactors abroad, with Export-Import Bank financing and with the U.S. in possession of a huge nuclear weapons stockpile of its own, the U.S. contribution to world Bomb proliferation will continue unabated, and official pronouncements against it will be hollow indeed.

Two items:
• In October 1977, *Nucleonics Week*, a key industry trade journal, announced that the DOE's Oak Ridge National Laboratory had designed a simple, cheap, "quick and dirty" reprocessing plant. The plans show that almost any country or private group with the desire and funds could, in four to six months, build a short-cut plant capable of producing 100 kg of plutonium per month from standard reactor spend fuel rods.[37]
• In July 1978, the U.S. House of Representatives upheld President Carter's decision to send 17,000 pounds of enriched uranium to India. This despite the fact that India had already exploded its own "nuclear device" and had refused to sign the U.S.'s non-proliferation treaty requiring IAEA inspectations of U.S. buyers' facilities.[38]

For three decades now the U.S. has manipulated nuclear technology for profit and as a tool of Cold War foreign policy.

The genie has long left the U.S. lamp. It will now take a world-wide movement to stop the proliferation of nuclear reactors and weapons.

Happily, other vendor nations have anti-nuclear forces at work. Throughout Europe, Japan, Australia, and Canada, strong popular pressure has developed to halt the spread of nuclear technology.

The U.S. exporters' argument that "if we don't sell them, someone else will," is simply not valid. One does not stop an evil by spreading it. By our stopping U.S. exports, we are acting in solidarity with anti-nuclear activists throughout the world.

A total embargo on reactor exports; an immediate halt to Export-Import Bank nuclear financing; economic sanctions against countries selling reactors abroad; and clear, unwavering pressure against those regimes buying them—these are minimal demands for calling a halt to this nightmare.

It is already very late.

Prepared by Anna Gyorgy and Harvey Wasserman

FOE/Australia, August 1977

Footnotes

1. Anthony J. Parisi, "U.S. Reactor Makers' Recovery in Doubt After 4-Year Market Dip," *New York Times,* 7 March 1978.

2. Irvin C. Bupp and Jean-Claude Derian, *Lightwater: How the Nuclear Dream Dissolved,* (New York: Basic Books, 1978), pp. 19-20. David R. Inglis, *Nuclear Energy: Its Physics and Its Social Challenge* (Reading, MA: Addison-Wesley Publishing Co., 1973), pp. 152-153.

3. "The goal of the United States-EURATOM Program, which included two of the four deferred-payment nuclear fuel contracts, (twenty-year loans at 4% interest including a ten-year grace period on principal repayments) was to persuade the Europeans to adopt American light-water reactor technology, so that American nuclear suppliers would benefit from exports; instead, it helped create the international competition which now threatens United States nuclear export markets."—Rep. Clarence D. Long (Md.), "Nuclear Proliferation: Can Congress Act in Time?" in *International Security,* 1978, p. 56. See also: Bupp and Derian, *op. cit.,* pp. 15-41.

4. Brazil was first among Third World countries to work actively for bomb technology. Rich in uranium, it has been trying to become an independent nuclear power since 1946. In 1951 Brazil accepted France's offer of a reprocessing plant, and soon after tried to buy a centrifuge for uranium production from the Federal Republic of Germany. The U.S., as the occupying power in post-war West Germany, prevented this and later Brazilian attempts to acquire German equipment.–"The Peaceful Bomb," West German radio program aired 24 May 1977, written by Frederico Fullgraf, produced by WDR/SFB. Summary by Michael Lucas, Berlin.

5. Statement of Janet Hieber, Environmental Policy Center, 28 March 1977, before the Banking, Finance and Urban Affairs Committee, U.S. House of Rep. Subcommittee on International Trade, Investment and Monetary Policy. p. 7. "The Oak Ridge plant alone uses about ½ million dollars worth of electricity per day. The cost of uranium ore is up from $6 per lb. in 1973 to $40 per lb. in 1976 largely as a result of AEC/ERDA enrichment and stockpiling policy." Ratepayers, domestic utilities and taxpayers are paying for the stockpiling practice.

6. John J. Berger, *Nuclear Power, The Unviable Option* (Palo Alto CA: Ramparts Press, 1976), pp. 153-154.

7. Hieber, *op. cit.,* p. 2.

8. *Ibid.,* p. 3. The contracts for 45 non-preferred foreign customers were made contingent on the U.S. going ahead with plutonium reprocessing

and plutonium recycle—the use of "mixed ox-ides" of P-239 and U-235 as reactor fuel. It was estimated that plutonium recycling could "stretch out our uranium reserves by 33% and make nuclear power 3 to 4% cheaper." —Leonard Ross, "How 'atoms for peace' became bombs for sale," New York Times Magazine, 5 Dec., 1976.

9. Bob Alvarez, "U.S. Nuclear Export Policies—1976-90: All Electric Kitchens and Starvation," Memorandum, Environmental Policy Center, 324 C St., S.E., Washington, D.C. 20003. p. 1. See also: IAEA, Market Survey for Nuclear Power in Developing Countries, 1974 edition, preliminary report, IAEA-165. USAEC, Nuclear Power Growth 1974-2000, WASH 1139, (74).

10. Warren H. Donnelly, Commercial Nuclear Power in Europe: The Interaction of American Diplomacy with a New Technology, Science Policy Research Division, Congressional Research Service, Dec. 1972, p. 32. Quoted in Clarence D. Long, op. cit., p. 55.

11. Clarence D. Long, op. cit., p. 59. Also: John W. Gofman and Egan O'Connor, "Atom-Bomb Proliferation: Business Wave of the Future?", 30 September 1976. Available from Committee for Nuclear Responsibility, MPOB Box 11207, San Francisco, CA 94101.

12. Clarence D. Long, who referenced "U.S. Financial Assistance in the Development of Foreign Nuclear Energy Programs," General Accounting Office (Report 10-75-63), 28 May 1975, p. 10.

13. Keike Kehoe, "Report to Environmental Policy Center: The U.S. Nuclear Industry," p. 1.

14. Gofman and O'Conner, op. cit. See also: David Burnham, "U.S. Export Ban on Nuclear Equipment Urged by Former Atomic Energy Chief," New York Times, 20 January 1976.

15. Inglis, op. cit., p. 153.

16. Ross, op. cit., (note 5).

17. Long, op. cit., p. 59. In 1977 the IAEA's safeguards budget was but 18% of the regular budget and only 14% of "total estimated resources," —IAEA "Summary of Estimated Programme Resources 1977."

18. Inglis, op. cit., p. 157. In early 1978 it was revealed that since 1974 the C.I.A. knew that Israel had produced atomic weapons, "partly with uranium it had obtained by clandestine means." "The C.I.A. document, a secret national intelligence estimate titled "Prospects for Further Proliferation of Nuclear Weapons," also predicted that Taiwan would be able to build a nuclear weapon by 1979, that South Africa could go forward with a nuclear-weapons program if seriously threatened and that Spain, Iran, Egypt, Pakistan, Brazil and South Korea would not be able to build bombs until at least 1984."—David Burnham. "C.I.A. said in 1974 Israel had A-bombs," New York Times, 27 January 1978. In March Burnham reported that according to a former C.I.A. official, the agency informed President Johnson in 1968 that the Israelis had nuclear weapons. Johnson told then-Director Helms that no one else should be told. (New York Times, 2 March 1978). See also: William Beecher, "U.S. Believes Israel has more than 10 nuclear weapons," Boston Globe, 31 July 1975; David Burnham, "U.S. Agencies Suspected Missing Uranium Went to Israel for Arms," New York Times, 6 November 1977.

19. Leonard Ross, op. cit.

20. Ibid.

21. Ibid.

22. Denis Hayes, Energy for Development: Third World Options, Worldwatch Paper 15, December 1977, p.17 (quote). Figures from Lindsay Mattison, Campaign to Stop Runaway Reactors, 9 June 1978. Center for Development Policy, 225 4th St., N.E., Washington, D.C. 20002.

23. Mattison, op. cit. For the fiscal year 1979, the Export-Import Bank has budgeted: $11 billion for loans, guarantees and insurance, half of which will go for energy-related exports ($5.7 billion). Of this amount, $1.6 billion is for nuclear exports; $1.6 for the liquid natural gas industry; $1.6 billion for conventional power generators; $0.9 billion for the oil industry (which really needs a break).

24. Clarence D. Long, quoted in Keiki Kehoe's report, op. cit., p. 2.

25. Hayes, op. cit., p. 16.

26. Richard J. Barber Associates, Inc., "LDC Nuclear Power Prospects, 1975-1990: Commercial, Economic and Security Implications," Springfield, Va. National Technical Information Service, 1975. From Denis Hayes, op. cit., p. 19.

27. Mattison, op. cit.

28. Denis Hayes, op. cit., p. 6. See also: Energy for Rural Development: Renewable Resources and Alternative Technologies for Developing Countries, National Academy of Sciences, Washington, D.C., 1976.

29. The Campaign to Stop Runaway Reactors is a program instituted by the Center for Development Policy, whose purpose is to focus on the siting of reactors in developing countries. The program will collect information on each reactor in the Third World for distribution to anti-nuclear organizations, human rights and church groups as well as anti-nuclear groups abroad. For more information contact: Center for Development Policy, 225 4th St., N.E., Washington, D.C. 20002.

30. Dan Ford, Union of Concerned Scientists, Cambridge, Mass. February 1978.

31. Hayes, *op. cit.*, p. 16.

32. Norman Gall, *Bulletin of the Atomic Scientists*, June 1976. From *Campaign to Stop Runaway Reactors*.

33. Anthony J. Parisi, *op. cit.* Also: Youssef M. Ibrahim, "U.S. Nuclear Industry Sees Bill as Threat to Exports," *New York Times*, 15 February 1978.

34. Zdenek and Barbara Rogers, *The Nuclear Axis: Collusion Between West Germany and South Africa* (NY: McMillan Publishing Co., 1977). Based on documents that disappeared from a collection of South African embassy files in West Germany, published by the African National Congress (ANC). The documents detail the sale of jet-nozzle uranium enrichment process by STEAG (Steinkohlen Elektrizitat Aktiongesellschaft) to UCOR (Uranium Enrichment Corporation) of South Africa. From review by Wilfred Burchett, *Guardian*, 20 September 1978, p. 20.

35. Michael Lucas, "Recent Developments in International Nuclear Relations," Berlin, 1 May 1978.

36. *Ibid.*

37. *Nucleonics Week*, vol. 18, no. 43, 27 October 1977. "U.S. Proliferation Policy Seen Shaken by Simple ORNL Reprocessing Design."

38. Maria Korchmar, "Carter, Congress Cave in on India Exports," *Critical Mass Journal*, July 1978, p. 8. Supporters of the export, mainly Joseph Nye, the State Department's under secretary for security assistance, science and technology, said U.S./India relations should take priority over proliferation fears.

Resources

BOOKS:

• John McPhee, *The Curve of Binding Energy*, (New York: Farrar, Straus and Giroux, 1973). The superb story of bomb developer-turned-safeguards-activist, Dr. T. Taylor.

• Theodore B. Taylor and Mason Willrich, *Nuclear Theft: Risks and Safeguards*, (Cambridge, Ma: Ballinger Publishing Co., 1974).

• Office of Technological Assessment (OTA), *Nuclear Proliferation and Safeguards*, (New York: Praeger, 1977).

ARTICLES:

• Citizens Energy Project: Report on Proliferation ("Seeding Mushroom Clouds"), 1413 K St., N.W., Washington, D.C. 20005. $1.00.

• Richard Wilson, "How to have nuclear power without weapons proliferation," *Bulletin of the Atomic Scientists*, November 1977, pp. 39-44.

• See also: materials referred to in footnotes.

Chapter 2: The International Story

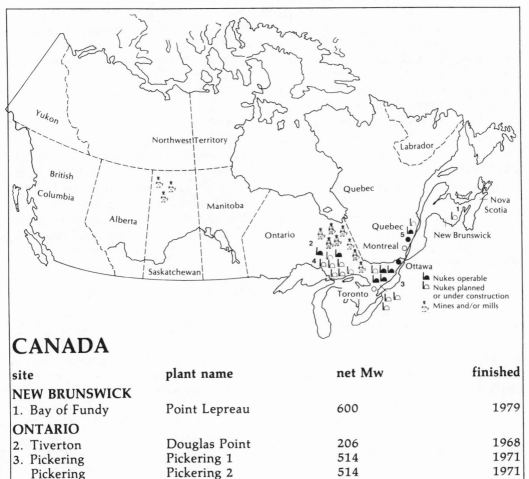

CANADA

site	plant name	net Mw	finished
NEW BRUNSWICK			
1. Bay of Fundy	Point Lepreau	600	1979
ONTARIO			
2. Tiverton	Douglas Point	206	1968
3. Pickering	Pickering 1	514	1971
Pickering	Pickering 2	514	1971
Pickering	Pickering 3	514	1972
Pickering	Pickering 4	514	1973
Pickering	Pickering 5	516	1981
Pickering	Pickering 6	516	1982
Pickering	Pickering 7	516	1982
Pickering	Pickering 8	516	1983
4. Tiverton	Bruce 1	746	1977
Tiverton	Bruce 2	746	1976
Tiverton	Bruce 3	746	1978
Tiverton	Bruce 4	746	1979
Tiverton	Bruce 5	769	1983
Tiverton	Bruce 6	769	1984
Tiverton	Bruce 7	769	1985
Tiverton	Bruce 8	769	1986
QUEBEC			
5. Becancour	Gentilly 1	250	1972
Becancour	Gentilly 2	600	1979

CANADA
The Canadian government has been involved with nuclear power since the wartime Manhattan Project that built the Bomb. Canadian and British scientists worked with U.S. and emigre physicists until 1946. Since then, a Canadian nuclear industry has developed that exports reactors as well as provides domestic nuclear power plants.

Uranium
Canada is rich in uranium which has been mined since the 1930s (at that time it was known as "pitchblende" and was mined for radium). Uranium exports grew during the 1950s, reaching a peak in 1959. In the 1960s, the U.K. and the U.S. stopped importing Canadian uranium, and the Canadian government began stockpiling it to keep the industry going. Their financial investment led them to take a major role in the international price-fixing cartel that was active from 1971-1976 (see p. 131). There were 24 mines active in 1959. Now there are 4: 2 at Eliot Lake in Ontario and 2 in Saskatchewan. Canada is a major uranium exporter. Sales are currently being negotiated with Japan and the Philippines.

As in the U.S., uranium mining in Canada poses great health hazards to miners, especially where company and province safety standards are lax. Health records from the Ontario Ministry of Health show that uranium miners between the ages of 40 and 57 were "four times as likely to die of lung cancer as the ordinary resident."[1] In addition to its effects on miners' health, mining has caused environmental damage. Radon from mine tailings has contaminated ground water and the Serpent River Basin in Ontario's Eliot Lake mining region.

Enrichment
Although the Canadian CANDU reactor does not use enriched uranium, there have been plans for a uranium enrichment facility at the James Bay hydroelectric project. Uranium would be enriched for export to countries with light-water reactors.

Wastes
CANDU reactors produce the same radioactive by-products as the U.S. light-water reactors—including plutonium. In fact, the spent fuel bundles from CANDUs contain about 3 grams of fissionable plutonium per kilogram of uranium—about twice or three times the amount produced per unit of electricity by U.S. light-water reactors.[2]

Canada has extensive reserves of thorium, and the CANDU reactor is being redesigned to take both plutonium and thorium fuels. At this time, there is no plutonium reprocessing or recycling going on in Canada, but a chemical process for reprocessing CANDU fuel bundles is planned, and reprocessing plants have been proposed for Ontario and Manitoba. The country has no atomic weapons program as it is part of the U.S./North American nuclear "umbrella."

Waste Storage—This is a problem in Canada as in every nuclear nation. In November 1977, the Department of Energy, Mines and Resources released a special report, "The Management of Canada's Nuclear Wastes." It rejected delaying nuclear construction because the wastes cannot (yet) be safely disposed of. Science would surely have the problem solved by 1995!

The Canadian Anti-nuke Movement
• The Canadian Coalition for Nuclear Responsibility (CCNR; Regroupement

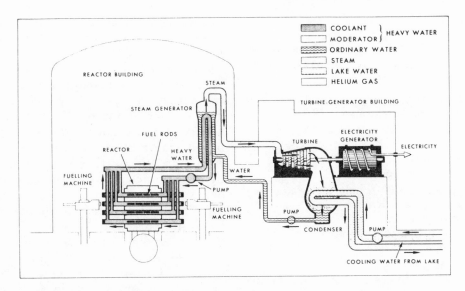

COOLANT ⎤
MODERATOR ⎦ HEAVY WATER
ORDINARY WATER
STEAM
LAKE WATER
HELIUM GAS

The Canadian Deuterium Uranium (CANDU) Reactor—This is unique among reactor designs in that it uses natural uranium as the fuel and heavy water as a moderator. (Source: *The Nuke Book*, p. 8)

pour la surveillance du nucleaire), formed in 1975 and represents more than 100 citizens' groups. Since 1975, CCNR has been calling for a full public inquiry into Canada's nuclear policies at the national level. They have gathered "tens of thousands" of names on a petition calling for such an inquiry. CCNR has been involved in a number of nuclear-related issues. They have a newsletter and written resources.

• Opposed to nuclear power in general and uranium mining especially is the Saskatoon Environmental Society founded in 1970. The SES has worked on a variety of environmental issues—for better timber cutting regulation, province-wide recycling of junk cars, preservation of historic buildings... They have a newsletter, periodic tabloids and some excellent resources.

• The Societe pour vaincre la pollution (S.V.P.; Society to conquer pollution) puts out an excellent newspaper, *journal l'environnement*. They also produced a 69-page study in 1976 on

nuclear power and Canada called "Tout ce que Vous Aimeriez ne pas Savoir sur l'Energie Nucleaire" (Everything you never wanted to know about nuclear energy...).

• In September 1977, 15 ecology and citizens' groups founded the anti-nuclear Common Front—Le Front Commun Anti-Nucleaire. They organized the first direct action against nuclear power in Canada—a demonstration on 22 October 1977 at the Gentilly nuclear and heavy water plants located between Montreal and Quebec. The demonstration called for an end to the nuclear industry, and the creation of a "new society that doesn't waste, that doesn't pollute, that doesn't dominate nature or people."

Footnotes

1. *CANDU: An Analysis of the Canadian Nuclear Program*, Part 1, p. 29.

2. *Ibid.*, p. 76.

Contacts:

CCNR
2010 MacKay St.
Montreal, Quebec P.

CCNR
54-53 Queen St.
Ottawa, Ontario P.

SES
P.O. Box 1372
Saskatoon, Saskatchewan, S7K3N9

S.V.P.
C.P. 65
Place d'Armes
Montreal, Quebec P.

Greenpeace (fights whale/seal slaughter, opposes nuclear power)
2108 West 4th Ave.
Vancouver, British Columbia
C.P. 1578

Resources

Two good resources on the Canadian nuclear industry are:

—*The Nukes Book: The Impact of Nuclear Development*, 2nd Edition, Pollution Probe, Ottawa Ecology Centre Associates, 1977.

—*CANDU: An Analysis of the Canadian Nuclear Program*, Parts 1 & 2, Pollution Probe Foundation, 1977. Available from SES.

Also

Fred H. Knelman, *Nuclear Energy, the Unforgiving Technology* (Edmonton, Alberta: Hurtig Publishers, 10560 105 St., 1976), $4.95.

Mining Fight in B.C.

In Canada, federal and provincial governments spent $4.8 million last year searching out and mapping potential uranium sources. Mining companies then use these maps to lay their claims. A similar program is going on in the United States. British Columbia is additionally encouraging exploration with a $5 million Mining Exploration Program, a revised mineral royalty scheme and new tax incentives.

In Canada, regulatory jurisdiction over uranium mining is spotty and muddled with both federal and provincial governments opting for control and much of the mining easily slipping through the broken web of enforcement. The federal government claims not only regulatory jurisdiction, but also is in the business of exporting uranium (and nuclear reactors) around the world, creating an obvious conflict of interest.

But as the uranium boom grows, so does grassroots resistance. Last December, more than 700 people attended an eight-hour public meeting in Clearwater, B.C., near the site of a proposed major open-pit uranium mine. Although the hearing was organized by the mining company to soothe residents' fears, testimony was almost unanimously opposed to the venture. In Grand Forks, not far from Genelle, B.C., a woman recently chased uranium explorers off her land with a shotgun. Groups are actively working against uranium mining in Saskatchewan and other Canadian provinces as well as other nations, especially Australia where recent federal legislation makes it a crime to demonstrate against certain uranium mines—one more show of government support for the uranium industry.

In British Columbia alone, opposition to uranium mining—at the very least a call for a moratorium until certain questions have been answered—has been voiced by the United Steelworkers of America, which represents almost all uranium miners in Ontario; the British Columbia Federation of Labor; the Canadian Association of Industrial Mechanical and Allied Workers, Canada's largest union; the B.C. Medical Association; the province's Fisherman's Union; the Sierra Club; the B.C. Conference of the United Church; 16 bands of Indians and various environmental groups.

"Uranium mining poses as many unsolved and serious threats to life and environment as do nuclear plants and weapons," says one representative of a B.C. environmental group. "Keeping uranium in the ground may be the most crucial part of the growing international anti-nuclear movement."

—Cathy Wolff

NUKES IN EUROPE

Some sites have more than one
nuclear power plant.

(Source: *Nuclear News*, 1 September 1976.)

Introduction to Nukes in Europe

European countries have been long-time customers and are now competitors of the U.S. atomic power industry. To varying degrees, the governments of Europe have committed their countries to nuclear-powered futures. But their plans have been understood and opposed.

A movement has grown in Europe against construction of nuclear power plants and related fuel cycle facilities, as well as the export of nuclear technology. Although the roots of this anti-nuclear fight are in local communities in many countries, the movement is an international one.

The U.S. public has heard little or nothing of the major anti-nuke/ecology movements in western Europe. Nor are most Europeans aware of the growing opposition to nuclear power in the U.S., or the weakened position of nuclear industry.

Communication on the grassroots level between people of different countries is difficult. But it is the only hope for stopping the spread of atomic power. The nuclear programs of western Europe and the U.S. support each other, even as they compete. The movement to stop nuclear power will be stronger and more successful when the connections between our fights are clearly seen and understood.

As with the national reports in this book, the international reports are samples—not all activities can be covered. They are also not "up to the minute." However, we hope that they will give you some background on where the European movement has been, and an idea of present directions that are being followed. The reports come from activists in Europe, or are taken from original materials from the country involved.

"I will always invest...   where others bear the risk..."
(Credit: *Forum Europa:* A Journal of Transnational Politics. Bonn, Fed. Repub. of Germany Nr. 3/4, 1976)

"Grab A Hold!" —Gorleben: This photo shows one of several hand-painted anti-nuclear billboards in the "alternative" playground in Gorleben, where the West German (FRG) government and nuclear industry plan to build a nuclear fuel reprocessing center along with temporary and permanent waste storage facilities. The land shown in the photo is part of a still unsold section of the construction site. It has been a gathering point for anti-nuke groups from surrounding country towns and from West German cities who have joined the fight to stop the government from carrying out its plans. The landscape appears desolate due to a fire in 1975, which many of the anti-nuclear townspeople suspect was the work of pro-nuclear forces. This spring a project was launched to reforest the land. The entire 66 acre tract has now been seeded with oaks, birches, and pine trees by people from all parts of West Germany and Berlin. This action was an expression of opposition to nukes and at the same time a real alternative to the destruction of the region by the reprocessing facility.

Chronology of European Anti-Nuclear Demonstrations and Occupations (by country)

This chronology of events in France, Switzerland, Germany and Italy is intended to give a rough idea of the international scope of the European anti-nuclear movement. It does not include all the demonstrations nor all the countries in Europe in which anti-nuclear opposition has developed, but rather lists the large demonstrations or smaller actions that have been important turning points in the movement.

FRANCE

1971
- 12 April   Fessenheim
1,300 people demonstrate against a nuclear power plant already under construction. it is the first anti-nuclear demonstration in Europe.

- 19 June   Lyon
3,500 people demonstrate in support of 7 anti-nuclear activists on trial for entering the firing control room of the Mont Verdun nuclear missile base and unfurling anti-nuclear banners.

- 10 July   Saint Valbas
15,000 people stage a "large, peaceful and happy march" against the Bugey I nuclear power plant on the Rhone River in Saint Valbas.

- 4 September   Bugey I
A 40-day sit-down strike of 30 anti-nuclearites begins at the Bugey I construction site.

1972
- 7 May   Fessenheim
10,000 people demonstrate against the local nuke. Opponents gather 50,000 signatures on petitions calling for a moratorium on all nuclear construction.

1973
- 6 May
Coordinated demonstrations in different parts of France—5,000 gather in Strasbourg, 3,000 in Paris.

1974
- May
EDF (the national electric utility) begins construction of the access road to a planned nuke site (Braud-Saint-Louis) without a permit. After a number of protests, farmers occupy the construction site, remove the concrete posts, and dump them in front of the local city hall where they hold a sit-down strike.

- 20 September   Markolsheim
Occupation begins against a lead factory planned by the German firm, Munich Chemical Works, on the French side of the Rhine River.

- 25 August
French and German participants hold a march against the Wyhl nuclear plant in Germany and the lead factory planned for Markolsheim.

- 20-29 August   Markolsheim
Occupation of the lead factory construction site. 100 occupy the first day; 1,000 the second.

- November
Anti-nuclear groups form throughout France following the French Research Ministry's announcement of plans to build 50 nuclear plants.

1976
- 3 July   Malville
20,000 demonstrate against the "Superphenix" fast breeder at the construction site. A group of demonstrators succeeds in getting over the fence and occupying the site. Two days later 5 squadrons of CRS (the French National Guard) invade and clear the site. Farmers then organize a "liberation march" with 5,000 participants.

- 17-18 July   Bugey I
An "information fair" is held on the Rhone River bank opposite the construction site. A film about the 1975 Wyhl occupation in Germany is shown.

- 24 July   Malville area
A 5 kilometer (3 mile) long caravan with cars and tractors follows a route through the towns and countryside that would be threatened by the Malville Superphenix.

- 8 August   Malville area
Farmers of Poleriou block nuclear reactor equipment passing through their town on route to Malville. 24 demonstrators are arrested, including West Germans and

Swiss. By evening 300 people gather and surround the police paddy wagon, forcing the release of all prisoners.

- 9 September
National Action Day against the construction of the "Superphenix" in Malville. A pirate anti-nuclear radio station broadcasts for a week without police interference.

- 15 December
1,000 engineers, physicists and technicians of CERN (the European Nuclear Research Center) send a letter to the French, Italian and West German governments demanding a construction moratorium on fast breeders.

1977
- 26 June
Demonstrations are organized in different regions of France in preparation for the large international demonstration at Malville on 31 July. In Nogent-sur-Seine, a nuke site outside of Paris, 10,000 people gather for an information fair.

- 30 June   Grenoble
150 anti-nuclearites demonstrate in front of the city hall to protest the shut-off of electricity to 300 Grenoblians who withheld 15% of their utility bills in an anti-nuclear withholding campaign. Members of the Socialist Party city government barricade themselves in their offices.

- 29 June   Grenoble
3,000 people demonstrate to protest a fascist group's attack on a local Grenoble Malville organizing committee meeting.

- 31 July   Malville
60,000 people from France and all over Europe come to Malville to demonstrate against the "Superphenix" fast breeder. Police attacks with tear gas, and offensive grenades result in the death of 31 year old school teacher, Vital Michalon; many demonstrators are wounded.

SPAIN

1976
- May   Basque Country
150,000 signatures are gathered to protest nuclear construction in Lemoniz.

1977
- 14 July   Bilbao
150,000 people in the Basque Country protest the Spanish government's extensive nuclear program which calls for over 12 nukes on the Basque coast alone. Simultaneously, 1,000 people in Caspe demonstrated against a nuke planned for their town.

1978
- 10 March   Lemoniz
100,000 demonstrate against the nuclear plant on site.

SWITZERLAND
1975
- 31 March to 14 June   Kaiseraugst
Occupation of the construction site of a nuke planned for Kaiseraugst. The occupiers are threatened with action by the courts, the police and the army. Farmers, their families and townspeople come from the surrounding area to actively support the illegal action. A friendship house, a kindergarten and small huts are built on the occupied site.

1976
- 18 December   Kaiseraugst
1,000 people gather at this site.

1977
- 1 January   Kaiseraugst
700 people demonstrate at the plant site.

- Spring   Kaiseraugst
An Easter anti-nuke march calls for a 4 year construction moratorium. Popular support for the march exceeds all expectations.

SPAIN and PORTUGAL

● 28-29 May   Kaiseraugst
7,000 anti-nuclear citizens gather at the site of the planned nuke. They march to Wabrig, site of a proposed nuclear storage facility, and hold a rally. The next day 3,000 anti-nuclear opponents gather in Leibstadt and march toward Aarau.

● 30 May   Goesgen
5,000 people gather to march to Goesgen. By the time they reach their destination, their numbers have swelled to 10,000, including 800 Germans who were holding a demonstration directly across the Rhine River. They see the Swiss march and cross the river to join it.

● 25 June   Goesgen
4,000 people attempt to block the access road to the Goesgen nuke site and are attacked by 350 combat equipped police. A day later the pirate radio station "Radio Active Free Goesgen" resumes broadcasting after being stopped by police two days before the attempted occupation of the access road.

● 6 June
2,000 people demonstrate in Basel and 2,500 in Zurich.

● 2 July   Goesgen
6,500 demonstrators once again attempt to occupy the access road to the Goesgen nuke. Four hours after the beginning of the action, they are attacked without provocation by the police with tear gas, dogs and water cannons.

1978
● 25 March   Aarau
A three-day-long mass hunger strike against Swiss atomic energy program, especially in Goesgen and Leibstadt.

● 1 April   Kaiseraugst
Demonstration and reforestation of site.

● 13 May   Lucens
March and rally to stop plans for converting a closed nuclear plant into interim waste storage depot.

ITALY
1976
● 30 January   Capalbio
Demonstration against planned nuke.

1977
● January
Residents of Capalbio block the Rome-Genoa rail link after it becomes known that ENEL, the state-run National Electric Corporation, plans to dispossess farmers of their land to build nuclear power plants. In Montalto, Capalbio, Orbetello and Tarquinia citizen initiative groups form and organize resistance.

● February   Montalto
2,000 people demonstrate.

● 20 March   Montalto
The citizen initiative groups of Montalto hold an information fair around a central theme of non-violence. Over 15,000 people attend.

● 3-4 February   Milan
National gathering of anti-nuclear groups in Milan. For two days 800 participants discuss "Nuclear Energy—Alternative Energy—New Development Forms."

FEDERAL REPUBLIC OF GERMANY
1971
● Beginning of anti-nuclear opposition in the Kaiserstuhl (Breisach).

1973
● Following local citizen opposition, the government decides against Breisach as a nuke site. Wyhl is chosen instead.

1974
● 20 September   Markolsheim (France)
Occupation of the lead factory construction site facing Wyhl, Germany. Many Germans join the occupiers.

1975
● 18 February   Wyhl
First occupation of the nuclear plant construction site, as land clearing begins.

● 20 February   Wyhl
Police clear the site brutally with water cannons.

● 23 February   Wyhl
Second Wyhl occupation. 28,000 citizens, Germans, French, Swiss, establish the occupation, which continues for more than a year, while construction comes to a halt.

● 25 February
Victory at Markolsheim. The lead plant will not be built.

● 21 March   Wyhl
Freiburg court orders halt to construction
at Wyhl site.

● 1 April
Occupation at Kaiseraugst, Switzerland.
Many Germans join the action.

1976
● 31 October   Brokdorf
6,000-7,000 people at first occupation of
nuke construction site. Expelled by police
the next morning.

● 13 November   Brokdorf
Second attempt at occupation of the nuclear plant site by 30,000; met with massive
police violence.

1977
● 19 February   Itzehoe and Brokdorf
50,000 demonstrate near the site and at
the nearby town. Symbolic occupation at
Grohnde by 100 people.

● 19 March   Grohnde
Second occupation attempt at Grohnde.
15,000 are met with police violence.

● June   Grohnde
Anti-atom village established next to site.

● July   Brokdrof
Anti-atom village established in Brokdorf.

● 24 September   Kalkar
Demonstration by 50,000 people against
the fast breeder reactor being built at
Kalkar.

1978
● February-March   Stuttgart-Hamburg
Boycott begins to hold back payment of the
portion of electricity rate used to support
nuclear power plant construction.

● 5 March   Schleswig-Holstein
Startling success of "greens" (environmentalist) candidates in local elections.

HOLLAND
1978
● 4 March   Almelo
International rally against the uranium
fuel enrichment plant.

—Material, other than for Germany, taken
from the *Die Internationale*, 28 August 1977. (J.
Reents, *Verlag Arbeiterkampf*, Lerchenstra. 75,
2000 Hamburg 50.)
—Prepared by Michael Lucas

Brokdorf, 13 November 1976—Water cannons used against anti-nuke demonstrators. (Credit: H. Morell, Hamburg, FRG)

site	plant name	net Mw	finished
ENGLAND, SCOTLAND, WALES			
1. Gloucestershire	Berkeley 1	138	1962
Gloucestershire	Berkeley 2	138	1962
2. Essex	Bradwell 1	150	1962
Essex	Bradwell 2	150	1962
3. Wales	Trawsfynydd 1	250	1965
Wales	Trawsfynydd 2	250	1965
4. Kent	Dungeness A1	275	1965
Kent	Dungeness A2	275	1965
Kent	Dungeness B1	600	1978
Kent	Dungeness B2	600	1978
5. Suffolk	Sizewell 1	290	1966
Suffolk	Sizewell 2	290	1966
6. Somerset	Hinkley Point A1	250	1965
Somerset	Hinkley Point A2	250	1965
Somerset	Hinkley Point B1	625	1976
Somerset	Hinkley Point B2	625	1976
7. Gloucestershire	Oldbury 1	300	1968
Gloucestershire	Oldbury 2	300	1968
8. Anglesey	Wylfa 1	590	1971
Anglesey	Wylfa 2	590	1972
9. Durham	Hartlepool 1	625	1978
Durham	Hartlepool 2	625	1979
10. Lancashire	Heysham 1	625	1979
Lancashire 2	Heysham 2	625	1979
11. Ayrshire	Hunterston A-R1	160	1964
Aryshire	Hunterston A-R2	160	1964
Aryshire	Hunterston B-R3	625	1976
Aryshire	Hunterston B-R4	625	1976
12. Cumbria	Calder Hall 1	50	1956
Cumbria	Calder Hall 2	50	1956
Cumbria	Calder Hall 3	50	1956
Cumbria	Calder Hall 4	50	1956
13. Dumfriesshire	Chapel Cross 1	50	1958
Dumfriesshire	Chapel Cross 2	50	1958
Dumfriesshire	Chapel Cross 3	50	1958
Dumfriesshire	Chapel Cross 4	50	1958
14. Cumbria	Windscale	32	1963
15. Dorset	Winfrith	92	1968
16. Highland	Douneray	250	1976

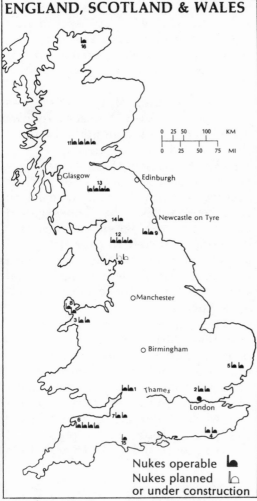

ENGLAND, SCOTLAND & WALES

Glasgow

Edinburgh

Newcastle on Tyre

Manchester

Birmingham

Thames

London

Nukes operable

Nukes planned
or under construction

Nuclear Power
In England, Scotland & Wales

At one time Britain led the world in civilian nuclear power production. Its first commercial power station was Calder Hall, built at Windscale in 1956. Subsequently, some dozen power plants were constructed—mostly gas-cooled reactors.

Britain's reactors have mainly been built away from population centers at remote seacoast or estuary sites in northern Scotland, northern Wales, east Anglia, and the Severn Estuary. When they were first built, there was no sign of public concern. Since expansion has usually been achieved by building second plants on the same site, until very recently there have been no siting disputes.

Nuclear power produces some 12% of the U.K.'s electricity (4% of its total energy). Plans call for a considerable increase over the next couple of decades—perhaps eightfold. However, the industry is in some disarray. The preferred reactor for the next phase of operations is the advanced gas-cooled reactor (AGR). Despite disasterously long commissioning lead times with the first few stations, the AGR program is going forward. Two plants have been given the go-ahead, in preference to the U.S. pressurized water reactor.

There are long-term plans for developing a fast breeder. Two breeders have already been tested at Douneray, and there is mounting pressure for the construction of a prototype commercial fast reactor.

The Windscale Nuclear Fuel Reprocessing plant in Cumbria on the northwest coast is the focus of current debate, partly because its expansion might be seen as a prerequisite to a breeder program.

The immediate justification for the proposed expansion is that it would enable British Nuclear Fuels Ltd. (a private but state-financed company) to reprocess Japanese fuel. A £600 million contract is at stake.

Opposition to Nuclear Power

The world's first large-scale anti-nuclear weapons movement was born here, the Campaign for Nuclear Disarmament (CND), which mobilized hundreds of thousands of people and gave us the ☮ peace sign. But no mass anti-nuke plant movement has emerged, partly because CND campaign was based on the idea of 'Atoms for Peace'—conversion of military nuclear technology to peaceful, "progressive" civilian use.

Britain's nuclear plants have been operating relatively safely for twenty years and they are felt to be substantially safer than the U.S. plants. No siting disputes have occurred. The only blemish in the U.K. AEA's book was the 1957 reactor fire at Windscale. (See p. 118).

Although a relatively well-developed "underground" alternative technology movement has emerged in the U.K., the environmental movement is nowhere near as powerful as that in the U.S. This is partly because British environmental planning law has seemingly been able to cope with some of the worst problems. The Clean Air Act, for example, stopped killer-smog in London very promptly and effectively.

Until 1975 there were few signs of opposition to nuclear power from conservationists and environmentalists led by the U.K. section of the Friends of the Earth (FOE). They first began objecting on grounds of safety, then economics, and finally proliferation.

Subsequent developments were much as in the U.S. FOE got sucked into fighting with authorities over technical issues, which culminated in a major involvement with the Windscale Inquiry.

In the autumn of 1975 there was public concern over Windscale following news of small accidents and leaks at the plant. The Windscale Inquiry was called by Parliament to assess the safety of the proposed expansion of nuclear fuel reprocessing there. Many existing organizations like the Conservation Society and the Town and Country Planning Association submitted evidence to the Inquiry. They joined with specifically anti-nuclear groups at local and national levels to form the "Windscale Appeal."

The Inquiry heard evidence over 100 days. Although there was much testimony about the dangers of plutonium that would be created in the reprocessing of spent fuel rods (many from Japan and other countries), Justice Michael Parker, who conducted the inquiry, found in his report that the risks were small. On 15 May 1978

John F. Carroll, Vice-President of Irish Transport and General Workers' Union, speaks at anti-Windscale demonstration, Trafalgar Square, London, 29 April 1978.

the House of Commons voted over-whelmingly to permit construction at the plant.

Few people expected this anti-nuclear effort to halt the Windscale program, but involvement in the inquiry did bring anti-nuclear activists together.

On the other hand, as in the U.S., many activists feel that involvement with public hearings consumes time and money and is essentially counter-productive. It absorbs effort that could just as well go into local organisation and direct action efforts.

In the last few months the pressure to opt for non-violent direct action has increased. The first large-scale actions here were the "Nuclear Excursion," a train ride to Windscale organized by FOE in 1976, and the parliamentary lobby by Energy 2000 (a coalition of trade unionists and environmentalists) in November 1977—each of which attracted 600 people. A small demonstration also took place in October 1976 in London's Trafalgar Square, the traditional place for demonstrations. However, as a result of the widespread publicity surrounding the Windscale Inquiry, the Friends of the Earth was able to organize a major rally in April 1978 which attracted 10,000 people.

Our first citizen occupation and a rally organized by SCRAM (Scottish Campaign to Resist the Atomic Menace) took place the following month in Torness, Scotland at the proposed site of an AGR reactor. Small demonstrations have also occured against proposals for uranium mining in Scotland's Orkney Islands and nuclear waste dumping near Loch Doon, Galloway. These actions were fueled by Scottish nationalist/separatist sentiment.

Workers Power not Nuclear Power

Although the scale of opposition to nuclear power is still small, there exists in Britain a unique opportunity to weld a coalition with the labor unions. In Britain trade unions are far more radical, independent, and progressive than in the U.S. This does not mean the task will be easy. Nearly all union bosses are pro-nuclear, believing that nuclear power will guarantee jobs and prosperity. But different attitudes are emerging at the grassroots "shop-floor" level, which in Britain has some degree of autonomy via elected "shop stewards," delegates responsible to their members.

There are several radical groups working with shop stewards on this issue. The Socialist Environment and Resources Association (SERA) is one. SERA uses the argument pioneered by the U.S. Environmentalists for Full Employment and others that we can get more jobs from conservation and soft energy than from nuclear energy. SERA's slogan is CREATE JOBS NOT PLUTONIUM. SERA has also pointed out that the security constraints in the nuclear industry tend to undermine many trade union rights such as disclosure of technical information to shop stewards for bargaining and health and safety purposes, and the right to take industrial action, pickets and strikes.

The conventional left and extreme left are still wary of the nuclear issue, fearing involvement in "single issue" populist politics, but things are slowly changing.

Overall, it seems possible that, because Britain has entered relatively late into the nuclear debate, we have the opportunity to create a radical broad-based movement which links environmental concerns with trade union issues. It is clearly vital in the U.K. context to win support from the trade union and labor movement. And the signs are that organized labor is

beginning to see that nuclear technology, just like all other technologies
generated by, in, and for capitalist (and
state capitalist) societies, is not necessarily going to benefit them or their
communities.

Indeed some groups of workers, for
example those at the Lucas Aerospace
Company, faced with the threat of
unemployment because of declining
orders for advanced aerospace, defense, and energy technology, are campaigning for conversion to alternative
technology production as a way to
safeguard jobs and better meet social
needs.

Dave Elliott
Spring 1978

Contacts in the U.K.

Friends of the Earth
9, Poland Street,
London W. 1.

Conservation Society,
12 London Street,
Chertsey, Surrey, KT16 8AA

Nuclear Information Network
29, St. James Street,
London WC1N 3ES

Political Ecology Research Group
36, Wharton Road,
Headington, Oxford

Greenpeace Ltd.,
47, Whitehall,
London W. 1

SERA (Socialist Environment and Resources Associates)
9, Poland Street,
London W. 1

SCRAM (Scottish Campaign to Resist the
Atomic Menace)
2a Ainslie Place,
Edinburgh, 3, Scotland

Publications

The best all-round source for U.K. developments in the anti-nuclear and alternative technology field is *Undercurrents* magazine, available on subscription ($9.00 air
mail) from 12 South St., Uley, Dursley,
Gloucestershire.

THE REPUBLIC OF IRELAND

Ireland may be the only Common Market (EEC) country where the trade
union movement will oppose the peaceful and military uses of nuclear power
and lead the resistance to a nuclear
Ireland.

Although the European Commission and Commissioner Brunner promised the Irish delegation during the
January 1978 EEC Nuclear Hearings
that they would *not* impose any nuclear
plans upon the Republic of Ireland,
and even though Edward Teller, nuclear proponent and Father of the H-
Bomb, has publicly supported a non-
nuclear Ireland, the Irish Minister for
Industry, Commerce and Energy,
O'Malley, recently indicated his approval of a nuclear power station in
County Wexford. He did so without
even the intention of holding a public
inquiry.

While farmers, fishermen and
Wexford County Councilors maintain
that the whole question of Ireland
being the last EEC member state to
adopt nuclear power should be subject
to public inquiry on a national level, the
go-ahead for the Carnsore Point
nuclear plant seems to already have
been given, Minister O'Malley extolls
the plant as a source of cheap, bound-
less, safe, and clean energy and as
creator of 2,000 construction and
several hundred permanent jobs. An
Agricultural Institute report tried to
allay fears about the nuclear power
plant by stating that a major accident is
unlikely to happen for at least 17,000
years. Dangers of radiation are coun-
tered with assurances that such
substances would only be released into
the atmosphere or sea occasionally,
and that these would be strictly
monitored , with no effect on people or
agriculture.

Local farmers in County Wexford
have begun to question the arbitrary

decisions being taken by Minister O'Malley and have sponsored local educational forums. The Irish Farmers' Association called the government's so-called planning procedures for the Carnsore Point plant "mere charades of democracy." A Wexford Nuclear Safety Association exists but its numbers are still quite small. Professor Robert Blackith leads resistance in the academic and scientific community. And Aldermen and Councilors on the Dublin City Council also oppose nuclear development in Ireland and have called on all political parties to state their positions.

The greatest hope for a growing Irish resistance to nuclear power comes from the Irish Transport and General Workers' Union, whose vice-president John Carroll has taken a firm anti-nuclear stand. It will now be up to the workers' movement in Ireland to determine how far workers will go in opposing their government's nuclear plans, which, besides the Carnsore plant, include plans for storing EEC nuclear waste in sparsely populated regions of the Irish Republic.

Here are a few excerpts from a speech made by John Carroll on 24 September 1977 at a rally during the demonstration against the fast breeder plant now under construction in Kalkar, West Germany.

The nuclear lobby throughout the Western world has spent extremely large sums of money on the support and development of nuclear technology, and the same lobby continues to use its political and financial muscle to influence national governments and regional authorities towards the erection of nuclear power stations and/or expansion of existing ones. This is done mostly through the multinational companies who have

vested interests in mining rights, technology development, reactor construction companies, energy supply sources, etc. and who are so interrelated and interwoven that it is almost impossible to disentangle the various financial, banking, investment and industrial interests that have control and influence over the nuclear scene and, indeed, over other energy supply systems as well.

And even though it is now fully established that there are major problems and dangers associated with nuclear reactors and the plutonium economy that defy solution, the same supporters of the nuclear lobby press ahead for the expansion of the nuclear programme, not because they are concerned, as they claim, with providing jobs and better living standards, but because they are seeking to get a massive return on their substantial holdings in nuclear investment stock and in the power that goes with the control and supply of any energy source.

If only a fraction of the monies already spent by companies, by banks and by governments had been invested in research and development of soft energy sources, the evidence of the amount of jobs that could thereby result would be beyond contradiction...

Unfortunately...not all trade unions are united in opposing nuclear development. Some are so influenced by the economic and social propaganda of the nuclear lobby that they believe jobs can only come from nuclear development.

The fact is that the type of social and economic policies pursued in Western societies makes it extremely difficult for many trade union officials to opt out of the nuclear race. On the other hand, there is a growing body of opinion amongst trade unionists that the gambles with peoples' lives and with the worsening of the environment consequent on nuclear activity, plus the terrible dangers associated with the nuclear arms race, are not worth the alleged value which is claimed for nuclear energy.

This has been recognized very much in Australia, from which I just recently returned. There, many many trade unionists are absolutely and fully opposed to the mining of uranium and its export to other countries for use in nuclear reactors, plus its use in the armaments industry...

John Carroll has warned the government that approval of a nuclear plant could lead to civil unrest and conflict. Knowing the violent background of Irish politics, the anti-nuclear movement in Europe is watching developments in this country very closely in the hope that anti-nuclear forces in Ireland will not be provoked to violence...

Already the Irish Friends of the Earth and Sean McBride of the International Peace Bureau have called for speedy development of alternative sources of energy—wind, wave, solar power, and biomass. Ireland's dependence on expensive imported oil for power plants could be dramatically reduced by setting up windmills at key locations. Irish ecologists maintain that a concentrated effort to insulate homes and buildings efficiently and stop heat losses would create far more jobs.

According to a booklet, *The Power That Corrupts: The Threat of Nuclear Power Promotion in Ireland*, put out by the Irish Conservation Society:

Officially, the generating authorities in Ireland keep an open mind on the type of reactor they want; there can be little doubt that what they really want is an American Light Water Reactor, and that virtually all their planning is directed on this assumption. Hardly anyone bothers to deny that these reactors have the worst safety record and the worst performance record (the two are interrelated)...

A new nuclear plant would cost, optimistically, some £400 million at current values. There are 675,000 dwellings in the Republic (in 1975), so that if the capital cost were employed in insulating existing dwellings some L500 would be available for each one....Domestic demand accounts for some 66% of electricity consumption though much of this is used for cooking. Very roughly, applying the cost of a single nuclear plant to insulation, better building standards, installation of solar panals or wind generators we could save fuel equivalent to the amount of electicity generated by somewhere between half and one-and-a-half nuclear plants...

Dr. Robert E. Blackith
(Dublin Univ. Press Ltd., 1976
pages 15, 10-11)

—Petra Kelly

Contacts in Ireland
Friends of the Earth/Ireland
17, Arbetus Place
S.C. Road
Dublin 8

Sweden

Until the fall of 1977, it looked like Sweden would be one of the world's major commercial nuclear powers. The country had five commercial reactors, five others in various stages of construction and three more on the drawing boards. The long-time Social Democratic leadership considered nuclear power to be the only alternative to imported oil. They planned that by 1985, the 13 plants would be providing 40% of Sweden's electricity.

Then the Social Democrats were voted out after 44 years in power by the more conservative Centrist Party, whose candidate for Prime Minister, Thorbjoern Faelldin, opposed nuclear construction. He vowed to eventually shut down Sweden's reactors and end the entire nuclear program.

However, as soon as the new government came to power, Faelldin's conservative and liberal coalition partners broke their silence on the nuclear issue and began campaigning for continuation of the program. Six major Swedish trade unions have pressured for new construction, claiming that more than 38,000 jobs would be lost if the nuclear program were completely abandoned.

When Faelldin gave the go ahead to start up the second Barsebaeck nuke several weeks after taking office, the anti-nuclear movement, which had been active in Sweden since 1973, took on new momentum.

The two Barsebaeck reactors are on the southwestern coast. Their location just 12 miles from Copenhagen, Denmark and the major Swedish city of Malmo puts them in close proximity to almost 3 million people—the biggest concentration of populace in Scandinavia. Barsebaeck, which opponents claim is "one of the worst placed nuclear power plants in the world," has become an international focus of anti-nuclear activism.

In June 1978, the Danish Environmental Protection Agency reported that a worst possible accident at Barsebaeck could lead to 20,000 long-term cancer deaths in the Copenhagen area.

The first opposition to Barsebaeck came from the Danish women's movement during the summer of 1974. On 7 August, about 6,000 people marched against Barsebaeck in the first all Scandinavian demonstration against the plant. On 10 September 1977, around 15,000 people marched up to 13 miles in driving rain and wind to protest the plants. It was the largest anti-nuclear

More than 7,000 people from all the five Nordic countries walked together in "Nordiska Atommarchen 1976." (Credit: Einar F. Anundsen/*MILJO*-magazine.)

demonstration ever held in Sweden, and a truly international event.

Uranium
Sweden has uranium deposits amounting to half the uranium in Europe. They are located at Ranstad, 300 km (190 miles) southwest of Stockholm. The local population has opposed mining, but future export of uranium continues to be an issue here.

Alternatives
As a result of pressures from both a dedicated group of alternative energy researchers and the anti-nuclear movement, the Swedish government is also taking moves toward replacing nuclear energy with wind and biomass energy. In May 1978, the Swedish parliament adopted a three year $200 million research program in wind power, biomass conversion, and energy use in buildings. Although the program does not represent a complete shift away from nuclear power, for the first time "soft" technologies will be receiving more money for research and development than nukes.
Contact: EKOTEKET
S. Jordbrovagen 179 VII
S-136 52 Handen Sweden

DENMARK
A strong anti-nuclear opposition has prevented nuclear power plant construction so far in Denmark. Danes have also been active in opposing nuclear power in neighboring Sweden. In 1978 the Danish government and parliament have to decide whether or not to go ahead with construction of nuclear plants. The Danish OOA (Organization for Information about Atomic Power) is organizing to defeat nuclear development.

From 25-27 August 1978, they sponsored two marches that they on simultaneously, beginning at probable reactor sites in Gyllingnaes in Jutland, and Hojstrup on Stevns. Fifty-thousand people participated in the "Atom March."

Contact: OOA, Skindergade 26/ DK-1159 Copenhagen, Denmark. (Tel. 45-1-110673 or 45-1-110973)

WISE
In February 1978 activists from all over the world came to Amsterdam to establish the "World Information Service on Energy" (WISE). WISE is an action-oriented information service supporting people and groups in the anti-nuclear movement. A better and more easily accessible flow of information that allows for international coordination of actions is an urgent priority for the movement.

The first issues of WISE appeared in May and July 1978. Subscriptions in North America are available for $5.00/year from:
Terry Provance
Mobilization for Survival
1213 Race St.,
Philadelphia, Pa. 19017

WISE
2e Weteringplantsoen 9
Amsterdam, Netherlands

NUCLEAR POWER IN THE NETHERLANDS (HOLLAND)

The Netherlands has been the scene of many creative and hopeful anti-nuclear actions. It is a Common Market member that has *not* accepted EEC industrial and nuclear energy as blindly as the other countries. The Netherlands has questioned many of the assumptions concerning growth that pervade economic EEC thinking. For this reason the anti-nuclear and alternative citizen-action groups have been able to gain more ground.

The Dutch government is now sharply torn by the nuclear issue. Many groups within the the various Dutch political groupings oppose construction of the three new power plants that would bring Holland's total to five.

Much of the activity has been concentrated around the "STOP KALKAR" Movement. Kalkar is a small German town near the Dutch border where a German, Dutch and Belgian consortium is building a fast breeder reactor. In this region, there have been many transnational demonstrations.

ALMELO

On 4 March 1978, 40,000 people came to an international anti-nuclear demonstration at Almelo, Holland. Almelo is the site of a centrifuge uranium enrichment plant owned and run by URENCO, a British, Dutch and West German consortium. One of the two plants at Almelo is completely owned by the FRG.

The centrifuge has been around for years, but now the Dutch government, witn considerable prodding from Germany, wants to enlarge the facility to make it function commercially. Enlargement of the plant is a crucial link in the FRG's planned international fuel production cycle. The post-war Treaty of Paris forbids enrichment plants on West German territory; thus the FRG's involvement in Almelo. URENCO's future plans are to fuel the whole nuclear power system of northwestern Europe and export to other continents as well.

Uranium enrichment is the key link between uranium mining and nuclear power plants. Increased facilities stimulate the spread of nuclear power, add to the danger of atomic weapons proliferation and intensify the pressure for continued uranium mining. In short, expansion of Almelo would be a step towards an all-out nuclear future.

The pieces of the URENCO puzzle are scattered all over the world. Sixty percent of the enriched uranium produced is to go to the FRG, to fuel its own nuclear reactors as well as for resale to Brazil. (See pp. 374-376). URENCO officials have visited Australia to talk about future deliveries of uranium ore. Recently they also visited Japan to negotiate the sale of enriched uranium to that country. The consortium has a similar enrichment plant at Capenhurst, U.K.

—Some of the material from the previous report came from *The Dutch Link*, no. 1, Jan. 1978, a bulletin published by the LEK "Landelijk Energie Kommittee," the umbrella group of the Dutch anti-nuclear movement. "It's purpose is to ease the flow of action-relevant information between the anti-nuclear movement in the Netherlands and English speaking areas worldwide." Contact: 2e Weteringplantsoen 9; Amsterdam, The Netherlands.

336

ALMELO: 4 March 1978. Demonstration Against Uranium Enrichment. Top left and bottom: People gather at Town Square. Center banner reads: "Atom State=Police State." **Top right:** Dutch police at the enrichment plant. At least 60 different political and theater groups and tens of thousands of people from Holland, Germany, and elsewhere gathered at Almelo. Unlike the demonstration at Kalkar, Germany, the Almelo protest was free of machine-gun-toting police. Note the straw shields and relatively lightly-equipped Dutch police. So far, the Dutch government has dealt with the domestic anti-nuclear movement with "repressive tolerance." Violent confrontation is avoided, dialogue and negotiation emphasized.

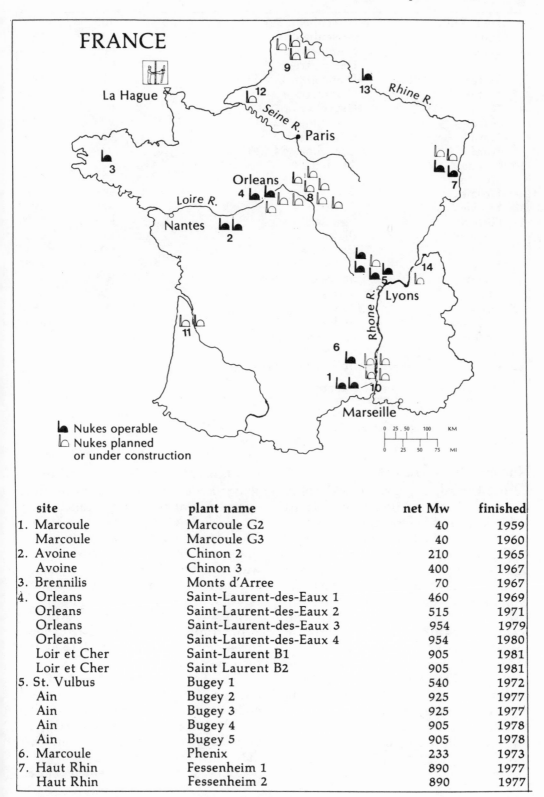

FRANCE

La Hague

Paris

Seine R.

Rhine R.

Orleans

Loire R.

Nantes

Lyons

Rhone R.

Marseille

la Nukes operable
lo Nukes planned
   or under construction

| 0 25 50 100   KM |
| 0   25 50 75   MI |

site	plant name	net Mw	finished
1. Marcoule	Marcoule G2	40	1959
Marcoule	Marcoule G3	40	1960
2. Avoine	Chinon 2	210	1965
Avoine	Chinon 3	400	1967
3. Brennilis	Monts d'Arree	70	1967
4. Orleans	Saint-Laurent-des-Eaux 1	460	1969
Orleans	Saint-Laurent-des-Eaux 2	515	1971
Orleans	Saint-Laurent-des-Eaux 3	954	1979
Orleans	Saint-Laurent-des-Eaux 4	954	1980
Loir et Cher	Saint-Laurent B1	905	1981
Loir et Cher	Saint Laurent B2	905	1981
5. St. Vulbus	Bugey 1	540	1972
Ain	Bugey 2	925	1977
Ain	Bugey 3	925	1977
Ain	Bugey 4	905	1978
Ain	Bugey 5	905	1978
6. Marcoule	Phenix	233	1973
7. Haut Rhin	Fessenheim 1	890	1977
Haut Rhin	Fessenheim 2	890	1977

	Haut Rhin	Fessenheim 3	905	1982
	Haut Rhin	Fessenheim 4	905	1983
8.	Loiret	Dampierre 1	905	1979
	Loiret	Dampierre 2	905	1980
	Loiret	Dampierre 3	905	1980
	Loiret	Dampierre 4	905	1981
9.	Nord	Gravelines B1	925	1979
	Nord	Gravelines B2	925	1979
	Nord	Gravelines B3	925	1980
	Nord	Gravelines B4	925	1981
10.	Drome	Tricastin 1	925	1979
	Drome	Tricastin 2	925	1979
	Drome	Tricastin 3	925	1980
	Drome	Tricastin 4	925	1980
11.	Gironde	Blayais 1	925	1981
	Gironde	Blayais 2	925	1981
	Loiret	Chinon B1	905	1981
	Loiret	Chinon B2	905	1982
	undesig.	undesig.	905	not set
	undesig.	undesig.	905	not set
12.	Calvados	Palvel 1	1,300	1982
	undesig.	undesig.	1,300	not set
	undesig	undesig.	1,300	not set
	undesig.	undesig.	1,300	not set
13.	Chooz	SENA (France/Belgium)	310	1967
14.	Creys-Malville	Superphenix	1,200	1985

Nuclear Power in France

France has an agressive nuclear policy of development at home and export abroad. The state-controlled Electricity of France (EDF) has an announced goal of 200 nuclear plants by the year 2000—an average of 6 new nukes a year! Already the country has the world's most complete fuel cycle with:
• The only large waste reprocessing plant for pressurized-water reactors in the world, at Cape de la Hague.
• An enrichment plant to supply the nuclear fuel for 200 plants, now under construction at Tricastin. An existing plant is at nearby Pierrelatte.
• A 250-Mw fast breeder reactor, the Phenix—named for the mythical bird that rises from its own ashes—is in Pierrelatte.

• A 1200-Mw fast breeder now under construction, the Superphenix (a much opposed joint project of France, owning half, Belgium, Spain, and Italy)... The Superphenix is being built near the small village of Creys-Malville. It was the scene of the most violent encounter of all international demonstrations against nuclear power (30 July 1977). Although the Superphenix is not finished, the EDF has ordered three more fast breeders of 1800 Mw for Chalon-sur-Saone.

The French Atomic Energy Commission (CEA) has a monopoly on all military and "peaceful" nuclear research. The EDF produces and distributes electricity. The ties between CEA, EDF, and the private companies that build reactors are extremely close.

French President Giscard d'Estaing's government is committed to a national policy of continued electrical energy growth. In July 1977 his Prime Minister Raymond Barre announced that "Growth is indispensible because we must have growth!"[1]

The parties of the left, Socialist and Communist, missed their chance for power when they lost the 1978 national election. Both parties support nuclear power plant construction and the continued development of an independent "force de frappe"—a French nuclear arms program.

When it comes to energy, the growth issue is crucial in France as in other industrialized countries. If postwar prosperity is to continue, how will the energy needed be provided? For the French government the answer has been atomic power. In the summer of 1977, just before the big demonstration at Malville, Giscard said he hoped that France's nuclear production of 4,000 Mw—amounting to 10% of the country's electrical consumption— would increase ten-fold to 40,000 Mw by the end of the century.

France As Vendor

France is a major nuclear vendor. Framatome has sold reactors to Belgium, South Africa, South Korea, and Iran. In 1977 the French government cancelled a deal to sell a reprocessing plant to South Korea, following great pressure from the U.S.[2] They are still expecting to ship a reprocessing plant to Pakistan, but have agreed to eschew further foreign sale of reprocessing technology because of U.S. pressure and the obvious proliferation possibilities. It is clear that Pakistan, for instance, does not need a fuel reprocessing plant for its two projected nuclear plants. It is interested in the plutonium product.

In February 1978 *The Elements* reported that authorities in Peking were considering launching "an ambitious nuclear energy program" and had approached France about a possible reactor purchase. Since the French nuke builder Framatome works under license to Westinghouse, the U.S. company would have to okay the deal.[3]

Ecologists
Have a Better Idea

An alternative to a nuclear-powered future for France is put forth by ecologists and members of various Amis de la Terre (Friends of the Earth) groups.[4] The ecologists' vision of the future developed out of opposition to nuclear power and a general eco-political awareness. They favor decentralization of political power as well as energy production and worker self-management. Their "ecological communities" would feature planned growth, public transportation and bicycles, windmills and solar collectors, recycling and integrated agriculture, as well as truly democratic neighborhood-based government.

In 1974 ecology took to the polls with the candidacy of ecologist and Third World affairs expert Rene Dumont for president. Although Dumont got only 1.3% of the vote, a new phenomenon was launched. And it took off. Neither right, center, nor left had ever questioned the idea of limitless growth. Politics did not speak to the ever-increasing degradation and annoyances of modern industrial life. The ecologists expressed the feelings of many French people, both urban dwellers and rural neighbors of nuclear plants.

In the 1976 municipal elections, Brice Lalonde of Friends of the Earth/ Paris got 7% of the vote in one Parisian district. In March 1977, he and Dumont ran again. Their program was titled "When you want it..." It went like this:

Having for five years put their hands to exploring several particular areas like pollution, energy and food, ecologists are now attacking all the problems of society. They have seen that neither pressure group practices nor mass demonstrations are sufficient to provoke the conversion of industrial societies. That is why they are now presenting themselves in the elections to propose directly to the French people a program that the traditional parties are not capable of taking on.

Here are the first proposals presented by the Paris Friends of the Earth for the formation of "Paris-Ecology" slates in the municipal elections...these proposals, which must be widely discussed, are the priming of a movement rather than a catalogue of electoral promises.

The ecologists had surprisingly

Paris—Ecology Proposals—1977 Elections

• Absolute priority to pedestrians over cars; wider sidewalks planted with trees; gardens and parks for children; free bicycles; river boats on the River Seine

• "The country returns to the town"... Planning of open spaces; roof gardens; gardens in some streets and abandoned lots; fruit trees; students study nature sciences one day a week in the gardens

• Clean air and water; eliminate industrial pollution; install filters; replace asbestos ceilings; clean the Seine; fight noise pollution

• Stop the French nuclear program; practice energy conservation; install insulation, solar and wind devices

• Control urbanization, lower rents, rehabilitate neighborhoods

• recycling

• attention to food and diet; cooking and shopping not restricted to women

• Free and preventive medicine; decentralized clinics

• A 30 hour maximum work week, including transportation—"It's impossible to participate in neighborhood life and communal administration if the work and travel hours are too long." Production of needed durable goods; reduced hours to help diminish unemployment

• Priority to artisans, small industries, especially for repair, upkeep, recycling

• Neighborhood cooperatives for daycare, laundries, cultural activities, etc. Broad community involvement

• The rotation of unpleasant tasks so that each Parisian only has to spend 12 hours a month doing them

• Have Paris neighborhoods establish special relationships with several rural villages for sharing of products, vacation home exchanges, festivals—"Ecology includes the right to nature at the same time as the right to the town"

• Neighborhood banks, investing locally

• A mayor for each neighborhood of 10,000 people; good local communication through neighborhood newspapers, cable TV, etc. Referenda on important issues; voter initiatives to place questions before all people. A Parisian council with proportional representation from all areas of the city

• Free urban mass transit

• Schools open to all for practical and intellectual training

• The (national) government should leave Paris; decentralization of government to medium sized-cities, cutting down on the concentration of power and luxury and the hostility of French people for Parisians, confused with the State. Parisian national army troops would be replaced by elected guardians of the peace.[5]

strong results: 12.5% of the first round in Paris, as high as 20% elsewhere, for a national average of about 10%. In the Malville area, ecologists were elected with 60% of the vote!

Direct Action
Against Nuclear Power

There have been a number of marches, rallies and protests against nuclear power in France. One plant with a lot of opposition is Nogent-sur-Seine, being built just thirty miles upstream from Paris. An accident there could pollute the capital's drinking water.

Anti-nuclear sentiment has run strongest among the local population of Alsace, the region bordering Germany on the Rhine River. It was there, in the town of Markolsheim, that citizens opposing the construction of a polluting lead factory occupied the site to prevent construction. The occupation lasted from 20 September 1974 until November. The occupiers built a "Friendship House" for themselves and their supporters from both sides of the river. They dug wells and brought in farm animals. The occupation was successful—in February 1975 the plant's permit was withdrawn by the French government. The first large nuke on the Rhine was the twin reactor at Fessenheim. This plant opened in 1975 only to be closed after a mysterious bombing. It reopened in 1976 under heavy guard. The plant gave people a clear idea of what nuclear power was all about. French people were active in opposing the construction of a nuclear plant at Wyhl—just north of Fessenheim on the German side of the Rhine. In February 1977, hearings took place near Wyhl that would determine the fate of the plant—at least for the time being— French Alsacians on the other bank were occupying the Gerstheim site. This nuke site was near a hydroelectric station that was using only one of three generators. Farmers and area residents moved quickly as word of construction came. Fifty farmers with their tractors led the march of occu-

The two month occupation at Gersheim ended in success. French farmers' tractors kept continual vigil.

piers onto the site. A group stayed there constantly for two months. Phone trees would alert people on both sides of the river, should the group be evicted. But their presence there— before construction had started— seemed to embarrass the government sufficiently and show them that there would be stiff and continued resistance to construction. The occupation ended when EDF said they had not planned to build there after all!

Malville

The major anti-nuclear struggle in France has been against the Super-phenix, being constructed on 400 acres of land near a small rural village in France's Rhone River valley in the southeastern department of Isere.

Local opposition to the plant grew as ecologists came in to explain to the locals the especially dangerous aspects of this plutonium-fueled and produc-ing reactor.

During the summer of 1976, 20,000 people attempted a non-violent oc-cupation of the breeder site. They came from all over France to an area that was still largely unaware of the nature of this project underway in their midst. In July 1976, demonstra-tors were able to get on the reactor site itself. Two thousand people camped for five days until they were roughly removed by the French National Guard, the CRS. The next day they were evicted from a new campsite on local residents' land. Shocked by the police attack on the non-violent ecolo-gists, local villagers offered them beds. In the weeks that followed, many pro-testors stayed in the area, educating the locals about the dangers from this new neighbor and helping to form Malville Committees.

Opposition continued to build all over France, as Malville Committees formed. In late winter a date was set for the next big Malville demonstra-tion.

The Battle of Malville

After more than a year of intense organizing and education, on 31 July 1977, 60,000 people from France, Ger-many and other European countries, came to Malville to protest the French government's Superphenix fast breed-er. Before the demonstration, pro-

A demonstrating farmer who has seen the sad reality: Nuclear Society=Police Society— Malville

testors were roughly searched; many were harassed at the German-French border. Martial law had been declared and the French national guard was out in force. They channeled the demon-strators into one small area, and even-tually attacked with tear gas and ex-plosive TNT-loaded grenades. A 31 year old French high school physics teacher was killed by a grenade; four people lost limbs and many others were badly injured.

The demonstration made people all over France aware of the dangers of nuclear power—both from nuclear plants and from the state's efforts to "defend" them.[6] But the action left many dubious about the success of violent confrontation in the movement against nuclear power.

The 1978 Elections

Many ecologists turned their attentions to the national French elections in early 1978. But their outcome was not encouraging and by summer the French press was announcing that the ecological movement was dead. What had happened?

One problem was that a great deal of energy went into the electoral effort, while local organizing suffered. Some ecology groups formed electoral alliances with centrist environmental groups, leading to campaigns that, although stressing an end to nuclear power, omitted the ideas of ecological reorganization of society that had been the essential and exciting points of discussion in the earlier programs. There was division over whether or not to support the left in the second round of elections. Some candidates called for support of the Socialist Party; others refused to endorse either right or left.

Overall, the ecology slates got less than 3% of the national vote. The ecologists received only 4% of the vote around Malville, where support had previously been high. The only place where the ecologists scored well was at La Hague, location of the fuel reprocessing and storage plant. There a local "green" slate, with strong support from the atomic workers' union (CFDT), got 12% of the vote.

Although the French press may have announced the end of the ecology movement, ecologists don't agree! A lack of media events doesn't mean that nothing is happening. Friends of the Earth activist Brice Lalonde asks: "To please the media, sympathizers, voters, militants, must we do forced labor to organize spectacular actions when they serve no purpose and when no one wants them?" He urged ecological action at home, in towns and cities. "Let us try to live and survive outside of the state and its commodities."[7]

Given the great diversity in the French ecology movement, many directions will undoubtedly be followed. Some people will continue to be involved in electoral politics, in coalitions and "green" slates. Others hope that the Socialist Party will change its ways, with the development over the next few years of some kind of "new left" that will take ecological issues into account. Meanwhile, ecologists are involved in projects around solar and alternative energy. There are also groups involved in "green radio"—illegal transmissions of neighborhood/ecology news and music. Such radio stations have been active in the Fessenheim area and have been attempted (and jammed) in Paris.

Clearly the vitality and consciousness of the French anti-nuclear movement will not be lost, although its form may change in the time to come.

Footnotes

1. Pierre Radanne, "The Battle of Malville—An Eyewitness Account," *WIN* Magazine, 22 September 1977.

2. Richard Halloran, "Seoul Officials Say Strong U.S. Pressure Forced Cancellation of Plans to Purchase a French Nuclear Plant," *New York Times*, 1 February 1976.

3. *The Elements*, February 1978, no. 37, p. 8.

4. The French Friends of the Earth is very decentralized. The Paris branch publishes books nationally, but does not direct provincial groups in any way. All FOE groups have separate fundraising and newsletters, unlike the FOE/U.S., which has a far more centralized setup.

5. "For Ecological Communities," from *La Baleine* ("the whale"), journal of FOE/Paris, no. 26-27. Proposals for the March 1977 municipal elections.

6. Anna Gyorgy, "France Kills Its First Protester," *The Nation*, 8 October 1977.

7. Brice Lalonde, "mouvement neo-cistercien recrute," *Le Sauvage*, September 1978, p. 16.

Resources

ARTICLES:
See footnotes for two articles on Malville.

Le Sauvage, 12 rue du Mail/ 75002 Paris.

BOOKS
Syndicat CFDT de l'Energie Atomique,*L'Electronucleaire en France*, Editions du Seuil, 1975.

Les Amis de la Terre (FOE), *L'Escroquerie Nucleaire*, Lutter/Stock 2, 1975.

Yves Lenoir, *Technocratie Francaise*, Collection Amis de la Terre, J.J. Pauvert, 1977.

Philippe Simonnet, *Les Nucleocrates*, Presses Universitaries de Grenoble, 1978.

FILM
Condamnes a Reussir (Sentenced to Success), 60 minute color film produced by Cine Information Documents, Paris. Available for rental/sales from: Green Mountain Post Films.

Contact
Amis de la Terre
117 Ave. de Choisy
75013 Paris

LA HAGUE

From May to October of 1976 the workers of the La Hague nuclear reprocessing plant in France went on strike following what was euphemistically described as a radical "deterioration of working conditions." The problems were the result of a shift from the reprocessing of conventional European nuclear plant fuel to spent fuel from light water reactors.

Redesigned to transform uranium fuel into plutonium for fast breeder reactors, the plant is supposed to service not only the reactors of France, but those of the other European nuclear countries as well.

As a result of the increase in cases of radioactive contamination at the plant, a number of serious accidents, work overloads, and the management's failure to assure the adequate technical functioning of the reprocessing equipment, the workers went on strike. Backed by the CFDT (Confederation Francaise du Travail), they demanded an overhaul of the entire installation and threatened to quit unless their demand was met. They further insisted that control of the plant remain with CEA (Commission d'Energie Atomique—like our AEC) as part of the public sector. The workers were unified in their opposition to Cogema, the company which had been created (by CEA) to run the plant for profit.

The Significance of the Strike

The strike at La Hague was one of the first European examples of workers' opposition to nuclear power at an indispensible link in the production chain—the processing of material from light water reactors to create fuel to start fast breeders. (It is important to note that once fast breeders get underway, there is no reprocessing plant to reprocess the plutonium that it creates—with the exception of one small research plant in the German Democratic Republic.)

During the strike, workers got together with local residents. Collective demonstrations, public information meetings and exhibitions were organized. The question of pollution in general and radioactivity specifically were discussed both in terms of their effects on workers in nuclear plants and on inhabitants in areas where atomic and reprocessing plants are located.

On the basis of the events at La Hague alone it is more than reasonable to assume that opposition from workers who have to handle radioactive power plant materials—for storage or reprocessing—will only increase as the nuclear industry develops throughout the world.

—Michael Lucas

Germany and Switzerland

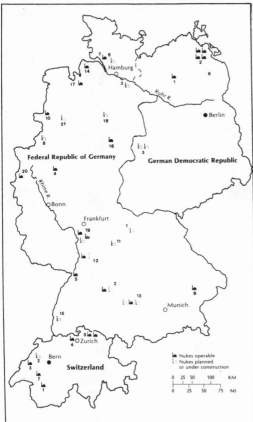

Federal Republic of Germany

West Germany has seen militant local and national action against nuclear power. And the anti-nuclear movement has seen an escalation of police power and a suppression of civil liberties unequalled in any Western country. Opposition to the government's nuclear program has been interpreted as treason and even terrorism against the state. In defending their nuclear program, the FRG has trampled on the rights of the population. It is a situation that we all must become aware of.

The country is very industrialized, with little open space in a territory the size of California's. Nuclear plants cannot be hidden from view in unpopulated areas. Nuclear construction has

been opposed as one part of a general degradation of modern life, as environmental quality is sacrificed for ever-increasing profit and growth.

The nuclear debate has been raging in Germany for the past few years. Citizen groups have multiplied with speed and enthusiasm. The basic model of citizen organization is the "Burgerinitiativen," the citizen initiative or citizen action group. There are at least 400,000 people in hundreds of these groups all over the country. They oppose nuclear power and are also active on other ecology issues affecting them locally.

Membership in these groups cuts across political and party lines. There are conservatives who oppose nuclear power as an example of undesirable

"In any case, we have never had such a high standard of living" - Atomic Plants, for whom?

site	plant name	net Mw	finished
GERMANY (DDR)			
1. Rheinsberg	Granesee region	70	1966
Lubmin, Greifswald region	Nord 1-1	440	1973
2. Lubmin	Nord 1-2	440	1975
Lubmin	Nord 2-1	440	1977
Lubmin	Nord 2-2	440	1978
3. Magdeburg	Magdeburg 1	440	1980
Magdeburg	Magdeburg 2	440	1980
GERMANY (DFR)			
1. Grafenrheinfeld	Grafenrheinfeld	1225	1979
2. Neckarwestheim	Neckarwestheim	850	1976
Neckarwestheim	Neckarwestheim	850	1981
3. Gessthact-Kruemmel/Elbe	Kruemmel	1260	1979
4. Hamm/Uentrop	Hamm	300	1977
5. Karlsruhe	Karlsruhe	52	1962
6. River Elbe	Brokdorf	1300	
7. River Elbe	Brunsbuettel	771	1976
8. Hamm/Uentrop	Hamm	1300	1981
9. Ohu	Isar	870	1977
10. Lingen	Lingen	256	1968
11. Obrigheim	Obrigheim	328	1969
12. Philippsburg	Philippsburg 1	864	1977
Philippsburg	Philippsburg 2	1250	1982
13. Gundremmingen	Gundremmingen A	237	1967
Gundremmingen	Gundremmingen C	1249	1981
Gundremmingen	Bundremmingen B	1249	1982
14. Stade	Stade	630	1972
15. Upper Rhine	Wyhl	1300	1979
16. Wuergassen	Wuergassen	640	1972
17. Esenshamm	Esenshamm	1230	1977
18. Grohnde	Grohnde	1294	1981
19. Worms	Biblis A	1146	1974
Worms	Biblis B	1240	1976
Worms	Biblis C	1228	1981
20. Kaerlich	Kaerlich	1228	1978
21. Kalker	Kalkar	282	1981
SWITZERLAND			
1. Berne	Muhleberg	306	1972
2. Graben	Graben 1	1140	1979
3. Kaiseraugst	Kaiseraugst	932	1976
4. Leibstadt	Leibstadt	955	1978
5. Doettingen	Beznau 1	350	1969
Doettingen	Beznau 2	350	1972
6. Ruthi	Ruthi	900	?
7. Daniken, SO	Goesgen	920	1978

progress. There are also many people active in left-wing, anti-capitalist groups such as the KB, or Communist League, which has been active against nuclear power, especially in northern Germany.

Most opponents of nuclear power identify with the political left. As progressives, they have been targeted as dissidents and terrorist-sympathizers by the Federal government. As anti-nuclear actions have grown in strength and influence, so has the escalation of military force. But the anti-nuclear movement in Germany has responded by challenging the state repression and organizing non-confrontational, politically clear tactics.

The Wyhl Story

The first international occupation of a nuclear power plant site took place in Wyhl* on 23 February 1975. This small rural village is near the Rhine River in the Kaiserstuhl area of southwestern Germany, well-known for its vineyards and fine wines. Local Burgerin-

*Wyhl is pronounced "veal" and is often misspelled, but this is how the locals spell it!

itiatives had organized against the plant since it was announced in 1971, but their petitions and demonstrations failed to stop utility plans.

On 17 February 1975 construction was finally to begin. Several hundred local activists—farmers, housewives, small merchants, students—went to the site, held a press conference, and proceeded to sit in front of the bulldozers, preventing construction for the day. Police responded with water hoses and arrests, but the local people were not ready to give up. Many stayed overnight, and the next week they returned with 28,000 supporters from all over Germany and from French Alsace, just across the river. Their numbers overwhelmed the unprepared police, who withdrew as people entered the site.

For more than a year, people occupied the construction site. They built a "friendship house," as had been done at the occupied lead plant site in Markolsheim. Local farmers supported the occupiers with food, and the new village became a local social center. After work people would gather there, and

On site at Wyhl—Local opponents celebrate announcement that the plant will not be built.

the Wyhler Wald Volkshochschule (Wyhl Woods People's High School) held frequent educational and social evenings. Local people became experts on all aspects of nuclear power and maintained a strong opposition to construction.

Construction has still not started at Wyhl. After more than a year's occupation, local groups agreed to leave pending a hearing and decision before a panel of judges. For more than a week in February 1977 the panel heard testimony about the dangers of nuclear power and the structural deficiencies of the Wyhl nuke design. Dr. Ernest Sternglass and Richard Pollard from the U.S. came to testify. Finally, the panel ruled against the plant. Still, the Volkshochschule continues to meet regularly. Its members oppose nuclear power everywhere. The Wyhl occupation became a model for citizen direct action and inspired occupation-type demonstrations from Malville, France to Seabrook, U.S.

Brokdorf

But subsequent attempts at site occupations to block nuclear construction in the FRG were met with violence and bloodshed. In northern Germany, at the Brokdorf site, local res-

Police Mass at Brokdorf—Although occupation attempts failed, construction at Brokdorf has been halted pending a "solution" to the storage of radioactive waste.

idents and their urban supporters met a barricaded, heavily fortified site with troops massed inside. As demonstrators left the 13 November 1976 demonstration, helicopters dropped tear gas cannisters. Had the Federal Republic declared open war on its citizens?

Grohnde

Similarly violent confrontation followed at the Grohnde nuke site on 19 March 1977. Demonstrators tried to cut through fences at the site; police attacked with water cannons and mace. Fleeing demonstrators were clubbed and more than 100 were arrested. (In early 1978 12 demonstrators went on trial with charges ranging from resisting police to attempted murder!)

Following the bloody demonstrations at Brokdorf, Grohnde, and Malville (attended by many Germans), anti-nuclear organizers tried to plan large demonstrations specifically to avoid police violence. With the actions against Kalkar and Almelo, they seemed to have succeeded.

Kalkar

A massive demonstration was called for 24 September 1977 to oppose construction of a fast breeder plant at Kalkar in northern Germany near the Dutch border.

> The Confederation of Citizen's Initiatives for the Protection of the Environment (BBU), in coalition with other German and a Scandinavian environmental group, organized the demonstration along strictly nonviolent direct action lines and proclaimed in no uncertain terms that any violence that erupted would be the responsibility of the state and federal government, and their police and battle ready military.

Police at Kalkar (*Frankfurter Allgemeine Zeitung*, Barbara Klemin)

The pre-demonstration publicity disseminated by the bourgeois media, government officials and by the police, resembled the witch-hunting and smear campaigns that consistently have dogged all large anti-nuclear actions since the movement's birth in Europe. "In Kalkar one can expect massive violence," cynically proclaimed the *Handelsblatt*, Germany's *Wall Street Journal*.[1]

But the press was wrong. The day went on as planned, despite massive police roadblocks, searches, and other forms of harassment. In all, around 50,000 people from ten countries made it to Kalkar, while another 10-20,000 never reached the march because they were stopped or delayed by police patrols. The day went well for those who did make it, with a strong non-violent show of opposition to the construction in spite of the massive police presence.

The Kalkar demonstration took place in particularly strained times poli-tically. For it went on as the government was tracking down the terrorist abductors of German industrialist leader (and former SS-Nazi) Hans Martin Schleyer. At least in the government's mind, there was some connection between the terrorist kidnappings and murders, and the mass mobilizations of the anti-nuclear activists.

...the government's campaign against terrorism continues to conveniently overlap its fight against all forms of popular opposition. For a long time the goverment and the police have gone to a great effort and expense to impose on the public mind the association of anti-nuclear agitation with terrorist activity. Such refrains have saturated the mass media to the point of boredom. The government's intention has been to deny the anti-nuclear movement's mass character by representing it as a conspiracy of "terrorists," "criminals," and

Anti-Atom Village at Gorleben

"communists." This slandering campaign has fallen short of its aims in the sense that although it continues to have some effect, it has failed dramatically to reverse the growth of the movement.[2]

Repression of Civil Liberties

Of all the countries in Europe, none is as intolerant and repressive of ecology/ anti-nuclear activism as the FRG. A West German booklet entitled "Campaign Against the Model West Germany" describes the development of the FRG within the last 20 years as "one of integration of all relevant organizations in the state, by guaranteeing a high standard of living providing that no disruptions are caused by social unrest, and through an extensive control of newsmedia and other forms of publicity."[3] Since German schools and universities are controlled by the state, academic jobs and all civil service jobs are subject to government scrutiny. Laws known as *berufsverbote* make government loyalty a prerequisite for employment. Teachers have been fired for talking against nuclear power with their students and have been disciplined for wearing buttons. There were 147,000 cases of identity and vehicle searches during the Kalkar demonstration—yet "only" 50,000 people attended the march. Thus everyone must have been searched at least twice!

Anti-Atom Villages

Despite government harassment, the ecology and anti-nuclear movements continue to grow in the FRG. There have been several examples of non-violent direct action. One was the founding of "Anti-Atom Villages" near nuclear plant sites, in a sort of off-site occupation that could keep pressure on nuke-builders and serve as a local information-education center. Such a village was founded near Grohnde during the summer of 1977. It began in June, just two months after the bloody clash when non-violent anti-nuclear activists occupied the site of cooling towers for the nuke. By July the occupiers had built a playground, friendship houses and huts, an information center, etc. Eviction finally came on August 23 when 1,300 police with tanks and buses cleared the area. Although the village did not have the same local support as at Wyhl, it was effective in expanding the anti-nuclear movement in the area.

A similar activity was planned for Gorleben—a 1978 "summer camp."

Gorleben

This town on the East German border in northern Germany is one of the focal points of the German movement because of its critical importance as a site for a reprocessing plant and nuclear waste disposal dump. As a reprocessing plant it will produce plutonium which can, of course, be used for nuclear weapons. Thus besides being essential to the FRG's commercial nuclear program, it is also part of the physical plant for a possible future military capability.

The International Connection—Like Barnwell and la Hague, Gorleben is strategically important for the international fuel cycle. For Germany, Gorleben may turn out to be the "high noon" of the anti-nuclear struggle. For if the government can succeed in building its dump and reprocessing facilities (to service countries of Europe, South America and the Far East), it's likely to win at nuclear power plant siting too.

If the U.S. reprocessing plant at Barnwell is defeated, then Gorleben

and other reprocessing plants around the world may to some degree be used as a bail-out for the international industry. In the meantime, the German government is strengthening its police and military fortifications at Gorleben and passing legislation in an attempt to prevent any and all public opposition in Luchow Dannenburg. It's crucial that opposition to Gorleben come from people all over the world.

Rate Withholding—
No Money for Nukes

"No Money for Nukes" (Keine Mark fur AKW) is a non-violent direct action economic campaign begun by anti-nuclear activists in Hamburg in early October 1977. Citizens are asked to withhold 10% of their electricity bills from the Hamburg Electric Company.

Electric Bill Boycott—No Money for Nukes— I'm With You: German rate witholding sign

The amount is equivalent to the money spent by the utility on nuclear-generated electricity. The campaign was developed as an alternative to confrontational demonstrations like Grohnde.

Households that want to participate can either withhold their money right away, or join a "waiting list" of people who have agreed to withhold their money when their number reaches 1,000. The reason for the list is that any response from the government will depend in part on the size and strength of the movement. The numner of households withholding had reached 420 by May 1978. The withheld funds are in an escrow account to be handed over to the utility when it agrees to stop its nuclear plant operations. So far the utility has ignored the campaign and urged the media to do likewise. They still keep sending a constant stream of pro-nuclear literature with utility bills, and some boycotters have gotten bills for false amounts.

"Nuclear Power Creates Jobs"

Only if and when the many local withholding campaigns come together on a national and international scale can the movement challenge the Federal Government's most important nuke projects, such as the reprocessing plant and radioactive garbage storage facilities planned for Gorleben. With this goal in mind, withholding activists met in January 1978. The different groups who attended exchanged experiences and discussed past and present withholding campaigns in Italy, Holland, Switzerland and France.[4]

Rate withholding campaigns are useful because they can involve people in non-violent direct action, because they are educational, and because they strike at the economic relationship between the population and the nuclear industry.

German Ecology Politics

Electoral "fever" has crossed the border between France and Germany. The anti-nuclear movement is beginning to get involved in eco-politics, following the successful campaign of ecologists in the 4 June 1978 municipal elections in Hamburg.

Not only are there progressive antinuclear parties, but a right-wing eco-party has formed as well. Activists have different views on the effects of such a turn-of-events.

In Frankfurt, an industrial city in central Germany close to the giant Biblis nukes, Daniel Cohn-Bendit, known as "Danny the Red" during his days in the Paris strikes of May 1968, ran on an ecology ticket in the October 1978 regional elections. In an interview appearing in a French ecology journal, the new "Danny the Green" was asked why he joined the ecology movement:

For me, the ecology movement is an attempt to reformulate all the critiques of society that have been put forward since the sixties. Analyses critical of a consumer society and daily life have reached the stage where we have been led to put together ecological projects...For me, being an ecologist is not a reconversion. It is, in trying to understand certain types of movements, the result, the clarification of what I thought before...Ecology comes before the economy. It questions economic industrial growth, no matter what the type of society, capitalist or socialist. Ideas about revolution, socialism, have to be seen again through the (sun) glasses of ecology...[5]

Danny and the ecology group he's part of did not spend their time pasting up posters. They had pre-election actions planned—a demonstration at Biblis, the largest nuke in Europe, a collective "fish-in" at the Main River that flows through Frankfurt to check out possible pollution, etc.

But others are fearful of this new direction. Activist Michael Lucas in (West) Berlin writes that "in the upswing of electorialism, a large portion of the energy, the imagination and political work that could otherwise go into extending the grassroots organizational structure of the movement through direct action tactics, will be channeled into campaigns to place radicals in parliament on a local and national level.... The electoral shift will leave a good number of people at the radical end of the anti-nuclear political spectrum more vulnerable to government repression. As the entire movement is pulled further to the right by the more powerful rightist forces it will be much easier for the government to criminalize and politically isolate more radical tendencies within the movement."[6]

***

How can activists help the German anti-nuclear movement? We can urge our government to stop shipping en-

riched uranium fuel to reactors in Germany (and for export in general). We can add Gorleben and Kalkar to the list of fuel cycle and breeder projects that must be stopped. We can lobby the State Department for sanctions against both the FRG and Brazil to pressure both contries to drop their agreement for FRG sale of the complete nuclear fuel cycle to Brazil. (See Brazil, pp. 374-376.) And we can try to get news from Europe, demanding an end to the press blackout of ecology news from abroad, and asking for German news from our ecology journals in this country.

Footnotes

1. Paper by Michael Lucas, "Kalkar," November 1977, p. 1. (West) Berlin, FRG.

2. *Ibid.*, p. 5.

3. "Campaign Against the Model West Germany," July 1978, p. 2.

4. Report from Michael Lucas, Spring 1978, Berlin. Information from: *BBU Actuell*, no. 2, January-February 1978. Subscriptions or single issues: Lorenzstr. 16-17, 1000 Berlin 45, FRG. Send material from the U.S. anti-nuclear movement to Michael Lucas c/o above address, for translation.

5. Charlotte Vinsonneau, "Danny le Vert," *Le Sauvage*, September 1978, p. 11. From interview: "Ecology means regionalism, and the autonomy of all movements. In the ecology movement, the type of alliance that we have achieved allows for autonomy of all groups in it and does not commit them to majority points of view. One of the fundamental points of the alliance was the right to have minority views included in the party program... To refuse the traditional politics of alliances that consist of uniting around a minimum common program, this is new. I would say even revolutionary. To vote for a slate this radical signifies not just being counted, but structuring a really open extra-parliamentary opposition."

6. Letter from Michael Lucas, 22 July 1978.

Resources:

PUBLICATIONS

Cultural Workers Collective, *Workbook on Nuclear Power*, see "Interview with Anna Gyorgy" and "Non-Violence Triumphant," a story of the Wyhl occupation by Alsacian activist Solange Fernex. ($3.75 from CWC, Box 302, No. Amherst MA, 01059.)

"Atomkraft—Nein Danke: The Anti-Nuke Movement in Germany and Western Europe," *Science for the People,* Sept./Oct. 1978, vol. 10, no. 5. ($1.25 from Science for the People, 897 Main St., Cambridge MA 02139.)

Campaign Against the Model West Germany, 36 page report in English. (Available from Campaign... c/o Evangelische Studentengemeinde (ESG), Querendburger Hoehe 287, 4630 Bochum 1, Bundesrepublik Deutschland.)

Was Wir Wollen. This is an excellent newsletter from the Wyhl region, with national and international European nuke and alternative energy news. In German with some French. (*Was Wir Wollen*, Wilhemstrasse 15, 78 Freiburg, FRG.)

FILMS:

More Nuclear Power Stations. 55 minutes; color; produced by Flip Films, Copenhagen. This documentary film from Denmark takes you inside German nuclear plants and waste storage facilities for a first-hand look at nuclear power.

Better Active Today than Radioactive Tomorrow. 65 minutes; black and white; produced by Nina Gladitz/Teldok, Freiburg. Tells the story of the citizens' occupation at Wyhl with first-hand footage and political insight.

Nuclear Reaction at Wyhl. 15 minutes; color. This film was made from an 8mm home movie shot during the Wyhl occupation.

These films are available for rental/sale from Green Mountain Post Films. Send for complete catalog: Box 177, Montague MA 01351 (Tel. 413/863-4754.)

Nuclear Power Stations in the Soviet Union

- ■ In Operation ▣ Under Construction
- □ Projected to 1980's   0 Miles 300

Source: *New York Times*, 14 January 1977, p. D5   The New York Times

Nuclear Power in the U.S.S.R.

The Soviet Union is the third largest producer of nuclear power plants, after the U.S. and Canada. In fact, the world's first industrial (as opposed to military) nuke went on-line near Moscow in 1954, and in 1973 the Soviet BN-350 was the only fast breeder in the world generating electricity for industry.

Despite this headstart over the West, Soviet civilian nuclear power during the 1950s and '60s suffered considerable delays, mostly due to bottlenecks in production of nuclear hardware. Thus by 1977, total nuclear generated electricity amounted to 7,000 Mw from 25 nukes, while the US. total was around 40,000 Mw.

However, faced with an impending energy shortage similar to that of the West, plus increasing international competition for nuclear markets and spheres of influence, the Soviet Union has recently made efforts to accelerate its nuclear program. According to its Commissioner for the Peaceful Uses of Atomic Energy, by 1980 the Soviet Union will have a nuclear electrical capacity of 30,000 Mw.[1] An extensive program of plant construction is planned at home, with exports to Eastern Europe and Cuba and other Third World countries.

Energy Situation

About 80% of the energy used in Russia is consumed in the Western industrialized urban centers. Meanwhile 90% of vast fuel reserves are east of the Urals, in Siberia and the far north. But exploitation of these resources is hindered by climate, geology, plus lack of transportation and all facilities.

Although the U.S.S.R. has enough oil now to export East and West, its own predicted growth will require imported oil by the 1980s.[2] Ever since Lenin defined communism as "soviet power plus electrification," electricity production has had a central place in Soviet five year plans. At present the Soviet economy is growing faster than energy production. The developing domestic energy gap is one of the pressures behind recent efforts to accelerate the industrial nuclear program.

Nuclear vs. Coal—Nuclear power is favored over coal for several reasons. There would be economic, structural and environmental problems with a vastly increased use of coal. A main argument of Soviet nuclear technocrats is that nukes do not produce substantial amounts of pollution. As in the west, coal is used in comparison.[3]

Exports—At a COMECON (see footnote 2) meeting in July 1977 in Warsaw, Soviet Prime Minister Kosygin presented an over-all energy strategy for Eastern Europe. By 1990, 40-50% of COMECON electrical needs would be met by nukes.[4] The final communique' of the conference stressed the need for a "crash development of hardware for atomic reactor construction."

Nuclear cooperation between Russia and its COMECON partners is for the most part based on a division of labor. According to this, nuclear reactors will be built in the U.S.S.R. As much as possible, the Soviets will continue to monopolize nuclear knowhow. Other COMECON countries will manufacture nuclear hardware. One exception to this general scheme is the production of reactors in the GDR.[5]

Western Connections

In 1965 the Soviets signed an agreement with France for cooperation in the development of nuclear energy. Similar cooperation treaties were signed with Holland, Belgium, Sweden, Finland, a number of Third World countries and with the U.S. and Canada as well.[6] The so-called Nixon-Brezhnev nuclear cooperation agreement of 1973 called for "strengthening of cooperation in the area of controlled thermonuclear fusion, breeder reactors and basic research in the properties of matter."[7]

Safety

As in the West, early decisions on the nuclear question were made without consultation with local populations, nor with adequate consideration of the health, environmental, and actual safety problems of nuclear power.

Although the Soviet authorities claim that their reactor technology is as modern as its Western counterpart, it is common knowledge in nuclear establishments throughout the world that Russian nuclear safety standards are behind those of the U.S. This may be one reason for the Soviet nuclear establishment's efforts to acquire Western nuclear plants. It may also be why the U.S.S.R.'s top nuclear technocrats must justify nuclear safety standards which, under the pressure of independent criticism and anti-nuclear opposition, have either been abandoned or seriously descredited in the U.S.

The lack of public debate on nuclear power in the U.S.S.R. has meant that the program was never subjected to the independent scientific criticism and public pressure that has characterized the American program since the late 1960s.

The Soviet nuclear establishment—both scientists dealing with purely technical matters and nuclear technocrats attempting to hold down costs—have been able to push through designs that as far as safety goes are inferior to Western models.

The best example is the 440-Mw Nowoworonesh reactor. This design has no separate emergency cooling system, just secondary pumps that duplicate the ones in the primary cooling system. Basically reactor design does not take into consideration the risk of a core meltdown.[8]

Another striking feature of the 440-Nowoworonesh is its lack of a steel reinforced concrete containment vessel. Commenting on the matter, Director of the State Committee on Atomic Energy, A.M. Petrossjanz has said: "We consider a containment vessel unnecessary. However, we will install one when our customers want us to."[9]

Finland has imported the Nowoworonesh 440. Worried about the absence of an emergency core cooling system, Finnish nuclear authorities—undoubtedly with Russian approval and technical cooperation—have installed a Westinghouse back-up system.[10] The Finns have also equipped their nuke with a containment vessel.

In 1973 Scandinavian countries protested construction of a Soviet-designed nuke in the GDR (East Germany). For if a serious accident occurred at the Greifswald plant, prevailing winds would carry radioactivity into Scandinavia. The protest cited the lack of both an emergency core cooling system and steel reinforcement of the reactor's containment vessel. In private conversations, Russian scientists told their Swedish colleagues that partly because Russian reactors did not have an adequate system against emissions of radioactivity, they had previously been installed in the sparsely populated zones of Siberia.

Fast Breeders

In 1970, ten U.S. scientists were given an inspection tour of Russian fast breeder installations. When they came home they reported that the supposed Russian advances in the breeder program were actually due to their comparatively substandard safety guidelines.[11] Many Western alterations that had been incorporated into breeder research and development designs for safety considerations were simply absent on the Soviet models.[12] Not surprisingly, there have been accidents.[13]

Waste Management

The U.S.S.R. forbids burial of radioactive waste underground, ocean dumping or disposal in open or underground waterways. These strict guidelines are the result of many years of indiscriminate burial of raw wastes and a tragic history of accidents. The most devastating was the 1958 explosion of radioactive waste buried in the southern Urals (see page 128).

As for spent fuel storage, the most recent Soviet reactors are built so that used fuel rods are deposited in temporary storage cellers directly beneath the plants. They can stay there for upwards of thirty years.[14]

The waste disposal plan of the Soviet Union involves glassifying highly radioactive waste in 200 liter containers and encasing the latter in concrete. Since 1954, low and middle level radioactive waste has been buried in deep rock formations. Like the DOE, the Russian atomic energy authorities are considering the use of salt domes for burial of highly radioactive waste.[15]

An Anti-Nuclear Movement?

So far there is no popular grassroots movement in the U.S.S.R. against the nuclear threat. The only signs of opposition have been "faint rumblings" among Soviet intelligensia, particularly among scientists, many of whom are quite aware of the dangers of nukes.[16]

The lack of a popular anti-nuclear movement can be partly blamed on the Soviet news blackout of Western anti-nuke movements, plus the complete lack of public discussion of nuclear power's technical and safety problems at home. Anti-nuke opposition may emerge first in countries like Czechoslovakia, Poland, Rumania, and East Germany, which are geographically closer to western Europe and have more access to nuclear-related news.

Nuclear Connections - East and West

Both the U.S. and the U.S.S.R. are attempting—or more precisely are being forced by the logic of their respective systems—to hold down and spread out the capital costs of their nuclear programs by imposing the nuclear solution on other countries.

In addition, both super-power nuclear establishments use the others' nuclear power programs to justify their own, and thus sell the necessity of nukes to their domestic populations. With a few relatively unimportant exceptions, every supplier nation since the birth of industrial nuclear development has been privy to and has participated in a *de facto* conspiracy of silence concerning the dangers of their own and each others' civilian nuclear programs. One example is the joint U.S.-U.S.S.R suppression of information about the explosion of atomic wastes in the Soviet Union in 1958.

The Soviet nuclear establishment uses the U.S. nuclear program as a crutch to justify the safety of their nuclear reactors and, as in the case of Finland's Russian-made nuclear reactors, to "patchup" technical and safety deficiencies with U.S. nuclear hardware. On the U.S. side of the political divide, one justification for the further development of nukes, both military and civilian, is the tried and true "We can't let the Russians get ahead of us." The 1978 Congressional allocation for continued funding of the fast breeder program was justified in exactly these terms and passed, despite Carter administration opposition and studies that have argued the technical, military, and commercial disadvantages of immediate fast breeder development.[17]

If the U.S. civilian nuclear power program is a threat to the health, safety, and well-being of every human being on this earth, it is clear that the Soviet nuclear program with its even lower technical, environmental, and safety standards is even more dangerous. The U.S. government and CIA are well-informed about the dangers of Soviet nuclear technology. But despite anti-Communist propaganda programs and support of dissident intellectuals, they have never spoken out against Russian civilian nukes. The obvious reason is that such action would only put into further question the already politically threatened U.S. nuclear program.

Strategies for Change

Given the competitive structure of the world market and the division of the world into competing national economies, it seems highly unlikely that civilian or military nukes could be definitively stopped in the U.S. without being more or less simultaneously halted in the Soviet Union and other technologically advanced nations. The anti-nuclear movements in the U.S., Japan, Europe, and Australia are faced not only with stopping nukes in their own nations, but also in those of the Soviet Union, Eastern Europe, and China.

One of the preliminary steps in the development of an effective international movement is the development of tactics and strategies to make information concerning the dangers of nuclear power available to people of Eastern block countries and the Soviet Union.[18] Making connections with Soviet and Eastern dissident groups and oppositional workers tendencies over the issue of nuclear power are possible approaches. To confront the international structure of the world-wide nuclear establishment, much more attention must be given in general to its international dynamics than has been the case up to now.

Edited from a longer report by Michael Lucas, August-Sept. 1978.

Footnotes

1. *Kernenergie,* (Nuclear journal published in the German Democratic Republic), May 1976.

2. At present the Soviet Union produces enough oil and natural gas to meet its own needs, those of its COMECON partners and to export to the West. Except for Poland with its coal and Rumania which has oil, the COMECON nations are dependent on the U.S.S.R. for energy. With the planned growth rates of COMECON this dependence is increasing and with it the pressure to accelerate its nuclear power timetable...From Western exports the Soviet Union gets 30% of its foreign currency reserves, which are needed in part to pay for basic food stuffs to feed its population. On the basis of currently accepted growth figures, it is predicted that Russia will have to import oil in the 1980s.

COMECON: The Council for Mutual Economic Aid; founded in Moscow in 1949. According to its statutes it aims to "unify and coordinate planned economic development among member states; accelerate their economic and technical progress; raise the level of industrialization in countries with underdeveloped industry; and steadily raise their productivity and their standard of living." COMECON partners as of 1978 include: U.S.S.R., People's Republics of: Poland, Hungary, Rumania, Bulgaria, Czechoslovakia, also Cuba and the GDR. Yugoslavia has been "associated" since 1964.— Jorg Hallerbach,*Hammer, Sichel und Atom*, mimeo to be published.

3. Sozialistisches Osteuropakomittee, *Kernkraftwerke in Osteuropa* ("Nuclear Power in Eastern Europe"), May 1978, p. 5. This pamphlet is an excellent source of information about the energy and nuclear situation in the Soviet Union and the Eastern block. Many facts taken from here. (Henceforth referred to as KOE). See also: Jeremy Russell, "Die Energiesituation in der Sowjetunion und Osteuropa," *Europa— Archiv* 1976, 3, p. 96.

4. KOE, *op. cit.*, p. 13. See also: *The Petroleum Economist* (London) 8 August 1977. In Czechoslovakia by 1990 there are supposed to be 10 nuclear power plants in operation planned to cover 70% of electricity output. In Hungary, 15% electric output is to be covered by nukes by 1980. In Poland by the year 2000 8,500 Mw or 13% of electrical output are to be nuclear. In Bulgaria the goal for nuclear electricity at the end of the century is 50%.

5. A giant nuclear industrial complex ("Atomnash") is under construction by the Zimljansker Reservoir in Wolgodonsk in the U.S.S.R. It will make reactors and hardware. Although construction will go on until 1982, production has already begun in some sections. In Czechoslovakia, the Skoda Werde that makes cars also produces hardware for fast breeders. Nuclear engineers, technicians and other workers are trained in Obninsk.—KOE, *op. cit.*, p. 18. Also: "Werk fur Kernkraftwerke," *Sowjetunion heute*, ("Factories for Atomic Power Plants," *Soviet Union Today*), 2 February 1976, p. 14; and 1 October 1975.

6. KOE, *op. cit.*, p. 19; *Pravda* 19 May 1965, *Osteuropa* December 1967, p. 53 & p. 922. Nuclear cooperation treaties with the Third World include: a treaty with Afganistan for assistance in building an atomic power plant (1963); an agreement with Egypt in 1964 to buld the first African nuclear research center as well as agreements with Iraq, Ghana, Lybia and other nations.

7. American-Soviet Communique, 25 June 1973.

8. For a fuller account of Soviet reactor safety, see Joseph Lewin, "The Russian Approach to Nuclear Reactor Safety," *Nuclear Safety*, vol. 18, no. 4, July/Aug. 1977. The nuclear establishment makes no secret of its concern about holding down reactor costs by maximizing the size of its reactors. Igor Glebow, Director of the Research Institute for Energy Machine Construction commented in an interview: "Building large complexes is not technocratic whim, but is based on giving utmost attention to questions of economics. It is easier and cheaper to build a structure to house 2 units with 1200 Mw than, for example, for 8 with 300 Mw. The fewer machines there are, the easier they can be serviced."—*Hammer, Sichel und Atom, op. cit.* "The closer the capacity of reactors comes to the 1000 Mw threshold, the more competitive they will be."—From an article in *Soviet Union Today*, 1 February 1977, pp. 17-18. See also: K. Fuchs and G. Schumann, *Die Bedeutung der Kernenergie bei der Deckung des kuenftigen Energiebedarfs in Energietechnik*, 27th year, no. 5, May 1977, p. 190.

9. Joseph Lewin, *op. cit.*, p. 442. See also Jorg Hallerbach, *op. cit.*

10. KOE, *op. cit.* p. 21. Also: Amory Lovins, *Soft Energy Paths*, p. 209-210.

11. KOE, *op. cit.*, p. 25. Also: Holger Strohm, *Friedlich in die Katastrophe*, (Hamburg, 1977), p. 336.

12. *Ibid.*

13. For example, in July 1973, a leak in the steam generators of the operating BN-350 demonstration breeder in Schetschenk on the Caspian Sea allowed water to contact the highly volatile liquid sodium coolant. The nuke exploded.—KOE, *ibid.; Financial Times,* 25 February 1974.

14. KOE, *ibid*, p. 27. Also: "Geringste Gefahr U.S.S.R./Kernenergie," *Spiegel*, 6/31.1.77.

15. Hallerbach,*op. cit.*

16. At the 250th anniversary of the Soviet Academy of Sciences in October 1975, the 82-year-old atomic physicist Pjotr Kapiza, one of the fathers of Soviet Atomic energy, warned in a speech that a 1000 Mw nuclear plant could have the effect of a 20 kiloton bomb in the event of an accident. He also said the "nuclear waste is highly radioactive and safely dealing with it involves technical problems for which there is not generally recognized solution." Kapiza warned that with the world-wide proliferation of plutonium, safeguards against nuclear blackmail and nuclear weapons proliferation become all the more difficult. Although Kapiza's speech was printed in the Journal of the Academy of Sciences, one of the most independent institutions in the Soviet Union, it was not reported in the press. Nevertheless, the speech was considered important enough that an article appeared in *Izvestia* specifically to refute Kapiza. However, the article did not directly refer to the scientist.—*Nucleonics Week*, Vol. 1, (1976) no. 20.

17. See, for example, Senator Frank Church's speech "The Nuclear Dilemma: Energy, the Atom and Survival," delivered at Wroxton College, England, 18 June 1977. (Reprinted in *Alternative and Long Range Energy Strategies* Additional Appendices, 1977, p. 2112; Joint Hearing before the Select Committee on Small Business, 9 December 1976.)

18. On 4 September 1978, simultaneous antinuclear demonstrations occurred in Washington D.C. and in Moscow. Seven Americans held up a red and white banner and handed out leaflets in Red Square while at the same time 11 persons among tourists taking a regular morning tour of the White House left the tour path, jumped over a rope and walked slowly to the center of the White House Lawn where they unfurled a large banner saying "No nuclear weapons, no nuclear power." The two contingents of demonstrators—in Red Square and on the White House Lawn—were promptly arrested.—*Stars and Stripes*, 5 September, 1978.

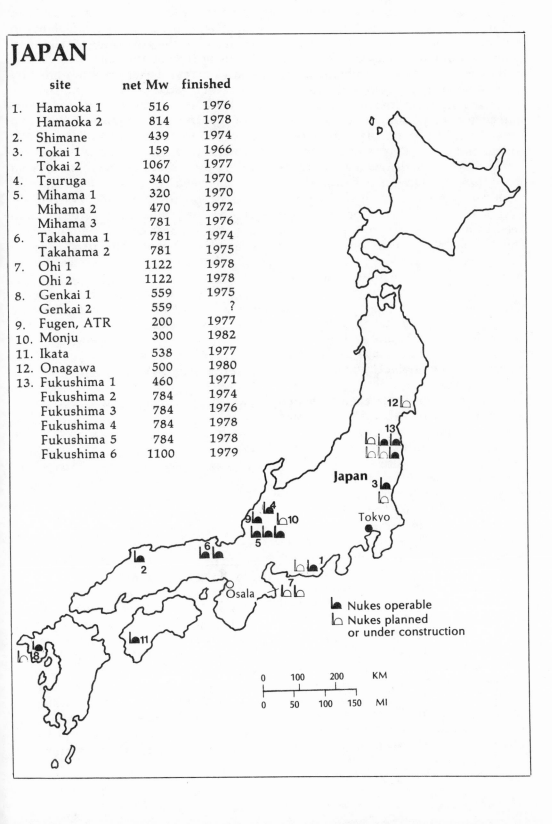

JAPAN

site	net Mw	finished
1. Hamaoka 1	516	1976
Hamaoka 2	814	1978
2. Shimane	439	1974
3. Tokai 1	159	1966
Tokai 2	1067	1977
4. Tsuruga	340	1970
5. Mihama 1	320	1970
Mihama 2	470	1972
Mihama 3	781	1976
6. Takahama 1	781	1974
Takahama 2	781	1975
7. Ohi 1	1122	1978
Ohi 2	1122	1978
8. Genkai 1	559	1975
Genkai 2	559	?
9. Fugen, ATR	200	1977
10. Monju	300	1982
11. Ikata	538	1977
12. Onagawa	500	1980
13. Fukushima 1	460	1971
Fukushima 2	784	1974
Fukushima 3	784	1976
Fukushima 4	784	1978
Fukushima 5	784	1978
Fukushima 6	1100	1979

Japan

Tokyo

Osala

Nukes operable
Nukes planned
or under construction

0	100	200	KM
0	50	100	150	MI

Nuclear power is fast becoming the number one environmental issue in Japan.

The list of problems is long. The densely-populated, heavily-industrialized nation has been overwhelmed by a depressing array of ecological catastrophes ranging from mercury, cadmium and chromium poisoning, to pollution-caused asthma, to people keeling over unconscious in Tokyo's summer smog.

Through it all, the Japanese government has insisted on pushing ahead with an aggressive nuclear program, despite the fact that plant performance records have been among the worst in the world. In response, public outcry has forced a drastic drop in the government's nuclear projections, and could soon bring a halt to new construction altogether.

Twenty commercial reactors were scheduled to be on line at the end of 1978, placing Japan alongside the U.S., Britain and the Soviet Union in nuclear megawattage.

The first Japanese reactor opened at Tokai in 1966. A British gas-cooled model, it remains the only major plant of non-U.S. design in the archipelago.

Despite the national "nuclear allergy" contracted at Hiroshima and Nagasaki, the Japanese people apparently welcomed the "peaceful atom." According to the *Japan Times*, Tokai was greeted as "a symbol of the peace-loving nation that renounced war under constitution." In the midst of unprecedented industrial expansion, communitites throughout Japan competed for nukes and the tax job benefits they were told to expect. The story is much the same as in the U.S. where people in small towns have often welcomed nukes with open arms.

In March 1970, the first full-scale plant opened at Tsuruga. A second opened within the year at Mihama. In 1971 the government announced plans for sixteen more plants, and added three more to the list in 1972. By 1976 there were a dozen operable plants in Japan, with the government talking in terms of fifty by the year 2000. All the plants except Tokai were designed by General Electric or Westinghouse.

With an annual electric consumption growth rate well over 12%, and projections for an overall economic growth rate of 7%, Japan's nine privately-owned utilities were totally sold on the need for nukes. Japan has no coal or oil to speak of. With strong assurances from U.S. reactor producers, the Japanese governmental-industrial complex committed itself to being 25% dependent on nuclear electricity by 1985.

In the public's mind, however, the romance with the atom had already been tarnished.

Prospect of a Radioactive Sea...and More

In 1971, fishermen working the seas around Tsuruga began catching abnormally large trepangs (sea cucumbers). Cobalt-60 was subsequently found in the sea water, in mussels, and in pearl oysters near the plant's coolant outlets. Later it was also found in seaweed.

Area residents were greatly alarmed. Japanese eat five to six times as much seafood as Westerners; they rely on it for 50% of their protein. There could be no more basic threat to Japanese life than a radioactive sea.

The bad news began to pile up. In March 1971, radioactive gas was detected leaking from the Tsuruga stacks. In June there was an iodine-131 leak, prompting the removal of 14 fuel rods.

In June 1973, highly radioactive waste water leaked from a storage room at Fukushima I. Someone failed to shut a drainage valve, and nearly three cubic meters of "hot" water were misrouted.

In July 1974, Kansai Electric asked Westinghouse to replace the steam generator of one of Kansai's two Mihama reactors. Mihama I had experienced four major shutdowns in less than four years.

In September 1974, 21 of 55 U.S. nukes were closed for an emergency safety check, prompted by a leaky bypass pipe at Illinois' Dresden I plant. Japanese authorities decided to inspect their 6 boiling water reactors because of their similarity in design and manufacture to the U.S. plant. They found alarmingly similar defects at Tokyo Electric's Fukushima I and at Hamaoka.

In January 1975, 23 U.S. plants shut down for a second emergency check, this time because of an emergency core cooling system problem—again at Dresden. The Japanese checked their BWR's and once again found critical problems, this time at Tsuruga and at Fukushima I, which was just about to reopen.

At the same time, Kansai's Mihama II was shut because of "wall thinning" of tubes in the reactor cooling system— a possible cause of radioactive releases. In May, further inspections at Mihama II revealed a serious problem that required removal of half the 121 fuel assemblies. Called "bowing," or fuel rod bending, the problem greatly angered Kansai officials, who had been assured by Westinghouse that fuel rod technology had been perfected. Although they would publically deny it, Kansai officials soon asked Westinghouse for a refund on their Mihama I reactor, which (as of late 1978) has remained shut since 1975.

A month prior to the Mihama II bowing discovery, ten workers at the construction site of the Tokai reprocessing plant were exposed to potentially fatal cobolt-60 radiation.

At Takahama, reactor Unit II was shut for a month because jellyfish had fouled the coolant intake pipe. The plant is designed to suck in 50 tons of seawater per second, and swarms of jellyfish attracted by warm waste water had clogged the intake pipes at both Takahama I and II. The problem required removal of more than 20,000 jellyfish per day.

While the environmental problems at Japanese plants began to take on a nightmarish quality, some severe economic factors also came into play. Assured by U.S. industry that the technology would pay for itself, Japanese utilities in fact found themselves with a fleet of white elephants. Twice in 1974, seven of eight operable reactors were shut down simultaneously. At one point, in the fall of 1975, only one out of twelve "operable" plants was actually generating. From April until September of 1977, six of Japan's fourteen reactors remained inactive. The year's overall operations produced a dismal capacity factor of under 47%. Construction costs are considerably higher in Japan than in the U.S.. With its catastrophic operating record, the Japanese reactor program had lost much of its luster.

MUTSU vs. Fishermen

Economic factors aside, no single recent incident has contributed more to Japanese disaffection with nuclear power than the MUTSU.

MUTSU is an 8,214-ton surface ship built by the Japan Nuclear Ship Development Agency as a national showpiece at a cost of $133 million. Begun in the late sixties, it was the only Japanese reactor built without British or U.S. guidance, although Westinghouse was called in at the end for an advisory check.

The project was meant to mark Japan's emergence into the age of independent atomic technology. The project was originally welcomed by the local government of Mutsu Bay, a fishing community in the remote northern reaches of Honshu, Japan's main island. Many felt MUTSU would be a boon to the depressed local economy.

But as the ship was being built, local residents began harboring doubts about the unfamiliar nuclear intrusion. By 1972, when MUTSU was ready to sail, there was enough public opposition to force Japanese courts to keep the ship firmly anchored in port. Fears that radioactivity would destroy fishing and scallop cultivation brought local people into open, angry protest. Even the government's request to set sail under conventional power and fire the reactor only at sea was not enough.

Finally, in August 1974, the government had had enough. Moriyama Kinji, head of the Science and Technology Agency, announced arrogantly "I will never yield to the pressure of demonstrations and red flags. I consider them 'congratulations' on our departure."

But on 25 August, 300 small fishing boats swarmed around the nuclear ship. While 20,000 people cheered from shore, the fishing people lashed their armada into a giant blockade. When one of them managed to thread a mooring rope through the MUTSU's anchor chain, the ship became an atomic prisoner.

Twelve hours later, Maritime Safety Board patrol boats tried slashing their way through the barricade, only to be beaten back. A tugboat tried hauling the ship out, but the fisherman chopped through the dragline with hatchets.

Finally, at night, rising typhoon winds forced the blockade to disperse. The MUTSU limped out of port, and the fishing people vowed to keep it out.

As the MUTSU proceeded to sea and fired its reactor, three "Banzai" cheers came from the 58-man crew.

But no sooner did it go critical than radioactivity was detected leaking from the top of the reactor. At 1.4% of capacity, the radiation indicator showed .2 milliroentgens, a level expected only at 100% capacity. At that rate the radiation level would have reached as much as 400,000 times the maximum standard.

Technicians soon surmised that the top reactor shield was inadequate to stop fast neutrons, and plugged it with 75 pounds of boron-treated rice balls. Later they filled crew members' socks with polyethylene and covered the reactor with these. Finally, there was no choice but to shut down the reactor. The crew members were now prisoners on a radioactive ship.

Meanwhile, the Mutsu Bay fishing people began laying sand bags at the harbor mouth. The MUTSU drifted

25 August 1974—Small fishing boats blockade the nuclear ship MUTSU. Courtesy of Kyoto News Service.

helplessly for 51 days before an agreement was reached. The ship was then allowed to return on the condition that a new home port be found within six months and the old facilities dismantled. The ship docked safely. At least ten cities then turned down offers to serve as a new home port.

But by mid-1978 plans were under way to move the MUTSU to Sasebo, near Nagasaki, and to use a massive subsidy to the area's depressed shipbuilding industry. Immediately, however, the plan was greeted with mass demonstrations and the threat of another blockade.

The original MUTSU incident poked a big hole in Japan's nuclear credibility. A national opinion poll taken before MUTSU's 1974 cruise revealed that 44% of the Japanese public thought nuclear power "dangerous;" afterwards, the figure had soared to 77%. "The MUTSU fiasco really hurt us," admitted a high Tokyo Electric official. "Our years of efforts to persuade local people have been absolutely shot."

Opposition Spreads

Indeed, strong pockets of resistance forced the government to cut back drastically on the number of new sites for construction and to expect a fight every step of the way. Typical of the struggles is the one in Kashiwazaki, a farming and fishing area on the Japan Sea. Known as Japan's "rice bowl," the region is also noted for its ornamental carp. The lush countryside is dotted with small gardens, thatched roofs, rice paddies and fish ponds. In the fall the leaves of the many hardwood trees become a riot of New England-like color.

In the late 1960s, the Kashiwazaki community invited Tokyo Electric to build at least one reactor five kilometers outside Kashiwazaki City.

Among other things, the company had told them that radioactivity from the plant would aid both rice cultivation and the coloring of the carp!

Construction was to begin in 1972, but local fishing people began holding out for more money for their fishing rights. Meanwhile, radical students from Tokyo appeared in the community to talk about the dangers of nuclear power. The deeply conservative locals at first resented the intrusion, but gradually the new information—and visits from several scientists—began to have an impact.

In the meantime, the company shifted its exact plant site five times. Local concerned citizens grew suspicious and conducted their own geological survey. They found extensive evidence to indicate severe earthquake displacements occurring as recently as 30,000 years ago. Tokyo Electric had claimed the activity was 300,000 years old—apparently a deliberate lie. The plant suddenly became an insult, and the local community has been fighting it—successfully—ever since.

It was also later discovered that right-wing Prime Minister Kauei Tanaka had been involved in shady land dealings at the site, a fact that contributed strongly to his downfall and disgrace.

The story of the Kashiwazaki fight is typical of what has happened to nuclear power in Japan. Reactor orders have been cut way back, and utility companies have been forced to make a serious reevaluation of their nuclear commitments. The original 1985 projections of 60,000 megawatts have been slashed to well below 40,000, and industry critics doubt that even that will be attained.

The industry has not given up, however. Japan is still pressing forward with its plans for a reprocessing facility at Tokai and is still strongly committed to nuclear power.

Indeed, a recent court decision may guarantee even further polarization on the nuclear issue. In August 1973, residents living near the proposed Ikata nuke brought suit against the government in the Matsuyama District Court. Over the course of nearly five years, the suit involved many of Japan's top scientists. It also witnessed a dubious shifting of judges at key points in the trial, so that, as the decision came down in the spring of 1978, at least one key judge had heard only a very small portion of the testimony.

It therefore came as no great surprise to nuclear opponents that the verdict was in favor of continued atomic expansion. "For many people the Ikata decision meant the end of legal channels," says Dr. Sadao Ichikawa, an important scientist in the Japanese movement.

The Ikata case did much to spread popular knowledge about nuclear power. But the decision may lead to an escalating conflict over specific nuclear sites around Japan.

One important factor in the fight may be a small flower, known as the spiderwort. Methods pioneered by Dr. Ichikawa have turned the spiderwort into a highly reliable tool for monitoring emissions from active plants. Ichikawa and co-workers have already used the plant at various locations around the archipelago to produce evidence that some reactors are more dangerous than their owners have been willing to admit. (See pp. 85-87).

At the same time, however, major Japanese corporations have joined in partnership with General Electric and Westinghouse to export reactors and their components to Third World nations.

Like GE and Westinghouse in the U.S., the drastic cutback of domestic reactor orders has forced the Japanese producers to look abroad for nuclear markets.

But the fight in small communities around Japan continues. With the Ikata decision behind them, with a growing network of locally-based struggles like that of Kashiwazaki making it increasingly difficult for the industry to find reactor sites, and with a growing national consciousness of the dangers of atomic energy, nuclear opponents have become increasingly confident of their ability to turn the Japanese nuclear industry into one big MUTSU, under blockade.

Contacts:
Organizations active against nuclear power:
• Gensuikin (Japan Congress Against A- and H-Bombs)
4th floor Akimoto Bldg. 2-19 Tsukasa-cho Kanda, Chiyoda-ku, Tokyo, Japan.
• Jishu-Koza
4-2 3-chome
Asahi-cho
Akishima, Tokyo, Japan
People's Research Institute on Energy and Environment, (Newsletter)
B. Kaikan, Shinjuku 7-26-24
Shinjuku-ku, Tokyo, Japan (160)
• Environmental Book Center, (Newsletter)
1325 Kamoi-cho, Midori-ku
Yokahama, 226, Japan
• NAMAZU Collective, (Newsletter)
2-12-2 Asahimachi, Abeno
Osaka, Japan
Barefoot Gen ("Hadashi No Gen") This is a cartoon story book about a boy called Gen living in Hiroshima at the time of the first atomic bombing. The book has been read by more than 5 million Japanese people. The first volume of 5 has now been translated into English. It is available for $3.80 from: War Resisters League, 339 Lafayette St., New York, N.Y. 10012

AUSTRALIA

Leaders of the anti-uranium movement in Australia head the October 22 march in Sydney. They represent a broad spectrum of groups: the Black Land Rights movement, the Labor Party, Teachers Federation, Railways Union, and others.

Uranium Mining in Australia

Uranium first became an object of interest in Australia in 1944, although the exploration which led up to the discovery of the country's present massive reserves began in 1967. By 1976 it was known that Australia had 27% of the world's "reasonably assured" reserved of uranium.

The first phase of uranium mining in Australia was done to supply the British government's nuclear weapons program. Mines were opened in the Northern Territory, in South Australia and Mary Kathleen in Queensland. Operations were phased out following the 1963 Test Ban Treaty, and the mines closed. The interests involved were subsidiaries of Conzinc Riotinto of Australia (CRA) and a few smaller companies, along with the Australian Atomic Energy Commission (AAEC). CRA is a subsidiary of the London based Rio Tinto-Zinc Corporation (RTZ), which also has uranium interests in the USA, Canada, South Africa and Namibia.

The vast bulk of known uranium reserves lie in a little square about 90 miles wide in the northern part of Australia's Northern Territory. It lies about 136 miles west of Darwin and borders on the Arnhem Land Aboriginal Reserve and the proposed Kakadu National Park. Over 75% of the reserves are contained in the Ranger and Jabiluka deposits. The RTZ, Getty Oil Co., and Canadian firms are among the major owners. The mining companies operating in Australia are represented by two powerful lobbies—the Australian Mining Industry Council and the Australian Uranium Producers Forum.

Uranium mining and waste disposal have been the subject of dispute over the past 20 years. Residues left behind in the Rum Jungle mining complex in the Northern Territory will continue to pollute the local environment for at least 100 years. Waste buried in South Australia was inadequately covered in several places, and there are now proposals for Japan to bury its waste at Yerlirrie in Western Australia, 300 miles north of Kalgoorlie.

Aborigines, the Government's Position, and the Fox Report

The top end of the Northern Territory is the traditional home of several Aboriginal tribes. Past experience has shown that destruction of land vital to the Aboriginal culture and the introduction of alcoholism and prostitution inevitably accompany mining ventures. The Aborigines of the Northern Territory are the only ones who have retained their culture—and 72% of Australian uranium is in this region. Money could not compensate them for the damage mining would do there.

Time To Speak Out—The following are brief excerpts from a statement made by Silas Roberts, then Chairman of the Aborigine Northern Land Council, to the Ranger Uranium Inquiry on 27 May 1976.

> There are too many people who are not Aborigines who speak about us and try to tell the world what we want and what we think. It is time for us to speak out and I do so now after having thought about what I am going to say with other members of my Council who have been a great help to me...

> Aborigines have a special connection with everything that is natural. Aborigines see themselves as part of nature. We see all things natural as part of us...Our connection to all things natural is spiritual. We worship spiritual sites today...

In my travels throughout Australia, I have met many Aborigines from other parts who have lost their culture. They have always lost their land and by losing their land they have lost part of themselves...

If mining has to go on and our government says so, there is not much we can do about it. How can we who follow aboriginal tradition say we will allow anything that hurts our land? But we have always been the ones to move over...

We Aborigines are not so interested in money as white people are. Our main interest is our life style and our culture which of course includes our land...

> "Uranium Deadline"
> *Friends of the Earth*, Vol. 1, #4
> August/September 1976

The Mary Kathleen mine located in Queensland was reopened in late 1974 by a CRA/RTZ subsidiary, but mining was delayed in the Northern Territory by the Labour Government's (1972-75) decision to set up a Commission of Inquiry into the mining proposals of Ranger Uranium Mines Pty. Ltd. in the Northern Territory. The "Fox Commission" under Justice Fox and two other Commissioners was appointed in July 1975. Over 18 months it took in 12,000 pages of transcripts and heard evidence from 160 people. In June 1976, the Commission announced that it would issue two separate reports. The first would deal with the international issues and the question of whether Australia should export its uranium at all. The second would deal with the local issues involved.

The first Fox Commission report appeared in October 1976 and consisted of a carefully detailed discussion of the hazards encountered at each stage of the nuclear fuel cycle, followed by a slightly ambiguous set of 16 findings and recommendations. These were easy to misinterpret and initially some of the media did so by reporting that the Commission had given a "green light" to uranium mining. The Liberal-Country Party coalition government elected in November 1975 certainly saw it that way. Following the second local report, the government ignored the Commission's recommendations for a full-scale public debate, etc., and on 25 August 1977 lifted the four year old ban on uranium mining.

The Commissioners, seeing how the government had misinterpreted the first report, prefaced their final recommendations carefully: "By proceeding as we have done, we have not meant to imply that a decision favourable to uranium development in Australia will or should be made." Justice Fox himself handed down the Second Report stating that it was "not fit for red or green light reporting." Reactions varied. Following publication of the report, the Sydney *Morning Herald* proclaimed "Uranium: Future Still Obscure," *The National Miner* attacked the report, while the *Northern Territory News* proclaimed "August for Uranium Start."

In June of 1977 the Australian Labour Party, the Opposition in Parliament, had passed a resolution calling for an indefinite moratorium on uranium mining. This meant that if they were in power there would be at least a three year delay to allow time for public debate. Following the Fox Commission's Ranger Reports the Labour Party went through a long debate and finally declared itself against any future uranium development in Australia until safeguard problems had been overcome. It added that a future Labour government would not be bound to honor any new uranium contracts entered into by the government under Prime Minister Frazier. However, the Labour Party was defeated in December 1977 national elections, thus forcing a continuing national movement outside of government.

Union Action

Trade Unions have taken stronger stands against nuclear power in Australia than in any other country faced with nuclear related development. In September 1977 the Australian Council of Trade Unions (ACTU) called for a referendum to be held on the issue of uranium mining within a year. This was to be preceded, it said, by a full public debate with both sides being allowed equal amounts of money and access to the media. It should be noted that in passing this resolution, the ACTU came within 60 votes of also calling for an indefinite moratorium. Had that happened, there would now be a complete union ban on the handling (mining, transportation, and loading) of uranium. The unions gave the government two months to make up its mind; meanwhile, they would cooperate with the government by continuing to honor existing contracts. One week before the union ban was due to be imposed, the ACTU announced that it would defer taking any action until after the December election. The majority of the ACTU's Executive Board is pro-uranium, but the Board is ruled by the decisions of the Congress. The referendum proposal was a compromise sought by the right-wing pro-mining lobby to counter the more radical and left-wing support of a total ban on all uranium-related work. Opposition to mining is very strong in the union movement; thus there was no chance of the pro-mining forces winning a straight "yes or no" vote.

In May 1976 the Australian Rail-

June 1977: Anti-uranium demonstrators tried to prevent the loading of 200 tons of yellowcake destined for the U.K. via the U.S.A. 400 people were arrested at this dock at Glebe Island, Sydney.

ways Union (ARU) called a one day strike following a dispute over the handling of sulphur destined for the Mary Kathleen mine. Opposition to uranium mining has also been expressed by the Builders Federation (better known for their "Green Bans"— refusal to work on projects deemed by the union to be ecologically destructive), the Metal Trade Unions and the Waterside Workers.

Following police violence on 2 July 1977 against demonstrators who went to the Melbourne docks to protest the presence of a ship carrying uranium oxide to West Germany, the Victoria branch of the Waterside Workers refused to handle any more ships carrying yellowcake.

The Trade and Labour Councils— union groups—have declared themselves against uranium mining, but not all unions are affiliated to it. Other groups declaring themselves against further uranium mining include the Australian Council of Churches, which has called for a five year moratorium to be accompanied by a full public debate, and environmental groups like the Australian Conservation Federation.

The Movement Against Uranium Mining

Many groups opposed to uranium mining are affiliated with the Movement Against Uranium Mining (MAUM) which was set up in 1974. Local groups usually work with the Friends of the Earth at the state level under a variety of names—the Campaign Against Nuclear Power, Campaign Against Nuclear Energy, Uranium Action Group. In Sydney and Melbourne, feminists have created Women Against Nuclear Energy (WANE) groups. As Australia is such a large country—roughly the same size as the continental U.S., but with a population of under 14 million— organizing is largely focused at the state level and goes on in the main cities and towns. Fully 70% of all Australians live in the ten largest cities, with almost half the population living around Sydney and Melbourne.

Recent efforts have been focused on the demand for a five year moratorium on uranium mining to be accompanied by a fully informed public debate and the setting up of the Campaign Against Mining Aboriginal Land (CAMAL) in Melbourne.

MAUM groups have organized non-violent protests in many cities, focusing strongly on Hiroshima Day, August 6. In April 1977, between ten and twenty thousand people sat down near the offices of CRA in the center of Melbourne. A meeting in Sydney drew 2,000 people. Then in July, 300 demonstrators were brutally assaulted by state police while picketing the docks in

Melbourne. Protests in Sydney in August accompanied Prime Minister Frazier's visit to the university there following his announcement lifting the ban on uranium mining. After the protests he called for files to be kept on demonstrators, but the Labour government of New South Wales said it would not pass on such information to the Federal authorities. Two weeks later street marches were banned in Queensland, one of the country's six states.

On the weekend of Hiroshima Day 1977, 20,000 people marched peacefully in Melbourne; 15,000 in Sydney; 5,000 in Adelaide; 3,000 in Perth. To show how remarkably the movement has grown—two years previously, a Hiroshima Day rally in Sydney was attended by only a dozen people! More demonstrations were held countrywide on October 22, with the government of Queensland arresting 418 of the marchers in Brisbane, including a Senator and several church leaders, for defiance of the newly imposed law banning street marches.

For the past three years there has been a uranium bike ride from Melbourne and Sydney to Canberra, following various routes, spreading the word about the dangers of nuclear power throughout the most heavily populated part of Australia.

In November 1976 an Atom Free Embassy was set up near the two small reactors at Lucas Heights, 23 miles south of Sydney, which have a capacity of 100 and 10 megawatts. The latter has been operating for 18 years now, and the AAEC wants to replace it with a new, larger one. The Atom Free Embassy—a teepee construction—became a form in microcosm of the constructive alternatives to nuclear power, with emphasis on alternative sources of energy, until an unknown arsonist burned it down in May 1977.

FOE Exposes Cartel
The best known action of Friends of the Earth/Australia was probably their publication in August 1976 of documents revealing the existence of a uranium cartel that had been set up in

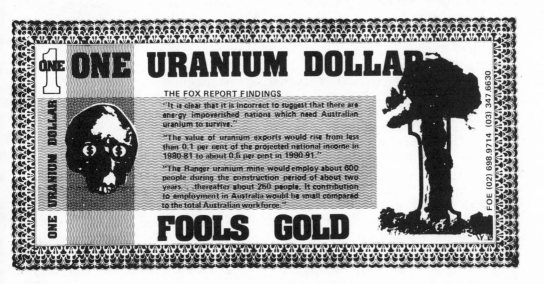

May 1977: Cyclists block bridge in Canberra at end of interstate bicycle ride against uranium mining. More than 1,000 cyclists converged on the city to protest government uranium policies. (Credit: A. Byron)

1973 by three governments and 29 corporations to fix the price of uranium at a higher level than the prevailing $4 per pound. (It was eminently successful—the price rose more than tenfold in four years!)

One consequence of FOE's revelations was a series of anti-trust actions against cartel members initiated by the Westinghouse Corporation in the U.S. after it had to renege on a number of contracts made some years before to supply uranium oxide to customers in the U.S. and Sweden. The company's customers in turn took legal action against Westinghouse for breach of contract. The Australian media—effectively controlled by four men—ignored the leak. It received more attention in North America. The Canadian and Australian governments both passed laws preventing Westinghouse access to documents needed to effectively prosecute the cartel.

The MAUM is probably the largest organization to emerge in Australia since the days of opposition to Australia's active support of U.S. intervention in Vietnam. MAUM's opponents have launched an expensive well-oiled propaganda attack, bringing over a number of pro-nuclear American scientists and speakers as well as Japanese and other delegations. Nevertheless, the debate continues.

It is essential for the success of the movement that links be made with other groups in other countries who are struggling against the spread of nuclear power as well as the proliferation of nuclear weapons. Another important angle is to connect the corporations who are involved in Australia with their other interests in Canada, South Africa and Namibia, and the U.S.—where most of the non-communist world's currently known uranium reserves are located. For example, the Rio Tinto-Zinc Corporation has subsidiaries in Canada (Rio Algom), the U.S. (the Rio Algom Corporation with a mine in Utah), South Africa

(Palabora), Namibia (Rossing Uranium) and Australia (Mary Kathleen Uranium). It is in turn supported by the Anglo-American Corporation of South Africa and Rothschilds Bank in West Europe, besides having interlocking directorates with other banking concerns, mining interests, and insurance groups in those countries where it has subsidiaries.

—from reports by
Peter D. Jones & Alastair Machin
Australia

Update

With strong legislation to protect itself against the opposition of unionists and environmentalists, the Australian government has given the green light for large-scale uranium mining.

Legislation that turns Australia into a police state, as far as opposition to the nuclear industry is concerned, was forced through in June 1978 by Frazier's conservative government. A package of six bills, including the so-called Environmental Protection (Nuclear Codes) Bill restricts civil liberties, imposes secrecy regulations, and erodes the land rights of the Aborigines. And they make inadequate provision for waste disposal and safeguards.

Uranium mining has now been brought under an amended version of the Atomic Energy Act of 1953, a piece of repressive legislation dating from the Cold War period. Trade unionists or environmentalists will now be liable to 12 months in prison or fines of 10,000 Australian dollars for demonstrating or even speaking against the Ranger mining project. The Nuclear Code bill covering all aspects of the nuclear industry officially regulates environmental, health and safety aspects. But it enables the governor-general (representative of the British crown, and aligned with conservative interests) to give ministers sweeping powers to deal with emergency situations.

Over the past two years Australian delegations have been negotiating with the U.K., Federal Republic of Germany, Finland, Japan, U.S., France, Brazil, the Philippines, and the Anglo-German-Dutch URENCO enrichment company. Deals were clinched recently to export uranium valued at $600 million to Finland and the U.K. The simultaneous go-ahead for mining in Australia (and in Canada) plus the planned expansion of URENCO facilities, look like part of a coherent plan.

—World Information Service
on Energy (WISE), No. 2. July 1978

Contacts:

Movement Against Uranium Mining
51, Nicholson St.
Carlton. Victoria. 3065

Movement Against Uranium Mining
277 Brunswick St.
Fitzroy. 3065.

Friends of the Earth
423, Crown St.
Surry Hills. NSW 2010.

Women Against Nuclear Energy
62 Regent St.
Chippendale.

MAUM puts out a journal called *Uranium Deadline*, and the mining issue is also covered in the FOE publication *Chain Reaction*.

Flash:

In September 1978, Galarrwuy Yunupingu, chairman of the Northern Land Council, agreed to requests by six Aboriginal communities to reconsider before signing an agreement opening work at the Ranger uranium mine. This reconsideration will delay mining until sometime in 1979. The government and industry had hoped to begin in July-August 1978.

Brazil

It has not been possible to organize any movement of popular dissent in Brazil against the construction of nuclear plants given the lack of rights to free assembly and free association under Brazil's military regime. Nevertheless, the opposition outside the country has been very effective in this important struggle.

Holland was going to supply Brazil with enriched uranium. In September 1977, various Dutch organizations, together with the Brazilian Committee (which includes Brazilian exiles and Dutch citizens) began to mobilize public opinion against the nuclear agreement. These organizations jointly engaged in a public protest in March 1978 at Almelo, Holland that coincided with the visit of Brazil's president. (See p. 335) Subsequently, the agreement was provisionally suspended.

The Brazilian military regime is now apparently trying to obtain an alternative source of enriched uranium from England. A new campaign has started to mobilize British public opinion.

One of the most active Brazilian exiles is Marcio Moreira Alves, formerly a federal deputy from the opposition party, Movimento Democratico Brasileiro (MDB), and now a professor at the Graduate Institute of Economics in Lisbon. At the Almelo, Holland demonstration, former Representative Moreira Alves gave the following speech:

"Dear Friends:

We have come here today from different parts of Holland, of Europe, and other countries all over the world. In many respects we have different opinions and interests, just as our own origins differ. But we are tied both by a mandate and by fear. We are the self-nominated leaders of the future, of generations yet to be born. We fight for the cause of life, both in the rich societies of the northern hemisphere as well as poor countries of the Third World. And we are afraid.

"As a Brazilian, I would like to speak now about the specific reasons for my presence here today. As you know, the Brazilian military dictatorship negotiated, under the most secret conditions, a long term nuclear agreement with the German Federal Republic. The negotiations were carried out under the strictest security measures, without consulting the people of Brazil. Debate was not allowed before the signing of the agreement, and those who dared to oppose the agreement—mainly scientists and professors—suffered a series of reprisals ranging from being branded as 'traitors' to direct police persecution (action against them).

"As far as Brazilian public opinion can tell, this agreement involves $10 billion to purchase the technology for eight plants to generate nuclear energy, one plant for uranium enrichment, and another one to reprocess the nuclear fuel used in the production of plutonium. These two last plants are referred to, in military jargon, as the 'highly sensitive part of the agreement' since it is the part which will give the Brazilian dictators the capability to produce nuclear arms.

"In the first stage of this nuclear agreement now being implemented is the delivery of two reactors at a cost of 3.7 billion marks, with 2.8 billions earmarked for other equipment. This corresponds to 2.3% of Brazil's GNP, or, three times the amount the government annually allocates to the Ministry of Health.

"These enormous expenditures are essential in order to be able to attend to the needs of the our people. The number of abandoned children in our streets is estimated to have reached 10 million, or the equivalent of the population of Belgium. Infant mortality in Brazil is twelve times that of Holland, and even in cities like Sao Paulo—the richest city in the country—45% of the deaths in the first year of life are directly or indirectly related to hunger. More than 50% of the people in this 'model city of independent industrialization' and approximately 72% of the surrounding municipalities are classified as undernourished. Only 30% of the Sao Paulo area houses are connected to the public sewage system and only 53% have running water.

"Brazilians still die of infantile paralysis, of the bubonic plague, and of smallpox—diseases which, in each case, are perfectly controllable by vaccinations or common medication.

"Not only the most basic human needs of our people continue not to be taken care of because of lack of funds, but recently, some of the needs of national capitalists and foreign investors have been neglected: the construction of a rail line for exporting iron from the mines in the interior of the country to the nearest port at Rio. This project was also suspended for lack of funds.

"At the same time, billions of dollars are detoured for this nuclear adventure. Why? Is it due to the pressure of the demand of energy which can not be supplied from other sources? No. These nuclear plants will be constructed in a country whose hydro-electric resources are more than sufficient to take care of the demands generated by an annual growth rate of 10% (of national industrial output), at least until 1990, and whose gigantic hydro-electric reserves in the Amazon region have not even been appraised.

"From the Brazilian point of view the only justification for this nuclear problem is the acquisition of nuclear capacity for the military. If this were to happen, the immediate consequence

would be the multiplier effect: Just as in the recent past some underdeveloped countries considered the State iron and steel works a sign of national independence, some will consider the atomic bomb a status symbol. Argentina will almost surely be the first, given that they are considerably ahead of Brazil in nuclear technology, and following will be Iran, Pakistan, and Indonesia, etc.

"Arguments in favor of the Brazil-Germany agreement stress the transfer of technology, nuclear shield, and the lack of danger from the plants in relation to the neighboring population and the environment. Each of these arguments is false. Let's begin with the last. It is the intention of the German industries to construct in Brazil the same kind of plants that they could not build in Germany because of opposition...This came from the "Initiative of Citizens" via both legal processes and mass demonstrations. We would be used as their guinea pigs, and further, we are going to pay for that privilege! With regard to the plants themselves, within three years their generating capacity would be reduced 35%; over seven years it would drop 65-70% due to the wearing down of materials exposed to high levels of radiation. In 25 years it would have to be abandoned, thereby creating a permanent and incredible danger of contamination.

"The first Brazilian nuclear energy plant, now almost completely constructed, has been located on top of a geological fault in one of the most beautiful tourist areas of the country.

"Since to date no one knows for sure how to dispose of nuclear waste or what to do with nuclear plants which are no longer operative, it cannot be assumed that in dealing with this imported problem, Brazil will be any more effective in solving these problems that those countries in which public opinion and democratic institutions can exercise some form of control over the capitalists, who are delirious in their desire for profits, and the military, who are thirsting after power.

"In regard to the transfer of technology, the principal reason for our being here today is that this transfer will not take place. The Germans will acquire, thanks to this deal with Brazil, not only the possibility of filling in the technological gap in this field but also independent access to prospecting and exploration. The Brazilians will have only middle-level technicians like the ones who can now operate the local Volkswagon factories, but who are not able to create a new Volkswagon. And they will always and indefinitely depend on the supply of enriched uranium produced here in Almelo. This is why our efforts can prevent it. This is also why we *have* to prevent it."

Nuclear Power in the Philippines

Without final legal approval, construction has begun on a 600-megawatt Westinghouse PWR on the Bataan Peninsula, 45 miles from Manila The plant's cost is an inflated $1.09 billion. The U.S. Export-Import Bank plans a loan of $664 million to finance the deal. This reactor sale has been termed "a textbook case in the dangers of exporting reactors, including health and safety hazards, inappropriate technology, unjust development strategies, potential weapons proliferation, a government subsidy for the reactor industry, human rights violations, and so on." Despite martial law in the Philippines, there is a growing underground movement against this plant. And for good reasons:

• There are an average of 2 earthquakes a day in the Philippines; recent surveys indicate the plant site is *directly* on a fault. Active volcanoes are not far away; fittingly, a major geothermal project is planned near the nuke site. The Bataan area is also subject to typhoons and tidal waves.

• The plant is designed to serve U.S. interests. Indications are strong that the electricity is slated for the U.S. Subic Naval Base, Clark Air Force Base, and the largely U.S.-owned Bataan Export Processing Zone.

• Reactor opponent Ernesto Nazareno was arrested and tortured on 2 May 1978; on 14 June he disappeared and is feared dead. Such human rights violations are common in a country with martial law since 1972 and some 20,000 known political detentions. At hearings on the plant, 50 soldiers stood guard. What sort of public safeguards will be possible in such an atmosphere?

• Westinghouse is now offering the Filipinos a turbine design whose dangers have led to some $200 million in suits here.

• A relative of Dictator Marcos helped negotiate the deal. He's been charged with dubious financial practices; the Dept. of Justice is investigating.

• When asked about the nuclear waste problem, a high Philippine government official responded: "We have plenty of ocean."

(From *Report of the National NO NUKES Strategy Conference*, Louisville KY, 16-20 August 1978.)

Legal interventions and Congressional inquiries concerning this sale have started. For information on how to help stop the sale contact:
Campaign on Runaway Reactors
225 4th St. N.E.
Washington, D.C. 20002 (202-547-1656)

Friends of the Filipino People
553 30th St. #4   11 Garden St.
Oakland CA 94609   Cambridge MA 02138

See: "Scams and Schemes in the Philippines," *Not Man Apart*, May 1978.

Nuclear Power in South Africa

South Africa has the ability to manufacture and launch nuclear weapons. The country has definite nuclear resources and, with the help of the Western powers, has developed the technology to use them. The U.S., the U.K., France and the Federal Republic of Germany (West Germany) have seen nuclear cooperation with South Africa as being in their own best interests. They have helped the South African government to develop its nuclear potential, and have bought from it uranium oxide for their own commercial reactors and nuclear weapons programs.

Together, South Africa and Namibia have an estimated 26% of the world's known uranium reserves. Much of this uranium is in Namibia— formerly known as Southwest Africa, now illegally occupied by South Africa. A number of foreign companies are involved in prospecting there, or are taking part in current production.

Details of South Africa's nuclear potential are hard to track down because under the South African Atomic Energy Act of 1948, all substances containing more than 0.006% uranium are controlled by the government and information is kept under a blanket of strict secrecy.

In the early 1960s, South Africa saw nuclear power as the solution to its energy needs, despite the fact that plants can only be built along the coast because of the large supplies of water needed for cooling. In May 1976, a French consortium was awarded the contract for South Africa's first nuclear power station at Koeberg, 20 miles north of Cape Town on the Atlantic Seaboard. The first unit of the power plant is supposed to be completed in November 1982, the second a year later. U.S. business is also involved in the Koeberg deal, as West-

inghouse (USA) holds 15% of the capital in the French company Framatome.

South Africa says that the electricity generated from these pressurized water reactors will be used to supply energy to industries in the Western Cape that are now dependent on fossil fuel—coal brought from the Transvaal or Natal, a thousand miles away. But South African nuclear development cannot be justified in purely commercial terms. Beside the massive investment required for uranium enrichment, nukes themselves are extremely expensive. Given the country's abundant coal reserves that because of the exploited Black labor sell at the lowest price in the world, a nuke in South Africa costs four times more than a coal-fired power station. Economics alone would not seem to justify a nuclear program.

Foreign expertise has been crucial in South Africa's nuclear research program. The U.S. Atoms for Peace programs helped a lot. A large number of South Africans studied abroad and by 1964 the country had a well-trained corps of nuclear scientists and 83 more South Africans were attending foreign schools—mainly in France, the U.S., and the U.K. Also came American fuel for a research reactor, the SAFARI-1 at the National Research Center at Pelindaba, near Johannesburg.[1]

By 1965, France was a close third behind the U.S. and U.K. in assistance to the South African nuclear program. More recently nuclear cooperation between the two countries has also increased.[2]

South Africa's relations with West German companies in developing its nuclear capacity are, as is the case with France, largely shrouded in secrecy. But German interest in South Africa goes back almost 20 years. Most of the cooperation between the two countries has been in the field of uranium enrichment. Secret documents taken from South African embassy files in Bonn in 1975 revealed that the FRG and South Africa had been cooperating in nuclear matters, particularly enrichment. It seems evident that the FRG is responsible for South Africa's formidable nuclear capacity, with all its military implications.

Since 1962 it has been assumed that South Africa is capable of making an atomic bomb. The country's government has never signed the Nuclear Non-Proliferation Treaty and has made an effort to develop relationships with other non-signatories of the Treaty.[3]

With so much of the world's uranium supplies, South Africa naturally has a number of potential clients. The sole South Africa marketing outlet for the processed uranium oxide is the South African Nuclear Fuels Corporation (NUFCOR), established in 1967 by the uranium-producing gold-mining companies. Present and potential customers for South Africa's uranium are the U.K., France, Iran, Japan, West Germany, and Israel.

Conclusion

"...it is clear that the South African regime hopes to take advantage of its position as a major producer of uranium, and eventually of enriched uranium, to involve the major industrialized countries more closely in the apartheid economy and thereby to strengthen their vested interest in support of the status-quo in South Africa."
—United Nations Special Committee Against Apartheid. Report of Subcommittee on the Implementation of U.N. Resolutions and Collaboration with South Africa 1975.

South Africa has nuclear resources that the Western industrialized powers, Japan, and Iran sorely want. For its part, the South African regime can and is using its uranium and nuclear technology to gain allies off the African continent. But reliance on South African uranium cannot give any country "energy independence."

There is a war going on now in South Africa. As the struggle for freedom and self-determination heightens in the white-ruled country, uranium will continue to be an important international lever for the white regime, and the specter of its nuclear weapons capability may become established fact.

This information edited from a fascinating paper by Peter D. Jones, Australia.

Footnotes

1. The U.S. supplied heavy water (leased) for the SAFARI-1 research reactor, and enriched uranium for a light-water reactor. The ten-year agreement to supply this uranium was renewed in 1967. A special agreement exists between the U.S., South Africa and the IAEA, limiting SAFARI-1 to peaceful uses. South African import of other enriched uranium would cancel the deal.

2. By 1970 the French were supplying South Africa with enriched uranium, but the U.S./South Africa relationship continued.

3. In 1974, the vice-president of the South African Atomic Energy Bureau, Dr. Louw Alberts, repeated that South Africa had the technology and resources to produce an atomic bomb, adding that "our nuclear program is more advanced than that of India." India of course exploded an atomic bomb in 1975.

Convert Rocky Flats
U.S. PROPERTY
NO
TRESPASSING
Rocky Flats Truth Force
Photo: Robert Godfrey
recycled

Chapter 1:

Development of a Movement

Development of a Movement

Inseparable from the growth of a nuclear program has been the movement to stop it.

The movement has taken many forms and adopted many tactics, all with some degree of success. Of late, the headlines have been dominated by mass civil disobedience actions aimed at the physical shut-down of nuclear power plants. These have been organized by groups like the Clamshell Alliance, Abalone Alliance, and others.

But in fact, the anti-nuclear movement dates back to the fifties when citizen groups such as Women's Strike for Peace, SANE and others opposed the government's atomic bomb testing policies. Through letter writing, leafletting, and demonstrations, the anti-bomb groups were able to attract attention to the issue, and are in large part responsible for what limits have been set on nuclear bomb testing throughout the planet.[1]

The government, however, had other plans for the atom. One was the "Plowshare" program, which called for the use of "peaceful" atomic explosions to dig canals, underground storage systems, and other mammoth excavations.

Another, of course, was the use of atomic reactors to generate electricity. By and large, the government and utilities industry had expected to carry on unopposed with plans to dot the map with dozens of reactors. But serious questions about radiation began prompting citizen action, much of it highly effective.

Early Opposition

As early as 1959, for example, a citizens' group called the Massachusetts Lower Cape Committee on Radioactive Waste Disposal forced the AEC to stop illegal dumping of radioactive wastes into the nearby Atlantic. The spot the AEC had chosen was just 12 miles off Boston and 30 from Provincetown, at the tip of Cape Cod. The next year, the group beat back an attempt to build a nuclear waste reprocessing center on Cape Cod. They proved that a "handful of earnest souls" could create a "hurricane."[2]

In 1962, citizens won a victory against New York's mammoth Consolidated Edison, forcing the utility to cancel plans for a nuclear reactor at Ravenswood, Queens, in the heart of one of the most heavily populated cities on earth.[3]

Two years later, residents of northern California forced cancellation of a reactor planned for Bodega Head. Pacific Gas & Electric had already begun excavation on the coastal site when citizens groups demonstrated that the site lay directly above an earthquake fault. The reactor was abandoned, leaving begind a huge hole as a monument to the project.[4]

Also in the early sixties, citizens in rural Pennsylvania successfully fought "Project Ketch," a Plowshare project which would have employed a 24-kiloton bomb to create a deep storage cavern for natural gas. The explosion, which would have occurred under state forest land, was ultimately cancelled.[5] Such explosions did go on in Colorado until passage of a statewide referendum in 1974 (see p. 443).

Also defeated by referendum was a nuclear plant on Oregon's coast. In 1966 the town of Eugene voted in favor of the project, which would be largely financed through the local municipal utility. After a 16-month campaign, however, the town reversed itself and voted to kill the project.[6]

Intervention

By the early 1970s, the issue of nuclear weapons had somewhat faded from the public eye. But widespread construction of atomic power reactors had prompted the birth of hundreds of small energy groups across the U.S. Many were engaged in legal interventions in the AEC's regulatory proceedings which determined the granting of construction permits and operating licenses. It was here many citizens hoped to stop the construction of nuclear plants in their backyard.

Lawyers such as Myron (Mike) Cherry from the Midwest, Gus Speth from the South, David Pesonen of California, Anthony Roisman in Washington, and others took on the AEC and utility legal teams. Intervention organizers such as June Allen of Virginia, Mary Sinclair of Michigan, Diana Sidebotham of Vermont, Judith Johnsrud of Pennsylvania, Irene Dickinson of New York, Kay Drey of Missouri, Dorothy Jones of California, Katherine Quig of Illinois, and Helen Mills of Georgia played key community roles. They had their effect. They forced numerous new safety requirements upon the industry, collected invaluable information on the nuclear question, and got it out to the press. By doing this work, they bought precious time for the general public to consider the implications of atomic construction. Lengthy interventions against the Calvert Cliffs (MD), Vermont Yankee, Indian Point (NY), and Midland (MI) reactors led to a series of legal challenges and precedents that laid the groundwork for all future debate on nuclear energy.

But the interventions had their costs. They were expensive, complex, and technical, virtually incomprehensible to the average citizen. Events often took place in Washington, D.C. hearing rooms, removed from the public eye. Citizen groups that formed to support the legal challenges found themselves in a constant struggle to raise the tens of thousands of dollars that a legal intervention can demand.

Partly due to the demands of the process, intervention groups tended to be mainly middle-class, with educated, professional people involved. Most of these efforts were spearheaded by women, many of whom continue to play leading roles in the movement today. But because of its expense and the limitations of its forum, legal intervention tended away from general public participation. The proceedings were demanding, lengthy, specialized and usually went on during the day, thus preventing the participation of most working people.

Although intervenors had succeeded in making the anti-nuke case, and in slowing down the industry juggernaut, the process seemed incapable of bringing it to a halt. After all, judge and jury were first the AEC, which had been designed to promote as well as regulate the industry, and then the Nuclear Regulatory Commission, which has *never* denied a domestic construction permit.

As the struggle escalated, intervenors from around the country began to coordinate their efforts, and a movement began to grow, helped along by several dedicated people who travelled great distances to spread the word about the problems of nuclear power.

Citizen Activists

One such activist was Leo Goodman, first Secretary of the United Auto Workers' (UAW) Atomic Energy Committee. A close friend of Walter Reuther, Goodman had coordinated the UAW intervention against the Fermi I fast breeder reactor. Goodman labored for many years at the UAW's Washington office, building up extensive files on the AEC and atomic industry, the first of their kind outside of corporate headquarters.

Another key anti-nuclear pioneer has been Larry Bogart, editor for years of the newsmonthly *Nuclear Opponents.* In the early days he was one of the very few citizens who questioned in print the benefits of the "peaceful atom."

And Dr. Ernest Sternglass. A University of Pittsburgh professor, Sternglass became a nuclear opponent when he discovered—in the midst of doing some industry-sponsored research—that there were concrete links between atomic energy and the incidence of cancer, leukemia, and birth defects. When he went public with his findings, the industry attacked him, and has been on the assault ever since. Stern-

glass, said one writer in 1971, "is one of the most vigorously refuted and generally maligned critics that the AEC has ever had—and the most influential."[7]

In 1969, Drs. Gofman and Tamplin were having their run-in with the AEC hierarchy (see pp. 17-19). They soon took their discoveries about radiation and health to the public, which prompted still more activity among citizens' groups increasingly concerned about the accelerating spread of reactors. For by the early seventies, reactor orders had reached the level of some 30 per year.

In the midst of that rapid expansion, the AEC held lengthy "rule-making" hearings on the controversial emergency core cooling system. The hearings were largely brought about by the efforts of Dr. Henry Kendall of the Union of Concerned Scientists. He in turn involved consumer advocate Ralph Nader, who soon leapt to the forefront of the anti-nuclear drive. Nader's student-based "Public Interest Research Groups" went on to lay crucial groundwork in public education and state-level lobbying. In 1974 Nader convened the first national anti-nuclear gathering, "Critical Mass '74," held in Washington, D.C. Subsequent conferences were held in 1975 and 1978.

Meanwhile, the nuclear issue had split apart the nation's oldest environmental group, the Sierra Club. In the early sixties David Brower, then president of the prestigious 200,000-member organization, left after it refused to take a firm stand against atomic energy. In 1975, the Sierra Club finally did formally oppose nuclear power plants. But in the meantime, Brower had formed Friends of the Earth. FOE took a strong anti-nuclear line and became instrumental in developing a world-wide network of ecology activists.

Another group of broad scope was National Intervenors (NI), a coalition formed in the early seventies and active during the ECCS hearings. Functioning as a clearinghouse for nuclear and legislative information, the NI counted some 130 member groups by 1974.[8]

But by the time of Nader's 1974 Critical Mass conference, impatience was growing over the legal intervention process. In the spring of that year, Sam Lovejoy had toppled a 500-foot utility weather tower in Montague, MA (see pp. 393-395) as an act of civil disobedience against proposed nuclear construction there. That act was no secret to the 1,200 participants at Critical Mass. Their tolerance for the AEC as judge and jury in atomic matters was already wearing thin. New tactics were clearly on their way.

Citizen Initiatives

The key in many activists' minds was taking the case directly to the public rather than relying on a court of government and industry "experts." One tool for "going to the people" became the citizen initiative, a legislative process legal in 17 states, most of them in the West. Through this process, laws can be passed by referendum vote. Grassroots organizers decided it was time to take the case to the people.

In 1972, Joyce and Ed Koupal, citizens of southern California, put a Clean Environment Act initiative on the state ballot. The bill included a five-year moratorium on atomic construction. It was defeated 2 to 1, a setback which Koupal attributed to the use of the word "moratorium," which had "negative connotations" in the public mind because of the Vietnam war. Others attributed the defeat to lack of time for general education, and to the extraordinary amounts of money poured in by the industry.

In 1974, nuclear opponents in western Massachusetts did substantially better. That November they questioned voters in three Connecticut Valley counties on proposed twin reactors at Montague. In winning 47.5% of the vote they stunned even their supporters, who had anticipated a far lower anti-nuclear showing at such an early stage of opposition. In addition, some 33% of the voters registered their willingness to dismantle reactors operating nearby at Rowe, MA and Vernon, VT, the first such vote taken in the U.S. Observers had predicted a 10% showing at best on that controversial proposal.

In 1976, nuclear opponents stepped up their initiative efforts. In the spring, another nuclear initiative went onto the ballot in California. This bill called for a complex series of health and environmental restrictions on reactor operation. The proposal was defeated publicly, 2 to 1. In the fall, similar resolutions went onto the ballot in Arizona, Oregon, Washington, Montana, Colorado, and Ohio. Though pre-election polls showed nuclear opponents "substantially ahead" in Oregon, Washington, and Colorado, all six initiatives went down to defeat, losing in Oregon 56-42, in Montana 60-40, and by 2 to 1 and more in the other four states.

As usual the industry poured in millions of dollars, which analysts cited as a major factor in the outcome. "In all cases," commented *New Age* magazine, "the industry poured in from ten to one hundred times as much money as the proponents had to spent. In all cases they protrayed the proposed reforms as being a blanket ban on nuclear construction, and went to great expense to convince the electorate that the bills would cost them jobs and money."[9]

But nuclear opponents were also

forced to realize that there were other causes for their defeat beyond being outspent, reasons that focused on economic issues. Dr. Gofman, in an article entitled "But Did They Really Want To Win?" that appeared in *Mother Jones* magazine soon after the referendum, criticized the propositions for being unclear and contradictory in their meaning. The initiatives focused on health and safety reforms which were often difficult to understand. In some cases, voters were shown to have voted against the initiative falsely thinking that they were casting a vote against nuclear power. Proposition 15 supporters claimed that the nuclear industry could meet the safety requirements—that there could be "safe nuclear power." The movement would have done better, said Gofman, to make the vote a clear yes-no choice on atomic energy.

At the same time, he said, the economic implications of the issue had been ceded to the industry, which claimed loudly that stopping atomic power would cost the public jobs, blackouts, and higher electric bills. "With a combination of facts, half-truths and outright lies," said Gofman, "industry effectively hammered out a case aimed at the average voter's economic self-interest." The key to stopping nuclear power, Gofman said, was to build an anti-nuclear case "for both safety reasons and economic ones."[10]

CWIP Clipped

Gofman's criticisms were borne out by the CWIP vote in Missouri. While the anti-nuclear initiatives were going down to defeat, Missouri voters were opposing nuclear construction—on economic grounds—by a margin of 2 to 1. The Missouri initiative opposed Construction Work in Progress (CWIP), a billing procedure by which utilities charge consumers for construction projects *while they are being built.*

Missouri utilities claimed that without CWIP, nuclear construction would be essentially halted.[11]

But Kay Drey of the Citizens for Reformed Electric Rates and a host of anti-nuclear activists were able to use the referendum to question the economic benefits of atomic energy. Why, they asked, if atomic energy was so cheap, did utilities have to charge for it even before the plants were built?

The voters responded overwhelmingly and banned CWIP from Missouri, with the resulting cancellation of at least one reactor. The issue has caught on elsewhere. As the huge amounts of capital needed to build reactors have become increasingly difficult to find, utilities have been forced to request CWIP rate hikes. And the anti-nuclear movement has used the issue. In New Hampshire, for example, CWIP rates used to build the Seabrook plant have become a hot political issue thoughout the state, and were a major issue in the 1978 gubernatorial race. Because of popular pressure, the state legislature voted in Spring '78 to ban CWIP. The ban was vetoed by Gov. Meldrim Thomson, a strong supporter of the plant. At some point, observers say, either Thomson will be gone or the legislature will override the veto. Then construction at Seabrook could come to a grinding halt.

Local Votes

Meanwhile, the initiative process has also met with some success—but on the local level. In March of 1978, voters in Kern County, California, overwhelmingly rejected plans for a reactor complex in the town of Wasco. The county had gone 2 to 1 against the 1976 anti-nuclear Proposition 15. But when it came to having reactors in their backyard, local voters were not so anxious to allow nuclear development to go ahead. Their vote effectively killed the project.

Within two months, California was experiencing a *de facto* moratorium. In 1976, just prior to the Proposition 15 vote, the state legislature had moved to undercut the referendum by passing three bills aimed at nuclear safety. Designed to preempt anti-nuclear sentiment in the state, one clause of the bills called for a halt to further nuclear construction unless the nuclear waste problem were solved.

Just after the 1978 Kern County vote, nuclear proponents moved to get an exemption from the 1976 ordinance. The San Diego Gas & Electric Company was anxious to move forward with a reactor project at Sundesert, on the Arizona border. The company felt rising costs were making time run out for the project, and it demanded an exemption so that construction could proceed.

But the Kern County vote, coming as it did in one of California's most conservative areas, indicated a strong tide against nuclear power. In its wake, moves to exempt the Sundesert project died. And with Sundesert went the last firm near-term plans for new nuclear construction in California. Although the two anti-nuclear referenda had been defeated, they had nonetheless helped to raise enough questions and enough legal barriers to nuclear construction to indirectly bring about a halt to new atomic proliferation within the state.

Direct Action

But the process had been slow and expensive, and it had no effect on reactors already near completion. For that, the movement would have to find new tactics.

In February 1975, some 28,000 West German, French and Swiss nuclear opponents overran a nuclear site at Wyhl, on the West German side of the Rhine River. Construction was blocked. The action inspired nuclear opponents throughout the world. It seemed that by force of numbers, nonviolent direct action might succeed as a "last resort" against nuclear power where intervention and referenda had failed.

In August 1976, the first American occupiers marched onto the Seabrook construction site. Three weeks later, their numbers had grown to 180. Then in April, 1977, more than 2,000 Clamshell occupiers marched onto the site, where construction had now started in earnest. By this time, occupations were also in the works at Diablo Canyon, California, where twin reactors were 99% complete, and at Trojan, in Oregon, where the nation's largest single reactor was already in operation.

By this time also the movement against nuclear weapons was reviving and began to play an important role in anti-nuclear activities. The Philadelphia-based Mobilization for Survival—founded in 1977, called for the "funding of human needs" through a halt to nuclear power and weapons development. During the 1977 August 6-9 "Hiroshima and Nagasaki Days" the Mobilization joined the Eastern Federation of Nuclear Opponents and Safe Energy Proponents in a broad grassroots effort, coordinated through the "telephone grapevine." The anniversary was marked by more than 100 simultaneous demonstrations and balloon releases at nuclear sites throughout the U.S. It was the first coordinated nationwide grassroots action atomic reactors and weapons in U.S. history.

At the same time, important breakthroughs were being made with organized labor. Through the efforts of groups such as the Washington-based

Environmentalists for Full Employment (EFFE), a new rapport began to develop between environmentalist groups and unions. EFFE's 1977 pamphlet *Jobs and Energy* was widely circulated. It documents the claim that conservation, recycling and solar energy offer better hope for the employment picture than atomic energy.

The study and organizational work done by EFFE, Sun Day '78, Barry Commoner, and others, paved the way for possible labor-environmentalist coalitions. In 1977, for example, EFFE coordinated the endorsement of the AFL-CIO's long-fought for Labor Law Reform Act by more than two-dozen leading environmentalists and groups. Grassroot organizations such as the Clamshell Alliance gave support for striking miners during the '77-'78 winter's national coal strike and endorsed the J.P. Stevens boycott, local strikes and other key union efforts. The opposition to the Barnwell reprocessing plant has supported and worked with striking farmers.

In response, local union chapters are increasingly open to nuclear opposition arguments. Internationals such as the UAW, Sheetmetal Workers, and Machinists Union have become strong proponents of solar energy.

By early 1978, the years of organizing and coalition-building were bearing fruit. In the spring, major civil disobedience actions at the Barnwell-Savannah River weapons-waste facility in South Carolina, and the Rocky Flats plutonium factory in Colorado, drew hundreds of participants and national media coverage.

A Clamshell rally on June 25 drew more than 18,000 members of the general public, making it the largest U.S. anti-reactor action ever. The turnout, which included representatives from organized labor, over-whelmed even its organizers.

And even more dramatically, the action at the site was followed by another occupation—this one starting three days later at the Nuclear Regulatory Commission, which was in the process of evaluating a suspension in construction at Seabrook. After a dramatic three-day action, in which some 250 nuclear opponents camped on the street in front of the NRC (fifty were arrested in a non-violent "die-in" during the occupation), the Commission decided to suspend construction at the site.

The suspension brought the anti-nuke movement full circle. The decision was clearly the culmination of years of hard work by legal intervenors and their supporters. When the ecstatic NRC occupiers danced in the Washington street following the NRC decision to suspend construction, they danced for both legal intervention and direct action.

The victory, however, proved temporary as most knew it would. The Public Service Company of New Hampshire (PSCo) was badly hurt both politically and financially by the halt. But within three weeks, the NRC (with EPA help) had voted to allow construction to start again.

Meanwhile, hundreds of additional arrests had occurred at Diablo Canyon, Trojan, the Satsop reactor under construction in Washington, and at the Bailly construction site in Indiana.

The Politics of Direct Action

Although to some extent the growth of a direct-action oriented wing of the anti-nuclear movement was a logical outgrowth of the disappointments and frustrations of intervention and legal action, there were important differences between the new activists and the earlier intervenors. The differences were in background, political orientation, and ways of organizing to 'get the job done.'

In the mid to late 70s, as the nuclear program spread across the country, people who had been politically active in the late 60s began to get involved in the nuclear issue. The new nuclear opponents found the same kinds of cover-ups, lies, vested corporate interests and inhumanity involved in nuclear power as in the war issue. In fact, nuclear power seemed in many ways to be "the Vietnam war brought home." By aiding the nuclear industry while assuring the public it had nothing to fear, the government was supporting an energy source that could prove as lethal as any war.

One important lesson learned during the Vietnam war days was that citizen action—at all levels—does bring change. And the way that people act has a lot to do with the kind of change they'll get.

The large Vietnam-era actions were most often organized by a small group of men; people were then asked to join as "the masses." Although the huge anti-war demonstrations had immense effect, it was to a large degree the daily work of thousands of people across the country doing the less glamerous leafletting, speaking, filmshowing, etc. that made them possible and helped turn the tide of public opinion against the Vietnam involvement.

Both the anti-war movement and the earlier civil rights movement demonstrated the power of individual and especially collective civil disobedience. It was this tactic that broke through racist barriers in the South and "raised the social cost" of the Vietnam War to the point where policymakers had to take notice.

A New Consciousness

The anti-nuclear movement has always attracted women, who are angered and moved to action by the dangers presented by nuclear power.

Most intervention efforts have been organized by women. As the direct action oriented groups and alliances formed, women were naturally involved there too. The new groups stress democratic decision-making and open participation. They are consciously non-sexist and non-hierarchical. Responsibilities are shared, with no elected "officers" or designed leadership. People who do the work make decisions, and, given varying (volunteer) time commitments, people share the organizational work and direction setting.

To work towards this democracy, Alliances organized themselves with care, encouraging maximum participation from all involved. Some techniques used at meetings have included: rotating facilitators rather than permanent chairpersons; breaking into small groups to discuss questions before coming to a decision; consensus-decision-making; evaluation sessions following meetings. Agenda may be drawn up by a designated group in advance, with times allotted by meeting members according to the importance or immediacy of an issue. Sometimes a meeting will decide that everyone present must have a chance to speak on an issue before anyone can speak for the second time.

Affinity Groups

Organization by affinity groups has evolved as one important way to insure maximum participation and group support. The term comes from the Spanish Civil War era (1936-1940) when small "grupos de afinidad" were the basic form of Anarchist organization. But small groups have U.S. roots too. Their use has long been practiced by the Quakers and American Friends Service Committee.

Organizing affinity groups is a way of getting things done while paying attention to group process and internal dynamics. Groups are large enough to feel strong and active, small enough to give people a chance to participate more or less equally.

The methods of organization that have been adopted and developed by the anti-nuclear movement in the new direct action alliances do not pretend to solve the problems of sexism, dominance and authoritarianism that are such an integral part of our society. But they are an expression of intent and interest in building a society where people do not dominate and abuse either nature or each other.

Support and Solidarity
The anti-nuclear movement is evolving politically, with increased understanding of the economic, political and social system that has brought us nukes. As this awareness grows, so will the possibility for increased cooperation and solidarity with people working for change in different areas. At this point some outreach has been made to organized labor, but little to the unemployed as a group. Feminist and health organizations should become close allies in the fight against nuclear power. The elderly have their own needs; a reorientation of the economy away from weapons and nuclear power plants towards immediate social needs would help them too.

Since the U.S. anti-nuke movement grew up in rural America, connections with U.S. Black and Third World urban groups are weak. In early 1977 the National Association for the Advancement of Colored People (NAACP) came out with a declaration of support for nuclear power and expanded gas and oil exploration, a stand cheered on by Mobil Oil, among others. The NAACP's statement was a real shock to anti-nuke environmentalists. They

then made a big effort to reach members of NAACP groups and others in the Black community, talking about the dangers of nuclear power, the cost and job advantages of conservation and alternative energy. The incident showed that the anti-nuclear movement has to address the needs and interests of all U.S. citizens.

Civil Disobedience
It is important that the anti-nuke movement involve people coming from different places in our society. Some organizers have expressed fear that direct action tactics like site occupations are alienating to many working and older people who cannot participate in an extended illegal act. But for now, "CD" is seen by many others as a fruitful tactic which has the necessary support of thousands of citizens among the general population. For every citizen willing to occupy, the movement can claim hundreds of supporters. Thus far, the direct action wing has been self-disciplined with a strong and growing commitment to civil disobedience. None of the now thousands of arrests at nuclear sites around the U.S. have been marred by violence and serious injuries.

The citizen commitment to stopping nuclear power faces the prospect of almost infinite growth. Should legal remedies ultimately fail and nuclear construction continue, it seems inevitable that the number and size of direct actions against the institutions that support it will grow.

Moving On
In the movement against nuclear power, direct actions are really the "tip of the iceberg." People are opposing nuclear power in a variety of ways that spread the truth about this source of energy. For the "movement" is just that—a movement of ideas,

information, resources and activities all around the country and the world. Through coordinated and diversified action, groups and individuals are proving once again that we have the power to change the course of human events.

In the following chapter, Up From the Grassroots, we will hear from a very few of the many U.S. groups that are actively working for a non-nuclear future. Their stories reflect the differences and similarities, strengths and weaknesses of our movement. Together they reflect the spirit, energy, dedication, and perseverence of the citizen-in-action against atomic energy.

Footnotes

1. Ruth Rae, "Women Against Nukes, An Old Story," *Workbook on Nuclear Power*, (Cultural Workers' Collective, Box 302, N. Amherst, Mass. 01059. $3.75.)

2. Jane Sherman Lehac, "Eve's Fight Against the Atom," *Poughkeepsie Journal*, 17 November 1974.

3. Richard Curtis and Elizabeth Hogan, *Perils of the Peaceful Atom*, (New York: Ballantine Books, 1969), pp. 125-126.

4. Lynton K. Caldwell, Lynton R. Hayes, Isabel M. MacWhirter, *Citizens and the Environment: Case Studies in Popular Action*, (Bloomington, Ind. and London: Indiana Univ. Press, 1976), pp. 195-204.

5. Richard S. Lewis, *The Nuclear-Power Rebellion*, (New York: Viking Press, 1972), p. 207-220.

6. Caldwell, Hayes, MacWhirter, *op. cit.*, pp. 204-210.

7. Lewis, *op. cit.*, p. 60.

8. *National Intervenors Newsletter*, September 1974.

9. "Six States Reject Nuclear Safeguards Initiatives," *New Age*, December 1976, p. 8.

10. John W. Gofman, "But Did They Really Want to Win?" *Mother Jones*, February/March 1977.

11. One critic has said that CWIP "is analogous to having General Motors require you to start paying for your new car 5 to 10 years before you receive it." *New York Redbook 1975*, (Albany, NY: Williams Press, 1976), pp. 919-920. From "Nuclear Energy, Rockefeller, and Big Business," Peter Salmansohn, Masters Thesis, June 1976, p. 81, with thanks.

Resist Nuclear Madness!

Rocky Flats Truth Force

Chapter 2:
Regional Reports: Up From the Grass Roots

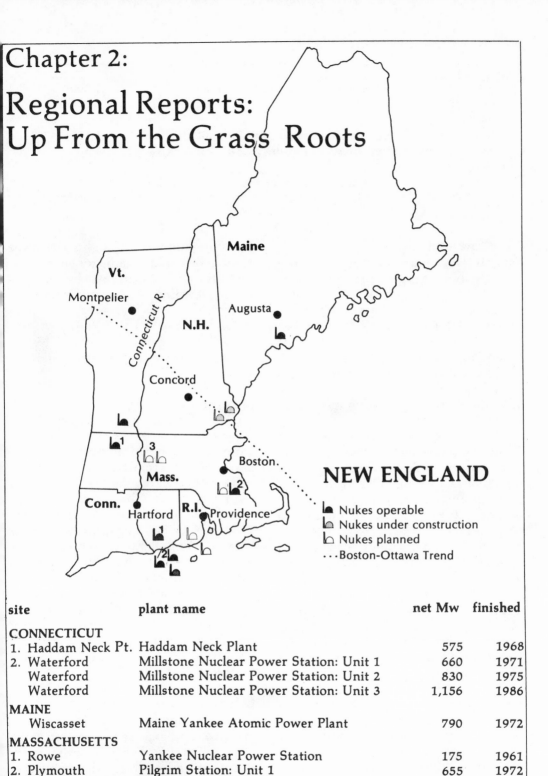

Maine

Vt.

Montpelier

Connecticut R.

N.H.

Augusta

Concord

Mass.

Conn.

Hartford

R.I.

Providence

Boston

NEW ENGLAND

Nukes operable
Nukes under construction
Nukes planned
···Boston-Ottawa Trend

site	plant name	net Mw	finished
CONNECTICUT			
1. Haddam Neck Pt.	Haddam Neck Plant	575	1968
2. Waterford	Millstone Nuclear Power Station: Unit 1	660	1971
Waterford	Millstone Nuclear Power Station: Unit 2	830	1975
Waterford	Millstone Nuclear Power Station: Unit 3	1,156	1986
MAINE			
Wiscasset	Maine Yankee Atomic Power Plant	790	1972
MASSACHUSETTS			
1. Rowe	Yankee Nuclear Power Station	175	1961
2. Plymouth	Pilgrim Station: Unit 1	655	1972
Plymouth	Pilgrim Station: Unit 2	1,180	1984
3. Montague	Montague: Unit 1	1,150	1988
Montague	Montague: Unit 2	1,150	1990

NEW HAMPSHIRE			
Seabrook	Seabrook Nuclear Station: Unit 1	1,200	1983
Seabrook	Seabrook Nuclear Station: Unit 2	1,200	1985
RHODE ISLAND			
Charlestown	New England Power (NEP): Unit 1	1,150	1984
Charlestown	New England Power (NEP): Unit 2	1,150	1986
VERMONT			
Vernon	Vermont Yankee Generating Station	515	1972

New England

The six New England states are in a very serious energy squeeze. This is reflected in the region's electric rates which average the highest in the nation outside of New York City. In recent years, imported oil has met 88% of New England's energy needs, compared to 43% for the rest of the nation. New England alone is now importing 40% of all the oil brought into this country.

The only known coal deposits in the region lie underneath cities and populated areas, making them environmentally and socially disastrous to remove in any quantity. Test drilling for oil and natural gas has been launched off the New England coast, but presents its own environmental problems, including disruption of rich fishing grounds.

The Northeast has energy needs different from other regions. For example, 40% of New England's energy is used for staying warm—residential and commercial space heating—as opposed to 13% for the rest of the nation.

But New England is rich in alternative sources of energy: wood, small-scale hydro, mountain and offshore wind. Even in New England, solar energy could provide 40-60% of a building's annual heat requirements.

Individuals, especially in northern New England, are increasingly turning to wood heat to defray skyrocketing winter heating bills, and a few communities and industries have retooled old hydro dams for electricity.

In the mid-50s, private electric utilities in New England became interested in atomic power. The second commercial nuke in the U.S. was Yankee Atomic, a 185-megawatt plant in Rowe, Massachusetts, that came on-line in 1960. The utility group that built the Rowe plant went on to invest in other nukes in the region.

The six-state region is around 35% dependent on electricity generated from the seven operable plants. Three more nukes are under construction and five more are planned, including a twin-reactor at Charlestown, Rhode Island, site of a defunct Naval Station. That project has sparked controversy because the federal General Services Administration turned the site over to the private utility without public hearings or an impact statement. Federal lands are supposed to first be offered to other government departments and the Department of the Interior was interested in making the old Naval Station a bird sanctuary!

Intervention—Vernon

Organized opposition to nuclear power in New England began in February 1971, when citizens and scientists from Vermont and western Massachusetts formed the New England Coalition on Nuclear Pollution (NECNP). Based in Brattleboro, Vermont, the group raised money to hire regulatory law expert

Anthony Roisman to intervene in operating licensing hearings for the Vermont Yankee plant.

The intervention resulted in some safety additions to the plant. The most important was the year-round use of cooling towers (recently modified to allow once-through use of the Connecticut River for plant cooling in winter, over NECNP/citizen protest).

Despite the intervention, Vermont Yankee went on-line in 1973 under a unique "temporary" operating license made possible by special Congressional action pushed by former Vermont Senator Aiken.

However, appeals and questions initiated by NECNP continued through the court process. The group and the state of Kansas joined a Natural Resources Defense Council (NRDC) case that has heavy implications for the nuclear industry. The NRDC and others challenged Vermont Yankee's lack of plans for permanent disposal of radioactive waste. They held that numerical values assigned by the NRC to represent the effects of the uranium fuel cycle were incorrect and did not reflect the true health dangers. In the summer of 1976, the Washington D.C. District Court of Appeals ruled in their favor, and for over two months all licensing of new nuclear plants was suspended. Although the Supreme Court overturned the Court of Appeals ruling and licensing was reinstated, the high court sent the question back to the lower court. **In late 1978-early 1979, the Court of Appeals will consider the whole question of uranium fuel cycle health effects, to determine if the NRC's calculations are right. If the court finds the NRC has been inaccurate (and it should, since the effects of radon gas have been grossly underestimated), the license of every nuclear plant in the country is in jeopardy. New hearings could be called plant by plant to examine their health effects in terms of the entire nuclear fuel cycle.**

Other appeals are still pending, but the Vernon nuke continues operation—more or less. The plant has been shut down repeatedly, including 19 times during its first 17 months of operation. It has suffered faulty fuel rods, a cracked torus (see Dictionary), and releases of radioactive material—including the accidental dumping of 83,000 gallons of tritium-contaminated waste water into the Connecticut River in summer 1976.

Despite its record of shutdowns, Vermont Yankee today is actually one of the most efficient plants in the country, according to its official annual production of power record.

Direct Action—Montague

On the last day of 1973, Northeast Utilities (NU), a Connecticut-based holding company of private utilities and a few small municipalities, officially announced their plans to build a twin 1150-megawatt nuke at Montague. This rural town in western Massachusetts is just 30 miles east of the old Rowe plant and 15 miles south of Vermont Yankee.

After learning of NU's plans, some Montague residents formed NOPE, Nuclear Objectors for a Pure Environment, in the fall of 1973. Then two months after NU's "Christmas present" announcement came a dramatic direct action against nuclear power. On 22 February 1974, Washington's Birthday, organic farmer Sam Lovejoy took a crowbar to the support structure of a weather-monitoring tower NU had put up at the site. With its bright blinking lights, the 550-foot tower symbolized the impending nuke. Lovejoy felled 349 feet of the tower and turned himself in to the local police. He presented a statement in which he took full responsibility for the action.[1]

KENTUCKY DILLS

ORGANIC CRASHING TOWER PICKLES

In an unusual support/education action, friends of Lovejoy packed and sold 2,000 quarts of organically grown dill pickles. The back label carried a message of nuke dangers and Sam's action.

Lovejoy went on trial in September 1974 on charges of malicious destruction of personal property, a felony that could mean five years in jail. He presented expert witnesses to testify to the dangers of nuclear power and the legitimacy of civil disobedience. The packed nine-day trial ended with the judge ordering acquittal because of a "faulty indictment" (the tower was "real" instead of "personal" property, meaning the charge should have only been a misdemeanor, not a felony).

Although the jury was deprived of most of the expert testimony, it was learned after the trial that Lovejoy would have been found "not guilty," since jury members said they had been convinced his action was not "malicious." Lovejoy's action galvanized local public opinion and demonstrated that not everyone thought the planned nuke was a good idea. Nuclear power had become a controversial issue.

Soon after the tower was felled, NOPE founded the Nuclear Objectors (NO) Party. A slate of candidates—including Sam as a town meeting member—ran in May for Montague Town offices on an anti-nuclear platform. Their 7½% of the vote showed a core of committed opposition, which was to grow.

In June the Franklin County AEC (Alternative Energy Coalition) formed to oppose construction at Montague, taking the issue from the town to the county level. On Hiroshima Day August 6, this "new" AEC launched a signature drive to put two nonbinding referenda questions on the fall '74 ballot. Door-to-door canvassing helped spread public awareness of the issue. People began to realize that you didn't have to live on top of a nuke to be affected by it, and that you didn't have to be a physicist to understand the problems of nuclear power.

In the November 1974 elections, 47½% of the voters in the State Senatorial District opposed nuclear construction at Montague and 33½% said yes to dismantling the other plants! The group went on to sponsor a variety of public meetings and actions and opened an office for public information and resources on nuclear and solar energy. (Several years later NU opened its own local "nuclear information office," complete with green and white GO NUKES bumperstickers. Business has been notoriously slow.)

The day after Lovejoy's acquittal, NU announced a one-year delay in construction plans. Six months later—on the first anniversary of the tower toppling—came a second delay, for three more years. Then, in the spring of 1977—with state and federal hearings on site suitability nearing and a low-cost, high-energy citizen intervention campaign in full swing—NU delayed the project four more years.

The utility had just been refused about two-thirds of a $90 million rate hike by the Connecticut Public Utilities Commission. The PUC harshly advised NU to sell its stock in Seabrook (12%) and cancel Montague. Along with NU's financial problems, its excess electric generating capacity and reduced electric growth demand projections contributed to the postponing of the Montague project.

No Nukes in Seabrook

Meanwhile, an intervention battle was going on in New Hampshire's seacoast, where plans for another twin 1150-megawatt nuke were well underway. Intervenors in the Seabrook plant licensing included the N.H. Audubon Society, the Seacoast Anti-Pollution League (SAPL), the N.H. Society for the Protection of Forests, NECNP, and several individuals. According to the Audubon Society "there probably isn't a worse place in the United States for building a nuclear plant than the Seabrook site."

The 715-acre site is a rock outcropping in a delicate marshy estuary, the breeding grounds for birds and marine life and the location of an ancient Chumash cemetery. The cooling tunnels of the planned nuke would suck in a billion gallons of ocean water a day and return it to the ocean 30° F hotter. This issue became the main environmental argument against the plant and has led to repeated postponements of its construction.

Directly north and south of the site are bathing beaches that attract up to 100,000 people on summer weekends. The only access road is a two-lane highway. Quick evacuation in case of an accident would be a cruel joke.

When first proposed in 1968, the plant carried a price tag of under $900 million. By 1978 it was to cost at least $2.5 billion, more than three times the worth of the "Public Service" Co. (PSCo) of N.H., 60% owner and main sponsor of the plant. Initial company promises that the plant would mean no new rate hikes were forgotten by 1978 when PSCo received a $32 million rate hike, the largest in its history, much of it to help finance the nuke's construction. But intervenors showed that PSCo didn't need the power—rather it was for the New England grid and New York City.

The site is also near Boston-Ottowa fault lines. A local resident, Dolly Weinhold ("Earthquake Dolly") became interested in this aspect and presented evidence at licensing hearings that led to the strengthening of the plant. But despite extensive evidence presented on these points and more, the NRC's Atomic Safety and Licensing Board granted PSCo a conditional construction permit at the end of June 1976. The condition was final Environmental Protection Agency approval of the controversial cooling system, an approval that later was first denied, then awarded, then challenged by a court ruling and finally approved again.[2]

Enter Clamshell

Within days of the licensing decision, around 40 people from New Hampshire and Massachusetts anti-nuke groups, local citizens, and other interested individuals met on the New Hampshire seacoast. Since the NRC's approval had shown once again that the licensing of nukes was rigged, the group discussed more direct forms of political action, including civil disobedience.

The group named itself the Clamshell Alliance, wrote a Founding Statement, and made plans for education and protests against the plant.

Inspired by the citizen occupation that had blocked construction in Wyhl, West Germany, the Clams planned a first civil disobedience action for 1 August. Members of the fledgling Alliance did not expect thousands of people. But they did hope that their action would be the start of a new campaign that would make people aware of the dangers of nuclear power and the necessity for action.

The first Clams were mainly from the Seacoast and New Hampshire. Around the site, local opposition was strong. Two Seabrook town meetings voted against the plant. On 10 April 1976 the Concerned Citizens of Seabrook held a march—the first direct action taken against Seabrook—and on August 5th they demonstrated against the beginning of construction.

1 August 1976—

22 August 1976—

"The Last Resort"—Several Seabrookers were among the first 18 people to get arrested at the plant site. As the 18 N.H. residents walked down the railroad tracks onto the site, 600 people rallied in support. (By "chance," this first U.S. "occupation" was on the 30th anniversary of the creation of the AEC!)

Three weeks later the Clam returned ten times stronger—180 people went on the site, 179 were arrested. (Here Christina Platt is photographed while blind activist Fred Zapinsky waits his turn.) A support rally attracted 1,200 people. Local and Native American speakers spoke and sang. Joe Leinen brought greetings from Wyhl.

23 October 1976—

Alternative Energy Fair, Hampton Beach—The fair on the cold, windy public beach across from the Seabrook site attracted more than 3,000 people. Speakers included Leo Goodman; theatre groups, musicians, exhibits presented the nuclear problem and solar solution.

Affinity Groups

The Clam practices of affinity group organization and preparation for non-violent direct action were set with these first two Seabrook occupations. The affinity group, 10-20 people who had usually trained together, brought internal self-reliance, support, and unity to the civil disobedience actions. The small group structure allowed for democratic decision-making as well as a means of internal security against provocateurs. The nonviolence training sessions gave prospective occupiers a chance to prepare personally and as a group for the action. The training was influenced a great deal by the early involvement of American Friends Service Committee members in the Clam.

Growing

During the winter of 1976-77, the Clam grew quickly into a loose coalition of 35 New England groups. It laid plans for another occupation of the Seabrook site (30 April 1977). From its beginning, the Clam tried to achieve a non-hierarchical organization. Decision-making was by consensus, with no action taken until all could agree. A

30 April 1977—

On site—early morning
(N.E. photos: Lionel Delevingne)

coordinating committee with representatives from affiliated groups met regularly. Standing committees were formed with all groups urged to participate. Meanwhile, local groups continued their anti-nuclear/alternative energy education and projects in their own neighborhoods or states. This decentralization has been an organizational strongpoint of the Clam that has allowed for autonomous grassroots work, while pulling people together from throughout the region for major Seabrook-focused actions.

30 April - 13 May 1977 Occupation

The April 30 occupation was far less of a symbolic action than the two previous ones had been. For 24 hours, 2,000 people occupied the construction parking lot. The occupation was well organized. Trained affinity groups approached the site from six directions. Their meeting on-site was powerful and dramatic.

On Sunday, May 1, 4,000 people attended a rally at Hampton Beach State Park sponsored by the Concerned Citizens of Hampton Falls and Seabrook. As they listened to speeches and music, arrests began at the plant site.

The 1,414 arrests took many hours, with some people held in army trucks overnight. But the demonstration did not end with the arrests. More than half of those arrested refused to pay bail and were held for two weeks in five national guard armories. Said one tenant of the armory experience, "It was like the state had given us five free conference centers."

One small corner of
Somersworth armory

NOOKS

by Peg Averill (NYC 339) and Ginster (Ithaca AG)   more tomorrow!

About Nooks

Near the end of our incarceration, Richard Ginn came up with the idea of a comic strip on the occupation. We brainstormed through lunch and after dinner and traded bits of overheard conversation, funny moments and even fantasized conversations between Governor Thomson and other state officials. We planned to do Nooks as a daily strip which could be picked up by our support people, xeroxed and sent to all the other occupiers through our inter-armory mail. We showed the first around to occupiers and guards in our armory, and the response was good. After the second strip, we were on our way out, but it was fun while it lasted, and we added the comic strip to the ever-expanded list of improvised entertainment—including song, dance, and theatre—in our armories.

—**Peg Averill**

Peg Averill, a member of the WIN staff, was in Somersworth armory.

WIN June 16&23, 1977

The incarceration finally ended when the state and occupiers agreed to a mass trial. Demonstrators received a group verdict of guilty and were released on personal recognizance pending appeal in Superior Court. (There are still more than 1,200 cases pending. More than 200 people have spent time in jail, mainly those who decided not to appeal their convictions to a higher court.)

The Clamshell's April action inspired the formation of similar direct action groups and federations across the country. The method of organization—an alliance of autonomous local groups with actions carried out by trained "affinity groups" seemed to offer nuclear opponents the participation, support, democratic decision-making and attention to personal commitment that could allow for successful non-violent direct action.

Public Education

Although the Clamshell is known for its nonviolent civil disobedience actions, Clams devote much time to public education. The Alliance has purchased and fixed up a van with alternative energy displays, "The Great New England Power Show," which goes to town and county fairs around the region. Clam members frequently appear at schools, civic clubs, and on media talk shows. One group in northern New Hampshire is buying and retooling an old hydro dam; another group has put together a play for schools and fairs. The Clam opposes rate hikes in New Hampshire and elsewhere in New England.

Seabrook: 25 June 1978

June 25th saw the largest anti-nuclear plant rally yet in the U.S. More than 18,000 people came on site for an all-day rally sponsored by the Stop Sea-

brook Team of intervenor groups and the Clam. Many fine speakers and musicians contributed their time and talents.

The sloop Clearwater and others held a "boat picket" around the offshore drilling platform (drilling the nuke's cooling tunnels). The event was to have been an occupation/restoration attempt. Instead, the Clam accepted a state offer of land on the site for the action. Six thousand people camped with their affinity groups on the site and welcomed the public to two days of public education—information booths and exhibits on nuclear power, conservation, and alternative energy sources.

In the days that followed, many Clams went to Washington to demonstrate at the NRC (see p. 387).

In August 1978, the "Seabrook Saga" continued as the cooling tunnels once again were approved and construction resumed August 14. On that day, six Clam members chained themselves to a giant crane on the site; another six walked down the front road of the site, and six more chained themselves to a sign in front of the site. A new civil disobedience campaign against the Seabrook nuke had been launched. "Wave actions"—small but more frequent acts of civil disobedience—were organized by local Clam-affiliated groups. Within weeks, about 60 people had been arrested at the site in the course of several small actions.

As these actions continued, the Clam also turned more seriously toward planning a large boat and land blockade of the Seabrook Reactor 1's pressure vessel whenever it might be moved north from its storage location in Massachusetts.

25 June 1978—

Footnotes

1. Excerpts from Lovejoy's statement: "...In the long-established tradition of challenging the constitutionality of particular events, I readily admit full responsibility for sabotaging that outrageous symbol of the future nuclear power plant...Positive action is the only option left open to us...It is my firm conviction that if a jury of 12 impartial scientists was empanelled, and following normal legal procedure they were given all pertinent data and arguments: then this jury would never give a unanimous vote for deployment of nuclear reactors amongst the civilian population. Rather, I believe they would call for the complete shutdown of all the commercially operated nuclear plants...Through positive action and a sense of moral outrage, I seek to test my convictions..."—22 February 1974. Besides waking up people to the impending danger, Lovejoy had also hoped to disrupt Northeast Utilities' meteorological data collection by knocking down the tower. The AEC required a year's data on wind speed and direction (needed for radiation and dispersal estimation for evacuation planning) before a construction license could be applied for. But shortly after the tower toppling, the AEC changed its regulations, now requiring only 90% of a year's data! For Sam's story and the case against nuclear power, see Green Mt. Post's award-winning film, *Lovejoy's Nuclear War*.

2. The Seabrook construction permit marked only the second time in federal licensing of domestic nukes that there was a split vote (two to one). The lone dissenter was Ernest Salo, a marine biologist who cited possible danger to sea life from the cooling system.

Contacts—a few of many local and statewide groups. Contact closest to find group nearest you.

Maine:

*Nuclear Reaction   Safe Power for Maine
Box 8265   P.O. Box 774
Portland 04104   Camden 04843

Vermont:

New England Coalition on Nuclear Pollution
(NECNP)
Box 637
Brattleboro 05301   (newsletter)

Vermont Public Interest Research Group
(VPIRG)
26 State Street
Montpelier VT 05602

New Hampshire:
Clamshell Alliance
62 Congress St.
Portsmouth 03801

Seacoast Anti-Pollution League (SAPL)
5 Market St.
Portsmouth 03801

Massachusetts:
*Boston Clamshell Coalition
1151 Mass. Ave.
Cambridge 02138 (Tel. 617/661-6204)

Energy Policy Information Center (EPIC)
3 Joy St.
Boston 02108 (Tel. 617/523-0376)

*Western Mass. Alternative Energy Coalition
(AEC)
85 Main St.
Amherst 01002 (Tel. 413/253-9998)

Mass PIRG
120 Boylston St.   233 N. Pleasant St.
Boston   Amherst 01002

Connecticut:
*Connecticut Clamshell Coalition
P.O. Box 6346
Hartford 06106

Rhode Island:
Rhode Islanders for Safe Power
63 Boon St.
Narragansett

*Rhode Island Clamshell c/o AFSC
2 Stinson St.
Providence

*affiliated with the Clamshell Alliance

Resources

• The Clamshell Alliance has a catalog of resources for education/organizing that are available to groups at reasonable bulk prices. Included are posters (including the Ionizing Woman on p. 84), buttons, the famous NO NUKES bumpersticker and a variety of literature (mainly oriented towards New England). Also available are two pieces entitled: "What is the Clamshell Alliance?" and "How Does the Clamshell Work?" Write for catalog: Re-Source Inc., P.O. Box 127, Astor Station, Boston MA 02123.

• The *Clamshell Alliance News* is a bi-monthly newsletter with national and international distribution. Subscriptions are $3/yr. from the Portsmouth NH office.

• For the story of Seabrook through April '77 see *The Last Resort*, a one hour film by Green Mountain Post Films, Box 177, Montague MA 01351 (413-863-4754).

• For a listing of major articles about Seabrook and the Clamshell Alliance, write for Seabrook bibliography, Re-Source Inc. (address above)

NEW YORK

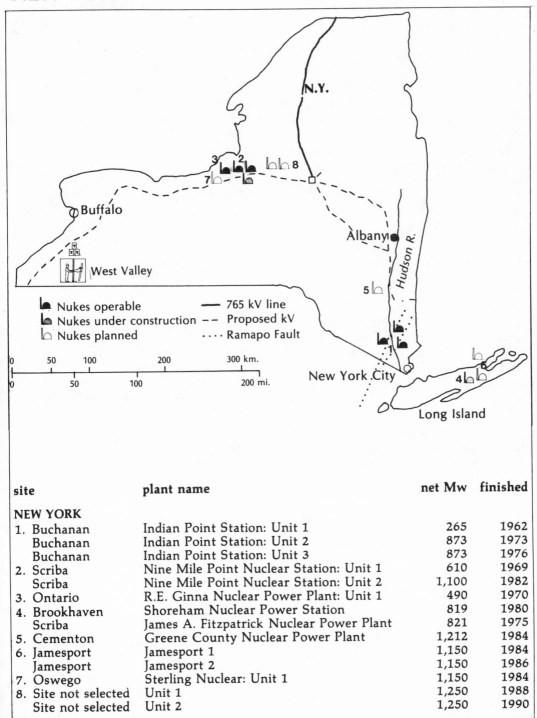

site	plant name	net Mw	finished
NEW YORK			
1. Buchanan	Indian Point Station: Unit 1	265	1962
Buchanan	Indian Point Station: Unit 2	873	1973
Buchanan	Indian Point Station: Unit 3	873	1976
2. Scriba	Nine Mile Point Nuclear Station: Unit 1	610	1969
Scriba	Nine Mile Point Nuclear Station: Unit 2	1,100	1982
3. Ontario	R.E. Ginna Nuclear Power Plant: Unit 1	490	1970
4. Brookhaven	Shoreham Nuclear Power Station	819	1980
Scriba	James A. Fitzpatrick Nuclear Power Plant	821	1975
5. Cementon	Greene County Nuclear Power Plant	1,212	1984
6. Jamesport	Jamesport 1	1,150	1984
Jamesport	Jamesport 2	1,150	1986
7. Oswego	Sterling Nuclear: Unit 1	1,150	1984
8. Site not selected	Unit 1	1,250	1988
Site not selected	Unit 2	1,250	1990

Long Island Safe Energy Coalition

A Brief History—The first organized effort to prevent construction of a nuclear power plant on Long Island was in the Huntington area. An environmental journalist named Ann Carl had written enthusiastically about the potential of nuclear power to replace dirty oil and coal plants. The response to Ann's column included communications from scientists who had direct experience with nuclear power technology, who were the first to warn Ann that something was wrong with the "peaceful atom." Dr. Carl gathered her friends and neighbors together in the Lloyd Harbor Study Group to investigate the pros and cons of atomic power; they became among the first citizen groups to intervene in the AEC hearing process, in 1967-68. The Long Island Lighting Company responded by relocating its proposed nuke to Shoreham, about 30 miles east of Huntington and Lloyd Harbor. The Lloyd Harbor Study Group kept after LILCO and the AEC in the Shoreham hearings, but plans were approved and construction began in September 1972. The LHSG has remained in the front lines of the hearings-and-litigation strategy against nuclear power, carrying lawsuits through federal courts, etc.

As LILCO's plans for two 1,150-megawatt reactors sited for rural Jamesport became generally known in early 1976, several citizen groups in the East End's environmental network felt they'd have to take a stand. The Long Island Farm Bureau brought nuclear opponents together that spring around the issue of power lines planned to cross farmlands. An alliance known as Prevent the Plants began sending out mass educational mailings to local communities on the eastern end of the island. The anti-nuke education drive was marked by a "counterpunch" newspaper advertising campaign in local weeklies: whenever LILCO published an ad explaining why nuclear power was good for farmers, for children, for outdoors people or for whomever, the same graphic of children playing, a farmer out in the field, or a young couple on bicycles would reappear the following week with a Prevent the Plants/Suffolk for Safe Energy ad explaining why it wasn't true.

The Long Island Safe Energy Coalition emerged in June of 1976 with groups from the entire island participating in a "Village Square day" action. A rally in Riverhead's Grangebel Park drew close to a hundred persons, as well as about twenty construction workers employed at LILCO's Shoreham site. The LILCO workers were offered an opportunity to speak and present their views and concern with those gathered. This allowed for a respectful human interaction of seemingly opposing groups. From the rally, people caravaned to the gates of the Shoreham nukes construction site for a balloon release.

Public demonstrations are one means of voicing citizen opposition to nuclear power. A picket line, accompanied by several truckloads of live ducks and locally grown potatoes and cauliflower, formed outside the Holiday Inn to protest the State Siting Board and NRC hearings on Jamesport taking place there.

As the hearings dragged on, so did the separate meetings of SFSE* and LISEC. Each anti-nuke group wondered what to do next. Finally, LISEC called for an island-wide strategy conference on 26 February 1977 in the first issue of its newletter *Chain Reaction*. There Ann Carl spoke of the need for direct action. Having spent ten years of her life in hearings and courtrooms, she was frustrated by the attitudes and rulings of the government

*Suffolk for Safe Energy

and its corporate allies. Dr. Charles Raebeck, co-chairperson of SFSE offered an idea for a mass gathering, a picnic of resistance on the beach ("On the Beach") near the Jamesport site. The picnic took place 17 September 1977 and attracted a thousand people, despite stormy weather.

Safe 'n Sound Forms—One of the workshops at LISEC's strategy conference was on alternate energy and conservation. The facilitator of the discussion invited all participants from the mid-Suffolk area to join in making alternate energy a reality. Those who responded formed a group called "Safe 'n Sound" (as in, safe energy on the Long Island Sound). Raising funds through recycling and concerts, Safe 'n Sound has done extensive petitioning and propagandizing on nuclear power in Shoreham and surrounding areas, and has launched a program to bring materials and advice for weatherproofing and solar space-heating to the many hidden low-income communities of Suffolk County.

Rate-Hike Fight—Long Island citizens' response to LILCO's continuous escalation of our electric bills has taken a variety of forms. The Long Island Ratepayers Association, one group protesting the rate hikes, is focusing on future public ownership of LILCO. The legislatures of Suffolk and Nassau Counties have joined together to fight the utility in court battles. Meanwhile, LISEC and other local groups continue to organize a rate-hike strike.

The withholding campaign gained some publicity when the Public Service Commission granted LILCO a $60 million rate increase in January 1978. In response to the announced rate hike withholding campaign, the public relations department of LILCO stated that the company would not act against those withholding until the amount withheld equalled or surpassed the amount of a billing period. Until then, what was withheld would appear as the balance due. LILCO will have to take individual cases to court for non-payment.

Households withholding a dollar as symbolic protest have already received notice from either the PSC, LILCO or both advising them to find another means of protest.

In May 1978 LILCO requested another $170 million rate-hike...

THEY BEAT US AT MONOPOLY...Now the bosses of LILCO want to play another game with you...and your grandchildren...and their grandchildren. (Credit: Van Howell)

Geographical Awareness—Confronted with the threat of several nukes on the island, we soon realized that the Long Island Sound is being used as a massive cooling basin for nuclear reactors. On the mainland, nukes are already operating along rivers that flow into the Sound and Atlantic Ocean. More are proposed, and a third is under construction at the Millstone site. (Now halted, at least temporarily.)

Hearing news of Vermont Yankee leaking 83,000 gallons radioactive liquid into the Connecticut River (in July 1976), which flows south to the Sound and Atlantic, we soon realized the holistic nature of the environment. Looking around, we find nukes up along the Hudson River too! This will add to the nuclear impact on Long Island Sound.

Citizens of Long Island have twice released balloons from the Shoreham nuke site to dramatize the spread of radiation that would be released in a "routine emission" or an accident. Returns came from Milford and Meriden, Connecticut as well as from Chilmark, Massachusetts on Martha's Vineyard.

From Long Island we are seeking contact and a working relation with persons and groups around L.I. Sound, up the Connecticut and Hudson rivers and also south along the mainland coast, where nukes may someday operate. We here on Long Island will work in concert with worldwide efforts.

The watershed and air paths of Our planet connect us all in this struggle for health and a sunny future. **NO NUKES!**

LISEC
November 1977

Some Area Contacts For Long Island

North Shore Coalition for Safe Energy
Box 18
Great Neck   11022
516/482-1551

Peacesmith Energy Project
90 Penn. Ave.
Massapequa   11758
516/785-8836

Long Island Safe Energy Coalition
Box 972
Smithtown   11787
516/653-6590 (Suffolk)
516/333-5044 (Nassau)
(LISEC has an excellent newsletter called *Chain Reaction*. A one-year subscription is $2.50.)

Safe 'N Sound
Box 60
Shoreham   11786
516/744-1942

Suffolk For Safe Energy
Box 2000
Riverhead
516/369-1050

Concerned Citizens of Montauk
Box 915
Montauk   11954

The Mid-Hudson Valley and Catskill Area

Background—North of New York City and south of Albany, the mid-Hudson—Catskill safe energy groups are confronting a host of energy problems. A rising awareness of our mutual concerns and need for interdependence is binding the forces opposing nukes, 765 kV power lines, and pumped storage facilities. This awareness is also leading to renewed support for municipal ownership of local and regional utilities.

New York now generates about 13% of its electricity at nuclear plants—Indian Point, Nine Mile Point (2), and Ginna. Plans are to add up to 12 more generating facilities in the mid-Hudson Valley alone. Sites under active consideration by the Power Authority of the State of New York (PASNY) and the private utilities include Cementon, Red Hook, Lloyd, Athens, and Stuyvesant.

Con Edison has announced its plans to build at two prime sites in southern Columbia/Duchess counties on the Hudson River. These are in the towns of Livingston and Red Hook/Clermont. Local opposition has greatly increased, and many of the local landholders around the sites have joined in a lawsuit to stop Con Ed from continuing their site surveys. Congressman Hamilton Fish and N.Y. State Assemblyman Maurice Hinchey have also joined the suits.

The mid-Hudson—Catskill region is largely rural. The low population density makes it attractive to nuke-builders, who are denied access to the large population centers that they seek to serve. The mix of rural and industrial sites along the Hudson River resembles the Rhine River area in Germany where strong opposition to the nukes has emerged. (See: International Story, page 297.) There is a growing awareness here of the global nature of the nuclear threat.

Active Groups—There are many safe energy groups operating in the area. Local groups have held informational meetings and workshops, shown films, provided speakers. They have held rallies and demonstrated in New York City and Albany. They have participated in memorial programs to Karen Silkwood, held concerts, plays, and puppet shows. And they have intervened in the legal process through hearings and in the courts. Nonviolent civil disobediance has been discussed as a "last resort." One affinity group from the Mid-Hudson Valley joined the April '77 Seabrook plant site occupation.

Citizens opposed to pumped storage facilities include those long active to save Storm King on the Hudson River and those more recently brought into the struggle by plans to locate another pumped storage plant high on the Esopus River at Prattsville. This plant would inefficiently use the excess power generated by the nuke planned for Cementon.

Citizens are beginning to understand the connections between nukes, pumped storage and high voltage power line grids.

Alliances—Lately, needed attention has been paid to organizing these various groups behind a unified action program. Affiliations and alliances have now been formed between groups opposing nukes, pumped storage facilities, and high-tension lines. As of this writing, two People's Power Assemblies have been held under the auspices of the People's Power Coalition. These and other activities, like the formation of the kV Alliance, serve to focus regional energy concerns.

Municipal Ownership—Municipal ownership of utilities has existed in New York State since the 1930s. More than 47 communities in New York now

Balloon release at Cementon, N.Y. nuke plant site, 6 August 1977.   Credit: Tobe J. Carey

have some sort of municipal ownership, which simply means that the local municipality has taken back its franchise for the generation or distribution of electrical power within its borders. The movement for municipal ownership has caught on with citizens burdened by profit-fat electric bills. We want to regain control of our franchises and effectively cut rates by doing away with profits.

Solar Alternatives/Conservation— Safe energy systems are beginning to dot the countryside. Most of these have been privately built and consist of solar heating and wind energy systems for individual homes. Some large industrial concerns with headquarters in the area, like IBM, have made substantial conservation measures pay off. They have in some cases reduced energy consumption by up to 40%. And everywhere homes are being insulated and retrofitted for wood burning and other renewable energy systems.

Local Government Action—Town and country governments have been enlisted in the fight against nuclear power in the region, with more than 15 townships passing resolutions against the placement of a nuclear facility within 50 miles of the township. Three local counties have offered similar resolutions. The Woodstock town board is now actively collecting these resolutions to be presented to the governor as an expression of more than 450,000 citizens. The governor is on record as opposing any new nuclear facilities being located in New York State until the waste problem can be adequately dealt with. Groups and individuals are now doing whatever is in their power to see that he lives up to that promise.

The Fight Goes On... The fight for safe energy goes on in New York, with the mid-Hudson/Catskill region bearing

its share of the struggle. Our optimism stems from the growing numbers of citizens fighting for a safe energy future.

November 29, 1977
Tobe J. Carey
Woodstock Nuclear Opponents
PO Box 604
Woodstock, NY   12498

A Brief History of the North Country (N.Y.) 765 kV Powerline Struggle

> ...a group of North Country people have seen that each generation must win its own freedom, and they have taken the first proud steps to hold that freedom and to protect their land. (from a statement of the Ft. Covington-Bombay Residents)

Since 1973, people in northern New York have been fighting the construction of a 765,000 volt powerline: this is the largest line ever planned for the Northeast, indeed, only one such line exists anywhere in the United States. The line would run through 150 miles of upstate farmland and woods, and all along that route farmers, teachers, native peoples, small business people, homesteaders, students and local legislators have come together to fight the Power Authority of the State of New York (PASNY).

Initially, the movement against the line focused on court fights against PASNY, and UPSET (formed in 1974) obtained intervenor status in the Public Service Commission hearings on the line. Extensive effort went into educating local people (and downstate people) on the issue of extremely-high voltage (EHV) lines and nuclear power plants: door-to-door canvassing and petitioning, booths at county fairs and field days, floats in parades, letter writing.

Completed tower, Holland Patent, N.Y.

In the fall of 1976, as clearing work began for the line, 500 people walked the six miles from Ft. Covington to Bombay, at the very northern end of the line, to express their opposition. In December of 1976, the first three farm women went to jail for blocking construction of the line. Since then, over forty people have been arrested: for sitting on bulldozers, for sitting in elm trees, for parking tractors in front of PASNY machinery.

In March of 1977, 1,000 people walked a three-mile stretch in the Elm Creek Valley in Edwards, New York (about the center point of the route) in opposition to the line. And, in August of 1977, two groups of people began from the north and south ends of the line and met in the middle ten days later. Once again, 1,000 people came together to say "no" to 765s and nukes. The people of Northern New York

have little experience in civil disobedience—or even in attempting to change the plans of big government and big business. But having learned what they have about EHV lines and nukes, they have felt compelled to play Paul Revere for the rest of their compatriots and warn others about the massive powerline grid planned for New York State, the Northeast and the entire country. Not only are 765 kV lines on the drawing board, but 1,000 kV, 1,500 kV and 2,000 kV (that's 2,000,000 volt) lines, lines which may more readily be built once the present 765 kV line is given final certification. In a sense, the fight over the Ft. Covington-Marcy 765 line is a generic fight.

One last word of warning: check your state planning maps, if you find large powerlines planned chances are a nuclear plant or some other large generating station will be built nearby. These lines are the backdoor method for rationalizing the construction of centralized power plants.

Power to the People, not to PASNY!

People from throughout the country (and from Europe and Australia as well) are writing to us for information about EHV lines: we have, in a sense, become the grandparents of the powerline fight. We seem to be the only organization with extensive literature, including scientific material, on the EHV line issue. That no government agency or utility company can supply any conclusive evidence on the impact of these lines supports our demand that there be an immediate construction mortorium until adequate scientific research can be done. Everywhere these lines are being built, people are resisting them: both because of their inherent adverse impact on the environment and people, and because they will serve as transmission facility for large, centralized power plants, especially nukes. We are happy to serve as a clearinghouse for powerline information.

Contact:
Upstate People for Safe Energy Technology (UPSET)
P.O. Box 571, Canton, N.Y. 13617
Ellen Rocco, (315) 355-2512

Why We Oppose 765 KV Lines

Prima Facie Reasons

1. Adverse impact on agriculture: loss of land, soil compaction, interference with drainage, destruction of houses and barns, contamination from herbicides (Tordon, a dioxin-containing herbicide, is the primary herbicide used to clear right-of-ways), possible biological effects on crops and livestock.
2. Permanent degradation of land: lowering of land value and erosion of tax base.
3. Visual and psychological pollution:
4 towers per mile, each tower about 175 feet tall, each tower base taking up ¼ acre of land.
4. Adverse health and safety effects: cardiovascular stress on humans and animals caused by the powerful electric field; production of nitric oxide and ozone, both toxic pollutants; destruction of ozone layer, leading to increased skin cancer; creation of induced shock; constant psychological nuisance of audible noise, visible light, and radio-TV interference; creation of a magnetic field which may interfere with migration of birds, flight patterns of bees; possible effects on global weather patterns.

The Nuclear Connection—While in the instance of the Ft. Covington-Marcy 765 kV line, Quebec hydropower will be carried to New York City,

Jane Standing Still, Iroquois woman, tells PASNY they cannot cut the elm tree—she "will not be moved."   Credit: Doug Jones

that power will only use 1/5 the carrying capacity of a 765. Eventually, the line will also serve large generating stations in the north country: and according to planning maps, those will be nuclear power plants.

Lines of this magnitude are built to transport power long distances from centralized power plants to large urban consumers. We are opposed to nuclear power plants in particular because: they represent a physical menace to present and future generations, and the construction of nuclear generating stations discourages energy conservation and decentralized energy systems, both of which we consider essential to our survival.

Exploitation of Native North American People—We are opposed to the construction of the 765 kV line because of its connection with the James Bay Hydroelectric Project. That project which will flood 63,000 square miles of Cree and Inuit Indian lands in Canada, will eventually provide the power to be shipped to New York City along the proposed line. Similarly, once the 765 kV project in New York State is finished, the St. Regis Mohawk Reservation along the St. Lawrence will be triangulated with EHV power lines. We do not wish to be responsible for this disruption of, and safety threat to, the lives of native North American people.

Social and Economic Impact—
1. There will be no economic or social benefit to the North Country, save a very few short-term jobs.
2. There will be economic and social distress created in the North Country: aside from damage to farming and degradation of non-farming land (resorts), there may be a growth in unemployment and welfare roles (as landowners are deprived of traditional means of livelihood).

3. There is no long-range benefit to New York City consumers: even PASNY estimates only a $4.92/annual savings per consumer, and that estimate was based on figures from the early 1970s.
4. Those who truly stand to gain from the construction of the powerline are investors in nearly $200 million worth of *tax-free* bonds which will finance the project.
5. The line will increase our energy dependence on foreign nations.
6. The powerline will further entrench wasteful energy policies by encouraging further subversion of the democratic process, and discouraging development of alternative energy sources.

The Politics of PASNY—The Power Authority was never required, nor did it offer, to prove need for this line, and throughout the application and hearing process PASNY has obstructed rational inquiry into possible health and safety hazards, as well as inquiry into adverse agricultural impact.

The one PSC Commissioner to dissent from certification, Harold A. Jerry, stated that the PSC had been "terrorized" by PASNY. He further asserted that certification before the completion of health and safety hearings would "damage seriously public confidence in the procedural fairness, environmental concern, and judicial independence of the Public Service Commission."

Further, PASNY has consistently used "scare" tactics against individual landowners in an effort to make people submit to their authority.

And, while PASNY claims this project will create jobs and help New York State industry, the steel for the towers was purchased in Italy, the transformers were purchased in England, and the cable was purchased in Sweden.

Decisions by other public bodies, such as the Department of Environmental Conservation and the Agricultural Resources Commission, strongly indicates that they have also been "terrorized" by the Power Authority.

EMPIRE STATE TO BE FEDERAL NUKE-WASTE DUMP?

"There is a distinct possibility that New York State officials are secretly planning with federal Department of Energy officials to make New York the site of a radioactive waste repository...

"New York State is facing a cost of several hundred million dollars to dismantle (decommission) the defunct West Valley nuclear fuel reprocessing plant and to provide for some sort of disposal of the 600,000 gallons of highly radioactive waste stored there. The state, of course, does not want to spend that sort of money and its officials along with several local members of Congress have been trying to get the federal government to bail them out.

"The Feds, on the other hand, are embarrassed that while the nuclear industry is constantly claiming that there is no radioactive waste problem, they are clearly not on the verge of establishing any place to put the stuff.

"Salt deposits in western New York are among the sites which the Feds have been eyeing as possible disposal sites and it appears that New York and the Feds may be negotiating some deal whereby the federal government will take over West Valley but will use the facility to receive radioactive wastes from nuclear plants within and outside of the state and to prepare those wastes for disposal somewhere in western New York. Such a move could eventually result in New York becoming a national or regional nuclear waste dump and would certainly provide further impetus to the construction of more nukes in the state."

Chain Reaction, Vol. 2, No. 1
Midwinter, 1978

The Rockefeller Connection

"Since the beginning of the Atomic Age, perhaps no man has been so influential in the development of nuclear power as Nelson A. Rockefeller. Starting even before his key role as governor of New York State, Rockefeller was involved in promoting President Eisenhower's "Atoms for Peace" Program. As governor, he created a multimillion dollar network of governmental bodies designed for the express purpose of creating a huge nuclear energy industry, along with a system of nuclear-powered electrical generating plants. His most visible work as Vice-President has been in the form of a proposal which would guarantee $100 billion in loans to induce private industry to undertake risky energy projects, particularly in the nuclear field."

—Peter Salmansohn
(From "Nuclear Energy, Rockefeller, and Big Business," June 1976, p. 89)

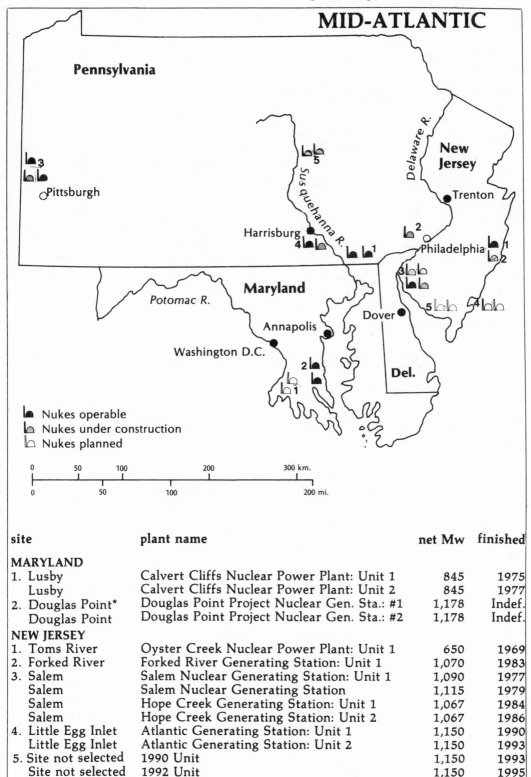

MID-ATLANTIC

Pennsylvania

New Jersey

Delaware R.

Susquehanna R.

Pittsburgh

Harrisburg

Trenton

Philadelphia

Maryland

Potomac R.

Dover

Annapolis

Washington D.C.

Del.

Nukes operable
Nukes under construction
Nukes planned

| 0 | 50 | 100 | 200 | 300 km. |
| 0 | 50 | 100 | 200 mi. | |

site	plant name	net Mw	finished
MARYLAND			
1. Lusby	Calvert Cliffs Nuclear Power Plant: Unit 1	845	1975
Lusby	Calvert Cliffs Nuclear Power Plant: Unit 2	845	1977
2. Douglas Point*	Douglas Point Project Nuclear Gen. Sta.: #1	1,178	Indef.
Douglas Point	Douglas Point Project Nuclear Gen. Sta.: #2	1,178	Indef.
NEW JERSEY			
1. Toms River	Oyster Creek Nuclear Power Plant: Unit 1	650	1969
2. Forked River	Forked River Generating Station: Unit 1	1,070	1983
3. Salem	Salem Nuclear Generating Station: Unit 1	1,090	1977
Salem	Salem Nuclear Generating Station	1,115	1979
Salem	Hope Creek Generating Station: Unit 1	1,067	1984
Salem	Hope Creek Generating Station: Unit 2	1,067	1986
4. Little Egg Inlet	Atlantic Generating Station: Unit 1	1,150	1990
Little Egg Inlet	Atlantic Generating Station: Unit 2	1,150	1993
5. Site not selected	1990 Unit	1,150	1993
Site not selected	1992 Unit	1,150	1995

*Utility is negotiating to cancel

PENNSYLVANIA			
1. Peach Bottom	Peach Bottom Atomic Power Station: Unit 2	1,065	1974
Peach Bottom	Peach Bottom Atomic Power Station: Unit 3	1,065	1974
2. Pottstown	Limerick Generating Station: Unit 1	1,065	1983
Pottstown	Limerick Generating Station: Unit 2	1,065	1985
3. Shippingport	Shippingport Atomic Power Station	60	1957
Shippingport	Beaver Valley Power Station: Unit 1	852	1976
Shippingport	Beaver Valley Power Station: Unit 2	852	1982
4. Middletown	Three Mile Island Nuclear Station: Unit 1	819	1974
Middletown	Three Mile Island Nuclear Station: Unit 2	906	1978
5. Berwick	Susquehanna Steam Electric Station: Unit 1	1,050	1980
Berwick	Susquehanna Steam Electric Station: Unit 2	1,050	1982

The Potomac Alliance

The Potomac Alliance is a coalition of concerned citizens from the Washington, D.C. metropolitan area who oppose reliance on nuclear power and favor the use of safe, clean, economical, renewable energy alternatives. The Alliance formed in the summer of 1977 following Clamshell Alliance's April 30th Occupation of Seabrook nuclear plant site by the Washington, D.C. affinity group. "Although based in the Nation's capital, our goal is to reach Washington area residents in direct action and education campaigns, maintaining the ideals of non-violence, decentralization and consensus decision-making." —Gina Moreland. February 1978.

Potomac Alliance protested Helmut Schmidt's visit to the U.S. (the West German Chancellor authorized the multi-million dollar sale of the entire nuclear fuel cycle to Brazil), released balloons at nearby nuclear plants, co-sponsored a large teach-in on nuclear power, and has been sending speakers to parishes and schools. Members regularly leaflet NRC, DOE, and other government agency workers on their lunch hours with the facts of low-level radiation and the government cover-up. With the cooperation of Washington peace and social justice groups, Potomac Alliance organized a candlelight vigil in front of the White House during the Barnwell and Rocky Flats actions to remind President Carter of his "nuclear energy as the last resort" and "zero nuclear weapons" campaign pledges.

One Alliance leaflet presented the evacuation problem that could face the city in case of a nuclear accident at one of the 14 reactors now in application or being built within a 100 mile radius of the city:

...no evacuation plans have been made available to the public, and no dry runs of evacuating the city have been conducted. If a nuclear accident occurred at one of these plants, over 3 million residents would have to be evacuated from the Washington metropolitan area within a few hours time.

How can people successfully evacuate if they do not know what the evacuation plan for the city is? In fact, the Potomac Alliance, a local citizen action coalition which opposes nuclear power, has been unable to locate a single D.C. or federal public official who knows what the evacuation plans for the city are, or if, in fact, there are any. TRY IT YOURSELF!

The Potomac Alliance
P.O. Box 9306
Washington, D.C. 20005

Pennsylvania

Over the years one of the most active groups in the country has been ECNP, the Environmental Coalition on Nuclear Power, a coalition of groups and individuals in Pennsylvania and neighboring states interested in electric power problems and their impact on society, the economy and the environment. Member groups have led public political opposition that has defeated the following projects:

• the AEC Plowshare Project Ketch (1967-1968), a plan to explode over 1,000 nuclear bombs underground in central Pennsylvania.
• a proposal to locate the demonstration breeder reactor in Northeastern Pa.; now referred to as the Clinch River Breeder Reactor.
• energy parks (1975), the national test case for nuclear energy centers
• leasing of state-owned game lands for uranium prospecting (1974-)
• commercial low-level radioactive waste disposal site proposed by Chem-Nuclear (1976)

In litigation and intervention, ECNP member groups have obtained the following:
• cancellation of 2 Newbold Island Reactors (NJ) on the Delaware River, in 1973 which reversed the AEC urban siting policy.
• delayed for five years the construction at Hope Creek, the alternative site for Newbold Island
• establishment of AEC policy of requiring cooling towers on inland water bodies (1974 Peach Bottom case)
• requirement of additional iodine hold-up systems, (1973 Three Mile Is. Unit 1)
• forced the NRC to vacate the radon number (74.5 curies) from the standard S-3 table, summary of the Environmental Effects of the Nuclear Fuel Cycle, and to admit under oath that the total number of curies attributable to Radon-222 will amount to billions of curies (premature deaths) per annual fuel requirement per reactor. This is still in litigation on grounds of NEPA and other violations.
• caused cancellation of Fulton MTGR I

and II in 1975 in consequence of intervention delay
• forced cancellation of Summit I and II, Delaware (1977)
• Appeal Board Decision remanding Three Mile Island II to the Appeal Board for reconsideration of the aircraft crash probability and risk assessment issue. In a stinging dissent, one member argued not only for reopening the proceedings, but also that the license had been illegally issued, and that the plant should be shut down.

ECNP is represented on the Governor's Energy Council Advisory Committee, and Task Force to Develop the State Comprehensive Energy Policy. We have also arranged or participated in numerous briefings and hearings before local, state and federal agencies and legislative bodies. ECNP was instrumental in the founding of the Eastern Federation of Nuclear Opponents and Safe Energy Proponents. For more information contact:
Judith Johnsrud
433 Orland Avenue
State College, Pa. 16801

From *Report of the National NO Nukes Strategy Conference*, Louisville KY, August 1978.

The SEA Alliance

The Safe Energy Alternatives (SEA) Alliance is a coalition of anti-nuke, pro-safe energy activists founded in July 1977. The Alliance includes 18 local groups in New Jersey, Delaware, and Eastern Pennsylvania.
Contact them at:
324 Bloomfield Avenue
Montclair, NJ 07042

The SOUTHEAST
and PUERTO RICO

Nukes operable
Nukes under construction
Nukes planned

Puerto Rico

site	plant name	net Mw	finished
ALABAMA			
1. Decatur	Browns Ferry Nuclear Power Plant: Unit 1	1,065	1974
Decatur	Browns Ferry Nuclear Power Plant: Unit 2	1,065	1975
Decatur	Browns Ferry Nuclear Power Plant: Unit 3	1,065	1977
2. Dothan	Joseph M. Farley Nuclear Plant: Unit 1	820	1977
Dothan	Joseph M. Farley Nuclear Plant: Unit 2	820	1980
3. Scottsboro	Bellefonte Nuclear Plant: Unit 1	1,213	1980
Scottsboro	Bellefonte Nuclear Plant: Unit 2	1,213	1981
ARKANSAS			
Russellville	Arkansas Nuclear One: Unit 1	850	1974
Russellville	Arkansas Nuclear One: Unit 2	912	1978
FLORIDA			
1. Florida City	Turkey Point Station: Unit 3	693	1972
Florida City	Turkey Point Station: Unit 4	693	1973

2. Red Level	Crystal River Plant: Unit 3	825	1977
3. Ft. Pierce	St. Lucie Plant: Unit 1	802	1976
Ft. Pierce	St. Lucie Plant: Unit 2	802	1983
GEORGIA			
1. Baxley	Edwin I. Hatch Nuclear Plant: Unit 1	786	1975
Baxley	Edwin I. Hatch Nuclear Plant: Unit 2	795	1978
2. Waynesboro	Alvin W. Vogtle, Jr. Plant: Unit 1	1,110	1985
Waynesboro	Alvin W. Vogtle, Jr. Plant: Unit 2	1,110	1986
LOUISIANA			
1. Taft	Waterford Generating Station: Unit 3	1,113	1981
2. St. Francisville	River Bend Station: Unit 1	934	1983
St. Francisville	River Bend Station: Unit 2	934	1985
MISSISSIPPI			
1. Corinth	Yellow Creek: Unit 1	1,285	1985
Corinth	Yellow Creek: Unit 2	1,285	1986
2. Port Gibson	Grand Gulf Nuclear Station: Unit 1	1,250	1981
Port Gibson	Grand Gulf Nuclear Station: Unit 2	1,250	1984
NORTH CAROLINA			
1. Southport	Brunswick Steam Electric Plant: Unit 1	821	1977
Southport	Brunswick Steam Electric Plant: Unit 2	821	1975
2. Cowans Ford Dam	Wm. B. McGuire Nuclear Station: Unit 1	1,180	1979
Cowans Ford Dam	Wm. B. McGuire Nuclear Station: Unit 2	1,180	1981
3. Bonsal	Shearon Harris Plant: Unit 1	900	1983
Bonsal	Shearon Harris Plant: Unit 2	900	1986
Bonsal	Shearon Harris Plant: Unit 3	900	1989
Bonsal	Shearon Harris Plant: Unit 4	900	1987
4. Davie County	Perkins Nuclear Station: Unit 1	1,280	1985
Davie County	Perkins Nuclear Station: Unit 2	1,280	1987
Davie County	Perkins Nuclear Station: Unit 3	1,280	1990
5. Site not selected		1,150	Indef.
Site not selected		1,150	Indef.
Site not selected		1,150	Indef.
SOUTH CAROLINA			
1. Hartsville	H.B. Robinson S.E. Plant: Unit 2	712	1971
2. Seneca	Oconee Nuclear Station: Unit 1	887	1973
Seneca	Oconee Nuclear Station: Unit 2	887	1974
Seneca	Oconee Nuclear Station: Unit 3	887	1974
3. Broad River	Virgil C. Summer Nuclear Station: Unit 1	900	1980
4. Lake Wylie	Catawba Nuclear Station: Unit 1	1,145	1982
Lake Wylie	Catawba Nuclear Station: Unit 2	1,145	1983
5. Cherokee County	Cherokee Nuclear Station: Unit 1	1,280	1984
Cherokee County	Cherokee Nuclear Station: Unit 2	1,280	1986
Cherokee County	Cherokee Nuclear Station: Unit 3	1,280	1989
TENNESSEE			
1. Daisy	Sequoyah Nuclear Power Plant: Unit 1	1,148	1978
Daisy	Sequoyah Nuclear Power Plant: Unit 2	1,148	1979
2. Spring City	Watts Bar Nuclear Plant: Unit 1	1,177	1979
Spring City	Watts Bar Nuclear Plant: Unit 2	1,177	1980
3. Oak Ridge	Clinch River Breeder Reactor Plant	350	Indef.
4. Hartsville	A, Unit 1	1,233	1983
Hartsville	A, Unit 2	1,233	1984
Hartsville	B, Unit 1	1,233	1983
Hartsville	B, Unit 2	1,233	1984
5. Site not selected	Phipps Bend, Unit 1	1,233	1984
Site not selected	Phipps Bend, Unit 2	1,233	1985

VIRGINA			
1. Gravel Neck	Surry Power Station: Unit 1	822	1972
Gravel Neck	Surry Power Station: Unit 2	822	1973
2. Mineral	North Anna Power Station: Unit 1	907	1978
Mineral	North Anna Power Station: Unit 2	907	1979
Mineral	North Anna Power Station: Unit 3	907	1982
Mineral	North Anna Power Station: Unit 4	907	1983
PUERTO RICO			
Arecibo	North Coast Power Plant **CANCELLED**	583	Indef.

North Anna Environmental Coalition

Was N-Plant Danger Covered Up? High-ranking staff members of the Nuclear Regulatory Commission knew the Virginia Electric and Power Co. was building two nuclear power plants on potentially unsafe ground at North Anna, but failed for several months to alert the NRC board which had authority to stop the construction, according to a Justice Department memorandum released yesterday.

The Washington Star
1 October 1977

The North Anna Environmental Coalition, headed by its president, June Allen, has been fighting construction and operating licenses for nuclear plants near Charlottesville, Virginia. Four reactors are planned by the Virginia Electric Power Company (VEPCO) for the North Anna site. The Coalition's citizen intervenor efforts have brought out much information about North Anna's safety problems.

In August 1973, the Coalition—not the AEC—made public the fact of a geological fault beneath the four reactors.

In October 1977, Ms. Allen testified before the Senate Subcommittee on Nuclear Regulation of the Committee on Environment and Public Works on the history of the fault discovery and cover-up:

...At North Anna, a construction permit should have been denied in 1970, and is no more defensible now just because this is seven years and close to two billion dollars later. A major siting mistake was made in 1968. In 1969, seismic researchers had to be rescued from the treacherous mud. Nevertheless, excavation for the four-reactor site began in December of 1969. By February of 1970, the site was in trouble. The wall of the excavation for Reactor 1 was collapsing. Rock slides were serious enough for the site geologist to call Stone & Webster in Boston to talk with their lead geotechnical engineer...

...*Is this installation even marginally safe?* Are Virginians protected from the consequences of a wet, sinking, highly fractured site beneath defective equipment by a proceeding that lets a fault off on a technicality?

The age of the fault is almost irrelevant next to the cumulative problems at this "unhappy site" and there is nothing in the record to give confidence in NRC-AEC approval of it at any stage of the licensing process, where the guiding principles appear to range from careless ignorance to obvious collusion.

Is this Subcommittee content to conclude that it is just too late for unfortunate Virginia, that so massive and expensive a mistake as North Anna must operate? Did not a similar outlook lead to the Teton Dam tragedy? Surely our government can do better by its people than resign them to technological blunders.

The Coalition would ask of Congress an in-depth investigation of the nuclear situation in Virginia, preceded by a recommendation that licensing proceedings on all Virginia reactors be re-opened and the Nuclear Regulatory Commission be instructed to abide by its own regulations regarding license revocation.

After a review of consultants' evidence proving the site unsafe for nuclear construction, Allen concluded:

The impression is inescapable that high level NRC policy is strictly promotional with events manipulated to expedite licensing...

On 1 April 1978, the NRC granted a full-power operating license to North Anna reactors 1 and 2.

For information contact:
June Allen
North Anna Environmental Coalition
Box 3951
Charlottesville, Va. 22903

The Catfish Alliance
The Catfish Alliance began in the summer and fall of 1977, as activists from 8 southern states established a decentralized coordinating communications network. In September the group met at the Monte Sano State Park near Huntsville, Alabama, and issued the following declaration:

Monte Sano Declaration—We the citizens of the Southern States stand in alliance to:
• oppose the development of nuclear power;
• make known to our fellow citizens the complete facts regarding nuclear power and solar energy and the great potential in energy conservation, to reassert our inherent democratic right to decide and direct our lives and the future of our communities;
• take responsibility for our regional energy development to tap our inexhaustible source of solar energy and develop a decentralized solar economic base of permanent job opportunities to benefit our people rather than those who exploit us for profit;
• bring to the forefront of our consciousness to live in harmony with our Earth as good stewards.

To further this purpose, we found the Catfish Alliance and commit our lives, fortunes, and sacred honors.

The south-wide coordinator for the Catfish Alliance is Darryl Wiley, P.O. Box 6306, Dothan, Alabama 36301.

People wanting to be added to the mailing list to receive a regional newsletter should contact: Alliance-Tallahassee, P.O. Box 20049, Tallahassee, Florida 32304 (tel. 904/644-1257 or 576-2483).

Key Contacts

Catfish Alliance
P.O. Box 6306
Dothan, Ala. 36301

Palmetto Alliance
18 Bluff Rd.
Columbia, .S.C. 29201

Oystershell Alliance
1808 Robert St.
New Orleans, La. 70115

East Tennessee Energy Group
1538 Highland Ave.
Knoxville, Tenn. 37916

Catfish Alliance-Tallahassee
c/o P.O. Box 20049
Tallahassee, Fla. 32304

American Friends Services Committee
P.O. Box 2234
High Point, N.C. 27261

Georgians for Clean Energy
110 E. Maple St.
Decatur, Ga. 30030

Coastal Citizens for Clean Energy
P.O. Box 9891
Savannah, Ga. 31401

**Palmetto Alliance
G.R.O.W.**

TVA: Federalized Nuclear Monster, and Growing

The Tennessee Valley Authority (TVA) provides electricity to 2.5 million people in a seven state region in and around Tennessee. TVA is the largest electric utility in the U.S.; it is the largest consumer of strip-mined coal; it is the largest uranium customer in the U.S.; and TVA is the leading proponent of nuclear power among U.S. utility companies. TVA's promotional rate structures, which reward large electricity consumers with lower per unit rates, pro-energy growth advertising and other methods which encourage electricity use, have created a situation in which the average residential consumer uses about 14,000 kwhs per year, almost twice the national average. Forty percent of homes in the TVA region are electrically heated, an extremely inefficient method of space heating, compared with 10% nationwide.

Already TVA supplies the power for the gaseous diffusion plant at Oak Ridge, TN and most of the power for the Paducah, KY and Portsmouth, OH uranium enrichment facilities as well. Overall, TVA produces two-thirds of the energy used by enrichment plants *worldwide*. At present this is the most lucrative part of the nuclear fuel cycle, and the enriched uranium market may, in fact, be what's holding the U.S. nuclear industry on its feet. TVA-land is also the home of the Clinch River Breeder Reactor, which will manufacture plutonium for use as nuclear fuel. It appears that TVA, along with Third World markets (see "Nuclear Proliferation," Feb. '78 *People & Energy*), is keeping the nuclear industry alive in the U.S.

TVA officials are now proceeding with plans to double generating capacity by 1983, despite the fact that conservation measures have already slowed the area's electricity demand growth rate substantially. While utilities in most parts of the country are reevaluating their commitment to nuclear power, TVA has plans to have 17 nuclear power plants in operation by 1983.

TVA is unique among electric utilities because it is owned and controlled by the federal government. Other utilities are investor-owned, municipal or rural electric cooperatives. Established in the 1930s as a 'progressive' attempt to counter increasing monopolization of the electric utility industry, TVA's original goal was to provide cheap, abundant electricity to raise the standard of living in the underdeveloped Tennessee Valley. Its early accomplishments were great—within a decade the poor, eroded countryside had been converted into lush farm and dairy lands.*

Today TVA stands in isolation from its constituency and cheap, abundant electricity has become an end in itself, whatever the environmental costs. A recent study determined that TVA ranked worst of 15 large utilities in overall water and air pollution.** TVA consistently uses cheap, but highly polluting high sulfur coal and has resisted installation of pollution control devices. In 1975, when a federal court ordered TVA to comply with the Clean Air Act, General Manager Lynn Seever declared that the agency would appeal the decision to the Superior Court saying, "If we lose the case there, we will try to get the law changed. We don't give up easily."

TVA is able to skirt compliance with federal emission standards because of its status as a federal corporation, which effectively exempts it from all avenues of external control. As an interstate corporation, no one state has jurisdiction to regulate it; thus, while other utilities must have their expansion plans approved by State Regulatory Commissions, TVA's customers have little input into decision-making. The local power Boards are appointed, rather than elected, and the three TVA directors are appointed to their 7-year terms by the President of the U.S. What this boils down to is that TVA's directors are answerable to Washington rather than anyone in the Tennessee Valley. As isolated political appointees, TVA's Board members are unduly subject to outside pressures, such as the relentless pressures from the faltering nuclear industry.

The absence of mechanisms for affecting TVA operations has frustrated citizens' attempts to change TVA's high growth policies and heavy nuclear emphasis. The TVA structure may represent a model for 'Nationalization' of the entire electric utility industry, so that the government can bypass citizen opposition in bailing out the nuclear industry in this country.

—Nancy Jacobs
People & Energy, March 1978

Contact:
Faith Young
Concerned Citizens of Tennessee
110 Pembroke Ave.
Nashville, Tennessee 37205

Taking Charge: A New Look at Public Power, Environmental Action Foundation, 724 Dupont Circle Bldg., Washington D.C. 20036
**The Price of Power/Update*, Council on Economic Priorities, New York, N.Y. 10011.

BARNWELL: Drawing the Line Against a Plutonium Economy
29 April - 1 May 1978

These are scenes from the first anti-nuclear civil disobedience action in the South. It focused on the Barnwell spent fuel reprocessing plant, complete but not operating. Participants demanded an end to both the commercial and federal plutonium economy—no reprocessing and no breeder reactor. Fifteen hundred people gathered at Barnwell on 30 April 1978. The next day, 285 people were arrested at the gates.

From a statement by the Palmetto Alliance: "The corporations that own the Barnwell Plant are known as criminals by most countries of the world. In America we know them as Standard Oil and Gulf. This year the taxpayers gave the Barnwell Plant $14 million to keep the operation financially viable.

"The Barnwell Nuclear Fuel Reprocessing and Waste Storage facility has often been called the jugular vein of the nuclear industry; however, it may be more appropriately called the rectum. The Barnwell plant is the only commercial nuclear fuel reprocessing facility in America. It has the capacity to handle the spent fuel from every nuclear reactor presently functioning in America. Without reprocessing of spent fuel there will be no plutonium. The Barnwell facility has been complete for 3

Mother and Son Demonstrate
(Photos: Lionel Delevingne)

years but has never functioned. Its operation has been held up pending the outcome of hearings on the use of plutonium as a nuclear fuel. The intervention effort has been instrumental in keeping the Barnwell Plant from opening for the last 3 years. However, federalization of the plant would effectively end the intervention process."

Contact:
Palmetto Alliance
18 Bluff Rd.
Columbia, S.C. 29201

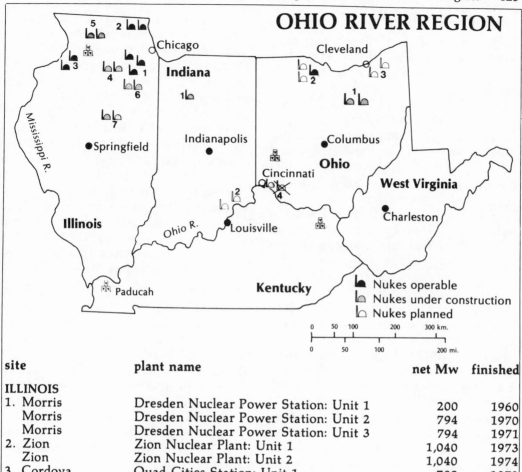

OHIO RIVER REGION

site	plant name	net Mw	finished
ILLINOIS			
1. Morris	Dresden Nuclear Power Station: Unit 1	200	1960
Morris	Dresden Nuclear Power Station: Unit 2	794	1970
Morris	Dresden Nuclear Power Station: Unit 3	794	1971
2. Zion	Zion Nuclear Plant: Unit 1	1,040	1973
Zion	Zion Nuclear Plant: Unit 2	1,040	1974
3. Cordova	Quad-Cities Station: Unit 1	789	1973
Cordova	Quad-Cities Station: Unit 2	789	1973
4. Seneca	LaSalle County Nuclear Station: Unit 1	1,078	1979
Seneca	LaSalle County Nuclear Station: Unit 2	1,078	1980
5. Byron	Byron Station: Unit 1	1,120	1981
Byron	Byron Station: Unit 2	1,120	1983
6. Braidwood	Braidwood: Unit 1	1,120	1982
Braidwood	Braidwood: Unit 2	1,120	1983
7. Clinton	Clinton Nuclear Power Plant: Unit 1	933	1981
Clinton	Clinton Nuclear Power Plant: Unit 2	933	1988
INDIANA			
1. Westchester	Bailly Generating Station	645	1983
2. Madison	Marble Hill Nuclear Power Station: Unit 1	1,130	1982
Madison	Marble Hill Nuclear Power Station: Unit 2	1,130	1984
OHIO			
1. Berlin Heights	Erie: Unit 1	1,260	1986
Berlin Heights	Erie: Unit 2	1,260	1988
2. Oak Harbor	Davis-Besse Nuclear Power Station: Unit 1	906	1977
Oak Harbour	Davis-Besse Nuclear Power Station: Unit 2	906	1985
Oak Harbor	Davis-Besse Nuclear Power Station: Unit 3	906	1987
3. Perry	Perry Nuclear Power Plant: Unit 1	1,205	1981
Perry	Perry Nuclear Power Plant: Unit 2	1,305	1983
4. Moscow	Wm. H. Zimmer Nuclear Power Sta.: Unit 1	810	1979
Moscow	Wm. H. Zimmer Nuclear Power Sta.: Unit 2	**CANCELLED**	1989

Ohio River Valley

Background—About three years ago, Public Service Co. of Indiana (PSI) announced its intention to build a twin reactor light water nuclear plant at Marble Hill, Indiana. Marble Hill is a wooded bluff overlooking the Ohio River. The plant site was eight miles downriver from Cinncinatti, Ohio, and 28 miles upriver from the Louisville, Kentucky city water system's intake pipes.

For many years Madison has been subject to the sooty exhaust gases of the Cliffty Creek coal-burning electrical station on the edge of town. Madison residents had fought long and hard to get emission control equipment for that plant. They formed an organization called Save the Valley to fight in the courts and educate the citizens of the valley to the dangers of coal-fired plants. As Save the Valley continued its work, a pattern began to emerged. Vast tracts of land were being bought up on both sides of the river from Ashland, Kentucky to Carbondale, Illinois as sites for future power plants and industrial development. Residents and environmentalists began to refer to the Ohio as "Power Plant Alley." Advertising rhetoric of the 1930s was being modeled into reality as the Ohio Valley prepared to become "the Ruhr* of America."

At first the members of Save the Valley were inclined to look with favor on the proposed Marble Hill nuke, as were many environmentalists from across the country. The first resistance came, as so often happens, from the people who were to be removed from the fertile bottom land of the plant site. Soon, people began educating themselves and recognized the special dangers of nuclear power. After some debate, Save the Valley decided to oppose the plant.

Since that time, Save the Valley and many other concerned organizations and individuals have worked their way through the now-familiar frustrations of the NRC hearing process. Within the past year, the metropolitan government of Louisville and the state government of Kentucky have joined as intervenors—and now as litigants—claiming that the plant is a health threat. The state owns the river, and therefore is refusing PSI a permit to discharge into the Ohio River. The legality of Kentucky's claim is being challenged. In the meantime, PSI has announced its intention to build two additional reactors at Marble Hill.

The Paddlewheel Alliance—Early in 1977, as word of the approaching Seabrook occupation passed through our communities, several Valley citizens set off on foot for Washington, D.C. They carried petitions and letters from the mayor and county judge to President Carter requesting a nuclear moritorium in the Ohio Valley. Their action on the eve of the Seabrook Occupation was the seed around which the Paddle wheel Alliance has grown.

Recognizing that all legal means tried thus far have failed, Paddlewheel is attempting to build a dramatic, popular opposition to Marble Hill and the power plant proliferation in the region. Paddlewheel (PWA) is a direct action organization modelled after the Clamshell Alliance. We now have an active membership of several hundred people as well a considerable, though unfocused, support from many other Indiana and Kentucky citizens.

There are PWA local groups in the following towns in Indiana: Richmond, Madison, Indianapolis, Evansville, Bloomington, Columbus, Muncie, Clarkville; and in these Kentucky towns: Louisville, Lexington, Bowling Green, and Henderson/Evansville.

*The German industrial heartland on the Rhine River bordering France.

Many thousands of valley residents have played a role in supporting a safe energy future. They are all heroes.

We are in touch with most of the Alliances around us and are particularly interested in expanding our contacts up and down the Ohio River. We plan to continue supporting direct actions, public campaigns, national actions, litigation, and other non-violent means to ensure a safe energy future for the Valley.

The main Paddlewheel contact address is:

Paddlewheel Alliance
1426 Highland Ave.
Louisville, Ky. 40204
502/584-7506

Citizen's Statement—30 April, 1977—
"We are walking from Louisville to Washington to symbolize the frustration and anxiety citizens across the nation are experiencing each time a nuclear reactor is proposed for their area of the country. In our area the citizens face the possibility of 100 to 200 power plants located on the Ohio River, of which 20% are projected to be nuclear.

"The continued lack of representation within the bureaucracies and the lack of due process of law within the Nuclear Regulatory Commission hearing offers the public no redress of grievance. It is for this reason that citizens of New Hampshire and others across the country have determined that civil disobedience is the only remaining alternative.

"It is our hope that this walk will focus attention on the April 30 occupation of a nuclear power plant site at Seabrook, New Hampshire. We want our walk to say to governmental leaders that the people of the United States should not have to resort to acts of civil disobedience in order to be heard, and we want it to further symbolize the sincere desire to avoid the type of confrontation that in the past has divided the country. Prosperity and harmony for our country and world can only be achieved through a united effort of citizenry and government."

The Jefferson County, Kentucky Judge/Executive sent a note with the walkers, which concluded: "There is no reason—other than profits for a utility—that the NRC has to rush ahead to license the plant at Marble Hill...Our citizens are walking to Washington as personal witnesses against the mistakes that are being made in our area."

L.J. Hollenbach, III

The Bailly Alliance

The Bailly Alliance opposes construction of the Bailly, IN reactor, the Morris Waste Dump, Zion nukes, and plans to work against the LaSalle, Dresden and Braidwood plants. Civil disobedience took place at the Morris Waste Dump on 19 August 1978. The Bailly Alliance also works with other anti-nuke groups in its area.

Contacts
Bailly Alliance
711 S. Dearborn; Rm. 548
Chicago, IL 60605
Prairie Alliance
P.O. box 2424, Sta. A
Champaign, IL 61820
Ohioans for Utility Reform
P.O. Box 10006
Columbus, OH 43201
Firelands Coalition for Safe Energy
P.O. Box 135
Berlin Heights, OH 44084
Citizens Against a Radioactive Environment (CARE)
3960 Winding Way, Cincinnati, OH

NORTHERN MID-WEST

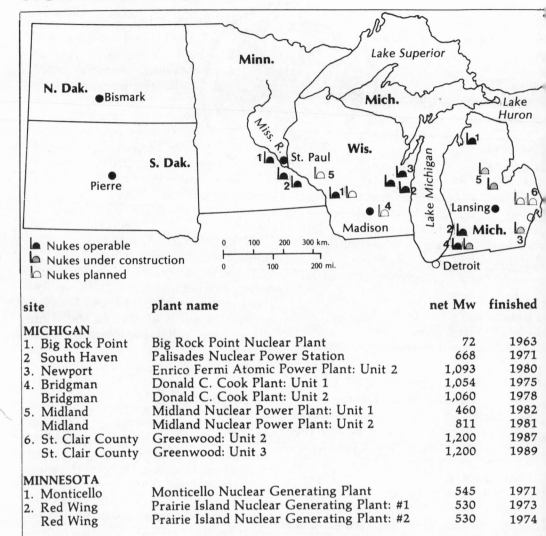

site	plant name	net Mw	finished
MICHIGAN			
1. Big Rock Point	Big Rock Point Nuclear Plant	72	1963
2 South Haven	Palisades Nuclear Power Station	668	1971
3. Newport	Enrico Fermi Atomic Power Plant: Unit 2	1,093	1980
4. Bridgman	Donald C. Cook Plant: Unit 1	1,054	1975
Bridgman	Donald C. Cook Plant: Unit 2	1,060	1978
5. Midland	Midland Nuclear Power Plant: Unit 1	460	1982
Midland	Midland Nuclear Power Plant: Unit 2	811	1981
6. St. Clair County	Greenwood: Unit 2	1,200	1987
St. Clair County	Greenwood: Unit 3	1,200	1989
MINNESOTA			
1. Monticello	Monticello Nuclear Generating Plant	545	1971
2. Red Wing	Prairie Island Nuclear Generating Plant: #1	530	1973
Red Wing	Prairie Island Nuclear Generating Plant: #2	530	1974
WISCONSIN			
1. La Crosse	La Crosse (Genoa) Nuclear Generating Station	50	1969
2. Two Creeks	Point Beach Nuclear Plant: Unit 1	497	1970
Two Creeks	Point Beach Nuclear Plant: Unit 2	497	1972
3. Carlton	Kewaunee Nuclear Power Plant: Unit 1	535	1974
4. Site not selected	Haven Nuclear Plant: Unit 1	900	1987
Site not selected	Haven Nuclear Plant: Unit 2	900	1989
5. Durand	Tyrone Energy Park: Unit 1	1,150	1984

The League Against Nuclear Dangers (LAND)

Background—Land was organized in May 1973 in response to a threat from the Wisconsin utilities (Wisconsin Electric, Wisconsin Power & Light, and Wisconsin Public Service Corp.) to construct 4,000 Mw of nuclear power by 1981 in the town of Rudolph in central Wisconsin. Now, five years later, one version of the utilities' Advance Plans mentions the *possibility* of 1,800 Mw in Rudolph by 1992; other versions have completely dropped the site. In the meantime, state agency action has prevented the siting of the same reactors at an alternate site, Lake Koshkonong, 30 miles south of Madison. Presently, the utilities are considering still another site—Haven on Lake Michigan—for the reactors.

LAND's success in arousing public awareness of the dangers inherent in nuclear technology is attested to by 13,000 signatures on the Clean Energy Petition from the Wisconsin 7th Congressional District—more than for any district in the nation.

One principle that has always guided our activity is Einstein's basic contention that "to the village square we must carry the facts of atomic energy... From there must come America's voice." We have always assumed that the ordinary American citizen *can understand* the basic issue and that, having understood, has a *constitutional right* to voice a decision.

LAND is a truly "grassroots" organization. The people on the land initiated the organization and have consistently sustained activity. But while the roots continued to be fed by local determination, they were also nourished by a world-wide information network. Now the fruits of our labor belong to the global fission fight and our "community"—like radioactivity itself—knows no borders, geographic, economic, political, philosophical. The truth is like that, democratic.

The Land Story—In the beginning it looked like a hopeless David & Goliath confrontation, but the first public meetings revealed our strength and gave our struggle direction. Utility VPs from the "big city" came in their $200 suits with their slick colorful "infor-

mation," proclaimed blanket "no risk" assurances of nuclear safety, and arrogantly declared that "public opinion" would have no effect on plant siting. They made a bad mistake—*and* cooked their own goose. They grossly underestimated the intelligence of their audience and insulted the dignity of people aware of constitutional rights. Their lies and arrogance were too gross. Murmurs of anger rose from the packed school gym, and LAND was born.

But anger is not enough. We needed knowledge to sustain, justify, and spread the anger. Fortunately, some of our early members were familiar with the hazards of nuclear weapons and fallout testing, and some had ties with members of the first fission fighters in eastern states. We contacted the national fission opponents organizations, *Nuclear Opponents*, National Intervenors, the Committee for Nuclear Responsibility, and the Lake Michigan Federation, who assisted us generously with literature and speakers. We found some funding through a University of Wisconsin-Stevens Point lecture series to help pay honorariums and traveling expenses for about a dozen speakers in quick succession. Now the issue was out in the open air of skepticism, and LAND support spread throughout the state.

Money has always been our largest problem, but auctions, candy and bake sales, paper drives manage to sustain publication of a newsletter, reprints of articles, brochures, research papers. No one in LAND is paid wages—although many of us have put in countless 14-hour days.

Knowledgeable speakers whetted our appetite for more facts. I cannot stress enough the necessity for us to *constantly* educate and reeducate ourselves! Only through *in depth* knowledge will we gain the self-confidence to address the public effectively. Only through the torturous route of constant reading, searching, and thinking will we and the public learn that utility "experts" are really only poorly informed PR agents at best; that at worst, the better-informed nuclear proponents are masters of evasion and cover-up.

We started a LAND library of every periodical, study, or book we could find. (In 1973 there weren't many.) This proved expensive and the burden was absorbed by individual members pooling resources. We regularly read more than a dozen important periodicals, a half-dozen newspapers and countless "newsletters." In addition we are alert to nuclear news in dozens of other publications. Federal and state agency hearing reports are collected also. We are fortunate to have access to all federal documents at the UW-Stevens Point Library.

In an unprecedented action, we requested the Public Document Room materials for operating reactors from the AEC in order to find out what goes on. The AEC complied (in part) by assigning the University the Document Room (i.e., materials) for the Point Beach plants. (I urge all nuclear opponents to familiarize themselves with Public Document Rooms. Don't be dismayed by the jargon and the volume of paper. Many important facts lie there awaiting discovery.)

For instance, we discovered an AEC Inspection Report critical of radiation monitoring, which led us to investigate the woefully inadequate means of assessing radiation dose to the public. Here, too, we discovered the special hazards to nuclear workers, the inadequacy of evacuation planning, and much more. Cover-ups became apparent. For instance, a public news release that there was no "inadvertent" release of radioactivity to the public during the

shutdown of Point Beach turned out to mean that the *containment* was "purged" of 1,400 curies of radioactive gas *on purpose*, and that over 7,000 gallons of primary to secondary leakage occurred. (Be on the alert for the real meaning of every modifier.)

Being knowledgeable is one thing; giving it to others is the most difficult and necessary follow-up. We have tried to do this on all levels and in as many directions as possible. Other methods have been an outcome of our handicaps (primarily economic) and our advantages (primarily our talented membership who within our loose organization have felt free to develop their own ideas). We have not evaluated the relative importance of activities, but one thing is clear: Nuclear proponents cannot survive public scrutiny; every public confrontation reveals truths about nuclear hazards which would otherwise remain hidden forever in document rooms and executive suites.

Besides our billboards, street petitioning and polling drives, parades, and countless "letters to the editor," "going public" has also meant active participation at all levels of government, from the town meeting to state and federal legislatures. Much of LAND's success must be credited to the watch-dog persistence of the citizens in the town of Rudolph, who reversed an initial approval of the proposed plant by the chairman and zoning board by demanding a referendum vote. County Board of Supervisors' opposition to the plant has increased from 8% to 41%. **People can be made to change their minds.**

As for the nuclear issues: I think groups tend to place concerns in a too-narrow focus (i.e., *only* on the waste problem or reliability). We have continued to pursue the low-level radiation dose problem and the nuclear

Demonstrators outside nuclear moratorium hearings in Madison.

worker hazards. The industry has no answers to these and they are problems which absolutely cannot be avoided (unlike those *possible* problems such as meltdowns, sabotage, etc.).

The unique characteristics of LAND are difficult to summarize but among the most meaningful are:

• We are truly grassroots in origin and membership: we are housewives, farmers, businesspeople, PhD's, grade school students, teachers. People of all political, religious, social, and economic positions have learned to work together. The issue transcends all differences.

• Our efforts have no boundaries of time, space, depth. When "our site" was rejected 2½ years ago we did not stop working, because "site citizens" whose first concern was their land have grown to see nuclear power as a global problem. When our search for information led us into the unknown, we did our own research—on radiation monitoring, evacuation, worker hazards, and cancer incidence. Citizen researchers can successfully challenge the "technological experts" and PR agents.

• We have been willing to work very hard, day after day. We have had to learn many new things: how to run a mimeograph, how to write a news release, how to blow up ballons, paint signs, and interpret documents. We have not hesitated to do whatever

seemed necessary at any time.

• The core leadership of LAND has been sustained by a love of the land, by a respect for life, and a belief that the will of an informed public will not allow the fission proponents to destroy our world. This land is our land!

Organizing—Here are some of the ways we have found to "go public" We speak to anyone who will listen: in classrooms from junior high school to college; to senior citizens and ladies auxiliaries; to farmers and Chambers of Commerce; at state hearings whether on rate increases, land use, or nuclear moratoriums; to county boards and church groups; on radio and television. Many LAND members have carried the message informally to their own clubs, neighborhoods, friends, relatives. We are not shy.

We have asked for debates with proponents. We challenged local utility managers and the local (utility-sponsored) pro-nuclear group to a neighbor-to-neighbor debate. They disqualified themselves! We arranged a high-level debate with John Gofman and the AEC Director, Dixie Lee Ray. The AEC bowed out. After utilities gave all the usual assurances of nuclear safety (no cancers, no accidents, no damage to foods, etc.) we presented the Assurance of Safety document for their signature at a public occasion. They, of course, refused to sign. These challenges were extremely effective— they shattered the pro-nuclear "expert" myth and shocked the public.

We have used signs of all kinds. Billboards have announced that the town of Rudolph opposed nuclear power and favors solar development. "Burma Shave"-type-signs along the roads are reminders that: NUCLEAR LEAKS/CAN CAUSE/HUMAN FREAKS. Once we erected a street banner proclaiming "nuclear power poisons." It was hung by city employees with city

permission on utility poles traditionally used for this purpose. The
utility was shocked and ordered it torn
down. A scandal erupted in the
mayor's office, with the upshot being
that the banner (rescued on its way to
the dump) was rehung on the main
street only a half block from the
nuclear-loving utility! All this publicity
came our way as a bonus, thanks to the
the arrogant stupidity of the utility
corporation.

Here are examples of our street
actions. One was called "project information." We asked citizens five simple
factual questions about nuclear plants.
We then explained the answers and
the people were given an opportunity
to sign the Clean Energy Petition.

We also picketed with signs: at a
county board meeting, after LAND
had been denied access; at the local
utility office; at state nuclear moratorium hearings; at a state college where
the director of the AEC was speaking
after having claimed she was too busy
to debate Dr. Gofman; at a protest of
an alternate plant site.

We use the newspapers, which regularly receive our news releases. Fortunately, some area newspapers have
resisted corporate pressure to reject
our news. Newspapers who have consistently refused to publish us are
likely to find a picket or two handing
out news releases in front of the publishing firm.

We could only afford one advertising campaign, but it brought us hundreds of inquiries and members. The
ad featured a 30-mile "impact area"
radius of the proposed plant. It was
printed in three area Shoppers' Guides.
We also started a series of "atomic
quizzes"—questions and answers that
included documentation using mostly
official documents. Although our funds
ran out, we have kept up a constant
flow of "letters to the editor." These

The very controversial street banner—LAND

often take the form of public debate, as
utilities still attempt to discredit us.
But happily we have always had the
last word in such encounters! When
utilities attack our sources, we notify
the scientists concerned, who have
retaliated by sending in their own
statements. Public relations agents
cannot stand up to real facts. Our
letters have publicly demonstrated
LAND's ability to document our statements, and since they are often written
by "non-experts," they have proved
that people with common sense **can**
understand the nuclear issues.

Wisconsin Farmers
Oppose NSP Nuclear Plans

It was late August 1977. The Sheriff's
deputies pulled into the farm drive-
way, nose-to-nose with the battered
pick-up blocking the entrance to the
farm. The real estate agents pulled up
nearby in their Cadillac, parked along
the edge of the country road, and sat
waiting with the windows rolled up.
The deputies emerged from their un-
marked car in official uniforms and
moved toward a bearded farmer
dressed in a blue work shirt and jeans.

The Sheriff's deputies carried papers ordering the farm's occupants to
let the real estate agents enter and
assess the farm lands and buildings.

The region's utility, Northern States Power Company (NSP) had gotten 40 acres of the Falkner Farm condemned to be used for the proposed Tyrone Nuclear Power Plant.

Henry Falkner's dairy farm is located in the green, rolling hills of west-central Wisconsin. He has worked his farm for about 38 years with the help of his sons. He has around 30 head of cattle and 152 acres of land in Dunn County. NSP first tried to seize the whole farm in Dunn County, but Henry and Clara Falkner held out against NSP, beating them back to 40 acres.

NSP began its land acquisition in 1969 wihout revealing that the land would be used for a nuclear power plant site. NSP warned owners that failure to sell immediately would lead to condemnation and lower prices. They told one farmer that his neighbors were "dealing behind his back," and used other divide-and-conquer techniques. Three families, the Ciders, Bauers, and Falkners have held fast against all NSP tactics.

But this August afternoon, the deputies toted pistols on their hips. The battle had moved from the hearing rooms and courtrooms to the farmer's home. One of the deputies pulled out a court order and began describing it to Bob Falkner, one of Henry Falkner's sons. Bob referred the deputy to his father, Henry, who was digging potatoes behind the farm buildings. A television crew from Channel 13 in Eau Claire and supporters from the Northern Sun Alliance in Eau Claire braved the drizzle to observe the confrontation.

Henry's other sons arrived shortly with their neighbor, Stan Cider, one of the two residents remaining within the abandoned village of Tyrone and a veteran of the struggle with NSP. Stan Cider and Francis Falkner demanded to know what the deputies wanted. The Deputy explained the court order again, and Francis stated his disagreement with it. He argued that he had a constitutional right to privacy and advised the assessors to keep off the land.

The deputies went back to their car to radio for reinforcements. The cloudy skies became grayer and rain splashed down off and on as the parties waited. Lucille and Clara Bauer arrived from a a neighboring farm that had been inspected earlier that day by the same assessors.

Lucille explained that these assessors had previously undervalued the Bauer farm. Although land without buildings sells for at least $700/acre in the area, the Bauers were only offered $350/acre for 200 acres of farmland with a house, barn, and other farm buildings.

One assessor had even claimed that the Bauer farm buildings were about to topple. An indignant Lucille Bauer insisted that the assessors be accompanied by the sheriff's deputies to ensure that no one was hurt by the alleged falling buildings. The assessors traversed the property without injury, their Cadillac followed into the corn-field by a caravan that included the TV crew and local supporters.

When the Sheriff arrived at the Falkner farm, followed by an official sheriff's car from the next county, the confrontation began once again. The Sheriff alternately explained, cajoled, and invoked the court order. The farm family resisted, refusing to accept responsibility for anything that might happen if the assessors entered the farm. Finally, the assessors themselves emerged from the Cadillac in their city suits and followed the uniformed Sheriff to the edge of the farm to try their persuasive powers. But the Falkner family remained firm in its opposition. The Sheriff was unwilling to enforce the court order by arresting local farmers in front of a television camera, so the assessors quietly returned to town without assessing the Falkner's land.

The Falkner's have spent thousands of dollars on extensive battles in administrative proceedings and Wisconsin court actions, and the family is determined to oppose further action towards the illegal theft of their land by NSP. Neither they nor the Bauers and Ciders will leave their land voluntarily.

Citizens for Tomorrow was formed by Tyrone area farmers in 1972 to save the land from becoming a nuclear energy park. The Northern Sun Alliance is organizing support groups to help pervent any evictions. Supporters can contribute or offer help.

Kitty Tucker
Environmental Policy Center
Washington, D.C.
August 1977

Northern Sun Alliance
P.O. Box 8794
Minneapolis MN 55408

Citizens for Tomorrow
Rte. 1, Box 191
Rock Falls, WI 54764

League Against Nuclear Dangers (LAND)
RR 1, Rudolph, WI 54475

"If you kill our farms, your cities will die.."

Farmers and Allies Fight Power Lines in Minnesota

People are resisting the spread of high-tension power lines in the states of New York, Wisconsin, Ohio, Nebraska, Washington, and Texas. Perhaps the bitterest battle to date has been in Minnesota, where two power companies are building an 800 kV direct current line that begins at a coal burning plant in Underwood, North Dakota and travels east through rural Minnesota farm land.

If this line operates, it will ultimately be administered by the Mid-Conti-

nental Area Power Pool (MAPP). As such it will be an essential part of an energy grid that already includes at least two operating nuclear power plants. Given present technology, high tension lines are a necessary part of nuclear plant operation.

The line is an example of planned energy development running counter to local needs and desires. And it has sparked a significant public opposition movement. In the western part of the state more than 100 people, mostly farmers, have been arrested for alleged illegal activities while protesting construction of the line.

Farmers oppose the line because it cuts through their farms—many of which have been in their families for generations. Since studies on the long-term effects of exposure to electrical fields created by the lines have not been done, the farmers would in effect be "unwilling experimental subjects."[1] Farmers oppose the taking of their land for the line's right-of-way by eminent domain; few have picked up the money that the utilities have offered for their land.

The farmers also challenge the companies' claim of a need for the powerline. The line would feed into the Northern States Power electrical grid, which had a 1000 Mw surplus in summer '77, enough to cover the line. In addition, growth of electrical demand in the area was overestimated.[2]

Although the power companies (Cooperative Power Association and United Power Association) call their structure "democratic" because they have local boards of directors, farmers maintain that there was never an informed discussion about the powerline decision by the local board of directors or the general membership, "let alone by the people directly affected...The farmers felt that the decisions came down from Washington and the local REA (Rural Electrification Administration) just followed orders."[3] "Some people believe that CPA-UPA are just a cover as a way of getting energy to St. Louis and Chicago because those cities can not have any more pollution produced near them."[4]

The farmers learned about the line in the summer of '74. After legal efforts to halt the line failed, farmers resorted to non-violent obstructionist tactics. They stopped the line in Pope County in December 1976. A moratorium on building was declared until after the state Supreme Court ruled on the issue.

The farmers are supported by the Pope County government and business community. County commissioners as well as 21 mayors have come out in support of the farmers; one mayor has been arrested. Throughout the state, there has been widespread sympathy for the farmers. In a poll reported in April 1978, 63% of people asked sided with the farmers in their fight; 35% favored the electric power cooperatives.[5]

When the Minnesota Supreme Court ruled in favor of the line at the end of September 1977, construction resumed and the farmers stepped up their opposition.

On October 8th, members of the Movement for a New Society gave a workshop on non-violence for some 80 farmers. A whole range of imaginative tactics ensued, such as driving up and down dusty roads in front of surveyor's sights, blocking surveyor's trucks with abandoned trucks and 1000 pound boulders, spreading manure with a favorable wind, riding horses to block surveyors and then preventing arrests by riding slowly to let others get

away. After the snow fell, snowmobiles were used to encircle surveyors and to snatch tripods.

The two power coops responded with court injunctions prohibiting interference as well as six $500,000 suits for obstruction by individual farmers and unnamed others.[6]

In the fall of 1977, the first urban supporters came out to join the farmers. Many of the city people were young "long-haired" radicals, former anti-war activists. The farmers had made contact with potential supporters through a food coop that linked rural producers with urban stores.

By all accounts the new help was welcome. "We don't care how they look or what they did in the past," said farmer Alice Tripp to a St. Paul newspaper, "It's time to forget our differences and work together to stop the corporations and bureaucracies from rolling over us."[7] In November 1977, six people from the Twin Cities (St. Paul/Minneapolis) stood in for farmers at the Tripp farm and were arrested for blocking construction. Farmers had been scared by the huge lawsuits filed against those who had first blocked construction crews. The support of radicals and a wide spectrum of environmentalists from the cities gave new momentum to the struggle.

The fight is still going on, even as the companies attempt to complete the line by spring '79. There have been night-time raids on completed towers. Seven tower legs were torched through in one evening in July '78. During the first two weeks of August, four of the 150 foot towers were unbolted and destroyed as they hit the earth. So far the protests have again delayed completion of the line, at great cost to the companies.[8]

Given the unyielding opposition of the local people and their supporters, it is questionable whether the companies will ever be able to guarantee use of the line even if it is completed under armed guard.

Contacts

General Assembly to Stop the Powerline
Lowry, MN 56349

Twin Cities Northern Sun Alliance
1513 East Franklin Ave.
Minneapolis, MN 55404

Footnotes

1. Don Olson, "Hold That Line!", *Soil of Liberty*, North Country Anarchists and Anarcho-Feminists, Vol. 4, No. 1&2, May-June 1978. p. 4. See also: Paul Brodeur's *Zapping of America* and Louise Young's *Power Over People*.

2. *Ibid.*

3. "The Rural Electrification Administration was a New Deal Program of the 30s to bring electricity to rural America which could not be profitably served by private utilities. Initially eligible for 2% interest loans, they now pay closer to market rates for capital...Each local REA has a board of directors elected by the membership and each board elects one member to sit on the board of directors of CPA or UPA. Throughout this struggle, CPA and UPA have continually pointed to this as a democratic structure, controlled from below. While the boards are the ultimate decision makers, discussions with a few farmers who had been on local boards revealed the old story of their being at the mercy of the greater technical expertise and information of management and especially of the general manager." *Ibid.*, pp. 2-3.

4. *Ibid.*, p. 4.

5. *Ibid.*, p. 5.

5. *Minneapolis Tribune*, 2 April 1978.

6. *Ibid.*

7. *St. Paul Pioneer Press*, 4 December 1977.

8. Spring '78 estimates ranged up to $43.5 million for costs stemming from vandalism, delay and other protest-related expenses. Final costs for the entire project could be as much as $1.2 billion.

(Credit: *Soil of Liberty*)

Detroit Safe Energy Coalition

SECO was born in early 1977 to educate about nukes and organize for direct action against nuclear power. The group is made up of neighborhood affinity groups with a coordinating committee of one person from each group. SECO believes in direct action, working at the neighborhood level to awaken people to nuclear power dangers. "Legislators are influenced more by lobbyists than by facts and respond slowly to polite public opinion." SECO has worked with other groups, including the Friends of the Earth in Ann Arbor and PIRGIM (Michigan's Public Interest Research Group).

Contact

SECO, Box 1074, Detroit MI 48231
Great Lakes Energy Alliance, P.O. Box 1069-A, Bay City MI 48706

MID-WEST

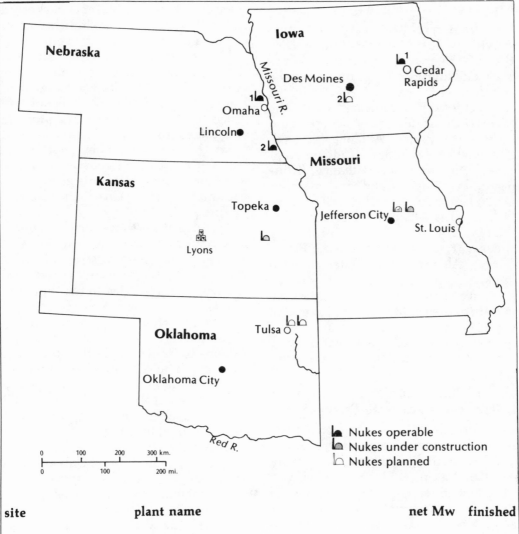

site	plant name	net Mw	finished
IOWA			
1. Palo	Duane Arnold Energy Center: Unit 1	538	1975
2. Vandalia	Vandalia Nuclear Project	1,270	Indef.
KANSAS			
Burlington	Wolf Creek Generating Station: Unit 1	1,150	1983
MISSOURI			
1. Fulton	Callaway Plant: Unit 1	1,120	1982
Fulton	Callaway Plant: Unit 2	1,120	1987
OKLAHOMA			
Inola	Black Fox Nuclear Station: Unit 1	1,150	1984
Inola	Black Fox Nuclear Station: Unit 2	1,150	1986
NEBRASKA			
1. Fort Calhoun	Ft. Calhoun Station: Unit 1	457	1973
2. Brownville	Cooper Nuclear Station	778	1974

Midwest

Introduction for Midwest—Anti-nuke activity in the Midwest, (along with that of the rest of the country), has been building in momentum over the last decade. In the past year much of this activity has coalesced with the formation of alliances which now include the Prairie Alliance (Illinois), Paddlewheel Alliance (Indiana-Kentucky), Northern Sun Alliance, (Minnesota-Wisconsin) and its member group Northern Thunder (Wisconsin), Dekalb Area Alliance for Responsible Energy (DAARE, Illinois), Sunflower Alliance (Kansas), and the Great Plains Energy Alliance (now Federation) in Iowa, Missouri, Kansas and Arkansas. All share a commitment to using a wide variety of non-violent means to replace the development of nuclear power with programs of conservation and conversion to safe, renewable energy sources.

Great Plains Federation/ Missourians For Safe Energy

Background—Missouri currently has no nuclear power stations operating, but two are under construction. In July of 1973, the Union Electric company of St. Louis announced they would build twin 1,150-megawatt nukes on 7,187 acres already purchased in southeastern Callaway County. (They had assembled the land under false pretenses. Their agents came in and bought it indirectly, spreading rumors it was being bought for a nudist colony!)

Early opposition was legalistic. Intervention by the St. Louis Coalition for the Environment and the Kansas City based Mid-America Coalition for Energy Alternatives did very little to slow down the licensing process. Opposition from local Fulton area citizens did not draw enough interest to set up any ongoing anti-nuke organization. Friends of the Earth and other environ-

mental groups in Columbia expressed opposition and concern, but this didn't catalyze a mass protest movement.

The first direct action opposition to the Callaway construction came in the summer of 1975 when a handful of Kansas City activists took a canoe trip down the Missouri River and stopped and talked to local residents in each town they came to. They ended their trip with a balloon release near the plant site. The core of this group later became the Kansas City People's Energy Project (KC PEP).

In April of 1976 an alternative energy symposium was held outside Columbia. The film *Lovejoy's Nuclear War* was shown, sparking a spontaneous workshop that led to the founding of Missourians for Safe Energy. It turned out that many people in the Columbia area were concerned and anxious to fight the plants, but needed a vehicle to do so. During the summer of 1976 there were study group meetings and self-education increased both the concern and the credibility of the nuclear opponents.

In April 1976 actual construction of the plants began. Then, in late July and early August, the Continental Walk for Disarmament and Social Justice made its way across our region. The focus of the Walk in Missouri was nuclear power, and folks in Kansas City, Columbia, Fulton and St. Louis linked up and walked. A "die-in"* was held in Kansas City at the offices of Kansas City Power and Light. Leafletting, parades and several showings of the Lovejoy film drew interest in Fulton and Columbia.

The Great Plains Alliance Forms—November 1976 marked our first large-scale protest, a 38-mile three-day

---

*A die-in is a demonstration which uses the theatrical technique of a mass of people going through the agonies of dying and then falling still on the ground to illustrate the lethal potential of nuclear technology

march from Columbia to the plant site. At its climax this march brought together local opponents, Missourians for Safe Energy, KC PEP, and People for Disarmament and Social Justice of St. Louis, and it led to the founding of our alliance. November 1976 also marked the electoral victory of an initiative proposition barring the utilities from charging for Construction Work in Progress, CWIP). Now they could not pay for nuclear construction with rate hikes, and Missouri ratepayers do not have to pay for plants before they actually produce electricity.

Originally billed the Sho-Me Alliance, it soon became clear that our focus extended beyond the bounds of Missouri. For one thing, Kansas City nuclear opponents were starting to shift their concerns towards the Wolf Creek plant being built by Kansas City Power and Light and Kansas Gas and Electric near Burlington, Kansas. The Wolf Creek Station, about a year behind Callaway in construction, is a single 1,150-megawatt plant identical in design to the Callaway Station. They are both SNUPPS—Standard Nuclear Unit Power Plant System—plants. Nuclear opponents from Iowa City, Ames, and Cedar Rapids, Iowa expressed interest in joining forces with us. So the Great Plains Alliance was born.

The Alliance decided to stage a region-wide event on 30 April to 1 May 1977 to coincide with the occupation of Seabrook and other nuclear protests around the country. A ten-acre field about three miles from the Callaway reactor site was located for a Safe Energy Fair—combining solar displays, music, food, camping and nuclear protest. Despite a torrential downpour, about 400-500 people turned out. A march to the reactor site Saturday afternoon drew a counter demonstration of about 40 people, mostly plant workers.

An evaluation after the Fair led us to feel that for the most part, decentralized actions done in a coordinated fashion region-wide would yield more results and less burnout.** During the summer of 1977, much effort went into public education through film showings, booths at fairs, canvassing, etc. On August 6 - 9, the Alliance coordinated petitioning with the National Clean Energy Petition and staged several projects, notably one at Burlington, Kansas. Put together by the Wolf Creek Nuclear Opposition and KC PEP, this event drew 150-200 people and included a balloon release and another die-in.

As the movement has grown, the Great Plains Alliance has become the Great Plains Federation of Nuclear Opponents and Safe Energy Proponents. The Sunflower Alliance has formed in the Kansas area and is focusing on the Wolf Creek project with an eduation and direct action campaign. Throughout the region an effort is being made to broaden the base of nuclear opposition. Coalitions with labor unions, ratepayer groups, and appropriate technology proponents are being built around areas of mutual concern.

Demonstrations such as those held on Karen Silkwood Memorial Weekend (12-13 November 1977) and those planned for the spring and summer of 1978, punctuate our concern and draw attention to the movement. But our movement includes more—the full-time activities of education and outreach work, film showings, public meetings, newsletter production, etc. These actions are building a new consensus to stop nuclear power in the Great Plains region.

Mark Haim, MSE

**Burnout is a no-nuke term for organizer/activist over-exhaustion. It is a condition to be prevented by not taking on more than any one person or group can do! (Ed.)

Great Plains Federation Statement of Purpose
Adopted: 11 September 1977

We are united in active non-violent opposition to the development and maintenance of nuclear power plants anywhere. "Non-violence" should be understood as a respectful non-destructive and fair attitude toward our fellow humans.

Alliance members and other individuals and groups use a wide variety of methods such as education, legislative, court and regulatory action, referendum, petitioning, demonstrations, and other forms of public protest in their efforts toward this common goal. We support and welcome all efforts toward these ends.

We support and encourage conservation of our natural resources—which means doing better, not doing without—and widespread conversion to safe, clean, and renewable energy sources such as solar and wind power. These sources are best used in a decentralized manner under local control.

Nuclear power poses an unnecessary threat to our health, safety and the quality of our society. Our concern for all life requires us to take action.

Local Groups in the Great Plains Federation

*Citizens United for Responsible Energy
1342 30th Street   CURE
Des Moines, Iowa 50311
515/277-0253

*Coalition for the Environment
6267 Delmar
St. Louis, Mo. 63105
314/727-0600

Free Environment
Activities Center IMU
University of Iowa
Iowa City, Iowa 52242
319/353-3888

Kansas City Peoples Energy Project
4311 Holmes
Kansas City, Mo. 64110
816/753-5370

Missourians for Safe Energy
811 Cherry St. Rm 319
Columbia, Mo. 65201
314/449-LIFE

People for Disarmament and Social Justice
6340 Southwood Apt. 3S
Clayton, Mo. 63105

Peoples Power Project
Box 3179
St. Louis, Mo. 63130

*Wolf Creek Nuclear Opposition
c/o Francis Blaufuss
Westphalia, Kansas 66093

*Kansans for Sensible Energy (KASE)
1340 N. Hillside
Wichita, Kansas 67208

*These groups have not formally joined the GPF but have worked with us and attended our meetings.

The following are addresses of contacts around which new local groups are forming. (as of summer 1978).

SW Missouri Contact
Jim Butler
916 S. Missouri
Springfield, Mo. 65806

Missouri Ozarks Contact
Ozark Area Community Congress
c/o David Haenke
Box 67-2
Caulfield, Mo. 65626

Northern Arkansas Contact
James H. Diggs
Rt. 1, Box 87
Eureka Springs, Ark. 72632

Oklahoma/Citizens' Action for Safe Energy (CASE)

Public Service Company of Oklahoma (PSO) plans to build two nuclear power plants (Black Fox 1 and 2) near Inola, a small town thirteen miles east of Tulsa. Plans are underway to convert Camp Gruber, now largely a public hunting area in eastern Oklahoma near the Arkansas border, into a huge energy-producing complex. In May 1973, when PSO announced their plans, the plant's cost was put at $450 million. They're now quoting $1.5 billion—some experts say $2.5 billion is more accurate. This money will be paid for by increased rates to the electricity consumers if the proposed nuclear plants are built.

Citizen's Action for Safe Energy, Inc. (CASE) evolved as a result of the study of nuclear power (both pro and con) by a few Oklahoma citizens. In the fall of 1975, CASE informed the AEC of its intention to intervene in the public hearings required by law to be held, and it requested information concerning date and place of the hearings. Instead of writing, the AEC sent a representative from Washington, D.C. to meet with CASE representatives. He tried to persuade CASE not to intervene in the public hearings. But our representatives knew of real reasons why a nuclear power plant should not be built in Inola and felt that both sides of this issue should be aired in public hearings—not the least of which reasons were PSO's estimates of construction costs, which were less than half the cost of plants proposed in other states!

CASE has secured the services of attorneys and expert witnesses to represent us in the hearings. We believe that we have a very strong case against the proposed Black Fox nuclear power plants. Had no one intervened, PSO would already be building them. We believe our side of the issue must be heard, not only the NRC, but also by the public at large.

The Black Fox project may be in trouble.

In 1974 the Oklahoma Corporation Commission refused to grant PSO's requested rate increase. This denial forced the utility to delay their Black Fox plants for one year.

In addition, the utility must have a firm commitment for a water supply of 44 million gallons per day. The plants would require 28,000 gallons of water per minute for cooling. For two years, CASE members in Tulsa have been trying to prevent Tulsa city commissioners from signing a water contract with PSO for Lake Oolagah water or sewage effluent water.

We wish we could report that we have won our fight—that Black Fox has been routed! But, we fear it will be a long, drawnout battle. Perhaps the fight will not be ended until solar is cheap enough to take the place of nuclear. That is what we're pushing here. CASE has sponsored numerous workshops teaching people to "do-it-yourself." We're organizing for "Sun Day," 3 May 1978, in the belief that this will greatly help our cause. There is much solar activity in Oklahoma. Where two years ago there was only one solar architect in Tulsa, now there are about twenty!

God Bless all our efforts to stop nuclear power everywhere!

Carrie Dickerson, Chairperson
CASE
P.O. Box 924
Claremore, Ok. 74017

**Stop
Black Fox**

TEXAS

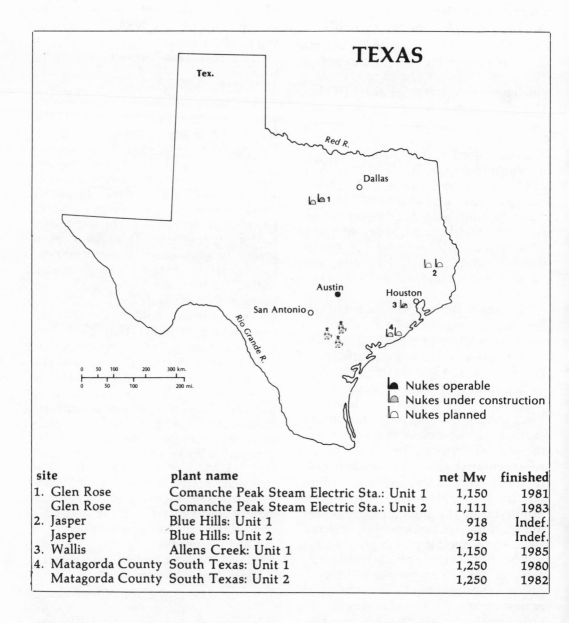

site	plant name	net Mw	finished
1. Glen Rose	Comanche Peak Steam Electric Sta.: Unit 1	1,150	1981
Glen Rose	Comanche Peak Steam Electric Sta.: Unit 2	1,111	1983
2. Jasper	Blue Hills: Unit 1	918	Indef.
Jasper	Blue Hills: Unit 2	918	Indef.
3. Wallis	Allens Creek: Unit 1	1,150	1985
4. Matagorda County	South Texas: Unit 1	1,250	1980
Matagorda County	South Texas: Unit 2	1,250	1982

Nukes operable
Nukes under construction
Nukes planned

Armadillo Coalition of Texas

Texas is the location of a major nuclear weapons manufacturing plant, large uranium mining and milling operations, five reactors under construction, and it is now being considered for a national nuclear waste dump.

In January of 1978, 10 groups in five Texas cities formed the Armadillo Coalition of Texas, although ACT had already seen the light as early as the summer of 1977 when a few friends formed the first group in Ft. Worth. Since the winter meeting, the new organization has grown to include 19 groups in eight cities with a total membership of about 500 people.

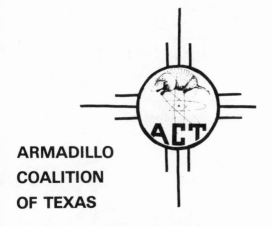

ARMADILLO COALITION OF TEXAS

We are in the process of building the foundation for what we hope will become a much larger movement. We've concentrated on educating the public and have put out a newsletter, appeared on radio and TV, and held small demonstrations. This strategy has been successful; we've gained new members with every presentation and have managed—even with our limited numbers—to put the utilities on edge. We're just now beginning to feel confident enough to call for a state-wide demonstration, and are thinking more seriously about increasingly dramatic tactics to stop nuclear power.

Armadillo Coalition of Texas (ACT)
P.O. Box 828
Fort Worth, Texas 76101
Newsletter for ACT, *ACT NOW*: $5/year.

Lone Star Alliance

This is a statewide organization of local groups in North Texas, Austin and San Antonio. It formed following the state's first anti-nuke rally in late May, 1978, at the Comanche Peak plant site. Each participating group sends two representatives to monthly open meetings. Decisions are reached by consensus. Major concerns are legislative drives for banning both waste disposal sites in Texas and nuclear waste transport through the state. This region would be a major transport crossroads for waste of the WIPP project if approved in New Mexico.

Contacts:

Lone Star Alliance
c/o Todd Samusson
2521 Enfield
Austin, TX 78703

ACT (see above)

Texas Mobilization for Survival
c/o A.F.S.C.
600 West 28th #102
Austin, TX 78705

Citizens Concerned About Nuclear Power
c/o Coral Ryan
106 13th St.
San Antonio, TX 78215

MOUNTAIN STATES & THE SOUTHWEST

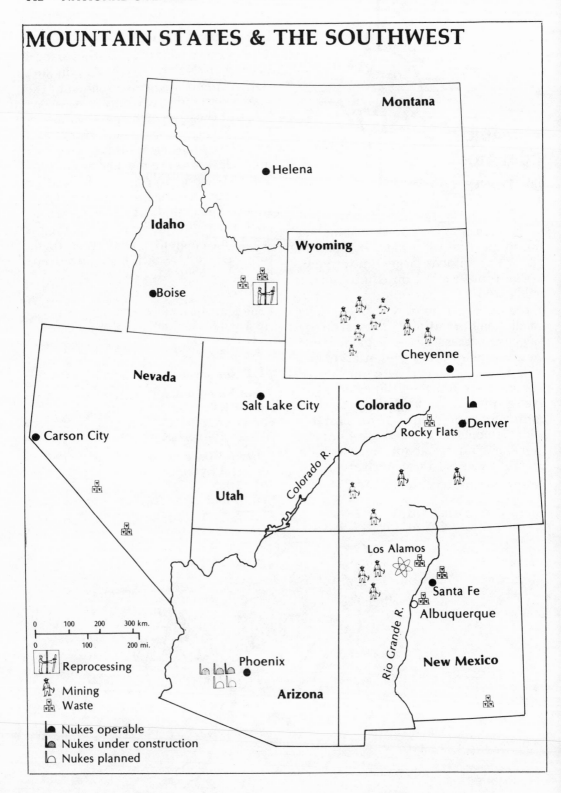

Montana

●Helena

Idaho

Wyoming

●Boise

Cheyenne
●

Nevada

Salt Lake City
●

Colorado

● Carson City

Denver
●
Rocky Flats

Utah

Colorado R.

Los Alamos

Santa Fe
●
Albuquerque

Rio Grande R.

New Mexico

| 0 | 100 | 200 | 300 km. |

| 0 | 100 | 200 mi. |

Reprocessing

Mining

Waste

Phoenix
●

Arizona

Nukes operable
Nukes under construction
Nukes planned

ARIZONA			
Wintersburg	Palo Verde Nuclear Generating Station: Unit 1	1,237	1983
Wintersburg	Palo Verde Nuclear Generating Station: Unit 2	1,237	1984
Wintersburg	Palo Verde Nuclear Generating Station: Unit 3	1,237	1986
Wintersburg	Palo Verde Nuclear Generating Station: Unit 4	1,237	1988
Wintersburg	Palo Verde Nuclear Generating Station: Unit 5	1,237	1990
COLORADO			
Platteville	Ft. St. Vrain Nuclear Generating Station	330	1978

Underground Testing in Colorado

Fall, 1974—"The Atomic Energy Commission detonated two underground nuclear blasts in Colorado—Project Rulison and Project Rio Blanco—both technological failures and economic disasters. The former, detonated in 1969, cost over $11 million and produced $1.5 million of gas, which was radioactive. The latter used $12 million in government funds alone and has produced no gas. If the $79 million spent on the three Plowshare underground nuclear blasts (including Project Gasbuggy in New Mexico) had been spent on insulating Colorado homes, annual savings in gas alone would be five times as much as the projected annual gas production of the three wells.

"The AEC plans more than 40,000 blasts in our state. Efforts to control these plans have failed."

—from a leaflet put out by People for Rational Energy Sources 3 So. Cook St. Denver, Co. 80209

The Initiative in Colorado

—On 5 November 1974, a 60% majority of Colorado voters passed Amendment Ten, which prohibits all underground nuclear explosions in Colorado unless they have the prior approval of voters by a direct popular vote at regular state elections. If Colorado citizens do give approval to a nuclear blast according to the provisions of Amendment Ten, the sponsors of the blast would be required to provide full and complete insurance against all seismic and radiological damage. To place this initiative on the ballot, the sponsors obtained 69,710 signatures.

Rocky Flats

The Rocky Flats Nuclear Weapons Facility was established in 1952 under the auspices of the U.S. Atomic Energy Commission (AEC) as a second facility (the first was at Hanford, Washington) for the manufacture of nuclear weapons components and for the conduct of nuclear research. Rocky Flats makes several plutonium component assemblies for hydrogen bombs each day. It is at present the only plant doing this in the country, although other federal facilities could be tooled up to do it. These plutonium component assemblies must be purified every so often and therefore are returned periodically to Rocky Flats from U.S. military installations around the world.

The Rocky Flats plant cost $250 million to build. Since then, more than $40 million has been spent to repair damage from fires and make safety improvements, $20 million to buy a buffer strip of land around the perimeter, and $130 million is now being spent for construction of new plutonium-recovery and water-recycling facilities.

The Dow Chemical Company was awarded the management contract of the plant at its inception. Following a number of management problems, Dow did not bid to renew its contract in 1975 and Rockwell International was given management responsibility. Currently the plant employs 2,800 workers with an annual payroll of $40

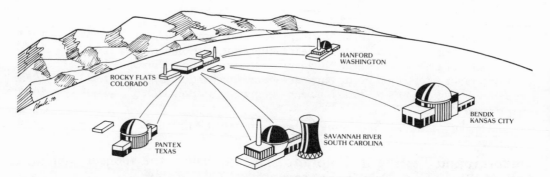

The Rocky Flats Plant, which manufactures plutonium triggers for nuclear warheads, is a vital link in a nuclear weapons production chain that includes: receipt of bomb grade plutonium from Hanford and Savannah River; dismantling of weapons at Pantex; fabrication of electric and electro-mechanical parts at Kansas City...(Credit: *Local Hazard/Global Threat*, Rocky Flats Action Grp.)

million. In the past 22 years about 9,000 workers have been employed. The Lamm-Wirth Task Force on Rocky Flats reported that "some 170 people have been exposed to 'significant' dose rates during the course of their employment at the Rocky Flats plant."

In 1974 the American Friends Service Committee and Environmental Action of Colorado brought together people from various peace, environmental, women's, etc. communities to form a new coalition, the Rocky Flats Action Group. RFAG's goals are to: close the plant, participate in the anti-nuclear/disarmament effort, and end nuclear weapons proliferation and the export of nuclear technology to developing countries. The campaign has included demonstrations, vigils, citizen education, and pressuring of government agencies. The decision to make Rocky Flats a national issue led to the April 1978 demonstration and a symbolic blockade of the railroad, which ships wastes.

(Source: "The Plutonium Situation at Rocky Flats," Nuclear Information Center) Newsletters available from:

RFAG c/o AFSC
1428 Lafayette St.
Denver, CO 80218

RFAG c/o Environmental Action
2239 E. Colfax
Denver, CO

Cactus Alliance

Over the weekend of 1-2 October 1977, people from the states of Colorado, New Mexico, and Nevada came together with the intention of forming a regional alliance of groups working against all aspects of nuclear energy *and* weaponry. We were successful and are happy to share with you the results. Naming ourselves the Cactus Alliance, we identify with our western mountain states region, as well as with the struggle throughout the United States and the world.

The Cactus Alliance is a coalition of citizens dedicated to the betterment of life through the advancement of the ideals and values of respect for life and health, and of sensitivity to the earth and its systems. These bring us into opposition with:

- the high cost and risks, especially health risks, of nuclear energy,
- the introduction of radioactive wastes into the environment, and
- the production, proliferation, and use of nuclear weapons.

We actively support the alternatives of strict conservation practices, the redirection of technology to meet human needs, and the full development of alternative energy sources along with decentralization of energy systems. To this end we pledge to further our goals by means of education, communication, direct action, and community organizing. Recognizing the importance of cooperative regional action, we of the western intermountain states are working together.

For the Alliance,
Judi Bartlett-Lagorio
CACTUS ALLIANCE
312 Mountain Road, N.E.
Albuquerque, N.M. 87102

Kathy Partridge (national contact person)
980 Pleasant St.
Boulder, Col.

New Mexican Say No! To DOE

In public hearings held by the Department of Energy in Carlsbad, Santa Fe and Albuquerque in April 1978, New Mexicans stood up to DOE officials. When the DOE gave a strong, propagandized presentation as an introduction, people expressed their concern that the DOE *not* attempt to dominate the hearing, and then proceeded to make it a true public hearing.

Some of the groups represented at the Albuquerque hearing included: the American Civil Liberties Union (ACLU), La Lucha Nuclear newsletter, the Southwest Research and Information Center, Citizens Against Nuclear Threats, Socialist Workers Campaign, New Mexico PIRG, and the Sierra Club.

Several citizens and various local groups expressed dissatisfaction with a myraid of issues concerning the proposed Waste Isolation Pilot Project, (WIPP). The few people who spoke in favor of the site were mainly scientists from Los Alamos laboratories and people from the Carlsbad business community. Citizens in opposition spoke of the many problems with the proposed site near Carlsbad: loss of state revenue and jobs from potash mining and natural gas and oil extraction, the impossibility of retrieving wastes (despite DOE reassurances to the contrary), the spectre of maintaining the site for a minimum of 25,000 years, and more. People directed many specific blasts at the report by John Deutch of the DOE research office regarding the feasibility of WIPP. Citizens questioned over and over the credibility of the DOE itself as plans for the site have escalated from dumping "simple" transuranic wastes to disposal of a limited number (1000) of commercial spent fuel assemblies—and potentially more! Folks also forced Deputy Secretary of DOE, John O'-Leary, to address the issue of New Mexico's current major waste dumps—some 90,000,000 tons of uncovered, eroding radioactive uranium mill tailings.

The most exciting event of the jammed Albuquerque session occurred when Junio Lopez, claiming to represent thousands of irate New Mexicans from the northlands, damned the project as "pouring poison into the side of Mother Earth." Almost all in the crowd of 300 exploded with approval as he exclaimed: "We will, if necessary, bodily defend our Mother Earth from that poison!" The DOE will never again be able to say that the people of New Mexico want the WIPP. Instead, it is now clear to all that if the DOE is successful and the site is constructed, it will be here totally against the will of the people.

Terry Mulcahy and
Judi Bartlett-Lagorio
CACTUS ALLIANCE

Major Victory in New Mexico

The first major victory in the anti-nuclear movement in New Mexico came 3 April 1978 when Chem-Nuclear of Bellevue, Washington announced plans to abandon its proposed nuclear waste disposal site outside the scenic town of Cimarron.

The company named four reasons for dropping its license application: 1) projections that the state would not approve the permit application within 15 months (the company hoped for reprocessing to begin within 6 months); 2) the DOE report recommending the federal government take over the licensing of low-level radioactive wastes; 3) requirements placed on the company by the Environmental Protection Agency for additional geohydrologic work costing the company about $500,000; 4) the owner of the land proposed for the burial refused to renew the contract allowing Chem-Nuclear to operate on the property with an option to buy later.

What Chem-Nuclear didn't say was that the local citizenry of Colfax County had organized to stop the waste burial site. The town invited the Cactus Alliance to hold its January meeting in Cimarron with free housing and the community center for meetings. In mid-February the Cimarron Chamber of Commerce voted 32-0 against the site.

In the state where the nuclear industry began and which is home to nuclear research, uranium mining and proposed burial sites, this victory in Cimarron is extremely significant for the entire anti-nuclear movement.

by Craig Simpson
Cactus Alliance
reprinted from *WIN* magazine, April 27, 1978.

The Southwest—
A Native American Perspective

The earth is our mother. We Hopis are very concerned because it involves all of us in this country. Once we start tearing up our mother's heart, bad things will happen. We may poke her body, her feet, all over, but when we start poking her heart, there's going to be a big convulsion, and something is going to happen. We are going to have to stop this strip mining.

Thomas Banyaca,
Spokesman for Hopi Traditionals

On a world scale, Indian tribes own one-fifth of the world's known uranium reserves. Tribes are also the fourth leading producer in the world, producing 13% of the world's uranium.

New Mexico accounts for approximately 42% of the total U.S. domestic production of uranium oxide. This production is in the area known as the "Grants Uranium Belt," 100 miles long and 20 miles wide, stretching from Gallup to Rio Ruerco in northwestern New Mexico. The majority of mines are located in the vicinity of Ambrosia Lake. The Grants Uranium Belt includes Navaho-allotted lands, the Navajo community of Canoncito and the entire reservation and pueblos of Laguna, Acoma, Jemez, and Zia. It also includes federal, state, and private lands.

There are 30 uranium ore mines operated by as many as 13 different companies and 5 uranium concentrate (yellowcake) mills, each operated by a different company. As of 1977, 19 more mines are planned to open by 1985, and an unspecified number more after that.

Of all the enemies Indian tribes have come up against, there is nothing to compare with what confronts us presently. Wealthy and affluent multi-national corporations are invading Indian Lands for the search and exploitation of any and all mineral treasures to be found.

U.S. companies are backed by a national energy policy that demands the increased use and dependence upon uranium and the nuclear fuel cycle and coal, and for a decreased use of oil and gas. The Southwest also contains over half the nations's low sulfur coal. Within the next 20 years, all reservations with known reserves will one day face the choice of signing a lease and having some control over the development process, or of standing by and watching the forced and armed expropriation of the uranium reserves—unless tribes exercise their inherent sovereign powers and maintain their control over their economies. The Department of the Interior, designated as trustees of Indian lands, has been involved for years with industry's attempt to gain control of Indian land in order to exploit its resources.

The Laguna Experience—At one time, the Lagunas were a self-sustaining, self-employed, independent people, capable of surviving through traditional agricultural means. Then the uranium boom came to Laguna. The mine itself was the first impact. As it slowly expanded, more manpower was required, and eventually hundreds of Lagunas were employed by Anaconda. The mine now dominates the Paguate Valley and its people. Many Lagunas have made the mine their way of life and given up former agricultural practices.

The area around Paguate Village was once one of the most beautiful places on the reservation. Since 1953, when the mine first started production, the depth and size of the mine has increased at a dramatic rate. It is now the world's largest open-pit uranium mine. Some pits are 250 to 300 feet deep and a quarter of a mile wide in places. Everywhere one looks there are exposed areas of uranium and low-grade stock piles. Waste piles dwarf the surrounding areas. Every day, an army of monsters (huge diesel-powered shovels) and a fleet of forty dump trucks haul out a daily average of 6,000 tons of crude uranium ore. This has been accomplished by adding a fourth shift to make a twenty-four hour day and a seven-day work week.

Presently, the mine rests at the southeastern foot of the village, a mere 500 yards away. The constant release of radon gas mixed with the dust pollution is affecting older residents in the village. Eye cataracts and respiratory disorders are common problems.

There are 700 Laguna workers in the mine. Some have been working with Anaconda from the beginning. What will be the long-term effects upon their bodies after so many years of exposure on the job? Working many years at one job and at the mine have caused lethargy and indifference leading to depression, alcoholism, and suicide. There is not one contributing factor to the drinking and death, but many factors, including job pressures and loss of dignity due to loss of the land.

Contracts and agreements of any kind between tribes and a company inevitably result in a faster acculturation process and the destruction of traditional culture. All aspects of tribal life show drastic and long-lasting effects, many irreversable.

Other effects are also obvious, like the change of fertile farmlands and beautiful mesa country into gaping, radioactive pits. The land is the heart and soul of the People. No matter how much royalties we receive from leasing our land or how many jobs the mine creates, it is not worth those returns to have our land gouged and permanently destroyed. Indian lands will be left with the ugly remains of the first stage of the nuclear fuel cycle.

Within this year (1978) a "San Juan Basin Uranium Study" is to be conducted to detail the possible dangers that 70 mines and 10 mills will have on the Basin area. One need not be an expert to reasonably predict that within the next twenty years large parts of the Southwest will become saturated with radioactive wastes and poisons in the air and water. Radon gas emissions will accumulate in the atmosphere. Surface and ground water will become polluted through the leeching and leakage of tailings and waste ponds. The constant exploratory drilling will also have its effect. Life as we see it today may not exist in the near future.

Can the arid southwest land survive the overwhelming number of open-pit and underground mines and mills planned by the corporations? Already there is evidence of ground and surface water contamination in the Ambrosia Lake-Milan-Grants district. Water contamination has also been noted on the Laguna reservation where the mine is located. Evidence indicates an alarming amount of radon gas and radon daughters escaping into the atmosphere during mining and milling of uranium. In addition, the mining and milling processes use thousands of acre feet of water per year draining the rivers and underground aquifers. This will lower the water table making an already parched land even dryer.

In addition to uranium production, coal is most abundant here and is slated for increased production. This unwarranted and indiscriminate waste of beauty and life leaves many native people sad. It is frustrating to try and comprehend the actions taken by the destroyers, the imperialists.

To the Native American, as well as all natural people, we possess a unique and profound relationship with the Earth and the rest of the universe. Indian religion views the destruction of the earth as sacrilege. The land and the people are one and the same. Without the land, the People wander about like lost souls. The Earth, in its natural form, is in its most beautiful state. Any disturbance upsets the balance of the whole.

—from articles prepared by the National Indian Youth Council
201 Hermosa, N.E.
Albuquerque, N.M. 87108

Contacts

The Cactus Alliance includes the following groups:

Citizens Against Nuclear Threat (CANT), Albuquerque, N.M.

War Resisters League, Albuquerque, N.M.

New Mexico PIRG, Albuquerque, N.M.

CANWIN, Santa Fe, N.M.

Alternatives, Las Vegas, N.M.

Sagebrush Alliance, PO Box 7339, Las Vegas, Nev. 89101

Rocky Flats Action Group, Denver, Col.

Mobilization for Survival, Boulder, Col.

Catholic Worker House, Colorado Springs, Col.

EARS Collective, Denver, Col.

For information on Rocky Flats contact:
Rocky Flats Action Group, 1428 Lafayette St, Denver, Col.
Rocky Flats Truth Force, 972 Pleasant St., Boulder, Col.

Wyoming: Wyoming's seven uranium mills process 40% of the nation's yellowcake. (DOE 1/1/78)
Contact:
Wyoming Outdoor Council, Box 1184, Cheyenne WY 82001

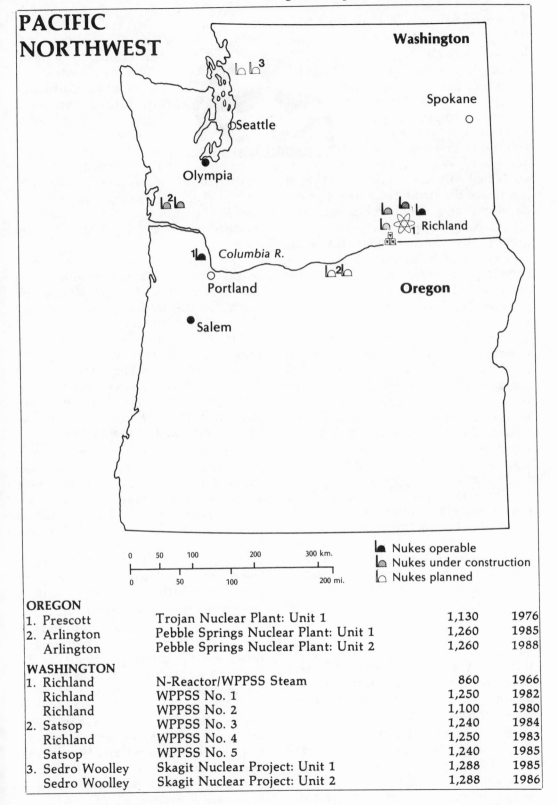

PACIFIC NORTHWEST

Washington

Spokane ○

○Seattle

● Olympia

Columbia R.

Richland

1● Portland

Oregon

●Salem

| 0 | 50 | 100 | 200 | 300 km. |
| 0 | | 50 | 100 | 200 mi. |

🝆 Nukes operable
🝆 Nukes under construction
🝆 Nukes planned

OREGON

1. Prescott	Trojan Nuclear Plant: Unit 1	1,130	1976
2. Arlington	Pebble Springs Nuclear Plant: Unit 1	1,260	1985
Arlington	Pebble Springs Nuclear Plant: Unit 2	1,260	1988

WASHINGTON

1. Richland	N-Reactor/WPPSS Steam	860	1966
Richland	WPPSS No. 1	1,250	1982
Richland	WPPSS No. 2	1,100	1980
2. Satsop	WPPSS No. 3	1,240	1984
Richland	WPPSS No. 4	1,250	1983
Satsop	WPPSS No. 5	1,240	1985
3. Sedro Woolley	Skagit Nuclear Project: Unit 1	1,288	1985
Sedro Woolley	Skagit Nuclear Project: Unit 2	1,288	1986

Crabshell Alliance in Washington

The Crabshell Alliance is located entirely within the borders of Washington State. There are local groups in Bellingham, Seattle, Olympia, Grey's Harbor Co., Pulman, Centralia, and the University of Washington.

CRABSHELL ALLIANCE

Crabshell Alliance is not a coalition of groups as the name connotes, but has developed as a membership organization which cooperates with other groups that have similar concerns. However, each Crabshell local has complete autonomy regarding issues which are of exclusively local concern.

The Nuclear Situation—Present nuclear generating plants in Washington are located entirely on the Hanford reservation, which is in sparsely populated eastern Washington. The facilities at Hanford and those planned for the future in the state are operated by the Washington Public Power Supply System (WPPSS). The aim of WPPSS, which is composed of 22 public utility districts, is to finance and construct five nuclear power plants before 1983.

There is also a plant planned for northwest Washington on the Skagit River that is being financed by a separate utility group. It has been successfully fought through the courts thus far by the Skagitonians Concerned About Nuclear Power (SCANP).

Crabshell has chosen to focus on the twin Satsop reactors located near Elma (between Aberdeen and Olympia), primarily because of their location. It is the only nuclear WPPSS site under construction in western Washington, where the population is most concentrated.

Background—The history of the Washington anti-nuclear movement is much like that of other states. It began as a legal battle in the sixties and early seventies and culminated in the anti-nuclear Initiative 325, which called for a moritorium on the construction of nukes until certain safeguards were assured. The initiative was defeated in November 1976 after a campaign carried out (primarily) by the Coalition for Safe Energy (CASE). After the defeat of Initiative 325, groups specifically opposed to nuclear power quickly began to lose energy.

The April 1977 occupation at Seabrook inspired some people from Olympia and Seattle—including a few from CASE—to form the Crabshell Alliance. In May, they drew up a declaration and immediately began planning a July demonstration near the Satsop reactor site. The demonstration drew about 700 people and brought more people into the Alliance. Crabshell was thereby greatly expanded, both in area and in membership.

Organizing—In the late summer and early fall of 1977, the Crabshell focused mainly on educating members about nuclear power and on developing an effective regional and local structure. All locals (Grey's Harbor, Olympia, etc.) are autonomous, non-hierarchical groups connected by a "SEA group," whose primary function is communication and "urgent" decision-making, as yet undefined.

Actions—Crabshell demands a complete halt to all construction and operation of nuclear power plants. To reach this goal, our emphasis remains on direct action. During September and October 1977, we did small actions exclusively, like going to WPPSS meetings and reading statements of opposition in front of press and tv cameras. We will continue these small actions, but we have also gotten involved in some major events.

• Crabshell joined a coalition that planned a demonstration against the Trident nuclear submarine held 21 May 1978. The event drew 4,000 people, of whom 300 were arrested for entering the base.

• In January, the Seattle local sponsored a large one day teach-in on nuclear energy that emphasized the role of direct action and drew attention to the spring (1978) occupation of Satsop. At this event and others, we provided pledge cards reading: "I will occupy the Satsop when 2,000 others pledge to do so." The occupation has been planned for June 24-25, the weekend of the fourth Clamshell occupation of Seabrook, N.H.

Paul Finley, Crabshell Alliance (Olympia), P.O. Box 7027, Olympia WA 98507 (Crabshell) 1114 34th Ave., Seattle WA 98122
Monthly newsletter: *Planned Emissions*

Oregon/Trojan
Decommissioning Alliance

Background—In December 1975 the Portland General Electric Company opened the 1300-megawatt Trojan nuclear power plant. Located on the Columbia River about 40 miles from Portland, Trojan is the largest operating nuke in the U.S.

Opposition to Trojan has been active since 1974. In November 1976, Oregonians narrowly rejected a Nuclear Safeguards Initiative proposal requiring that controversies over the safety of nuclear power plants, disposal of nuclear wastes, and complete liability insurance be resolved prior to approval of any new nuclear installations in Oregon. Utility advertising against it was intensive and expensive.

During the summer of 1977, the Trojan Decommissioning Alliance (TDA) formed. The state-wide antinuclear coalition issued its own Declaration of Nuclear Resistance which demanded:

• "...an immediate and permanent halt to the construction and operation of nuclear power plants;

•...[that] a supply of energy is a natural right and should in all cases be controlled by the people. Private monopoly must give way to public control;

• ...[that] in concert with public ownership, power supply should be decentralized, so that environmental damage is further minimized and so that control can revert to the local community and the individual."

The declaration called for a national focus on the development of "solar, wind, tidal, geothermal and other forms of cleaner renerable energy in concert with the perfection of an efficient system of recycling and conservation." Another demand concerned jobs—"any job lost through cancellation of nuclear construction or operation (must) be immediately compensated for in the natural energy field."

Non-Violent Direct Action—The Trojan plant has been the site of three nonviolent actions organized by the TDA. In August and November 1977, around 200 people trained in civil disobedience were arrested when they refused to stop blocking the Trojan plant's gates.

At the occupiers' first trial in December 1977, a jury acquitted the 96 defendants after hearing several days of testimony on the dangers of nuclear power. Lon Topaz, former director of the Oregon Department of Energy, testified that he believed the Trojan plant to be an "imminent danger" to the public. He said it should be shut down immediately.

Other expert witnesses at that trial included Dr. Rosalie Bertell, then a senior researcher at the Roswell Park Memorial Institute for Cancer Research in Buffalo, N.Y., and Dr. Ernest J. Sternglass, a world famous researcher on the effects of routine low-level radiation from nuclear power plants.

A few weeks after the acquittal verdict, the Oregon Department of Energy issued a report saying that according to its analysis of the latest data, the Trojan Plant could be shut down for the next ten years, and the electric utilities could save money and maintain reliable customer service at the same time.

In early April 1978, 500 delegates to the state-wide Democratic party platform convention voted overwhelmingly to support closure of the Trojan nuclear power plant. This marked the first time a state party platform has taken a stand against nuclear power.

This setback for the Trojan plant came on the heels of another defeat for the state's pro-nuclear electric utilities in mid-March ('78), when the Oregon Energy Facility Siting Council voted to oppose on-site storage of more than four-years-worth of nuclear waste at Trojan. A spokesperson for Portland General Electric Company, main owners of Trojan, complained that such a restriction would mean shutdown of the plant in 1982 when pres-

ently authorized on-site storage space runs out.

In the summer of 1978, the TDA continued its campaign to shut down Trojan with a third non-violent site occupation. Concerned citizens blocked entrances to the plant from 6-9 August: "We are taking action in self-defense, in defense of the people of the Northwest, and for children and grandchildren who are already burdened by the nuclear wastes generated by Trojan and other nuclear reactors." Over 200 people were arrested during the four-day action.

The Trojan nuke was shut down in March 1978 for a fuel change. Six months later it remained shut, following discovery that the nuke's control building didn't meet earthquake standards.

Contact

Trojan Decommissioning Alliance
215 SE 9th Ave.
Portland, OR 97242
503/231-0014
348 W. 8th Ave.
Eugene, OR 97401

Hanford Conversion Project
4312 S.E. Stark
Portland, Oregon 97215
Formed in July 1978 by anti-nuke and disarmament groups. Focus on conversion of Hanford Reservation to socially useful projects.

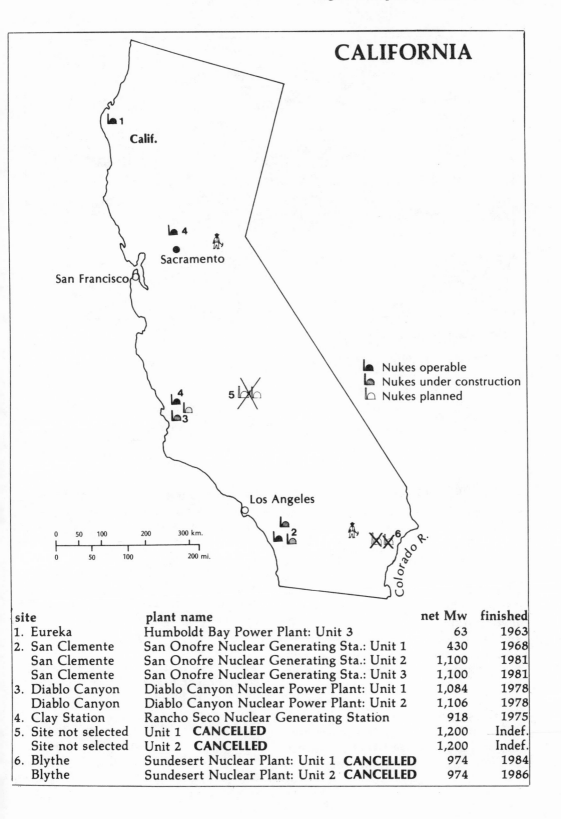

CALIFORNIA

Calif.

Sacramento

San Francisco

🔲 Nukes operable
🔲 Nukes under construction
🔲 Nukes planned

Los Angeles

Colorado R.

site	plant name	net Mw	finished
1. Eureka	Humboldt Bay Power Plant: Unit 3	63	1963
2. San Clemente	San Onofre Nuclear Generating Sta.: Unit 1	430	1968
San Clemente	San Onofre Nuclear Generating Sta.: Unit 2	1,100	1981
San Clemente	San Onofre Nuclear Generating Sta.: Unit 3	1,100	1981
3. Diablo Canyon	Diablo Canyon Nuclear Power Plant: Unit 1	1,084	1978
Diablo Canyon	Diablo Canyon Nuclear Power Plant: Unit 2	1,106	1978
4. Clay Station	Rancho Seco Nuclear Generating Station	918	1975
5. Site not selected	Unit 1 **CANCELLED**	1,200	Indef.
Site not selected	Unit 2 **CANCELLED**	1,200	Indef.
6. Blythe	Sundesert Nuclear Plant: Unit 1 **CANCELLED**	974	1984
Blythe	Sundesert Nuclear Plant: Unit 2 **CANCELLED**	974	1986

Citizens help redirect energy policy

(Credit: PANP)

Mothers For Peace—
San Luis Obispo

Background—San Luis Obispo Mothers For Peace (MFP) formed in 1969 out of concern for the waste of life resulting from the war in Vietnam. We still concern ourselves with the issues of peace—disarmament, amnesty, and meeting human needs. We have traditionally operated with a loose structure; our members are people who show interest and support our activities.

In late 1972 we began to educate ourselves about nuclear energy with books, speakers, tours of nuclear facilities and study sessions. Our concern developed from the connection we saw between nuclear weapons and nuclear power. When, in November 1973, the Pacific Gas and Electric Co. (PG&E) submitted their application for an operating license for the Diablo Canyon plant, the MFP filed as intervenors. In addition to the legal intervention against Diablo specifically, we are against nukes in general and for energy alternatives—conservation and the many forms of solar power.

The Story of the Diablo Canyon Nuclear Power Plant—PG&E announced its plans to build a nuclear plant on the Nipomo Dunes, several miles south of Diablo (Devil's) Canyon, in 1963. The Sierra Club objected to the site because of the fragile ecology of the dunes, but did not object to nuclear power *per se,* nor to a relocation of the project in Diablo Canyon, 12 miles southwest of San Luis Obispo. In the summer of 1966 this new site was formally chosen, and the Sierra Club membership became split over the issue.

The Scenic Shoreline Preservation Conference formed in 1966 to conduct "environmental litigation and education" and to intervene against the construction permits for the Diablo Canyon plant.

Site work began in June 1968 on a 750 acre site on the coast over a Chumash Indian cemetary in one of the few remaining totally undeveloped sections of coastline.

The AEC's (now NRC) Atomic Safety and Licensing Board (ASLB) issued a construction permit in April 1968 for Unit I and in December 1970 for Unit II. But because of the NEPA decisions requiring environmental impact statements, all plants granted construction permits after 1 January 1970 needed further environmental hearings to regain their permits. Thus additional environmental hearings on Diablo were held during 1973. At that time the ASLB refused to hear the issue of earthquake hazards. The Diablo plant's new construction permit was issued in June 1974.

The Diablo Intervention—When the MFP filed as intervenors in November 1973, the issues to be covered in the AEC hearings included: the effects of low-level radiation; radiation release as a result of accident; the untested ECCS; the lack of evacuation routes and emergency plans; problems associated with fuel and waste transportation and disposal of radioactive wastes; and the possiblility of sabotage. In January of 1974, the earthquake problem—seismicity—was also included. Other contentions raised by Scenic Shoreline Preservation, the Ecology Action Club (a student group at California Polytechnic State Univer-

sity in San Luis Obispo), and The Center for Law in the Public Interest included the effects of the thermal plume, cost benefit analysis, the need for power, energy conservation, nuclear fuel shortages, and plant reliability.

For almost three years, until August 1976, the MFP carried on the legal fight *pro se*—on our own without benefit of lawyers' arguments. We also acted alone in our educational and public information campaign against Diablo. Happily, both circumstances have changed.

In August 1976 the Los Angeles-based non-profit law firm, Center for Law in the Public Interest, took on the Diablo Canyon case. In October 1977 the Washington D.C. firm Wilmer, Cutler and Pickering announced that they would co-represent the intervenors with the Center. Then in January 1977 People Against Nuclear Power—since re-named People Generating Energy (PGE)—formed as a nonviolent direct action group. And, in June 1977, the Abalone Alliance was founded.

It is with the slimmest of hopes of stopping the plant from operating that the MFP continues its intervention. However, we do see it as a good means of bringing matters of fact to the public's attention, and we have been somewhat successful in obtaining modifications of the plant to make it "safer."

In April 1975, the Mothers filed a motion with the NRC's ASLB to deny PG&E permission to acquire and store nuclear fuel assemblies until a valid operating license was issued, which would not be until security and seismicity issues had been litigated. The hearing on this in December 1975 was the first ever held on a license to hold and store fuel. The NRC placed the burden of proof upon PG&E to prove that their storage methods would protect

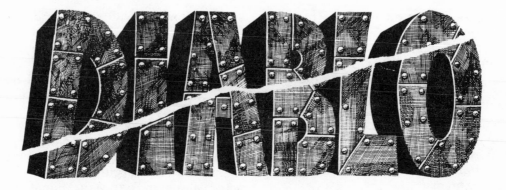

health and safety. The utility made profound structural changes in the new fuel-storage methods and the Board ruled in their favor. The intervenors appealed this decision, but fuel shipments began in February 1976 despite the pending appeal. That spring the Appeal Board ruled against the intervenors.

Diablo at Fault—The most important item in our intervention, and the fact that should keep Diablo from ever operating, is the presence of an active earthquake fault system less than three miles from the plant, which is now completed.

In 1967-8, PG&E had surveyed only 3/4 of a square mile around the site, even though earthquakes had been recorded in the area. The plant was designed to withstand a great earthquake on the San Andreas fault 48 miles from the site (8.5 on the Richter scale, ground acceleration of 0.19 g at plant site); or a large earthquake on the Nacimiento fault, 20 miles away (magnitude 7.25, ground acceleration of 0.12 g). When two geologists working for Shell Oil discovered the Hosgri fault in 1971, PG&E dismissed it as inconsequential.

In 1973 and 1974, the Scenic Shoreline Preservation Conference and the Mothers for Peace filed motions asking for stop work orders pending more extensive seismic studies. The Board denied both motions, saying that seismic issues would be discussed at hearings for the operating license (granted when plants are completed, before they start-up), and that continued construction would pose no hazard to the health and safety of the public. The Board also stated that its future judgement would not be affected by economic considerations—the fact that the plant would then be completed—at a cost of $1.255 billion! (Units I and II, PG&E figures.)

Studies by the U.S. Geological Survey published in 1975 indicated that the Hosgri-San Simeon fault system may be 200 miles long and capable of an earthquake of 7.5 on the Richter scale, (ground acceleration at plant 0.75 g.) Clearly this was a serious threat to the safety of a nuclear plant *and* the surrounding population.

Memos released in June 1977 show that the NRC pressured the Geological Survey to change its predictions by asking it to "consider additional facts." The NRC also tried to upgrade its previous view of how great a shock the plant might be able to resist, and it devised a plan whereby PG&E could seek an "interim license" that might be easier to approve than a normal operating license.

In August 1977—with seismic studies far from complete—PG&E did apply for an interim license to operate, with no specific final date given, based on the supposed "need for power" caused by the prolonged drought. This was the first time a utility had applied for a full-powered open-ended interim license. In this way, PG&E tried to exempt itself from meeting all the safety requirements of a regular operating license.

And more faults—Now a new fault has been discovered—the San Miguelito fault. California Bureau of Mines and Geology studies revealed the fault in late March 1978; intervenors were informed in early May. The fault's significance is not fully known, but it is accepted as active, and it may run as close as 1½-2 miles to the plant.

PG&E is no longer pursuing the interim license. We think this is because they were pressured not only by the Center for Law, but also by NRC staff, who made it clear to the utility that the license wouldn't come as fast as assumed. We believe that without our determined opposition and the help of the Center for Law and its excellent scientific consultants, this message would not have been given to PG&E.

The Mothers and Coalitions

For years MFP has seen the need for coalitions with allied groups. We knew there were others who cared but weren't attracted to our group. Mothers *is* in fact mostly mothers, and our meeting times and actions were and are influenced by the fact that most of us have young children. We also have some grandmothers and women who are not mothers in our midst. Although our name was never intended to exclude men, only a few participate as regularly active members. Many men do help with specific projects.

Finally, the Mothers were charter members of the Abalone Alliance.

Other Activities, Accomplishments and Things—As a direct result of MFP efforts, the local school board has

adopted a plan for radiological emergencies. We do not delude ourselves that this assures the safety of school children in case of an accident at the plant, or one involving radioactive materials in transit.. But at least the hazard has been admitted, and the need for some citizen response is recognized.

WHAT DO YOU DO IN CASE OF A NUCLEAR ACCIDENT.

KISS YOUR CHILDREN GOOD-BYE.

"Our famous poster is seen all over the U.S. at rallies and demonstrations."

In February 1976 Jane Fonda joined us in a rally to call public attention to the arrival of the first shipment of fuel at Diablo Canyon.

One of our most successful educational efforts was a forum held in 1974. After the County Board of Supervisors turned us down twice, we interested a large number of physicians in joining us in sponsoring a two-day educational event. On October 17th, some 4,000 people packed the California State Polytechnic University gym to hear Drs. John Gofman and Edward Teller debate nuclear energy. The following day featured debates from opposing viewpoints on various topics—health considerations, safety aspects, waste disposal, economics, and alternatives.

We participate in the electoral process by campaigning as individuals for candidates who share our priorities. We lobby our elected officials at the local, state, and national levels.

We are continuing our efforts to inform the public. Members speak at civic and school groups upon request. We make literature available at all kinds of public events. We invite the public to share films and speakers with us. Members and spokespersons for the group have appeared on local radio and television programs.

The official mailing address for the Mothers for Peace is:

Mothers for Peace
c/o Raye Fleming
1746 Chorro St.
San Luis Obispo CA 93401

Any questions may be addressed there, as well as to either of the undersigned who have put this information together: Liz Apfelberg & Jane Swanson.

Abalone Alliance
People Against Nuclear Power

People Against Nuclear Power is the San Francisco affiliate of the Abalone Alliance. Past actions we've been involved in include a demonstration against Carter's nuclear policy and a "plutonium tour" of Bay Area locations of stored plutonium.

We helped with support work and coordination for the Abalone Alliance's first non-violent occupation at Diablo Canyon on 7 August 1977. One thousand five hundred people came to a support rally; 47 people were arrested including two who were later revealed to be police agents.

We have done a lot of educational work, organizing teach-ins at colleges and communities across the state. Our theater collective performs at various events throughout the Bay Area. We had two actions at PG&E headquarters in which we attempted to carry an information rack of literature on nuclear power and alternative energy into their Energy Expo. We also had an action at their recent annual stockholders' meeting.

The work of PANP is done by collective groups doing media, outreach, theater, finance, non-violent training, local actions, education, and alternative energy. We also have a speakers' bureau. We are planning to continue working with other Abalone groups as well as other organizations and individuals in organizing nonviolent direct actions against the Diablo nuke. By joining hands across the nation and the world, we, as a people's movement, can and will stop the proliferation of nuclear power plants.

Peace and NO NUKES
Steve Leeds, PANP

The Abalone Alliance started a statewide clearinghouse (for communications purposes) in January.

Abalone Alliance Clearinghouse
452 Higuera
San Luis Obispo CA 93401
People Against Nuclear Power
1360 Howard St., 1st floor
San Francisco CA 94103

Chapter 3:

"Educate, Agitate, Organize"*

Goals

People who consider themselves part of the anti-nuclear movement naturally share one goal above all—to see a non-nuclear future in the U.S., and as soon as possible. But beyond this priority come a range of other objectives. The most obvious of these is replacing nuclear power with conservation and safe, renewable energy sources. Another is to have energy that everyone can afford.

Many people are also concerned about the future patterns of power production and distribution. We want to see safe, decentralized energy production, contolled by the communities it serves. Energy sources should be developed for public need, not private profit.

Many nuclear opponents see atomic energy as an expression of basic societal problems—like centralized power, white-male-capitalist decision-making, a permanent war economy. We want to see the kinds of long-term changes that will ensure that "mistakes" like nuclear power development never happen again. And until people (instead of corporate owners) have more control over the way the economy runs, what is produced and distributed, and by whom, and until people control education, community life and culture, and all the other features of daily life, then there is no guarantee that things *will* change.

Goals develop over time, and those of the anti-nuke movement are no exception. Hopefully, the focus of the movement will broaden out so that substantive structural changes can be demanded and won, even beyond a halt to nuclear plant construction and operation.

Strategy

The anti-nuclear movement in the U.S. has adopted one basic strategy in its effort to stop nuclear power. That is to create enough public pressure so that the government and nuclear industry will find it too costly—both politically and financially—to proceed

*from Syracuse Peace Council Stationery

with their nuclear designs. Local oppositions wage desperate fights against nuclear power, project by project. Taken as a whole, this opposition is forging a movement that will be heard!

This strategy has been used before. Social movements in the U.S. built the political pressure that forced adoption of the Limited Test Ban Treaty, the Civil Rights Act, and helped end the Vietnam War. In all cases reforms were made (to alleviate pressure from the movements), but basic problems remained. As we organize to stop nuclear power we must learn from the past, and try to build our movement in such a way that our work can go on beyond ending nukes to address further basic questions. The long-term goal would be to make our world a better place to live and work with self-management and personal freedom. The satisfaction of basic human needs and potentials would be the guiding themes of daily life.

The current strategy of pressure for change is being implemented through a variety of tactics. The most basic is public education, but there are many others.

Debates and teach-ins help spread the word...

Education

Education is really the name of the safe energy movement. The information that convinced me that nuclear power and weapons were a bad bargain has also convinced my friends. The problem is getting access to this information, and using this information to counteract the massive propaganda campaigns launched by government and industry.

Kitty Tucker
Eastern Federation, 1978

Public education is the force that will turn the tide, and make nuclear power a thing of the past. For the facts about nuclear power are enough to convince people that it's a bad deal all the way around—except for those who have a personal (usually financial) stake in atomic energy. Public pressure will have to work on them.

People opposed to nuclear power are generally not rich. They cannot buy TV and newspaper ads to get their message across. But, having educated themselves by means of many fine books, papers and films on the subject, they use a variety of creative methods to get the facts about nuclear power out to the public.

The list of ways groups of people have gone about educational work is long. Wisconsin's LAND report mentions some (see p. 426). Nuclear opponents speak everywhere, sponsor public meetings and debates, show films, write and distribute literature, set up literature tables at fairs and shopping centers, talk on radio and TV shows,

How to raise money, educate and have fun too.

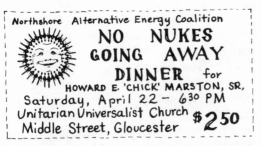

Northshore Alternative Energy Coalition

NO NUKES GOING AWAY DINNER for

HOWARD E. 'CHICK' MARSTON, SR.

Saturday, April 22 – 6:30 PM
Unitarian Universalist Church $2.50
Middle Street, Gloucester

Chick Marston, age 76, was going to jail in April-May '78 for 20 days for his part in the 1977 Seabrook occupation.

hold pot-luck suppers with a speaker or film and "literature bake sales" (something to read along with the cookies). Many of these essentially educational activities also bring in funds, allowing the group to continue and expand its activities. Many of these methods have been used by a wide variety of social groups and churches. And why not! It is good for people to get together and have some fun while they find out what's going on.

Pressure Politics

This set of tactics involves organizing for political clout within the existing system. Pressure politics can range from petitioning legislators, to lobbying, to the use of referenda, to running safe energy candidates for office. Interventions would also come under this category. Basically, citizens try to find "pressure points"—places where citizen pressure can successfully be applied—either for immediate change, for delay in the nuclear program, or for some educational value. Working "within the system" in this way can lead to minor reforms, cause welcome delays, and can expose the rigidity, corruption, and vested interests that abound in government regulatory circles.

The main obstacles to stopping nuclear proliferation will in fact be political pressure groups. To

counter them will require arousing the American people to the imperatives of the proliferation issue. **If there is one thing I have learned in fourteen years in Congress, it is that the finest oratory on the floor of the Congress is as nothing compared to a flood of letters from the folks back home.** But such grass roots pressure requires arousing the public—scarcely easy in view of the complexity of the issue and the distasteful vision of the future that people are asked to ponder.

—Rep. Clarence D. Long
International Security, p. 76

Political pressure from the grassroots at the right time (early!) has achieved important results. For example, early action by Pennsylvania's Environmental Coalition on Nuclear Power (ECNP) in 1969-71, led Governor Milton Shapp to oppose siting of a breeder reactor in the state. In 1975, ENCP led a strong and successful opposition to energy park siting—the clustering of up to 10-20 nukes in one location—in the state.

The Power of the Pen—From LISEC's newsletter *Chain Reaction*, Mid-winter '78, vol. 2, no. 1

Public Take-Over

The movement towards municipal power speaks directly to the question of control of resources. Publicly controlled power puts decision-making closer to community residents. Bills are lower because there are no profits going to stockholders, no fat executive salaries and useless fancy advertising. Publicly controlled utilities can also get low-interest loans to restore or build renewable energy systems for electrical generation.

Direct Action

Many people believe that nuclear power must be opposed by direct action, beyond educational efforts or legal tactics alone. Direct actions range from educational canvasses, to rallies, marches, and demonstrations, and sometimes include actions aimed at specific targets—such as the occupation of a nuclear site or facility. Direct actions are aimed at raising the social and political costs of pursuing the nuclear program, while simultaneously further educating the public about their dangers.

Balloon Rising

hundreds of helium balloons with notes attached will be released from nuclear sites to demonstrate who a similar release of radio-activity would affect.

Balloon Rising   Aug. 6 th

A good educational form of direct action. Let the balloons fly, see where they (and radiation in case of accident) come down. Between Aug. 6-9 '77, ballons were set off from more than 100 nuclear plant sites. Attached cards were returned from hundreds of miles away.

Direct actions raise the "cost" of nukes to their corporate, utility and government boosters by saying, essentially, "As you continue to pursue this energy program, more and more people will become aware and discontented, and will then demonstrate and even actively disrupt your efforts. Ultimately your legitimacy and power in all areas will come into question." The powers-that-be understand such pressures much better than they understand ethical arguments. In due course they will come to see that the "pursuit of nukes" must cease.

Direct action catches the ear of the press... Seabrook 30 April 1977

As long as utilities continue to invest our money in nuclear power, as long as the government continues to subsidize it, as long as rural areas are sacrificed to the energy-waste of urban America and the safe job producing alternatives to nuclear power are suppressed, the movement against nuclear energy will grow. And with it, the number and size of direct actions.

Direct action must be appropriate to particular situations. There is no one "pattern" that guarantees success. For example, although the Wyhl occupation led people to try and stop other plants physically, only one (Gerstheim) was similarly blocked. The conclusion here would seem to be that

So far, direct actions against nuclear power in the U.S. have been very consciously non-violent. This comes from many participants' philosophical beliefs and from tactical considerations as well. For there is no point in opponents "attacking" nuclear facilities. We would be quickly disposed of. And it is not *our* wish to in any way cause a nuclear accident or problem—on the contrary, we are trying to prevent them! **Our non-violence is a way of saying that we reject the violence of nuclear power and the economic system behind it.**

physical take-overs are most effective in halting a project before construction begins, when the utility and government have nothing physical to "defend." For as soon as there is "private property" on the site, the confrontation escalates to a new order. For sites where construction is under-way, new tactics may be necessary to avoid a violent confrontation. One approach is to focus on other centers of nuclear power power—banks, utility companies, and government agencies, for example. Boycotts and rate withholding campaigns are other forms of direct action.

Culture and Politics

Direct actions are a time to integrate a little grassroots culture with our politics. Artists, musicians, theater groups and performers of all kinds make important contributions to the movement for safe energy. Their talents can help spread the word about nuclear power. Information can be passed in ways that are creative and fun—like puppet shows. Local talent and nationally known performers can also

One creative direct action was the Plutonium Path Caravan that wound its way from Savannah River, Georgia to Rocky Flats, Colorado, graphically showing people the movement of plutonium across the country. This action and the occupation of the railroad tracks used to bring plutonium into the plant followed many months of public education, including a slide show shown to church, civic, social service and community action groups all over Colorado and throughout the country.

A SHORT GUIDE TO ORGANIZING

AGAINST RATEHIKES, ETC.

Organizing means talking with people and getting them to do things.

THE FIRST THING YOU HAVE TO DO IS get ten or a hundred rate-witholding leaflets. These are available from LISEC – we have enough contacts throughout the island so we can probably arrange prompt delivery to you. If you give us a small donation for larger quantities, it will make our jobs that much easier. If you take the one inserted in this Chain Reaction to a printer yourself, that's even better – get as many copies as you can handle. Too many is better than too few, so long as you get them OUT!

THE SIMPLEST AND MOST IMMEDIATELY EFFECTIVE WAY TO ORGANIZE RATEHIKE RESISTANCE is just to give out a lot of leaflets to everyone you know. Just say 'Listen, did you hear your next LILCO bill's going to be almost 10% higher? A lot of people all over the island say   they won't pay the increase.' Hand them a leaflet. 'Here's why, and here's where you sign up if you want to take off that part your next payment.' Try to reach people who see a lot of other people – anyone active in a club or organization, grocers and shopkeepers, delivery boys and LILCO meter-readers. Be prepared to take signed pledges on the spot, and send those you get to LISEC as soon as you can.

IF YOU'RE STILL SHY (and we all feel like fools until we get used to these things), just sneak little stacks of leaflets into public places – bars, libraries, etc. In any case, make sure you at least get one to each of your friends and relatives.

IF YOU BELONG TO AN ORGANIZATION, SPEAK UP AT THE NEXT MEETING. Give your group the option of passing a resolution putting it on record against the ratehike, and keep open your own option of just passing leaflets out to everyone. See if anyone can take a bunch to pass on to clients, co-workers, etc.

A FEW ORGANIZATIONS MAY BE WILLING to not only go on record against the ratehike, but also put the witholding campaign into all their community outreach. Get it in the newsletter, at least, even if the group didn't bother to officially endorse it.

IF YOU REALLY WANT TO GO ALL-OUT, here are a few suggestions. You can start a local group of your own – call it   the Riverbottom Citizens for Affordable Energy, or whatever – and get a couple of like-minded friends involved. Then you're in a position to really start organizing your community against LILCO.

AFTER YOU HAVE 6-10 ACTIVE MEMBERS, you can start community organizing in a more organized way. By then, LISEC will be able to give you standardized forms for volunteer sign-up sheets, contact-responses forms for house-to-house canvassing, suggestions for small fund-raising events, etc. BUT MAKE SURE YOU EMPHASIZE ACTION – not funds and organizational details – at the beginning stages. If you want to sound authoritative, read 'The Poverty of Power' by Commoner. Toss out a few of his ideas and GET PEOPLE MOVING!!!! Don't get hung up in endless philosophical discussions at meetings. Set up a study group as a sideline for that. Good luck, and let us know what happens.

Van Howell
(from *Chain Reaction*,
LISEC, Winter 1977)

Theater for No Nukes—Hampton Beach NH, 23 October 1976

raise a lot of money for the movement. Already, many "stars" have donated their time and energy to help keep the grassroots movement growing.

Alliances for Change

Still another tactic for attaining a non-nuclear future is one that so far has not been examined thoroughly enough by the anti-nuclear movement. And that is the formation of alliances with other groups in order to work together in combined political strength to achieve social/political change. The anti-nuclear movement has natural allies— among them people who are solar advocates, consumer groups, utility reform groups, labor unions and unemployed workers who need the jobs that conservation and alternative energy will bring. A lot of groups would be interested in seeing the resources now committed to nuclear development go into other far more pressing social needs—rebuilding the central cities, providing daycare centers, better social services to the elderly, etc.

The anti-nuke movement touches many aspects of the U.S. and world economy. We need to work with others who are interested in changing the priorities of the federal government away from "defense" and highway spending, toward meeting people's real needs. And we need to learn about and support people's efforts to stop nuclear power in other countries. For atomic energy is clearly an international problem. As Americans we have a special responsibility to stop nuclear energy, since it was the U.S. government that started this mess.

Where Do I Start?

Well, by reading this book, you've begun. The best way to fight nuclear power is to study up and start talking. Convince your friends and neighbors. Talk to any groups you are part of. Tell your children about the energy choices that face them too.

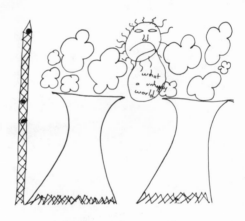

Drawing by Sequoya Frey, age 7

Look into solar alternatives in your community. Practice energy conservation and support local attempts to take over power production and distribution. Check out the sources of radiation nearest your home. Write letters, join or form an activist group. Be aware and be active. Demonstrate. Our future depends on it.

Remember!
Better Active Today
Than Radioactive
Tomorrow!